"In *The Fathers on the Future*, Michael Svigel makes a unique, biblical, and long-lasting contribution to the field of patristic eschatology. Taking seriously the nearly universal theological and exegetical ideas of the Ante-Nicene Fathers regarding the Last Days, this meticulously researched yet practical work revives the past from its shadows, shedding light on our current understanding of the future. This is a must-read for anyone interested in Christ's second coming as seen through the eyes of those closest to the apostles—with strong relevance for us today."

—Steven D. Aguzzi, Theology Department
Duquesne University

"Throughout the centuries, Christians have discussed and debated varying eschatological views. One way to renew a vision of the future is to review visionaries from the past. Michael Svigel's provocative retrieval of 'Irenaean premillennialism' does not fit seamlessly into modern systematic taxonomies. Readers from all eschatological commitments will find their horizons broadened, allowing rays from the early church to illumine the variegated contours of 'last things.'"

—Paul Hartog, Professor of Theology
Faith Baptist Theological Seminary

"Michael Svigel has penned a masterful tome that deserves to stand on every theologian's bookshelf. Combining high-end scholarship with clear, readable prose, this book refutes the mistaken notion that premillennial and pretribulational theology arose only in the nineteenth century. Rather, these important doctrines find their grounding in the pages of Scripture and the first generations of ancient Christian writers. More broadly, *The Fathers on the Future* reminds us of the centrality of eschatology for Christian life and thought. Svigel reclaims eschatology from the end-times quacks and repositions it as the rightful culmination of God's unfolding drama of redemption."

—Bryan Litfin, Professor of Bible & Theology
Rawlings School of Divinity, Liberty University

"I have been hoping for years that someone would highlight the futurist, premillennial eschatology of Irenaeus and the significance of this great theologian for current discussions and debates over eschatology. And here it is! Michael Svigel offers us a masterful discussion of eschatology, rooted in Scripture, and also in interaction with the most significant early church theologian who addressed eschatology—Irenaeus."

—Michael J. Vlach, Professor of Theology
Shepherds Theological Seminary

T0283459

"My friend and colleague, Dr. Michael Svigel, has done all of us in ministry a huge favor in writing his newest book *The Fathers on the Future*. In his inimitable, down-to-earth, yet substantive style, Michael leads us on a tour of the past to listen to the ancient church fathers and hear their voices on eschatology and the end times. This excellent volume combines Michael's immense scholarship with his keen understanding of the pulse of current ministry culture and shows us a calm and compelling hermeneutic of our times. You need this book."

—Mark M. Yarbrough, President
Dallas Theological Seminary

THE FATHERS ON THE FUTURE

A 2nd-Century Eschatology for the
21st-Century Church

THE FATHERS ON THE FUTURE

A 2nd-Century Eschatology for the
21st-Century Church

MICHAEL J. SVIGEL

The Fathers on the Future:
A 2nd-Century Eschatology for the 21st-Century Church

Hendrickson Publishers
3 Centennial Drive
Peabody, Massachusetts 01960
www.hendricksonpublishers.com

ISBN 978-1-4964-8766-7

Printed in the United States of America

Third Printing — December 2024

Library of Congress Cataloging-in-Publication Data

Names: Svigel, Michael J., 1973- author.
Title: The fathers on the future : a 2nd-century Eschatology for the
    21st-century church / Michael J. Svigel.
Description: Peabody, Massachusetts : Hendrickson Publishers, 2024. |
    Includes bibliographical references. | Summary: "A fair and balanced
    introduction to Christian eschatology, this book provides a fresh
    defense of the premillennial, futurist, and pretribulational positions.
    Integrating biblical, theological, and historical sources, it takes a
    new look at Christian hope and addresses lingering questions and debates
    with innovative insights and answers"-- Provided by publisher.
Identifiers: LCCN 2024016690 | ISBN 9781496487667 | ISBN 9781496487674
    (kindle edition) | ISBN 9781496487681 (ebook) | ISBN 9781496487698
    (ebook other)
Subjects: LCSH: Eschatology--History of doctrines--Early church, ca.
    30-600. | Theology, Doctrinal--History--Early church, ca. 30-600. |
    Fathers of the church.
Classification: LCC BT819.5 .S96 2024 | DDC 236--dc23/eng/20240517
LC record available at https://lccn.loc.gov/2024016690

I dedicate this volume to seven men whose personal mentorship and friendship impacted my life over the last several decades, without whom I would not be where I am—or who I am—today.

Brian L. Dent

Charles C. Ryrie

J. Lanier Burns

Charles R. Swindoll

D. Jeffrey Bingham

Glenn R. Kreider

John Adair

Memento de cetero.

Tertullian, *Ad Scapulam* 3

CONTENTS

Go Deeper Excurses
WWW.FATHERSONTHEFUTURE.COM

The main content of this book is supplemented by a number of "Go Deeper Excurses" available online at www.fathersonthefuture.com. Many of these excurses are of a highly technical nature and provide important technical support for the arguments of this book. Some are merely supplemental, further explaining various secondary matters of interest to some readers.

Acknowledgments

I want to extend a special thanks to Patricia Anders: With insightful queries and thoughtful changes, her firm but gentle hand in the laborious editing process moved this book from טוב to טוב מאוד.

I also thank the erstwhile members of my "menternship" group at Dallas Seminary who helped immensely in the preparation of the online excurses at www. fathersonthefuture.com: Michael Banks, Christopher Reynolds, Autumn Bogner, and, of course, Jack Riniker, who shepherded the project toward completion.

Errors of fact and form are still my own, but my editors significantly reduced their number.

A Note on Translations

Unless noted, quotations from Irenaeus's *Against Heresies* (cited as Irenaeus, *Haer.*) are from Alexander Roberts and James Donaldson, eds., *The Ante-Nicene Fathers*, vol. 1, *The Apostolic Fathers, Justin Martyr, Irenaeus* (Edinburgh: Christian Literature Publishing Company, 1885; reprint, New York: Scribner's, 1899). I will not indicate page numbers when citing this edition, just book, chapter, and section: e.g., *Haer.* 2.2.2 indicates book 2, chapter 2, section 2. Occasionally for books 1–5 of *Against Heresies*, I will refer to the modern translations cited as "Unger," including St. Irenaeus of Lyons, *Against the Heresies*, vol. 1, book 1, ed., trans., and annotated by Dominic J. Unger, rev. by John J. Dillon, Ancient Christian Writers: The Works of the Fathers in Translation, vol. 55 (New York: Newman, 1992); St. Irenaeus of Lyons, *Against the Heresies*, book 2, trans. and annotated by Dominic J. Unger, rev. by John J. Dillon, with introduction by Michael Slusser, Ancient Christian Writers: The Works of the Fathers in Translation, vol. 65 (New York: Newman, 2012); St. Irenaeus of Lyons, *Against the Heresies*, book 3, trans. and annotated by Dominic J. Unger, with introduction and rev. by Matthew C. Steenberg, Ancient Christian Writers: The Works of the Fathers in Translation, vol. 64 (New York: Newman, 2012); St. Irenaeus of Lyons, *Against the Heresies*, books 4 and 5, trans. and annotated by Dominic Unger, with introduction and rev. by Scott D. Moringiello, Ancient Christian Writers: The Works of the Fathers in Translation, vol. 72 (New York: Newman, 2024). Unless noted, quotations of Justin Martyr's 1 Apology, 2 Apology, and Dialogue with Trypho are from Thomas B. Falls, *Justin Martyr: The First Apology, the Second Apology, Dialogue with Trypho, Exhortation to the Greeks, Discourse to the Greeks, the Monarchy or the Rule of God, The Fathers of the Church: A New Translation*, vol. 6 (Washington, DC: Catholic University of America Press), 1948.

The translations of other fathers of the church will be indicated by the following abbreviations in parentheses after the quotation:

ANF: *The Ante-Nicene Fathers*. The volume containing the particular writing will be indicated after the citation; thus (*ANF* 2) refers to volume 2 of the *ANF* series.

NPNF[1]/NPNF[2]: *Nicene and Post-Nicene Fathers*, Series 1/Series 2. After the series, the particular volume within which the writing occurs will follow. Thus NPNF[1] 2 indicates series 1, volume 2.

Unless noted, translations of Irenaeus's *Demonstration of the Apostolic Preaching* (cited as Irenaeus, *Epid.*) are from Irenaeus of Lyons, *On the Apostolic Preaching*, edited and translated by John Behr, Popular Patristics Series, vol. 17 (Crestwood, NY: St Vladimir's Seminary Press, 1997).

Unless noted, all translations from the Apostolic Fathers are from Rick Brannan, trans., *The Apostolic Fathers in English* (Bellingham, WA: Lexham, 2012). This includes all quotes from 1–2 Clement, the letters of Ignatius, Polycarp's *To the Philippians*, Martyrdom of Polycarp, Didache, Barnabas, the Shepherd of Hermas, the Epistle of Mathetes to Diognetus, and Fragments of Papias.

Unless noted, for Eusebius's *Ecclesiastical History* (*Hist. eccl.*), I am using Eusebius of Caesarea, *The History of the Church: A New Translation*, translated by Jeremy M. Schott (Oakland: University of California Press, 2019).

Unless noted, all quotations from the Septuagint (LXX) indicated with (Brannan) are from Rick Brannan et al., eds., *The Lexham English Septuagint* (Bellingham, WA: Lexham, 2012).

Translations marked NETS are from Pietersma, Albert, and Benjamin G. Wright, eds. *A New English Translation of the Septuagint (Primary Texts)*, translated by Kenneth Atkinson (Oxford: Oxford University Press, 2007).

Unless otherwise noted, English Scripture quotations come from the New Revised Standard Version, Updated Edition. Copyright © 2021 National Council of Churches of Christ in the United States of America. All rights reserved worldwide.

Translations marked NASB refer to the New American Standard Bible®, Copyright © 1960, 1971, 1977, 1995, 2020 by The Lockman Foundation. All rights reserved.

Scripture quotations marked (ESV) are taken from the Holy Bible, English Standard Version (ESV®), copyright © 2001 by Crossway, a publishing ministry of Good News Publishers. Used by permission. All rights reserved.

Scripture quotations marked (NRSV) are taken from the New Revised Standard Version of the Bible, copyright © 1989 by the Division of Christian Education of the National Council of the Churches of Christ in the United States of America, and are used by permission.

Scripture quotations marked (NIV) are taken from the Holy Bible, New International Version®, NIV®. Copyright © 1973, 1978, 1984, 2011 by Biblica, Inc.™ Used by permission of Zondervan. All rights reserved worldwide. www.zondervan.com. The "NIV" and "New International Version" are trademarks registered in the United States Patent and Trademark Office by Biblica, Inc.™

ABBREVIATIONS

Apostolic Fathers

1 Clem.	1 Clement (Letter of the Romans to the Corinthians)
2 Clem.	2 Clement (An Early Christian Sermon)
Barn.	Epistle of Barnabas
Did.	Didache (The Lord's Teaching through the Twelve Apostles to the Nations)
Diogn.	The Epistle of Mathetes to Diognetus
Ign. *Eph.*	Ignatius, *Letter to the Ephesians*
Ign. *Rom.*	Ignatius, *Letter to the Romans*
Ign. *Smyrn.*	Ignatius, *Letter to the Smyrnaeans*
Pol. *Phil.*	Polycarp, *Letter to the Philippians*
Herm. Vis.	Shepherd of Hermas, Visions
Herm. Mand.	Shepherd of Hermas, Mandate
Herm. Sim.	Shepherd of Hermas, Similitude

Church Fathers and Greek Philosophers

Arist. *Apol.*	Aristides, *Apologies*
Leg.	Athenagoras, *Legatio pro Christianis*
Res.	Athenagoras, *On the Resurrection*
Civ.	Augustine, *De civitate Dei*
Exp. Apoc.	Cassiodorus, *Exposition of the Apocalypse*
Hist. eccl.	Eusebius, *Historia ecclesiastica* (*Ecclesiastical History*)
Haer.	Irenaeus, *Adversus haereses* (*Against Heresies*)
Epid.	Irenaeus, *Epipidexis tou apostolikou kērygmatos* (*Demonstration of the Apostolic Preaching*)
Vir. ill.	Jerome, *De viris illustribus*
De Trin.	John of Damascus, *De Trinitate*
Fid. Orth.	John of Damascus, *De Fide Orthodoxa*
A.J.	Josephus, *Antiquitates judaicae*
B.J.	Josephus, *Bellum judaicum*
C. Ap.	Josephus, *Contra Apionem*
1 Apol.	Justin Martyr, *Apologia i* (*First Apology*)
2 Apol.	Justin Martyr, *Apologia ii* (*Second Apology*)
Dial.	Justin Martyr, *Dialogus cum Tryphone* (*Dialogue with Trypho*)

Mart. Pol.	Martyrdom of Polycarp
Pol. *Phil.*	Polycarp, *To the Philippians*
Res.	Methodius of Olympus, *De resurruectione*
Cels.	Origen, *Contra Celsum*
Princ.	Origen, *De principiis (Peri archōn)*
Adv. Marc.	Tertullian, *Adversus Marcionem*
Apol.	Tertullian, *Apologeticus*
Prax.	Tertullian, *Adversus Praxean*
Pud.	Tertullian, *De pudicitia*
Res.	Tertullian, *De resurrectione carnis*
Autol.	Theophilus, *Ad Autolycum* (*To Autolycus*)
Exp. Apoc.	Tyconius, *Exposition of the Apocalypse*
Comm.	Vincent, *Commonitorium*

Old and New Testament Pseudepigrapha, Deuterocanonical Books, and Nag Hammadi Tractates

Apoc. Paul	Apocalypse of Paul
Apoc. Mos.	Apocalypse of Moses (Greek Life of Adam and Eve)
As. Mos.	Assumption of Moses
2 Bar.	2 Baruch
1 En.	1 Enoch
2 En.	2 Enoch
Jub.	Jubilees
1 Macc	1 Maccabees
2 Macc	2 Maccabees
Pss. Sol.	Psalms of Solomon
Sib. Or.	Sibylline Oracles
Sir	Sirach/Ecclesiasticus
T. Ash.	Testament of Asher
T. Ben.	Testament of Benjamin
T. Dan	Testament of Dan
T. Gad	Testament of Gad
T. Iss.	Testament of Issachar
T. Jos.	Testament of Joseph
T. Jud.	Testament of Judah
T. Levi	Testament of Levi
T. Naph.	Testament of Naphtali
T. Reu.	Testament of Reuben
T. Sim.	Testament of Simeon
T. Sol.	Testament of Solomon
T. Zeb.	Testament of Zebulun
Wis	Wisdom of Solomon

Secondary Literature

ANF	*Ante-Nicene Fathers*
AUSS	*Andrews University Seminary Studies*
BASOR	*Bulletin of the American Schools of Oriental Research*
BBR	*Bulletin for Biblical Research*
BDAG	Danker, Frederick W., Walter Bauer, William F. Arndt, and F. Wilbur Gingrich. *Greek-English Lexicon of the New Testament and Other Early Christian Literature.* 3rd ed. Chicago: University of Chicago Press, 2000 (Danker-Bauer-Arndt-Gingrich)
BDB	Brown, Francis, Samuel Rolles Driver, and Charles Augustus Briggs. *Enhanced Brown-Driver-Briggs Hebrew and English Lexicon.* Oxford: Clarendon Press, 1977
Bib	*Biblica*
bRev	*Biblical Review*
bSac	*Bibliotheca Sacra*
BZAW	Beihefte zur Zeitschrift für die alttestamentliche Wissenschaft
BZNW	Beihefte zur Zeitschrift für die neutestamentliche Wissenschaft
CBQ	*Catholic Biblical Quarterly*
CH	Church History
CTJ	*Calvin Theological Journal*
ECF	Early Church Fathers
EVQ	*Evangelical Quarterly*
ETL	*Ephemerides Theologicae Lovanienses*
ExpTim	*Expository Times*
FH	*Fides et Historia*
HNT	Handbuch zum Neuen Testament
HUCA	*Hebrew Union College Annual*
HZ	*Historische Zeitschrift*
JAJ	*Journal of Ancient Judaism*
JBL	*Journal of Biblical Literature*
JBQ	*Jewish Bible Quarterly*
JETS	*Journal of the Evangelical Theological Society*
JQR	*Jewish Quarterly Review*
JSJ	*Journal for the Study of Judaism*
JSNT	*Journal for the Study of the New Testament*
JSNTSup	Journal for the Study of the New Testament Supplement Series
JSOTSup	Journal for the Study of the Old Testament Supplement Series
JTS	*Journal of Theological Studies*
L&N	Louw, Johannes P., and Eugene Albert Nida, eds. *Greek-English Lexicon of the New Testament: Based on Semantic Domains.* 2nd ed. New York: United Bible Societies, 1996
LCL	Loeb Classical Library
MAJT	*Mid-America Journal of Theology*

MSJ	*The Masters Seminary Journal*
Neot	*Neotestamentica*
NRTh	*La nouvelle revue théologique*
NovT	*Novum Testamentum*
NovTSup	Supplements to Novum Testamentum
NPNF¹	*Nicene and Post-Nicene Fathers*, Series 1
NPNF²	*Nicene and Post-Nicene Fathers*, Series 2
NTS	*New Testament Studies*
OTE	*Old Testament Essays*
PTR	*Princeton Theological Review*
RTL	*Revue théologique de Louvain*
rThom	*Revue thomiste*
SBJT	*Southern Baptist Journal of Theology*
SC	Source chrétiennes
SJT	*Scottish Journal of Theology*
SSNTMS	Society for New Testament Studies Monograph Series
SVTP	Studia in Veteris Testamenti Pseudepigraphica
TDNT	*Theological Dictionary of the New Testament.* Edited by Gerhard Kittel and Gerhard Friedrich. Translated by Geoffrey W. Bromiley. 10 vols. Grand Rapids: Eerdmans, 1964–1976
TQ	*Theologische Quartalschrift*
TrinJ	*Trinity Journal*
TUGAL	Texte und Untersuchungen zur Geschichte der altchristlichen Literatur
TynBul	*Tyndale Bulletin*
VC	*Vigiliae Christianae*
VCSup	Supplements to Vigiliae Christianae
VE	*Verbum et Ecclesia*
VoxP	*Vox Patrum*
VT	*Vetus Testamentum*
WTJ	*Westminster Theological Journal*
WUNT	Wissenschaftliche Untersuchungen zum Neuen Testament
ZAW	*Zeitschrift für die alttestamentliche Wissenschaft*
ZNW	*Zeitschrift für die neutestamentliche Wissenschaft und die Kunde der älteren Kirche*

1

Putting Eschatology (Back) in Its Place

Nothing ordinarily so repairs the soul, and makes a
person better, as a good hope of things to come.

John Chrysostom, *Homily 2 on the Statues*

For some reason, the study of eschatology tends to attract a disproportionate number of—let me be blunt—hacks and quacks. End-times hacks produce mediocre, uninformed, trite work for the purpose of self-promotion or money. They ride the end-times circuits tickling ears with sensationalistic narratives, usually resting their interpretations of Scripture on current events or far-fetched conspiracy theories. Or they flood the market with cheap paperback books with red, orange, yellow, and black covers, usually repeating the same worn-out words they used in previous editions of their end-times yarns—sometimes with updates to fit their interpretations with the latest current events.

Many of these hacks can be classified as end-times quacks. A "quack" is a person who acts as if he or she possesses training, knowledge, and credentials they never earned and do not have. Their lack of training in biblical languages, extra-biblical literature, history of interpretation, doctrinal development, and experience in theological method leads to all sorts of strange—even bizarre and dangerous—doctrines. Hacks and quacks tend to fall into the ditches of date-setting or sign-seeking. They promote outlandish theories, badly argued conclusions, and outright errors of observation and interpretation of Scripture. They contain almost no historical reflection or awareness of their own idiosyncrasies.

Once you push through the swarm of hacks and quacks, though, you reach another level of what I just call "pop eschatology." These trained scholars, pastors, or other qualified men and women write popular-level treatments of the end times—usually with a subdued sensationalist bent. They avoid date-setting and sign-seeking, but sometimes they shift into low gear and rough it through the off-roads of speculation. They might even do some "this-*could*-be-that" reasoning regarding current events. For the record, I have nothing against popular level books per se, but sometimes they tend to be campy, presenting debatable issues as dogma and giving the impression that unclear matters of eschatology in Scripture are clear and unquestioned. In short, they place an exclamation point (!) on matters that should have a period (.), a question mark (?), or even ellipses (. . .).

A step away from pop-eschatology will bring you to informative introductory texts written for college and seminary students. Several of these are presented as merely descriptive surveys of various options in eschatology, sometimes including gentle critiques and the politely held view of the author. Other times, these are written from specific perspectives that argue for a particular eschatological viewpoint, perhaps in line with the author's denominational confession. In many cases, though, these didactic and dispassionate treatments of eschatology are part of larger systematic theologies, for which eschatology is the necessary concluding locus of theology.

Then we move into the genre of eschatology in which I place this volume—the intermediate-to-advanced academic treatment. Unlike the handful of excellent handbooks on various eschatological themes for serious students, I write this book from a particular perspective. This book is thus *prescriptive*, not merely *descriptive*. I am not just giving the reader options in eschatology; I am making a case for a form of premillennial, futurist eschatology that in many cases will differ from those reading this book—sometimes at the macro level, often in the details. But as I do, I hope to rekindle interest in the serious study of eschatology, drawing people out of hackery and quackery, even if they do not fully adopt the views presented in this book.

Beyond Eschatological Agnosticism and Amnesia

Back in Bible college, I had a professor—a staunch premillennialist—who said to a class of students mostly uninterested in the subject, "I'd rather you be a convinced amillennialist than an eschatological agnostic!" Eschatological agnostics are those who (1) do not know much about eschatology, (2) do not believe that anything beyond the fundamentals of Christ's return can be affirmed with any confidence, and (3) really do not care enough about it to spend time working out the details.

Since my college days in the 1990s, it seems the number of "eschatological agnostics" has only multiplied. The days of jam-packed annual prophecy conferences in local churches appear to be over—or they are at least taking a long hiatus. Part of the cause of recent eschatological agnosticism, I believe, is a reaction to its overemphasis in previous decades. Or they want to dissociate themselves from embarrassing excesses among sign-seekers, date-setters, and other sensationalistic approaches.

However, a neglect of eschatology by churches and academic institutions has left laypeople open to deception by fringe elements of Christianity. If Christian leaders do not answer the eschatological questions of their flocks, the sheep will seek answers from websites, podcasts, and unreliable or deceptive sources. Shepherds will lose important teaching opportunities to put those questions in the context of the bigger picture of God's redemptive narrative.

Yet even those who have maintained an interest in eschatology face another problem: eschatological amnesia; that is, they have forgotten the past. I hope to help remedy this situation as I make my case for what I am calling a "contemporary Irenaean premillennial eschatology." That is, I believe Irenaeus of Lyons (writing c. AD 180) along with the earliest fathers of the church were more right than wrong in their basic eschatological expectations. I argue that their second-century eschatology is an appropriate foundation and framework for a biblically defensible, theologically balanced, and historically informed eschatology.

I wrote this book for three kinds of readers. First, I wrote for those who want to better understand an eschatological perspective based on biblical, theological, and historical foundations, regardless of whether they will ultimately embrace it. Second, I wrote for those who do not know what they believe about eschatology and are exploring various options with an attitude of grace and charity. And third, I wrote for those interested in an alternative to the hard-and-fast models of premillennialism, amillennialism, and postmillennialism; or futurism, preterism, idealism, historicism; or covenantalism, dispensationalism, new covenant theology, or something in between. By looking back to the earliest church fathers as the foundation and framework for exegetical insight and theological vision I provide a new approach to eschatology today—new to contemporary readers, that is, but ancient in its original perspective.

Perspective and Distinctives of This Eschatology

I understand this book as one voice in a much bigger dialogue on these topics—a dialogue among disputants that has been ongoing for nearly two thousand years. My contribution is not intended to be a supercilious "final word" on these matters, like a conciliar definition, authoritative decree, or confessional standard. Rather, I view this book as a response to recent contributions from various eschatological traditions—including my own—and hopefully a conversation promoter for further dialogue. To this end, I would like to point out up front several distinctives of this eschatology.

A Recovery and Priority of Classic Sources

In keeping with Irenaeus's name (which means "peace"), this book seeks to represent his eschatological tradition with an irenic rather than polemical posture. Though I engage with secondary sources from a variety of perspectives, the purpose of this eschatology is not to respond to every single possible objection or to refute every counterargument or even to address every issue. Instead, I hope to present a comprehensive (not exhaustive) treatment of an Irenaean premillennial eschatology, addressing the issues with exegetical, theological, and historical evidence and arguments.

When appropriate, I will directly dialogue with secondary sources and contemporary scholarship, but my intention is not to entertain every possible alternative interpretation. In some matters, I may direct readers to more thorough treatments that warrant deeper technical discussions while presenting the results of my own research. At other points, I may interact with a handful of representative perspectives on important topics to demonstrate the range of views. As I do so, my goal is to treat opposing views fairly. On occasion, though, I will correct aberrant views from the history of interpretation and call out perspectives that lead us in bad theological and practical directions. Irenaeus would have done (and did do) the same.

As a child of the paleo-orthodoxy movement, influenced by twentieth-century programs of *ressourcement* (a return to the sources) and particularly the renaissance of Protestant patristic scholarship, my integrative theological method will involve a recovery and reincorporation of classic sources for the constructive study of eschatology.[1] Though I will interact with modern commentaries and theologies as well as Reformation- and post-Reformation-era contributions, I will primarily engage with ancient patristic as well as medieval sources in grappling with eschatological issues. This will be especially important when establishing the boundaries of explicit orthodox eschatology—that which has been believed everywhere, always, and by all. Admittedly, the explicit affirmations necessary for an orthodox eschatology are few and almost always noncontroversial.

Beyond mere orthodoxy, however, I frequently refer to classic sources to demonstrate that a particular interpretation or perspective is not without historical precedent or even pedigree. At times, an ignorance of the history of biblical interpretation and the development of doctrine has led Christians to level hasty charges of "novelty," "heterodoxy," or even "heresy" against views that were sometimes merely regarded as "peculiar"—at other times, even seen as "acceptable" or "common." Thus understanding the actual history of the diversity of permissible opinions within historic mainstream Christianity will reveal the contemporary options in eschatology.

Additionally, I will at times place special weight on a discernible early, widespread position within mainstream Christianity—that is, between about AD 50 and 200—as a means of shining light on the probable apostolic teaching concerning a particular issue. This priority for the most ancient, first- to second-generation sources is driven by the theological conviction and methodological presupposition that the original apostolic-prophetic teaching on a matter is authoritative, even if later eras of church history saw the dominance of different views. Through the lens of history, I hope to maintain a broad "catholicity" regarding the essential dogmas of orthodox eschatology while striving to retrieve an original "apostolicity" within its details.

A Dialogical and Integrative Theological Method

As a conservative Protestant theologian, the beginning and center point of my theological method is the canon of the Old and New Testaments as the inspired standard for all matters of faith and practice. My approach to asking and answering interpretive and theological questions, however, involves a dialogue with numerous resources. This dialogical approach means:

- *Reading Scripture in its original Hebrew, Aramaic, or Greek languages.* Many of the arguments presented in this book depend on original language vocabulary, grammar, and syntax. I do not assume all readers will have knowledge of these biblical languages, but as an intermediate-to-advanced eschatology, I will be interacting with original languages as necessary.

---

1. *Ressourcement* in eschatology has only just begun. In 2000, in the context of modern eschatological urgency and awareness, Hort urged, "Ce contexte exige donc des théologiens qu'ils procèdent à un profond ressourcement de leur discours eschatologique." Bernard Hort, "Millénarisme ou amillénarisme? Regard contemporain sur un conflit traditionnel," *RL* 31 (2000): 34.

- *Reading Scripture in light of its earliest historical-cultural-theological context.* My basic approach to biblical interpretation is to read the Bible the way it was meant to be read. This means understanding words, phrases, and concepts in their original historical sense. This also acknowledges the fact that the original authors and readers had a theological context within which their words were to be understood, and we should keep that theological context in mind while reading these texts.

- *Reading Scripture with the methodological presupposition that it is true in all it affirms and therefore does not contradict itself.* This study assumes the classic Christian view of Scripture, as confessed in the creed, that the Holy Spirit "spoke through the prophets," and that all Scripture is "God-breathed" (2 Tim 3:16). Thus Scripture is assumed to be true, the *norma normans non normata*—that Scripture is its own infallible interpreter as we read Scripture in light of Scripture.

- *Reading the whole of Scripture in light of its parts and its parts in light of the whole.* Because Scripture is true in all it affirms, individual passages must be understood in light of the larger canonical narrative. Also, this narrative must be true to these parts. Pitting one part of Scripture against another—or pitting the whole against the parts—is not acceptable.

- *Reading Scripture in light of the trinitarian creation-fall-redemption narrative centered on the person and work of Christ in his first and second comings.* Jesus Christ is the center of my theology and thus the center of the "big picture" of Scripture. Both the Old and New Testaments point to Christ's person and work in his first and second advents.

- *Reading Scripture in dialogue with the pastors and teachers of the church who have gone before.* The Spirit of God not only gave "apostles and prophets" to the church for its edification, but also "evangelists, pastors, and teachers" (Eph 4:11–16). Thus to neglect the historical contributions beyond the foundational inspired texts would be to neglect a good gift from God. Though an individual insight or even a corporate consensus are not regarded as binding or infallible, they should be considered and consulted in our own engagement with the sense of Scripture.

- *Reading Scripture with a view toward its redemptive and life-changing purpose.* Paul tells us that inspired Scripture was given not only to instruct us for salvation through faith in Christ (2 Tim 3:15) but also to equip us with all we need to accomplish "every good work" (3:16–17).

As I navigate various eschatological issues, my integrative method encourages me to discern a kind of "convergence" of evidence. That is, I will demonstrate, where possible, the intersection of exegetical, historical, theological, philosophical, and practical considerations. When these lines of evidence and arguments point in the same direction, I will regard the conclusions to be stronger than when only one or two arguments affirm a position, or if the various considerations seem to point in several plausible directions.

Simply put, beginning with the basic eschatology of Irenaeus of Lyons (ca. AD 180), this book revisits several of its features in light of eighteen hundred years of developments and debates. The result is a fresh defense of Irenaeus's foundation and framework, with a modification of some of its details in light of further reflection. Thus my treatment begins with an assumption that Irenaeus and his second-to third-century colleagues represented an early, widespread, and well-developed eschatology inherited from "the elders"—those who had been close associates of the apostles. I then explore some of the features of that early eschatology, clarifying obscure points, strengthening some elements, and correcting a few missteps.

Unfortunately, in the history of doctrinal development, the promising Irenaean tradition of eschatology was disinherited in its adolescence, replaced by eschatological narratives that fit better the new situation of Christendom and its long, fifteen-hundred-year dominance in the church. This book, then, is in many ways a retrieval of that early Irenaean eschatology—a return from exile of that dispossessed and disenfranchised heir apparent of apostolic teaching. That theology has, of course, grown more mature through the centuries, but its development has been slow. At times, it has developed some unseemly disfigurements that must be addressed in light of later reflection.

The Irenaean Foundation and Framework

In 1900, the German engineer and automobile maker, Ferdinand Porsche—yes, *that* Porsche—designed the first hybrid car consisting of an internal combustion engine that generated power to drive four electric wheels. And just two years before that, in 1898, he had contributed to the design of an all-electric motor vehicle while working for a company in Vienna. For almost a century, those electric and hybrid vehicles, the Egger-Lohner C.2 Phaeton (1898) and the Semper Vivus or Lohner-Porsche Mixte (1900)—along with a handful of similar siblings by turn-of-the-century designers—were little more than relics from a forsaken past. For most of the twentieth century, manufacturers focused on the internal combustion engine, fueled by gasoline. Only in the latter part of the twentieth century did engineers pick up serious research and design on hybrid and all-electric vehicles.

Occasionally, manufacturers look back to the early history of vehicles for inspiration. In fact, in the early 1970s, the designers of NASA's Lunar Roving Vehicle (LRV) or "moon buggy" drew inspiration directly from the all-electric design of the Lohner-Porsche. Today, the enthusiastic return to hybrid and all-electric vehicles suggests that it looks like civilization took a wrong technological turn in 1900. What if instead of shifting attention to the gas-burning motors of most of the past hundred years, our brightest engineers had developed hybrid and electric technology? One wonders what kind of world we would live in today had Porsche's original all-electric or even hybrid model remained the foundation upon which all twentieth-century automobiles were developed. Battery technology alone would be a century ahead of where it is today.

About seventeen hundred years before Porsche, in the late second century, Irenaeus of Lyons presented to the Christian church of his day a compelling vision of the future. It served as a fitting climax to his trinitarian creation-fall-redemption narrative centered on Christ's person and work in his first and second coming. It provided a powerful rebuke against over-spiritualizing heretics who had denied or downplayed bodily resurrection and the redemption of the physical world, false teachers who had reduced the Christian hope to a post-death heavenly home-going. In his day, Irenaeus instructed orthodox Christians in a well-developed eschatological narrative that incorporated both Scripture and the teachings handed down to him from his own teachers—the disciples of the original apostles. At the same time, he left many details unaddressed and several questions unanswered.

By the third century, influential voices in the church with a more "spiritual" understanding of the Christian hope had put Irenaeus's eschatology on the defensive. And by the fourth and fifth centuries, the church catholic—both East and West—all but forgot the dramatic, striking image of earthly redemption contained in Irenaeus's account of the coming of Christ as judge and king. For over a thousand years, the church's thinkers—bishops, monks, professors, reformers, and preachers—built on an eschatological foundation and framework quite different from that of Irenaeus's second-century model.

> **Go Deeper Excursus 1**
>
> *Who Was Irenaeus of Lyons and Why Does He Matter?*

In those ensuing centuries, Irenaeus's eschatological edifice was not so much refuted as it was abandoned. We find no later church father or medieval theologian who dismantles his evidence and arguments piece by piece or demolishes it with a dynamite argument. Instead, those laborers simply focused their attention on a different structure built on another foundation, while either ignoring, shrugging off, or even ridiculing the ideas of Irenaeus and his premillennial forerunners, colleagues, and descendants. One wonders, then, what eschatology would look like today had the church's thinkers given their attention to developing Irenaeus's eschatology further—filling in the framework, answering questions, and resolving problems.

Like the modern engineers who returned to Porsche's idea of all-electric and hybrid vehicles, this book returns to the foundation and framework of Irenaeus's eschatology. Because Irenaeus himself did not work out every detail or solve every problem, this book will not simply parrot his positions uncritically. Rather, his positions on eschatological questions will serve often as our starting point and sometimes as our point of departure.

Irenaeus of Lyons was born about AD 130 and likely raised in Smyrna, western Asia Minor (modern-day Turkey).[2] At the time, Polycarp, a disciple of the apostle John, was bishop of Smyrna. In fact, as a child, Irenaeus had been a "hearer" of the esteemed Polycarp (Eusebius *Hist. eccl.* 5.20.5). Irenaeus was certainly in a unique historical position to have known and conversed with students of the original disciples of Jesus. Throughout his writings, Irenaeus leans on the insights of those teachers for his own theological reflection.

---

2. Paul Parvis, "Who Was Irenaeus? An Introduction to the Man and His Work," in *Irenaeus: Life, Scripture, Legacy*, ed. Sara Parvis and Paul Parvis (Minneapolis: Fortress, 2012), 14–15.

Irenaeus's eschatological vision includes many details, which we will explore and fill out in due course. However, we will see that his eschatological perspective may be described as premillennial and futurist, as he believed in a seven-year tribulation period at the end of the age, climaxing in the return of Christ as king, the resurrection of the righteous as well as a remnant of mortal survivors of the antichrist's reign left to repopulate the earth, followed by a thousand-year intermediate kingdom, and concluding with the resurrection of the wicked and ushering in of the eternal renewed creation. Though he claimed to have received this foundation and structure of his eschatology from his previous generation—the students of the apostles—this eschatology took different paths after the second century.

A Brief History of Eschatological Developments[3]

From the beginning, Christian perspectives on details surrounding the second coming of Christ have been in flux. This fact alone should cause us to take a deep breath before we plunge into its depths. And it should also keep us from hurling charges of heresy or false teaching at people who hold positions different from us— because it is very likely the position we hold ourselves was once a minority view or arose from eschatological speculation sometime after the apostolic period. While Christians have agreed on foundational doctrines like the future return of Christ, the resurrection, and the restoration of all things (see chapter 3), if there ever was a universal consensus on the *details* of eschatology, it was short-lived. Although a thoroughgoing account of important developments in eschatological expectations throughout Christian history is impossible, let me present a general survey of some of the chief heads of debate to serve as a backdrop for a much more detailed discussion of the topics in the following pages.

The Patristic Period (100–500)

In the period immediately following the age of the apostles (AD 30–100), the early church continued to anticipate the soon return of Jesus Christ. The persecutions they experienced at the hands of pagan, Roman, and Jewish opponents and critics represented for them the birth pangs of the end times. By persevering through these earthly trials, the faithful saints could expect to be rewarded in the coming kingdom (see Did. 16.3–8, c. AD 50–70).

Along with this expectation of the soon return of Christ as judge and king, many early Christians understood the prediction of the thousand-year reign of Christ on earth in Revelation 20 as a future earthly period that would follow Christ's return and the resurrection of the righteous (premillennialism). In the second century, however, orthodox Christians also explored different interpretations of the

3. This historical overview of eschatology is adapted, with gracious permission from the publisher, from my own treatment of the same in Michael J. Svigel, "The End Times in Retrospect," in *Exploring Christian Theology*, vol. 3, *Church, Spiritual Growth, and the End Times*, ed. Nathan D. Holsteen and Michael J. Svigel (Minneapolis: Bethany House, 2014), 180–91.

details of the end times, including a less literal interpretation of the millennium (amillennialism).

In any case, early Christians expected a literal bodily resurrection of the dead. Just as Jesus Christ's body had been miraculously restored to life, gloriously transformed, and rendered immortal, Christians can also look forward to a day when their own bodies will be raised, restored, and glorified. Numerous early Christian apologists defended the doctrine of the resurrection against scoffers and critics, sometimes in whole treatises dedicated to the hope of resurrection.

Without abandoning the central expectation of the literal return of Christ, a real bodily resurrection, and the future judgment of the world, many Christians' earlier expectations of a thousand-year earthly kingdom waned over the centuries. By the fourth century, this anticipation of a millennium gave way to a widespread belief that Christ's kingdom had in some sense already commenced at Christ's ascension. Perhaps, some thought, the church itself was fulfilling kingdom prophecies and promises. Maybe the victory of the gospel over paganism and the conversion of the emperor to Christianity indicated that the expectations of the kingdom of God were being realized in current history between the ascension of Christ and his future return.[4]

The Medieval Period (500–1500)

If you were a medieval peasant eking out a living through constant labor, your eschatological expectations might be as simple as your daily life. An antichrist would one day appear, perhaps as the head of an army of Arabs or Turks or maybe an apostate emperor or king.[5] Nevertheless, Jesus would ultimately return as judge to destroy the wicked, raise the dead, and hold everybody accountable for their thoughts and deeds. Of course, many believed they were at the brink of meeting their maker at any moment through physical death. In such a context, personal eschatology—what happens to us when we die—seemed more relevant than what might or might not happen to the world leading up to Christ's second coming.

Official church doctrine emphasized the classic content of the creed—that is, "the resurrection of the dead and the life of the world to come."[6] Bodily resurrection continued to be maintained. Anselm of Canterbury (1033–1109) reasoned that "human nature was created in order that hereafter the whole man, body and soul, should enjoy a blessed immortality."[7] Coupled with this expectation of a resurrection into an immortal life was an enduring expectation of a renewed creation.[8] Yet,

---

4. See J. N. D. Kelly, *Early Christian Doctrines*, rev. ed. (New York: HarperCollins, 1978), 459–89.

5. See Adriaan H. Bredero, *Christendom and Christianity in the Middle Ages: The Relations between Religion, Church, and Society*, trans. Reinder Bruinsma (Grand Rapids: Eerdmans, 1994), 97–98.

6. *The Constantinopolitan Creed* (381).

7. Anselm of Canterbury, *Why God Became Man*, preface in Eugene R. Fairweather, ed. and trans., *A Scholastic Miscellany: Anselm to Ockham*, The Library of Christian Classics, ed. John Baillie, John T. McNeill, and Henry P. Van Dusen (Louisville: Westminster John Knox, 1956), 100.

8. Anselm, *Why God Became Man* 1.18, Fairweather, *Scholastic Miscellany*, 130.

increasingly, the idea of the "world to come"—that is, the breaking in of another world into this one—was replaced by the idea of each individual departing this world at death and "going to" another world. Hugh of St. Victor (1097–1141) taught that there were five places in the universe created by God: "Heaven is the highest place; after heaven, paradise; after paradise, the world; after the world, the purgatorial fire; and after purgatory, hell."[9]

Many in the patristic period expected that believers' glorification, heavenly ascent, and blessedness in the presence of God awaited the future resurrection and renewal of the world.[10] In the medieval period, however, this idea was displaced by many who taught that the "saints"—apostles, martyrs, and other more "perfect" Christians—were admitted into the highest heaven immediately rather than having to await resurrection and final judgment.[11]

Though it never seemed to completely die out, the belief in a literal earthly millennial reign of Christ held by many teachers of the earliest centuries was for the most part pushed into the shadows of medieval Christianity.[12] Most medieval theologians followed the teachings of Augustine that "the thousand-year rule of the saints as the period of the church's present existence on earth, from its founding until judgment day."[13]

As both the church and society in Western Europe deteriorated in the late medieval period (1200–1500), apocalyptic expectations took on darker and more radical forms. Around the year 1200, an Italian monk named Joachim of Fiore divided history into three distinct "ages" or "dispensations":

THE AGE OF THE FATHER:	THE OLD TESTAMENT (RULE OF ISRAEL)
THE AGE OF THE SON:	THE NEW TESTAMENT (RULE OF THE CHURCH)
THE AGE OF THE SPIRIT:	THE NEW AGE (RULE OF THE RIGHTEOUS)

Joachim predicted that the "Third Age" would begin in the year 1260. Although no epochal event occurred in 1260 that could be identified as a fulfillment of this calculation of the end, a sect known as the Fraticelli (Italian for "Little Brethren") or Spiritual Franciscans regarded themselves as the fulfillment of these predictions.

---

9. Hugh of St. Victor, *On the Sacraments of the Christian Faith* 1.8.2, Fairweather, *Scholastic Miscellany*, 302.

10. Louis Berkhof, *The History of Christian Doctrines* (Carlisle, PA: Banner of Truth Trust, 1969), 259–60.

11. Jaroslav Pelikan, *The Christian Tradition: A History of the Development of Doctrine*, vol. 3, *The Growth of Medieval Theology (600–1300)* (Chicago: University of Chicago Press, 1978), 33 34.

12. Cf. Berkhof, *History of Christian Doctrine*, 263; Pelikan, *The Christian Tradition*, 3:43.

13. Bredero, *Christianity and Christendom*, 97.

In fact, when certain popes challenged the claims of the Spiritual Franciscans, con-demning them as false teachers, they responded by labeling their papal opponents "antichrists."[14] This labeling of the reigning pope as antichrist would be repeated throughout the late middle ages by such forerunners of the Reformation as John Wycliffe and John Hus.[15]

The Protestant Period (1500–1700)

The anxiety many felt in the waning years of the medieval period (1300 to 1500) erupted into outright warfare in the sixteenth century. Roman Catholic dogmas that had been rarely challenged in the past were now open to reconsideration. At-tempts to wind the church back to an earlier age of purity affected numerous areas of theology, even eschatology.

Most of the mainline Reformers like Martin Luther, Ulrich Zwingli, and John Calvin maintained the medieval church's amillennial perspective as well as the expectation of the coming of Christ to judge the world.[16] These Reformers explic-itly rejected the idea of an earthly millennium preceding the Day of Judgment—a rejection expressed in the Lutheran Augsburg Confession of 1530: "They condemn others also, who now scatter Jewish opinions, that, before the resurrection of the dead, the godly shall occupy the kingdom of the world, the wicked being every-where suppressed."[17] Similarly, the Reformed Second Helvetic Confession of 1566 condemned "Jewish dreams that there will be a golden age on earth before the Day of Judgment, and that the pious, having subdued all their godless enemies, will possess all the kingdoms of the earth."[18]

At the same time, however, many of these Protestant leaders saw events of their own day as fulfillments of end-times prophecies. In fact, so tumultuous and wide-spread were the events of the Reformation that many saw them as clear signs of the soon return of Christ.[19] Thus Martin Luther believed the pope was the antichrist,[20] and in 1520, he outlined the false doctrines and practices of the Roman Catho-lic Church under the papacy.[21] Though John Calvin allowed that true churches

---

14. See Timothy George, *Theology of the Reformers* (Nashville: Broadman & Holman, 1988), 37–38.

15. Jaroslav Pelikan, *The Christian Tradition: A History of the Development of Doctrine*, vol. 4, *Reformation of Church and Dogma (1300–1700)* (Chicago: University of Chicago Press, 1983), 109.

16. Berkhof, *History of Christian Doctrines*, 263, 268.

17. Philip Schaff, ed., *The Creeds of Christendom with A History and Critical Notes*, vol. 3, *The Evangelical Protestant Creeds, with Translations*, 4th ed., Bibliotheca Symbolica Eccle-siae Universalis (New York: Harper & Brothers, 1877; repr., Grand Rapids: Baker, 1977), 18.

18. See Schaff, *Creeds of Christendom*, 3:257.

19. C. Arnold Snyder, *Anabaptist History and Theology*, rev. student ed. (Kitchener, On-tario: Pandora, 1997), 154.

20. Bernard McGinn, *Antichrist: Two Thousand Years of the Human Fascination with Evil* (San Francisco: HarperCollins, 1994), 202–3.

21. Martin Luther, *To the Christian Nobility of the German Nation Respecting the Ref-ormation of the Christian Estate*, 3.23, in Henry Wace and C. A. Buchheim, eds. and trans.,

continued to exist within the dominion of the Roman Catholic Church, like Luther and other Reformers he, too, regarded the papacy as an institution of the antichrist.[22]

After the dust settled following the violent and tumultuous early days of the Reformation, the rhetoric also died down, leaving only one important element of medieval eschatology greatly affected: the Roman Catholic doctrine of purgatory didn't survive the purifying flames of Reformation.[23] Besides that element of Roman Catholic personal eschatology, the general contours of medieval eschatology remained intact: the return of Christ as judge of the living and the dead, the resurrection of the body on Judgment Day, the reward of eternal life for the righteous, and the punishment of eternal hell for the wicked. These views became settled and dogmatized in the various Protestant denominational confessions of faith and continue to prevail in these traditions to the present day.

While mainline "magisterial" Reformers like Luther, Zwingli, and Calvin tended to hold similar conventional amillennial views, early in the sixteenth century, a number of politically and doctrinally radical preachers sparked controversy and conflict with a militant form of millennialism. Anabaptists such as Melchior Hoffman and self-proclaimed prophets such as Jan Matthys insisted that end-times prophecies were being fulfilled before their eyes and that they had been entrusted to establish the millennial kingdom on earth—through force, if necessary.[24] Their utopian millennial dreams, however, ended as apocalyptic nightmares. The tragic events of the city of Münster, Germany, in the 1530s serve as an example of just how out of control their twisted eschatology could get. After one Jan Beukelsz took control of the city in 1534, he attempted to institute a polygamous society governed by twelve apostle-like elders, declaring himself the end-times "King of Righteousness," intending to reign over the millennial kingdom from Münster. Within a year, he and his co-regents were captured or killed, putting an end to extreme millennial madness among radical reformers.

In the calm after the storm of Reformation, many level-headed Protestants in the sixteenth and seventeenth centuries continued to reexamine the doctrine of the end times in light of Scripture, history, and, yes, current events. Some of these Presbyterians, Lutherans, Congregationalists, and Anglicans began to entertain a postmillennial view of eschatology, envisioning a spiritual golden age of Christianity that would result in universal peace and righteousness prior to a final rebellion and the return of Christ. This was likely the predominant view of Puritan leaders like John Owen,[25] influencing the religious, social, and political thinking of Colonial America in the eighteenth century. Kenneth Newport notes that the "vast

---

First Principles of the Reformation or the Ninety-Five Theses and the Three Primary Works of Dr. Martin Luther (London: Murray, 1883), 73.

22. John Calvin, *Institutes of the Christian Religion* 4.2.12, trans. Henry Beveridge, 2 vols. in 1 (Grand Rapids: Eerdmans, 1989), 2:313–14.

23. *Thirty-Nine Articles* 22, in Schaff, *Creeds of Christendom*, 3:501.

24. Crawford Gribben, *Evangelical Millennialism in the Trans-Atlantic World, 1500–2000* (New York: Palgrave Macmillan, 2011), 20–22.

25. See Gary L. Nebeker, "John Nelson Darby and Trinity College, Dublin: A Study in Eschatological Contrasts," *FH* 34.2 (2002): 94.

majority" of seventeenth-century Protestants were postmillennial—that is, "that the literal return of Jesus to the earth will begin only after the 1,000 years during which the spiritual kingdom of Christ will advance."[26]

The Modern Period (1700–Present)

In the modern period, the critical attitude toward traditional beliefs and practices brought on by the Enlightenment affected core doctrines of the faith, including the Trinity, the incarnation and virgin birth, and the resurrection of Christ. The new liberal theologians and critical biblical scholars reduced the Christian faith to an ethical philosophy centered mostly on Jesus' moral teaching about brotherly love and social justice. Such a reformulation (not reformation) of the Christian faith and message gave little room to classic doctrines like the return of Christ, the resurrection of the body, or even eternal life. The late-eighteenth-century liberal theologian, David Friedrich Strauss, gave voice to the abandonment of eschatology this way: "Our superior scientific knowledge renders us but a poor service in demonstrating the simple preposterousness of such a conception."[27] Even those Christian thinkers who retained some vestiges of a Judgment Day regarded the concept of "hell" to smack of superstition, a view no longer tolerable to the sophisticated and scientific mind.[28]

In other liberal circles, the spiritual postmillennialism of the seventeenth and eighteenth centuries—manifested especially among New England Puritan theologians—underwent a transformation.[29] With the increase in secularism, the Christ-centered spiritual and moral dimensions of the achievable millennium gave way to a social and political hope of global social and economic transformation.[30] For example, Walter Rauschenbusch (1861–1918) attempted to reinterpret classic Christian eschatology in light of his Social Gospel: "The social gospel seeks to develop the vision of the Church toward the future and to co-operate with the will of God which is shaping the destinies of humanity. It would be aided and reinforced by a modern and truly Christian conception about the future of mankind. At present no other theological influence so hampers and obstructs the social as that of eschatology."[31] In Rauschenbusch's mind, a premillennial view of eschatology that expects Jesus himself to step into history and usher in the kingdom of God apart from human effort stands as an obstacle to true progress in the world.[32]

---

26. Kenneth G. C. Newport, *Apocalypse and Millennium: Studies in Biblical Eisegesis* (Cambridge: Cambridge University Press, 2000), 40.

27. David Friedrich Strauss, *The Old Faith and the New: A Confession*, 2nd English ed., trans. from the 6th German ed. by Mathilde Blind (London: Asher, 1873), 36.

28. Cf. Alister E. McGrath, *Christian Theology: An Introduction* (Oxford: Blackwell, 1994), 469.

29. See Berkhof, *History of Christian Doctrines*, 264.

30. McGrath, *Christian Theology*, 469.

31. Walter Rauschenbusch, *A Theology for the Social Gospel* (New York: Macmillan, 1922), 210.

32. Rauschenbusch, *Theology for the Social Gospel*, 224.

While people living in the 1800s might interpret the amazing advances in science, psychology, and technology as a sign that the world would only get better and better, that optimism in humanity's progress would suffer in the twentieth century. A man or woman born in 1900 might live to witness a number of shocking events that would first dampen and then destroy these hopes: World War I, the Great Depression, Fascist and Communist ideologies, World War II, the Holocaust, the atomic bomb, environmental disasters, economic crises, global terrorism, energy shortages, world hunger, incurable diseases, and population explosion.

The optimism and hope that fueled liberal theology's confidence in human achievement gave way to pessimism and despair, which fueled a new kind of expectation about the future. In the late 1800s and early 1900s, a movement known as "dispensationalism" emphasized a futurist premillennial eschatology. Soon, they believed, the tribulation would commence, during which the antichrist would establish a worldwide empire that would only be destroyed by the second coming of Christ.

A renewed emphasis on the end times throughout the nineteenth and twentieth centuries often led students of the Bible to seek signs of the end in current events and sometimes to speculate about the date of Christ's return. The interest in end-times prophecy, fueled by the radical changes in global politics, culture, and religion, led to the publication of countless books on prophecy, the founding of numerous ministries promoting eschatological viewpoints, and the increase in evangelistic and missionary efforts to win as many to Christ as possible before his return.

The sometimes fanatical obsession with the end times often led more traditional Protestants, who held an amillennial or postmillennial perspective, to respond negatively to the popular premillennial excitement. The result was increasing disunity among churches, pastors, theologians, and Christians over the details of end-times events and the practical implications with regard to the church's role in society. Should Christians continue to work at progressively improving society to bring about lasting peace and justice in the world, as some postmillennialists and amillennialists taught? Or should they focus on saving as many souls as possible prior to the inevitable coming of the time of tragic judgment of the earth, as the premillennialists proclaimed? Such differences in eschatology among evangelicals continue to the present day.

2

THE DRAMA OF CREATION, FALL, AND REDEMPTION

This, beloved, is the preaching of the truth, and this is the manner of our redemption, and this is the way of life, which the prophets proclaimed.

Irenaeus, *Demonstration* 98

Eschatology begins not in the Bible's final pages, but in its first. Like Beethoven's rousing Ninth Symphony, God's work of creation begins with a boom, builds with intensity, and reaches a majestic finale that summons all creation to its feet in uproarious applause. The overarching structure of the score is the trinitarian creation-fall-redemption narrative centered on the person and work of Jesus Christ in his first and second comings.

In the early stages of the narrative, the future movements are anticipated, sometimes foreshadowed. As the story unfolds, the narrative often looks back at the themes of creation, rebellion, exile, and promise—all the while looking forward to the ultimate restoration. Toward the end of the narrative, Scripture looks back at the beginning, rehearsing the episodes of creation, fall, and the work of redemption like nagging questions that finally receive their long-hoped-for answers.

Though this story of creation, fall, and redemption has been variously articulated throughout history, all variations recount the same major movements, directed by the same Triune God, centered on the same incarnate Savior. In the following chapter, I set forth a rendition of the story familiar to many, but with some additional insights from the second-century fathers. This classic recounting of the story provides the context that helps us understand God's future acts of ultimate redemption and restoration.

God's Unaltered and Undeterred Plan for Creation

God does not have a "Plan B." God's plan and purpose for all creation in general—and for humanity in particular—anticipated the rebellion and resulting descent into corruption. The fact that God has no "Plan B" has an important methodological implication: we can better understand the beginning of the story in light of its ultimate end, and we can understand the end of the story in light of its beginning. As we open the pages of Genesis and look at what God was doing with humanity and the initial created order, we can fill in some gaps by looking far ahead at what

God will do ultimately through renewed humanity and the restored creation. The account of the creation of the world and of humanity introduces God's plan: the fulfillment of the *imago Dei* mission. In the eschaton, then, we will see the ultimate fulfillment of this plan.

Whatever one decides regarding the chronology and details of the first chapter of Genesis, one thing is clear: God was in the process of "forming and filling" the previously "formless and empty (תהו ובהו)" world. After forming the world by separating day, night, sky, land, and sea (Gen 1:1–10), God began filling these with sun, moon, stars, birds, fish, and animals (Gen 1:11–25). One may be tempted to conclude that Genesis 1 presents the work of forming and filling as a *fait accompli*, but we discover that while God may rest from his work (Gen 1:31), he actually handed off the responsibility to continue the unfinished work of forming and filling to the crowning work of his creation—humanity. In short, while God began the process of taking the world from a formless and empty condition to its formed and filled intention, work still needed to be done.

Thus God created human beings with a capacity and calling to further his plan of ongoing forming and filling: "Then God said, 'Let us make humans in our image, according to our likeness, and let them have dominion over the fish of the sea and over the birds of the air and over the cattle and over all the wild animals of the earth and over every creeping thing that creeps upon the earth'" (Gen 1:26). With the creation of humanity came a provision of blessing as well as a mission: "God blessed them, and God said to them, 'Be fruitful and multiply and fill the earth and subdue it and have dominion over the fish of the sea and over the birds of the air and over every living thing that moves upon the earth'" (Gen 1:28).

Over the centuries, much debate has centered on what it means that God created humanity in the image of God, according to his likeness—the *imago Dei*.[1] Some have tied it to humanity's rational, moral, or religious capacities—that is, linking the *imago Dei* to human nature that distinguishes them from all other beings: animal or angelic (the structural view).[2] Others explain the image as somehow reflecting their personal relationships (the relational view). Without denying some element of truth to these, the best approach that fits the context of Genesis 1 understands the *imago Dei* in terms of function: humans created with the capacity and the calling to exercise dominion and authority under the supreme authority of God (Ps 8:6).[3]

Jewish commentator, Nahum Sarna, writes, "The characterization of man as 'in the image of God' furnishes the added dimension of his being the symbol of God's presence on earth. While he is not divine, his very existence bears witness to

---

1. See a survey and evaluation of various views in Marc Cortez, *Theological Anthropology: A Guide for the Perplexed* (London: T&T Clark, 2010), 14–40. Erickson summarizes the various views into three categories: substantive, rational, and functional. See Millard J. Erickson, *Christian Theology*, 3rd ed. (Grand Rapids: Baker Academic, 2013), 460–67.

2. Douglas Redford, *The Pentateuch*, vol. 1, Standard Reference Library: Old Testament (Cincinnati: Standard, 2008), 17.

3. See especially a helpful excursus on the meaning of "image of God" in Kenneth A. Mathews, *Genesis 1–11: An Exegetical and Theological Exposition of Holy Scripture*, New American Commentary, vol. 1a (Nashville: Holman Reference, 1996), 164–72. Cf. Eugene F. Roop, *Genesis*, Believers Church Bible Commentary (Scottdale, PA: Herald, 1987), 31.

the activity of God in the life of the world."[4] Humans were created, as it were, to be God's "right-hand man." In the overarching purpose of progressively transforming "formless and empty" to "formed and filled," God intended for humanity to fully realize that work by his power and through his provision; thus the need to be "blessed" to accomplish it (Gen 1:28).[5]

What would have occurred had Adam and Eve done what they had been tasked to do as God's imagers? What was the "*imago Dei* mission"? Adam and Eve were given a chain of commands, each dependent on the preceding.[6] They were to be fruitful, multiply, fill the earth, subdue it, and have dominion over all the world. The ultimate purpose was—and thus still is—for humans to "have dominion," the purpose for which they were created according to God's image (Gen 1:26–27). To accomplish this required a multitude of humans spread across the face of the earth. To "be fruitful and multiply and fill the earth (פרו ורבו ומלאו את־הארץ)" is straightforward. It relates to the *imago Dei* mission to carry on God's creation plan to continue to fill the earth, and it requires humans to procreate. Sexual reproduction, therefore, had always been part of God's plan for humanity.[7]

The command to "subdue" the earth, however, presents an interesting question. The verb "to subdue (כבש)" means "to subjugate."[8] It occurs fourteen times in the Old Testament, always in contexts in which some condition or enemy is brought under subjection by force. It refers to conquering enemies, thereby subduing a land or nation (Num 32:22, 29; Josh 18:1; 2 Sam 8:11; 1 Chr 22:18; Zech 9:15), to humans capturing and subjecting others to slavery or violence (Jer 34:11, 16; 2 Chr 28:10; Esth 7:8; Neh 5:5 [2x]), and to conquering sin (Mic 7:19). The Septuagint's translation of כבש, κατακυριεύω ("to exercise lordship over"), is a bit too restrained in its interpretation of the term. Kidner rather suggests "that there was a state of travail in nature from the first, which man was empowered to 'subdue' (1:28) (perhaps little by little as he spread abroad to 'fill the earth'). . . . The ordering influence of *the* Man,

---

4. Nahum M. Sarna, *Genesis*, The JPS Torah Commentary (Philadelphia: Jewish Publication Society, 1989), 12. Cf. Ian Hart, "Genesis 1:1–2:3 as a Prologue to the Book of Genesis," *TynBul* 46.2 (1995): 322; R. Kent Hughes, *Genesis: Beginning and Blessing*, Preaching the Word (Wheaton, IL: Crossway, 2004), 37.

5. On the nature of the blessing, see Paul Krüger and Matthew Haynes, "Creation Rest: Genesis 2:1–3 and the First Creation Account," *OTE* 30.3 (2017): 677.

6. It seems to me that Sailhamer's assertion that "the imperatives 'Be fruitful,' 'increase,' and 'fill' should not be understood as commands here, since the introductory statement identifies them as a 'blessing'" depends on a false dichotomy. John H. Sailhamer, "Genesis," in *The Expositor's Bible Commentary: Genesis–Leviticus*, ed. Tremper Longman III and David E. Garland, vol. 1, rev. ed. (Grand Rapids: Zondervan, 2008), 71. The invitation of humanity into the outworking of God's plan of ordering and filling—requiring obedient action—is itself a blessing; and the ability to carry out the work requires the provision and blessing of God. Kidner provides a proper balance: "To bless is to bestow not only a gift but a function." Derek Kidner, *Genesis: An Introduction and Commentary*, vol. 1, Tyndale Old Testament Commentaries (Downers Grove: InterVarsity, 1967), 56.

7. Paul J. Kissling, *Genesis*, The College Press NIV Commentary (Joplin, MO: College Press, 2004), 130–31.

8. Ludwig Koehler et al., *The Hebrew and Aramaic Lexicon of the Old Testament* (Leiden: Brill, 1994–2000), 460.

Christ Jesus, shows what was its full potential, one day to be realized everywhere and for ever (Rom. 8:19)."[9]

That the mission of humanity was to progressively order and fill creation, thus subduing it, seems evident upon a careful reading of the text. But the question of the actual condition of the world, which Kidner describes as in "a state of travail . . . from the first" may be overstated. We are simply not told in Genesis 1–3 what the actual condition of the world outside paradise was. God pronounced it as "very good (טוב מאד)" (Gen 1:31), yet this language cannot bear the weight of "perfect"— that is, beyond the capacity for improvement.[10]

Thus, while Genesis 1 presents a "good" picture of God's original work of creation, we must understand it as "good" in the sense of a builder who has established a strong foundation and framing but still requires additional labor to bring it to completion. "Good," even "very good," is not yet "best." The "good" physical creation was in a "raw" condition that required the work of humanity to "subdue it." What does this subduing mean and how would it be accomplished? While some may imagine a world in travail that requires a kind of initial redemption, I believe it is preferable to imagine a "good" world requiring a glorification to a more "perfect" condition.

In this sense, then, the perfect condition to which the world was to be conformed is none other than the perfect conditions present in paradise. When we couple the command to "be fruitful and multiply and fill the earth and subdue it and have dominion" (Gen 1:28) with the additional commands in paradise, we get a complete picture of the *imago Dei* mission. God placed Adam in the garden "to till it and keep it (לעבדה ולשמרה)" (Gen 2:15). Though infinitives, these take the force of imperatives: Adam is "to work" (עבד) and "to keep" the garden of Eden.

It should be noted that the material "dust" from which Adam was formed came from outside the Garden of Eden, after which he was then placed in the garden. This is made particularly clear when, after the fall, God sent Adam and Eve "from the garden of Eden, to till the ground from which they were taken" (Gen 3:23). It is also evident from the language of "garden (גן)" that this divinely established paradise was localized; the word indicates an "enclosure," separated from the area around it and distinct in quality.[11] Thus the quality within the garden was "heaven on earth" or, perhaps better, earth transformed into the quality of heaven. Krüger and Haynes sum up the situation well: "As humanity fulfilled its instruction to multiply and fill

---

9. Kidner, *Genesis*, 1:78.

10. That טוב does not imply "perfect" in the sense of "complete" and beyond all improvement is proved by the fact that God's progressive acts of creation during the creation week in Gen 1 are declared to be טוב, but evidently not "complete," or they would not require additional days of creation to add to the work. Further, both plant and animal life were regarded as טוב (Gen 1:12, 21, 25), yet they were created with the capacity for growth and reproduction, demonstrating that they were not created in their complete condition without the possibility of development—from "good" to "better." With the creation of Adam, regarded as "good," God judged that it was "not good" (לא־טוב) that Adam was alone; it took the creation of Eve to bring him to completion. In fact, Adam and Eve alone were not "perfect," or God would not have instructed them to be fruitful, multiply, and fill the earth.

11. Cf. BDB, 171.

the earth, this blessing would move forward to spill out beyond the borders of the garden of Eden to the rest of the earth as well. . . . In so doing, they will need to subdue the land that is outside of the garden so that it becomes like the land that is within the boundaries of the garden."[12]

Around AD 180, second-century apologist Theophilus of Antioch describes God's establishment of paradise "in the East" (*Autol.* 2.19 [*ANF* 2]), so that Adam "might be in a better and distinctly superior place" (2.23). Thus, while the rest of the world was created "good," paradise was superior in quality. He explains, "The things which were in paradise were made of a superior loveliness and beauty, since in it the plants were said to have been planted by God" (2.24). Theophilus also describes God's intention in placing Adam in paradise: "And God transferred him from the earth, out of which he had been produced, into paradise, giving him means of advancement. . . . For man had been made a middle nature, neither wholly mortal, nor altogether immortal, but capable of either; so also the place, paradise, was made in respect of beauty intermediate between earth and heaven" (2.24). Irenaeus of Lyons also explains:

> A place was prepared for him, better than this earth—excelling in air, beauty, light, food, plants, fruit, waters, and every other thing needful for life—and its name was paradise. And so beautiful and good was the paradise, [that] the Word of God was always walking in it: He would walk and talk with the man prefiguring the future, which would come to pass, that He would dwell with him and speak with him, and would be with mankind, teaching them righteousness. But the man was a young child, not yet having a perfect deliberation. (*Epid.* 12)

In this context, Adam was given explicit permission to eat "of every tree of the garden (מכל עץ־הגן)" (Gen 2:16), which necessarily includes the tree of life "in the midst of the garden (בתוך הגן)" (2:9). Only the "tree of the knowledge of good and evil" was forbidden to him (Gen 2:17). This is the sole negative command given to humans in the original created order (לא תאכל). Prior to their temptation and sin of eating from the forbidden tree, Adam and Eve were free to eat from all the other trees, including the "tree of life."

Commentators have taken different perspectives on whether a single bite would have imparted immortality to humans or if people were expected to eat from the tree continually to sustain their lives forever.[13] If only one bite would have imparted everlasting immortality, then Adam and Eve had clearly not eaten from the tree of life prior to the fall. However, in light of how the tree of life functions later in the redemption narrative and the church fathers' general understanding of the account suggests the tree of life was intended to impart physical life and health through constantly drawing from its sustenance.

Furthermore, in agreement with a common reading in the Christian tradition, I believe Adam and Eve had, in fact, eaten from the tree of life before eating from the tree of the knowledge of good and evil. As a consequence of eating from the tree

---

12. Krüger and Haynes, "Creation Rest," 680.
13. Sarna, *Genesis*, 18–19.

of the knowledge of good and evil, they were then banished from *continuing* to eat from the tree of life; the result, of course, was death. Perhaps, then, their extraordinarily long lives—and those of their descendants

Go Deeper Excursus 2

Had Adam and Eve Eaten from the Tree of Life?

for several generations—was a result of the residual effects of having eaten from the physically rejuvenating tree of life.

In keeping with Irenaeus's assertion that the paradise in Eden prefigured the future (*Epid.* 12), access to the tree of life was expected to be restored when paradise returns during the future kingdom. At that time, as we see in Revelation 22:2, the tree of life will function as was intended from the beginning: "On either side of the river is the tree of life with its twelve kinds of fruit, producing its fruit each month, and the leaves of the tree are for the healing of the nations." This continual crop of fruit implies that even in a redeemed creation with a redeemed humanity, people will continue to receive sustenance from the tree of life.

From the start, the mission of God's imagers called to order and fill the world was one of "edenification"—transforming or "terraforming" the world from its natural state to one in which the entire world would gradually become like the Garden of Eden. As Carl Delitzsch wrote long ago, "As nature was created for man, it was his vocation not only to ennoble it by his work, to make it subservient to himself, but also to raise it into the sphere of the spirit and further its glorification."[14]

Everything outside the advancing boundaries of paradise would be in a natural "good" condition. But everything within the space of paradise was of a higher quality, heaven on earth: physical, yes, but "heavenized," raised to a new creation by the infusion of the substance of the spiritual realm. Absent the fall, paradise would have progressively expanded outward as humanity obeyed the commands to be fruitful, multiply, fill the earth, subdue it, exercise dominion, work the garden, and continue eating from the tree of life as they themselves grew from their natural condition to that of a glorified being.

Yet that grand trajectory was derailed by the temptation of Satan, humanity's subsequent plunge into sin and death, and their ejection from paradise. Irenaeus provides a brief but potent account of the fall of humanity after disobeying the one commandment: "This commandment the man did not keep, but disobeyed God. . . . Then God cursed the serpent, which bore the Devil—a curse which fell upon that animal itself and the angel hiding in it, that is, Satan; and He put the man far from His face, making him then dwell by the road into the paradise, since the paradise does not receive sinners" (*Epid.* 16).

God's Gracious Governance from Adam to Noah

After the fall and banishment from paradise, humanity is still instructed to be fruitful and multiply, to fill the earth, and to subdue it (Gen 1:28; 9:1, 7; 35:11). They still

---

14. Carl Friedrich Keil and Franz Delitzsch, *Commentary on the Old Testament*, vol. 1, trans. James Martin (Edinburgh: T&T Clark, 1866; repr., Peabody, MA: Hendrickson, 1996), 52.

bear the image and likeness of God (Gen 1:26–27; 9:6; Jas 3:9). God's disposition of mercy and grace was already at work. Prior to the fall, God said, "In the day that you eat of it you shall die" (Gen 2:17). After the fall, Adam and Eve experienced exile from the source of life and fellowship with their Creator, but they were still permitted to live for nearly a thousand years. Though God would have been justified in ending human existence at the very instant of their disobedience, he preserved humanity from physical death. This gracious preservation—permitting the continued existence of those first humans and their posterity—is itself a promise of God's plan of future redemption.

Though God graciously bestowed a conscience on fallen humanity—a law "written on their hearts" (Rom 2:15) providing a sense of right and wrong—the events leading up to the Noahic deluge (the flood) demonstrated that the conscience can be seared not only at an individual level (1 Tim 4:2; Titus 1:15) but also at a societal level. In the latter case, the fabric of society itself unravels. In Genesis 6, we see that humanity descended from conscience-driven autocracy to conscience-seared anarchy, so "the wickedness of humans was great in the earth" and "every inclination of the thoughts of their hearts was only evil continually" (Gen 6:5).

The response to this was catastrophic judgment (Gen 6:6–7), from which only Noah and his family, by God's covenantal action, received grace (Gen 6:8). Of the days of Noah, Irenaeus writes:

> The things of wickedness overabounded, while those of righteousness decreased, until, when a judgement came upon the world from God, by means of a flood in the tenth generation after the first-formed, Noah alone was found righteous. He, because of his righteousness, was himself saved, together with his wife and three sons and the three wives of his sons, being shut up inside the ark together with all the animals which God commanded Noah to bring into the ark—for when the destruction of everything took place, both of men and of the other animals, that were upon the earth, that which was kept in the ark was saved. (*Epid.* 18–19)

So thoroughly did this judgment wipe sinful society from the earth that Peter could refer to its result as a kind of second creation. Against scoffers who mocked the notion of a coming judgment, Peter refers in 2 Peter 3:5 to the original creation described in Genesis 1, when God separated water from water to create the expanse of the "heavens" and separated the land from the waters below to form "the earth" (Gen 1:6–10). Peter then says that by the water that had been separated above and below, "the world of that time was deluged with water and perished" (2 Pet 3:6). The word *perished* (ἀπόλλυμι) implies utter destruction; the ordering and filling described in Genesis 1 was reversed in judgment and returned to its state of abysmal "formlessness and emptiness." So absolute was this destruction that Peter refers to the post-flood world as "the present heavens and earth (οἱ . . . νῦν οὐρανοὶ καὶ ἡ γῆ)." We are, as it were, living in the "second" heavens and earth, not the same ordering of creation that prevailed between Genesis 1 and 6.

After the deluge, God promised never again to destroy all life with a flood (Gen 8:21). With this unconditional promise, however, God also grants Noah (and presumably other patriarchs as they spread throughout the earth and establish various "nations") the administrative authority to exact retribution on evil doers (Gen 9:6). Romans 13 reflects that this same administrative responsibility resides in established human governments and that God established this system of authority to reward the good and punish the wicked. Irenaeus describes this means of external accountability established after the flood this way:

> For since man, by departing from God, reached such a pitch of fury as even to look upon his brother as his enemy, and engaged without fear in every kind of restless conduct, and murder, and avarice; God imposed upon mankind the fear of man, as they did not acknowledge the fear of God, in order that, being subjected to the authority of men, and kept under restraint by their laws, they might attain to some degree of justice. . . . Earthly rule, therefore, has been appointed by God for the benefit of nations . . . so that under the fear of human rule, men may not eat each other up like fishes; but that, by means of the establishment of laws, they may keep down an excess of wickedness among the nations. (*Haer.* 5.24.2)

Seen from this perspective, the family unit represents the most basic level of human government. Where individual conscience fails, the external accountability of family must step in. When the family fails to restrain wickedness, human government is meant to step in to enforce just laws that promote righteousness and punish wickedness. However, history has demonstrated that whole societies and nations can be corrupted, falling so far from natural law and justice that they promote wickedness and punish righteousness. In fact, this is the state of the world in which Abram is called into a special relationship with God.

God's Theocratic Rule

With Noah and his family after the flood, God establishes a new order. With that restart, God left humanity with both a promise and a command: he promised never again to destroy the world with a flood (Gen 9:11), and he reiterated his command that humans were to multiply and spread abroad across the face of the earth and to exercise dominion over it (9:1, 7).

Yet shortly after this fresh start, as humans began to grow in number, they collaborated in a way that revealed both distrust of God's promise and disobedience of his command. Genesis 11 tells us that a united humanity settled in a plain in Shinar, the region of modern-day Iraq, and began construction on a tower using "brick for stone and bitumen for mortar" (Gen 11:3), "a tower with its top in the heavens" (11:4). Josephus is probably correct in his observation that the tower was built from stone sealed with bitumen "that it might not be liable to admit water" and was built "too high for the waters to be able to reach" (Josephus, *A.J.* 1.4.2–3).[15] Instead of spreading over the face of the earth, as instructed, humans gathered in one place to preserve their common language and thus their homogonous ethnicity

---

15. Translation from William Whiston, *The Works of Josephus: Complete and Unabridged* (Peabody, MA: Hendrickson, 1987), 35.

and culture. They engaged in a project born of unbelief and disobedience, intending to perpetuate their fame: "Let us make a name for ourselves" (Gen 11:4).

In response, God confused their language, which led to division and scattering over the face of the earth and a cessation of the construction project (Gen 11:8–9). The resulting diversity of language, culture, and ethnicity cannot itself be seen as the judgment. Had humanity obeyed the command to multiply over the face of the earth, the natural effect would have been a diversifying of language, culture, and ethnicity. Had they not lost sight of the one true God, their differences would have been a harmonious hymn sung in praise of God. The nations instead departed from God, forgetting his holiness, justice, grace, and mercy.

As the budding nations began to drift farther from God, he ordained numerous nations that could serve under his providence to hold other nations accountable on an international scale. If one nation departed too severely from God's natural law, then God could raise up another nation to judge it (Isa 10:5; Jer 18:7–10). Yet what would prevent all nations from so completely departing from him that the result would be a total apostasy—a deterioration into wickedness and injustice so complete that every leader's conscience is seared and every government so corrupt that all people deserve just judgment?

To prevent this, God establishes a theocratic arrangement with a single nation that shifts the focus of his moral governance to a particular historical expression of divine rule. This establishment of a theocracy—a nation ruled by God himself—did not itself rule out human sub-rulers operating under God's government: patriarchs like Abraham and Jacob, Moses the legislator, a line of priests, a tribe of prophets, and a dynasty of kings. Their very offices were established on the basis of God's revelation and within a covenantal context that involved blessings for faithfulness to their calling and judgment for unfaithfulness. Josephus writes:

> Some legislators have permitted their governments to be under monarchies, others put them under oligarchies, and others under a republican form; but our legislator [Moses] . . . ordained our government to be what, by a strained expression, may be termed a Theocracy, by ascribing the authority and the power to God, and by persuading all the people to have a regard to him, as the author of all the good things enjoyed either in common by all mankind, or by each one in particular, and of all that they themselves obtained by praying to him in their greatest difficulties. (Josephus, *C. Ap.* 2.164–166)[16]

This theocracy began with a covenant with a man summoned from Ur of the Chaldeans—Abram (Gen 12:1–3). The contrast between the failure of humanity at the Tower of Babel (Gen 11) and the covenantal promises to Abram are worth noting. Humanity had been instructed to spread over the face of the earth (Gen 9:1, 7); instead, they doubled down in disbelief and disobedience in order to "make a name" for themselves (וְנַעֲשֶׂה-לָּנוּ שֵׁם) (11:1–4). In contrast, Abram's father, Terah, departed from the same region of Shinar (11:31), and when God called Abram to leave his home and country to go to a foreign land so God could bless him and "make [his]

---

16. Whiston, *Josephus: Works*, 803–4.

name great (ואגדלה שמך)" (12:1–2), he obeyed (12:4). The result was that through Abram ultimately all the world would be blessed (12:3).

The Abrahamic Covenant

The introduction of the Abrahamic covenant deserves some closer examination. Four primary passages detail the stipulations of this covenant: Genesis 12:1–3; 13:14–17; 15:1–21; and 17:1–19. These passages point to a covenant that included personal aspects that Abraham himself was to enjoy in his own lifetime: blessing (Gen 12:2), a great name or reputation (12:2), the mediator of blessing to others (12:2–3), a promise of retributive protection (12:3), and a child who would be his heir (12:2; 15:4).

In addition to these personal aspects, the covenant included national aspects that looked beyond Abraham's own generation to future generations of his descendants. These included the blessing of his descendants to becoming a "great nation" (Gen 12:2; 17:4–8), a specific body of land that would be the perpetual home of that nation (12:1; 13:14–15; 15:7; 17:8), and the extension of this covenant promise to his posterity, or "seed" forever (17:7). The personal and national aspects of the Abrahamic covenant led to universal aspects that involved mediated blessings to many nations (Gen 12:3; 17:4–6).

Though both the Hebrew זרע and Greek σπέρμα may denote an individual "offspring" or multiple "offspring," the stipulations of the covenant leave no doubt that the ultimate fulfillment of the promise would involve a vast multitude of descendants (Gen 15:5). And the land promise reiterated in this passage also has in view a nation of a great population occupying a specific territory (Gen 15:18).

In Abram's own lifetime, however, he received the full extent of neither the land nor the blessings. And the fulfillment of the "seed" or "offspring" promise was realized through an individual, Isaac, who then became the heir of the Abrahamic covenant: "I will establish my covenant with him [Isaac] as an everlasting covenant for his offspring after him" (Gen 17:19). Then Isaac's own son, Jacob, became heir of the covenant, even though he was Isaac's second-born son:

> And the Lord stood beside him [Jacob] and said, "I am the LORD, the God of Abraham your father and the God of Isaac; the land on which you lie I will give to you and to your offspring, and your offspring shall be like the dust of the earth, and you shall spread abroad to the west and to the east and to the north and to the south, and all the families of the earth shall be blessed in you and in your offspring. Know that I am with you and will keep you wherever you go and will bring you back to this land, for I will not leave you until I have done what I have promised you." (Gen 28:13–15)

After God renamed Jacob "Israel," Jacob became the father of the twelve patriarchs, who in turn became the fathers of the tribes of Israel, who constituted the promised nation. After centuries of bondage in Egypt, God then redeemed the people and led them back to the land promised to Abraham, Isaac, and Jacob, establishing them as a proper theocracy in the land with a law and structure of governance suitable to that calling. Irenaeus sums up the legacy of blessing from Shem (Noah's son) to Israel: "And so, in this way, the original blessing [given to] Sem passed to Abraham, and from Abraham to Isaac, and from Isaac to Jacob, the Spirit assigning the inheritance to them, for He was called 'the God of Abraham and the God of Isaac and the God of Jacob.' And to Jacob there were born twelve sons, from whom the twelve tribes of Israel are named" (*Epid.* 24).

The Mosaic Covenant

The law of Moses provides a contextualized expression of moral, civil, and ceremonial obligations to regulate God's theocratic means of administration. As such, it reflects an explicit and objective form of the unwritten moral sense that accompanies individual conscience, which itself developed into ethics, piety, and judicial forms throughout humanity. The law, then, is a revealed ethic, religion, and legislation for God's theocracy, the nation of Israel. It functions to keep God's established nation genuinely theocratic, preventing it from losing its identity and becoming like all the other nations. The law becomes the external conscience of the theocratic kingdom and thereby could also serve as the conscience of all kingdoms through the mediation of Israel's theocratic call.

Strictly speaking, the law of Moses in whole and in its parts was inseparable from a special covenant relationship with the nation redeemed from Egypt—the physical descendants of Abraham, Isaac, and Jacob. Obedience to the stipulations of the law would result in blessings in the land for that generation; disobedience would result in curses and ultimately exile from the land (Lev 26:1–46; Deut 11:8–32; 28:1–68). While the promise to Abraham of offspring, land, and blessing formed the seed of the theocratic arrangement whereby God would assert his mediated dominion over the world, the root system that developed over the course of the next generations would support generation after generation of branches of varying qualities. Some generations were more faithful to the covenant than others. When the law was added "because of transgressions" (Gal 3:19)—to hold back wickedness and promote truth, holiness, and justice among the people—some generations proved more righteous by the standards of that law than others. God established the sacrificial system with the law as an acknowledgment that the nation as a whole would never be fully righteous or able to keep the stipulations of the covenant as articulated by Moses: "Now, therefore, if you obey my voice and keep my covenant, you shall be my treasured possession out of all the peoples. Indeed, the whole earth is mine, but you shall be for me a priestly kingdom and a holy nation" (Exod 19:5–6)

Once the nation of Israel was established, God used Israel as his means of exercising judgment on the wicked nations that had deviated so far from God's natural law as a fulfillment of their role in promoting righteousness and holding back wickedness. Any consideration of the God's command to Israel to obliterate the Canaanites in their conquest of the promised land must consider Israel's unique role in God's administration of his rule over fallen humanity and his program of redeeming that world from sin, death, and the devil. As God's theocratic agent, Israel began functioning as God's chosen means of exercising judgment on the

Canaanite nations, whose evil had reached an intolerable pitch despite the witness of conscience.

The Davidic Covenant

Where conscience failed prior to the flood, human government was established to hold back wickedness and promote righteousness. When human nations deviated from God in disbelief and disobedience, God raised up his own theocracy of Israel first through the nation-forging promise to Abraham and then through the organizing effects of the Mosaic law. From God's initial promise, the theocratic rule was mediated through patriarchs, legislators, judges, prophets, and kings.

With the calling and anointing of David and his eventual establishment as king over Israel, God's kingdom centered on an individual, who himself was promised offspring who would always reign on his throne and over the kingdom of Israel (2 Sam 7; Jer 33:20–21). From that point forward, God's theocracy would forever be mediated by the Davidic king, through whom God would mediate the rule of Israel; Israel, in submission to its king, would thereby realize the fulfillment of the Abrahamic promise and blessing in the land, and through that nation, all the nations of the earth will be blessed.

Yet the problem with Israel's king and the nation itself was the problem of all humanity since the ejection of Adam and Eve from paradise: sin and death. This is why the prophets began looking forward to a time when God would establish a perfect king over a completely righteous nation under a new covenant who would bring to completion all the covenantal promises of the Old Testament. This future king would embody God's covenant: "I have given you as a covenant to the people, a light to the nations" (Isa 42:6; 49:8).

This covenant would reunite the divided kingdom of Israel and Judah (Jer 31:31). It would involve a total restoration of the nation—a complete cleansing of their sins, a transformation of their hearts, and a saving knowledge of God from the least to the greatest (Jer 31:33–34; 32:40; 59:21; Ezek 16:60–62). The nation of Israel would be restored and the city of Jerusalem rebuilt (Jer 31:35–40; 49:8; 50:4–6; Ezek 37:25–27). Their descendants would multiply and be known as blessed throughout the world (Isa 61:8–9; Ezek 37:26). In fact, the blessings of Israel would bring peace and blessings to nature and the whole world itself (Ezek 34:23–31).

Thus the full realization of the covenant under the Davidic king fulfills all God's promises and sums up all his covenants. It becomes the means of fulfilling the original *imago Dei* mission by which God establishes his kingdom over the entire world through his image-bearers, who will finally exercise dominion over the whole earth. That new humanity—the perfect Son of Man with those perfected by him and through him as the second Adam—becomes the means of ultimately transforming the world from chaos to order, from emptiness to fullness, from wickedness to righteousness, from death of life. It includes the Abrahamic promise of blessing to all the nations of the world through the mediation of Abraham's offspring—particularly the ultimate "seed" to whom the promise was intended, along with those united to him by faith. It establishes a perfect theocratic rule through the coming promised Messiah, son of David. And it fully realizes God's original purpose of fellowship with humanity—God with us—and the edenification of the world through his image-bearers.

Irenaeus articulates this expectation thusly: "He is the expectation of the nations, of those who hope in Him, for we expect Him to reestablish the Kingdom" (*Epid.* 57). At that time, even nature itself will be redeemed from chaos and restored to harmony, as was intended from the beginning. Commenting on the prophecy of Isaiah that states that "the wolf shall live with the lamb; the leopard shall lie down with the kid; the calf and the lion will feed together" (Isa 11:6), Irenaeus writes, "But concerning the concord and peace of the animals of different species, who [are] opposed by nature and enemies of one another, the elders say that it will truly be so at the advent of Christ, when He is going to reign over all" (*Epid.* 61).

But how will God accomplish these future things in keeping with his promises and the unfulfilled realization of the *imago Dei* mandate? We begin to tackle this difficult question in the following chapters.

3

INTRODUCTION TO FUTURE THINGS: THE THREE "R"s OF ESCHATOLOGY

Let us consider, beloved, how the Master
continually points out to us the resurrection that
is coming, of which he made the first fruit by
raising up the Lord Jesus Christ from the dead.

Clement of Rome, *Letter to the Corinthians* 24.1

The biblical drama of creation, fall, and redemption looks forward in hope—hope of the coming of a perfect Davidic king who will bring justice and righteousness not only to Israel but also to the world. It leaves the believer longing for hope in victory over sin, death, and the forces of chaos. The story of the Old Testament leaves readers longing for a sequel that will tie up the loose ends and bring the promises to fulfillment and the drama to a climax. The believer still hopes for the restoration of paradise, the fulfillment of the *imago Dei* mission, and the renewal of intimate fellowship with the Almighty.

The New Testament introduces that final chapter of the grand narrative in the person and work of Jesus the Messiah—the son of David, son of Abraham, son of Adam, Son of God (Matt 1:1–17; Luke 3:23–38). Yet his birth, life, teaching, death, and resurrection mark the beginning of the end, not the end itself. With the advent of the Messiah, promises and prophecies are fulfilled but many more are yet to come. The angel Gabriel declared to Mary that the baby born to her "will be great and will be called the Son of the Most High, and the Lord God will give to him the throne of his ancestor David. He will reign over the house of Jacob forever, and of his kingdom there will be no end" (Luke 1:32–33; cf. 1:54–55).

While every Christian believes that this future hope centers on the Lord Jesus Christ, not all agree on exactly how that future hope will come to pass. In this chapter, I will examine the most vital aspects of future things on which all orthodox Christians agree, and then I will introduce the issues on which disagreement has dogged the church almost from its beginning.

Three Things on Which All Christians Agree

As I write this, I am staring at a line of books along the back of my desk written by dozens of biblical scholars and theologians, each defending the author's own unique perspectives on eschatology. If I left my office and walked across campus to the library, I would find shelf after shelf of volumes chronicling centuries of discussion and debate on the end times. Whole books are devoted to sorting out the nature of the millennium of Revelation 20, whether prophecies in the Old Testament will be fulfilled in the future literally or are being fulfilled spiritually in the church, whether there will be a single end-times antichrist or if we should expect many antichrists. The list of disputed matters goes on and on, from the timing of the rapture of the church in 1 Thessalonians 4:17 to the identity of the two witnesses in Revelation 11.

No wonder many Christians throw in the towel. The task of sorting through all the options can feel daunting. However, if we take a few steps back from the swirling chaos of end-times controversy, we will discover a few major issues the church has believed, confessed, and taught from the beginning. In fact, to apply the words of the fifth-century Christian teacher Vincent of Lérins, we can discern a handful of doctrines related even to eschatology that have been believed "everywhere, always, by all" (Vincent, *Comm.* 2.6 [*NPNF*[2] 11]). And while creeds, confessions, and doctrinal statements may differ on other issues, on these things they agree.

These three essential truths of orthodox Christian eschatology constitute the faith "once and for all handed on to the saints" (Jude 1:3): (1) the *return* of Christ as judge and king to bring all things to completion and to reign forever; (2) the *resurrection* of the dead when the righteous are raised bodily to eternal life and the wicked raised bodily to eternal condemnation; and 3) the *restoration* of all creation when all sin, suffering, death, and devil will be banished forever. The return, resurrection, and restoration constitute the common foundation on which all Christians stand and upon which all eschatological diversity is built.

The Return of Christ as Judge and King

When the disciples witnessed the ascension of Christ into heaven, two angels appeared among them and said, "Men of Galilee, why do you stand looking up toward heaven? This Jesus, who has been taken up from you into heaven, will come in the same way (ἐλεύσεται ὃν τρόπον) as you saw him go into heaven" (Acts 1:11). The term τρόπος indicates the manner in which something is done.[1] Thus the passage asserts that the manner of Jesus' "coming (ἔρχομαι)" will be an inverted mirror image, as it were, of his ascension. Just as Jesus' ascension was physical and literal, so will his coming. This is emphasized by the use of terms for seeing: Christ will return in the same way they "saw (ἐθεάσασθε)" him ascend.[2]

In the last book of the Bible, likely written toward the close of the first century, the apostle John writes, "Come (ἔρχου), Lord Jesus!" (Rev 22:20). That first generation of Christians clung to the hope that one day Jesus would return from heaven, just as he promised: "If I go and prepare a place for you, I will come again (πάλιν

---

1. BDAG, 1016–17.

2. Whatever we may rightly say about Christ "coming" in the sense of fulfilling the role of mediating a theophanic visitation in judgment (see chapters 16 and 17) and associate this with first-century events described in the Olivet Discourse, Acts 1:11 speaks of a bodily, observable, personal return, not a "coming" in judgment mediated through various means of retributive justice.

ἔρχομαι) and will take you to myself, so that where I am, there you may be also" (John 14:3). The apostle Paul noted that followers of Christ were "to wait for his Son from heaven, whom he raised from the dead—Jesus" (1 Thess 1:10; Phil 3:20). Believers should be waiting for "the blessed hope and the manifestation (ἐπιφάνειαν) of the glory of our great God and Savior, Jesus Christ" (Titus 2:13). Paul prays that his readers will be found holy and blameless "at the coming (ἐν τῇ παρουσίᾳ) of our Lord Jesus with all his saints" (1 Thess 3:13). And Peter encouraged his readers: "Set all your hope on the grace that Jesus Christ will bring you when he is revealed (ἀποκαλύψει)" (1 Pet 1:13). A cluster of terms are commonly used for the future, visible, personal, and glorious return of Christ: ἔρχομαι ("coming"), ἐπιφάνεια ("appearing"), παρουσία ("presence"), and ἀποκάλυψις ("revelation").

It appears that even during the first-century apostolic period, though, people had grown skeptical about this future, visible, personal return of Christ. Peter refers to scoffers asking sarcastically, "Where is the promise of his coming (παρουσίας)?" (2 Pet 3:4). In response, Peter reminds his readers that the coming of Christ in judgment will be "like a thief" (2 Pet 3:10). It will be unexpected; therefore, they are to be ready and waiting, leading lives of holiness and godliness (3:11–12).

Even today, some have slipped into the error of rejecting a future, visible, personal return of Christ in a number of ways. Perhaps, they say, Jesus "returned" in a spiritual sense when the Holy Spirit came in a special way to God's people on Pentecost (John 14:16–20; Matt 28:20). Or maybe Christ "returns" individually to each of us as we become believers; that is, he "comes" to us and takes residence in our lives (Acts 9:3–5; Col 1:27). Or maybe John 14:3 is not Christ's promise of a personal, visible return to take us to be with him; perhaps it refers to Christ coming to each of us when we die to usher us into the heavenly realm. Though all these things are true—Christ does dwell with us by the power of the Spirit, he does take residence with us when we are converted, and he does usher us into his presence upon death (2 Cor 5:8)—these things do not constitute what Scripture means by the second coming of Christ.

That Christians of every generation since the first century have eagerly anticipated the future, physical, personal coming of the Lord is clear and unambiguous. The first-century handbook for newly planted churches known as the Didache (c. 50–70)[3] says, "Be ready, for you do not know the hour in which our Lord comes" and "the world will see the Lord coming upon the clouds of heaven" (Did. 16.1, 8). And the anonymous writing historically known as the Epistle of Barnabas, written either in the late first or early second century, writes, "Upon coming his Son will abolish the time of the lawless one and will judge the ungodly and will change the sun and the moon and the stars" (Barn. 15.5). Around the middle of the second century, Justin Martyr begins his discussion of the second coming of Christ with Trypho, his Jewish respondent, in the following manner: "If such power is shown to have accompanied and still now accompanies His Passion, just think how great shall be His power at His glorious Advent (παρουσία)! For, as Daniel foretold, He

---

3. On dating and genre of the Didache, see Michael J. Svigel, "*Didache* as a Practical Enchiridion for Early Church Plants," *BSac* 174.1 (January–March 2017): 77–94.

shall come on the clouds as the Son of Man, accompanied by his angels" (*Dial.* 31). And earlier, with reference to prophecies of the coming Messiah, Justin says, "Some of these and similar passages from the Prophets refer to the first coming of Christ, in which he is described as coming in disgrace, obscurity, and mortality; other passages allude to His second coming when He shall appear from the clouds in glory" (*Dial.* 14).

And finally, in the late second century, Irenaeus writes, "All the prophets announced His two advents: the one, indeed, in which He became a man subject to stripes, and knowing what it is to bear infirmity . . . and came down to them that He might deliver them: but the second in which He will come on the clouds, bringing on the day which burns as a furnace, and smiting the earth with the word of His mouth, and slaying the impious with the breath of His lips" (*Haer.* 4.33.1). Later, Irenaeus makes the claim that this belief in the physical, visible, and personal return of Christ as judge and king constitutes the universal faith of all Christians throughout the world, a claim that can be substantiated by surveying the literature of the second century (*Haer.* 5.20.1).

Thus the earliest church knew nothing whatsoever of "full preterism," the view that all biblical prophecies were fulfilled in the first century—a modern view unheard of in the history of the church and contrary to the teachings of the church universal. The language of the Nicene-Constantinopolitan Creed (AD 381) serves as a summary of the faith of the whole church up to and including the fourth century, as well as a touchstone for all future articulations of orthodox eschatology. At some time in the future, Christ "will come again with glory to judge the living and dead."[4]

The Resurrection of the Dead—Both Righteous and Wicked

Though the concept of a future bodily resurrection is found throughout the New Testament, the Old Testament contains hints, allusions, and a few express indications of that hope of a restoration of physical, bodily life after death. For example, Isaiah 26:19 states, "Your dead shall live; their corpses (נבלתי) shall rise. Those who dwell in the dust will awake and shout for joy! For your dew is a radiant dew, and the earth will give birth to those long dead" (26:19).[5] Later, in Daniel 12:2, we are told that at the end of the world "multitudes who sleep in the dust of the earth (אדמת־עפר) will awake: some to everlasting life, others to shame and everlasting contempt."[6]

By the time we reach the New Testament, the concept of bodily resurrection is already firmly established in Judaism. In Paul's testimony before Felix, he summed

---

4. *The Constantinopolitan Creed*, in John H. Leith, ed., *The Creeds of Christendom: A Reader in Christian Doctrine from the Bible to the Present*, 3rd ed. (Louisville: John Knox, 1982), 33.

5. Cf. Geoffrey W. Grogan, "Isaiah," in *The Expositor's Bible Commentary: Proverbs–Isaiah*, rev. ed., ed. Tremper Longman III, Garland David E., vol. 6 (Grand Rapids: Zondervan, 2008), 635.

6. The physicality of this resurrection of the righteous and wicked is underscored by the use of "corpse (נבלה)" and "dust of the earth (אדמה־עפר)," which cannot refer merely to an immaterial "life after death" as the sum of eschatological expectations.

up the eschatological expectations not only of early Christians but also of most Jews: "I believe everything that is in accordance with the Law and that is written in the Prophets, and I have the same hope in God as these men themselves have, that there will be a resurrection of both the righteous and the wicked" (Acts 24:14–15). Though the resurrection language, especially as it relates to Christ's resurrection from the tomb, dominates the New Testament, a primary passage for understanding the Christian teaching concerning the future bodily resurrection is 1 Corinthians 15. There Paul directly challenges those who try to redefine the resurrection in a merely spiritual direction: If there is no such thing as bodily resurrection, then Christ himself has not been raised bodily; and if that is true, then the Christian faith is a lie and all hope is lost (1 Cor 15:12–19). Paul then directly ties Jesus' bodily resurrection to the expectation of the future bodily resurrection of all (15:20–28). By means of the resurrection accomplished at Christ's return, death itself will be conquered.[7]

After establishing bodily resurrection as an essential aspect of the Christian hope (1 Cor 15:29–34), Paul then attends to some lingering questions regarding the nature of the resurrection body (15:36–42). Along the way, Paul contrasts our current mortal, perishable, natural body with the future immortal, imperishable, supernatural or "spiritual" body (15:42–54). Paul's language of "spiritual body (σῶμα πνευματικόν)" has sometimes led interpreters to assume he meant a nonphysical resurrection, that we are destined to be immaterial, ghostly, spiritual beings like angels. However, the same adjective πνευματικός ("spiritual") is used to describe Christians in this life who are mature, empowered and led by the Spirit. Thus Paul says, "Brothers and sisters, I could not speak to you as spiritual people (ὡς πνευματικοῖς) but rather as fleshly, as infants in Christ" (1 Cor 3:1); and elsewhere, "If a person is caught in any wrongdoing, you who are spiritual (πνευματικοὶ) are to restore such a person in a spirit of gentleness" (Gal 6:1 NASB).

Paul's contrast between the present mortal body and the future body after the resurrection is a contrast between quality and power, not substance. F. F. Bruce writes, "The present body is animated by 'soul' and is therefore mortal; the resurrection body is animated entirely by immortal and life-giving spirit, and is therefore called a spiritual body."[8] Further, when Paul says "flesh (σὰρξ) and blood cannot inherit the kingdom of God" (1 Cor 15:50), he does not thereby mean that the resurrection body will be immaterial. He uses the phrase "flesh and blood" to denote a merely mortal, perishable condition, which he clarifies with the appositional statement: "nor does the perishable inherit the imperishable" (15:50). After his own resurrection, Jesus affirmed that he was not a mere ghost: "Look at my hands and my feet; see that it is I myself. Touch me and see, for a ghost (πνεῦμα) does not have flesh (σάρκα) and bones as you see that I have" (Luke 24:39).

Later, in the early second century, Ignatius of Antioch wields this encounter against docetic heretics who denied Jesus' fleshly body in the incarnation. He paraphrases this encounter recorded in Luke 24:39, drawing from it some theological

---

7. See chapter 9 for a detailed discussion of the order of bodily resurrection in 1 Cor 15.

8. F. F. Bruce, *1 & 2 Corinthians*, The New Century Bible Commentary (Grand Rapids: Eerdmans, 1971), 152. See also C. K. Barrett, *A Commentary on the First Epistle to the Corinthians* (New York: Harper & Row, 1968), 372–73.

implications: "For I know and believe he was in the flesh even after the resurrection. And when he came to those with Peter, he said to them, 'Take hold. Touch me and see that I am not a bodiless demon.' . . . And after the resurrection he ate with them and drank with *them* as fleshly, although being united spiritually with the Father" (Ign. *Smyrn.* 3.1–3).

In defining the nature of the resurrection body, the classic Christian faith has strived (though not always successfully) to avoid two ditches—the hyper-spiritual and the hyper-carnal. On the one hand, the church has avoided a view of the resurrection body that dissolves its physicality in a way that renders the resurrection body merely spiritual—like an angel. On the other hand, the church has avoided a view that renders the body merely a healthier version of the present mortal body. Beth Felker Jones strikes a great balance regarding the orthodox view of the resurrection of the body:

> **Go Deeper Excursus 3**
>
> *Bodily Resurrection in the History of the Church*

> Resurrection is not reanimation or resuscitation. When we meet the resurrected Jesus, we meet someone who has been transformed. He has not just been brought back to life. He has been raised to a new kind of life. Resurrection is also not about souls going to heaven. Instead, resurrection is for whole people, body and soul together. The church has sometimes highlighted this truth—the resurrection is about hope for bodies—by confessing belief in the resurrection of the "flesh." Flesh is a strong word, one that works against any tendency to cut our hope off from muscles and marrow. In the resurrection, we have meaty hope, hope that extends into every part of creation and every aspect of human being.[9]

The Restoration of Creation and the Banishment of Sin, Suffering, Death, and the Devil

All orthodox Christians have always embraced the hope that this world will not remain in its fallen, corrupt condition dominated by pain, injustice, disease, warfare, deception, and all other manner of evil. We all look forward to the blessedness of the world to come, even if we may understand differently the details of how the world will ultimately arrive at that condition.

Turning to the words of Paul, he tells us that "the sufferings of this present time are not worth comparing with the glory about to be revealed to us" (Rom 8:18). That Paul is not speaking simply of "dying and going to heaven" is clear in the context. He speaks of a restoration of all creation in connection with the future resurrection. Romans 8:19 says, "For the creation waits with eager longing for the revealing of the children of God." All creation—visible and invisible, physical and spiritual—has suffered the effects of decay and corruption since the fall (Rom 8:20–21; cf. Gen 3).

---

9. Beth Felker Jones, *Practicing Christian Doctrine: An Introduction to Thinking and Living Theologically* (Grand Rapids: Baker Academic, 2014), 226.

Yet that bondage to corruption is not the end of the story. Just as our physical bodies will one day be resurrected, so too creation will partake of a glorious restoration and renewal (Rom 8:21). Jesus refers to this future restoration of creation as "the renewal of all things" (Matt 19:28). Peter calls this period of restoration the "seasons of refreshing" that come with the return of Christ (Acts 3:20).[10] And Paul explicitly ties the refreshing, renewal, and restoration of creation to the resurrection (Rom 8:22–23). Paul's language in Romans 8 connects all three "Rs" of the universal eschatological expectations embraced by all Christians, everywhere, at all times: the *return* of Christ leads to the *resurrection*, which ultimately brings to completion the process of the *restoration* of creation.

The late first-century Epistle of Barnabas points forward to a future age in this world in which the *imago Dei* mission will be ultimately fulfilled through redeemed humanity. Establishing the principle that God will "make the last things like the first things (τὰ ἔσχατα ὡς τὰ πρῶτα)" (Barn. 6.13), the author affirms that those believers who are being made alive "by the faith of the promise and the word" . . . "will live" in order to "exercise dominion over the earth" (6.17). For the author of Barnabas, this rule is not a present spiritual reality nor realizable in our current mortal condition. Rather, he ties the original creation mandate to "increase and multiply and rule over the fish" to a future condition in a future age. He says, "Who is able now to rule over beasts or fish or birds of the sky?" (Barn. 6.18). The answer to his rhetorical question is "no one." Thus he concludes, "Therefore, if this [rule over creation] does not occur now, then he has told us at what time: when we ourselves have been perfected (ὅταν καὶ αὐτοὶ τελειωθῶμεν) to be made heirs of the Lord's covenant" (6.19).[11]

Taken all together, we see that in the present age, we are not now able to rule over creation (Barn. 6.18), nor are we able to keep the present Sabbath in purity and holiness (16.6). However, these things will be fulfilled in the coming age when several conditions will converge: we will be made perfect, inherit the Lord's covenant, experience vindication, and receive the promise—that is, when all lawlessness will be banished and all things will be made new. These things follow the Lord's return (Barn. 15.5).

In the early second century, Polycarp writes in his letter to the church in Philippi, "If we are pleasing to him in the present age, we will also receive the one to come, just as he promised to raise us from the dead, and that if we lead lives worthy of him, we will also reign with him, if indeed we believe" (Pol. *Phil.* 5.2). Though the phrase "the present age" can be contrasted with place of the departed saints in the intermediate state—"with the Lord (παρὰ τῷ κυρίῳ)," regarded as an actual "place (τόπον)" (see Pol. *Phil.* 9.2), the reference to the "age to come (τὸν μέλλοντα)" and its correspondence to the promised resurrection from the dead and the reign with Christ places this anticipated "age (αἰών)" in the future—a period of time coming upon the earth, not a place to which departed saints are going.[12] Thus Polycarp

---

10. See detailed discussions in chapters 7 and 8.

11. See my deeper discussion of Barnabas's view of the future restoration as it relates to the millennium in Go Deeper Excursus 7.

12. BDAG refers the phrase ὁ αἰὼν μέλλων, "the coming age," to "the Messianic period" (32). Loew and Nida, 647, define the term as "a unit of time as a particular stage or period of history."

expected that faith and faithfulness in this present era would be rewarded in "the coming age," the time of the resurrection of the dead, during which the resurrected saints would reign with Christ.[13] It is not surprising that Polycarp's disciple, Irenaeus of Lyons, writes concerning this future restoration: "But when this present fashion of things passes away, and man has been renewed, and flourishes in an incorruptible state, so as to preclude the possibility of becoming old, then there shall be the new heaven and the new earth, in which the new man shall remain continually, always holding fresh converse with God" (*Haer.* 5.36.1).

Though the later patristic and medieval periods saw a deemphasis on the restoration of creation and an overemphasis on eternity in a heavenly, spiritual realm, this foundational teaching never dropped away completely. In the late eleventh century, Anselm of Canterbury argued that in connection with the resurrection and glorification of the elect, creation itself must be renewed and restored: "We believe that the material substance of the world must be renewed, and that this will not take place until the number of the elect is accomplished, and that happy kingdom made perfect, and that after its completion there will be no change" (*Cur Deus Homo* 1.18).[14]

Elsewhere, I have summarized the classic Christian expectation of the coming restoration of all things in the following way: "As far as the dark stains of sin and death, suffering and pain, evil and tragedy have—infected this universe, the cleansing blessings of His life will wash it all away—forever. Though we struggle today with the excruciating pain of a dying world, one day that death will be vanquished permanently by the invincible force of Life itself (Rev. 21:4)."[15]

Diverse Perspectives on Future Things

The return of Christ, the resurrection of the body, and the restoration of all things—these doctrines have been believed, confessed, and taught everywhere, always, and by all. They are clearly affirmed in Scripture, embraced by all orthodox Christians throughout church history, and serve as the foundation of all truly Christian eschatology.

However, within these broad boundaries of basic orthodox eschatology, the church has long borne with a diversity of doctrines and opinions regarding the details and order of future events. The first major point of departure among orthodox

---

13. Whether Polycarp conceived of this era as limited to a distinct period of time, to an eternal condition, or to both is not clear from this passage. However, Polycarp did regard the resurrection and kingdom as an age that was coming upon this world, contrasted with the present; he did not view the resurrection and reign as a present spiritual reality or something to which the faithful went upon their deaths.

14. Translation from Sidney Norton Deane, *St. Anselm: Proslogium; Monologium; An Appendix in Behalf of the Fool by Gaunilon; and Cur Deus Homo* (Chicago: Open Court, 1926), 217.

15. Michael J. Svigel, "When He Returns: Resurrection, Judgment, and the Restoration," in *Exploring Christian Theology*, vol. 3, *The Church, Spiritual Growth, and the End Times*, ed. Nathan D. Holsteen and Michael J. Svigel (Minneapolis: Bethany House, 2014), 195–96.

Christians is the question of the nature and timing of the coming kingdom—often
called the "millennium"—as it relates to the return of Christ. Also included in this
discussion is the nature, duration, and timing of the coming judgment, the "Day of
the Lord" or the "tribulation," not to mention the details of its purpose and whether
the church of that time will be present during the entire period of judgment. These
variables have led to numerous diverse perspectives regarding the coming kingdom,
usually plotted among three large traditions known as premillennialism, postmillennialism, and amillennialism.

These terms—though ubiquitous in modern writings on eschatology—are
sometimes a hindrance to precise thinking on the matter of the coming kingdom.
Part of the problem is that it centralizes one passage of Scripture, Revelation 20,
which alone in the Bible mentions the "millennium" (Latin for "thousand year").[16]
This gives the false impression that the whole discussion rests on how one interprets
that text in all its symbolic glory. The fact is, the Old and New Testaments have
much to say regarding the messianic age and the restoration of creation, and, as
we will eventually see, Revelation 20 does little more than tie up a few loose ends.

Another problem with using the terms "premillennial," "postmillennial," and
"amillennial" to differentiate eschatological views of the coming kingdom is that
these terms categorize an eschatology based on the answer to a specific question:
"When will Christ physically return as king relative to the future, earthly millennium described in Revelation 20?" The premillennialist, answers, "He will return
before the millennium of Revelation 20." The postmillennialist, answers, "He will
return after the millennium of Revelation 20." The amillennialist says, "Revelation
20 does not describe an earthly, future millennium."

Using these modern terms can lead to all sorts of confusion. For instance, despite the "a" prefix (which basically means "no" or "not"), all amillennialists who
have Revelation in their Bibles hold to a "millennium" in fulfillment of Revelation
20, but they tend to understand it as symbolizing a present, spiritual, or heavenly
reality. Thus, with regard to the timing of the return of Christ relative to the millennium, "amillennialists" are technically "postmillennial" because Christ will return
after the completion of the spiritual kingdom that has been taking place since
Christ's ascension. And if an amillennialist holds that the present rule of Christ
through his church advances his kingdom in the world to a large degree, that es-

---

16. The idea of a thousand-year golden age prior to the eternal condition is not unique
to Rev 20. In the first-century *Book of the Secrets of Enoch,* often called 2 Enoch, after an
account of the creation of six days, God revealed to Enoch that the days of creation also
represent and anticipate periods of a thousand years of history, with the eighth period actually representing "a time of not-counting, endless, with neither years nor months nor weeks
nor days nor hours"—that is, eternity (2 En. 33.1). Translation from Robert Henry Charles,
ed., *Pseudepigrapha of the Old Testament,* vol. 2 (Oxford: Clarendon, 1913), 451. Drawing on
this concept of the "world week," the unknown author of the Epistle of Barnabas explicitly
refers to a thousand-year "day" preceding the "eighth day" of a new world (Barn. 15). Thus
outside Rev 20, the idea of an intermediate thousand-year earthly kingdom had already been
circulating in an undeveloped form. It is hardly likely, though, that the early church would
have developed a robust millennialism based just on these noncanonical writings, regardless
of how popular they were in the first century.

chatology begins to look a lot like postmillennialism, but with the view that we are presently in that heavenly/earthly kingdom. Similarly, both premillennialism and postmillennialism can hold many of the views of amillennialism with regard to a present, heavenly, spiritual reality of the reign of Christ—a partially realized eschatology. Thus they can agree even on a partial binding of Satan (usually referred to as "restraining"), a spiritual resurrection occurring for the saints throughout the church age, the assumption of their souls to heaven upon death, and even a present realization of some aspects of prophecies in the present era related to antichrists, false prophets, and tribulations.

In other words, the terms "amillennial," "premillennial," and "postmillennial" are good at answering narrow questions regarding the chronological relationship between the future return of Christ and the reign symbolized in Revelation 20 (before or after) and perhaps its nature (heavenly or earthly). However, the terms tend to reinforce an either/or approach to eschatology while reducing a complex set of questions regarding the coming kingdom to just a couple issues related to Revelation 20 and the order of two—albeit important—events. Perhaps it would be preferable to refer to the various views of the kingdom as either "chiliastic" or "nonchiliastic." Thus a chiliast (from Greek for "one thousand") expects a future earthly kingdom between Christ's physical return to earth and the full realization of the new creation. Yet, how then would we categorize the postmillennialist who also holds to a literal earthly kingdom prior to the new creation but absent Christ's physical presence on earth?

In light of these definitional difficulties, it would be best not to create new terms and new confusion. Instead, I will strive to be explicit, clear, and consistent in my use of terms. I will use "premillennial" in reference to the position that expects Jesus to return physically and personally to earth prior to a future earthly intermediate kingdom, which will then be followed by the condition called the new creation. The term "postmillennial" will refer to the position that a future earthly intermediate kingdom will be followed by the physical and personal return of Christ as judge and king, which will be immediately followed by the new creation. And I will use "amillennial" for the view that the intermediate kingdom began at Christ's ascension and will conclude at his physical return to earth, at which time he will usher in the new creation.

Yet none of these three categories are monolithic. Within each, we can discern a diversity of emphases and perspectives. Amillennialism has often been associated with the notion of a "realized eschatology," a term that has been used since C. H. Dodd in 1935 in reference to the thesis that the Gospels portray Jesus' ministry as a fulfillment of the kingdom of heaven as opposed to a future, unrealized kingdom at the end of the age.[17] While the key to amillennialism is that Christ's ascension and enthronement commenced the reign described in Revelation 20, it does not answer the subsequent question regarding the nature of that reign and how its effects are felt. Is it strictly heavenly and entered upon death? Is it soteriological, spiritual, and moral, entered by faith, spiritual resurrection/regeneration, and living according to

---

17. See C. H. Dodd, *The Parables of the Kingdom* (London: Nisbet, 1935).

the kingdom ethic? Is it both soteriological and ecclesiological, entered by baptism and virtually indistinguishable from the church on earth? Does the presence of the kingdom in the world through the church also involve a mandate to manifest that kingdom in the world as the church influences culture, society, and government? And would that, then, make a "heavenly kingdom" rather earthly? This spectrum of emphases has led to a variety of "amillennialisms" rather than a single monolithic "amillennialism."

The same can be said about the broad category of postmillennialism. Within that tradition, we can find what we might call "militant" postmillennialism, in which the proponents view themselves as the means by which judgment will be exercised upon the world. They bear arms and stage a revolt they hope will result in the establishment of a perfect Christian society free from doctrinal and moral corruption. Another shade of postmillennialism may be termed "political" postmillennialism, in which proponents view their mission as one of gradual Christianization of the world by political and social activism. Driven by Christian convictions, they attempt to influence governments toward Christian principles with the goal of one day establishing Christian nations. When all the nations of the world are converted to Christ and their laws and institutions promoting Christian values, that will constitute the "millennium." A third form of postmillennialism might be called "evangelistic" postmillennialism. In that form, the millennial golden age does not come by violent revolution or political victory. Rather, at some point in the future, the Holy Spirit will be poured out in a great wave of conversions and awakenings such as the world has never seen. Individuals, families, communities, cities, and nations will repent and believe the gospel. Whole religions will convert to Christ, and through those conversions the world will become Christian.

Finally, premillennialism has also enjoyed a variety of perspectives. Some, like "carnal chiliasm," have exaggerated the earthiness of the future earthly kingdom, suggesting that resurrected saints will themselves have children, indulge in sensual delights, gorge themselves on unlimited amounts of food and drink—essentially "party" for a thousand years as a reward for their holiness and self-control in this life. Thankfully, such an extreme view of the millennium was never the main view; it was held by heretics who had bigger theological problems than their eschatology. A major form of premillennialism includes resurrected, glorified saints ruling with Christ in the coming millennium over a world increasingly populated by mortal survivors of the coming earthly judgment. Thus, the millennium will have two kinds of humanity living side by side: mortal and immortal. The mortals may be subject to death, especially if they harbor rebellion or sin; they certainly engage in marriage and have children. Other forms of premillennialism emphasize the spiritual nature of the future kingdom: fellowship with angels, growth in spiritual delights, increase in glory, and eventual admission into the heavenly realms. Sometimes, that form includes only resurrected, glorified saints populating the kingdom.

As can be seen, the borders of these distinct traditions—premillennial, amillennial, and postmillennial—can be rather porous. The more "earthy" amillennialism is, the more it begins to look like political or evangelistic postmillennialism: this world transformed by the values of the coming kingdom. And as both postmillennialists and premillennialists wrestle with the present aspect of the spiritual kingdom—and almost all do—their descriptions of the "already" character of the kingdom sound like the spiritual, soteriological, moral, and even ecclesiological variations of amillennialism. And some forms of historicist premillennialism— which views the book of Revelation as progressively being fulfilled throughout history—anticipate a deterioration of the world, especially as the return of Christ draws near. Yet other forms of premillennialism that view the increasingly severe wickedness and judgment in the book of Revelation as referring to a distinct period of the future known as the tribulation can be open to a relative success of the gospel in this present age, like evangelical postmillennialism, or a constant conflict until the end, as in some forms of amillennialism. In short, it is precarious to make sweeping generalizations about postmillennialism, amillennialism, and premillennialism. And stereotyping those who identify with one of these traditions is less than helpful. Though it is not possible to hold all three simultaneously, even when we plant our feet in one tradition, we may legitimately draw insights, perspectives, and even positions from the other two.

With the exception of extreme and marginal variations of each of these broad views, all share the same basic belief in the return, resurrection, and restoration, and proponents of each ought to acknowledge one another as orthodox Christians. Postmillennialist Loraine Boettner explains this point well:

> While Post-, A-, and Premillennialists differ in regard to the manner and time of Christ's return . . . , they agree in regard to the *fact* that He will return personally and visibly and in great glory. Each alike looks for "the blessed hope and appearing of the glory of the great God and our Saviour Jesus Christ" (Titus 2:13). Each acknowledges Paul's statement that, "The Lord himself shall descend from heaven, with a shout, with the voice of the archangel, and with the trump of God" (1 Thess. 4:16). . . . They also agree that at His coming He will raise the dead, execute judgment, and eventually institute the eternal state. No one of these views has an inherent liberalizing tendency. Hence the matters on which they agree are much more important than those on which they differ. This fact should enable them to cooperate as evangelicals and to present a united front against Modernists and Liberals who more or less consistently deny the supernatural throughout the whole range of Bible truth.[18]

---

18. Loraine Boettner, *The Millennium* (Phillipsburg, NJ: P&R, 1957), 18.

4

THE KINGDOM OF GOD IN BIBLICAL
AND THEOLOGICAL PERSPECTIVE

*The predicted blessing, therefore, belongs unquestionably
to the times of the kingdom, when the righteous shall
bear rule upon their rising from the dead; when also
the creation, having been renovated and set free, shall
fructify with an abundance of all kinds of food, from
the dew of heaven, and from the fertility of the earth.*

Irenaeus, *Against Heresies* 5.33.3

In the previous chapter, I presented the threefold foundation of orthodox eschatology—the return of Christ, resurrection of humanity, and the restoration of creation—and also introduced the three major traditions regarding the coming kingdom coexisting within that orthodox eschatology—amillennialism, premillennialism, and postmillennialism. In this chapter, I answer a question: "What is the kingdom?" How one answers this question will set parameters on issues related to the timing and character of the coming kingdom in the Old and New Testaments, its relationship to the future return of Christ, and its place in the overarching plan and purpose of God.

In the middle of the last century, George Eldon Ladd noted, "There are few themes so prominent in the Bible which have received such radically divergent interpretations as the Kingdom of God. . . . The perplexing fact is that when we turn to the Scriptures, we find an almost equally bewildering diversity of statements about the Kingdom of God."[1] When we look to Scripture for the use of "kingdom (ממלכה/βασιλεία)," we see the term used in the following distinct—though often related—ways:

1. God's universal sovereign rule over all creation, all nations, and all people (Ps 22:28; Dan 4:3, 34; 6:26). This kingdom is characterized by divine virtues of justice (Ps 45:6), grace, compassion, mercy, universal goodness, glory, power, faithfulness, and holiness (Ps 145:8–13).

2. Human, earthly kingdoms (e.g., Gen 10:10; Ps 68:32; Matt 4:8; Luke 4:5, etc.), even though these "kingdoms of the earth" are under the sovereign rule of God (#1 above) (2 Kgs 19:15; 2 Chr 20:6; 36:23; Dan 2:37).

---

1. George Eldon Ladd, *The Gospel of the Kingdom: Scriptural Studies in the Kingdom of God* (Grand Rapids: Eerdmans, 1959), 15–16.

3. The people of Israel as a whole—God's unique "kingdom of priests" (ממלכת כהנים) under God's direct, unique theocratic rule, intended to acknowledge and reflect #1 above (Exod 19:6; Num 24:7).

4. The kingdom of Israel under a human king—Saul or David and his dynasty (Deut 17:18; 1 Sam 13:13; 2 Sam 3:10; 7:16; 1 Kgs 2:12), which was nevertheless viewed as the kingdom of YHWH mediated through that human ruler among his special theocratic nation (#1 and #3 above) (2 Chr 13:8).[2]

5. The divided kingdom of Israel in the north (1 Kgs 11:31) or Judah in the south (2 Chr 11:17).

6. The messianic kingdom, which seems to combine elements of the previous expressions of the kingdom, particularly #1, #3, and #4 (Isa 9:7; Dan 2:44; 7:14, 18, 22, 27 [cf. Dan 4:3, 34; 6:26]; Mic 4:8; Mark 11:10; Luke 1:33).

7. A spiritual and ethical way of life in keeping with God's values, priorities, virtues, and standards—the rule of God in the minds and lives of those submitting to him (Matt 5:3, 10; 6:33). This form of the kingdom is realizable in the present through proclamation and faith (Matt 13:24, 31, 33, 44, 45, 47; 19:14; John 18:36; Rom 14:17).

8. The imminent coming kingdom brought about by the preaching first of John the Baptist and then of Jesus—the "gospel of the kingdom" (τὸ εὐαγγέλιον τῆς βασιλείας) (Matt 3:2; 4:17, 23; 9:35; 10:7; Luke 4:43; 10:9; Acts 8:12), which may be identified with or related to #6–7 above as the means by which those aspects of the kingdom are more fully realized (Matt 24:14).

9. Closely associated with #6–8, the term "kingdom" sometimes refers more strictly to the future eschatological kingdom under Jesus and fully manifested in the world (Matt 7:21; 8:11; 13:41, 43; 20:21; Mark 14:25; Luke 13:28–29; 21:31; 22:16; 22:30; Acts 1:6; 1 Cor 15:24; 2 Tim 4:1).

10. The present church as that body fulfilling the spiritual and ethical life of faith (#7) and foreshadowing the coming eschatological kingdom (#9) (Matt 16:18–19; 21:43; 25:34; 26:29; John 3:3–5; Col 1:13).

11. On occasion, the eschatological term seems to refer to a kingdom in the realm of heaven itself, apart from and "above" the earth, though necessarily under the universal rule of God over all things (#1) (2 Tim 4:18).[3]

Given the distinct yet often complementary ways in which the kingdom of God/kingdom of heaven are presented in the Old and New Testaments, it seems best not to select one aspect of the kingdom and force other passages to conform

---

2. Whether the phrase in 2 Chron 13:8 was God's perspective on the matter or a theory of theocracy advanced by Abijah to rally the troops does not change the fact this was a common view and consistent with the promise of perpetuity in the Davidic covenant (2 Sam 7).

3. References to the "kingdom of heaven" (ἡ βασιλεία τῶν οὐρανῶν), especially in Matthew, are not necessarily references to a kingdom located in the heavenly sphere, as a passage like Matt 11:12 indicates.

to it—either a future, earthly rule; a heavenly realm; or a spiritual, ethical domain.[4] Rather, a better approach is to understand these various aspects—realizable in diverse times and places, means and manifestations—with a general definition that accommodates numerous specific applications.

In fact, we have such a definition in Scripture itself: the kingdom of God, in its most general sense, is God's will realized on earth as in heaven, as found in the Lord's Prayer (Matt 6:10). Ladd writes:

> The confidence that this prayer is to be answered when God brings human history to the divinely ordained consummation enables the Christian to retain his balance and sanity of mind in this mad world in which we live. . . . But when we pray, "Thy Kingdom come," we also ask that God's will be done here and now, today. . . . We should also pray, "Thy kingdom come, Thy will be done" in my church as it is in heaven. . . . "Thy kingdom come, Thy will be done" in my life, as it is in heaven.[5]

Thus the "kingdom of God" can be more or less present as the values and priorities of heaven are impressed upon this world. In this sense, the kingdom of God was originally manifested in the Garden of Eden, with plans for expanding it into the rest of the world and the universe, as we discussed in chapter 2. The kingdom was partially and imperfectly realized in both the preservation of creation by God's grace and mercy (e.g., conscience, family, human government) and the redemptive work of God's covenant-forging relationships with particular people (e.g., theocratic rule under the patriarchs and judges). The kingdom finds a more stable and fixed expression in the establishment of Israel as a theocracy and the covenant of law as a contextualized theonomy. It is personally realized as individual believers embrace and practice divine virtue and power.

In the economy of the incarnation, Christ himself as the God-man is not only the mediator of the kingdom of God, but he is also in himself a microcosm of the kingdom (Luke 11:20; 17:21). That is, Christ embodies both king and kingdom fully and perfectly. His body, the church, in its present stage also embodies the kingdom in a partial and imperfect way. Yet the more the church lives up to its calling, the more the kingdom of God is expressed and experienced: God's will done on earth as in heaven.[6]

Upon the return of Christ, we begin to see the ultimate manifestation of God's values and priorities in the earthly realm: the return of the garden of God. Even

---

4. Cf. Ladd, *Gospel of the Kingdom*, 22–23.
5. Ladd, *Gospel of the Kingdom*, 23.
6. See helpful accounts of the multifaceted nature of the "kingdom of God" and its relationship to the theocracy of Israel, to Jesus, to individual believers, to the church, and to the future in J. Mark Beach, "The Kingdom of God: A Brief Exposition of Its Meaning and Implications," *Mid-America Journal of Theology* 23 (2012): 53–76; G. Goldsworthy, "Kingdom of God," in *New Dictionary of Biblical Theology*, ed. T. Desmond Alexander and Brian S. Rosner (Downers Grove, IL: IVP, 2000), 615–20; George E. Ladd, "Kingdom of God (Heaven)," *Baker Encyclopedia of the Bible* (Grand Rapids: Baker, 1988), 1269–78; Christopher Morgan and Robert A. Peterson, eds., *The Kingdom of God,* Theology in Community (Wheaton, IL: Crossway, 2012); and Andrzej Napiórkowski, "Is the Kingdom of Heaven the Church of Jesus Christ?," *Vox Patrum* 33 (2013): 547–57.

then, the kingdom of God, manifested in the theocracy centered and sourced in the king, Jesus, and mediated through his kingdom advances throughout the world. The process of complete transformation of creation and its bondage to corruption endures until the entire earth is edenified and the whole world, including all people and things in it, is transformed "as it is in heaven." Bruce Waltke notes, "In light of the war between the particular kingdom of God under the direct rule of the triune God and of the universal kingdom under the restricted rule of Satan, the Lord's Prayer teaches the church to hope for a future when the particular kingdom will become coextensive with the universal kingdom."[7]

Thus, though multilayered, the "kingdom of God" is not many things but one thing—God's will accomplished on earth as in heaven—more or less manifested in any particular time or place as the priorities, values, and virtues of heaven are realized in the earthly realm. Morgan and Peterson rightly note, "A deeper look at Jesus' words reveals that he views the kingdom as multifaceted. He speaks of the kingdom as both present and future, as including both salvation and judgment, as encompassing both rule and locus. In addition, the kingdom pertains to human beings, angels, and the heavens and earth."[8]

The Return of Paradise and the Coming Kingdom

Though multifaceted and realizable to varying degrees in the present age, the "kingdom of God/kingdom of heaven" in its fullest sense will be fully present in the world when Christ returns. As we have mentioned, this return of Christ, resurrection of the dead, removal of evil, and restoration of creation correspond with the climax of the grand narrative of humanity's loss of access to paradise and the ultimate return of paradise in the transformation of this world (chapter 2). At this point, a closer look at the relationship between the coming kingdom and the return of paradise is necessary, as second-century church fathers understood these to be one and the same thing.

Go Deeper Excursus 4

"Your Will Be Done" as "Your Kingdom Come"

In Luke 23:42, the penitent thief crucified beside Jesus implored him, "Jesus, remember me when you come in your kingdom." To this request, Jesus replied, "Truly I tell you, today you will be with me in paradise (ἐν τῷ παραδείσῳ)" (23:43). That the departed righteous went to paradise was a common belief in the first century.[9]

7. Bruce K. Waltke, "The Kingdom of God in the Old Testament: Definitions and Story," in *The Kingdom of God*, ed. Christopher W. Morgan and Robert A. Peterson, Theology in Community (Wheaton: Crossway, 2012), 55.

8. Christopher W. Morgan and Robert A. Peterson, introduction in *The Kingdom of God*, ed. Christopher W. Morgan and Robert A. Peterson, Theology in Community (Wheaton, IL: Crossway, 2012), 20. Cf. John Bright, *The Kingdom of God: The Biblical Concept and Its Meaning for the Church* (New York: Abingdon-Cokesbury, 1953), 238; Patrick Schreiner, *The Kingdom of God and the Glory of the Cross*, Short Studies in Biblical Theology (Wheaton, IL: Crossway, 2018), 20.

9. See the discussion of its possible origins and background in Martin Goodman, "Paradise, Gardens, and the Afterlife in the First Century CE," in *Paradise in Antiquity: Jewish*

The term ὁ παράδεισος ("paradise") appears two other times in the New Testament, both with the definite article, as here, indicating a particular, well-known concept. In 2 Corinthians 12:2–4, Paul recalled when he had been "caught up into paradise (ἡρπάγη εἰς τὸν παράδεισον)," which he parallels with the phrase "caught up into the third heaven (ἁρπαγέντα . . . ἕως τρίτου οὐρανοῦ)" (12:2). In Paul's understanding, the place called paradise is theoretically able to sustain both physical and spiritual beings, as he expresses uncertainty about whether he had been snatched up into paradise "in the body or out of the body" (12:2).[10]

The third place where paradise appears is Revelation 2:7, where Jesus promises, "To the one who overcomes, I will give them to eat from the tree of life, which is in God's paradise (ὅ ἐστιν ἐν τῷ παραδείσῳ τοῦ θεοῦ)." The present tense ἐστιν immediately suggests the tree of life—from the paradise of Eden—continues to exist in this heavenly realm. This comports well with Paul's earlier statement that paradise accommodates both physical and spiritual beings (2 Cor 12:2).

By the time the term is used in the New Testament as something that continues to exist in the heavenly realm, the term "paradise" had already been used as the place where the first people were placed—distinct from the rest of the created world from which they had been formed. In the Septuagint, "paradise" first appears in Genesis 2:8—"The Lord God planted a paradise in Eden (παράδεισον ἐν Εδεμ) in the east, and he put there the man whom he had formed." And in 2:9, the text further states that God caused numerous trees, good for eating, to grow from the earth, including "the tree of life in the midst of paradise (τὸ ξύλον τῆς ζωῆς ἐν μέσῳ τῷ παραδείσῳ)." Here, according to ancient Christian teaching, humans where originally intended to enjoy fellowship with God and other spiritual and physical beings, to eat from the trees—especially the tree of life—and to grow in their immortality.

The second-century apologist, Theophilus of Antioch, describes God's establishment of paradise "in the East" (*Autol.* 2.19), that Adam "might be in a better and distinctly superior place" (2.23 [*ANF* 2]). Thus while the rest of the world was created "good," paradise was superior in quality. He explains, "God, then, caused to spring out of the earth every tree that is beautiful in appearance, or good for food. For at first there were only those things which were produced on the third day,— plants, and seeds, and herbs; but the things which were in paradise were made of a superior loveliness and beauty, since in it the plants were said to have been planted by God" (2.24). Theophilus describes God's intention in placing Adam in paradise: "And God transferred him from the earth, out of which he had been produced, into paradise, giving him means of advancement, in order that, maturing and becoming perfect, and being even declared a god, he might thus ascend into heaven in possession of immortality. For man had been made a middle nature, neither wholly

and Christian Views, ed. Markus Bockmuehl and Guy S. Stoumsa (Cambridge: Cambridge University Press, 2010), 57–63.

10. That this paradise in the third heaven is to be identified with the paradise in Eden is explained by Ambrose in his work *On Paradise* (1.1–2) written around AD 375. See John J. Savage, introduction in *St. Ambrose: Hexameron, Paradise, and Cain and Abel*, trans. John J. Savage, *The Fathers of the Church: A New Translation*, vol. 42 (Washington, DC: The Catholic University of America Press, 1961), ix.

mortal, nor altogether immortal, but capable of either; so also the place, paradise, was made in respect of beauty intermediate between earth and heaven" (2.24).

Therefore, when Jesus promises the overcomers that they would eat from the tree of life (Rev 2:7), which is in God's paradise, he draws together the original garden of paradise from which humanity had been ejected and barred (Gen 3:24), the present place in the heavenly realm where paradise continues, and a future place of sustenance and fellowship with God. Jesus' use of the future tense ("I will give," Rev 2:7) suggests an eschatological restoration of paradise; his use of the present tense ("which is in paradise") suggests its present existence. This fits well with Paul's assertion of being caught up to paradise, to a place called the "third heaven," which could sustain both bodily and spiritual beings. This, in turn, is similar to the original paradise of Eden, where both the first humans and the "face of the Lord" (προσώπου κυρίου, מפני יהוה), who walked in the garden (περιπατοῦντος ἐν τῷ παραδείσῳ, מתהלך בגן) (Gen 3:8, 10), enjoyed fellowship with each other.[11]

That paradise continues to exist in a supercelestial realm is asserted in diverse ways in the apocryphal literature composed between the testaments. First Enoch 20.1 calls Gabriel "one of the holy angels, who is over paradise (ὃς ἐπὶ τοῦ παραδείσου)."[12] And in his apocalyptic journey to the east, Enoch encounters the "paradise of righteousness (τὸν παράδεισον τῆς δικαιοσύνης)," which still contains the tree of wisdom (1 En. 32.3–6). In another member of Enochian literature, *The Book of the Secrets of Enoch*, often simply called 2 Enoch (c. AD 30–70), we get a glimpse of the popular view of the relationship between the "third heaven" and paradise to which Paul himself referred. When Enoch recounts his ascent to the "third heaven," he enters paradise. He notes, "I saw all the sweet-flowering trees and beheld their fruits, which were sweet-smelling" (2 En. 8.2). Also, in this paradise of the third heaven stands the tree of life, "adorned more than every existing thing" (8.3). Enoch describes this place as "between corruptibility and incorruptibility"— that is, both physical and spiritual, mortal and immortal (8.5). When Enoch comments on the sweetness of paradise, the angels respond, "This place, O Enoch, is prepared for the righteous . . . for eternal inheritance" (2 En. 9.1).[13]

In keeping with this early understanding, in the late second century, Irenaeus of Lyons says that Enoch kept his body but was translated to paradise; Elijah, too, was "taken up." This view, he says, had been handed down to him from the apostles through his own teachers: "Wherefore also the elders who were disciples of the apostles tell us that those who were translated were transferred to that place ["paradise, from which Adam was expelled"]. . . . and that there shall they who

---

11. Later, the "paradise of God" or "paradise of the Lord" is sometimes used to compare earthly gardens to that original Edenic condition (Gen 13:10; Isa 51:3). Or it simply refers to any lush garden on the earth (Num 24:6 LXX; 2 Esd 12:8 LXX [cf. Neh 2:8]; Eccl 2:5; Song 4:13; Sir 24:30; 40:17, 27; Jer 36:5; Joel 2:3).

12. Translation from R. H. Charles and W. O. E. Oesterley, *The Book of Enoch* (London: Society for Promoting Christian Knowledge, 1917).

13. Interestingly, in the extreme north of the third heaven also exists the place of torments for the wicked as an eternal inheritance. Thus the place of both the righteous and the wicked are "above" in the heavenly realm (2 En. 10).

have been translated remain until the consummation [of all things]" (*Haer.* 5.5.1). For this teaching, we can assume that Irenaeus is referring to the oral teaching he received from people such as Polycarp or Papias. The fact that Irenaeus mentions Paul's catching up to paradise in 2 Corinthians 12:4 suggests that paradise was still regarded as the place of the righteous saints awaiting the consummation even in Irenaeus's day.[14]

Even the Old Testament prophets foresaw a time when the promised land, despite its erstwhile desolation in judgment, would not only be restored but glorified to a condition comparable to the Garden of Eden. Isaiah 51:3 (LXX) says, "Even now I will comfort you, Zion, and I have comforted all her deserted places, and I will make her deserted places like a garden and the western places like a garden of the Lord (ὡς παράδεισον κυρίου, MT כגן-יהוה)" [Brannan]). Of the flourishing of the world in the future kingdom, Ezekiel writes, "The land that was desolate shall be tilled, instead of being the desolation that it was in the sight of all who passed by. And they will say, 'This land that was desolate has become like the garden of Eden'" (Ezek 36:34–35).[15] The prophets' vision of the future appears to have involved the return of paradise and its unleashing upon this world, resulting in a gradual but steady redemption and transformation of the earth, beginning in Jerusalem and spreading throughout all creation.

Some in the early church expanded on this idea of an eschatological restoration of creation as a kind of second coming of paradise. After explaining that when Adam transgressed, "the sin in which man was concerned brought even upon" the animals, Theophilus of Antioch anticipates the great eschatological reversal: "When, therefore, man again shall have made his way back to his natural condition, and no longer does evil, those also shall be restored to their original gentleness" (*Autol.* 2.17 [*ANF* 2]). We should catch glimpses here of Isaiah's imagery in Isaiah 65, which portrays a new harmony between humanity and beasts and among beasts themselves. Theophilus also taught a restoration of paradise on earth and a return of humanity to this Edenic state—through improved by resurrection and immortality. This will occur "after the resurrection and judgment" (*Autol.* 2.26).[16] Furthermore, Irenaeus of Lyons also noted that God's personal presence with Adam and Eve in paradise was "prefiguring the future, which would come to pass" in the coming kingdom (*Epid.* 12).

In light of this, another passage in the Gospels that bring together both paradise and the coming kingdom deserves our attention: the account of Christ's transfiguration on the "holy mountain" (2 Pet 1:18), which Peter associates with "the power and coming of our Lord Jesus Christ" (1:16). Peter is likely reflecting on

---

14. Ambrose of Milan, *On Paradise*, 11.53, also asserts that "the just are caught up into paradise, just as Paul 'was caught up into paradise.'"

15. Also see the imagery in Isa 41:18–19; 58:11; 60:13; Ezek 31:8–9.

16. That paradise will return to earth in the coming kingdom from its sojourn in the third heaven is seen in Irenaeus of Lyons, *AH* 5.36.1–2, where a distinction is made between those who dwell in the earthly city, those who are admitted by virtue of spiritual progress, to paradise, and those who are taken up to the highest heaven. Also see Basil (*De Paradiso, Oratio* III), Cyril of Jerusalem (*Cat.* 2.7), and John of Damascus (*De fide orthodoxa* 2.11).

Jesus' statement, "Truly I tell you, there are some standing here who will not taste death before they see the Son of Man coming in his kingdom" (Matt 16:28). This prophecy has been variously interpreted throughout history.[17] However, an early and enduring tradition was that this promise of "seeing" the kingdom coming in power and glory was fulfilled immediately on the Mount of Transfiguration, a contextual connection made in all three Synoptic Gospels (see Matt 16:28 [cf. 17:1–8]; Mark 9:1 [cf. 9:2–8]; Luke 9:27 [cf. 9:28–36]).

In that scene of the vision of the coming kingdom, Jesus took Peter, James, and John up on a high mountain where he was transfigured before them (Matt 17:1–2). Like Moses who had ascended the mountain to which the Lord God had come down, Jesus' face began to shine like the sun, and his clothing became a radiant white (17:2). The allusions to Moses and the people of Israel meeting with God on Mount Sinai are not coincidental. Just as Moses gathered the people of Israel to the mountain in order to hear God speak to Moses in the midst of a thick cloud and trust him (Exod 19:9), Jesus also brought his three disciples to the mountain where a thick cloud formed, and they, too, heard the voice of God urging them to trust Jesus (Matt 17:5). Like the Israelites, the disciples' response to the voice of God was paralyzing fear (Exod 19:16; Matt 17:6). Just as Jesus' face glowed like the sun (Matt 17:2), Moses' face glowed after leaving the cloud of the presence of God (Exod 34:29–35). These clues suggest that the same event that occurred on Sinai with Moses and the people of Israel occurred also with Jesus and the disciples. When Moses was in the cloud on the mountain, he saw things from another realm. In fact, the tabernacle itself was built according to the plan shown to Moses on the mountain (Exod 25:9; 26:30). This pattern included cherubim on the ark of the covenant (25:18–20) and curtains embroidered with cherubim (26:1). The lampstand was to be fashioned with shapes of flowers with blossoms, suggesting a garden (25:33–35), just as Moses had seen on the mountain (25:40).

Many have noted the similarities between the original paradise of God in Eden and the imagery of Mount Sinai and the tabernacle based on the pattern shown on that mountain. In fact, the paradise of Eden is often understood as itself a kind of tabernacle or temple—a sacred space where heaven and earth intersect and God meets with his people.[18] The paradise of Eden had to have been on a mountain, because "a river flowed out of Eden to water the garden; and from there it divided and became four rivers" (Gen 2:10).[19] It had only one entrance, suggested by the fact that the cherubim stationed at the east prevented entrance to the garden and

---

17. See, for example, the range of interpretations in W. D. Davies and Dale C. Allison Jr., *A Critical and Exegetical Commentary on the Gospel according to Saint Matthew*, vol. 2, International Critical Commentary (London: T&T Clark, 2004), 677–79.

18. See discussions in G. K. Beale, "Adam as the First Priest in Eden as the Garden Temple," *SBJT* 22.2 (2018): 9–24; Meredith Kline, *Axis of Glory: A Biblical and Theological Analysis of the Temple Motif in Scripture* (New York: Peter Lang, 2010), 48–49; Yonatan S. Miller, "Sabbath-Temple-Eden: Purity Rituals at the Intersection of Sacred Time and Space," *JAJ* 9.1 (2018): 50–51; and Lisa Schachter, "The Garden of Eden as God's First Sanctuary," *JBQ* 41 (2013): 73–77.

19. Rita Nakashima Brock and Rebecca Ann Parker, *Saving Paradise: How Christianity Traded Love of This World for Crucifixion and Empire* (Boston: Beacon, 2008), 15.

the tree of life (3:24). The tree of life itself is reflected in the imagery of the blossoming golden lampstand in the midst of the sanctuary (Exod 25:31–40), providing constant light, a symbol for life (John 1:4).[20]

The text of Exodus also gives us clues that the descent of God to Mount Sinai was more than just a personal theophany: that is, God coming down and appearing in a glorious form to Moses and the Israelites. Rather, it appears to have been a kind of temporary superimposing of the heavenly realm onto the earthly realm. In Exodus 24, we read, "Then Moses and Aaron, Nadab and Abihu, and seventy of the elders of Israel went up, and they saw the God of Israel. Under his feet there was something like a pavement of sapphire stone, like the very heaven for clearness. God did not lay his hand on the chief men of the Israelites; they beheld God, and they ate and drank" (Exod 24:9–11).[21] Regardless of how we understand the "pavement of sapphire stones" under the feet of the theophanic form,[22] it seems that with the theophany came a transformation of the physical environment—the heavenly realm was superimposed upon the earthly realm, temporarily transforming this world. Eugene Carpenter captures the significance of the image well: "The biblical author-editor has done a superb job of meshing a matrix of reality that includes the interpenetration of the divine world into the natural world."[23] Besides standing in the presence of God and experiencing a transformation of their physical environment, the elders also "ate and drank," a kind of covenant meal reminiscent of the disciples' communion with Jesus as a foretaste of the coming kingdom.[24]

Returning to the Mount of Transfiguration, it appears that something similar to the meeting between God and the elders of Israel occurred.[25] Just as on Mount

---

20. See Daniel T. Lioy, "The Garden of Eden as a Primordial Temple or Sacred Space for Humankind," *Conspectus* (2010): 35.

21. It may also be appropriate to see parallels between the theophanic visitation on Mount Sinai and the highly stylized description of Eden, the Garden of God, in Ezek 28:11–15.

22. Several commentators point out the symbolism of heaven or the sky, in which case the celestial realm was under God's feet—at the ground level of Moses and the leaders of Israel—suggesting that heavenly and earthly realms had overlapped. See discussion of the language and symbolism in Walter C. Kaiser Jr., "Exodus," in *The Expositor's Bible Commentary: Genesis–Leviticus*, rev. ed., ed. Tremper Longman III and David E. Garland, vol. 1 (Grand Rapids: Zondervan, 2008), 508.

23. Eugene Carpenter, *Exodus*, ed. H. Wayne House and William D. Barrick, vol. 2, Evangelical Exegetical Commentary (Bellingham, WA: Lexham, 2012), 148.

24. See comments in H. D. M. Spence-Jones, ed., *Exodus*, vol. 2, The Pulpit Commentary (London: Funk & Wagnalls, 1909), 234; Seung-In Song, "Seeing the Johannine Last Meal as a Covenant Meal (John 13 and Exodus 24)," *Biblica* 100.2 (2019): 286–87. For arguments against a covenantal interpretation of the meal, see E. W. Nicholson, "The Interpretation of Exodus XXIV 9–11," *VT Vetus Testamentum* 24.1 (1974): 77–97. Contra Nicholson, see John W. Hilber, "Theology of Worship in Exodus 24," *JETS* 39.2 (1996): 183–84. I would contend that even if the eating and drinking of leaders of Israel who had ascended the mountain indicates a covenant-fellowship meal on Mount Sinai, when read in its canonical-theological context, its divine inclusion in the theophanic experience may be seen as pointing backward to eating freely in the paradise of God, forward to the spiritual food and drink of eucharistic fellowship, and ultimately forward to the food and drink that comes from the River of Life and Tree of Life in the restored paradise.

25. In fact, the parallels between the Mount of Transfiguration and the theophany on Mount Sinai are striking. Chilton contends, "*It is beyond reasonable doubt that the Trans-*

Sinai, during the meeting on the Mount of Transfiguration, the heavenly and earthly realms intersected. Moses and Elijah appeared. Moses himself had died and had gone to the place of the departed righteous (Deut 34:5). Elijah, however, did not die but had been caught up in a whirlwind to heaven (2 Kgs 2:11). Where had Moses and Elijah been prior to appearing on the Mount of Transfiguration with Jesus? Many first-century Jews would have answered, "In the heavenly realm, in paradise."[26]

Jesus confirms this general belief in his response to the request by the thief on the cross—"Jesus, remember me when you come in your kingdom" (Luke 23:42). Jesus replied, "Truly I tell you, today you will be with me in paradise" (23:43). Evidently, some relationship between the Messiah's "kingdom" (23:42) and "paradise" (23:43) exists, or Jesus' response to the man's desperate plea makes little sense. Some see the relationship as one of distinction: the thief asked to be resurrected in the (future) kingdom, but Jesus offers him immediate access to a heavenly paradise.[27] Others see the relationship as one of parallelism: the thief asked for access to the (heavenly) kingdom, and Jesus confirmed this request, suggesting paradise and heaven are the same.[28] Yet these apparently separate and mutually exclusive approaches are reconciled when we view the coming kingdom of the messianic age as the restoration of paradise from its present place in the heavenly realm to this earth. When paradise is again unleashed on this earth and God's will is quite literally accomplished "on earth as it is in heaven," then the kingdom will fully come. Thus the understanding of paradise planted on the earth, paradise removed from the earth, and paradise restored to the earth provides a framework for understanding how

---

figuration is fundamentally a visionary representation of the Sinai motif of Exod. 24" [italics original]. See Bruce D. Chilton, "The Transfiguration: Dominical Assurance and Apostolic Vision," *NTS* 27.1 (1980): 122.

26. The Jewish perspective regarding "paradise" varied in the first century, though they all tended toward similar ideas of its continued existence and future restoration. J. Osei-Bonsu summarizes the situation this way: "The word 'paradise', originally a loan word from Old Persian (*Pairi-daeza*) and meaning a nobleman's park, or garden, was adopted into Greek and Hebrew. The LXX used this word to translate the Garden of Eden in Gen. 2–3. It was believed that as a result of Adam's sin, paradise was removed and hidden at the very end of the earth (1 En. 60:23), in the east (2 En. 31:1; 43:3; 1 En. 32:2) or in the north (1 En. 77:3). Other Jews believed that paradise was hidden on a high mountain or in heaven: in the third heaven, according to 2 En. 8:1–8, or in the seventh heaven, according to Asc. Isa. 9:7. It was believed that paradise, which existed in a hidden form, would be restored to humankind in the age to come (cf. 2 Bar. 51:10f.) when the Messiah would "open the gates of paradise" (T. Levi 18:10). But in some strands of Judaism, it was believed that the souls of some righteous people went to this hidden paradise at death: paradise houses the souls of the departed patriarchs, according to 1 En. 70:4; T. Ab. 20A; Apoc. Mos. 37:5, as well as the souls of the elect and the righteous (1 En. 60:7f., 23; 61:12; 70:4)." See J. Osei-Bonsu, "The Intermediate State in the New Testament," *Scottish Journal of Theology* 44 (1991): 176.

27. Norval Geldenhuys, *Commentary on the Gospel of Luke: The English Text with Introduction, Exposition and Notes*, The New International Commentary on the Old and New Testament (Grand Rapids: Eerdmans, 1952), 611. Cf. Frédéric Louis Godet, *A Commentary on the Gospel of St. Luke*, trans. Edward William Shalders and M. D. Cusin, vol. 2 (New York: Funk, 1881), 335.

28. James R. Edwards, *The Gospel according to Luke*, ed. D. A. Carson, The Pillar New Testament Commentary (Grand Rapids: Eerdmans, 2015), 691. Cf. Trent C. Butler, *Luke*, vol. 3, Holman New Testament Commentary (Nashville: B&H, 2000), 396.

the kingdom of God can be regarded as both heavenly and earthly, spiritual and physical, present and future, realized, realizable, and unrealized, already and not yet.

Rather than seeing the various references to paradise—in Eden, in the third heaven, as the place of departed righteous, as a future reality in this world—as separate or contradictory perspectives, these distinct concepts can be reconciled when traced through the story of redemption. As such, "the paradise of God" is understood as a created realm that exists in an intersection between heaven and earth, spiritual and physical. When we put together the pieces of the puzzle of paradise, we get the picture that the original paradise garden planted by God on the earth, where the tree of life had been planted, did not cease to exist after the exile of humanity. Rather, paradise was removed from this world, taken up to an inaccessible realm. There it remains in the present age: after the fall, prior to the future restoration. Yet, when we catch a glimpse of the ultimate restoration of all things in the symbolic imagery of Revelation, we see that it will return with the coming kingdom concurrent with the transformation of this world (Rev 22:1–2). Thus Jesus' promise will be fulfilled: "To everyone who conquers, I will give permission to eat from the tree of life that is in the paradise of God" (2:7).

In this light, the vision of the new Jerusalem descending from heaven is best seen as a symbol for the return of Eden after its long exile in the heavenly realm. This recalls Old Testament Eden passages, especially Ezekiel 28:13. Jean Delumeau observes, "The images of the cosmic mountain on which Ezekiel locates the garden of Eden and of the precious stones with which he fills it will be applied in the Johannine Apocalypse to the messianic Jerusalem."[29] Many also see imagery of paradise in the vision of Ezekiel's temple.[30]

Grant Macaskill notes that the New Testament language and imagery presents "a belief in a present paradise, where the righteous dead reside and to which, in some sense, the church is spiritually connected in its fellowship with God through the spirit; but this does not eclipse or contradict an expectation of a future earthly paradise, when Christ's reign is perfected and the hopes of the Church fully realized."[31] Patristic scholar Christopher Hall sums it up well: "Christ will return one day with all the inhabitants of paradise to consummate his reign on earth. In the meantime, those who die confessing (with the believing thief) faith in Christ's kingdom can rest assured they will be with Christ in paradise during the strange, unexpected in-between time between Jesus' first and second coming."[32]

Simply put, paradise—the intersection of the heavenly and earthly realms— once occupied space in this world prior to the fall "in Eden, in the east" (Gen 2:8). After the fall, this paradise, along with the tree of life, was taken up into the "third heaven" (2 Cor 12:2, 4) and became the place of departed saints (Luke 23:43) as well

---

29. Jean Delumeau, *History of Paradise: The Garden of Eden in Myth and Tradition*, trans. Matthew O'Connell (New York: Continuum, 1995), 5.

30. Brock and Parker, *Saving Paradise*, 24.

31. Grant Macaskill, "Paradise in the New Testament," in *Paradise in Antiquity: Jewish and Christian Views*, ed. Markus Bockmuehl and Guy G. Stroumsa (Cambridge: Cambridge University Press, 2010), 81.

32. Christopher A. Hall, "Christ's Kingdom and Paradise," *CT* 47.11 (November 2003): 79.

as those who, like Enoch or Elijah, had been assumed bodily into heaven. In certain instances, the heavenly and earthly realms intersect, and humans catch a glimpse of paradise (e.g., Exod 24:1–11; Matt 17:1–8) or they are taken up to paradise (2 Cor 12:1–4). In the coming kingdom in the future, paradise will return to earth, which will then be progressively transformed into the quality of paradise itself (Isa 51:3; Ezek 36:34–35; Rev 2:7; 22:1–2). Thus the coming kingdom is to be identified with the return of paradise to earth.

5

The Earliest Fathers and the Coming Kingdom

When his Son comes, he will abolish the season
of the lawless one, he will judge the ungodly, and
he will change the sun and the moon and the
stars, then he will truly rest on the seventh day.

Epistle of Barnabas 15.5

Before exploring the Old and New Testament teaching on the coming kingdom, this chapter—together with its technical excurses—will set forth the eschatological expectations of the earliest church fathers from about AD 50 to about AD 200. In subsequent chapters, then, I make the case that the basic second-century eschatology of Irenaeus of Lyons best matches the teaching of Scripture based on careful exegesis. The Irenaean premillennial eschatology also provides the best climax of the trinitarian creation-fall-redemption narrative centered on the person and work of Christ in his first and second comings.

A Survey of Early Premillennialism Prior to Irenaeus

On the general history of early millennialism, Bernard Hort, former professor of systematic theology at the Faculté universitaire de théologie protestante de Bruxelles, writes:

> The hope in a thousand-year reign of happiness preceding the final denouement of history was widely shared by the first Christians. . . . It still clearly dominates in Saint Irenaeus. It will be profoundly relativized from the fourth century onward in favor of a symbolic reading of the book of Revelation. This reversal will be carried out mainly under the influence of Saint Augustine, though also by Tyconius, who appears to us in this matter to have been a true "Augustine before Augustine." The rejection of a literal understanding of Revelation 20 became the dominant position of the Church and then, after the Reformation, of the main churches.[1]

This snapshot sums up what can be called the "traditional view" of the course of millennial views in church history. Already in 1690, English theologian Thomas

---

1. Translated from Bernard Hort, "Millénarisme ou amillénarisme? Regard contemporain sur un conflit traditionnel," *Revue théologique de Louvain* 31 (2000): 35.

Burnet concluded that "the Millenary doctrine was *Orthodox* and *Catholick* in those early days. For these Authors do not set it down as a private opinion of their own, but as a *Christian doctrine,* or an *Apostolical Tradition*."[2]

This traditional view of an early, widespread, and well-developed millennialism has been challenged particularly by those from theological traditions or confessions that have officially rejected "chiliasm" or "premillennialism." Such challenges are addressed in Go Deeper Excursus 5, "Ancient and Modern Challenges to Early Premillennial Testimonies." In the rest of this chapter, I will first attend briefly to the testimonies of first- and second-century Christian writings, demonstrating that when they are not silent on the issue, the earliest church fathers express a premillennial eschatology.

The Probable Premillennialism in Didache 16

The Didache, or, more fully, the Teaching of the Twelve Apostles, is an early Christian writing that may be regarded as a handbook for newly appointed leaders of newly established churches.[3] With regard to date and provenance of the Didache, the twentieth century has seen a trend in scholarship willing to date the present form of the work to the first century, perhaps as early as from AD 50 to 70[4] but before AD 100.[5] Though both Egypt and Syria have been considered as viable candidates for the place of the Didache's composition or redaction, the general sense among scholars is that the work most likely originated in Syria or its environs.[6]

> **Go Deeper Excursus 5**
>
> *Ancient and Modern Challenges to Early Premillennial Testimonies*

---

2. Thomas Burnet, *The Sacred Theory of the Earth* (London: Walter Kettilby, 1690), 175. Burnet's view of the future earthly millennium, however, was more consistent with modern-day postmillennialism.

3. See Michael J. Svigel, "*Didache* as a Practical Enchiridion for Early Church Plants," *BSac* 174.1 (2017): 77–94.

4. See Jean-Paul Audet, *La Didachè: Instructions des Apôtres*, Ebib (Paris: Gabalda, 1958), 187–206; Aaron Milavec, *The Didache: Faith, Hope, and Life of the Earliest Christian Communities, 50–70 CE* (New York: Newman, 2003); and John A. T. Robinson, *Redating the New Testament* (Philadelphia: Westminster, 1976), 96–100, 322–27. In 2010, O'Loughlin accurately noted, "The broad consensus today is for a first-century date. This could be as early as 50 . . . or as late as 80 or 90." Thomas O'Loughlin, *The Didache: A Window on the Earliest Christians* (Grand Rapids: Baker Academic, 2010), 26.

5. Cf. Marcello Del Verme, *Didache and Judaism: Jewish Roots of an Ancient Christian-Jewish Work* (New York: T&T Clark, 2004), 5; Willy Rordorf and André Tuilier, eds., *La doctrine des douze apôtres (Didachè): Introduction, texte critique, traduction, notes, appendices, annexe et index*, 2nd ed., Sources Chrétiennes (Paris: Cerf, 1998), 94–97, 232–33; or, as Audet, *La Didachè*, 187, puts it, "une date plus haute que le IIe siècle." Dating the Didache in the first century, of course, is not a new suggestion; cf. Joseph Langen, "Das älteste christliche Kirchenbuch," *HZ* 53.2 (1885): 193–21.

6. Cf. Audet, *La Didachè*, 206–10. Rordorf and Tuilier, *La doctrine des douze apôtres*, 97–99. For a helpful survey on date and provenance of the Didache, see Clayton N. Jefford, *The Sayings of Jesus in the Teaching of the Twelve Apostles*, VCSup, vol. 11 (Leiden: Brill, 1989), 3–17.

Though the last lines of the original ending of the text are missing, Didache 16, the so-called Mini Apocalypse sets forth a futurist eschatology with a time of distress under an antichrist-like figure prior to the return of Christ (Did 16.3–5). Then, at Christ' return, the resurrection of the dead will occur (Did 16.6). Yet the text includes an important parenthetical statement clarifying that the resurrection at Christ's coming will not include all the dead—righteous and wicked—"rather, as it has been said, 'The Lord will come, and all his saints with him' " (Did 16.7). In Go Deeper Excursus 6, *The Eschatology of Didache 16*, I make a case that the best explanation for this clause is that the author expected that only the righteous ("saints") would be resurrected at Christ's return. The wicked would not be resurrected until a later time, which would render the eschatology of Didache 16 premillennial (cf. Rev 20:4–5, discussed in great detail in chapters 12 below).

I content that this premillennial reading of Didache 16 is not merely plausible but probable. Thus, Philip Schaff's conclusion from over a century ago represents a balanced position that still holds true:

> The resurrection here spoken of is restricted to the saints (xvi. 7). This may be understood in a chiliastic sense of the *first* resurrection (ἡ ἀνάστασις ἡ πρώτη, Rev. xx. 5); but the author of the *Didache* says nothing about a Millennium, and of a *general* resurrection after it. We have, therefore, no right to commit him either to the chiliastic or to the antichiliastic school, but the greater probability is that he was a Chiliast, like Barnabas, Papias, Justin Martyr, Irenaeus, Tertullian, and the majority of ante-Nicene fathers.[7]

The Epistle of Barnabas and the Eschatological Sabbath

The book conventionally titled "Epistle of Barnabas" was probably written sometime in the late first or early second century, perhaps in Egypt.[8] If the letter was associated in some way with Alexandria,[9] we can assume that it was either written from Alexandria to a group elsewhere in Egypt, or written to a group in a nearby region such as Palestine, or even from Palestine to Alexandria.[10]

---

7. Philip Schaff, *The Oldest Church Manual Called the Teaching of the Twelve Apostles* (New York: Scribner's, 1885), 77.

8. See discussion on the place of origin in Ferdinand-Rupert Prostmeier, *Der Barnabasbrief*, Kommentar zu den Apostolischen Vätern, ed. Norbert Brox, G. Kretschmar, and Kurt Niederwimmer, vol. 8 (Göttingen: Vandenhoeck & Ruprecht, 1999), 119–30. The issues are quite complex and the evidence "does not justify dogmatic statements about the origin and background of the epistle." Robert A. Kraft, *The Apostolic Fathers: A New Translation and Commentary*, vol. 3, *Barnabas and the Didache*, ed. Robert M. Grant (Camden, NJ: Nelson, 1965), 54.

9. This is the general scholarly consensus. See Holmes, *The Apostolic Fathers*, 271–72.

10. Barnard favors the view that the book was probably written from Alexandria to a group of Jewish-Christians somewhere in middle Egypt between about AD 117 and 132. Leslie W. Barnard, "The Problem of the Epistle of Barnabas," *Church Quarterly Review* 159.2 (1958): 212. Though I lean toward an Alexandrian origin for this letter, I think the plausibility of a Palestinian destination in the late first century may have been overlooked in scholarship.

The purpose of the letter was to show the true Christian interpretation and application of the Old Testament law in light of the Christ event and current events, demonstrating that God has always been

Go Deeper Excursus 6
The Eschatology of Didache 16

interested in moral application rather than external ritual. In the course of the author's attempt to explain Old Testament passages through a New Testament lens, he approaches the fourth commandment—to keep the Sabbath holy—in an allegorical sense, applying it eschatologically to a future age, in fact, to the seven-thousandth "millennium" of human history. This age would commence after Christ's return.

After a thorough reexamination of the evidence and arguments, I argue that Barnabas 15 presents a form of chiliastic (premillennial) eschatology.[11] The full technical argument can be found in Go Deeper Excursus 7, "The Chiliasm of the Epistle of Barnabas."

However, even a cursory reading of Barnabas 15 demonstrates that the issue is not really whether the author of Barnabas sets forth a premillennial eschatology; he does. That is, in Barnabas 15 the eschatological thousand-year "sabbath" follows—it does

Go Deeper Excursus 7
The Chiliasm of the Epistle of Barnabas

not precede—the return of Christ. The eschatological sabbath in Barnabas is not a present reality associated with Christ's current heavenly session (as in amillennialism), nor does the eschatological sabbath arrive prior to the physical return of Christ (as in postmillennialism). So, without question, Barnabas presents a premillennial return of Christ. The real issue is how the author conceives of that future eschatological sabbath in terms of its character and chronology. Is it a symbol for the new creation with no distinction? Or is it a unique period of a thousand years distinct from—but related to—the establishment of the subsequent new creation?

As the excursus demonstrates, Barnabas 15 distinguishes between the future seventh-thousand-year sabbath rest and the eighth day as a dawn of a new world (Barn. 15.8). In the eschatological expectation of Barnabas, while the resurrected,

---

It certainly would help explain the letter's concern over the first (or, perhaps, the second) Jewish revolt and the destruction (or reconstruction) of the temple in Jerusalem. Though by no means conclusive, the way the author refers to Syrians, Arabs, and Egyptians suggests that he wrote to or from Judea or Samaria, situated in the midst of these surrounding nations (Barn. 9.6).

11. That Barnabas did not actually embrace a future millennium, believing the seventh and eighth days were merely symbolic and pointed to the same period, is argued by many today, though not by all. So influential has this interpretation become that Paget suggests in a brief summary of the eschatology of Barnabas, "Final redemption appear to involve a return of Christ (7.9f.) and possibly a millennial kingdom (chap. 15)." James Carleton Paget, "The *Epistle of Barnabas*," in *The Writings of the Apostolic Fathers*, ed. Paul Foster (London: T&T Clark, 2007), 79. See Jean Daniélou, *The Theology of Jewish Christianity* (London: Barton, Longman & Todd, 1964), 396–401; D. H. Kromminga, *The Millennium in the Church* (Grand Rapids: Eerdmans, 1945), 29–40; Ferguson, "Was Barnabas a Chiliast?," 157–67. In support of the view that Barnabas was a chiliast, see J. W. Mealy, *After the Thousand Years: Resurrection and Judgment in Revelation 20*, JSNTSup, vol. 70, ed. Stanley E. Porter (Sheffield: JSOT Press, 1992), 48. Beale says Mealy's view is merely "plausible." G. K. Beale, *John's Use of the Old Testament in Revelation* (Sheffield: Sheffield Academic, 1998), 150.

glorified saints will have been made able fully to enjoy a sanctified rest during the thousand-year sabbath after Christ's return, the rest of the world will still need renewal through its liberation from a bondage to corruption. This work of the seventh-day sabbath, then, will be the beginning or starting point for the new world, represented by the eternal eighth day. Thus the author presented the outline of a fairly well-developed eschatology of progressive cosmic renewal that would occur throughout the future millennial period, culminating in the new creation. In this sense, the author of Barnabas was consistent with the Irenaean premillennialism that followed later in the second century.

The Indirect Testimony of Papias and Apollinaris of Hierapolis

Little is known directly about Papias of Hierapolis. He was born in the latter part of the first century and had direct contact with many of the original disciples of the first-generation followers of Jesus (Eusebius, *Hist. eccl.* 3.39.3–4). He also had brief yet influential contact with the apostle John and other eyewitnesses of Jesus (cf. Irenaeus, *Haer.* 5.33.4).[12] In any case, Papias was a contemporary and associate of Polycarp of Smyrna, who himself had personally heard the teachings of the apostle John.

The work for which Papias was well known, *Exposition of the Sayings of the Lord* (Λογίων κυριακῶν ἐξηγήσεως), has been mostly lost to us save some brief excerpts and quotations from later fathers. Originally it was comprised of five books of comments on the sayings of Jesus that Papias had collected from oral teachings from his own elders and colleagues. Regarding Papias's eschatology, Eusebius reports, "He says that a thousand-year period will occur after the resurrection of the dead, and that the kingdom of Christ will be set up corporeally on this very earth" (*Hist. eccl.* 3.39.12 [Schott]).

Likely drawing on the writings of Papias of Hierapolis, Irenaeus of Lyons relays that the material, earthly blessings predicted in the Old Testament belong

> to the times of the kingdom, when the righteous shall bear rule upon their rising from the dead; when also the creation, having been renovated and set free, shall fructify with an abundance of all kinds of food, from the dew of heaven, and from the fertility of the earth: as the elders who saw John, the disciple of the Lord, related that they had heard from him how the Lord used to teach in regard to these times, and say: The days will come, in which vines shall grow, each having ten thousand branches, and in each branch ten thousand twigs, and in each true twig ten thousand shoots, and in each one of the shoots ten thousand clusters, and on every one of the clusters ten thousand grapes, and every grape when pressed will give five and twenty metretes of wine. And when any one of the saints shall lay hold of a cluster, another shall cry out, "I am a better cluster, take me; bless the Lord through me." In like manner [the Lord declared] that a grain of wheat would produce ten thousand ears, and that every ear should have ten thousand grains, and every grain would

---

12. See a discussion on Eusebius's ancient attempt to challenge this personal relationship between the apostle John and Papias in Go Deeper Excursus 5: *Ancient and Modern Challenges to Early Premillennial Testimonies.*

yield ten pounds of clear, pure, fine flour; and that all other fruit-bearing trees, and seeds and grass, would produce in similar proportions; and that all animals feeding [only] on the productions of the earth, should [in those days] become peaceful and harmonious among each other, and be in perfect subjection to man. (*Haer.* 5.33.3)

The words attributed to Jesus are probably best understood as hyperbolic, but the general picture of extreme fruitfulness is consistent with the Old Testament collage of images of the coming kingdom (discussed in chapter 6 below), as well as the narrative of the restoration of Edenic conditions along with the release of the physical creation from its bondage to corruption.[13] While Irenaeus introduces this hyperbolic image of the coming kingdom as coming from "the elders who saw John, the disciple of the Lord," in the next section it becomes clear that his primary source is Papias, likely from his *Exposition of the Sayings of the Lord*.[14] Irenaeus writes,

And these things are borne witness to in writing by Papias, the hearer of John, and a companion of Polycarp, in his fourth book; for there were five books compiled by him. And he says in addition, "Now these things are credible to believers." And he says that, "when the traitor Judas did not give credit to them, and put the question, 'How then can things bring forth so abundantly be wrought by the Lord?' the Lord declared, 'They who shall come to these [times] shall see.'" (*Haer.* 5.33.4)

Jerome also relays in the fifth century that Papias of Hierapolis "published the Jewish opinion of one thousand years"; that is, "that after the resurrection the Lord will reign in the flesh with the saints" (*Vir. ill.* 18).[15] In this same work, we are told that Papias's later successor to the episcopacy of Hierapolis, Apollinaris, also held to the same premillennial view: "a view shared by Irenaeus, Apollinaris, and others" (*Vir. ill.* 18). This Apollinaris was a well-known apologist, a contemporary of Melito of Sardis and also of Irenaeus (*Haer.* 4.26.1; 4.27; 5.16.1). None of Apollinaris's many works survived antiquity.[16]

---

13. For parallels and background imagery on this saying reported by Papias, see H. J. de Jonge, "BOTRYC BOHCEI: The Age of Kronos and the Millennium in Papias of Hierapolis," in *Studies in Hellenistic Religions*, ed. M. J. Vermaseren (Leiden: Brill, 1979), 37–49.

14. See Stephen C. Carlson, "Fragments of Papias," in *The Cambridge Companion to the Apostolic Fathers*, ed. Michael F. Bird and Scott D. Harrower (Cambridge: Cambridge University Press, 2021), 339.

15. Unless noted, for Jerome's *Illustrious Men (Vir. ill.)*, I am using the translation of Thomas P. Halton, *Saint Jerome: On Illustrious Men*, The Fathers of the Church: A New Translation, vol. 10 (Washington, DC: Catholic University of America Press, 1999).

16. Apollinaris of Hierapolis (c. AD 160–180) is not to be confused with the fourth-century Apollinaris Laodicea, the instigator of the heresy of Apollinarianism, as Daley does (*Hope of the Early Church*, 80). That Jerome is referring to the earlier Apollinaris is made clear by grouping him with Irenaeus "and others" rather than with the latter Victorinus and Lactantius. After mentioning that Jerome lists the second-century Apollinaris of Hierapolis as among the chiliasts mentioned by Jerome, Philip Schaff notes, "Jerome mentions Irenæus as the first, and Apollinaris as the last, of the Greek Chiliasts . . . but this is a palpable error, for Barnabas and Papias were Chiliasts before Irenæus; Methodius and Nepos long after Apollinaris. Perhaps he meant Apollinaris of Laodicea, in Syria." Philip Schaff and David Schley Schaff, *History of the Christian Church*, vol. 2 (New York: Scribner's, 1910), 740n4.

The Premillennialism of Justin Martyr

In *Dialogue with Trypho*, Justin relays a question from his Jewish interlocutor Trypho: "But, tell me truthfully, do you [plural] really believe that this place Jerusalem shall be rebuilt (ἀνοικοδομηθῆναι τὸν τόπον Ἱερουσαλημ), and do you actually expect that you Christians will one day congregate there to live joyfully with Christ, together with the patriarchs, the prophets, the saints of our people (καὶ τοῖς ἁγίοις τοῦ ἡμετέρου γένους) and those who became proselytes before your Christ arrived?" (*Dial.* 80.1 [Falls]).

In response to Trypho's incredulous question, Justin clarified that he "with many others" (καὶ ἄλλοι πολλοί) are of the same mind on those things (*Dial.* 80.2). Yet he also acknowledged that many who are pure and pious Christians are not of the same mind, presumably differing on some of the eschatological details (80.2). Yet Justin also noted that others were merely "Christians in name" and that they were heretics because they rejected the central doctrine of the resurrection of the dead and asserted that the soul ascended straight to heaven upon death (80.3–4). In contrast, Justin writes, "But I and every other completely orthodox Christian feel certain that there will be a resurrection of the flesh, followed by a thousand years in the rebuilt, embellished, and enlarged city of Jerusalem (καὶ σαρκὸς ἀνάστασιν γενήσεσθαι ἐπιστάμεθα καὶ χίλια ἔτη ἐν Ἱερουσαλὴμ οἰκοδομηθείσῃ καὶ κοσμηθείσῃ καὶ πλατυνθείσῃ), as was announced by the Prophets Ezechiel, Isaias and the others" (80.5 [Falls]).

In support of this doctrine of a millennium, which Justin alleged was the proper opinion, he quotes first from Isaiah 65:17–25, tracking closely with the text of the Septuagint (*Dial.* 81). He notes that Isaiah spoke here "concerning the millennium (περί τῆς χιλιονταετηρίδος)," and he identifies this millennium with Isaiah's reference to "the new heavens and new earth" (Isa 65:17), the restoration of Jerusalem and God's people (65:18–19), the banishment of sorrow (65:19), the birth of children and an extraordinary long lifespan (65:20, 23), the building of homes and experience of prosperity (65:21–22), the intimate fellowship between God and his people (65:24), and the restored harmony of creation itself (65:25).

Justin also sees a veiled reference to the thousand years hidden in the Isaianic phrase, "For as the days of the tree of life, so will be the days of my people; the works of their hands will be multiplied" (Isa 65:22 LXX).[17] Justin notes that Christians understand this to point symbolically to the thousand years (*Dial.* 81.3), reasoning that if Adam ate from a tree and died prior to reaching a thousand years, constituting a "day" in God's reckoning (Gen 2:17), and that if a day of the Lord is like a thousand years (Ps 89:4), then the reference to the "days of the tree of life" in Isaiah 65:22 pointed to a future thousand-year period.

Yet in the conclusion of this section, Justin seems to indicate the real authoritative source of this millennial doctrine: the apostle John. He asserts, "Moreover,

---

17. The Hebrew Masoretic text of Isa 65:22 does not have the modifier "of life." Justin takes advantage of the interpretive rendering of the Septuagint, which reads τὰς ἡμέρας τοῦ ξήλου τῆς ζωῆς.

a man among us named John, one of Christ's Apostles, received a revelation and foretold that the followers of Christ would dwell in Jerusalem for a thousand years, and that afterwards the universal (καθολικὴν) and, in short, everlasting resurrection and judgment would take place" (*Dial.* 81.4). Thus Justin presents a straightforward premillennial expectation: the coming of Christ, the resurrection of those who believed in him, the thousand-year period of rebuilding and blessing centered in Jerusalem, concluded with the final resurrection and judgment of all. He also pulls together several Old Testament texts from the collage of images of the coming kingdom and understands them in a fairly straightforward literal fashion.

With Justin's testimony around the middle of the second century, we also have the first indication of a different view of eschatology, though we cannot be sure exactly which details were rejected. In Justin's view, there are three categories—the complete heretics blaspheme by "asserting that there is no resurrection of the dead, but that their souls are taken up to Heaven at the very moment of their death" (*Dial.* 80). Here, it does not appear that the rejection of a millennium per se makes one a heretic in Justin's mind, but a rejection of the bodily resurrection coupled with the teaching that salvation consists only of ascending to the highest heaven upon death. Therefore, the second category—the pious Christians with whom Justin disagrees on eschatological matters—cannot be those who reject the resurrection. Rather, they must reject other details of eschatology in Justin's list: "a thousand years in the rebuilt, embellished, and enlarged city of Jerusalem" (*Dial.* 80.5). But even here, we cannot be sure whether Justin's Christian detractors disagreed with the doctrine of the millennium itself or with the more literal interpretation of the prophets and the Jerusalem-centered character of the coming kingdom. That is, were they actually amillennial or were they premillennialists who held to a more spiritual nature of the coming kingdom? This cannot be known for sure.

What can be known is that Justin regarded the third group—his own—to be the proper and probably majority opinion on the matter. That is, right-minded Christians on all points agreed with his premillennial eschatology, with a kingdom centered in Jerusalem in fulfillment of Old Testament prophecies of the coming kingdom. Falls' note on this passage that "the belief in the millennium was not as general as Justin's words," pointing out that "the only other early supporters of this doctrine were Papias of Hierapolis and Irenaeus," is misleading.[18] It neglects the likely premillennial eschatology of the Didache and that of Barnabas (see above), does not account for the indirect testimony of Apollinaris of Hierapolis (see above), and assumes that the second category of detractors to which Justin refers disagreed on the millennium itself rather than its nature and character.

Later, in *Dialogue* 113, Justin draws a parallel between Christ and Joshua: "Just as he, not Moses, conducted the people into the Holy Land and distributed it by lot among those who entered, so also will Jesus the Christ gather together the dispersed people and distribute the good land to each, though not in the same manner. For, Josue gave them an inheritance for a time only, since he was not Christ our God, nor the Son of God; but Jesus, after the holy resurrection, will give us an inheritance

---

18. Falls, *Justin Martyr*, 277n5.

for eternity. . . . After His coming the Father will, through Him, renew heaven and earth (τὸν οὐρανὸν καὶ τὴν γῆν καὶ δι οὗ ὁ πατὴρ μέλλει καινουργεῖν)" (*Dial.* 113). This last portion links the coming millennial kingdom with the expected renewal of creation, consistent with the narrative of progressive edenification we have advanced throughout this book.

It should be noted that Justin Martyr's relationship to the so-called center of chiliastic expectations—Asia—is shaky. Born in Samaria around AD 110, Justin spent his youth seeking meaning in various competing philosophical schools of his day: the Stoics, the Peripatetics, the Pythagoreans, and finally the Platonists, the followers of Socrates and Plato (*Dial.* 1). His wanderings brought him to western Asia Minor where he met a man near Ephesus who would change his life. The old man engaged Justin in philosophical and theological matters, eventually leading him to faith in Christ (*Dial.* 7). Justin soon left Asia and arrived in Rome, where he established himself as a teacher there until his martyr's death. While it may be that Justin received his initial instruction in premillennial eschatology in Asia Minor toward the beginning of his life as a Christian, he still maintained that eschatology while in Rome during the composition of his *Dialogue with Trypho,* where he expressed no indication that it would have been unacceptable or entirely out of place.

The Millennialism of Irenaeus and Beyond

Irenaeus of Lyons (c. AD 130–200) was a disciple of Polycarp, who had been a direct disciple of the apostle John. As evidenced mostly by the eschatological exposition in the final of his five-book *Against Heresies,* Irenaeus's eschatology was unambiguously futurist (holding to a future tribulation period coming upon this earth) and premillennial (holding to a literal earthly kingdom following the return of Christ and preceding the eternal state). His eschatology also involved a number of fairly "earthy" elements consistent with the emphases of his own teachers and contemporaries in the second century but scorned by later theologians. These included a literal rebuilt temple in the tribulation, a future fulfillment of Daniel's seventieth week (Dan 9:27), a real conversion and restoration of the remnant of ethnic Israel under Christ, literal antichrist and false prophet figures, and even, as we will see, a literal assumption of at least a portion of the church prior to the future tribulation.

Understandably, post-Reformation amillennial theology did not think too highly of Irenaeus's premillennialism, which has played little role in the theological development and formulation of much Protestant theology. Christopher Smith writes, "Recent scholarship, echoing the sentiment which led to the suppression of these final chapters [of *Against Heresies*], . . . has either conveniently ignored this aspect of Irenean [*sic*] theology, or sought to excuse it as a gratuitous anomaly or pardonable excess."[19] Because the final chapters of *Against Heresies,* in which Irenaeus elaborates on the details of his eschatology, were only rediscovered in the late sixteenth century, late medieval scholars as well as Protestant Reformers had no

---

19. Christopher R. Smith, "Chiliasm and Recapitulation in the Theology of Ireneus," *VC* 48.4 (1994): 313.

access to these texts to inform their own eschatological reflection. By the time his eschatological exposition was published, many Protestant Reformers had solidified their amillennial—indeed, *anti*-millennial—eschatologies, which would eventually be codified in Protestant confessions.

Irenaeus's eschatology in both its broad strokes and details presents a narrative consistent with his predecessors, colleagues, and heirs of Christian tradition.[20] Irenaeus writes as though his eschatological perspectives reflected the views of the hearers of the apostles, that he was faithfully transmitting the traditional teachings passed down from those apostles through his own teachers, and that he expected most of his readers to be content with his perspectives, if not in support of them.

> **Go Deeper Excursus 8**
>
> *The Coming Kingdom in Irenaeus, Tertullian, and Hippolytus*

Irenaeus presents both the framework of his eschatology and its details in a way that exhibits long, careful thought. His words do not come across as off-the-cuff remarks on matters for which he had no time to reflect. When we reach the final book of *Against Heresies*, Irenaeus's eschatology is not in its infancy, nor is it a bumbling toddler or awkward teen. Rather, it has entered young adulthood with a level of internal continuity and consistency expected of a theology reflectively received, relayed, and adapted to his anti-gnostic context, not adopted passively from a previous text or teacher nor concocted ad hoc to address the over-spiritualizing hermeneutic of the Valentinian gnostic heretics of his day.

A more detailed examination of Irenaeus's view of the coming kingdom is found in Go Deeper Excursus 8, *The Coming Kingdom in Irenaeus, Tertullian, and Hippolytus*. Readers are also encouraged to read through Book 5 of *Against Heresies* on their own to get a feel for both the full content and tone of Irenaeus's exposition of last things. In the following chapters where I interact with specific biblical texts as well as eschatological issues, I will revisit many passages from Irenaeus and his contemporaries. The following, however, is a brief preview and summary of some of the more prominent points of Irenaeus's view of the coming kingdom.

According to Irenaeus, at the close of the future seventieth week of Daniel (Dan 9:27; cf. *Haer.* 5.25.4; 5.30.4), Christ will come to destroy the antichrist's reign during the second half of the seven-year tribulation. Christ will then usher in his earthly kingdom—"the hallowed seventh day" during which the Old Testament promises to Abraham would be restored (*Haer.* 5.30.4). This first phase of the eternal reign of Christ will thus last a thousand years, similar to the thousand-year eschatological sabbath in Barnabas 15 (*Haer.* 5.28.3). During the millennial period, the righteous will be resurrected to reign with Christ (*Haer.* 5.26.2), while the mortal survivors of the tribulation period who were not glorified would be among those who repopulate the earth (*Haer.* 5.35.1). While Irenaeus understood the present church to constitute the "spiritual seed of Abraham," he may have also understood that the literal descendants of Abraham would be regathered from among the nations in fulfillment of Old Testament prophecies (*Haer.* 5.32.2; 5.34.1). Thus, rather

---

20. Robert M. Grant, *Irenaeus of Lyons*, The Early Church Fathers (London: Routledge, 1997), 1.

than affirming an either/or approach to biblical prophecy, Irenaeus employed a both/and approach that allowed for partial, spiritual fulfillment of prophecies in the church today while expecting a complete, literal fulfillment at Christ's return.

Go Deeper Excursus 9

The Advent and Advance of Amillennialism

Irenaeus's grand, comprehensive vision of the future involves the whole person as well as the whole creation. It takes seriously the earthly imagery of the Old Testament, foresees a restoration not merely of Jerusalem and Israel according to the promises but of all people and all nature—from animals to angels. The Godward journey of humanity, derailed at the fall, will be restored. Even resurrection itself in the intermediate kingdom is not the final chapter of the story but the beginning of a new story that never ends (see further discussion in chapter 21). The resurrected saints will grow from glory to glory and will eventually be admitted into the presence of the glorious Father to experience the beatific vision. Brian Daley writes, "Irenaeus seems to imply the possibility of growth and advancement toward closer union with God even after the judgment, until at last all distinctions disappear. . . . Such a relationship, Irenaeus implies, is neither static nor limited by human finitude: it is part of a history of growth, whose term is participation in the glory which is God's own life."[21]

Summary and Conclusion

This survey of voices—including the more technical Go Deeper Excurses—reveals a few important points regarding the early precedence of Irenaean premillennialism. First, when they were not silent on the issue of the millennium, first-century and second-century Christian texts espoused a premillennial perspective (Didache, Barnabas, Papias of Hierapolis, Justin Martyr, Irenaeus of Lyons, Tertullian, Hippolytus). This premillennial perspective was not isolated to one place but was geographically widespread (e.g., Didache in Antioch, Barnabas in Egypt, Papias in Asia, Justin and Hippolytus in Rome, Irenaeus in Gaul, and Tertullian in western North Africa). Also, premillennialism was presented in diverse texts and traditions—from the allegorizing of Barnabas to the careful, almost systematic articulation and defense by Irenaeus. By the time we reach Irenaeus in the late second century, premillennialism is fairly well developed, exhibiting all the signs of a well-thought-out eschatological system. From where did Irenaeus get such teachings? By his own words, he claims to have received them from his own teachers who had received them from the apostles themselves (*Haer.* 5.33.3; *Epid.* 61).

The first explicit hints at an eschatology different from that of Irenaeus come to us secondhand from the premillennialist fathers, Justin Martyr and Irenaeus. They regarded the differing opinion on the millennium among orthodox Christians as imperfect, with dubious origins (Justin) or, in the case of Irenaeus, as an effect of the unhappy influence of gnostic heretics who exhibited an over-spiritualized,

---

21. Brian E. Daley, *The Hope of the Early Church: A Handbook of Patristic Eschatology* (Grand Rapids: Baker Academic, 1991), 31, 32.

over-realized eschatology. Go Deeper Excursus 9, *The Advent and Advance of Amillennialism*, demonstrates that though Clement of Alexandria in the late second/ early third century does not explicitly address the millennial question, he has all the elements of an amillennial eschatology, and his successor in Alexandria, Origen, explicitly rejects premillennialism for an entirely spiritual interpretation of the prophecies of the coming kingdom. From that point on, amillennialism gains support while premillennialism wanes.

Though we could speculate on the reasons for the decline of premillennialism and the rise of amillennialism from the third to fifth centuries, based on the survey in this chapter and its technical excurses, five motivating factors seem to have contributed most. These are my own thoughts on potential explanations, each of which could probably stand for a full chapter-length treatment. First, premillennialism was increasingly viewed as less sophisticated, too naive; Eusebius's remarks about Papias's simple mindedness point in this direction (*Hist. eccl.* 3.39.13).

Second, the rising influence of a Middle and Neo-Platonism between Clement and Augustine, though resisting outright gnostic dualism, nevertheless tended to exalt the spiritual and heavenly over the physical and earthly.[22] The earlier incarnational eschatology that involved a redeemed creation in real time and space seems to have lost ground to these philosophical pressures.

Third, the growing popularity of a more spiritual, allegorical approach to the interpretation of all Scripture—and especially Old Testament prophecy—made the older, earthy interpretations of Papias, Justin, Irenaeus, and Hippolytus unacceptable. This is evidenced by the dispute between Dionysius and the followers of Nepos described in Excursus 9, *The Advent and Advance of Amillennialism*.

Fourth, the political changes in the empire and the relationship between church and state no longer accommodated the older premillennial narrative that saw the present world system as entirely given over to Satan and the age to come as a radical reversal. With the Christian empire, it became increasingly obvious to many that the kingdom had somehow arrived—or that Christ's heavenly millennial reign was finally transforming the world and that the church was an extension of that present rule.[23]

Finally—and on this matter we must be careful neither to exaggerate it nor to downplay it—an increasing anti-Judaism and anti-Semitism made the more Jerusalem-centered aspects of early premillennialism *a priori* unfavorable. Chiliasm became known as a "Jewish" view (cf. Origen, *Princ.* 2.11.2; Eusebius, *Hist. eccl.*

---

22. See, e.g., relevant discussions in A. H. Armstrong, "Dualism: Platonic, Gnostic, and Christian," in *Neoplatonism and Gnosticism*, ed. Richard T. Wallis and Jay Bregman, Studies in Neoplatonism: Ancient and Modern, vol. 6 (Albany: State University of New York Press, 1992), 48–51; Robert M. Berchman, "Origen and the Reworking of the Legacy of Greek Philosophy," in *The Oxford Handbook of Origin*, edited by Ronald E. Heine and Karen Jo Torjesen (Oxford: Oxford University Press, 2022), 27–33; and John M. Dillon, *The Middle Platonists, 80 B.C. to A.D. 220*, rev. ed. (Ithaca, NY: Cornell University Press, 1996), 43–51.

23. Cf. Timothy P. Weber, "Millennialism," in *The Oxford Handbook of Eschatology*, ed. Jerry L. Walls (Oxford: Oxford University Press, 2008), 370.

24.2). In increasingly anti-Semitic circles, that alone would have been enough to guarantee its rejection.[24]

Century	Premillennial Witnesses	Amillennial Witnesses
First	Possibly the Didache (Syria) Barnabas (Egypt)	
Second	Papias of Hierapolis (Asia) Justin Martyr (Italy) Apollinaris (Asia) Irenaeus of Lyons (Gaul)	Unknown detractors (Rome?) Clement (Alexandria)
Third	Tertullian (Africa) Hippolytus (Italy) Commodianus (Africa) Victorinus (Pettau) Nepos (Egypt)	Origen (Alexandria) Caius (Rome) Dionysius (Alexandria)

With this historical survey behind us, we may now ask how strong is the biblical and exegetical argument for an Irenaean premillennial eschatology. Though in the next several chapters we explore the concept of the coming kingdom in the Old and New Testaments—with particular attention to key passages and especially Revelation 20—we have not left our interest in the early fathers behind. As we turn to the words of the inspired authors, we will also continue to listen to the voices of the second-century fathers for insight into the earliest understanding of these texts by those who were the spiritual children and grandchildren of the original disciples of Jesus.

---

24. Horner writes, "In light of the theological anti-Judaism that flowed forth with dominant influence out of Augustine's eschatology, it is easier to understand how premillennialism suffered Cinderella-like belittlement as a consequence." Barry E. Horner, *Future Israel: Why Christian Anti-Judaism Must Be Challenged*, NAC Studies in Bible and Theology (Nashville: B&H Academic, 2007), 150–51.

6

THE COLLAGE OF THE COMING
KINGDOM IN THE OLD TESTAMENT

If, however, any shall endeavor to allegorize prophecies
of this kind, they shall not be found consistent with
themselves in all points, and shall be confuted by
the teaching of the very expressions in question.

Irenaeus, *Against Heresies* 5.35.1

As valuable as the writings of Irenaeus of Lyons may be for illustrating an early, well-developed view of the coming kingdom popular in his second-century context, Irenaeus's writings are not inspired, infallible Scripture. He was neither a prophet nor an apostle. Though he had access to oral traditions from the apostles as well as written texts from early disciples of the apostles lost to us today, Irenaeus and the other fathers consistently pointed back to Holy Scripture as the primary source and ultimate standard for their theology.

In keeping with this patristic emphasis on the authority and sufficiency of Scripture, in this chapter, I begin our pursuit of the biblical concept of the coming kingdom with an exploration of the coming kingdom in the Old Testament. From here, I will explore how the New Testament handles those Old Testament expectations (chapters 7–9), and then examine Revelation 20 in light of a biblical theology of the coming kingdom (chapters 10–13). The result will be an articulation and defense of a "contemporary" Irenaean premillennial eschatology, modified at some points in light of exegetical considerations.

We saw in chapter 4 that the biblical concept of the kingdom of God—that is, God's will accomplished on earth as it is in heaven—is multifaceted. Ridderbos distilled these various iterations to two major distinctions: (1) God's universal power and dominion over all creation, all nations, and all people and (2) God's particular theocratic relationship with Israel.[1] In our exploration of the concept of the coming kingdom in the Old Testament prophets, we will see that in the eschaton these two distinctions merge into one. However, the Old Testament presents the coming kingdom in often strange, sometimes bewildering language and imagery that has led many to conclude that the picture is so blurred by figurative language that nothing clear can be asserted about the coming kingdom. This leads to a question: What are we seeing in the Old Testament prophecies of the coming kingdom?

---

1. Herman Ridderbos, *The Coming of the Kingdom*, trans. H. de Jongste, ed. Raymond O. Zorn (Philadelphia: Presbyterian and Reformed, 1962), 4.

What Are We Seeing in Old Testament Prophecy?

When approaching the poetic and figurative language of the Old Testament prophets, where do we draw the line between symbol and reality? This problem becomes acute when we consider the nature of much of the Old Testament's prophecies of the coming kingdom. What do we do with all the vivid details? How should we read the symbols? In short, when we read the Old Testament prophecies of the coming kingdom, what, exactly, are we looking at? At the risk of oversimplification—but for the purpose of clarity—let me suggest three possible answers to this question that lie on a spectrum: the *fantastic*, the *figurative*, or the *photographic*, with mediating positions between.[2]

The *fantastic* approach views the language as simply a means of instilling awe, wonder, and the virtues of faith, hope, and love. In this view, the text does not correspond with an actual present or future reality. On the other end of the spectrum, the *photographic* approach sees the language as having a one-to-one correspondence with reality—as if the prophet was looking directly at future events and simply describing them in the best language he had at his disposal. The *figurative*—the view adopted in this book and by a great number of commentators throughout history—sees much (though not all) of the poetic and prophetic language as symbolic or metaphorical but corresponding to actual referents in the future.

Go Deeper Excursus 10

What Are We Seeing in Old Testament Prophecy: Fantasy, Photo, or Figure?

In the end, we must take care to avoid the two extremes of uncritically viewing the language of Old Testament as an exact "photo" of future events or as a vague "fantasy" of spiritual truths unconnected to the future. Rather, what we are "seeing" in the prophetic literature of the Old Testament is most often a stylized, picturesque "figure" of real events, sometimes with poetic or abstract imagery but always pointing to real future conditions. How literally or figuratively we take particular words and images must be determined by context, usage in Scripture, and how the language would likely have been understood at the time. Also, we must take into consideration how clearer passages address similar future events and conditions and the overarching narrative of Scripture.

Go Deeper Excursus 11

The Coming Kingdom in the Old Testament: Detailed Analysis of Key Passages

In the following pages, I present synthetic summaries of the much more detailed examination of all major passages related to the coming kingdom in the Old Testament. The full, detailed discussion of these passages from Isaiah to Zechariah can be found in Go Deeper Excursus 11, *The Coming Kingdom in the Old Testament: Detailed Analysis of Key Passages*.

---

2. These roughly correspond with Oswalt's distinctions between "literalistic" (photographic), "spiritualistic" (fantastic), and "figurative" (figurative). See his comments on Isaiah 11:6–9 in John N. Oswalt, *The Book of Isaiah, Chapters 1–39*, The New International Commentary on the Old Testament (Grand Rapids: Eerdmans, 1986), 283.

The Coming Kingdom in Isaiah

The coming kingdom portrayed in picturesque, figurative kingdom oracles in the book of Isaiah entails a glorious future. In an undefined time in the future (Isa 2:1; 9:1), God's people, having suffered just judgment for their covenant unfaithfulness (Isa 1:2–24; 27:7–11; 31:6–9), will turn again to God in repentance and will be called back from their places of exile around the world to be restored to their own land in a kind of ultimate exodus (Isa 2:1–4; 4:4; 11:11–12; 27:12–13; 30:18–19; 32:16–18; 35:10; 41:8–9; 43:5–7, 11–17; 49:9–13; 52:11–12). This restoration will be through the enthronement of the anointed and Spirit-empowered king in Jerusalem—the ultimate Servant of the Lord—who will rule with justice, righteousness, peace, and equity, along with a plurality of rulers reigning with him (Isa 2:4; 9:6–7; 11:1–16; 16:4–5; 32:1; 42:1; 52:13; 53:1–12; 60:15–18).

This new condition of the nation of Israel under their king will be an "everlasting covenant"—indeed, the king himself will be "a covenant for the people" (42:6; 49:8; 55:3; 50:21; 61:8). Through him, the nation of Israel will increase beyond its borders, all nations will flock to Israel to learn their ways (Isa 2:2–3; 25:6; 42:3–4; 45:22; 49:1, 6; 60:21–22), and all the world will be blessed as they all come to know God (14:1–2; 42:1; 60:2–14). The blessing will extend beyond the peoples of the world as nature itself—plants and animals—will be tamed and flourish (4:2; 11:6–9; 27:2–36; 30:23–24; 40:5; 44:2–3; 62:8–9; 65:25). The world will be progressively terraformed to the quality of the paradise of Eden (9:7; 11:6–9; 26:15; 32:15; 35:1–2, 6–7; 51:3). Children will be born healthy (11:8; 49:17–21; 54:1–2; 61:9; 65:20, 23), joy and jubilation will replace sorrow and sadness (12:1–6; 35:10; 51:11; 52:7–9; 61:10–11; 65:19), and suffering and death will first become but a trickle, then a dripping, and then it will be swallowed up forever (25:7–8; 26:19; 35:5–6; 65:20). This messianic age itself will be so radically different from the present world that it will be called "a new heaven and a new earth" (65:16–17)—a renewal of such an exceedingly high quality that it cannot even be compared to the present time of suffering. Geoffrey Grogan writes, "The message of Isaiah is strongly eschatological. There are many passages in which the prophet deals with the future destiny of Israel and of the Gentiles, a special feature being the range of material that has Jerusalem-Zion as its focus."[3]

Even if much of the language and imagery of the coming kingdom in Isaiah can be taken less literally and more figuratively, the repetition, details, consistency, and insistency on its truthfulness make it difficult to dismiss as mere "fantasy" or simply as visions with an affective purpose or moral imperative. The earliest Christians, too, saw many passages as referring to an era on this earth when the Messiah will return to establish his kingdom. What, though, becomes of this language and imagery of the coming kingdom in the other prophets? In the next two sections, we will more rapidly explore the coming kingdom in the rest of the Old Testament

---

3. Geoffrey W. Grogan, "Isaiah," in *The Expositor's Bible Commentary: Proverbs–Isaiah*, rev. ed., ed. Tremper Longman III and Garland David E., vol. 6 (Grand Rapids: Zondervan, 2008), 450–51.

prophets. We will see that the impressionistic picture they paint is consistent with the established language and imagery of Isaiah.

The Coming Kingdom in Jeremiah to Zechariah

The rich collage of images of the coming kingdom in Isaiah presents us with a compelling picture of a messianic reign of righteousness, justice, prosperity, and peace centered in Jerusalem in a restored kingdom to Israel, but its scope and scale will be much greater than even the most majestic manifestation of that historical kingdom under the Davidic monarch. Rather, its power and influence will fill the earth, and all creation itself will be transformed. Progressively, all things will be restored and renewed, culminating in a creation that far exceeds all hopes and dreams. Ultimately, even death itself will be swallowed up by the victory of God through his Messiah reigning by the power of the Spirit, and all nations will be redeemed and bask in the glory of the one true God.

How does this Isaianic vision of the coming kingdom develop in the rest of the prophets from Jeremiah to Zechariah? We will see that they paint the same collage of the coming kingdom, often using many of the same terms and images but sometimes adding their own unique details and descriptions. This presents us with a clearer picture of the Old Testament expectation of the coming kingdom as we move into the hopes in the hearts and minds of the Jewish people in the inter-testamental and New Testament periods.

The Coming Kingdom in Jeremiah

The picture of the coming kingdom in Jeremiah matches that of Isaiah in all its major points. After experiencing tribulation for their wickedness (Jer 3:1–13; 20:37; 30:4–7), both Israel and Judah will be called back to God (30:3, 10–11; 31:27–28, 31; 46:27–28; 50:4). In their repentance (3:13), they will experience a second exodus that exceeds even the first out of Egypt (3:14–18; 16:14–15). They will be restored to the land promised to their fathers as a united people and blessed beyond measure in descendants, abundance, and prosperity (3:14; 23:3; 30:3, 18–20; 31:4–7; 33:6–7). Repeatedly, God promises his restored people, "You shall be my people, and I will be your God" (Jer 30:22; 31:31–34; 32:38). They will be ruled over by a righteous branch from the line of David—a king who will reign in wisdom, justice, and righteousness (23:5–6; 30:8–9, 21; 33:15–16), and he will have rulers who reign with him (3:15; 23:4). The cities will be rebuilt—especially Jerusalem—and the borders of the land will be fully established (3:17; 31:38–40; 32:36). This restoration will be called a "new covenant," not like the first covenant associated with the first exodus. It will involve the complete conversion of the remnant of Israel and Judah, the law inscribed on their hearts, and a universal saving knowledge of God, which will result in faith and obedience (31:31–34; 32:39–41; 50:5). At that time, the ark of the covenant will not only be forgotten but never rebuilt, indicating a change from worship focused on a temple and sacrifices (3:16). However, the line of David and the line of Levi will be particularly preserved from generation to generation from

Isaiah's day to the time of restoration as a guarantee that both the throne and the nation will be preserved (33:17–26).

The Coming Kingdom in Ezekiel

Prophesying during the time of the Babylonian captivity in the sixth century BC, the scattering of the people of Israel and Judah are accomplished facts in Ezekiel's day. However, according to his kingdom oracles, the destruction of the nation and the diaspora are not permanent realities. As proclaimed by Isaiah and Jeremiah before him, Ezekiel foretells a time when Israel and Judah will be regathered from among the nations, reunited, and restored to their own land (Ezek 11:17–18; 20:34; 28:25; 34:13–34; 37:15–22; 39:26–28). This will come after repentance and cleansing from their previous sins (11:18; 16:61–63; 20:34–38; 36:25). Echoing the "new covenant" language of Jeremiah 31:31–34, Ezekiel foresees a time when the Spirit will be poured out upon Israel, when they will have a new heart, which will enable them to trust and obey the Lord (11:19–20; 16:60; 36:26–27; 37:26; 39:29). Then, God says, "They shall be my people, and I will be their God" (11:20; 34:30–31; 37:23). The Davidic king—the Messiah—will be ruler over the people and the nation at that time (34:23–24; 37:22–24). This future kingdom will be centered in Jerusalem (20:40), where Israel themselves will become an offering to the Lord (20:41–42). The restoration of the nation will be like a resurrection from the dead (37:1–28); in fact, Ezekiel may also be suggesting an actual resurrection of the dead in connection with the restoration (37:12–14). In any case, in the restoration, God will comfort, nourish, bless, and prosper the people of Israel and the land with many descendants and bountiful provisions (34:15–16, 26–29; 36:9–11, 28–30; 37:25–28). The land itself will flourish and become like the Garden of Eden, and harmony in creation will be restored (34:25; 36:33–35).

The Coming Kingdom in Daniel

Through apocalyptic visions, dreams, and revelations mediated by angels, Daniel prophesies of a coming destruction of current world powers opposed to God and his people (7:9–12). These powers will be replaced by God's own kingdom, which will be ruled by a perfect administration of a coming king and holy rulers—the Messiah and his co-regents seen already in previous kingdom oracles (2:44–45; 7:13–14, 27). This kingdom, centered in Jerusalem, will involve the abolishing of sin and the ushering in of everlasting righteousness (9:24). It will gradually grow to cover the whole earth and all nations, and it will never be destroyed (2:45; 7:14).

The Coming Kingdom from Hosea to Zechariah

Consistent with the collage of imagery of the coming kingdom in the major prophets, the minor prophets foresee a time of future restoration of God's people after a time of judgment and scattering (Hos 1:9–11; 3:4–5; Joel 2:18–29; Mic 3:12–4:3; Zeph 2:7; Zech 10:6–12). This restoration will be accomplished through the rule of a coming Davidic king who is God himself ruling (Hos 1:10; 3:5; Amos 9:11–15;

Mic 5:2–3; Zeph 3:14–15; Zech 9:9–10). The people of Israel will know the Lord, and they will experience blessing of offspring, peace, security, prosperity, and bounty in the land (Hos 2:16–17, 20–21; Joel 2:19, 21–25; Amos 9:11–15; Mic 4:4–8; Zeph 3:11–16; Zech 8:1–19; 9:17). Jerusalem and the holy land will be established forever as the center of the future global kingdom (Joel 2:18, 32; 3:1–2, 20; Amos 9:15; Obad 19–21; Mic 4:6–8; 5:4–5; Zeph 3:20; Zech 9:9–10). The people themselves will experience spiritual renewal and refreshing, as the Spirit of God is poured out upon them (Joel 2:28–31; Zeph 3:9–10; Zech 12:10–14). Creation itself will be restored to a state of harmony and bounty (Mic 4:1–3; Zech 2:4; 14:5–8).

Conclusion: The Coming Kingdom in the Old Testament Prophets

To sum up, even granting profoundly figurative language and deeply symbolic imagery to the prophetic oracles and apocalyptic visions of the Old Testament, a fairly consistent, comprehensive, and compelling picture of the coming kingdom emerges. It includes a perfectly righteous king—the long-awaited descendant of David—who will defeat the enemies of God and of his people. He will establish his throne in Jerusalem, which will become the center of his glorious kingdom of justice, peace, and prosperity. The remnant of Israel who had been dispersed in judgment will be restored in blessing under a new, eternal covenant of peace. All nations will submit to the rule of the Messiah and find their fullest blessing united to that future kingdom. All nature itself will be tamed, and all the earth will be transformed until it becomes like the Garden of Eden itself—a veritable return of paradise. Ultimately even death itself will be conquered, including a resurrection from the dead. This kingdom will have no end.

Terry Briley writes, "As the prophets look to the future, they anticipate a better world. Jeremiah envisions it on the basis of a new covenant (31:31ff.). To that picture Ezekiel adds God's renewal of human hearts and the bestowal of his Spirit (36:24ff.). Isaiah's contribution to the prophetic vision of the future is the creation of new heavens and a new earth."[4]

The eschatological hope of the coming kingdom in the Old Testament gives no indication of an escape from this world and a flight to heaven; nor does it anticipate an utter annihilation of this world and its replacement with a new creation *ex nihilo*. Rather, as Donald Gowan rightly notes: "The OT does not speak of the end of the world, of time, or of history. It promises the end of sin (Jer. 33:8), of war (Mic. 4:3), of human infirmity (Isa. 35:5–6a), of hunger (Ezek. 36:30), of killing or harming of any living thing (Isa. 11:9a)."[5] And Robin Routledge writes, "The prophets look forward to a time, beyond judgment, when God will deliver and restore his people and usher in a new age, an era of salvation and peace, where his reign will be established over

---

4. Terry R. Briley, *Isaiah*, vol. 2, The College Press NIV Commentary (Joplin, MO: College Press, 2000), 309.

5. Donald E. Gowan, *Eschatology in the Old Testament*, 2nd ed. (Edinburgh: T&T Clark, 2000), 2.

the whole earth."[6] Bill Arnold sums up Israelite eschatology as follows: "The present cosmos, created as 'good' by YHWH but temporarily marred by injustice, infirmity, war, and sin, and in general by evil will be reclaimed and redeemed by God. . . . It longs for, indeed expects, a period in which Yhwh triumphs over evil, redeems his people Israel, and finally rules the world in peace and salvation."[7]

> **Go Deeper Excursus 12**
>
> *Expectation of the Coming Kingdom in the Intertestamental Period*

While details will continue to be debated concerning the order of events, the limits of figurative language and whether some passages relate to an idealized fulfillment after the exile or a promised restoration dependent on contingencies that were never met, not all the passages can be set aside. Thus first-century Jews would have had a fairly clear picture of the coming kingdom. The general contours of the Old Testament's picture of the coming kingdom are confirmed in the language and imagery of the literature of the Second Temple (intertestamental) period, which is explored in greater detail in Go Deeper Excursus 12, *Expectation of the Coming Kingdom in the Intertestamental Period*.

The Reception of the Coming Kingdom in the New Testament

Moving from biblical studies to eschatological studies, the issue is not what the Old Testament promises of the coming kingdom actually were; the question is what becomes of the Old Testament promises of the coming kingdom with the advent of Jesus Christ. Are the promises set aside with the rejection of the Messiah by the majority of Israel—especially their religious and political leaders? That is, were the conditions for a full realization of the Old Testament blessings of the coming kingdom simply not met, so ethnic Israel forfeited their inheritance, which would now be given to others? Are the very earthy, physical blessings of the coming kingdom spiritualized by the New Testament in some way? Are earthly promises about universal peace and the reconciliation of nature transformed into allegories about the reconciliation of hostile

> **Go Deeper Excursus 13**
>
> *Hoekema's and Merkle's Approaches to Old Testament Restoration Prophecies*

peoples and their peace with God and one another? Are the Old Testament promises fulfilled spiritually *in Christ* and therefore through their union with Christ in the church? Or are they simply culturally meaningful symbolic images of the future new creation cast in terms of preexilic, exilic, and postexilic ideals of restoration? In other words, did the prophets simply lack the full palette of colors needed to paint a more glorious and precise picture of the new creation, so they utilized the limited palette available to them in their pre-Christian context? For representative

---

6. Robin Routledge, *Old Testament Theology: A Thematic Approach* (Downers Grove, IL: InterVarsity, 2012), 273. Cf. excellent summaries in Routledge, *Old Testament Theology*, 278; and Ridderbos, *Coming of the Kingdom*, 5–6.

7. Bill T. Arnold, "Old Testament Eschatology and the Rise of Apocalypticism," in *The Oxford Handbook of Eschatology*, ed. Jerry L. Walls (Oxford: Oxford University Press, 2008), 24–25.

amillennial approaches to what happens to the Old Testament collage of the coming kingdom in the New Testament, see my interaction with the approaches of Anthony Hoekema and Benjamin Merkle in Go Deeper Excursus 13.

A Case for the Classic Both/And Approach

A major problem with the common amillennial approaches to Old Testament restoration prophecies is that they tend to present a false choice. *Either* these prophecies are literal and refer in a kind of univocal way to a future restoration of Israel, *or* they are symbolic and find their fulfillment spiritually in New Testament realities. Merely demonstrating a spiritual application of Old Testament prophecies to the church in the present age does not actually rule out a future fulfillment. Counterexamples from the New Testament, which I will present shortly, demonstrate that the either/or approach is unsatisfactory.

Also, the Old Testament visions and prophecies that had already been fulfilled in the Old Testament are themselves fulfilled in a figurative sense—that is, the prophecy or vision uses figurative language to point to an actual future reality. They are not mere symbols for spiritual truths or fables to communicate moral principles. And while it may sound like we are honoring Christ most by interpreting these restoration passages as being fulfilled *in him* and thus *in his body, the church*, it is not less honoring to add that these promises are fulfilled not only *in him and his church* in the present but also will be fulfilled *through him and his church* in the future. Such a both/and perspective is not less Christocentric but more.

The New Testament also applies Old Testament historical people, things, and events as fulfilled spiritually in Christ and the church. This does not mean that such people, things, and events did not exist in the real world in the past, or that they were cyphers that pointed to spiritual realities but had no reality of their own. Rather, the use of typology depended on the reality of historicity. In the same way, there is nothing incongruent in seeing real people, things, and events related to the future restoration of Israel as also serving as types for present spiritual realities.

Finally, a close examination of particular New Testament passages that depend on the collage of Old Testament terms and images for the restoration of Israel provides an important anchor for this discussion. It is absolutely correct that the New Testament must inform our understanding of how Old Testament prophecies are to be interpreted and fulfilled. But as we draw such methodological conclusions, we must consider all New Testament passages, not just a handful that seem to support a preconceived hermeneutic driven by an *a priori* either/or approach. What such an exploration of passages reveals is that the New Testament actually supports a both/and approach to Old Testament passages: they will be fulfilled literally in the future full manifestation of the coming kingdom, while they are also fulfilled spiritually in the church today during its partial manifestation. Only the both/and approach fully satisfies the actual New Testament evidence.

Michael Vlach rightly pushes back against the tendency among many Christians who claim the New Testament "*transforms* or *transcends* the storyline begun in the OT" and urges rather that "unfulfilled promises at Jesus' first coming do not need to be spiritualized. They look forward to literal fulfillment at His return."[8] While I affirm Vlach's pushback against an over-spiritualizing, I would also lend a gentle nudge against what appears to be a slight "under-spiritualizing" in Vlach's approach. That is, a classic both/and approach to Old Testament prophecy allows for a present partial, spiritual manifestation or application of the original promises of the coming kingdom—not an allegorical or metaphorical treatment of the prophecies, but an actual experience of their promises in a partial but real sense today. Instead of saying "the Old Testament promises are not spiritualized but literally fulfilled in the future," I believe the more biblically, theologically, and historically faithful way of stating it is to say that the Old Testament promises are not merely spiritualized for the church today but will also be literally fulfilling in the future.

In surveying how the Old Testament prophecies are treated in the New Testament, we must be careful not to fall into the error of "cherry picking"—that is, gathering a few examples that support one's hermeneutical or eschatological presupposition while ignoring or suppressing evidence of a different approach. We cannot simply cite a few examples of the New Testament applying Old Testament prophecies spiritually to the church and draw sweeping hermeneutical rules from those few examples. Nor can we cite a few cases of the New Testament applying Old Testament prophecies literally to support a universal literal hermeneutic.

The fact is, while the New Testament does interpret Old Testament prophecies in a spiritual manner, it also interprets Old Testament prophecies literally. Sometimes it provides more than one interpretation of a single prophecy, or it interprets a prophecy both spiritually and literally in different passages. In the modern era, especially since the twentieth century, many theologians have tended to cast eschatological perspectives as an either/or prospect. Those who favor a symbolic, spiritual, and present interpretation of the text are not alone. Those who favor a literal, physical, and future interpretation do the same thing in an equal-but-opposite direction.

- *Either* the kingdom is future, *or* the kingdom is present.

- *Either* the church is presently the new, spiritual Israel, *or* Israel will be restored literally in the future.

- *Either* the Old Testament promises are currently fulfilled spiritually in Christ and the church, *or* they will be fulfilled physically through Christ in the future.

- *Either* the symbol of the wolf living with the lamb points to the spiritual reconciliation among peoples in the church, *or* it refers to a literal harmony of animals in the coming millennium.

- *Either* the binding of Satan in Revelation 20 refers to the present restraint of Satan's ability to deceive the nations, *or* it refers to a future binding in which Satan will be utterly banished from this world.

8. Michael J. Vlach, *He Will Reign Forever: A Biblical Theology of the Kingdom of God* (Silverton, OR: Lampion, 2017), 16–17.

The earliest Christian expositors felt no obligation to choose between such alternatives. Rather, they appear to have applied a hermeneutical principle of "both/ and," perhaps modeling this approach after the explicit and implicit teachings of the New Testament itself. For example, in 1 Corinthians 10, Paul refers to Israel's literal, historical experiences of the exodus in ways that establish a typological pattern applicable to the Christian's redemptive experiences (1 Cor 10:1–5). Although those events actually occurred in history, Paul asserts, "Now these things occurred as examples (τύποι) for us" (1 Cor 10:6). And, again, "These things happened to them to serve as an example (τυπικῶς), and they were written down to instruct us" (10:11). In the passage between these bookends, Paul draws practical, moral applications for the church today, "on whom the ends of the ages have come" (10:11).

Paul's typological applications to the present church do not negate the fact that the historical events recorded in Scripture *occurred in the real world—literally and physically*. Paul felt no need to employ an either/or approach in the interpretation and application of these passages. For example, *either* these things happened to Israel in the past, *or* they were written as moral examples and warnings for our present spiritual well-being, as if they were mere allegories or morality fables. For Paul, the events in Israel's redemptive history were actual, historical events *and* they continue to carry spiritual, moral application for us today. In fact, that application was intended in God's original orchestration of the events, as well as in moving his people to record them as they did in holy Scripture.

In the same way, biblical prophecies—in their sometimes earthy, this-worldly details—may be conceived as having a both/and rather than an either/or interpretation and application. We see several examples of this in the New Testament. First, regarding the resurrection of the dead, instead of presenting this as *either* a literal, future resurrection of the body in the age to come *or* as a present, spiritual resurrection of the regenerate believer, the New Testament presents resurrection in a both/and sense. Christians are resurrected spiritually and morally by grace through faith through the Triune God's work of regeneration (John 5:25; Rom 6:4; Eph 2:1–6), *and* they will be resurrected physically and literally in real history in the age to come (John 5:28–29; Rom 8:11; 2 Cor 4:14). In fact, the literal, future resurrection is the primary emphasis in redemptive history; the spiritual resurrection and present standing of the believer in Christ is viewed in terms of a firstfruits, a down-payment, a promise of even greater things to come.

Another example relates to the new creation, or the "new heavens and new earth." We have seen earlier that this theme is found already in the Old Testament (Isa 65:17; 66:22), connected with the restoration of Israel and an age of global peace and prosperity. This future-oriented expectation of the new heavens and new earth is in no way set aside by the coming of Christ and the giving of his Holy Spirit. In fact, 2 Peter indicates that this new creation is the object of the Christian's future hope (2 Pet 3:13). Paul also anticipates this future renewal and restoration of all creation in connection with the resurrection of the body (Rom 8:18–25). Yet the enduring fact of a literal, physical new creation in the future does not stop Paul from applying the "new creation" concept spiritually to the Christian today.[9] In 2 Corinthians

---

9. Though the Old Testament foundation uses the merism "new heavens and new earth" in reference to the "new creation," Shillington rightly notes that "Paul has adopted the term

5:17, he writes, "So if anyone is in Christ, there is a new creation: everything old has passed away; look, new things have come into being." This language is drawn loosely from Isaiah 65:17.[10] In Galatians 3, Paul also draws on "new creation" language, with the prophecy of Isaiah 65:17 as the background. Just as the wicked world will pass away under God's judgment (Isa 65:1–16), so the believer's world of wickedness has passed away spiritually by the cross of Christ, "through which," Paul says, "the world has been crucified to me, and I to the world" (3:14). Then, just as the judgment of the world was to give way to a new heaven and new earth—a new creation—which includes a glorious restoration of Jerusalem and Israel (Isa 65:17–25), so the New Testament believer, incorporated into the church, experiences a spiritual "new creation" already, and in this spiritual sense the church may be called the "Israel of God" (Gal 6:15–16).[11] Yet we have already seen that this application of the prophetic language and imagery to the church in a spiritual sense does not preclude a both/and literal interpretation of the prophetic texts in the future. Just as we have been spiritual resurrection, we will be physically resurrected in the future. Just as we are already called the spiritual "new creation" and spiritual "Israel," we may anticipate a literal, future new creation and a physical restoration of Israel.

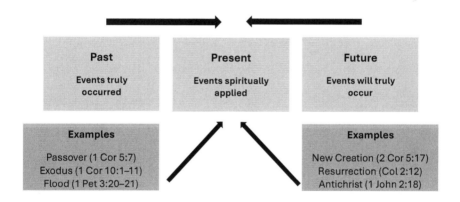

This both/and approach is also observed in Paul's treatment regarding the "mystery of lawlessness" already active in the world (2 Thess 2:7), manifested in the presence of false messiahs and false prophets throughout history. Yet this present

---

from apocalyptic Judaism and adapted it to his new insight on the significance of the death and resurrection of Jesus Christ for the world (e.g., 2 Esdras 7:75; 2 Baruch 32:6; Jubilees 4:26; 1QS 4:25; cf. Rev. 21:1; 1 Enoch 45:4–5; 72:1; 91:15–16)." V. G. Shillington, *2 Corinthians*, Believers Church Bible Commentary (Scottdale, PA: Herald Press, 1998), 130. These apocryphal texts themselves draw from the language of imagery of Isa 65–66.

10. For a discussion of Paul's thought regarding the relationship of the creation and new creation in Rom 8, 2 Cor 5, and Gal 6, see Christina Hoegen-Rohls, "Κτίσις and καινὴ κτίσις in Paul's Letters," in *Paul, Luke and the Graeco-Roman World: Essays in Honour of Alexander J. M. Wedderburn*, ed. Alf Christophersen, Carsten Claussen, Jörg Frey, and Bruce Longenecker, JSNTSup, vol. 217 (London: Sheffield Academic Press, 2002), 114–22.

11. However, see discussion on whether the "Israel of God" refers to the church in Richardson, *Israel in the Apostolic Church*, 74–84.

reality does not rule out the expectation of a future "lawless one" who will embody all godless rebellion (2 Thess 2:3). This may also be John's meaning in 1 John 2:18, when the apostle refers to the singular "antichrist" who is coming in connection with "the last hour," while asserting that many "antichrists" have appeared, marking their own day as "the last hour." Rather than treating these assertions as mutually exclusive either/or options—*either* the antichrist/man of lawlessness will appear literally in the future *or* the spirit of antichrist/mystery of lawlessness is fulfilled in the present—the New Testament seems open to a more sophisticated both/and perspective: the antichrist/man of lawlessness is *both* a present, spiritual reality *and* the antichrist/man of lawlessness figure will be a literal, future eschatological person.

This both/and versus either/or approach to prophecy was founded on the pattern of the New Testament itself, but it continued to be the governing principle in the early church and endured in some fashion even into the modern era. It appears to be a mostly modernistic presupposition—likely a product of polarizing eschatological polemics—that the belief in a present spiritual interpretation of Old Testament prophecy necessarily rules out a future, literal fulfillment; or that a belief in a future, literal fulfillment of Old Testament prophecies necessarily rules out a present, spiritual application to the church today.[12]

An interesting account—whether apocryphal or not—is extant in which the late first-century emperor Domitian interviewed descendants of Christ's brothers. In a record of that interrogation, we read, "And when they were asked about Christ and what kind of kingdom he had and where it was and when it would appear, they gave the statement that it was not worldly nor would it be upon the earth, but that it would be in the heavens and angelic (οὐ κοσμικὴ μὲν οὐδ᾽ ἐπίγειος, ἐπουράνιος δὲ καὶ ἀγγελικὴ τυγχάνοι), and that it would come at the completion of time, when he would come in glory to judge the living and the dead and reward each person according to the way one lived one's life" (Eusebius, *Hist. eccl.* 3.20.4 [Schott]). This has sometimes been read as evidence for an amillennial or antichiliastic view of the kingdom in the late first century. However, that interpretation can be sustained only if one presupposes an either/or approach to the matter of the kingdom. If, however, one is open to a both/and view of the kingdom, then this passage would easily fall in that category. The kingdom of Christ was—in the time of Domitian—not of this world, but it would—in the future—appear at the end of the age.

Irenaeus of Lyons represents the classic both/and approach to Old Testament prophecy when he writes, "But concerning the concord and peace of the animals of different species, who [are] opposed by nature and enemies of one another, the elders say that it will truly be so at the advent of Christ, when He is going to reign over all. For this makes known, in a figurative manner, [how] men of different races and dissimilar customs are gathered in one place in a peaceful concord by the name of Christ" (*Epid.* 61). That is, Isaiah's prophecy of the wolf and lamb dwelling together will be fulfilled literally and physically in the future kingdom; but it is also fulfilled in a spiritual sense today in the reconciliation among believers in the church.

---

12. For another modern advocate of a more "both/and" versus "either/or" approach, see, e.g., Vlach, *He Will Reign Forever*, 16.

Similarly, Irenaeus seems to apply the promise of the salvation of the "seed of Abraham" both spiritually to the church in the present as well as physically to the literal descendants of Abraham who "will be saved" from among the nations (*Haer.* 5.34.1). Irenaeus envisions a future, literal fulfillment of the restoration of the actual sons of Abraham, despite the fact that the church—the spiritual seed of Abraham—experiences a spiritual fulfillment of these promises today. For Irenaeus, fulfillment of these prophecies was not an either/or prospect but a both/and reality.

Certainly, as an earthly, millennial eschatology began to fall out of favor after the second century, such a both/and approach gave way to an interpretation that saw the promises of the Old Testament fulfilled only in the church, in heaven, or in some future eternal state. An appeal to a precedent of "Protestant interpreters"[13] as the default position for a spiritual interpretation of the Old Testament prophecies is irrelevant. The reformers simply adopted the approach of their medieval and late patristic forefathers without much critical thought. Only in the post-Reformation era did scholars begin to question the sufficiency of such an approach.

By providing these examples of both New Testament and second-century writers who appealed to a both/and approach to Old Testament prophecy, I have not thereby made the interpretation of Old Testament prophecies simple. Each passage must be analyzed in its original historical context and in its broader canonical context. Yet I have demonstrated that the both/and approach is not novel. I have also shown that the either/or approach that seems to underlie so many disputes between especially amillennial and premillennial interpreters in particularly the nineteenth and twentieth centuries represents a "false choice." Expositors in the ancient church followed the New Testament approach of allowing for both a literal, future fulfillment as well as a spiritual, present fulfillment of Old Testament promises (e.g., resurrection, new creation, etc.).

Those who demonstrate that the New Testament sometimes—or even often— applies language and imagery from the Old Testament collage of the coming kingdom to Christ and the church do not thereby rule out an ultimate literal fulfillment of these promises through Christ and the church to Israel, the world, and all creation.

---

13. Kim A. Riddlebarger, *A Case for Amillennialism: Understanding the End Times* (Grand Rapids: Baker, 2013), 50.

7

THE MESSIAH'S PROMISE OF
RENEWAL AND RESTORATION

*He promised to drink of the fruit of the vine with His
disciples, thus indicating both these points: the inheritance
of the earth in which the new fruit of the vine is drunk,
and the resurrection of His disciples in the flesh.*

Irenaeus, *Against Heresies* 5.33.1

The previous chapter introduced the concept that the New Testament sometimes applies Old Testament promises of the coming kingdom spiritually to the church. However, this present spiritual application of future prophecy does not exhaust what the New Testament writers do with language and imagery of the coming kingdom. In the next several chapters—including important technical exegetical excurses—I examine New Testament passages regarding the coming kingdom, in which I demonstrate that the New Testament writers continued to promote the expectation of a fulfillment of a restoration of Israel in the land while pushing this expectation to the future return of Christ. In the present age between Christ's ascension and his return, the Spirit partially mediates aspects of the coming kingdom in and through the church. Thus the second-century Irenaean "both/and" eschatology provides an effective framework for explaining the present and future realities of the kingdom of God.

In this chapter, I look at what becomes of the Old Testament promises of the coming kingdom first in Jesus' teaching during his earthly ministry (Matt 19:23–30 [Luke 22:28–30]; Matt 24:29–35 [Mark 13:24–31]). In chapter 8, I explore the promise of the coming kingdom as anticipated by Jesus and Peter in the book of Acts (Acts 1:3–7; 3:19–21). Then, in chapter 9, I examine the anticipation of the coming kingdom in two key passages by Paul (Rom 11:25–27; 1 Cor 15:22–26). Only after this survey of the language and imagery related to the New Testament understanding of the expectation of the coming kingdom can we approach the question of the millennium in Revelation 20 in chapters 10–13.

The Expectation of the Coming Kingdom in Matthew
19:23–30 (Mark 10:28–31; Luke 22:28–30)

For an examination of this pericope, I will work primarily from the fullest account in Matthew 19:23–30 and supplement it with parallel statements in Mark 10:28–31 and Luke 22:28–30.[1] The first thing to note is the correlation between several terms and images and the Old Testament expectation of the coming kingdom expressed in the prophets: the kingdom of heaven/kingdom of God (Matt 19:23–24; Luke 22:29), the renewal of all things (Matt 19:28), the Son of Man sitting on his glorious throne (Matt 19:28), the enthronement of those who followed him (Matt 19:28; Luke 22:30), the administration over the twelve tribes of Israel (Matt 19:28; Luke 22:30), the reward of a hundredfold blessing (Matt 19:29; Mark 10:30), eating and drinking at the table (Luke 22:30), and the reception of eternal life (Matt 19:30; Mark 10:30). This clustering of concepts would have brought to the minds of Jesus' first-century Jewish hearers snapshots from the collage of the coming kingdom in the Old Testament prophets discussed in chapter 6.

Already in this passage the kingdom of God/kingdom of heaven (the terms are used synonymously in Matt 19:23–24) is connected to the "renewal of all things" (19:28). In the complementary account in Luke 20:28–30, Jesus says, "You are those who have stood by me in my trials, and I confer on you, just as my Father has conferred on me, a kingdom, so that you may eat and drink at my table in my kingdom, and you will sit on thrones judging the twelve tribes of Israel." Thus the "regeneration" and the "kingdom" are coextensive.[2] The term does not therefore mean "the kingdom in heaven" per se but the kingdom that originates from heaven and has its source of authority from the heavenly realm.

What is meant, then, by "the renewal of all things" (Matt 19:28 NRSVue)?[3] The Greek noun παλιγγενεσία is used only here and in Titus 3:5, where people are saved "by the washing of regeneration (παλιγγενεσίας) and renewing (ἀνακαινώσεως) by the Holy Spirit." Though it may be tempting to conflate the meaning of these two verses, to do so would fail to do justice to their distinct contexts. In Jesus' promise, ἐν τῇ παλιγγενεσίᾳ refers to a period of time during which something will happen;[4] thus a faithful gloss would be "during the period of the regeneration." This is reinforced by Jesus' use of ὅταν ("when"), the time that this period of regeneration will occur: "When the Son of Man is seated on the throne of his glory (ἐπὶ θρόνου δόξης αὐτοῦ)." We must again reject the hasty conclusion that Jesus is referring to his ascension to heaven to sit at the right hand of the Father. In the only exact parallel of θρόνος δόξης in the New Testament, Jesus himself indicates when he will sit on the "throne of his glory": "When (ὅταν) the Son of Man comes in his glory and all the angels with him, then (τότε) he will sit on the throne of his glory

---

1. On the connection with Luke 22:28–30, see David C. Sim, "The Meaning of παλιγγενεσία in Matthew 19:28," *JSNT* 15.50 (1993): 3.

2. Cf. Herman Ridderbos, *The Coming of the Kingdom*, trans. H. de Jongste, ed. Raymond O. Zorn (Philadelphia: Presbyterian and Reformed, 1962), 271; Sim, "The Meaning of παλιγγενεσία," 3.

3. Outside the New Testament, παλιγγενεσία "always implies either the rebirth of the world (the "new world" in Jewish apocalyptic) or the rebirth of the individual." Fred W. Burnett, "Παλιγγενεσία in Matt. 19:28: A Window on the Matthean Community?," *JSNT* 5.17 (1983): 64.

4. See Friedrich Blass and Albert Debrunner, *A Greek Grammar of the New Testament and Other Early Christian Literature*, trans. and rev. R. W. Funk (Chicago: University of Chicago Press, 1961), 107 (§200).

(καθίσει ἐπὶ θρόνου δόξης αὐτοῦ)" (Matt 25:31).[5] I concur with Sim, who concludes that "παλιγγενεσία in Mt. 19.28 means not just the new age but the total re-creation of the cosmos which accompanies the new age."[6]

What would this time of παλιγγενεσία—the "age to come" (Mark 10:30) and the "kingdom" (Luke 22:30)—have meant to Jesus' first-century Jewish hearers and Matthew's first-century Jewish-Christian readers? They would most likely have understood Jesus as referring to the collage of images of the coming kingdom found in the Old Testament prophets, received by subsequent generations, and developed in the intertestamental Jewish apocryphal and apocalyptic writings in terms similar to the language Jesus used in Matthew 19:23–30.[7]

Moving to the image of the "Son of Man" taking his seat on his glorious throne, this language points back to Daniel 7 and the manifestation of the ultimate kingdom of God that topples world empires.[8] The corporate interpretation of the Son of Man fits well with Jesus' promise that the disciples will sit on twelve thrones "judging the twelve tribes of Israel."[9] Several questions arise with this statement. Does "judging" (κρίνω) mean to inflict punitive justice (Ezek 35:11; 36:19), to distinguish between the righteous and wicked (Ezek 34:20–22), or simply to administer just governance (Isa 2:4; 11:3–4; Jer 22:16)? Eschatological passages of the Old Testament involve all these ideas. The context of the promise, its association with Jesus as the coming messianic king, and the period of the "judging" as the time of the "renewal of all things" would most naturally lead to the positive understanding of "judgment" in the sense of administrating justice (cf. Pss. Sol. 17.26–29). This may, of course, involve administration of punitive judgments, but it primarily involves deciding disputes (cf. Isa 2:4; 11:3, 4; Jer 22:16).

The phrase "the twelve tribes of Israel" would have been understood by the original hearers as referring to the actual, historical tribes of Israel.[10] As Meier insists in connection to this passage, "'Israel' in Mt always means the actual OT

---

5. See Burnett, "Παλιγγενεσία in Matt. 19:28," 64–65; and Sim, "The Meaning of παλιγγενεσία," 4.

6. Sim, "The Meaning of παλιγγενεσία," 11.

7. Sim, "The Meaning of παλιγγενεσία," 5. Sim, 5–7, points to numerous texts that support this idea: 4 Ezra 5:55; 7:30–32; 7:75; 14:10–11; 2 Bar. 32:6; 44:12; 57:2; 85:10; 1 En. 45:4–5; 72:1; 91:16; and Jub. 1:29.

8. On the reference to the Son of Man—not only here but elsewhere in the Synoptic Gospels—see Ridderbos, *Coming of the Kingdom*, 31.

9. See, e.g., Richard A. Horsley, *Jesus and the Powers: Conflict, Covenant, and the Hope of the Poor* (Minneapolis: Fortress, 2011), 205–11, who argues for a more positive understanding of "judge." In contrast, Llewellyn Howes argues for a judgment that separates the righteous from the wicked, restoring a remnant of the tribes of Israel. See Howes, "Judging the Twelve Tribes of Israel: Q 22:28, 30 in Light of the Psalms of Solomon and the Community Rule," *VE* 35.1 (2014): 1–11.

10. Ridderbos, *Coming of the Kingdom*, 36. However, Ridderbos, 199, sees in the assignment of the twelve apostles over the "twelve tribes of Israel" an indication that they themselves, in a sense, constitute the restoration of Israel, and the new people of God—the church—continues the covenant with Israel. He does understand this language as depending on the Old Testament cluster of imagery related to the coming kingdom. Cf. John Bright, *The Kingdom of God: The Biblical Concept and Its Meaning for the Church* (New York: Abingdon-Cokesbury, 1953), 226.

people Israel, and not the church."[11] The mention of the "twelve tribes" would have signaled to Jesus' original Jewish audience a reference to the reunification and restoration of all the nation of Israel, thus the eschatological "second exodus." That this is connected eschatologically to the coming kingdom is reinforced by the language of Luke 22:29–30. Though just the twelve disciples are mentioned in direct connection with the restored tribes of Israel, the broader context of the pericope extends the blessing—both in the present age between Christ's advents and the future age to come—to all who follow Christ as the disciples followed him (Matt 19:29–30; Mark 10:30–31).

Regarding the promise of "eternal life," then, this pericope also associates it with the coming of the Son of Man and the "regeneration."[12] In Jesus' preaching, eternal life is not only a present spiritual experience but more fully a future reality. In Mark 10:29–30—the Synoptic parallel of Matthew 19:29–30—Jesus says, "Truly I tell you, there is no one who has left house or brothers or sisters or mother or father or children or fields for my sake and for the sake of the good news who will not receive a hundredfold now in this age (νῦν ἐν τῷ καιρῷ τούτῳ)—houses, brothers and sisters, mothers and children, and fields, with persecutions—and in the age to come eternal life (ἐν τῷ αἰῶνι τῷ ἐρχομένῳ ζωὴν αἰώνιον)." This fits well with Jesus' contrast between the present world and the world to come, the latter related to the resurrection (Luke 20:34–36).

The pericope of Matthew 19:23–30 shares many similarities with the same apocalyptic expectations expressed in the first- to second-century AD writing 1 Enoch 37–71 (*Book of Parables*). The author notes that God will judge sinners on the "day of suffering and tribulation" (1 En. 45.2), but on that day, God's elect one "shall sit on the throne of glory" and execute judgment (45.3). Sinners will be cut off (45.2, 6), but those deemed righteous will have places of rest (45.3); they "shall grow strong within them when they see Mine elect ones, and those who have called upon My glorious name" (45.3). At this point, God will cause his elect one "to dwell among them" (45.4)—that is, the dwellers of the earth who have been granted rest because of their righteous deeds.[13] At that time, God "will transform the heaven and make it an eternal blessing and light," he "will transform the earth and make it a blessing," and on this transformed, blessed earth, he will cause his elect ones "to dwell upon it" (45.5) along with his "righteous ones" (45.6). Relying on Isaiah's imagery of the "new heavens and new earth" (Isa 65:17), the author of 1 Enoch paints a picture of a renewed, glorified creation in which righteousness dwells under the reign of the "elect one" and an apparent co-regency of the "elect ones" over the righteous ones on the earth who had been separated from the wicked. This mirrors the cluster of images in Matthew 19 as well as the general expectation of the coming kingdom in both the Old Testament and the second-century Irenaean eschatology.

---

11. John P. Meier, *Matthew* (Collegeville, MN: Liturgical, 1980), 223.

12. See Burnett, "Παλιγγενεσία in Matt. 19:28," 65. Burnett, 72n41, supports this with reference to Matt 12:32, urging that "the Evangelist conceived of the new age in temporal terms (cf. Mark 3:29; Luke 12:10)."

13. On the distinction between the "righteous" and "elect," see also 1 En. 58.1–3.

Anthony Hoekema once complained against premillennialism that Jesus teaches in Matthew 25:31 that at his coming he will usher in the eternal state, not an intermediate state.[14] However, this assertion presents a false choice, because when we read Jesus' words in the context of the first-century understanding of the coming kingdom and the messianic age, the period immediately following Christ's return is itself the means by which Christ ushers in the new creation. It is a renewal of creation, of expanding the boundaries of paradise, of progressively subduing the earth, which was always intended in the *imago Dei* mission (see chapter 2). We must not envision a sudden and instantaneous transformation of all creation at the moment of Christ's return—from bullets and bombs to birds and butterflies in a matter of seconds. On the contrary, the classic second-century Irenaean eschatology has a vital purpose for the millennial kingdom: the gradual renewal of the heavens and earth resulting in the full manifestation of the new heavens and the new earth. In this sense, the period of progressive liberation of all creation from the bondage to corruption is distinct—not separate—from the coming age, the "regeneration" (Matt 19:28).

Irenaeus of Lyons so read this pericope as referring to the future physical kingdom on earth after the bodily resurrection from the dead (*Haer.* 5.33.1–2), noting that "these are [to take place] in the times of the kingdom, that is, upon the seventh day, which has been sanctified, in which God rested from all the works which He created, which is the true Sabbath of the righteous" (5.33.2).

The Expectation of the Coming Kingdom in Matthew 24:29–35 (Mark 13:24–31; Luke 21:25–33)

In response to his disciples' marveling at the beauty of the temple that had been renovated by Herod, Jesus prophesied, "Not one stone will be left here upon another; all will be thrown down" (Matt 24:2). Detecting end-of-the-world type language, the disciples asked, "Tell us, when will this be, and what will be the sign of your coming and of the end of the age?" (24:3).

Earlier, the disciples had heard Jesus' description of the "age to come," the "renewal of all things," and the "kingdom" associated with the coming of the Son of Man (discussed above, Matt 19:23–30). Jesus' words concerning the catastrophic destruction of the temple would have triggered in their minds imagery of the coming "day of the Lord"—the period of judgment, purification, and conflagration in preparation for the establishment of the coming kingdom (see chapters 15–17 in this book). The disciples thus conflated the destruction of the first-century temple, the end of the age, and the coming of the Son of Man. Later revelation would distinguish between the destruction of that particular first-century temple as the end of the old covenant era and a future time of judgment prior to the parousia. But the disciples' question at the time, even with its inaccuracies as to timing, was not absurd.

Jesus then describes a number of "signs" drawn from classic "day of the Lord" imagery—some of which seem to apply to events imminent in the first century;

---

14. Anthony A. Hoekema, *The Bible and the Future* (Grand Rapids: Eerdmans, 1994), 185.

some of which seem to point to a distant, ultimate period of judgment.[15] In any case, in the portion of the discourse relative to a discussion of the coming kingdom, Jesus notes that "immediately after" the "tribulation" (μετὰ τὴν θλῖψιν) he just described, cosmic portents of the day of the Lord will be displayed (Matt 24:29; Mark 13:24–25). As we will see later in chapter 15 of this book, this language is drawn from repeated terms and images of the "day of the Lord" judgments in the Old Testament (e.g., Isa 13:10; 34:4; Joel 2:10; 3:4; 4:15; Ezek 32:7; Hag 2:6). Thus the events described beginning in Matthew 24:30 (paralleled in Mark 13:26) follow the judgments associated with the "day of the Lord" or "tribulation" (Matt 24:21; Mark 13:19).

Mark's version of the coming of the Son of Man simply states: "Then they will see 'the Son of Man coming in clouds' with great power and glory" (Mark 13:26). The image is drawn from the apocalyptic vision of Daniel 7:13–14, which itself relies on the picture of the coming kingdom in the Old Testament prophets.[16] Matthew's version of this same saying, though, adds another detail and Old Testament reference: "Then the sign (τὸ σημεῖον) of the Son of Man will appear in heaven, and then all the tribes of the earth will mourn, and they will see 'the Son of Man coming on the clouds of heaven' with power and great glory" (Matt 24:30). The mention that "all the tribes of the earth [or land] will mourn (κόψονται πᾶσαι αἱ φυλαὶ τῆς γῆς)" recalls language from Zechariah 12. We have seen in chapter 6 that the language of Zechariah 12 fits within the collage of images of the coming kingdom in the Old Testament. In that vision, the Lord promised to pour out a "spirit of compassion and supplication on the house of David and the inhabitants of Jerusalem" with the result that "they will look on me whom they have pierced" (Zech 12:10), and, in the Septuagint, "they will mourn for it with a mourning as for a beloved friend (καὶ κόψονται ἐπ᾽ αὐτὸν κοπετὸν ὡς ἐπ᾽ ἀγαπητὸν), and they will be grieved with a grief as for the firstborn." Verse 12—the more direct source for the quotation in Matthew 24:30—adds, "And the land will mourn, tribes by tribes (καὶ κόψεται ἡ γῆ κατὰ φυλὰς φυλάς)." The same convergence of passages in Matthew 24:30 is also found in Revelation 1:7: "Look! He is coming with the clouds; every eye will see him, even those who pierced him, and all the tribes of the earth will wail on account of him."

In Matthew 24:30, when Jesus refers to "all the tribes of the land" (πᾶσαι αἱ φυλαὶ τῆς γῆς), does he use φυλή in reference to the tribes of Israel, as in his source of the language in Zechariah 12 (and in Matt 19:28; Luke 2:36; 22:30; Acts 31:21; Rom 11:1; Phil 3:5; Heb 7:13–14; Rev 5:5; 21:12)? Or does he use it more universally for all peoples of the earth?[17] Or, does he use it in a figurative sense with reference to "spiritual Israel"?[18] In light of Jesus' earlier promise that the disciples would be involved in

---

15. This ultimate tribulation period will be discussed more in chapters 16 and 17.

16. See the discussion of the imagery of the coming kingdom in Dan 7:13–14, 26–27 in Go Deeper Excursus 11.

17. How one understands "tribes" in Matt 24:30 will affect whether one understands "tribes" in Rev 1:17 as referring to Israel or to Gentile nations (Rev 5:9; 7:9; 11:9; 13:7; 14:6). It should be noted that in Revelation, when "tribes" seems to be used in its broadest sense, it is always grouped with "peoples and languages and nations."

18. Whether the "tribes of Israel" in Jas 1:1 and Rev 7:4–8 refer to literal tribes of Israel or to "spiritual Israel" rests on theological—not exegetical—considerations.

administration over the "twelve tribes of Israel" (Matt 19:28), and in light of Matthew adding an allusion to Zechariah 12:12, it seems best to regard the reference to "all the tribes of the land" to the actual tribes of Israel. Given these contextual restraints, the burden of proof is on those who would opt for a universal or spiritual interpretation.

The next line—found in different forms in both Matthew and Mark—increases the likelihood that Jesus intended to instill in his listeners a hope for a future repentance and regathering of the tribes of Israel in keeping with the Old Testament collage of the coming kingdom. In fact, the specific complementary language in Matthew and Mark draws on the Old Testament Septuagint as well as other intertestamental literature that would have been well known during the first century.

Consider the language of Matthew 24:31. When the tribes of the land mourn and the Son of Man comes on the clouds of heaven, "he will send out his messengers (ἀποστελεῖ τοὺς ἀγγέλους αὐτοῦ) with a great trumpet (μετὰ σάλπιγγος μεγάλης), and they will gather (καὶ ἐπισυνάξουσιν) his elect (τοὺς ἐκλεκτοὺς αὐτοῦ) from the four winds (ἐκ τῶν τεσσάρων ἀνέμων), from one end of the sky to the other end (ἀπ᾽ ἄκρων οὐρανῶν ἕως [τῶν] ἄκρων αὐτῶν)." Mark's shorter version matches in all essential respects, but it does not mention a "great trumpet" associated with the ingathering of the elect; instead of "from one end of heaven to the other," it has "from the ends of the earth to the ends of heaven." Also, Mark has the Son of Man responsible for gathering the elect (ἐπισυνάξει); Matthew places this responsibility in the hands of the "messengers"—"Then he will send the messengers (ἀποστελεῖ τοὺς ἀγγέλους) and he will gather the elect (καὶ ἐπισυνάξει τοὺς ἐκλεκτοὺς) from the four winds (ἐκ τῶν τεσσάρων ἀνέμων), from the ends of earth to the ends of heaven (ἀπ᾽ ἄκρου γῆς ἕως ἄκρου οὐρανοῦ)."

Numerous commentators have hastily concluded that the "trumpet," "gathering," "angels," and "heaven" are none other than a references to what is often called the "rapture of the church" described in 1 Thessalonians 4:15–17 (cf. 2 Thess 2:1). However, upon careful reflection, one realizes that (1) the associations with the "rapture" in Matthew and Mark are plausible but not certain, and (2) Jesus' language actually points to a more precise background in the Old Testament and intertestamental literature that better explains the different variations in Matthew and Mark. First, related to the alleged associations with the "rapture," 1 Thessalonians 4:15–17 mentions the "coming of the Lord" (τὴν παρουσίαν τοῦ κυρίου) "from heaven" (ἀπ᾽ οὐρανοῦ) and those caught up "in the clouds" (ἐν νεφέλαις) to meet him "in the air" (εἰς ἀέρα); and 2 Thessalonians 2:1 presumably refers to this παρουσία in conjunction with "our being gathered together with him" (ἐπισυναγωγῆς). Similarly, Matthew and Mark both mention the "Son of Man coming upon the clouds of heaven [Mark: 'in the clouds']" (τὸν υἱὸν τοῦ ἀνθρώπου ἐρχόμενον ἐπὶ τῶν νεφελῶν τοῦ οὐρανοῦ [ἐν νεφέλαις]) (Matt 24:30; Mark 13:26) in conjunction with the gathering together of the elect (ἐπισυνάξουσιν [ἐπισυνάξει] τοὺς ἐκλεκτοὺς) (Matt 24:31; Mark 13:27). Also, 1 Thessalonians 4:16 says the coming and gathering will occur "with [or at] the trumpet of God" (ἐν σάλπιγγι θεοῦ; cf. 1 Cor 15:52), while at least Matthew's Gospel mentions sending forth his messengers or angels "with a great trumpet" (μετὰ σάλπιγγος μεγάλης) (Matt 24:31), a detail missing from Mark. It is therefore certainly reasonable to envision the Matthew and Mark passages to be referring to the same event as described in 1 and 2 Thessalonians.

At this point, however, some differences emerge that cast doubt on a correspondence of the two passages. While Matthew and Mark mention the Son of Man sending forth "messengers" or "angels" (ἀποστελεῖ τοὺς ἀγγέλους) (Matt 24:31; Mark 13:27),[19] 1 Thessalonians mentions the Lord descending from heaven "with [or at] the voice of the archangel" (ἐν φωνῇ ἀρχαγγέλου) (1 Thess 4:16). One could assume that the archangel's voice is the cause of sending forth the multitude of angels mentioned in Matthew 24:31 and Mark 13:27, but in both Matthew and Mark, the Son of Man sends forth the messengers/angels, not an archangel. Though the "trumpet" in Matthew is called the "great trumpet" (σάλπιγγος μεγάλης), the trumpet in 1 Thessalonians 4:16 is called "the trumpet of God" (σάλπιγγι θεοῦ). This may seem like a minor difference, but as we see the Old Testament background for the "great trumpet," it will become significant that 1 Thessalonians does not adopt that same language to make a connection with Matthew 24:31 firm. Neither Matthew nor Mark suggests that the "elect" gathered from the four winds or four corners of the earth/heaven are caught up into heaven. Rather, they are gathered together from the remote horizon on the earth. Neither Matthew nor Mark mentions the resurrection of the dead, which is, in fact, the primary focus 1 Thessalonians 4. Thus the connections between Matthew and Mark and 1 and 2 Thessalonians are plausible but superficial upon closer examination.[20]

More importantly, the specific language used in Matthew 24:31/Mark 13:27 actually points to the gathering of the remnant of repentant Israel scattered among the nations—the four corners of the earth—to restore them to their land after the day of the Lord for the commencement of the coming messianic kingdom. The following passages from the Old Testament and intertestamental literature makes this background clear.

Already in Deuteronomy 30, where Israel is warned that their covenant unfaithfulness will result in exile, Moses instills hope for a future after repentance:

> And the Lord shall heal your sins, and he will show mercy to you, and he will gather (συνάξει) you again from all the nations into which the Lord scattered you there. If your dispersion should be from one end of heaven as far as the other end of heaven (ἀπ' ἄκρου τοῦ οὐρανοῦ ἕως ἄκρου τοῦ οὐρανοῦ), from that place the Lord your God will gather (συνάξει) you and from that place the Lord your God will take you. And your God will lead you from that place into the land that your fathers inherited, and you shall take possession of it. (Deut 30:3–5 LXX)

The use of the idiom for the vast extent of the diaspora, ἀπ' ἄκρου τοῦ οὐρανοῦ ἕως ἄκρου τοῦ οὐρανοῦ (Deut 30:4), is similar to the idiomatic phrase in Matthew 24:31—ἀπ' ἄκρων οὐρανῶν ἕως [τῶν] ἄκρων αὐτῶν.

---

19. In the explanation of the weeds among the wheat (Matt 13:36–43), Jesus uses a similar image; but in this case, instead of the elect being gathered by angels, the wicked are carried away to judgment.

20. Craig Blomberg, *Matthew*, The New American Commentary, vol. 22 (Nashville: Broadman & Holman, 1992), 363.

In Isaiah 11:11–12, which is one of the primary passages of the Isaianic collage of images of the coming kingdom (see discussion in chapter 6 above), we read the following vivid description of the restoration of Israel to the land, including raising a "sign" (σημεῖον) toward the nations (cf. Matt 24:30):

> And this will happen on that day: the Lord will continue to show his hand to be zealous for those of the people who remain, who were left behind by the Assyrians and from Egypt and from Babylonia and Ethiopia and from Elam and from the east and out of Arabia. And he will raise a sign (σημεῖον) toward the nations, and he will gather (συνάξει) those of Israel who were destroyed, and he will gather (συνάξει) from the four wings of the land (ἐκ τῶν τεσσάρων πτερύγων τῆς γῆς) those of Judah who were scattered.

Likewise, Isaiah 27:12–13 says, "But as for you, gather (συναγάγετε) the children of Israel one by one. And this will happen on that day: They will trumpet with the great trumpet (τῇ σάλπιγγι τῇ μεγάλῃ), and those who have been destroyed in the country of the Assyrians and those who have been destroyed in Egypt will come and worship the Lord on the holy mountain, Jerusalem." Of note is the use of the phrase "with the great trumpet" (τῇ σάλπιγγι τῇ μεγάλῃ), which echoes the same expression in Matthew 24:31: μετὰ σάλπιγγος μεγάλης.[21]

Isaiah 41:8–9 includes language related to Israel as God's "elect" (cf. Matt 24:31; Mark 13:27). And Isaiah 43:5–7 says, "Do not be frightened, for I am with you; I will lead your offspring from the east, and I will gather (συνάξω) you from the west. . . . Lead my sons from a far land, and my daughters from the ends of the earth (ἀπ᾽ ἄκρων τῆς γῆς)." The phrase ἀπ᾽ ἄκρων τῆς γῆς referring to the far extent of the exiled Israelites is echoed in Mark 13:27—ἀπ᾽ ἄκρου γῆς. Similarly, the Septuagint of Zechariah 2:6 [2:10 LXX] reads, "'Flee from the land of the north,' says the Lord, 'because from the four winds of heaven (ἐκ τῶν τεσσάρων ἀνέμων τοῦ οὐρανοῦ) I will gather you together (συνάξω),' says the Lord." Zechariah's use of ἐκ τῶν τεσσάρων ἀνέμων τοῦ οὐρανοῦ for the extent of the dispersion from which Israel is regathered matches both Matthew 24:31 (ἐκ τῶν τεσσάρων ἀνέμων) and Mark 13:27 (ἐκ τῶν τεσσάρων ἀνέμων).

Further, in the tenth of the eighteen Jewish prayers known as the *Amidah* or *Shemoneh Esreh,* prayed daily even in the time of Jesus and the disciples,[22] we read

---

21. Meier conflates the different ways in which trumpets are used in the Old and New Testaments when he writes, "The trumpet is a traditional symbol for the last judgment (cf. Isa 27:13; 1 Thess 4:16; 1 Cor 15:52; Rev 8:2–11:15)." Meier, *Matthew*, 288. As will be seen below in the discussion of the "Day of the Lord" in chapter 15, this is definitely true much of the time. However, the "great trumpet" particularly is associated with the rescue and return of God's people to the land. It would be more accurate to say that trumpets are traditionally associated with eschatological events.

22. See Joseph Tabory, "The Rabbinic Traditions about the Establishment of the *Amidah*: Some Observations," in Nuria Calduch-Benages, Michael W. Duggan, and Dalia Marx, eds., *On Wings of Prayer: Sources of Jewish Worship: Essays in Honor of Professor Stefan C. Reif on the Occasion of His Seventy-Fifth Birthday,* Deuterocanonical and Cognate Literature Studies, vol 44 (Berlin: De Gruyter, 2019), 337–54. The modern version of the *Amidah* includes nineteen rather than eighteen prayers, but the name *Shemoneh Esreh*, indicating eighteen blessings, remains. In 2003, Instone-Brewer could speak of a "general consensus

the following request for the regathering of the exiles back to their land: "Sound the great shofar (בשופר גדול) for our freedom and raise a banner to gather (לקבץ) our exiles, and unite us together from the four corners of the earth (מארבע כנפות הארץ). Blessed are You, Lord, who regathers the scattered of His people Israel."[23] The mention of the "great shofar" (בשופר גדול) reflects the language of the Hebrew text of Isaiah 27:13: "And on that day a great trumpet (בשופר גדול) will be blown, and those who were lost in the land of Assyria and those who were driven out to the land of Egypt will come."[24] This passage is translated in the Greek Septuagint thusly: "And it shall come to pass in that day, that they shall blow the great trumpet (τῇ σάλπιγγι τῇ μεγάλῃ), and the lost ones in the land of the Assyrians shall come." When Matthew says, "And He will send forth His angels with a great trumpet (σάλπιγγος μεγάλης)," the most defensible background for that language is the regathering of the elect of Israel from the lands of their dispersion.

Finally, *Psalms of Solomon* 11:1–3 in the Septuagint says, "Blow ye in Zion on the trumpet (σάλπιγγι) to summon (the) saints, cause ye to be heard in Jerusalem the voice of him that bringeth good tidings (εὐαγγελιζομένου); for God hath had pity on Israel in visiting them. Stand on the height, O Jerusalem, and behold thy children, from the East and the West, gathered together (συνηγμένα) by the Lord; from the North they come in the gladness of their God, from the isles afar off God hath gathered (συνήγαγεν) them."[25]

The verbal and thematic parallels between Matthew 24:31/Mark 13:27 with Deuteronomy 30:3–5; Isaiah 11:11–12; 27:12–13; 41:8–9; 43:5–7; Zechariah 2:6; *Shemoneh Esreh* 10, and *Psalms of Solomon* 11:1–3 are too close to be coincidental. In these passages, we see those proclaiming a message (messengers/angels), calling the redeemed of Israel (the elect) from the four winds/ends of the earth/heavens, gathering them to the land of Israel, with the sounding of a great trumpet. In both the Old Testament and Jesus' teaching, this event of gathering Israel from the four winds comes after the time of tribulation, or the "day of the Lord," in commencement of the messianic kingdom. To Jesus' original first-century audience, this language and imagery would have naturally been understood as the restoration of Israel to the land.[26] In light of these facts, it does not appear that an eschatological in-gathering of the church at a resurrection or rapture is at all in view in this particular passage.

. . . that the Eighteen originates from the Second Temple period," though not necessarily in precisely the same form as we have them from the second century." David Instone-Brewer, "The Eighteen Benedictions and the Minim before 70 CE," *JTS* 54.1 (2003): 27.

23. Kimelman sees the tenth blessing as the first of a "series of national eschatological blessings (10–15)" that "delineates the order of redemption, commencing with the great shofar's blast of freedom which announces the ingathering of the exiles and culminating in the return of God to Zion." Reuven Kimelman, "The Daily Amidah and the Rhetoric of Redemption," *JQR* 79.2–3 (1988–1999): 175.

24. On the use of language from Isaiah in the tenth blessing, see Louis Finkelstein, "The Development of the Amidah," *JQR* 16.1 (1925): 13–14.

25. Translation from Robert Henry Charles, ed., *Pseudepigrapha of the Old Testament*, vol. 2 (Oxford: Clarendon, 1913), 643–44.

26. Cf. W. D. Davies and Dale C. Allison Jr., *A Critical and Exegetical Commentary on the Gospel according to Saint Matthew*, vol. 3, International Critical Commentary (London: T&T Clark, 2004), 364.

Conclusion on Messiah's Promise of Renewal and Restoration

Reading the two pericopae of Matthew 19:23–30 and 24:29–35 together, we see Jesus promising his disciples that after the Son of Man comes in glory and takes his throne "in the regeneration," they would sit on twelve thrones judging the twelve tribes of Israel (Matt 19:28; Luke 22:30)— the tribes reunited and restored to their land after they repented following the future day of the Lord (Matt 24:29–30), at which time the "great trumpet" of ingathering will be sounded, summoning the exiles of Israel from wherever they had been scattered (Matt 24:31; Mark 13:27). That future manifestation of the kingdom of God (Matt 19:23), associated with the "age to come" (Mark 10:30) and "eternal life" (Matt 19:29; Mark 10:30), is what Jesus calls "my kingdom," which he will confer upon his disciples (Luke 22:29–30).

The rest of Jesus' words regarding the parable of the fig tree and the warning that these things are so "near" that the present generation would not pass away until the things had most certainly taken place (Matt 24:32–35; Mark 13:28–31; Luke 21:31–32) appears to shift back to the larger discussion that includes prophecies that have fulfillments both in the first century (the destruction of the temple, the end of the old covenant "age," the establishment of the spiritual kingdom) as well as remotely at the parousia or coming of the Son of Man in glory. We may make sense of the phrase "until all these things have taken place (ἕως ἄν πάντα ταῦτα γένηται)" (Matt 24:34) if we understand the verb as an ingressive aorist, meaning "until all these things start to happen."[27] D. A. Carson also makes a case for what is essentially the same result:

> All that v. 34 demands is that the distress of vv. 4–28, including Jerusalem's fall, happens within the lifetime of the generation then living. This does *not* mean that the distress must end within that time but only that "all these things" must happen within it. Therefore, v. 34 sets a *terminus a quo* for the Parousia; it cannot happen until the events in vv. 4–28 take place, all within a generation of AD 30. But there is no *terminus ad quem* to this distress other than the Parousia itself, and "only the Father" knows when it will happen (v. 36).[28]

Comments on Matthew 24:29–34, Mark 13:24–31, and Luke 21:25–33 are noticeably missing in Irenaeus of Lyons, Justin Martyr, and other second-century writers. In his treatise, *On the Resurrection of the Flesh*, in the earliest years of the third century, Tertullian interacts with this pericope in his refutation of those who say the resurrection is either a present, spiritual reality when people believe or when they dye and go to heaven (*Res.* 22). In demonstrating that the resurrection is yet future, he quotes from Jesus' words in the Olivet Discourse, arguing that they have reference both to the events related to the destruction of the temple in the first

---

27. See Daniel B. Wallace, *Greek Grammar beyond the Basics: An Exegetical Syntax of the New Testament* (Grand Rapids: Zondervan, 1996), 558–59. For various interpretations of this passage, see Davies and Allison, *Matthew*, 366–68.

28. D. A. Carson, "Matthew," in *The Expositor's Bible Commentary*, vol. 9, *Matthew–Mark*, rev. ed., ed. Tremper Longman III and David E. Garland (Grand Rapids: Zondervan, 2010), 569.

century as well as to the future (a classic both/and approach): "[Jesus] discourses to them first of the order of Jewish events until the overthrow of Jerusalem, and then of such as concerned all nations up to the very end of the world" (*Res.* 22 [*ANF* 3]). Tertullian understands the "times of the Gentiles" to refer to the time of the calling of Gentiles to faith—"meaning, of course, those which were to be chosen of God, and gathered in with the remnant of Israel."

To underscore the fact that this has not come to pass and that we therefore await a future coming of Christ and future resurrection, Tertullian mentions several things that had not yet occurred: "Who has yet beheld Jesus descending from heaven in like manner as the apostles saw Him ascend, according to the appointment of the two angels? Up to the present moment they have not, tribe by tribe, smitten their breasts, looking on Him whom they pierced. No one has as yet fallen in with Elias; no one has as yet escaped from Antichrist; no one has as yet had to bewail the downfall of Babylon" (*De resurrectione carne* 22 [*ANF* 3]).[29]

The preceding examination of passages in Matthew 19 and 24 (and their parallels in Mark and Luke) reveals a use of language consistent with the collage of images of the coming kingdom in the Old Testament prophets. This includes language most naturally read in their contexts as a restoration of the tribes of Israel to their land associated with the future judgment and coming of the Son of Man. Jesus used terms and concepts that would have triggered in the minds of his hearers the picture of the coming messianic age set forth repeatedly and consistently in the prophets and continued in the intertestamental period. He did nothing to dissuade them from this expectation, though he certainly pushed it forward in connection with the glorious coming of the Son of Man.

At the same time, it cannot be denied that Jesus prepared his disciples for a spiritual form of the kingdom as a present reality even in his own day—one that would continue in the world prior to the glorious coming of the Son of Man. We therefore do not see a setting aside of the future promises of an earthly kingdom of restoration and renewal in favor of a present spiritual kingdom of repentance and reconciliation; rather, Jesus' teaching accommodates a both/and approach to the kingdom. However, we must consider the possibility that such an invitation to the tribes of Israel to experience restoration in the land in keeping with the Old Testament promises was contingent upon their repentance and acceptance of Jesus as their Messiah. Perhaps, it may be argued, Jesus' offer was valid only during the unique period of his earthly ministry; once the Jewish leaders and many of the people rejected Jesus, resulting in his execution, that marked a decisive turn from an earthly fulfillment to a more spiritual fulfillment in its stead. To consider this possibility, we must move to post-resurrection and post-Pentecost expectations of the coming kingdom.

---

29. That Tertullian expected some kind of future repentance of Israel is demonstrated in *Prax.* 17, *Pud.* 8, *Adv. Marc.* 5.9.

8

The Messianic Time of Restoration in the Book of Acts

*Then the Lord will come from heaven in the clouds, in
the glory of the Father. . . . Bringing in for the righteous
the times of the kingdom . . . and restoring to Abraham
the promised inheritance, in which kingdom the Lord
declared, that "many coming from the east and from the
west should sit down with Abraham, Isaac, and Jacob."*

Irenaeus, *Against Heresies* 5.30.4

In the previous chapter, I demonstrated that Jesus' eschatological language would have encouraged his hearers toward a continued expectation of the restoration of Israel in a future time of cosmic regeneration following his parousia in keeping with the Old Testament collage of images of the coming kingdom. In this chapter, I explore the book of Acts to discern what happens to this expectation of a coming kingdom after the Jewish leaders in Jerusalem rejected Jesus. The first passage will examine Jesus' own words prior to his ascension (Acts 1:1:3–7). The second will examine the words in Peter's sermon to his Jewish audience in Jerusalem (Acts 3:19–21).

The Expectation of the Coming Kingdom in Acts 1:3–7

In the wake of Jesus' teaching concerning the coming kingdom discussed in the previous chapter, we are left with three possibilities moving forward: (1) Jesus' offer of a physical, earthly kingdom in keeping with the Old Testament was genuine, but instead of responding in repentance and faith, they forfeited the restoration because of their hard hearts; (2) Jesus was delaying instruction about the true spiritual nature of the kingdom for a later time after his death and resurrection or the coming of the Spirit; or (3) Jesus' echoing of Old Testament promises and expectations was genuine, but the fulfillment would be delayed until his future coming as judge and king, while the spiritual form of the kingdom would be established between his first and second advents.

The prologue to the book of Acts addresses the first of these possibilities. Luke briefly notes that for forty days after his resurrection, Jesus was "speaking about the kingdom of God" (λέγων τὰ περὶ τῆς βασιλείας τοῦ θεοῦ).[1] The instruction

---

1. The phrase "kingdom of God," though common in Luke, occurs only six times in Acts (1:3; 8:12; 14:22; 19:8; 28:23, 31).

concerning the kingdom of God would have provided an excellent opportunity for Jesus to set the record straight regarding the nature of the kingdom, especially in light of the shocking rejection of the Messiah by religious and political authorities. Because the Old Testament promises regarding the coming kingdom were contingent upon Israel's repentance, one might argue that the failure of most Jewish people to embrace Jesus justly resulted in a kind of rescinding of the promises or at least a permanent failure to realize them.

During his post-resurrection instructions, Jesus told his disciples to remain in Jerusalem to await the baptism of the Holy Spirit, which they would experience "not many days" after his ascension (Acts 1:4–5). To any Jewish hearer informed regarding the Old Testament promises of the coming kingdom, the mention of the Holy Spirit would have brought to mind that collage of images associated with the restoration of Israel (Isa 11:2; 32:5; 42:1; 44:3–4; 59:20–21; Ezek 11:17–20; 37:12–13; Joel 2:28–29; Zech 12:10; Pss. Sol. 17:37–38). Given the close eschatological association between the Holy Spirit and the coming kingdom, the disciples' question is not out of place.[2] "So when they had come together, they asked him, 'Lord, is this the time (ἐν τῷ χρόνῳ τούτῳ) when you will restore (ἀποκαθιστάνεις) the kingdom (βασιλείαν) to Israel (Ἰσραήλ)?'" (Acts 1:6).[3]

In context, the phrase "at this time (ἐν τῷ χρόνῳ τούτῳ)" refers to the time of the coming of the Spirit (1:5). They expected that with the pouring out of the Spirit, the kingdom would also be restored to Israel as prophesied in the Old Testament.[4] Their question suggests they had these related promises in mind. It also reveals that nothing in Jesus' post-resurrection instruction "about the kingdom of God" had dissuaded them from an expectation of an earthly, physical kingdom.[5]

Commentators have softened the significance of the disciples' question in Acts 1:6 in a number of ways. John Bright asserts that the disciples demanded of Jesus "things which were not in his nature to deliver."[6] And John Stott, following Calvin, suggests the disciples were entirely mistaken in the assumptions underlying their question, and he alleges that "in his reply (7–8) Jesus corrected their mistaken notions of the kingdom's nature, extent and arrival."[7] Yet Darrell Bock observes, "There is no indication in Jesus' reply, however, that anything they asked was wrong except that they are excessively concerned about when all of this would take place."[8]

---

2. See John B. Polhill, *Acts*, The New American Commentary, vol. 26 (Nashville: Broadman & Holman, 1992), 84.

3. Wainwright observes, "The word 'Israel' is always used by him [Luke] with reference to the Jewish people." A. W. Wainwright, "Luke and the Restoration of the Kingdom to Israel," *ExpTim* 89.3 (1977): 76.

4. L. Scott Kellum, *Acts*, B&H Exegetical Guide to the Greek New Testament, ed. Andreas J. Köstenberger and Robert W. Yarbrough (Nashville: B&H Academic, 2020), 19.

5. Wainwright, "Luke and the Restoration," 76.

6. John Bright, *The Kingdom of God: The Biblical Concept and Its Meaning for the Church* (New York: Abingdon-Cokesbury, 1953), 93, cf. 199. See also William S. Kurz, *Reading Luke-Acts: Dynamics of Biblical Narrative* (Louisville: Westminster/John Knox, 1993), 74–75.

7. John R. W. Stott, *The Message of Acts: To the Ends of the Earth*, The Bible Speaks Today (Downers Grove, IL: IVP Academic, 1990), 20.

8. Darrell L. Bock, *Acts*, Baker Exegetical Commentary on the New Testament (Grand Rapids: Baker Academic, 2007), 63.

During Jesus' earthly ministry, when followers and disciples asked him questions based on false premises, he most often corrected their misunderstanding in no uncertain terms.[9] When we contrast such examples in which Jesus responds to "bad questions" with his response to the disciples in Acts 1:7, the allegation that he corrected their aberrant view of the nature and extent of the kingdom is difficult to maintain. Wainwright notes, "When Jesus is asked, 'Lord, will you at this time restore the kingdom to Israel?' (Ac 1[6]), he does not deny that he will perform this task, but merely indicates that it is not for his disciples to know the time of the event."[10] If one wants to make the case that the disciples' persistent expectation of a restoration of the kingdom to Israel was mistaken, that case will have to be made by some means other than Jesus' reply, which addressed only the timing of the event, not its nature.[11]

Even the language of the disciples' question suggests that they had in mind the kind of restoration of Israel envisioned by the Old Testament prophets. Wainwright notes, "Redemption in Luke's writings cannot be separated from restoration. The words ἀποκαθστάνειν ('restore') and ἀποκατάστασις ('restoration') are used in the Acts to describe events which will occur at the end of the age." He sees the Old Testament prophets as the proper background for understanding the passages in Acts regarding restoration.[12] The details of this background will be explored in more depth in the next section related to Acts 3.

Nevertheless, many commentators have opted for interpretations that see the Old Testament language taking on a different significance in the New Testament. Fuller argues that Luke-Acts establishes a theme of Israel's regathering that actually finds its fulfillment in the twelve disciples, who themselves constitute the restoration of Israel; thus the coming of the Spirit and the restoration of the kingdom to Israel are the same.[13] That is, either in the disciples' original question or in Jesus' answer, "Israel" and its restoration are applied to the twelve disciples and their ministry of proclamation that will occur with the coming of the Spirit at Pentecost. Yet this explanation does not take into consideration the previous background of Jesus' teaching concerning the disciples' reign over the twelve tribes of Israel in connection with the future coming of the Son of Man in glory at the time of the "regeneration" and the kingdom (Matt 19:28; Luke 22:30). Nor does it consider Peter's post-Pentecost statements regarding the "times of refreshing" and "restoration" that will come at Christ's return (Acts 3:19–21), which I will address in the next section.

---

9. For example, see Matt 12:10–13; 15:1–9; 16:1–4 (cf. 12:38–40); 17:10–13; 18:1–3 (cf. Luke 22:24–27); Matt 18:21–22; 19:7; 19:16–26 (cf. Luke 10:25–37; 18:18–26); Matt 20:20–22; 22:15–22; 22:23–33; 24:3–51; Luke 6:1–5; 6:6–11; 9:51–55; 14:1–6; 20:20–26, 27–40; 21:7–36; John 3:1–21; 4:19–26; 6:52–65; 9:1–3; 18:33–38.

10. Wainwright, "Luke and the Restoration," 76; cf. Göran Lennartsson, *Refreshing & Restoration: Two Eschatological Motifs in Acts 3:19–21* (Lund, SE: Lund University Center for Theology and Religious Studies, 2007), 289.

11. Cf. Robert C. Tannehill, *A Narrative Unity of Luke-Acts: A Literary Interpretation*, vol. 2 (Philadelphia: Fortress, 1994), 15.

12. Wainwright, "Luke and the Restoration," 76.

13. Michael E. Fuller, *The Restoration of Israel: Israel's Re-gathering and the Fate of the Nations in Early Jewish Literature and Luke-Acts*, BZNW, vol. 138, ed. James D. G. Dunn et al. (Berlin: de Gruyter, 2006), 257–63; cf. Polhill, *Acts*, 84–86.

After dissuading his disciples from seeking after knowledge about "times or periods" (Acts 1:7), Jesus pivots to a strong contrast: "But (ἀλλὰ) you will receive power when the Holy Spirit has come upon you, and you will be my witnesses in Jerusalem, in all Judea and Samaria, and to the ends of the earth" (1:8).[14] While the reference to "times or periods" (χρόνους ἢ καιροὺς) has strong eschatological connotations (1 Thess 5:1) and seems to push the timing of the restoration of the kingdom to Israel into the undetermined future, the pouring out of the Spirit is imminent—in just a few days. Thus Jesus' words are more naturally read as postponing the restoration of Israel to the second coming of Christ. In the present period between the coming of the Spirit and the return of Christ, the disciples will be witnesses of the resurrection and representatives of the spiritual kingdom of God.[15]

In other words, the issue in Acts 1:6 was not *whether* the kingdom would be restored to Israel, but *when* it would be restored.[16] Because "the apostles' question about restoration in Acts 1:6 implies similarity of meaning to 3:21,"[17] that passage will shed additional light on our understanding of the mind of the apostles in Acts 1:6.[18]

The Expectation of the Coming Kingdom in Acts 3:19–21

In John 16:12, Jesus said, "I still have many things to say to you, but you cannot bear them now." In light of these words, it could be claimed that Jesus postponed a correction of the disciples' too-Jewish understanding of the coming kingdom until the coming of the Spirit, who would guide them into the truth (John 16:13).[19] Therefore, it could perhaps be argued that the seemingly earthy, physical imagery of the coming kingdom in Matthew 19 and 24 and Acts 1 was still an effect of divine condescension to the weakness of his audience. That is, perhaps Jesus spoke to them in Old Testament terms because they were not yet ready for the reinterpretation and reapplication of those promises until the coming of the Spirit. If this were the case, we would expect the language to change after the coming of the Spirit in Acts 2.

However, Peter's address to his Jewish audience in Acts 3:19–21 and its connection to Acts 1:6–7 argues against that approach. That these passages are connected thematically by Luke is clear. Lennartsson notes, "The 'restoration of the kingdom to Israel' in Acts 1:6 correlates in meaning with the expression . . . in Acts 3:21. They do not represent two different meanings."[20] In Acts 3, Peter urges his Jewish

---

14. Kellum, *Acts*, 20, notes, "Ἀλλά creates a strong contrast to the previous statement. Instead of that which is out of their control, Jesus announces an empowerment and a ministry."

15. Robert C. Tannehill, "Israel in Luke-Acts: A Tragic Story," *JBL* 104.1 (1985): 76.

16. Bock, *Acts*, 60.

17. Lennartsson, *Refreshing & Restoration*, 78.

18. Though the fathers do not refer to this text frequently, when they do address the disciples' question and Jesus' answer, they refer the "times and seasons" to the future return of Christ. See Augustine, *Civ. Dei* 18.50, 53; Cyril of Jerusalem, *Catechetical Lectures* 15.4; and John of Damascus, *De Trin.* 9.75.

19. This seems to be implied in John Chrysostom's exposition of Acts 1 in *Homily 2 on Acts 1:6* (see *NPNF* 1.11:11, 14).

20. Lennartsson, *Refreshing & Restoration*, 78; cf. 89–90. Also see Tannehill, "Israel in Luke-Acts," 76.

audience to "repent" and "turn" so their sins may be wiped away (3:19). This in turn would lead to "seasons of refreshing" from the Lord's presence and the sending of the Messiah, who must remain where he is in heaven until the time of complete restoration long ago prophesied by God through the holy prophets (3:20–21). But what exactly is promised and prophesied in Acts 3:19–21? Because this passage stands as a crucial text for the enduring expectation of restoration in keeping with Old Testament promises, reinforced during Jesus' earthly ministry (e.g., Matt 19, 24) and still anticipated by the disciples prior to Christ's resurrection (Acts 1:6), we must take a close look at the language and syntax of this passage.

"Repent and Turn Again" (Acts 3:19)

Peter's exhortation in Acts 3:19 to his Jewish audience to "repent and return" (μετανοήσατε . . . καὶ ἐπιστρέψατε) is the same in Paul's preaching to both Jews and Gentiles (Acts 26:20); thus these responses cannot be seen as limited merely to Israel. Elsewhere in the New Testament, the call of "return" (ἐπιστρέφω) is particularly directed toward a Jewish audience perceived to have been unfaithful to Yahweh and their covenant. Drawing from the language of Isaiah 6:9–10, Jesus says, "'For this people's heart has grown dull, and with their ears they can barely hear, and their eyes they have closed, lest they should see with their eyes and hear with their ears and understand with their heart and turn (ἐπισρέψωσιν), and I would heal them'" (Matt 13:15; cf. Mark 4:12; Acts 28:27). The verb is used repeatedly for turning to God in faith and repentance.[21]

In the Old Testament prophets, the call to "return" (ἐπιστρέφω) is of particular significance. It first appears in this connection in Deuteronomy when Moses warns the people of their future apostasy, exile, repentance, and restoration: "And all these words shall find you in the end of days (ἐπ' ἐσχάτῳ τῶν ἡμερῶν), and you will return (ἐπιστραφήσῃ) to the LORD your God and listen to his voice" (Deut 4:27, 30).[22] It is used in reference to individuals—including Gentiles—turning to the Lord in repentance.[23] In 2 Chronicles 30:9, King Hezekiah sent messages to all Israel and Judea, calling them to turn to the Lord in repentance in hope of restoration. In the mouths of the prophets, the call to "return" is thus tied to repentance and the restoration of the kingdom (1 Sam 7:3).[24] Throughout Jeremiah's prophecy, God calls to Israel to return to him so he may forgive, heal, and restore them (Jer 3:12, 14, 22; 4:1; 15:19; Lam 5:21). In fact, this turning to the Lord is cast in the context of new covenant restoration (Jer 24:4–7). In this passage, as in Acts 3:19–21, turning to God is directly associated with the restoration of Israel (Jer 24:6; Acts 3:21; cf. Ezek 14:6; 18:30).

The immediate result of repentance and turning in Acts 3:19 is "for the blotting out of your sins" (εἰς τὸ ἐξαλειφθῆναι ὑμῶν τὰς ἁμαρτίας). In the Septuagint, the term ἐξαλείφω ("blot out") in connection with sin is used famously in Psalm

---

21. See Acts 9:35; 11:21; 14:15; 15:19; 26:18; 2 Cor 3:16; 1 Thess 1:9; 1 Pet 2:25.

22. Cf. Deut 30:8, 10; 1 Kgs 8:47–48; 2 Chr 6:24, 26, 37, 38; 15:4; 2 Esd 11:9; Jdt 5:19; Tob 13:6.

23. See 2 Kgs 23:25; 2 Chr 35:19; Ps 21:28 LXX; 50:15; 84:9; Job 22:23; 33:23; Sir 5:7; 17:25; etc.

24. Cf. Hos 3:5; Joel 2:12–14; Zech 1:3; Mal 3:7; Isa 6:10; 19:22; 45:22; 46:8; 55:7.

50:3, "According to the abundance of your compassion blot out my lawless deed (ἐξάλειψον τὸ ἀνόμημά μου)" (cf. Ps 50:11; 2 Macc 12:42; Pss. Sol. 13:10). When we arrive at the prophets, Isaiah 44:22 promises, "For see, I have blotted out (ἀπήλειψα, cf. Acts 3:19 [ἐξαλείψω]) your acts of lawlessness like a cloud and your sins like darkness; return (ἐπιστράφητι) to me, and I will redeem you" (cf. 43:1–28).

The call to repentance and turning, as well as the offer of forgiveness, also resemble the fifth blessing, *Teshuvah*, and sixth blessing, *Selichah*, of the *Shemoneh Esrei*. Although it is unknown if the later specific mishnaic forms of these daily prayers reach back to the first century, the content likely reflects expressed yearnings and expectations of the first-century Jewish faithful. The *Teshuvah* says, "Return us, our Father, to your law . . . and restore us in complete returning to your presence (והה זירנו בתשובה שלמה לפניך)." In the sixth blessing, the *Selichah*, the petitioners ask for forgiveness, appealing to God's gracious disposition as a pardoner of sins. Thus Peter's call for his hearers to repent and turn again would have been a familiar concept, saturated with expectations of a restoration of the nation of Israel in keeping with the collage of images from the Old Testament promises of the coming kingdom.

"Seasons of Refreshing from the Presence of the Lord"

Returning to Acts 3:19–21, contingent upon their repentance and returning, God would wipe away their sins, with two concurrent results (ὅπως ἄν): that "seasons of refreshing may come from the presence of [lit., "face of"] the Lord" and that "he may send the one appointed for you, Christ Jesus" (Acts 3:20).

In the phrase καιροὶ ἀναψύξεως ("seasons of refreshing"; Acts 3:20), the exact noun ἀναψύξις (a hapax legomenon in the NT) has no significant nominal parallel in the LXX (cf. Exod 8:11 LXX). Its related term, ἀναψυχή, is used in Psalm 65:12 (LXX) for the relief and revival that comes after tribulations. Its verb form, ἀναψύχω, is used in reference to the refreshment that comes by observing the seventh-day Sabbath (Exod 23:12). The association of the weekly Sabbath rest to the eschatological Sabbath rest in connection with the coming messianic age was established by the time of the writing of Acts. In light of this background, the "seasons of refreshing" most naturally bring to mind the messianic age of cosmic Sabbath rest for Israel and the world.

Kellum, following Barrett, insists that the plural καιροί ("seasons") in the first purpose clause distinguishes it from the "eschatological reign of Christ" that will come after his return, concluding that it indicates a period of similar "'refreshing events rather than a single event'; thus upon their repentance, they receive refreshing in the form of the coming of the Holy Spirit in the present age."[25] Yet the plural καιροί is already used in Acts 1:6 in Jesus' reference to the delay of the restoration of the kingdom of Israel with no significance related to multiple consecutive periods of time; it is used simply for a long period of time in Luke 22:24, the "times of the Gentiles," and "seasons of bounty" in Acts 14:17. In the Septuagint reading of Daniel 11:14, it simply refers to a duration of time in the future: "in those appointed times (ἐν τοῖς καιροῖς ἐκείνοις)" (cf. also 1 Macc 4:59; 11:14). The reference, then, to "seasons of

---

25. Kellum, *Acts*, 55.

refreshing" in Acts 3:21 does not necessarily refer to multiple successive "seasons" but to a long age or even to multiple seasons during which the world will be refreshed in keeping with the expectation of the coming kingdom in the Old Testament.

These "seasons of refreshing" will come "from the presence of the Lord (ἀπὸ προσώπου τοῦ κυρίου)" (Acts 3:20). Similarly, in 2 Thessalonians 1:6–10 Paul casts the coming of Christ as judge in terms of the Old Testament's portrayal of Yahweh's theophanic visitation in judgment (Isa 66:14–16; cf. 2 Thess 1:8).[26] While the wicked receive wrath and tribulation at Christ's coming, believers will receive ἄνεσις, "relief" (2 Thess 1:7). Though not the same terms, the nouns ἄνεσις in 2 Thessalonians and ἀνάψυξις in Acts 3:20 are in the same semantic domain.[27] The additional phrase ἀπὸ προσώπου τοῦ κυρίου, occurring in both 2 Thessalonians 1:9 in the context of judgment and Acts 3:20 in the context of refreshing, establishes a conceptually complementary link between these passages. When the Lord comes, his presence will bring eternal destruction for the wicked (2 Thess 1:9; cf. Ps 96:5 LXX; Pss. Sol. 12:6; 15:5), but seasons of refreshing and relief for the righteous (2 Thess 1:7; Acts 3:20–21).

Peter's reference to the "seasons of refreshing" may also recall themes in the daily *Amidah* prayers, especially those following the fifth and sixth blessings, regarding turning (תשובה) and forgiveness (סליחה) respectively. In the seventh prayer, requests are made for redemption, and the eighth prayer, רפואה, calls for healing: "Heal us, Lord. . . . Save us. . . . Bring complete healing for all our sicknesses." The ninth prayer, ברכת השנים, or prayer for a blessed year, asks for bountiful crops and blessing on the face of the earth, confessing God as the one who "blesses the years" (מברך השנים), which could loosely correspond to the plural "seasons (καιροὶ) of refreshing" in Acts 3:20.

From the perspective of the contemporary Jewish understanding of the concept in the first century, Lennartsson summarizes: "Regarding the expression *times of refreshing* (καιροὶ ἀναψύξεως) the common understanding would probably be a time of release from work, sitting in a cool breeze on a hot summer day. For someone familiar with the Biblical and Jewish tradition, there might have been a slight difference of nuance for a Greek speaker compared with an audience listening to a (reconstructed) Semitic original, and that is the association to the Spirit of God."[28]

"Refreshing" and "Restoration"—Concurrent or Consecutive?

Scholars debate whether the effects of the repentance in Acts 3:20–21 are concurrent or consecutive.[29] A concurrent view understands the passage to mean that if they repent (3:19), God will send Jesus the Messiah who will usher in the "seasons of refreshing," which are the same as the "times of restoration" prophesied in the Old Testament. On the other hand, a consecutive interpretation understands that

---

26. This Day of the Lord as a "mediated theophanic visitation in judgment" will be explored more fully in chapters 15 and 16.

27. L&N, 245–46.

28. Lennartsson, *Refreshing & Restoration*, 257.

29. Lennartsson, *Refreshing & Restoration*, 69, writes, "On this issue, there is a disparity of opinion among scholars. For some 'times of refreshing' in Luke's perspective is essentially still future, whereas for others it is present already in the time of Acts."

repentance (3:19) will result in God sending "seasons of refreshing," and then these seasons of refreshing will subsequently give way to the sending of the Messiah, who will then usher in "times of restoration."[30] In the concurrent view, it could be taken in a spiritual, realized way—the seasons of refreshing (= times of restoration) is a spiritual reality experienced by the church in this age; or it could be taken in a physical, unrealized way—the seasons of refreshing (= times of restoration) is a physical reality that will be experienced in the world after Christ returns. In the consecutive view, the "seasons of refreshing" could be taken as occurring in the present era of gospel proclamation prior to Christ's return, followed by the "restoration of all things" after Christ's return. Alternately, it could be understood as seasons of refreshing after Christ's return in an intermediate kingdom, which will give way to the "times of restoration of all things" in an eternal new creation.

Possible Interpretations of the Chronology of Acts 3:19–21

	1 **Fulfilled in the Present Age (Already)**	**2** **Fulfilled in the Future Age (Not Yet)**	**3** **Fulfilled in the Present and Future Ages (Already/Not Yet)**
A **Concurrent View** **(refreshing = restoration)**	Upon repentance, God's people and creation will be spiritually refreshed and restored, and then the Messiah will come.	Upon repentance, the Messiah will return to fresh and restore both his people and all creation.	Upon repentance, God's people will begin to experience spiritual refreshing and restoration, and then the Messiah will come and complete the refreshing and restoration.
	1 **Fulfilled in the Present Age (Already)**	**2** **Fulfilled in the Future Age (Not Yet)**	**3** **Fulfilled in the Present and Future Ages (Already/Not Yet)**
B **Consecutive View** **(refreshing → restoration)**	Upon repentance, God's people will first experience spiritual refreshing and as more repent, restoration will follow in this age, and then the Messiah will come.	Upon repentance, the Messiah will come and begin the process of refreshing (in cosmic Sabbath terms), which process will result in the complete restoration both of his people and of all creation.	Upon repentance, God's people will experience spiritual refreshing and restoration, and then the Messiah will come and fully realize the future refreshing of his people, which will culminate in the full restoration of creation.

---

30. Stott, *Message of Acts*, 39.

Whether the seasons of refreshing and times of restoration are concurrent or consecutive is an important matter eschatologically. Will the seasons of refreshing come first, lasting for a long period (either the period of the church age or a future golden age of the kingdom), followed by the sending of Christ as a result (as in amillennialism or postmillennialism)? Or will these things occur concurrently, as a result of repentance, turning, and forgiveness; that is, the coming of Christ and the seasons of refreshing will come together (as in premillennialism)?

In a detailed examination in Go Deeper Excursus 14, *The Case for Concurrent Periods in Acts 3:19–21*, I argue on both lexical and syntactical grounds for a concurrent futurist view.[31] That is, upon repentance, the Messiah will return to usher in seasons of refreshing, which is also the times for the restoration of all things prophesied in the Old Testament. However, in light of the both/and approach to prophetic Scripture, this futurist/concurrent interpretation of the ultimate referent to Peter's words in Acts 3:19–21 leaves open a present and partial spiritual realization of "refreshing" and "restoration" in the era between Christ's ascension and return.

Having narrowed the options to a futurist eschatology in which seasons of refreshing will be concurrent with Christ's return, is there a way to decide whether Peter anticipated future "seasons of refreshing" at Christ's return that would be distinct from the "times of restoration of everything" in Acts 3:21? Or does the text teach that the καιροί and χρόνοι are themselves concurrent, both referring to the same future period of time at the return of Christ? Lennartsson argues that "any significant difference of meaning based on the choice of the terms (χρόνοι and καιροί) seems unlikely."[32] After all, Jesus used these same two terms in his response to the disciples' questions regarding the time of the restoration of the kingdom to Israel (Acts 1:6–7), and the connection between these two passages has already been asserted.

Go Deeper Excursus 14

The Case for Concurrent Periods in Acts 3:19–21

To answer the question of what was intended by the "times of restoration of everything" in Acts 3:21, we must look more closely at that terminology and Peter's own reference to the Old Testament for clarification.

"Times of Restoration of Everything"

The disciples' question in Acts 1:6 and Peter's picture of seasons of refreshing/times of restoration in Acts 3:20–21 are closely connected.[33] With regard to the meaning of ἀποκατάστασις ("restoration"), Lennartsson provides a helpful survey of perspectives,[34] noting that "scholars do not offer any conclusive meaning of the word *apokatastasis* in Acts 3:21, nor of the idiom 'times of the restoration of all.'"[35]

---

31. Hans Conzelmann, *Acts of the Apostles*, Hermeneia: A Critical and Historical Commentary on the Bible (Minneapolis: Augsburg Fortress, 1988), 29.
32. Lennartsson, *Refreshing & Restoration*, 82.
33. Lennartsson, *Refreshing & Restoration*, 77–78.
34. Lennartsson, *Refreshing & Restoration*, 79–80.
35. Lennartsson, *Refreshing & Restoration*, 80.

His own approach for understanding the meaning of the phrase "times of restoration" is to examine contemporary messianism in the first century.[36]

However, Peter's own words in Acts 3:19–21 point to the source of his intended background for the language—the things "about which God spoke by the mouth of his holy prophets long ago (διὰ στόματος τῶν ἁγίων ἀπ᾽ αἰῶνος αὐτοῦ προφητῶν)" (3:21). Peter claims that the "times of restoration of all things" are precisely those of which (ὧν) God spoke (ἐλάλησεν ὁ θεὸς).[37] So, the question must be answered by looking at the canonical Old Testament prophets and what they said about seasons of refreshing and times of restoration associated with the coming of the Messiah.[38]

Acts 3:21 starts with a relative pronoun, indicating that the appointed Messiah must be welcomed or received in heaven "until (ἄχρι) times for restoring all things of which God spoke through the mouth of the holy prophets long ago." The preposition ἄχρι indicates that Christ's current session in heaven is temporary. Its end has already been suggested in verse 20 with the promise that upon the repentance and turning of the people, God would send (ἀποστείλῃ) the appointed Christ. That is, Christ will be sent from his current place in heaven, concurrent with the sending of times of refreshing (Acts 3:20). Already in Acts 1:11, the expectation of the coming of Christ from heaven had been established as a hope of the disciples. Furthermore, Matthew 19:28 and 25:31 (discussed in chapter 7) established a connection between the coming of the Son of Man in glory, his enthronement, and the time of the "regeneration." Thus when verse 21 refers to the present heavenly reception of Christ continuing until (ἄχρι) a particular condition or event, this has already been established. Now Peter is more direct. With the coming of Christ from heaven, the earth will experience "times of restoration of all things" (Acts 3:21). I have already

---

36. Lennartsson, *Refreshing & Restoration*, 84.

37. There is an equivocation with the relative pronoun ὧν in Acts 3:21, which can be either neuter plural or masculine plural. If neuter, its antecedent would be the word immediately preceding, πάντων, and the meaning would be "the times of restoration of everything, that is, everything concerning which God spoke through the mouths of the holy prophets" (Acts 3:21). If ὧν is taken as masculine, it could still refer to πάντων, but πάντων would then be understood as "all men," thus: "the times of restoration of all people, that is, all people concerning which God spoke through the mouths of the holy prophets" (Acts 3:21). It seems the former interpretation (neuter πάντων) would likely include the latter ("all people"), while the latter would not necessarily include the former. A third possibility is that ὧν is masculine and the antecedent is not πάντων but χρόνων, thus "the times of restoration of everything, that is, the times concerning which God spoke through the mouths of the holy prophets" (Acts 3:21). If this latter is the case, then both the first and second senses would be included, as the "times of restoration" would include the restoration of people and things—whatever was spoken by God through the prophets. Thus the syntactical question of ὧν and its antecedent may be of immediate exegetical significance, but it is not of weighty theological significance.

38. Lennartsson's able research and scholarship is commendable, but its pursuit of contemporary first-century meanings for the phrases does not seem to follow from Peter's own signaling toward the Old Testament as the interpretive key. I refer readers to his work on background language and imagery associated with messianic expectations, refreshing, and restoration from the Amidah, Psalms of Solomon, 1 Enoch, the book of Jubilees, the Qumran community, Ben Sira, the Assumption of Moses, the Testaments of the Twelve Patriarchs, 2 Baruch, 4 Ezra, and Josephus, as well as later Jewish and Hellenistic writings. Lennartsson, *Refreshing & Restoration*, 163–245.

established in Go Deeper Excursus 14 that this period most naturally concurs with the "seasons of refreshing" in 3:20.

The noun ἀποκατάστασις ("restoration") is a hapax legomenon in the New Testament. Its noun form does not appear in the Septuagint nor, for that matter, do we find it in the Apostolic Fathers. It does appear in various contexts in classical Greek literature.[39] None of these, however, shed any light on Peter's meaning recorded in Acts 3:21. For this we must turn to the verb forms of the term (ἀποκαθίστημι, ἀποκαταστάνω, and ἀποκαθιστάνω) found repeatedly in the Septuagint version of the Old Testament prophets. These, not surprisingly, correspond with passages that composed the collage of images of the coming kingdom in the Old Testament.

In Jeremiah 16:14–15, we read, "Therefore, behold, days are coming, says the LORD, and they shall no longer say, 'The LORD lives who brought the sons of Israel up out of the land of Egypt,' but 'The LORD lives who brought the house of Israel up out of the land of the north and out of all the countries, there where they had been driven.' For I will restore (ἀποκαταστήσω) them to their own land that I gave to their fathers" (cf. Jer 23:8). The verb is also used as a promise in connection with Israel's turning to God in repentance: "And I will fix my eyes upon them for good, and I will restore (ἀποκαταστήσω) them to this land. And I will rebuild them and never tear down, and I will plant them and never pluck up. And I will give them a heart that they may know me, that I am the LORD, and they shall become a people to me, and I will become a god to them, because they shall return (ἐπιστραφήσονται) to me with their whole heart" (Jer 24:6–7). Note the similar conditional promise as we find in Acts 3:19–21: if they return, they will be returned to their land (Jer 24:6; cf. 27:19). This future restoration appears to involve more nations than just Israel (Ezek 16:55). In the New Testament, the verb form is used in connection with the moral reforms at the coming of Elijah (Matt 17:10–11; cf. Mark 9:12).

In the daily prayers of the Amidah, blessing 11, ברכת הדין, closely resembles Peter's "times for restoring all things." The petitioners request, "Restore our judges like in the early times (השיבה . . . כבראשונה) and our counselors like in the beginning (כבתחלה)." They call for the removal of sorrow and pain with the restoration of righteousness and justice. The fourteenth blessing, בנין ירושלים, calls for the rebuilding and restoration of Jerusalem and for God to "return and rest in it (תשוב ותשכון בתוכה)," which could correspond thematically with Peter's promise of the return of the Messiah in conjunction with the "times for restoring all things" in Acts 3:21. The prayer also specifically asks for God to "establish the throne of David within it": that is, within Jerusalem (וכסא דוד . . . לתוכה תכין). Similarly, the fifteenth blessing focuses on the Davidic king specifically, asking that God would cause the "branch of your servant David [to] flourish," in conjunction with deliverance and restoration. What is particularly interesting with regard to the fourteenth blessing, בנין ירושלים, is that the prayer specifically recalls the promises of God himself, presumably from the prophets, "just as you said (כאשר דברת)," which is

---

39. Polybius, *Histories* 3.99.6–7; Diodorus Siculus, *Library* 12.36.2; Josephus, *A.J.* 11.63; Plutarch, *Caesar* 59.2.

similar to Peter's words, "of which God spoke through the mouth of the prophets" (ὧν ἐλάλησεν ὁ θεὸς διὰ στόματος τῶν ἁγίων . . . προφητῶν [Acts 3:21]).

In short, when Peter refers to the times for "the restoration of all things" spoken of in the prophets, the clearest referent in both the Old and New Testaments is the restoration of Israel in the land along with the transformation of creation in keeping with the Old Testament promises (see chapter 6). This also fits well with the expectation expressed in Matthew 19:28 and Romans 8:18–23, which corresponds to "all things" subjected to humanity, which has "not yet" occurred (Heb 2:6–8).[40]

Wainwright justly rejects Jervell's claim—dependent on Acts 15:16–18—that the restoration of Israel prophesied in Acts 3 was deemed spiritually fulfilled by the remnant of the Jewish believers in the church.[41] Jervell's argument was that because Cornelius—a Gentile—had been converted in Acts 10, James thus regarded the inclusion of the Gentile to signal the completion of the restoration of Israel. The words of James are as follows: "And with this the words of the prophets agree, just as it is written, 'After this I will return, and I will rebuild the tent of David that has fallen; I will rebuild its ruins, and I will restore it, that the remnant of mankind may seek the Lord, and all the Gentiles who are called by my name, says the Lord, who makes these things known from of old'" (Acts 15:16–18). James's words are a fairly close, if loose, quotation from the LXX of Amos 9:11–12: "On that day I will raise up the tent of David that is fallen and rebuild its ruins and raise up its destruction, and rebuild it as the days of old in order that those remaining of humans and all the nations upon whom my name has been called might seek out me" (NETS). The passage James quotes refers to the physical restoration of the land and its structures: "I will rebuild the tent of David" (ἀνοικοδομήσω τὴν σκηνὴν Δαυὶδ), "I will rebuild its ruins" (τὰ κατεσκαμμένα αὐτῆς ἀνοικοδομήσω), and "I will restore it" (ἀνορθώσω αὐτήν).

Of its twenty occurrences in the LXX, the verb ἀνοικοδομέω ("rebuild") refers to physical restoration seventeen times; three times, it is used in a figurative sense for God building a "siege" against someone (cf. Lam 3:5, 7, 9). It is never used for spiritual renewal. In the New Testament, it is used only twice in Acts 15:16, both quoting an Old Testament passage that uses the verb in an explicitly literal sense. Thus it is reasonable that James viewed the Second Temple period, with its postexilic restoration, as the fulfillment of Amos 9:11, with the result that "the remnant of the people may seek the Lord, and all the Gentiles who are called by my name" (Acts 15:17; cf. Tob 14:5–6). Even if James was applying the words of Amos 9:11 in a figurative sense—the rebuilding of the tent of David as a reference to the resurrection of Jesus, the son of David; and the rebuilding of the ruins as a reference to the Jewish remnant in the church—neither James nor Luke make any indication that this spiritual building (ἀνοικοδομέω) was meant to correspond with the earlier renewal (ἀνάψυξις) or restoration (ἀποκατάστασις) of all things in Acts 3:20–21. In fact, in James's paraphrase of Amos 9:11, Luke actually adds καὶ ἀνορθώσω αὐτήν ("and I

---

40. See Bock, *Acts*, 177. See also J. Richard Middleton, *A New Heaven and a New Earth: Reclaiming Biblical Eschatology* (Grand Rapids: Baker Academic, 2014), 24.

41. He cites J. Jervell, *Luke and the People of God* (Minneapolis: Augsburg, 1972), 51–52.

will restore it"), a phrase that was not part of the original text of the LXX. Had Luke wanted to make a clearer connection with the restoration of all things mentioned in Acts 3:21, he could easily have added a phrase with ἀποκαθίστημι/ἀποκαθιστάνω, the verb forms of ἀποκατάστασις. Nothing in the text of Acts 15:17 suggests any verbal or conceptual connection to a spiritual fulfillment of Amos 9:11. In any case, Wainwright points out the obvious problem with understanding Acts 3:21 as spiritually fulfilled in the remnant of Israel in the church: "The restoration of Israel in Ac 3²¹ is obviously expected to coincide with the parousia, and therefore Luke cannot have regarded it as already accomplished before the Jerusalem Council."[42]

Conclusion on the Coming Kingdom in the Book of Acts

In light of the preceding discussion, "the seasons of refreshing" and the "times of restoration of all things" both refer to the same future period after the return of Christ, during which not only Israel will be restored in repentance but all things will be progressively refreshed and restored, a gradual liberation of all creation from its bondage to corruption and its deliverance to the freedom of the children of God (Rom 8:18–23). At that time, the boundaries of paradise will eventually embrace the whole world and the *imago Dei* mission will be accomplished by the second Adam and his redeemed humanity.[43]

Cosmic redemption is therefore gradual and progressive—seasons of refreshing and times of restoration—not instantaneous. Hoekema seems to think an "in-between" aspect of the millennial period of premillennialism is actually its weakness: "The millennium of the premillennialists, therefore, is something of a theological anomaly. It is neither completely like the present age, nor is it completely like the age to come.[44] Rather, I contend that this is its greatest strength because it presents the future of redemptive history—*cosmic* redemptive history—as the fulfillment of that original *imago Dei* mission in which humanity was instructed to be fruitful, multiply, fill the earth, subdue it, exercise dominion, and work the garden, eventually terraforming the world itself (see discussion in chapter 2). This also fits best with the kingdom expectations of the second-century fathers (see chapter 5). Such a progressive transformation of creation would mean that the stage upon which such a program of redemption is to occur would necessarily involve a world neither completely like the present age nor completely like the eternal age. As such, it also allows for not only the big picture of the Old Testament promises to be fulfilled in a new creation but also its details.[45]

Even in this case, the biblical understanding of the nature of the messianic age and its relationship to the coming kingdom of God allows for a spiritual, realized, and—to a degree—realizable phase of the coming refreshing and restoration.

42. Wainwright, "Luke and the Restoration," 77.
43. Cf. the same conclusions by Lennartsson, *Refreshing & Restoration*, 288.
44. Hoekema, *The Bible and the Future*, 186.
45. The futurist view of the fulfillment of Acts 3:20–21 was also the understanding of Tertullian, *On the Resurrection of the Flesh*, 23.

In the present, when individuals repent and turn to God, forgiveness comes, and times of spiritual refreshing can come to individuals and to the church in seasons of renewal and repentance. Through that manifestation of kingdom values and virtues, spiritual and moral restoration occur in the lives of individuals, families, churches, communities, and, at times, even nations. However, these manifestations of the coming kingdom in the present, prior to the literal sending of the Son from heaven and the arrival to the appointed times and seasons for ultimate refreshing and restoration, will be marked by partial, imperfect, and temporary manifestations of the kingdom of God.

9

The Pauline Expectation of the Eschatological Kingdom

In due time the Son will yield up His work to the Father, even as it is said by the apostle, "For He must reign till He hath put all enemies under His feet. The last enemy that shall be destroyed is death." . . . The apostle, too, has confessed that the creation shall be free from the bondage of corruption . . . so as to pass into the liberty of the sons of God.

Irenaeus, *Against Heresies* 5.36.2–3

In chapter 7, I argued that Jesus' language in Matthew 19:23–30 and 24:29–35, along with parallels in the Synoptic Gospels, furthered the Old Testament expectation of a future regeneration of creation and restoration of Israel at the time of his parousia. In chapter 8, we saw this same expectation as both Jesus and Peter continued to anticipate a future restoration of the kingdom of Israel (Acts 1:3–7) and a concurrent season of refreshing and time of restoration of everything promised by the Old Testament prophets at the coming of Christ from heaven (Acts 3:19–21). In this chapter and Go Deeper Excursus 15, I examine the anticipation of the coming kingdom in two key passages by Paul: Romans 11:25–27 in connection with the eschatological salvation of "all Israel" and 1 Corinthians 15:22–26 in connection with the plan for the resurrection of the dead in relation to the coming kingdom.

The Expectation of the Coming Kingdom in Romans 11:25–27

Though we saw evidence of a continued expectation of a coming restoration of the kingdom to Israel in keeping with Old Testament promises in both the teachings of Jesus as well as the early preaching of Peter, some could reasonably argue that the book of Acts presents the climax of a tragic story of the dashed hopes of restoration of Israel because of their failure to repent.[1] With this possibility in mind, Paul's discussion of the then-current status and ultimate destiny of Israel in Romans 11 is instructive. Even as Paul witnessed the increasing resistance to the gospel from his fellow Jewish brothers and sisters, he continued to cling to the hope of a future restoration at the end of the age in keeping with the Old Testament collage of the coming kingdom.

---

1. See this view in Robert C. Tannehill, "Israel in Luke-Acts: A Tragic Story," *JBL* 104.1 (1985): 72, 76.

Paul wrote the book of Romans sometime during his third missionary journey, as recorded in Acts 18:23–21:17, during his stay in Corinth (Acts 20:2–3). This would have been just a few years prior to his words declaring the hearts of his Jewish compatriots resistant to God's word (Acts 28:25–28). Therefore, the reality of a hardening of the hearts of most of his fellow Jewish people was a fact Paul himself had to reckon with. Romans 9–11 follows Paul's discussion of the security of believers "in Christ" because of the certainty of God's call of the elect (Rom 8:1; 28–39). In response to Paul's rousing affirmation of the security of believers, the natural question arises: How secure are believers in Christ if God's chosen people, Israel—to whom he had made such lofty promises—have been rejected and cast off in judgment? Paul composes chapters 9–11 to clarify the actual situation regarding the state of his "own brothers and sisters," his "own flesh and blood": "Israelites" (Rom 9:3–4).[2]

That Paul is talking about the actual historical descendants of Jacob is demonstrated by the explicit description of "Israelites" (Ἰσραηλῖται) (Rom 9:4). While it can be argued whether the name Ἰσραήλ may refer figuratively to the Messiah (Isa 49:3) and applied to the body of Christ as spiritual "Israel" (Gal 6:16),[3] in no instance is the term Ἰσραηλίτης ("Israelite") used as anything other than "the ethnic name of a person belonging to the nation of Israel."[4] Paul avoids any misunderstanding when he describes his present "brothers and sisters" in the following specific terms: "to them belong the adoption, the glory, the covenants, the giving of the law, the worship, and the promises (αἱ ἐπαγγελίαι); to them belong the patriarchs, and from them, according to the flesh, comes the Christ" (Rom 9:4–5).

In Romans 9:6, then, Paul rejects the idea that "the word of God has failed" in light of the fact of widespread Jewish unbelief. Here, he establishes the theological principle that "they are not all Israel who are descended from Israel (οὐ γὰρ πάντες οἱ ἐξ Ἰσραὴλ οὗτοι Ἰσραήλ)" (9:6 NASB).[5] He is not in this case alleging that people outside the circles of the children of Israel or the descendants of Abraham are true "Israel" or true "children of Abraham." Rather, he is arguing the opposite: just because a person may be a physical descendant of Abraham, this does not guarantee that this physical descendant will also be an heir of the covenantal promise. For his example, he uses the selection of Isaac rather than Ishmael; even though both were children of Abraham, only Isaac received the promise (9:6–8). The argument,

---

2. The *TDNT*, 386, notes, "The issue here is one which arises out of the character of the Jews as the people of God. Can the new community trust God's Word when it seems to have failed the Jews (9:6)?"

3. *TDNT*, 387–88, notes, "The one passage where it is most probable that Ἰσραήλ has this new meaning is Gl. 6:16. Here Ἰσραήλ τοῦ θεοῦ is used of those who follow the rule of Paul, to whom circumcision and uncircumcision are of no account, and for whom the world is crucified by Christ. It should be noted, however, that this statement is used against those who think that the heritage of ancient Israel, especially circumcision, is a necessary prerequisite of Christianity and who believe that membership of the people of God is only possible on this condition. Here too, then, the expression is in a sense to be put in quotation marks."

4. L&N, 824. See Num 25:8 LXX; 25:14; 3 Kgdms 20:27; 4 Macc. 18:1; Jub. 47.3; John 1:47; Acts 2:22; 3:12; 5:35; 13:16; 21:28; 2 Cor 11:22.

5. Some manuscripts here read Ισραηλιται, a reading adopted by the NRSV based on the testimonies of D F G 614. 629. 1881ᶜ vgʷʷ.

then, is further extended to the next generation when only one of the two physical descendants of Isaac—Jacob and Esau—received the spiritual promise by election. Paul's point is not that someone *outside* the bounds of Israel becomes the true "spiritual Israel" or "eschatological Israel," but that *not all* within the bounds of Israel are heirs of the spiritual promises.[6]

Applying the principle of the "true spiritual Israel" within "physical Israel" to the issue in Paul's day, the point is that God is presently keeping his promise by continuing to call men and women from among the physical descendants of Israel; they thus constitute the "true Israel" according to promise, joined together with Gentiles to the "people of God" (Rom 9:23–26), applying an Old Testament restoration passage spiritually to the church (Hos 1:9–11). This inclusion of but a portion of ethnic Israel among the saved in the present age is in keeping with the Old Testament theme of the "remnant" that will be saved from among the throng of Israel (Rom 9:27) so that Israel will not be entirely wiped out (9:29). The reason, though, that most Israelites do not obtain a right standing with God in the present age while many more Gentiles are converting to Christ is that Israel had stumbled over the Messiah and failed to embrace his offer of salvation by faith (9:30–33). Paul returns to his original expression of a deep longing for his fellow Israelites, noting that his prayer is that they "may be saved" (Rom 10:1). He is speaking of ethnic Israelites who are, for the most part, in unbelief in their opposition to Christ because of their insistence on a righteousness from the law (10:2–21).

Finally, in Romans 11:1, Paul asks the driving question: "Has God rejected his people?" The context here—both what precedes and what follows—does not provide warrant for suggesting the referent for "his people" is broader than ethnic Israelites. He clarifies: "By no means! I myself am an Israelite, a descendant of Abraham, a member of the tribe of Benjamin. God has not rejected his people whom he foreknew" (Rom 11:1–2). The fact that Paul himself, an Israelite and a descendant of Abraham, is saved and part of the new covenant community of Christ proves that not all Israel has been rejected. In keeping with Paul's discussion in the previous two chapters, he says that God is presently preserving a remnant, and Paul himself is proof (Rom 11:2–6). So, Israel as a whole has not achieved what they were seeking by the law—a right standing with God—but a remnant of "the elect" have received it while "the rest were hardened (οἱ δὲ λοιποὶ ἐπωρώθησαν)" (Rom 11:7). The use of οἱ λοιποί indicates that the two groups—the elect and those who were hardened—are of the same broad category of "Israel." That is, part of Israel—the elect remnant, of which Paul is a representative—has received salvation, while another part of Israel— those who are hardened—has not. This is in keeping with the pattern of spiritual hardening of the majority of Israel, even in the Old Testament (Rom 11:8–10).

Paul then questions whether their stumbling is total and permanent: "So I ask, have they stumbled so as to fall?" (Rom 11:11). To this, he provides the same answer

---

6. Peter Richardson, *Israel in the Apostolic Church*, SNTSMS, vol. 10 (Cambridge: Cambridge University Press, 1969), 131–32. On Rom 9:6, the *TDNT*, 387, rightly rejects a hasty notion that "true Israel" is simply "spiritual Israel": "We are not told here that Gentile Christians are the true Israel. The distinction at R. 9:6 does not go beyond what is presupposed at Jn. 1:47, and it corresponds to the distinction between Ἰουδαῖος ἐν τῷ κρυπτῷ and Ἰουδαῖος ἐν τῷ φανερῷ at R. 2:28 f., which does not imply that Paul is calling Gentiles the true Jews."

as when he asked whether God has rejected his people: "By no means!" Rather, in God's plan of redemption, he has chosen to permit their stumbling, which involves a partial hardening of the nonelect in the present (11:5, 7). The result of this present condition of partial hardening is that salvation has come to the Gentiles, which provokes Israel to jealousy (11:11; cf. 10:19; 11:14). Then, arguing from the lesser to the greater, Paul says, "Now if their stumbling means riches for the world and if their loss means riches for gentiles, how much more will their full inclusion mean (πόσῳ μᾶλλον τὸ πλήρωμα αὐτῶν)!" (Rom 11:12). Paul has already established that, in the present, a partial remnant of Israelites—himself included—has been preserved and incorporated into the new covenant community of Christ, the church. It is this partial inclusion that Paul regards as the present "stumbling" and "loss" of the majority who are hardened. So, the "fullness" must refer to a level of conversion far beyond the present circumstances.

Paul then addresses his "gentile" audience exclusively: "Now I am speaking to you gentiles" (Rom 11:13)—that is, believers in Christ other than ethnic Israelites. This must be taken into consideration in reading the rest of the passage; references to the third-person plural from this point cannot refer to Gentiles or to Gentile Christians, only to ethnic Israelites—either believers or unbelievers. Paul says that he exults over his ministry to the Gentiles because it provokes his own people to jealousy and thus leads to their salvation. He uses the quite explicit phrase "those of my flesh (μου τὴν σάρκα)" in reference to his people, fellow Israelites "according to the flesh," which is similar to his reference at the start of this section: "my compatriots according to the flesh (τῶν συγγενῶν μου κατὰ σάρκα), who are Israelites (οἵτινές εἰσιν Ἰσραηλῖται)" (9:3–4).

He then uses another phrase that anticipates a future in which the present hardness comes to an end: "For if their rejection is the reconciliation of the world, what will their acceptance be but life from the dead?" (Rom 11:15). Whether the third-person plural pronouns modifying "rejection" and "acceptance" are subjective or objective genitives does not change the fact that Paul is imagining what kind of miraculous blessing the acceptance of Israelites will bring to the entire world, considering the present rejection brings reconciliation. Paul almost certainly uses the image of resurrection metaphorically for the "resurrection" of Israel, likely drawing from the famous image of national restoration in Ezekiel 37:1–28.

Paul piles on additional metaphors to illustrate this expectation of a dramatic change from the present condition of rejection of his fellow Israelites (the partial remnant excepted) to a future condition of full acceptance and inclusion of his fellow Israelites. He says, "If the part of the dough offered as firstfruits is holy, then the whole batch is holy" (Rom 11:16); that is, if the small number of Israelites currently believing is accepted as a holy offering, how much more the whole number of Israelites who will believe. Then he shifts to the analogy of a tree: "And if the root is holy, then the branches also are holy" (11:16). If the image of the "firstfruits/whole lump" is meant to parallel the image of the "root/branches," then the root represents the earliest entirely Jewish believers in Jesus of the original apostolic community, while the branches represent all the Jews who ultimately believe in Jesus through their ministry. Yet it could be that the "root" (ῥίζα) has a christological meaning, as in Romans 15:12, "the root of Jesse" (cf. Rev 5:5). The term "firstfruits" (ἀπαρχή) can have a christological meaning in 1 Corinthians 15:20, 23, though it is also used in reference to the earliest converts in a particular region (Rom 16:5; 1 Cor 16:15; 2 Thess 2:13). The term ῥίζα is used in the Septuagint of the coming Messiah (Isa 11:1, 10).

At this point, it is easy to get lost in the weeds of possible alternatives, distracted by the shifting metaphors. Instead, it is best to focus on the clear, nonmetaphorical assertions: Israel has not been rejected by God (11:1). In the present, there is a remnant of Israelites chosen by grace (11:5). The elect remnant has thus achieved a right relationship with God, while the rest were hardened (11:7). Yet Israel had not stumbled to the point of falling (11:11). In fact, if in their stumbling, riches have come to the world, then their full inclusion will mean much more (11:12). And if their present rejection means the world's reconciliation, then their acceptance will be like resurrection (11:15).

In this context, Paul introduces his two metaphors of the firstfruits/whole lump and root/branches. Then, speaking to a representative "gentile" interlocutor (cf. Rom 11:13), Paul introduces the illustration of the olive tree: "But if some of the branches were broken off, and you, a wild olive shoot, were grafted among the others to share the rich root of the olive tree, do not boast over the branches" (Rom 11:17). The "root" here must mean either Christ as the ῥίζα of Jesse/David (Rom 15:12), the original covenantal promises of the patriarchs (cf. Rom 9:4–5), or the "firstfruits" of Christ's ministry: the original Jewish believers in Jesus prior to the inclusion of the Gentiles. It is possible, however, to understand ῥίζα as all three in Paul's image. The deepest roots reach back to the patriarchs, promises, covenants, and all the foundational "oracles of God" (Rom 3:2; 9:4–5). From this root system, then, the Messiah, the Son of David, comes up the main trunk of the tree (Rom 9:5). The original apostolic community at the planting of the church is also included in the earliest stages of its growth when the entire body of the church was composed only of Israelites.

Yet instead of that tree growing by the incorporation of its natural branches in the conversion of all the Israelites throughout the world, Paul employs a striking image to reemphasize a point he has already made repeatedly: "some of the branches were broken off" (11:17). That is, some of the Israelites originally part of that nation who received the oracles of God were rejected because of their unbelief. In their place, "wild" branches—that is, Gentiles—were grafted in because of their faith (11:20). Paul, however, warns those who were grafted in not to boast over the original branches (11:18), presumably those that had been broken off (11:19), though it could also involve a kind of disrespect shown toward those believing Israelites who were part of the tree. In either case, the "natural branches" are undoubtedly a reference to ethnic Israelites. Thus the wild branches—the Gentiles—do not support the root; the root supports them (11:18). This makes the best sense if the "root" does not refer to Christ alone or to the nation or people of Israel as a whole (as they are represented by the branches), but to the patriarchs, promises, and covenants that established the messianic community and that guarantee its continued preservation.

Paul then warns his Gentile interlocutor: If the natural branches (Israelites) were broken off (rejected) because of unbelief while the Gentile stands because of faith (Rom 11:20), the Gentile may also fall under judgment for unbelief (11:21–22). Yet again, at the end of the illustration of the olive tree, Paul returns to his repeated hope and expectation of a full acceptance and restoration of Israelites into their own story of redemption. Even the Israelites, "if they do not continue in unbelief, will be grafted in, for God has the power to graft them in again" (11:23). Everything Paul has intimated about a future restoration reaches a climax here. If God can incorporate Gentiles, who entered into an alien covenant relationship as unnatural branches, "how much more will these natural branches be grafted back into their own olive tree" (11:24). In this past statement, Paul no longer operates in the hypothetical realm of potentiality. He states it in the future indicative: "They will be grafted back in (ἐγκεντρισθήσονται)" (11:24); the condition, though, as always throughout the Old and New Testament depictions of a future restoration of Israel, is their repentance and faith: "And those of Israel, if they do not continue in unbelief, will be grafted in (ἐγκεντρισθήσονται)" (11:23). The condition of faith in verse 23 places the restoration of Israelites back into covenant relationship with God in the realm of possibility; the power and promise of God will make sure that such a restoration comes to fruition (11:23–24).

Then, in verses 25–27, Paul emerges from the realm of metaphor into interpretation of the imagery. Recalling that the context is his assertion that Israelites can and will be restored to faith and reincorporated into the covenant community, Paul writes, "I want you to understand this mystery, brothers and sisters, so that you may not claim to be wiser than you are" (11:25). I take the phrase τὸ μυστήριον τοῦτο ("this mystery") as referring to the symbolism of the olive tree that came before;[7] what follows in verses 25–27 is thus the explanation of the metaphor: "A hardening has come upon part of Israel until (ἄχρι) the full number of the gentiles has come in. And in this way all Israel will be saved" (11:25–26). The notion that Israel has been hardened "in part" is not new (cf. Rom 11:5, 7).

Rather, the new idea is that an unknown number of Gentiles yet to be saved will be brought into the covenant community, at which point "all Israel will be saved" (11:26). This does not mean every Israelite who has ever lived will be saved, but that at some future time, circumstances will lead to the conviction and conversion of all the nation of Israel; for the first time in its history, every member of the Israelite community, not merely a remnant, will know the Lord. The company of the people of Israel and the company of the elect of Israel will be coextensive. Put another way, the millennia-long reality of a "true, elect Israel" within "Israel according to the flesh" will come to an end: all Israel according to the flesh will be the true, elect Israel.

The idea of a universal knowledge of God among the entire nation of Israel, though, rests upon the Old Testament promise of the new covenant and the coming

---

7. Contra Richardson, *Israel in the Apostolic Church*, 128, who understands the statement itself to be the mystery and its explanation in Rom 11:31. In the other two passages, Paul uses the phrase τὸ μυστήριον τοῦτο. The phrase introduces an explanation of a preceding image or illustration in Eph 5:32 (explaining the illustration in 5:25–31); and in Col 1:27, it introduces the explanation of the "mystery" mentioned briefly in the previous verse Col 1:26—"the mystery that has been hidden." That Paul's mention of "this mystery" in Rom 11:25 immediately follows a confusing illustration of the olive tree argues strongly that Paul is doing the same thing here: presenting the content of the "mystery" in the previous verses, followed by the explanation of the mystery with the phrase τὸ μυστήριον τοῦτο. Incidentally, the phrase is also used in reference to the preceding vision to be interpreted in Dan 2:18, 30, 47; 1 En. 16.3.

kingdom. Recall that the new covenant was tied explicitly to the coming kingdom with the promise, "I will be their God, and they shall be my people" (Jer 30:22; 31:33). The restored nation of Israel was to be characterized by universal saving knowledge of the Lord—from the least to the greatest (Jer 31:34). And for the first time in its storied history of redemption, all Israelites will be righteous, having hearts submissive to God (cf. Isa 11:9; 29:21). This universal saving knowledge of the Lord, the basis of an intimate relationship, will be wrought by forgiveness of sin: "For I will forgive their iniquity and remember their sin no more" (Jer 31:34).

That this Old Testament imagery of the coming kingdom and its restoration under the stipulations of the new covenant was on Paul's mind in Romans 11 is made clear by his quotation in 11:26–27. "And in this way all Israel will be saved, as it is written, 'Out of Zion will come the Deliverer; he will banish ungodliness from Jacob. And this is my covenant with them, when I take away their sins.'" Paul's citation comes from at least two texts from the Old Testament collage of the coming kingdom. The first part of the verse is drawn from the Septuagint of Isaiah 59:20–21, which, in context, says, "*The deliverer will come for the sake of Zion, and he will turn ungodliness back from Jacob. 'And this is my covenant with them,*' says the Lord. 'My spirit which is upon you, and my words which I put in your mouth, will not cease from your mouth or from the mouth of your descendants'" (portion quoted in Rom 11:26–27 in italics).[8] Though it may be tempting to understand Paul's prophecy, "out of Zion will come the Deliverer," as a reference to the first coming of Christ and the apostolic mission as the outworking of that coming, the preceding assertion, for which this verse is an explanation, makes this unlikely: "A hardening has come upon part of Israel until (ἄχρι) the full number of the gentiles has come in." The ἄχρι indicates the perpetuation of the hardness of heart of most of Israel, which will come to an end when the fullness of the Gentiles comes in, at which point "all Israel will be saved" (11:26). This places the coordinate set of events in an eschatological context, which connects the expectation of Romans 11:26–27 with the similar expectation of repentance and restoration of Israel described by Peter in Acts 3:19–21.

The second portion of the quotation from Romans 11:27 comes from Isaiah 27:9: "Because of this, the lawlessness of Jacob will be taken away. And this is his praise: *When I take away his sin,* when they make all the stones of the altars broken up like fine dust, and surely their trees will not remain, and their idols will be cut out just like a forest far away" (portion quoted in Rom 11:27 in italics).

It is also possible that the Septuagint of Jeremiah 31:33–34 (38:33–34 LXX) stands behind Paul's thought,[9] though the language is not precise: "'For *this is my*

---

8. Richardson, *Israel in the Apostolic Church*, 128–29, alleges that Paul breaks off the quotation in Isa 59:21 "just at the point where it becomes explicitly applicable to Christians." However, the promise in the rest of Isa 59:21 regarding the sending of the Spirit would in no way detract from Paul's argument or render the passage less directly applicable to unbelieving Israel, because the point is that unbelieving Israel will be converted and experience all the new covenant blessings promised to them.

9. Richardson, *Israel in the Apostolic Church*, 128n8, calls the assertion of this possible allusion "misleading."

covenant that I will establish with the house of *Israel* after those days,' declares the LORD. 'I will surely put my laws into their mind, and I will write them upon their hearts. And I will become a God for them, and they will become a people for me. And each one will not teach his fellow citizen, or each his brother, saying, "Know the LORD!" because *everyone* (πάντες) will know me, from the smallest of them to the greatest of them, because *I will be gracious to their injustices.* And I will by no means remember *their sins* any longer'" (possible portion alluded to in Rom 11:26–27 in italics).

Romans 11:26–27	Isaiah 59:20–21	Isaiah 27:9	Jeremiah 31:33–34 (38:33–34 LXX)
²⁶καὶ οὕτως πᾶς Ἰσραὴλ σωθήσεται, καθὼς γέγραπται, ἥξει ἐκ Σιὼν ὁ ῥυόμενος, ἀποστρέψει ἀσεβείας ἀπὸ Ἰακὼβ ²⁷καὶ αὕτη αὐτοῖς ἡ παρ' ἐμου διαθήκη, ὅταν ἀφέλωμαι τὰς ἁμαρτίας αὐτῶν.	²⁰καὶ ἥξει ἕνεκεν Σιὼν ὁ ῥυόμενος καὶ ἀποστρέψει ἀσεβείας ἀπὸ Ἰακώβ. ²¹καὶ αὕτη αὐτοῖς ἡ παρ' ἐμοῦ διαθήκη, εἶπεν Κύριος	⁹διὰ τοῦτο ἀφαιρεθήσεται ἡ ἀνομία Ἰακώβ, καὶ τοῦτό ἐστιν ἡ εὐλογία αὐτοῦ, ὅταν ἀφέλωμαι αὐτοῦ τὴν ἁμαρτίαν	³³ὅτι αὕτη ἡ διαθήκη, ἣν διαθήσομαι τῷ οἴκῳ Ἰσραήλ . . . ³⁴ὅτι πάντες εἰδήσουσίν με ἀπὸ μικροῦ αὐτῶν καὶ ἕως μεγάλου αὐτῶν, ὅτι ἵλεως ἔσομαι ταῖς ἀδικίαις αὐτῶν καὶ τῶν ἁμαρτιῶν αὐτῶν οὐ μὴ μνησθῶ ἔτι.

Romans 11:26–27	Isaiah 59:20–21 LXX	Isaiah 27:9 LXX	Jeremiah 31:33–34 (38:33–34 LXX)
²⁶ "Out of Zion will come the Deliverer; he will banish ungodliness from Jacob. ²⁷And this is my covenant with them, when I take away their sins."	²⁰ "The deliverer will come for the sake of Zion, and he will turn ungodliness back from Jacob. ²¹And this is my covenant with them," says the LORD.	⁹ "Because of this, the lawlessness of Jacob will be taken away. And this is his praise: When I take away his sin."	³³ "For this is my covenant that I will establish with the house of Israel . . . ³⁴because everyone will know me, from the smallest of them to the greatest of them, because I will be gracious to their injustices. And I will by no means remember their sins any longer."

In sum, as scriptural support for his claim that one day—after the fullness of the Gentiles has come into the covenant community of Christ—"all Israel (πᾶς

Ἰσραήλ) will be saved" (Rom 11:26), Paul reaches back into the Old Testament's cluster of passages related to the restoration of Israel and the establishment of the coming kingdom (see detailed discussions in chapter 6). He begins with a direct quote from Isaiah 59:20–21 and ends with the promise of the removal of sin from "Jacob" in Isaiah 27:9. Reflecting the language of "all Israel" in Romans 11:26 and the general image of the new covenant restoration, Paul may be alluding to concepts from Jeremiah, especially with reference to "Israel" (Jer 31:33 [38:33 LXX]) and the fact that "everyone (πάντες)" from Israel will know the Lord (31:34 [38:34 LXX]).

As the theological foundation of his expectation of a future restoration of Israel depends on their conversion, Paul appeals to God's unwavering faithfulness to his promises, thus bringing the discussion back to the original problem: How can we trust God's promises to the church if he failed to keep his promises to Israel? In Romans 11, Paul asserts that God will be proved trustworthy by his future faithfulness to the promises made to Israel in the Old Testament collage of images of the coming kingdom. Verse 1 began, "Has God rejected his people? By no means!" Verse 11 says, "Have they stumbled so as to fall? By no means!" With this confidence in the promises of God as a steady baseline throughout Romans 9–11, Paul concludes, "As regards the gospel they are enemies for your sake, but as regards election they are beloved for the sake of their ancestors (διὰ τοὺς πατέρας), for the gifts and the calling of God are irrevocable" (Rom 11:28–29).

Though many throughout history have attempted to generalize "Israel" in a broad sense as "the people of God" and see the small remnant of elect Jews in the church—or the Gentiles who replace them—as a fulfillment of the promise that "all Israel will be saved" (Rom 11:26), a careful reading of Paul's language, his explicit contrast between "Israelites" and "gentiles," his repeated reference to the events of revelatory and redemptive history that apply only to ethnic Israel, and the overall argument of Romans 9–11, make such a theologically anachronistic reading untenable. Rather, among writers who downplay or dismiss a future conversion or restoration of Israel, the passage is sometimes simply ignored; while other times, it is taken as evidence of Israel's future conversion.[10]

Yet even some who admit that the force of the language in Romans 11 points to a future conversion of ethnic Israelites tend to downplay the force of Paul's

---

10. Authors who have no room for a restoration of Israel or a more realistic fulfillment of the Old Testament promises of the coming kingdom often avoid passages like Acts 3:19–21 and Rom 11:25–27, failing to think through and incorporate their implications. Cf. Bright's *Kingdom of God*, in which Acts 3:19–21, Rom 11:25–27, 1 Cor 15:22–26, and Rev 20:1–10 play no real role in questions of the coming kingdom. Bright treats Acts 3:21 in the most general way: "The Kingdom of God moves on to its inevitable triumph: the unconditional surrender of the Foe, the restoration of all creation under the divine domain (Acts 3:21)." John Bright, *The Kingdom of God: The Biblical Concept and Its Meaning for the Church* (New York: Abingdon-Cokesbury, 1953), 233. Origen of Alexandria briefly wrestles with Rom 11:26 in light of his insistence that God has issued Israel a bill of divorce, apparently reconciling the two facts in light of the reality that just as Christ is Lord of the Sabbath, he is also Lord of divorce. Origen, *Commentary on Matthew* 14.20. Cf. Origen, *Against Celsus* 6.80; John of Damascus, *De Trinitate* 11.34.

quotations from the Old Testament prophets.[11] Hoekema writes, "Even if one were inclined to understand this passage as teaching such a future national conversion of Israel, he would still have to admit that Romans 11 says nothing whatsoever about Israel's being regathered to its land or about a future rule of Christ over a millennial Israelite kingdom."[12] This presupposes a particular hermeneutical principle that the passages Paul cites regarding the coming salvation of Israel are not intended to be understood in their original context. If this were the case, then we must ask why Paul would cite those particular passages. It seems less precarious to assume that he cited these passages in support of the future salvation of Israel precisely because of what they asserted in their original contexts.

In any case, Paul's forecasting of a future salvation of "all Israel" according to Old Testament promises of the coming kingdom actually fits well with the passages we have already seen than cast the same kind of expectation of restoration according to Old Testament prophets in Acts 3:19–21. Because Romans 11 was written well into the apostolic mission to both Jews and Gentiles, and because Paul had ample evidence of a hardening of Israelites against the gospel, Romans 11:26–27 argues that God's promises will nevertheless stand. The issue is not *whether* the picture of the coming kingdom in the prophets will be fulfilled, but *when*.

The Expectation of the Coming Kingdom in 1 Corinthians 15:20–28

Regarding the heart of this passage, Middleton writes, "The only debatable text sometimes cited by millenarians is 1 Corinthians 15:24–28, since it suggests a two-stage kingdom. However, nowhere else in Paul's writings does he suggest anything like a millennium in the sequence of events of Christ's return. The two stages of the kingdom in 1 Corinthians 15:24–28 most likely refers to the distinction between Christ's present rule (the 'already' of the kingdom) and the final state, which begins after evil is eradicated from the world (the 'not yet' of the kingdom)."[13] We must, of course, grant that nowhere in Paul's writings does he refer to a "millennium"— that is, a thousand-year intermediate kingdom. Yet it will be shown that a careful reading of 1 Corinthians 15:22–26 in light of previous dominical and apostolic teachings concerning the coming kingdom best aligns with the expectation of a multistage realization of the new creation: the first as the "seasons of refreshing/ times of restoration of all things" that occurs after Christ returns; and the second, at

---

11. Richardson, *Israel in the Apostolic Church*, 126–27.

12. Anthony A. Hoekema, *The Bible and the Future* (Grand Rapids: Eerdmans, 1994), 200.

13. J. Richard Middleton, *A New Heaven and a New Earth: Reclaiming Biblical Eschatology* (Grand Rapids: Baker Academic, 2014), 287n16. Cf. Hoekema, *The Bible and the Future*, 184. The claim that an intermediate kingdom is absent from Paul's writings, therefore 1 Cor 15:20–28 should not be read this way, is rightly criticized by Kreitzer as circular. L. Joseph Kreitzer, *Jesus and God in Paul's Eschatology*, JSNTSup, vol. 19 (Sheffield: JSOT, 1987), 138. Kreitzer is responding to the work of W. D. Davies, *Paul and Rabbinic Judaism*, 3rd ed. (London: SPCK, 1970).

the completion of this initial phase of the kingdom, when the world will have been fully edenified and the *imago Dei* mission realized through the second Adam. The symbol of the "thousand years" for this intermediate period of progressive renewal of creation prior to the full manifestation of the new creation is revealed later in Revelation 20. So, whether we call the time between the "parousia" (1 Cor 15:23) and "the end" (15:24) a "millennium" or an "intermediate kingdom" or the "first phase of the new creation" should not concern us at this point. Instead, we must ask whether 1 Corinthians 15:20–28 allows for, implies, or teaches such a span of time between the parousia and the end.

Two basic interpretations of this text are found in commentaries. The first, like Middleton describes, reads that passage as presenting two events separated by a single period of time of an unspecified length: (1) the resurrection of Christ, the firstfruits; and (2) the resurrection of all others at the parousia, corresponding to "the end" and the defeat of death itself. We will call this the "two-stage" interpretation, which is diagrammed as follows:

The Two-Stage Interpretation of 1 Corinthians 15:20–28

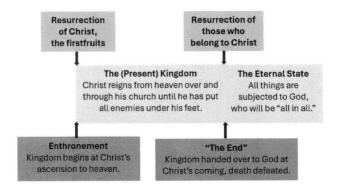

The second interpretation of 1 Corinthians 15:20–28 reads the passage as presenting three events separated by two periods of time of unspecified lengths: (1) the resurrection of Christ, the firstfruits; (2) the resurrection of those who belong to Christ at the parousia; and (3) the resurrection of all others, signifying the defeat of death itself at the end.[14] We will call this the "three-stage" interpretation, which is diagrammed as follows:

---

14. Lietzmann writes, "Die Auferstehung erfolgt nach 'Klassen'. Der Wortlaut legt es nahe, in v. 23 ζωοποιηθήσεται durchweg zu ergänzen, also ἀπαρχή Χριστὸς ἐζωοποιήθη, ἔπειτα οἱ τοῦ Χριστοῦ . . . ζωοποιηθήσονται, εἶτα τὸ τέλος ζοιηθήσεται als drei gleichartige Glieder zu fassen, wobei τέλος dem ἀπαρχή gut entspricht: drei τάγματα." Hans Lietzmann, *An die Korinther I/II*, HNT, vol. 9 (Tübingen: Mohr Siebeck, 1949), 80.

The Three-Stage Interpretation of 1 Corinthians 15:20–28

In Go Deeper Excursus 15, *The Case for a Three-Stage Resurrection in 1 Corinthians 15:20–28*, I demonstrate that Paul's language in 1 Corinthians 15:20–28 is best understood as teaching three stages of resurrection. However, the three-stage order of events set forth in this passage does not specify the length of the two intervening periods of time. Thus the passage does not explicitly teach a "millennium." Yet, when read in light of passages regarding the coming kingdom already examined earlier, 1 Corinthians 15:20–28 makes best sense from a premillennial perspective.

Paul then mentions the first stage in the resurrection of "all" the dead: "Christ the first fruits" (1 Cor 15:23). In Paul's perspective, this has already occurred (15:20). Jesus is the "first to rise from the dead" (Acts 26:23) and the "firstborn from the dead" (Col 1:18; Rev 1:5). Christ's unique, individual resurrection from the dead in a glorified resurrection body begins the multiphase process of universal resurrection of all the dead. In a very real sense, the resurrection of the dead has already begun, and regardless of one's eschatology, every view of resurrection has *at least* two distinct phases. No view of resurrection has a single, universal resurrection of all the righteous and all the wicked at once, because Christ—a member of the category of the righteous—has already been raised.

> **Go Deeper Excursus 15**
>
> *The Case for a Three-Stage Resurrection in 1 Corinthians 15:20–28*

Then, by using ἔπειτα . . . εἶτα ("then . . . then"), Paul describes three distinct phases of resurrection of all people by Christ. The first phase was Christ's resurrection (1 Cor 15:23); "then" (ἔπειτα) comes the second phase—"those who are Christ's" (ὁι τοῦ Χριστοῦ), which will occur "at his coming (the parousia)" (ἐν τῇ παρουσίᾳ); "then" (εἶτα) comes the third phase at "the end" (τὸ τέλος)—presumably including those unsaved wicked dead who remain after the resurrection of those who belong to Christ. Given the normal use of ἔπειτα/εἶτα . . . ἔπειτα/εἶτα to indicate events separated by spans of time (whether lengthy or brief), it is certainly possible that Paul supposed a space of time between not only Christ's resurrection and the resurrection of the righteous but also between the resurrection of the righteous and the resurrection of the wicked.

Reading the two ὅταν ("when") clauses as both occurring simultaneously at the parousia and resurrection of those who are his is not allowed, because Paul inserts a subsequent εἶτα ("then"), thus creating a third stage in the process of resurrection. Thus if an amillennial or postmillennial interpretation of this passage is to reckon responsibly with the presence of the subsequent εἶτα, the only alternative is to regard the gap between the second and third stages of resurrection—that is, between the righteous and the wicked—as one of mere moments, perhaps minutes or hours. But if there is no practical significance in the timing between the resurrection of the righteous and that of the wicked, then Paul's second εἶτα seems unnecessary—unless, of course, the gap is meant to indicate an intermediate period of Christ's earthly rule.

In light of these considerations, the better explanation that results in the least unresolved problems and unanswered question and best fits the form of the text, is that just as there is a lengthy period of time between Christ's resurrection and the parousia, there will also be a lengthy period of time between the parousia and the end. If so, then two events happen concurrent with the end, indicated by the two ὅταν clauses: (1) Christ hands over the kingdom to God the Father, and (2) he has (previously) abolished every ruler and every authority and power (15:24). Thus 1 Corinthians 15:25–26 makes the best sense when read in light of a future manifestation of the kingdom distinct from the present spiritual kingdom of the ascended Christ. In that future kingdom, "He must reign until he has put all his enemies under his feet," and "the last enemy to be destroyed is death."

Regarding the question of the identification of "the kingdom" in 1 Corinthians 15:24–28, it seems best to see the language of verse 24—"for he must reign until he has put all his enemies under his feet"—not only as a reference to his present enthronement as a partial realization of this promise in a spiritual sense in heaven but also with a view toward a future fulfillment of the expectation in a physical sense in this world. Thus the end must come many generations after the parousia. Though Paul does not specify how lengthy the span of time will be between the parousia and the end, it must be enough time to allow for resurrected humanity to liberate all creation progressively from its bondage to corruption described in Romans 8:19–23, which is contrasted with the "present time" (8:18) and associated directly with time of our resurrection (8:23). The process of subduing all creation and terraforming the world will take centuries, not decades, but Paul does not specify exactly how long; in fact, it is possible that at the time he himself did not know. Nevertheless, the time between the parousia and the end will need to be sufficiently long so that at the end, Christ, along with his resurrected co-regents, will have edenified all creation, subdued all enemies, destroyed all forms of death, and handed over that new, paradise-infused creation to the Father as a fait accompli. I do not take the phrase "when he hands over the kingdom to God the Father" (1 Cor 15:24) as indicating the eternal kingdom comes to an end. Rather, it signals that the responsibility given to humanity to edenify creation will be fulfilled; the Son will offer up creation to the Father as a "mission accomplished"—just as all things had been handed over to the Son by the Father (Matt 11:27).

Though the language of 1 Corinthians 15:20–28 could plausibly be read in keeping with amillennial, postmillennial, or premillennial eschatologies, the amillennial and postmillennial interpretations leave Paul's purpose in supplying the subsequent εἶτα ("then") clause without a good explanation from the text. That is, there is no reason for Paul to have included a second "then" unless he intended for the language of victory over all enemies including death, in verses 24–26 to explain the events accomplished between the parousia and the end, during the course of the future, earthly manifestation of the coming kingdom following Christ's return. This reading, too, is in keeping with the original *imago Dei* mission, the picture of the coming kingdom in the Old Testament, and the reiterations of those promises of restoration in the coming age seen in the New Testament. Therefore, the premillennial interpretation of 1 Corinthians 15:20–28, though not completely provable from that passage, is preferrable simply because it makes the most sense of the εἶτα clause and its concurrent ὅταν clauses. This interpretation also alleges that Paul affirmed a present, heavenly, spiritual aspect of the kingdom embodied in Christ, which would become manifested in the world at the parousia and realized throughout the world by means of the new humanity resurrected and glorified in him.

Turning to the second-century fathers, it is clear that Irenaeus of Lyons understood "the end" in 1 Corinthians 15:24 as a reference to the end of the period of the kingdom that will follow Christ's parousia, claiming the "disciples of the apostles" as the source of his understanding of that period of continued advancement throughout the kingdom age:

> The presbyters, the disciples of the apostles, affirm that this is the gradation and arrangement of those who are saved, and that they advance through steps of this nature; also that they ascend through the Spirit to the Son, and through the Son to the Father, and that in due time the Son will yield up His work to the Father, even as it is said by the apostle, "For He must reign till He hath put all enemies under His feet. The last enemy that shall be destroyed is death." For in the times of the kingdom, the righteous man who is upon the earth shall then forget to die. (*Haer.* 5.36.2).

Therefore, despite many attempts at arguing to the contrary, I find myself agreeing with the summary of Godet argued long ago—not because it is older, but because the newer commentators have failed to undo it:

> The apostle has thus assigned to the resurrection of the body its place in the system of the Christian salvation as a whole. He has brought out its three phases (Christ's resurrection, the resurrection of believers, the universal resurrection), and he has pointed out the correspondence between these phases and the three principal epochs of the Divine work (the consummation of salvation in Christ Himself, the inauguration of His Messianic kingdom, and the close of His whole work).[15]

---

15. Frédéric Louis Godet, *Commentary on St. Paul's First Epistle to the Corinthians*, trans. A. Cusin, vol. 2 (Edinburgh: T&T Clark, 1893), 375–76.

10

The Kingdom of Revelation 20:
Introductory Issues

In a still clearer light has John, in the Apocalypse, indicated
to the Lord's disciples what shall happen in the last times.

Irenaeus, *Against Heresies* 5.26.1

In the previous chapter, I argued that a close reading of 1 Corinthians 15:20–28 makes space for three stages of resurrection (Christ, then the righteous, then the wicked) with an intermediate kingdom between the resurrection of the righteous and the wicked. During that coming kingdom, the world will be progressively edenified prior to the final destruction of all God's enemies and of death itself at the end of the initial phase of the eternal kingdom. Regarding 1 Corinthians 15, Wilbur Wallis notes:

> The universal extent of resurrection, completed in a third stage, is the decisive matter in the entire discussion. Once the necessity of resurrection of all the dead is recognized, there is no necessary objection to a third order of resurrection. However, when a third order of resurrection is admitted, the parallel with the Apocalypse becomes obvious. It is therefore appropriate to bring together certain parallels between Paul and the Revelation. I believe these are sufficiently cogent to strengthen the assumption that Paul and the Revelation are in harmony.[1]

But in a canonical approach to theology, this relationship can also work in the other direction. If Revelation 20 teaches a first resurrection of the righteous followed by a long period of a messianic kingdom, which ends with a second resurrection of the wicked, then 1 Corinthians 15:20–28 is rightly read in harmony with this understanding. But if Revelation 20 teaches a present spiritual reign of Christ followed by a final bodily resurrection of all people at once—some to eternal life and others to eternal judgment—then that should also tip the balance of 1 Corinthians 15 in the opposite direction toward a single-resurrection interpretation.

The interpretation of Revelation 20, however, is not simple. For my general approach to Revelation, see Go Deeper Excursus 15, *Who, What, When, and How of Revelation: Pre-interpretive Issues*, where I argue that what John wrote is a close

---

1. Wilber B. Wallis, "The Problem of an Intermediate Kingdom in 1 Corinthians 15:20–28," *JETS* 18.4 (1975): 237.

approximation of the prophetic vision he actually experienced.[2]

Go Deeper Excursus 16

Who, What, When, and How of Revelation: Pre-interpretative Issues

As I explained in the beginning of this book, I am adopting as my basic foundation and framework the general Irenaean futurist premillennial eschatology. Thus with Justin, Irenaeus, and Hippolytus— and many others from the early church—I understand the book of Revelation to refer primarily to future things. With this perspective in mind, we may approach the major elements of that vision addressing the question of the timing and nature of the coming kingdom: the prophetic vision of the "thousand-year reign" portrayed in symbolic fashion in Revelation 20:1–10. For the rest of this chapter, I will begin this argument by discussing the relationship between chapters 19 and 20—that is, the chronological relationship between the vision of the second coming of Christ and his kingdom.

The Relationship between Revelation 19 and 20

Kreitzer presents what I regard as an overly optimistic appraisal of the actual situation when he writes, "It is generally recognized that the Apocalypse of John does indeed teach a future, earthly millennial Kingdom distinct from the Eternal Age which follows it."[3] Granting that amillennial, postmillennial, and premillennial perspectives understand the millennial period described in Revelation 20 as preceding the eternal age, not all see this thousand-year kingdom as "earthly," not all see it as future, and not all understand it as distinct from the eternal age.

Futurist premillennialists view the order of events envisioned in Revelation 19:11–21:8 as a linear progress beginning with the future return of Christ as judge (19:11–21), which results in the destruction of the antichrist and false prophet along with their forces of evil (19:19–21). After this, the great instigator of wickedness, Satan, is not cast with them into the lake of fire but bound in a temporary place in the spiritual realm for a span of a thousand years (20:1–3). During that time, a thousand-year reign is established on the earth under Christ and the resurrected saints (20:4–5). Some understand the thousand years to be literal while others understand it as representing a lengthy period of time. Regardless, after this earthly manifestation of the kingdom, Satan will be released for a brief, ultimate revolt, resulting in his judgment in the lake of fire (20:7–10). The bodily resurrection of the wicked results in their judgment and casting into the lake of fire (20:11–15). Finally, the new heavens and new earth, now devoid of all sin, suffering, death, and the devil, replaces the present world system (21:1–8).

Postmillennial interpreters view the events of Revelation 20:1–21 as "a vision setting forth in figurative language the age-long struggle between the forces of good

---

2. Cf. Theodor Zahn, *Introduction to the New Testament*, vol. 3, trans. John Moore Trout ct al. (Edinburgh: Clark, 1909), 389.

3. L. Joseph Kreitzer, *Jesus and God in Paul's Eschatology*, JSNTSup, vol. 19 (Sheffield: JSOT, 1987), 135.

and the forces of evil in the world, with its promise of complete victory"[4]: that is, a symbol of the victory of the gospel in the world throughout the church age and culminating in the victory of the truth over the forces of Satan, symbolically portrayed as being defeated like an army and cast into the fire. The result is a full binding of Satan, whose present activities are merely restricted (20:1–3). The outcome of the victory of the gospel will be the establishment of the kingdom in this world, in which Christianity is the dominant force of peace and justice (20:4–6). After this period, an apostasy will occur as Satan is released, but this will result in the final judgment and second coming of Christ (20:7–15). Finally, the new heavens and new earth will replace the existing world (21:1–8).[5] Variations on the details characterize the general postmillennial perspective, though they are usually seen as presenting a linear progress—usually in terms of highly symbolic language.[6]

In the amillennial position, however, the series of scenes do not necessarily imply a chronological order in their referents. Thus in the general amillennial approach, Revelation 20:1–21 do point forward to the ultimate return of Christ, destruction of the antichrist or the anti-Christian world system. However, scene 20:1–3 does not follow the events of the previous chapter chronologically; rather, with Revelation 20:1, a completely new vision opens,[7] rewinding the story of salvation history to the time of Christ's victory of Satan at the cross, which results in the binding of the dragon for a thousand years. The thousand-year duration is understood as a symbol for a long period of time between the ascension of Christ and his future return. Thus scene 20:4–6 is a present reality, and the resurrection of martyrs is a reference to spiritual resurrection either in soteriological regeneration or in entrance to heaven upon death.[8] Then, 20:7–15 follows this present spiritual millennial age and points again to the future judgment that will accompany Christ's return. Therefore, 20:7–10 refers to the same judgments as did 19:11–21 in a separate vision and from a different perspective.[9] Finally, upon the judgment of the anti-Christian world and the return of Christ, the bodily resurrection of both righteous and wicked will occur and the eternal new heaven and new earth will be ushered in (20:11–21:8).

---

4. Loraine Boettner, *The Millennium* (Phillipsburg, NJ: P&R, 1957), 30.

5. See, e.g., Marcellus J. Kik, *An Eschatology of Victory* (Phillipsburg, NJ: P&R, 1971), 254; Keith A. Mathison, *Postmillennialism: An Eschatology of Hope* (Phillipsburg, NJ: P&R, 1999), 87.

6. Samuel Hopkins, *A Treatise on the Millennium* (Edinburgh: John Ogle, 1794), 51; Boettner, *The Millennium*, 14.

7. See, e.g., R. Fowler White, "Reexamining the Evidence for Recapitulation in Rev 20:1–10," *WTJ* 51 (Fall 1989): 319–44. Also see William Hendriksen, *More Than Conquerors: An Interpretation of the Book of Revelation* (Grand Rapids: Baker, 1967), 22–31, who outlines the book of Revelation in seven separate cycles of visions, which he understands as presenting "progressive parallelism." These are Rev 1–3; 4–7; 8–11; 12–14; 15–16; 17–19; 20–22. Each section "rewinds," as it were, and retells aspects of the story already covered, ending a little farther in the eschatological narrative. Rev 19 ends and then Rev 20 rewinds to the beginning of the present spiritual kingdom and goes beyond the final judgment (pictured in Rev 19 as well as the release of Satan in Rev 20:7–10).

8. Anthony A. Hoekema, *The Bible and the Future* (Grand Rapids: Eerdmans, 1979), 227.

9. Sam Storms, *Kingdom Come: The Amillennial Alternative* (Fearn, SCT: Mentor, 2013), 431, 433.

On the surface, none of these three approaches to Revelation 19–21 is absurd. The amillennial reading has the advantage of acknowledging that the book of Revelation is not one single vision of chronological events but a series of visions, including scene changes that point to different aspects of past, present, and future realities. The issue is whether the change from Revelation 19 to Revelation 20 indicates such a change of visions. Nor should the hermeneutical approach of postmillennialism with its more symbolic interpretation of the appearance of Christ on the white horse shock our sensibilities. The book of Revelation—like all apocalyptic visions— consists of symbolic representations of reality; it is not a univocal picture of that reality itself (see Go Deeper Excursus 16). The question is whether Revelation 19:11–21 is a symbolic picture of the parousia or a symbolic picture of the victory of the church's gospel proclamation.

A Single Progressive Vision in Revelation 19:11–20:15

As seen above, one important feature of the amillennial interpretation of Revelation 20 is that of "recapitulation."[10] Sam Storms points to the disjunction between Revelation 19 and 20 as an "example of recapitulation in Revelation, in which the same period of time is described from differing vantage points with different imagery in order to secure a different, but still complementary, emphasis."[11] However, this solution that avoids a postmillennial or premillennial interpretation of Revelation 20 has not gone without significant challenges.[12] The eschatological stakes of the exegesis are rather high. If it can be established that Revelation 19 and Revelation 20 are two completely separate visions, then the millennium could refer to the spiritual kingdom established at the heavenly enthronement of Christ (amillennialism). But if Revelation 19:11–20:10 constitutes a single progressive vision, then Revelation 20 follows either the judgment on the antichrist and the return of Christ to earth (premillennialism), or it follows the victory of the church over anti-Christian worldviews and false religions (postmillennialism).

The arguments for or against recapitulations or progression in Revelation 19–20 have gone back and forth for some time, resulting in a kind of stalemate.[13] Both positions are at least plausible. However, in Go Deeper Excursus 17, *Revelation 19:11–20:10 as a Single Progressive Vision*, I establish a case for continuity between

---

10. See, e.g., G. K. Beale, *The Book of Revelation: A Commentary on the Greek Text*, The New International Greek Testament Commentary, ed. I. Howard Marshall and Donald A. Hagner (Grand Rapids: Eerdmans, 1999), 972–1038; R. Fowler White, "On the Hermeneutics and Interpretation of Rev 20:1–3: A Preconsummationist Perspective," *JETS* 42.1 (1999): 53–66.

11. Storms, *Kingdom Come*, 431n10.

12. See especially the work of Alan E. Kurschner, *A Linguistic Approach to Revelation 19:11–20:6 and the Millennium Binding of Satan*, Linguistic Biblical Studies, vol. 23 (Leiden: Brill, 2022).

13. See a description and summary of some arguments against the recapitulation view in Charles E. Powell, "Progression versus Recapitulation in Revelation 20:1–6," *BSac* 163.1 (January–March 2006): 94–109.

Revelation 19:11–20:10 by examining an exegetical question that has irked transla-
tors and commentators alike for centuries: the subject of the verb ἐκάθισαν ("and
they sat") in Revelation 20:4.

In Go Deeper Excursus 17, I present the case that the subject of "and they sat"
(καὶ ἐκάθισαν) in Revelation 20:4 is found in an ana-

Go Deeper Excursus 17

*Revelation 19:11–20:10 as a
Single Progressive Vision*

phoric reference to Christ and the armies of heaven
mentioned in Revelation 19:14, 19. Thus Revelation
19:11–20:11 must be seen as a single progressive vision
rather than two separate visions.

The implications for ancient and ongoing millennial debates are far-reaching.
Interpreters generally agree that if Revelation 19:11–21 and 20:1–10 are a single
progressive vision, then it follows that the consequent effects from the battle at
Christ's parousia (19:11–21) are the future millennial binding of Satan and the millennial reign of the saints (20:1–6). On the other hand, the nonsequential interpretation construes the events in 20:1–6 as occurring prior to the parousia (i.e., a
recapitulation).[14] In that framework, the millennial binding of Satan was established at Christ's first coming, and he continues to be bound in the interadvent age
(amillennialism).

However, because the subject of ἐκάθισαν ("they sat") is to be found most naturally in 19:11–21, an amillennial interpretation of Revelation 20 is highly improbable.
Revelation 19 and 20 are not two separate visions but one progressive vision. As
demonstrated in Go Deeper Excursus 17, the simplest explanation that accounts for
all the evidence is that the subject of ἐκάθισαν is Christ and the armies of heaven
(Rev. 19:14, 19). This also parallels the course of action in the climactic defeat of the
world powers and the enthronement of the saints in Daniel 7, which serves as a
background for the imagery of Revelation 19–20.

Why, then, do translations and commentators almost always overlook this
simple explanation? From my reading of the literature, I suggest five common reasons. (1) The chapter break at Revelation 20:1 has led interpreters to miss—probably
unintentionally—the prohoratic antecedent for ἐκάθισαν.[15] (2) Many have been
misled by translation glosses that render ἐκάθισαν ("and they sat") as if it were a
participle (e.g., καθήμενοι, "already seated"), thus concealing the problem from
many readers of less literal translations. (3) Some have simply accepted with little
challenge the common assertion among expositors and exegetes that ἐκάθισαν has
no antecedent. (4) Some have uncritically accepted the complex grammatical explanations provided by some commentators trying to explain the allegedly subjectless

---

14. For example, amillennialism locates the event of the ones who sit (ἐκάθισαν) on the
thrones ruling with Christ during the interadvent period between Christ's first and second
coming. Thus they situate it historically preceding the eschatological battle when the armies
of heaven accompany Christ in chapter 19. So, Stephen S. Smalley, *The Revelation to John*
(Downers Grove: IVP Academic, 2012), 505: "During the age of the Church, and beyond,
they share his salvation and participate in his judgment."

15. This point can be seen by the fact that most commentators are completely silent on
such a consideration. Their energies have been spent mostly focusing on solecisms or other
grammatical explanations.

verb, usually as an "impersonal plural."[16] (5) Exegetes who may have considered a potential prohoratic antecedent of ἐκάθισαν as Christ and the armies of heaven may have been consciously or unconsciously dissuaded from seriously considering this due to its negative implications for the common amillennial interpretation of Revelation 20.

Where does this leave us with regard to the interpretation of the timing of the thousand-year kingdom in Revelation 20? The amillennial interpretation—dependent, as it is, on Revelation 19:11–21 and Revelation 20:1–10 as separate visions—is rendered exegetically tenuous.[17] Though postmillennialists often see Revelation 19:11–20:10 as a single progressive vision, they interpret Revelation 19:11–21 not as the parousia but as the victory of the gospel over this world.[18] Warfield articulated this in its classic form: "In fine, we have before us here a picture of the victorious career of the Gospel of Christ in the world. All the imagery of the dread battle and its hideous details are but to give us the impression of the completeness of the victory. Christ's Gospel is to conquer the earth."[19] This is a novel view unheard of in the early centuries of the church and not followed by most commentators today.[20]

---

16. Fanning asserts that ἐκάθισαν "has no definite referent but indicates 'some (unidentified) individuals, people' (as in 16:15; 18:14; cf. Luke 16:4)." He then dismisses the prohoratic explanation as "highly unlikely" without providing any reasons for deeming it as such. Buist M. Fanning, *Revelation,* Zondervan Exegetical Commentary on the New Testament (Grand Rapids: Zondervan, 2020), 501. Cf. George Eldon Ladd, *A Commentary on the Revelation of John* (Grand Rapids: Eerdmans, 1972), 263.

17. I agree with Campbell's assessment of the recapitulation view of Rev 19 and 20: "This is a far from straightforward reading of the text, and if that is what John meant one might have expected him to make this clearer." R. Alastair Campbell, "Triumph and Delay: The Interpretation of Revelation 19:11–20:10," *EvQ* 80.1 (2008): 5.

18. Cf. Jay E. Adams, *The Time Is at Hand* (Philadelphia: P&R, 1970), 80–82. In the words of Alastair Campbell, "If chapter 19 is not intended as a description of the Parousia at all, but is rather a victory parade in which the fall of Babylon is celebrated, the millennium is set free to fulfil its true function." Campbell, "Triumph and Delay," 11. Campbell's treatment suffers from an overdependence on Roman backgrounds rather than attention to the use of Old and New Testament and intertestamental texts as the governing sources of interpretation (see discussion on approaches to Revelation above). Boxall, *Revelation,* 272, also argues against the longstanding consensus that Rev 19:11–21 pictures the second coming and argues instead that "it is essentially the battle fought and won on the cross, replayed with shocking mythological vividness." His arguments, though, rest on shaky ground; he claims the military imagery is unusual for early Christian parousia scenes (but the imagery of 1 Thess 4–5 and 2 Thess 1–2 is also quite strong). He notes that elements in other parousia scenes are missing from this scene (but when comparing each other scene, they are all missing elements of the others). He observes that angels associated with the parousia are missing (this is really a specific of the second problem; but if we realize all of Revelation is picturing aspects of the second coming, then angels are everywhere). These problems do not seem to me to be sufficiently potent to overthrow the earliest and most enduring interpretation of this passage. See Fanning, *Revelation,* 485.

19. Benjamin B. Warfield, *Biblical Doctrines* (New York: Oxford University Press, 1929), 647. That chapter originally appeared as Benjamin B. Warfield, "The Millennium and the Apocalypse," *PTR* 2 (1904): 599–617.

20. Johnson writes, "Early as well as modern interpretation has for the most part seen in vv. 11–16 a description of the second coming of Christ—an event to which the NT bears a frequent and unified witness." Alan F. Johnson, "Revelation," *The Expositor's Bible Commentary:*

Though the fathers of the church do not provide more than a few passing comments on Revelation 19:11–21, premillennialist Irenaeus of Lyons refers the passage to the future destruction of the antichrist and his regime by the glorious second coming of Christ (*Haer.* 5.28.2). In the fourth century, amillennialist Tyconius interpreted Revelation 19:11–21 as the future return of Christ and the armies that follow him in his return as the church: "*And his name is called the Word of God, and the armies which are in heaven followed him in white robes;* that is, the church, in bodies made white, imitates him and follows his footsteps" (Exp. Apoc. 7 [19:14]).[21] Tremper Longman has said of this passage, "Rev 19:11ff. clearly describes Christ's second coming and does so employing military imagery strongly reminiscent of Divine Warrior passages in the OT."[22]

The symbolic vision of Christ and his armies and their victory over the beast, the false prophet, and their armies may be seen as consisting of three "scenes" indicated by the phrase καὶ εἶδον ("and I saw"):[23] the appearance of Christ and his armies (Rev 19:11–16), the pronouncement of the angel (19:17–18), and the defeat of the beast and his armies (19:19–21).[24] The first scene begins with "heaven opened (τὸν οὐρανὸν ἠνεῳγμένον)" (Rev 19:11). The phrase is used for the visible manifestation of heavenly things (e.g., Matt 3:16; Acts 7:56), or of the literal downpour of rain (Gen 7:11; Ps 77:23 LXX), or the figurative pouring out of God's judgment (Isa 24:14; 64:1). In the New Testament, Christ says of himself, "Very truly, I tell you, you will see heaven opened and the angels of God ascending and descending upon the Son of Man" (John 1:51). This language reflects Jacob's dream at Bethel, when he saw a kind of stairway on earth reaching to heaven and angels "ascending and descending" followed by an actual theophanic manifestation (Gen 28:12). In this case, then, Jesus' words may suggest a similar actual manifestation and appearance of the Son of Man in glory. If so, he is making a connection to the second advent, as in Matthew 16:27—"For the Son of Man is to come with his angels in the glory of his Father, and then he will repay everyone for what has been done"—and Matthew 25:31—"When the Son of Man comes in his glory and all the angels with him, then he will sit on the throne of his glory." However, the phrase "heaven opened" is also used in a context in which the heavenly nature of a vision is intended (Acts 10:11; cf. Ezek 1:1 LXX). At least John intends the phrase to indicate the heavenly origin of his vision, if not a connection to Christ's future appearance as judge. As soon as heaven is opened, John sees a "white horse" (ἵππος λευκὸς) (Rev 19:11). A white horse also appeared earlier in 6:2, variously identified by commentators with interpretations

Hebrews–Revelation, vol. 13, rev. ed., ed. Tremper Longman III and David E. Garland (Grand Rapids: Zondervan, 2006), 757; Lenski, *Revelation*, 550; Grant R. Osborne, *Revelation: Verse by Verse*, Osborne New Testament Commentaries (Bellingham, WA: Lexham, 2016), 313.

21. Tyconius of Carthage, *Exposition of the Apocalypse*, trans. Francis X. Gumerlock, The Fathers of the Church: A New Translation, vol. 134 (Washington, DC: Catholic University of America Press, 2017), 173.

22. Tremper Longman III, "The Divine Warrior: The New Testament Use of an Old Testament Motif," *WTJ* 44.2 (1982): 298.

23. Fanning, *Revelation*, 485; Sydney H. T. Page, "Revelation 20 and Pauline Eschatology," *JETS* 23.1 (1980): 31–32.

24. Cf. Beale, *Revelation*, 948.

ranging from Christ to the antichrist.[25] Revelation 6:2 does not contain enough clues to arbitrate between the various positions. However, the interpretation of the rider on the white horse in Revelation 19:11 as Christ is certain,[26] which could mean the rider on the white horse in Revelation 6:2 is also a vision of Christ. On the other hand, these are two completely separate visions, and the symbols need not have precisely the same referents.[27] The clear christological title "Faithful and True" (cf. Rev 3:14) reflect a high Christology (21:5, 6; cf. 3 Macc 2:11). This high Christology is further underscored with the purpose of his appearance: he "judges and makes war in righteousness (ἐν δικαιοσύνῃ κρίνει καὶ πολεμεῖ) (Rev 19:11). The phrase "he judges in righteousness" appears in Psalm 9:9 with reference to a theophanic visitation of the Lord God in judgment: "And he will judge the inhabited world with righteousness (κρινεῖ τὴν οἰκουμένην ἐν δικαιοσύνῃ). He will judge the peoples with uprightness" (LXX). The language and imagery of the Psalm 9 depicting God's theophanic coming in judgment is applied to Christ as the ultimate theophanic judge. Beale points out that "Acts 17:31 also alludes to the same psalm texts in affirming the future day of judgment to be executed by Christ."[28] The same phrase for the "whole inhabited world" (οἰκουμένη) in the LXX of Psalm 9:9 is used in reference to the gathering of the kings of the whole world to Armageddon "for battle on the great day of God the Almighty" (Rev 16:14), a gathering assumed in the imagery of the gathered armies of the earth in Revelation 19:19–21. From its opening line, therefore, the imagery used in Revelation 19:11 points in the direction of the coming of Christ as judge, not to a victory over the world of sinners by the preaching of the gospel.

The symbol of the "armies of heaven" (Rev 19:14) has already been identified earlier in light of Revelation 17:14, which also provides additional context for the imagery of Revelation 19:11–21. In explaining the symbolism of the beast with seven heads and ten horns, the angel says, "The ten horns that you saw are ten kings who have not yet received a kingdom, but they are to receive authority as kings for one hour, together with the beast" (17:12). At least at the time of the writing of Revelation, the figures represented by the ten horns were not yet reigning. This places the events in the future from the perspective of Revelation 17. When the beast rises to power, those kings will have authority of a limited duration, symbolized by the "one

---

25. Warfield, *Biblical Doctrines*, 647, saw it as Christ and the victory of the gospel.

26. See the following parallels: "faithful and true" (Rev 19:11 || 3:14); "eyes like flames of fire" (Rev 19:12 || 1:14; 2:18); "called the Word of God" (Rev 19:13 || John 1:1); "two-edged sword from his mouth" (Rev 19:15 || 1:16; 2:12); "King of kings and Lord of lords" (Rev 19:16 || 17:14); "he will rule the nations with a rod of iron" (Rev 19:15 || Ps 2:9).

27. An apocalyptic "white horse" also appears in the vision of four chariots in Zechariah 6—chariots with red horses, black horses, white horses, and spotted horses (Zech 6:1–3). Henry Barclay Swete, ed., *The Apocalypse of St. John*, 2nd. ed., Classic Commentaries on the Greek New Testament (New York: Macmillan, 1906), 247, writes, "The Rider here is not the rider of *c. 6.*; there we see the Roman Imperator, or possibly the Parthian King (cf. Ramsay, *Letters to the Seven Churches*, p. 58), with his bow and wreath . . . ; here the Commander-in-chief of the host of heaven . . . with His sharp sword and many diadems; the superficial resemblance seems to emphasize the points of contrast. In any case no doubt is left as to the personality of the present Rider." Cf. Robert Henry Charles, *A Critical and Exegetical Commentary on the Revelation of St. John*, vol. 2 (Edinburgh: T&T Clark, 1920), 121.

28. Beale, *Revelation*, 951.

hour." Their reign will be directly associated with the reign of the beast (17:13). However, verse 14 gives us this short, proleptic promise: "They [the beast and ten kings] will wage war on the Lamb, and the Lamb will conquer them, for he is Lord of lords and King of kings, and those with him are called and chosen and faithful." This imagery corresponds to the image of the epiphany of Christ on the white horse with the "armies of heaven" accompanying him to destroy the beast and his armies in Revelation 19:11–21. Also, the language referring to the rider striking down the nations with the sword of his mouth (ἐν αὐτῇ πατάξῃ τὰ ἔθνη) and ruling them with a rod of iron (ποιμανεῖ αὐτοὺς ἐν ῥάβδῳ σιδηρᾷ) (19:15) reflects not only Psalm 2:9 but also Isaiah 11:1–4.[29] The latter messianic passage is also alluded to in 2 Thessalonians 2:8 in explicit reference to the parousia of Christ in judgment of the lawless one, "whom the Lord Jesus will destroy with the breath of his mouth, annihilating him by the manifestation of his coming (τῇ ἐπιφανείᾳ τῆς παρουσίας αὐτοῦ)." Thus Revelation 19:15, Isaiah 11:4, and 2 Thessalonians 2:8 triangulate on the parousia. The text also reaches the Apocalypse through the Psalms of Solomon 17:

> See, O Lord, and raise up their king for them, a son of David, for the proper time that you see, God, to rule over Israel your servant. And undergird him with strength to shatter unrighteous rulers. Cleanse Jerusalem from the nations that trample it in destruction, to expel sinners from the inheritance in wisdom, in righteousness, to rub out the arrogance of the sinner like a potter's vessel, to crush all their support with an iron rod (ἐν ῥάβδῳ); to destroy lawless nations by the word of his mouth (ἐν λόγῳ στόματος αυτοῦ), for Gentiles to flee from his face at his threat, and to reprove sinners by the word of their heart. (Pss. Sol. 17:23–27 [Brannan])

The remainder of Psalms of Solomon 17:28–51 describes the resulting messianic age in terms similar to the Old Testament collage of the coming kingdom. This, therefore, places the events in the future, in a context of actual eschatological judgment as expressed by the Old Testament and intertestamental imagery.

The image of the rider on the white horse with a robe dipped in blood (Rev 19:13) and treading "the winepress of the fury of the wrath of God the Almighty" (19:15) recalls similar imagery from Isaiah 63:2 and Joel 3:13. The passage in Isaiah 63:1–6 employs classic "Day of the Lord" imagery, which points to God's mediated theophanic visitation in judgment upon his enemies (see discussion on the Day of the Lord in chapters 15–17). While it does not lend itself easily to imagery referring to spiritual conquering of enemies with the victory of the gospel, it does reflect the kind of imagery of the coming of Christ as judge, when he personally takes the role of God coming in judgment. In the same way, Joel 3:13 is lifted from a Day of the Lord passage, when God gathers the nations together in the "Valley of Jehoshaphat" for judgment (Joel 3:12). That actual armies are intended is clear by the mention of

---

29. Granting the vision is saturated with symbolic imagery, leaving us with the faintest impression of what the actual event will look like, only a selective reading of the background texts under a heavy theological bias against punitive judgment can avoid the connection with real judgment and the destruction of enemies. See attempts at reading these texts in such a way in Mark Bredin, *Jesus, Revolutionary of Peace: A Nonviolent Christology in the Book of Revelation* (Milton Keynes: Paternoster, 2003), 200–16.

"warriors" and "soldiers" who are instructed to pound their plowshares into swords and their pruning hooks into spears (3:9–11). The judgment of God on the nations is pictured as a harvest and pressing of wine: "Go in, tread, for the winepress is full. The vats overflow, for their wickedness is great" (3:12–13). From that point, where Revelation 19:15 draws its language, Joel enters into a quick description of the "Day of the Lord." Again, such Old Testament imagery applied to Christ in the New Testament points to events of eschatological judgment mediated through worldly warfare and destruction; it is not in any way associated with spiritual warfare and the victory of the gospel.

In the next scene of the vision, an angel standing mid-heaven in the sun calls together birds to feast on the flesh of those who are to be slain (Rev 19:17). This language appears to rely upon Ezekiel 39:17, which, in its context, points to the eschatological battle of "Gog and Magog" (Ezek 39:17–20). In that context, the prophecy points to an actual invasion and defeat of enemies of Israel—armies consisting of "horses and chariots, with warriors and all kinds of soldiers" (39:20). Following this judgment in Ezekiel, Israel's fortunes are restored (39:21–29). This further argues in favor of Revelation 19:11–21 picturing in figurative terms drawn from the Old Testament actual events of judgment upon wicked nations associated with the second coming of Christ. These images, in their biblical usage, do not point to spiritual victory over the forces of Satan by the success of the gospel.

Finally, the showdown between the "beast and the kings of the earth with their armies" gathered against "the rider on the horse and . . . his army" (19:19). Recall that this beast and his allies had already been mentioned in 17:12–14: "They are to receive authority as kings for one hour, together with the beast. . . . They will wage war on the Lamb, and the Lamb will conquer them, for he is Lord of lords and King of kings, and those with him are called and chosen and faithful." Also, in the earlier vision of the bowls of the last plagues, the sixth bowl presents symbols of the providential gathering of these kings and their armies:

> The sixth angel poured his bowl on the great River Euphrates, and its water was dried up in order to prepare the way for the kings from the east. And I saw three foul spirits like frogs coming from the mouth of the dragon, from the mouth of the beast, and from the mouth of the false prophet. These are demonic spirits, performing signs, who go abroad to the kings of the whole world, to assemble them for battle on the great day of God the Almighty. ("See, I am coming like a thief! Blessed is the one who stays awake and is clothed, not going about naked and exposed to shame.") And the demonic spirits assembled the kings at the place that in Hebrew is called Harmagedon. (Rev 16:12–16)

Note that three figures—the dragon, the beast, and the false prophet—are mentioned as instigating the gathering of the armies of the kings of the earth to "the great day of God the Almighty" (16:14). Interjected in this scene of the vision is a quotation that points us to the parousia: "See, I am coming like a thief!" (16:15). This is language used in the New Testament of the sudden coming of the eschatological "Day of the Lord" (1 Thess 5:2; 2 Pet 3:10; Rev 3:3). That it is used in connection with the gathering of the armies of the earth to Armageddon points to a judgment of the actual nations through destruction. It does not agree with the notion that the victory of Christ over his enemies in Revelation 19:11–21 is spiritual, social, or political, accomplished by Christ but mediated through the church's successful proclamation of the gospel. The language and imagery of this vision cannot bear that kind of figurative interpretation.

Recalling, then, that the stage-setting vision for the last battle of "the great day of God the Almighty" (Rev 16:14) involved the behind-the-scenes working of the beast, the false prophet, and the dragon (cf. Rev 13), who had all lured the kings and their armies to the place of judgment, we see the appearance of Christ and his army dispensing with each member of the vision of Revelation 16:12–16 in turn.[30] First, the beast is captured, together with the false prophet, and they are summarily thrown into the lake of fire—the symbol for the place of eternal judgment—never to return (19:20). This leaves the kings and armies of the world, along with the dragon who had provided the beast and false prophet with their authority and power (cf. Rev 12:18; 13:2, 4, 11). The next verse says that the rest—the kings of the earth and their armies—were killed by the sword-like word from the mouth of the rider on the white horse: Christ (19:21). If we are correct in seeing a connection between the stage-setting vision of Revelation 16:12–16 and the outcome of that gathering in 19:11–21, then the only figure left in the vision is Satan. Ignoring the chapter break between 19 and 20, we see that the dragon is precisely the next (and last) figure to which the judgment attends.

All of this argues that the image of the coming of Christ as judge in Revelation 19:11–21 refers not to the victory of the gospel over all political, religious, and social obstacles, but to the physical, bodily return of Christ in the future. Mounce puts it well: "The Seer is not describing the gradual conquest of evil in the spiritual struggles of the faithful, but a great historic event that brings to an end the Antichrist and his forces and ushers in the long-awaited era of righteousness. History may offer examples of the triumph of right over wrong, but far from exhausting the truth of Revelation, they merely prefigure the actual consummation with its end to wickedness and beginning of universal peace."[31] And Fanning notes, "Even though this portrayal is highly symbolic with metaphors that are clearly not to be read with wooden literalism . . . it is not a reference to a transcendent, spiritual battle only."[32] To this question of the binding of Satan and the relevance of this to the coming kingdom we must now turn.

At the close of Revelation 19, then, the last remaining enemy in the vision is the dragon—Satan. We will devote the next chapter to the dragon's fate, which plays a pivotal role in establishing the chronology of the coming kingdom, as Fanning notes:

---

30. Swete, *Apocalypse*, 252, writes, "In *c.* 16. the forces are seen gathering for battle, but the battle is not yet begun; and there seems to be no reason why we should not find its consummation here." On Rev 16:12–16 as the stage-setting vision for the action climactic face off between the armies of earth and armies of heaven in 19:11–21, see, e.g., Gordon D. Fee, *Revelation: A New Covenant Commentary*, New Covenant Commentary Series (Eugene, OR: Cascade, 2011), 271.

31. Robert H. Mounce, *The Book of Revelation* (Grand Rapids: Eerdmans, 1977), 247.

32. Fanning, *Revelation*, 492.

If Satan's binding to prevent him from deceiving the nations 'any longer' (20:1–3) *follows* Christ's second advent when he defeats the nations assembled by Satan to resist him (16:13–14; 19:11–21), then it cannot be a restraint that operated during the symbolic "thousand years" of the church from Christ's first coming (or his cross, resurrection, and exaltation) to his second coming as the amillennial view portrays it. The events of 20:1–10 must be a repetition or recapitulation of visions that occurred earlier to avoid this chronological problem. For the issue of binding Satan, the focus of this question is whether Revelation 20:1–6 is a repeat of the events of Revelation 12:7–11 in a different symbolic form.[33]

---

33. Fanning, *Revelation*, 500.

11

THE BINDING OF SATAN IN REVELATION 20:1–3

When Satan is bound, man is set free.

Irenaeus, *Against Heresies* 5.21.3

It is often observed that Revelation 20:1–10 is the only passage in all of Scripture that mentions the thousand-year reign; therefore, premillennialism rests on a weak biblical foundation. It is not true, however, that futurist premillennialism as an approach to the coming kingdom rests entirely on those ten verses. In fact, even if Revelation 20 did not exist, something like a doctrine of a coming earthly kingdom in fulfillment of Old and New Testament expectations would still find a footing. In light of the teachings of the earliest church fathers (see chapter 5) and the interpretation of 1 Corinthians 15:20–28 as a multistage process of resurrection and its relationship to the kingdom that comes at Christ's parousia (see chapter 9), the basic structure of premillennialism would be intact.[1] Revelation 20:1–10 does introduce two images that strengthen the teaching: (1) the symbol of the binding and loosing of Satan at the start and end of the kingdom period and (2) the symbolic number of a thousand years to describe that period.

"Symbolic" is an important term here. Premillennialism does not rest on the thousand years as a strictly literal number. It may very well be a round number that indicates a very long period of time used to denote the duration of particular conditions unique to that period. Of course, nothing prevents the number from representing a literal thousand-year period either, but the literalness of the number is not what makes someone a premillennialist. Rather, premillennialists are those who believe the return of Christ as judge and king precedes the first phase of the eternal kingdom punctuated by the resurrection of the righteous at its commencement and by the resurrection and final judgment of the wicked at its conclusion, during which Satan is completely bound and banished.

What premillennialists see in Revelation 20:1–10, then, is a condensed reference to what the whole Old Testament and New Testament—not to mention intertestamental Jewish and early Christian writings—had been sketching for centuries. That is, the "millennium" is simply shorthand for a period on this earth during which Christ and his saints rule, wickedness is banished, creation is progressively

---

1. On the relationship between Rev 20 and Pauline eschatology, see Sydney H. T. Page, "Revelation 20 and Pauline Eschatology," *JETS* 23.1 (1980): 31–43.

transformed, nations are oriented to the worship and service of God and submission to Christ, nature is liberated from its bondage to corruption, and ultimately death itself is defeated. The "thousand years" in Revelation 20 serves as a symbol for that earthly stage upon which those events play out.

In the previous chapter, I made the case that Revelation 19:11–20:10 comprised a single progressive vision and that Revelation 19:11–21 employed symbolic imagery referring to the future second coming of Christ as judge and king. Now, as we move into the details of Revelation 20 itself, we first encounter the symbolic vision of the binding of Satan for a thousand years in Revelation 20:1–3. To what does this image refer, and when does this take place relative to the present period between Christ's ascension and return?

> **Go Deeper Excursus 18**
>
> *A Survey and History of Interpretations of Revelation 20:1–3*

Toward an Understanding of the Thousand-Year Binding of Satan

The key to answering the questions of the nature and timing of the binding of Satan in Revelation 20:1–3 lies in the language and imagery used in the passage. Premillennialists often note the severity of the language: it is not merely a chain but a "*great* chain" (ἅλυσιν μεγάλην); Satan is not merely "seized" but also "bound" (ἔδησεν) with the chain; not simply bound but "cast" (ἔβαλεν); not merely cast away but cast "into the abyss" (εἰς τὴν ἄβυσσον); and not merely banished to the abyss, but the abyss itself is "closed and sealed over him" (ἔκλεισεν καὶ ἐσφράγισεν ἐπάνω αὐτοῦ) (Rev 20:2–3). Had the vision been intended simply to portray particular limitations placed on Satan's activities, this imagery appears far too strong. For many readers, the extreme picture of binding and casting into the abyss does not seem to match the comparatively softer referent of specific limitations to Satan's power today.[2] On the strength of the language, Fanning observes, "This emphatic description makes the standard explanation of this 'binding of Satan' by amillennialists quite implausible."[3]

Challenged by the image of apparently absolute banishment, amillennialists usually respond in a way similar to R. C. H. Lenski who said: "The strong symbolism of being bound with a great chain and thrown into the abyss reveals how mighty was the foe who above all else intended to stop this heralding [of the gospel], and what was required to stop him, and how thoroughly he was stopped. Is the imagery too strong for you? Perhaps the Lord who uses it in this vision knows the dragon

---

2. Beasley-Murray writes, "The incarceration of the Devil is trebly circumscribed. He is bound up, locked in, and sealed over. The writer could hardly have expressed more emphatically the inability of Satan to harm the race of man." G. R. Beasley-Murray, *The Book of Revelation*, rev. ed., New Century Bible Commentary, ed. Ronald E. Clements and Matthew Black (London: Marshall, Morgan & Scott, 1974; repr., Grand Rapids: Eerdmans, 1981), 285.

3. Buist M. Fanning, *Revelation*, Zondervan Exegetical Commentary on the New Testament (Grand Rapids: Zondervan, 2020), 499n6.

better than you do, seeing that he conquered him on the cross at the cost of his own death."[4] Beale appeals to alleged parallel New Testament passages to argue that the language of binding, casting, and sealing—despite its apparent severity—actually does not communicate total banishment of Satan from the human realm. He writes:

> The *binding, expulsion, and fall* of Satan can be seen in other NT passages that affirm the same terms ("bind," "cast," etc.) that the decisive defeat of the devil occurred at Christ's death and resurrection (Matt. 12:29; Mark 3:27; Luke 10:17–19; John 12:31–33; Col. 2:15; Heb. 2:14). More precisely, the binding was probably inaugurated during Christ's ministry, which is more the focus of texts such as Matt. 12:29; Mark 3:27; and Luke 10:17–19. Satan's binding was climactically put in motion immediately after Christ's resurrection, and it lasts throughout most of the age between Christ's first and second comings. According to 20:7–9, the end point of the binding occurs immediately before Christ's final coming.[5]

Beale relies heavily on two suppositions that lead him to read the metaphors related to the binding of Satan as less severe than they seem on the surface: "If our understanding of the disjunctive temporal relation of 20:1–6 to 19:11–21 and our view of the 'keys' are correct, then Christ's work of restraining the devil's ability to 'deceive' is not a complete curtailment of all of the devil's activities but only a restraint on his deceiving abilities."[6] I have already spent considerable space noting the exegetical problems with regarding Revelation 19 and 20 as two completely separate visions (see chapter 10 and Go Deeper Excursus 17), so the first of Beale's protases is at least weakened if not dismissed. The second issue recalls Beale's assertion that the "key" of the abyss in the hand of the angel (Rev 20:1) refers to "the same as 'the key of death and of Hades,' which Christ holds in c. 1 because he has overcome death through his resurrection (1:18)."[7] The argument is that if Christ holds the keys of death and Hades by virtue of his own death and resurrection, that key—his death and resurrection—is what binds Satan. And since Christ died and rose again as part of his first advent, it is reasonable that the binding of Satan concurred with these events.

However, even if it were true that the angel's "key of the bottomless pit (τὴν κλεῖν τῆς ἀβύσσου)" is identical to Christ's "keys of death and Hades (τὰς κλεῖς τοῦ θανάτου καὶ τοῦ ᾅδου)," it does not necessarily follow that possessing the keys results in using them instantly. In any case, identifying the "key of the abyss" and the "keys of death and Hades" is a wrong turn for several reasons. First, by virtue of his death and resurrection, Christ holds "the keys" (plural) of death and Hades

---

4. R. C. H. Lenski, *The Interpretation of St. John's Revelation* (Columbus: Lutheran Book Concern, 1935), 576.

5. G. K. Beale, *The Book of Revelation: A Commentary on the Greek Text*, The New International Greek Testament Commentary, ed. I. Howard Marshall and Donald A. Hagner (Grand Rapids: Eerdmans, 1999), 985.

6. Beale, *Revelation*, 986. When Beale, 985, asserts that "context, and not the metaphor by itself, must determine what degree of restriction is intended," he means by this the context of the apparent macrostructure of Revelation, the alleged disjunctive relationship between Rev 19 and 20.

7. Beale, *Revelation*, 984.

(Rev 1:18). We should not make too much of this, but it does open the possibility that two different symbols are employed for two different referents. Second, had the vision of Revelation 20:1–3 intended to affirm the binding of Satan at the time of Christ's first advent, that connection could have easily been made by placing the action of binding in the hands of Christ, the actual holder of the keys. Or the language could have referred explicitly to the "keys of death and Hades" in the binding of Satan. As it is, in Christ's announcement that he holds the keys to death and Hades, he makes no connection between this fact and his victory over Satan. Nor does the passage referring to the victory over Satan connect it explicitly to Christ's keys of death and Hades. Absent such clear connections, the second leg of Beale's argument is placed in question.

The third, and more serious, problem with Beale's identification between Christ's keys and the angel's key is the use of the image of the "abyss," often translated as "bottomless pit" in Revelation 20:1 and also referred to in an earlier vision in 9:1. The terms "Hades" and "abyss" are not necessarily references to the same thing. The "abyss" is used to indicate *"the deep Underworld where even demons dread to go."*[8] In Romans 10:7, the term ἄβυσσος is used in contrast to "heaven" and "denotes the realm of the dead."[9] In his examination of the various uses of ἄβυσσος in the New Testament in light of its background in Old Testament, intertestamental, and other Greek literature, Kim Papaioannou draws close associations between the portrayal of the abyss in Luke 8:31, Revelation 9:1–3, and the banishment of Satan in Revelation 20:1–3. He concludes:

> The use of Abyss in Luke 8:31 parallels most closely the Abyss of Revelation albeit in a non-apocalyptic context. Thus the release in Revelation 9:1–11 of evil forces from the Abyss that leads to great harm to humanity is paralleled in Luke 8:26–39 by the demons wanting to remain "outside" the Abyss, and among the humans whom they cause to suffer. Likewise, the picture of the devil being bound and thrown into the Abyss (Rev. 20), so as not to deceive, is paralleled in a less apocalyptic and more temporal way in Luke's language of the binding of the devil and his forces in 11:24–26 and in the demons being "imprisoned" in the Abyss they dread to go in Luke 8:31.[10]

Each layer of intensifying restriction compounds the problems with interpreting the imagery as a partial restraint with a limited scope and scale.[11] In the first century, ἄβυσσος already carried with it not a mere limitation of activity in the

---

8. Benjamin M. Austin, "Afterlife," ed. Douglas Mangum et al., *Lexham Theological Wordbook*, Lexham Bible Reference Series (Bellingham, WA: Lexham, 2014), s.v. ἄβυσσος.

9. Kim Papaioannou, *The Geography of Hell in the Teaching of Jesus: Gehenna, Hades, the Abyss, the Outer Darkness Where There Is Weeping and Gnashing of Teeth* (Eugene, OR: Pickwick, 2013), 143.

10. Papaioannou, *Geography of Hell*, 172.

11. See especially the thorough study of the background of ἄβυσσος, including one of the most detailed textual, grammatical, and syntactical analysis of Rev 20:1–3 in Maria Emilia Schaller, Ἄβυσσος: *Un estudio en contexto: El significado del término "abismo" en el libro de Apocalipsis*. Serie Tesis de la Escuela de Graduados de la Facultad de Teología Universidad Adventista del Plata (Libertador San Martín, AR: Editorial Universidad Adventista del Plata, 2017), 328.

world but total banishment from the present world—the spiritual equivalent of solitary confinement. The abyss was the place from which the beast would arise when his time comes (Rev 11:7; 17:8). According to Luke's Gospel, the demonic hoard known as "legion" begged Jesus "not to command them to go away into the abyss" (Luke 8:31). This is usually associated with the "prison" in which the angels who had sinned prior to the flood were kept until the day of judgment (1 Pet 3:19; 2 Pet 2:4). The imagery in Revelation of the hoard of scorpion-like demons being released from this "abyss" indicates that prior to their release, they were unable to exercise any power in the world.

In fact, it may be that the release of the demonic swarm from the abyss in Revelation 9:1–3 is the Apocalypse's picture of the fulfillment of Peter's prophetic statement that the angels who sinned before the flood were committed "to chains of deepest darkness to be kept until the judgment (εἰς κρίσιν τηρουμένους)" (2 Pet 2:4). And Jude notes regarding those same pre-flood fallen angels that God "has kept in eternal chains in deepest darkness for the judgment of the great day (εἰς κρίσιν μεγάλης ἡμέρας)" (Jude 1:6). If this is the case, then the "day of judgment" is none other than the eschatological "Day of the Lord": the period of tribulation and testing upon the world that accompanies the coming of Christ as judge (see chapters 15–17). Just as the antediluvian demons were kept in the prison of the abyss or "Tartarus," to be released at the time of judgment (2 Pet 2:4; Jude 1:6; Rev 9), so Satan himself will be imprisoned in the same abyss or Tartarus for the period of the millennium, released only at its close to be judged in the lake of fire along with those who had already been so judged at the second coming of Christ.[12]

Another problem with the amillennial interpretation is that it artificially restricts the purpose of the binding and casting of Satan to the specific content of the ἵνα clause as the key for interpreting the symbolism of the binding. That is, when answering the question "What does the symbolism of binding/casting mean?" the answer is drawn from the purpose of the binding/casting: it simply means preventing Satan from deceiving the nations. Yet the text itself cannot bear this precision. The ἵνα clause explains the purpose for which the action in the previous clause was taken; it does not explain the symbolism of the action.[13]

However, a deeper problem with the amillennial interpretation lies in the background of the imagery itself. The binding and casting of Satan into the abyss in Revelation 20:1–3 draws on well-known contemporary language and imagery from 1 Enoch that would have indicated total incapacitation, not partial restraint. Even if we were to interpret the image of the ἄβυσσος as purely symbolic rather than as indicating the place to which Satan is banished,[14] still the interpretation of the symbol must match the meaning of the symbol itself as it would have been understood in its original context and to its original audience.

In the first century, Enochic literature—and particularly the so-called *Book of the Watchers* (1 En. 1–36)—was wildly popular in Jewish and Christian circles.

---

12. Cf. Matt Waymeyer, "The Binding of Satan in Revelation 20," *The Master's Seminary Journal* 26.1 (Spring 2015): 22; cf. 25–30.

13. Fanning, *Revelation*, 500n8.

14. Cf. Beale, *Revelation*, 987.

George Nickelsburg and James VanderKam describe 1 Enoch as "a collection of apocalyptic (revelatory) texts that were composed between the late fourth century B.C.E. and the turn of the era. The size of the collection, the diversity of its contents, and its many implications for the study of ancient Judaism and Christian origins make it arguably the most important Jewish writing that has survived from the Greco-Roman period."[15] Enochic literature enjoyed a popularity not unlike the *Lord of the Rings* or *Star Wars* in the modern day. That is, in Jewish-Christian circles, the language and imagery of Enoch were familiar and influential, even making a cameo appearance by name in Jude 1:14–15. Language and images from 1 Enoch appear indisputably in texts related to the spirits in prison in 2 Peter 2:4 and Jude 1:6, as well as in numerous other New Testament books and early Christian writings.[16] However, "from the Middle Ages to early modern period, the early Enochic pseudepigrapha were largely lost to the West."[17]

Several passages in 1 Enoch shed light on the language and imagery adopted and adapted in Revelation 20:1–3 with reference to the binding of Satan and his casting into the abyss as a prison for a season prior to his ultimate judgment. Those passages are fictional accounts of events related to wicked angels who rebelled in the days of Noah prior to the judgment of the flood. In 1 Enoch 10.4–6, we read: "To Raphael he said, 'Go, Raphael, and bind (δῆσον) Asael hand and foot, and cast him into the darkness; and make an opening in the wilderness that is in Doudael. Throw (βάλε) him there, and lay beneath him sharp and jagged stones. And cover him with darkness, and let him dwell there for an exceedingly long time. Cover up his face, and let him not see the light. And on the day of the great judgment, he will be led away to the burning conflagration.' "[18]

A little later, it continues: "And to Michael he said, 'Go, Michael, bind (δῆσον) Shemihazah and the others with him, who have mated with the daughters of men,

---

15. George W. E. Nickelsburg and James C. VanderKam, *1 Enoch: The Hermeneia Translation* (Minneapolis: Augsburg Fortress, 2012), vii.

16. George Njeri, "Surprise on the Day of Judgment in Matthew 25:31–46 and the Book of the Watcher," *Neotestamentica* 54.1 (2020): 89; James VanderKam, "1 Enoch, Enochic Motifs, and Enoch in Early Christian Literature," in *The Jewish Apocalyptic Heritage in Early Christianity*, ed. James C. VanderKam and William Adler, Compendia Rerum Iudaicarum ad Novum Testamentum, section 3, vol. 4 (Minneapolis: Fortress, 1996), 33–59.

17. Annette Yoshiko Reed, *Fallen Angels and the History of Judaism and Christianity: The Reception of Enochic Literature* (Cambridge: Cambridge University Press, 2005), 2. For most people for much of the history of the church, this background literature—which would have shed light on the original understanding of the binding of Satan in Rev 20:1–3—was unavailable. Just as adjustments to biblical interpretation and theology occurred in the Reformation with the recovery of ancient biblical texts and writings of early church fathers, perhaps some age-old assumptions about the original meaning of Rev 20:1–3 should have been revisited in light of the restoration of these important texts. Alas, Protestant Reformers mostly adopted and adapted the old Augustinian amillennial reading of the text, doubling down on the partial, limited binding of Satan in the present church age. This failure of recovery and reassessment led to the perpetuation of weak exegesis of the passage, which in turn codified an anti-premillennial eschatology for centuries. But if we read the passage in light of its original historical-theological-literary context, a blurry picture that can be manipulated in a number of ways becomes more focused and defined.

18. Translation is from Nickelsburg and VanderKam, *1 Enoch: The Hermeneia Translation*.

so that they were defiled by them in their uncleanness. And when their sons perish and they see the destruction of their beloved ones, bind (δῆσον) them for seventy generations in the valleys of the earth, until the day of their judgment and consummation (μέχρι ἡμέρας κρίσεως αὐτῶν, καὶ συντελεσμοῦ), until the everlasting judgment is consummated (ἕως τελεσθῇ τὸ κρίμα τοῦ αἰῶνος τῶν αἰώνων). Then they will be led away to the fiery abyss (εἰς τὸ χάος τοῦ πυρὸς),[19] and to the torture, and to the prison where they will be confined forever" (1 En. 10.11–13; cf. also 1 En. 54.1–6).

In *The Book of the Parables* (1 En. 37–71), we read:

> And I looked and turned to another part of the earth, and I saw there a deep valley with burning fire. And they brought the kings and the mighty and threw them into that deep valley. And there my eyes saw them making their instruments, iron chains of immeasurable weight. And I asked the angel of peace who went with me, "For whom are these chains being prepared?" And he said to me, "These are being prepared for the host of Azazel, that they might take them and throw them into the abyss of complete judgment, and with jagged rocks they will cover their jaws, as the Lord of Spirits commanded. And Michael and Raphael and Gabriel and Phanuel will take hold of them on that great day, and throw them on that day into the burning furnace, that the Lord of Spirits may take vengeance on them, for their unrighteousness in becoming servants of Satan, and leading astray those who dwell on the earth. (1 En. 54.1–6)

As in Revelation 20:1–3, these accounts from 1 Enoch portray demonic spirits bound and cast into prison, where they are held until the day of judgment and then cast into the fire. In every case, those bound spirits are utterly incapable of any influence on the earth. While acknowledging that the imagery is symbolic, our interpretation of Revelation 20:1–3 must be guided by the meaning of the symbols as they would have been understood in their first-century context. Simply put, in no way would first-century Jewish or Christian readers familiar with Enochic imagery have drawn the conclusion that the language and imagery of Revelation 20:1–3 portrayed anything other than Satan's total incapacity—utter removal from the inhabited creation. Because Satan and his demons are not, in fact, imprisoned in a place that is cut off from this present world, Revelation 20:1–3 must await a future fulfillment.[20]

Even since the modern restoration of 1 Enoch as a literary source for establishing the first-century meaning of terms and images of Revelation 20:1–10, many modern commentators completely ignore this background or grant it a mere passing comment in a footnote.[21] Even those few who do engage the passage in some

---

19. Note that the English translation renders χάος as "abyss."

20. Fanning, *Revelation*, 499–500; cf. see Grant R. Osborne, *Revelation: Verse by Verse* (Bellingham, WA: Lexham, 2016), 325.

21. For example, Ian Boxall, *The Revelation of Saint John*, Black's New Testament Commentary (London: Continuum, 2006), 278–79, briefly alludes to 1 En. 10:4–6, but it plays no role in his interpretation of the passage. Johnson, *Triumph of the Lamb*, 283, leans on Beale's view on the binding of Satan and its imagery. He does not address the Enochian background of Rev 20:1–3 at all. Leon Morris, *Revelation*, rev. ed., Tyndale New Testament Commentar-

detail do not sufficiently counter the weight of the Enochic background in their amillennial interpretations (see Go Deeper Excursus 19, *A Critique of Beale's Interpretation of Revelation 20:1–3*). When interpreters do not incorporate all exegetical evidence, their efforts in bridging the gap between text and interpretation will necessarily be aided by theological biases, confessional commitments, or other texts or doctrines alien to the actual context of Revelation 20:1–3.

Implications of the Binding and Loosing of Satan in Revelation 20

If one accepts that the binding of Satan for a thousand years is yet future and refers to a millennial kingdom on this earth, then two important issues emerge. First, why is there an intermediate period between the end-times judgments of Revelation 19:11–21 and the ultimate final judgment of Satan in Revelation 20:7–10? It seems it would make much more sense to have a single period of judgment on the earth, after which all sin, suffering, death, and devils are banished for good. Second, what is the purpose of releasing Satan and his second rebellion? To answer these questions, we must return to the big picture of God's story of creation, fall, and redemption and his original plan for humanity

> **Go Deeper Excursus 19**
>
> *A Critique of Beale's Interpretation of Revelation 20:1–3*

The exegetical evidence from Revelation 19:11–20:15 supports the second-century Irenaean premillennial understanding of a future earthly intermediate kingdom following the return of Christ as judge and king. At the commencement of that reign, Satan will be completely bound, and the righteous of every age will have been raised. The earth will then be progressively transformed, and the quality of paradise will eventually spread throughout the whole earth. Redeemed humanity will be involved in the renewal and restoration project, fulfilling the original *imago Dei* mission. By the end of the this period, the "new heavens and new earth" condition will have been accomplished as the whole world enjoys the blessing of a tamed, bountiful nature.

In Irenaean premillennial eschatology, however, the coming of Christ at the close of the future tribulation period will meet many followers faithful to him who maintained their testimony by refusing to worship the beast. Those who suffered martyrdom, of course, will be raised (Rev 20:4), but those who are still alive, found "in the flesh," will enter the kingdom in their mortal bodies. They will multiply on the earth, restoring the population of humanity generation after generation (*Haer.* 5.35.1).

---

ies (Grand Rapids: Eerdmans, 1987), 223–25, also makes no mention of any Enochic background. Jürgen Roloff, *Revelation: A Continental Commentary* (Minneapolis: Fortress, 1993), 226, acknowledges the Enochic background but does not develop its implications. Likewise, Stephen S. Smalley, *The Revelation to John* (Downers Grove: IVP Academic, 2012), 500–501, actually lists references for the background imagery of Rev 20:1–3 (e.g., Isa 24.21–22; 1 En. 10.4–12; 14.5; 54:3–5; 88.1; 2 En 7.1–2; Pr. Man. 2–4; 2 Bar. 56.13; Jub. 5.6; Sib. Or. 2.286–89; 2 Pet 2:4; Jude 1:6); nevertheless, hc does not actually engage with the implications of this imagery or explore what the vision of 20:1–3 is intended to communicate in light of it.

Yet after the "times of refreshing" and "regeneration" of all things (Matt 19; Acts 3) during this intermediate kingdom, Revelation 20:7–10 states:

> When the thousand years are ended, Satan will be released from his prison and will come out to deceive the nations at the four corners of the earth, Gog and Magog, in order to gather them for battle; they are as numerous as the sands of the sea. They marched up over the breadth of the earth and surrounded the camp of the saints and the beloved city. And fire came down from heaven and consumed them. And the devil who had deceived them was thrown into the lake of fire and sulfur, where the beast and the false prophet were, and they will be tormented day and night forever and ever.

Whereas the beast and the false prophet were consigned to the lake of fire immediately upon Christ's return (Rev 19:20), the dragon was captured and consigned to the abyss during the thousand-year kingdom (20:1–3). But why would God's plan call for the banishing of Satan, only for him to be released after a centuries-long reclamation and edenification project? Would this not be anticlimactic—indeed, rolling back God's plan of redemption rather than moving it forward? Would the battle of "Gog and Magog" otherwise constitute a *second* final Day of the Lord and a *second* second coming?

We will see in chapter 15 of this book that the Day of the Lord is itself reiterative. Just as there could be an ultimate Day of the Lord for Babylon and an ultimate Day of the Lord for Assyria, so there will be an ultimate Day of the Lord for the kingdom of the beast as well as an ultimate Day of the Lord for the rest of humanity and Satan.

Also, the image from Revelation 20 implies a failed attempt to rush the "camp" of Christ—presumably Jerusalem—from the remotest parts of the earth. But the earlier vision of Christ's return (Rev 16:14–16; 19:17–21) pictures the armies of heaven invading the realm of the beast and conquering them. In Revelation 19, Christ is the invader who instantly defeats the beast and the armies of the earth. In Revelation 20, Christ is the defender who instantly puts an end to a failed coup.

But what of that battle itself? First, we are told that Satan is released from his prison (Rev 20:7) and promptly engages in deceiving the nations (20:8)—the very reason he was imprisoned in the first place (20:3). The mention of "the nations at the four corners of the earth" (20:8) is a geographical idiom. It is used in Revelation 7:1 for the angels who are standing "at the four corners of the earth, holding back the four winds of the earth"—apparently a figure for the four directions of the compass. It is used in Testament of Asher 7.2 of the scattering of God's people "unto the four corners of the earth." In light of this, it is idiomatically parallel to the language used in Matthew 24:31 with reference to the gathering of the elect of Israel "from the four winds, from one end of the sky to the other end" (cf. Mark 13:27). The passing mention of "Gog and Magog" in apposition to the expression "the four corners of the earth" (Rev 20:8) confirms that the vision refers to people geographically remote from Jerusalem.

The terms "Gog and Magog" are never used elsewhere in the New Testament, and they are not directly connected to end-times events pictured previously in Revelation. However, they do have a background in the Old Testament as well as intertestamental expectations of end-times events. Ezekiel mentions an individual called "Gog, of the land of Magog, the chief prince of Meschech and Tubal" (38:2), and imagery from Ezekiel is reflected in the depiction of the coming of Christ and his armies in Revelation 19:11–21.[22] In Ezekiel 38–39, however, "Gog" refers to an individual, perhaps what we call the antichrist and his armies; thus the primary referent is the events depicted earlier in Revelation that climax at Christ's return in 19:11–21.

In Revelation 20:7–10, however, the appositional phrase "Gog and Magog" is used more as a geographical reference for nations scattered as far from the city of God as possible. Though in the book of Jubilees, "Gog" refers to a region in the north (Jub. 8.25), the *Sibylline Oracles* alternates between placing Gog and Magog in the region of Ethiopia (3.319) and associating it with the Marsians and Dacians in Europe (3.512).[23] The fact is, nobody really knows for sure where the "Gog and Magog" of Revelation 20:8 are supposed to be located geographically, but the sense is that the term refers to remote regions beyond the horizon, perhaps in the north.[24] This callback to the image of Gog and Magog would underscore the fact that Satan is not—and cannot be—reformed or redeemed. Despite his thousand-year incarceration to prevent him from deceiving nations as he had done prior to his banishment, he immediately engages in the same desperate attempt to deceive and topple the kingdom of Christ.

The vision of Revelation 20:7–8 presents us with a stark contrast in the history of redemption and its ultimate climax. Just as the angels will gather the elect of Israel scattered among the wicked nations from the four ends of the earth to establish the kingdom centered in Jerusalem (Matt 24:31; cf. Rev 7:1–8; 14:1–4), so Satan will gather the wicked scattered among the righteous nations from the four corners of the earth to attack the kingdom centered in Jerusalem (Rev 20:7–9). In that vision, the number of Satan's postmillennial army is described as "numerous as the sands of the sea" (20:8). The idiom "numerous as the sands of the sea" elsewhere in Scripture is used of large armies probably numbering in the thousands, not in the millions or billions (Josh 11:4; Judg 7:12; 8:10; 1 Sam 13:5).[25] Even if the number of those Satan was able to deceive were one million, in a world population numbering perhaps ten billion after a thousand years of human thriving and abundance, this great multitude of rebels would constitute .01 percent of the population. It would be wrong for us, then, to imagine an "Armageddon II" in the sense of a total apostasy in which only a remnant of righteous survive. Rather, Satan's final attempt at revolt may be more akin to a one-time wildly popular president who has trouble rallying enough supporters in his second bid for president.

---

22. See Rev 19:17. The language appears to rely on Ezek 39:17–20, which points to an eschatological battle.

23. Cf. also Walter A. Elwell and Barry J. Beitzel, "Magog," *Baker Encyclopedia of the Bible* (Grand Rapids: Baker, 1988), 1377–78.

24. J. J. Reeve, "Gog," in *The International Standard Bible Encyclopaedia*, ed. James Orr et al. (Chicago: Howard-Severance, 1915), 1273.

25. See comments in Hélène M. Dallaire, "Joshua," in *The Expositor's Bible Commentary: Numbers–Ruth*, vol. 2, rev. ed., ed. Tremper Longman III and David E. Garland (Grand Rapids: Zondervan, 2012), 939–40.

The frequently asked question, though, is where does this army of deceived rebels come from? This is not as problematic, however, as sometimes presented. In second-century Irenaean premillennialism, the intermediate kingdom will be populated not only by resurrected saints of all ages reigning with Christ in the heavenly and earthly realms, but also by mortal humans who are the original survivors of the future tribulation period. These survive because Christ's coming cuts short the days of the judgment; otherwise, "no one would be saved" (Matt 24:22; Mark 13:20). That is, there are survivors of the tribulation, remnants of the tribes of Israel and Gentile believers, who repopulate the world (*Haer.* 5.35.1). The descendants of these original survivors, having spread throughout the face of the earth, will constitute the nations of the millennial period. And because these are not resurrected, glorified saints, the potential exists for some of them to resist the lordship of Christ and his kingdom. They could harbor rebellion in their hearts while conforming externally to the mandates of the perfect kingdom and partaking of its blessings. This may be hard to believe until we reflect on the hardness of heart surrounding the great miraculous theophanic manifestations of God's power and glory throughout Scripture.

The fraction of the mortal population that harbored hardness of heart against Christ and his kingdom would naturally be driven to corners of the earth, as far away from its center as possible. Thus the image of Gog and Magog as the far reaches of the earth may be taken as a symbol for both geographical and spiritual remoteness. If someone in the coming kingdom despised God and his goodness and resisted the rule of Christ in their heart, they would find themselves retreating farther and farther away from the boundaries of the progressive edenification of the world, and instead delighting in spiritual darkness. When Satan is released from his prison, he goes to the places where such rebels would be seeking refuge from the presence of Christ and his saints—as far from Jerusalem as possible.

Another parallel exists between the opening and the concluding chapters of the Bible. In Genesis 3, the serpent was allowed into the Garden of Eden to test the first humanity after the order of Adam. Going to the woman, he deceived her (2 Cor 11:3) into disobeying God's command by enticing her to eat from the tree of the knowledge of good and evil (Gen 3:1–6). Upon offering that fruit to her husband, Adam was faced with a choice. He should have knocked the fruit from Eve's hand, crushed the head of the serpent, and banished it from the garden. Instead, he succumbed to the temptation and suffered the fate of exile and death (Gen 3:6, 17–24).

When we fast-forward to the final chapters of the Bible, we find a parallel scene. Christ (the second Adam)—along with both glorified saints and moral humans— has succeeded in bringing to near completion the original *imago Dei* mission. The mortal portion of humanity have filled the whole earth (Gen 1:26–27). Humanity has tended and kept the garden of paradise—returned from the heavenly realm to earth in the establishment of the kingdom—so that the whole world is nigh to being completely renewed by the conditions of Eden. That is, God's will is being done on earth as it is in heaven in the most ultimate sense.

At this point, then, the serpent is allowed back into "paradise." As he did at the beginning, Satan is able to deceive a portion of humanity (Rev 20:8), riling them up perhaps by fanning into flame a smoldering sense of injustice, inequity, oppression, or even slavery to a king they never met and a regime they never embraced. Whatever the means of deception, the army is roused and makes their way to Jerusalem (20:9). Yet at this point, the second Adam succeeds where the first Adam failed. Christ crushes the head of the serpent and banishes him from the garden into the lake of fire itself. The disobedience of the first Adam has been fully reversed by the obedience of the second Adam. As a result, wickedness and mortality are banished for good (Rev 20:10–15). This final victory over sin, death, and devil is represented by the advent of the new heavens and the new earth (Rev 21).

We may now return to the original problem of the release of Satan and the final battle of Gog and Magog in Revelation 20:7–10. Anthony Hoekema articulates the amillennial concern in the following terms:

> Why should believers, who have been enjoying heavenly glory during the intermediate state, be raised from the dead in order to return to an earth where sin and death still exist? Would this not be an anticlimax? Do not glorified resurrection bodies call for life on a new earth, from which all remnants of sin and of the curse have been banished? Why, further, should the glorified Christ return to an earth where sin and death still exist? Why should he after his return in glory still have to rule his enemies with a rod of iron, and still have to crush a final rebellion against him at the close of the millennium? Was not Christ's battling against his enemies completed during his state of humiliation? Did he not during that time win the final, decisive victory over evil, sin, death, and Satan? Does not the Bible teach that Christ is coming back in the fulness of his glory to usher in, not an interim period of qualified peace and blessing, but the final state of unqualified perfection?[26]

Similarly, Sam Storms argues:

> To insist, as the premillennialist must, that the natural realm will undergo a *dual renewal*, a preliminary and incomplete one prior to the millennial age and a final and perfect one after it, demands that we anticipate a similar *dual renewal* in the case of all Christians. It seems more reasonable to me that Paul's description of the day of redemption for both Christians and the created order (i.e., the second coming of Jesus) is identical with the advent of the new heavens and new earth portrayed in such texts as 2 Peter 3:10–13; Revelation 21:1ff.; and Matthew 19:28. If so, there is no place for a "millennium" subsequent to the return of Christ.[27]

This either/or approach is precisely what must be overcome. In classic Irenaean premillennialism, the either/or gives way to a more nuanced approach. Rather than seeing the millennium as an imperfect "gap" period between the present age and the new heavens and the new earth, the Irenaean approach sees the future millennial period as the multigenerational, progressive realization of the edenification of

---

26. Anthony A. Hoekema, *The Bible and the Future* (Grand Rapids: Eerdmans, 1994), 184–85.

27. Sam Storms, *Kingdom Come: The Amillennial Alternative* (Fearn, SCT: Mentor, 2013), 154.

creation. We are already participating in a spiritual and promissory sense in the new creation, and thus this reclamation process has already begun in the church. So also, the millennial period is, in fact, the early stages of the renewal of creation itself. It is the next step in the renewal of heaven and earth, culminating in the definitive final product—the new heavens and the new earth—at the completion of the reclamation and transformation process (see full discussion in chapter 13).

This is not a "dual renewal," but a single renewal of creation that takes time. This present world is filled with pollution, contamination, corruption, chaos, ecological systems teetering on the brink, destruction, suffering, and death. The Irenaean approach to the future millennium sees the redemption and transformation of this world as a grand reclamation project in which the *imago Dei* mission originally intended for humanity is fully realized. Thus, the wretched world to which Christ returns is gradually subdued, redeemed, and released from its bondage to corruption. It is the end of this process of subduing all enemies—spiritual, ecological, natural, and otherwise—that is the function of the coming kingdom established at Christ's return, the end of which results in the defeat of death itself and a handing over of that creation to God the Father by the second Adam as an offering: mission accomplished (1 Cor 15:24–28).

Though amillennialists often fault premillennialists for saying that mortality, sin, and death are present during the millennial period after Christ's return, this charge is grossly exaggerated. In the case of classic Irenaean premillennialism, outright sin, suffering, and death will be extremely rare during the millennium. Death will be thought a curse reserved only for the outright rebellious, of which there will likely be few (Isa 65:20). In fact, the mortal survivors of the tribulation will never grow old or die. Irenaeus put it beautifully: "For in the times of the kingdom, the righteous man who is upon the earth shall then forget to die" (*Haer.* 5.36.2). Instead, by participating in the means of immortality, eating from the tree of life returned now from the heavenly realm and planted permanently in the earth, humans will grow from glory to glory. Only those who are unregenerate and cut themselves off from God and the means of immortal life will suffer the effects of corruption and death.

It is not an exaggeration to say that the Irenaean premillennial model has far less sin, suffering, and death during the millennium described in Revelation 20:1–10 than amillennialism or postmillennialism. In fact, in amillennialism, as Christ is presently reigning over heaven and earth, every human born dies and sin reaches such a pitch of fury as to shock even the minds of the most godless ancients. In the postmillennial expectation, while righteousness will prevail in society and government, the mortal nature, temptation, sin, and death will still be universally present among humanity with no means of affecting supernatural transformation or healing of the dilemma of fallenness. The problem of "death" during the millennium is a problem all millennial views share; only in premillennialism is death subdued and virtually nonexistent in most places at most times during this golden age.

12

The Two Resurrections in Revelation 20:4–6

John, therefore, did distinctly foresee the first
"resurrection of the just" and the inheritance in the
kingdom of the earth, and what the prophets have
prophesied concerning it harmonize with his vision.

Irenaeus, *Against Heresies* 5.36.3

Patristic scholar Eric Osborn summarizes Irenaeus's teaching on resurrection succinctly: "Irenaeus, joining Revelation 20:1–21:4 and 1 Corinthians 15:24–8, speaks of two resurrections, the first being the resurrection of the just in the kingdom of the son (5.36.3) and the second being the general resurrection which follows the delivering of the kingdom by the son to the father. In the kingdom of the son man will continue to grow and progress towards perfection in Christ (4.11.1; 5.35.1), and the creation will be restored (5.33.3)."[1]

For Irenaeus, the first resurrection will occur when Christ returns to establish his earthly kingdom after overthrowing the kingdom of the antichrist. In reference to Daniel 2:34, 44–45, Irenaeus notes, "Christ is the stone which is cut out without hands, who shall destroy temporal kingdoms, and introduce an eternal one, which is the resurrection of the just (*justorum resurrectio*)" (*Haer.* 5.26.2; cf. 5.32.2; 5.33.4; 5.35.1). Irenaeus asserts that the apostle John "did distinctly foresee the first 'resurrection of the just' (*primam justorum resurrectionem*) and the inheritance in the kingdom of the earth (*in regno terrae*), and what the prophets have prophesied concerning it harmonize [with his vision]. For the Lord also taught these things" (*Haer.* 5.36.3; cf. *Haer.* 5.34.2). As far as the timeline relates to the future millennium, he writes, "It behooves the righteous first to receive the promise of the inheritance which God promised to the fathers, and to reign in it, when they rise again to behold God in this creation which is renovated, and that the judgment should take place afterwards" (5.32.1). Thus Irenaeus's second-century eschatology drew together 1 Corinthians 15:24–28, Revelation 20:1–10, the teachings of Jesus on the coming kingdom and resurrection, as well as the Old Testament prophets' expectations of the coming messianic age.

In his discussion with Jewish unbelievers, Irenaeus's predecessor, Justin Martyr, reflects the same eschatological expectations in the middle of the second century: "I and every other completely orthodox Christian feel certain that there will be a

---

1. Eric Osborn, *Irenaeus of Lyons* (Cambridge: Cambridge University Press, 2001), 137.

resurrection of the flesh, followed by a thousand years in the rebuilt, embellished, and enlarged city of Jerusalem, as was announced by the Prophets Ezechiel, Isaias and the others" (*Dial.* 80 [Falls]). Shortly thereafter, Justin affirms, "Moreover, a man among us named John, one of Christ's Apostles, received a revelation and foretold that the followers of Christ would dwell in Jerusalem for a thousand years, and that afterwards (μετὰ ταῦτα) the universal (τὴν καθολικὴν), and in short, ever-lasting resurrection and judgment would take place" (*Dial.* 81 [Falls]). Later, in con-trasting the temporary inheritance of the Holy Land under Joshua with the future, eternal inheritance under Jesus, Justin writes, "Josue gave them an inheritance for a time only, since he was not Christ our God, nor the Son of God; but Jesus, after the holy resurrection (μετὰ τὴν ἁγίαν ἀνάστασιν), will give us an inheritance for eternity (αἰώνιον)" (*Dial.* 113 [Falls]). The order is clear: after the holy resurrection (that is, the resurrection of the righteous), the millennial kingdom will take place, which will then be followed by the "universal" resurrection and judgment of all people (πάντων ἀνάστασιν γενήσεσθαι καὶ κρίσιν, *Dial.* 81).

As history progresses and later church fathers pivot away from the idea of an intermediate stage of the coming kingdom, the two-stage future resurrection (the first of the righteous, the second of the wicked) also falls out of favor. In its place, later fathers opt for a single, general resurrection of the righteous and wicked at the return of Christ. How do these later fathers reckon with the two resurrections described in Revelation 20:4–6? A couple of examples will suffice.

In the fourth century, Tyconius understood the reign of the souls of those who had been beheaded (Rev 20:4) as those who are currently with Christ at the right hand of the Father and presently reigning spiritually with him: (Exp. Apoc. 7 [20:4]). Yet Tyconius does not call the rising to heaven upon death itself the "first resurrection." Rather, "*This is the first resurrection*, indeed in which we rise through baptism, as the Apostle says: 'If you have been raised with Christ, seek the things which are above.' . . . Just as the first death is in this life through sin, so also the first resurrection is in this life through the forgiveness of sins" (7 [20:5]).[2]

In the early fifth century, Augustine also promoted the view that the first resur-rection refers to present spiritual regeneration while the second resurrection is the bodily resurrection of both the righteous and the wicked at Christ's future return as judge. Augustine explains it this way:

> For all these dead souls one living man died—a man utterly free from sin—with the intention that those who come alive by forgiveness of their sins live no longer for themselves, but for Him who died for all on account of our sins, and rose again for our justification. All this was to the end that, believing in Him "who justifies the impious," we might be rescued from unbelief like men quickened out of death and belong to the first resurrection which is here and now. For, no one belongs to the first save those who are to be blessed forever. To the second, however, of which Christ is about to speak, belong both the blessed and the damned, as He teaches

---

2. Tyconius of Carthage, *Exposition of the Apocalypse*, trans. Francis X. Gumerlock, The Fathers of the Church: A New Translation, vol. 134 (Washington, DC: Catholic University of America Press, 2017), 178.

us. The first resurrection is a resurrection of mercy; the last is to be a resurrection of judgment. (*Civ.* 20.6)[3]

Augustine further writes, "During the 'thousand years' when the Devil is bound, the saints also reign for a 'thousand years' and, doubtless, the two periods are identical and mean the span between Christ's first and second coming" (*Civ.* 20.9). He understands the thrones and those sitting on them in Revelation 20:4 as "the prelates who govern the Church here and now" (*Civ.* 20.9). Thus the souls of those who were beheaded are "the faithful departed" who are "not divorced from Christ's kingdom which is the temporal Church" (20.9). He sums up his view: "We conclude, therefore, that even now, in time, the Church reigns with Christ both in her living and departed members" (20.9).[4]

Modern Amillennial Interpretations of the Two Resurrections

The classic Augustinian amillennial view that the first resurrection is present and spiritual while the second resurrection is future and bodily continues to the present day.[5] However, another view among amillennialists has also taken shape. B. B. Warfield articulated the view that the thousand-year reign in Revelation 20:1–10 is "the 'intermediate state'—of the saints of God gathered in heaven."[6]

Modern voices for amillennialism continue to promote the view that the image of the first resurrection in Revelation 20:4–5 is in some sense spiritual, though the classic Augustinian view that it is a symbol for our regeneration avoids some problematic theological implications of the view that the first resurrection is actually the intermediate state.[7] Depending heavily on the work of Meredith Kline, Kim Riddlebarger sees the first resurrection in Revelation 20:4–6 as "a spiritual resurrection, specifically, the death of believers and their entrance into heaven, where they now reign with Christ until the thousand years are over. Christ then returns in glory to raise the dead, judge the world, and make all things new."[8] He continues,

---

3. Translation from *Saint Augustine: City of God, Books XVII–XXII*, trans. Gerald G. Walsh and Daniel J. Honan, The Fathers of the Church: A New Translation, vol. 24 (Washington, DC: The Catholic University of America Press, 1954).

4. Cassiodorus in the sixth century also represented this view in his exposition of the Apocalypse. Cass. *Exp. Apoc.* 20.4–6; 20.7–10; cf. 19.19.

5. Cf. arguments, especially drawing on Pauline reference to spiritual resurrection as a background to Rev 20, in Page, "Revelation 20 and Pauline Eschatology," 31–43.

6. Benjamin B. Warfield, *Biblical Doctrines* (New York: Oxford University Press, 1929), 649. Though Warfield has sometimes been categorized as a postmillennialist (cf. Loraine Boettner, *The Millennium* [Phillipsburg, NJ: P&R, 1957], 387), this is simply not true, at least not in the normal sense in which postmillennialism is defined. Warfield, *Biblical Doctrines*, 649–50, understood the symbol of the thousand years of Rev 20 fulfilled in the intermediate state between the advents of Christ; postmillennialists see the thousand years as commencing in the future when the gospel is victorious in the world.

7. Cf. William Hendriksen, *More Than Conquerors: An Interpretation of the Book of Revelation* (Grand Rapids: Baker, 1967), 230–32.

8. Kim Riddlebarger, *A Case for Amillennialism: Understanding the End Times* (Grand Rapids: Baker, 2013), 247.

"When believers are converted and then taste death, they participate in the first resurrection (a spiritual resurrection) so that they might be raised bodily at the end of the age. . . . When they die, they reign with Christ as they await the bodily resurrection at the end of the age. But when unbelievers die (the first death), they will experience the second death when they are raised unto everlasting punishment. . . . For Christians, death is really a resurrection unto life. For non-Christians, death entails a resurrection unto the second death."[9]

The source of Riddlebarger's view that led him to call death "resurrection" is an article by Meredith Kline.[10] Based on a word study in Revelation, Kline argues that the adjective πρῶτος ("first") modifying ἀνάστασις ("resurrection") in Revelation 20:5–6 does not necessarily mean "first in a series" but "first category."[11] I believe he is correct on this point. However, Kline then concludes that the "first resurrection" is not spiritual regeneration as in classic Augustinian amillennialism but the death of believers that ushers them into heaven. In short, the first resurrection is actually the first death.[12] He argues that for the second category of the wicked, the "second resurrection" is actually "the second death" to the lake of fire; so for the first category of the righteous, the "first resurrection" is actually "the first death" to heaven.[13]

However, the language and imagery of Revelation 20 actually leads to the conclusion that those thrown into the lake of fire had already been resurrected bodily prior to that event. The crowd standing before God's throne after the sea, death, and Hades had "given them up" (ἔδωκαν) (Rev 20:13) are described in terms used in 1 Enoch 51:1 of bodily resurrection: "And in those days shall the earth also give back that which has been entrusted to it. And Sheol also shall give back that which it has received, and hell shall give back that which it owes." These who are raised, in what can only be a picture of the "second" resurrection, are then thrown into the lake of fire, which is explicitly called "second death" (Rev 20:14). So, it is simply not true that the "second resurrection" is called "the second death"; the second (bodily) resurrection of the wicked occurs before casting them into the lake of fire. Kline's exegetical wire-crossing led him—and those who follow him—to state, "What for others is the first death is for the Christian a veritable resurrection!"[14] The problem with such a statement is that universally in Scripture and the early church, resurrection is the complete opposite of death.[15] In fact, death is the enemy defeated by resurrection (1 Cor 15:20–28).

9. Riddlebarger, *A Case for Amillennialism*, 247.
10. Meredith G. Kline, "The First Resurrection," *WTJ* 37.3 (1975): 366–75.
11. Kline, "The First Resurrection," 372.
12. Kline, "The First Resurrection," 370.
13. Kline, "The First Resurrection," 371.
14. Kline, "The First Resurrection," 371.
15. This precise point is leveled against Kline's thesis in R. Fowler White, "Death and the First Resurrection in Revelation 20: A Response to Meredith G. Kline" (Paper presented at the Eastern Regional Evangelical Theological Society Meeting, Capital Bible Seminary, Lanham, MD, April 3, 1992), 8–9; cf. also Sydney H. T. Page, "Revelation 20 and Pauline Eschatology," *JETS* 23.1 (1980): 31–43, who notes, "Like all attempts to relate the first resurrection to the intermediate state, [Kline's interpretation] faces the objection that the translation

Arguments for Two Physical Resurrections in Revelation 20

The real exegetical problem facing all amillennial interpretations of Revelation 20 concerns the phrase "the rest of the dead (οἱ λοιποὶ τῶν νεκρῶν)" in Revelation 20:5. In every instance of its plural form, οἱ λοιποί ("the remainder") followed by a plural genitive, as we have here, οἱ λοιποί refers to people or items of the same category.[16] The category in Revelation 20:5 is τῶν νεκρῶν ("the dead ones"). Logically, this category ("the dead ones") could be understood as referring either to "spiritually dead ones" or to "physically dead ones." The departure from the group "spiritually dead ones" would be accomplished by "spiritual resurrection." The departure from the group "physically dead ones" would be accomplished by "physical resurrection." At this point, categorical consistency is necessary. One does not depart from the category of "spiritually dead" by physical resurrection; and one does not depart from the category of "physically dead" by spiritual resurrection.

The phrase οἱ λοιποί ("the rest") indicates that the "souls" in verse 4 are a subset of the larger category of τῶν νεκρῶν ("the dead ones"). Already the use of the phrase "the souls of those who had been beheaded (τὰς ψυχὰς τῶν πεπελεκισμένων)" (Rev 20:4) employs imagery that convey the idea of physical death. One cannot conceive of a more direct and specific image for physically dead individuals than being "beheaded." In no instance in the ancient world does the term πελεκίζω, "to behead with an axe," refer to anything other than physical death.[17] So, the inspired vision uses a symbol pointing to physical death, not spiritual death. They had been beheaded because of the word of God and the testimony of Jesus (20:4). Therefore, these saints who have suffered physical death.

Because the vision uses this unequivocal symbol for physical death, it makes the most sense that ἔζησαν ("they lived/came to life") refers to physical resurrection. In fact, the aorist indicative of ἔζησαν most naturally means physical resurrection from the dead (Rom 14:9; Rev 2:8). Though it is used figuratively in the parable of the prodigal son, whose homecoming is described in terms of being "dead and has come to life (νεκρὸς ἦν καὶ ἔζησεν)" (Luke 15:32), in that context, it involves a background in which the lost son was presumed physically dead or "as good as dead." And in Revelation 13:14, the term is used in the vision of the beast "that had been wounded by the sword and yet lived (ἔζησεν)." Whether one believes the passage teaches that the beast had been wounded but survived or that he had died and been raised is really a theological, not an exegetical question. At least in the

---

of the soul of the believer to heaven at death is not spoken of as a resurrection anywhere else in the NT."

16. See Matt 25:11, "the rest of the virgins" were themselves a subset of the virgins; Luke 18:11, "the rest of the men" were themselves men like the self-righteous Pharisee; Acts 2:37; 1 Cor 9:5, "the rest of the apostles" were themselves apostles; 1 Cor 12:13, "the rest of the churches" were also churches; Gal 2:13, "the rest of the Jews" were also themselves Jews; Phil 4:3, "the rest of my co-workers" were also co-workers; 2 Pet 3:16, "the rest of the Scriptures" were also Scriptures; Rev 8:13, "the rest of the sounds of the trumpet" were themselves trumpet sounds like the previous; Rev 9:20, "the rest of the people" were themselves people; Rev 12:17, "the rest of her offspring" were themselves offspring like the former.

17. See BDAG, 794.

symbolism of the vision itself, "one of its heads seemed to have received a death blow (ὡς ἐσφαγμένην εἰς θάνατον), but its fatal wound (ἡ πληγὴ τοῦ θανάτου) had been healed" (Rev 13:3). The term σφάζω means to be murdered or slaughtered: "to slaughter, either animals or persons; in contexts referring to persons, the implication is of violence and mercilessness."[18] Though the symbol of being slaughtered could be taken as indicating something less than literal death in its real-world fulfillment,[19] in the vision itself, the language indicates a wound that causes actual physical death. Therefore, ἔζησαν in the aorist in Revelation 20:4–5 does not mean "continued to live" or "survived." It means "came to life": that is, they were resurrected. Without strong contextual proof to the contrary, it is most naturally read as indicating physical resurrection.

Therefore, it appears the text itself defines the category of τῶν νεκρῶν as "physically dead." This poses a problem for the amillennial interpretation that sees the first resurrection as spiritual, because categorical consistency requires that one is raised physically from physical death or the interpretation will result in the unfortunate dilemma of calling physical death resurrection. And because of the term "the rest" (οἱ λοιποί) demonstrates that the category does not change between the first resurrection and second resurrection, if the first resurrection is physical resurrection from physical death, so too the second resurrection must be physical resurrection from physical death. Logical consistency requires that the category does not change. The specific exegetical and theological issues are more fully explored in the Go Deeper Excursus 20, *A Detailed Examination of the Two Resurrections in Revelation 20*.

Go Deeper Excursus 20

A Detailed Examination of the Two Resurrections in Revelation 20

As demonstrated in Go Deeper Excursus 20, it is my conclusion that an amillennial interpretation of this passage (whether the first resurrection is viewed as the intermediate state or spiritual regeneration) fails to reckon seriously with the exegetical and theological implications of οἱ λοιποὶ τῶν νεκρῶν. The definitional inconsistencies on the one hand and universalist implications on the other inherent in an interpretation that fails to regard τῶν νεκρῶν ("the dead ones") as physical death and ἔζησαν ("came to life") as physical resurrection has not been lost on commentators. In a sermon delivered May 6, 1861, Charles Haddon Spurgeon articulated this puzzling problem with his customary wit:

> I once had the misfortune to listen to an excellent friend of mine who was preaching upon this very text, and I must confess I did not attend with very great patience to his exposition. He said it meant blessed and holy is he who has been born-again, who has been regenerated, and so has had a resurrection from dead works by the resurrection of the Lord Jesus Christ. All the while he was preaching, I could not help but wish that I could propose to him the difficulty to make this metaphorical interpretation agree with the literal fact—that the rest of the dead lived not till

---

18. L&N, 235.

19. But note that the beast "rises up out of the abyss," which suggests he comes from the place of the dead (Rev 11:7).

the thousand years were finished! For if the First Resurrection here spoken of is a metaphorical, or spiritual, or typical resurrection—why the next, where it speaks of the resurrection of the dead, must be spiritual, and mystical, and metaphorical too! Now, no one would agree with this.[20]

The classic nineteenth-century expositor Henry Alford describes the problem this way:

> If, in a passage where *two resurrections* are mentioned, where certain ψυχαὶ ἔζησαν ["souls lived"] at the first, and the rest of the νεκροὶ ἔζησαν ["dead lived"] only at the end of a specified period after that first,—if in such a passage the first resurrection may be understood to mean *spiritual* rising with Christ, while the second means *literal* rising from the grave;—then there is an end of all significance in language, and Scripture is wiped out as a definite testimony to any thing. If the first resurrection is spiritual, then so is the second, which I suppose none will be hardy enough to maintain: but if the second is literal, then so is the first, which in common with the whole primitive Church and many of the best modern expositors, I do maintain.[21]

In light of the lexical, exegetical, and syntactical considerations and striving for definitional consistency, narratival integrity, and theological orthodoxy, the classic Irenaean premillennial understanding of the two resurrections of Revelation 20 leaves us with the least problems.

Do Matthew 25:46 and John 5:28–29 Refute Premillennialism?

Despite the exegetical evidence in favor of a premillennial interpretation of Revelation 20:1–10, some consider "clearer" counterevidence of a single-stage resurrection in the Gospels as powerful enough to tip the balance in the direction of amillennialism.

Matthew 25:46

The context of Matthew 25:46 is the separation of the sheep from the goats, which Jesus says will take place when the Son of Man comes "in his glory, and all the angels with him," when "he will sit on his glorious throne" (Matt 25:31). Following this is an idealized description of a separation between the wicked and the righteous. To assert that this passage is clearer vis-à-vis the highly symbolic apocalyptic imagery of Revelation 20 seems to forget that Jesus is separating "sheep" and "goats"! Both passages are figurative and subject to the cautions related to the interpretation of apocalyptic/prophetic texts.

---

20. Charles Haddon Spurgeon, "The First Resurrection," Sermon 391 (May 5, 1861), in *The Metropolitan Tabernacle Pulpit Sermons*, vol. 7 (London: Passmore & Alabaster, 1861), 346.

21. Henry Alford, *The Greek Testament*, vol. 4 (Boston: Lee and Shepard, 1878), 732.

The first question that must be answered is whether Matthew 25:31–46 describes in detail actual events or if it is, as some suppose, a "parable."[22] That is, are we to imagine an event in which every human being who has ever lived—at least 100 billion, perhaps many, many more—stand before the Lord Jesus in some vast expanse? Or was Jesus painting a picture similar to the parable of the ten virgins (Matt 25:1–13) or the parable of the talents (25:14–30)? If Jesus is setting forth an actual event, the fulfillment of which will have a one-to-one correspondence with Jesus' description, then it would be proper to place it on a timeline and to harmonize it with other passages that establish a chronology of future reward and judgment (e.g., amillennial, premillennial, postmillennial, etc.). However, if Jesus' picture of the coming judgment is more "figure" than "photo," then such a precise reconciliation with a timeline of future events is not only unwarranted but impossible.[23]

Yet Matthew 25:31–46 does not bear the marks of an "apocalyptic vision" with symbolic images seen and heard, requiring an intermediary to provide an interpretation, as we find in apocalyptic material in Daniel, Zechariah, or Revelation. The pericope rather reads like a figurative prophetic word or an eschatological discourse employing similes, metaphors, and Old Testament judgment tropes. This approach, however, does not lend itself to using the passage for establishing a clear chronology of future end-times events.[24] The main features of the passage are the fact of the judgment, its totality, and its ultimate result in the separation of the righteous unto eternal life and the wicked unto eternal judgment.[25] One thing we can be sure about regarding the chronology is that the judgment in view will occur in conjunction with the coming of the Son of Man in glory and his eternal reign as king (Matt. 25:31).[26]

22. Roger L. Hahn, *Matthew: A Commentary for Bible Students* (Indianapolis: Wesleyan, 2007), 301; J. Dwight Pentecost, *The Parables of Jesus: Lessons in Life from the Master Teacher* (Grand Rapids: Kregel, 1998), 153; T. C. Smith, "Claims of Christ: The Parable of the Sheep and the Goats; an Exegesis of Matthew 25:31–46," *Foundations* 19.3 (1976): 204–22.

23. Lamar Cope, "Matthew XXV: 31–46 'The Sheep and the Goats' Reinterpreted," *NovT* 11.1–2 (1969): 43, calls it "a poetic picture of the Last Judgment." Lamar Cope, R. T. France, *The Gospel of Matthew*, The New International Commentary on the New Testament (Grand Rapids: Eerdmans, 2007), 960, says, "Its genre is closer to the majestic visions of divine judgment in the book of Revelation than to synoptic parables." Joachim Jeremias, *The Parables of Jesus*, trans. S. H. Hooke, rev. ed. (New York: Charles Scribner's Sons, 1963), 206, argues that this is not a parable but has parabolic elements in its use of figurative language. Cf. Larry Chouinard, *Matthew*, The College Press NIV Commentary (Joplin, MO: College Press, 1997), 444; Donald A. Hagner, *Matthew 14–28*, Word Biblical Commentary, vol. 33B (Grand Rapids: Zondervan, 2018), 740; and Stuart K. Weber, *Matthew*, vol. 1, Holman New Testament Commentary (Nashville: Broadman & Holman, 2000), 423.

24. Louis Barbieri's precise placement of this at the end of the tribulation prior to the millennium may be generally correct in a premillennial scheme, but the purpose of the eschatological message is not to establish a chronology. See Louis A. Barbieri Jr., "Matthew," in *The Bible Knowledge Commentary: An Exposition of the Scriptures*, ed. John F. Walvoord and Roy B. Zuck, vol. 2 (Wheaton, IL: Victor, 1985), 80.

25. Daniel J. Harrington, *The Gospel of Matthew*, Sacra Pagina Series, vol. 1 (Collegeville, MN: Liturgical, 2007), 310.

26. Hagner, *Matthew 14–28*, 746.

Almost no commentator understands Jesus to be describing a literal gathering of "all the nations" followed by a literal separation of one from the other, at least not in the precise manner envisioned in 25:32–33. The point of the figurative language is that there will be a reckoning for how people treat those in need. The passage does not actually mention resurrection of either the righteous or the wicked. Thus, from a premillennial perspective, it could be taken as a reference to the ultimate separation of the righteous and wicked throughout the kingdom period: from the initial judgment of the wicked at the earthly enthronement to the final judgment at the end of the millennial age. We are told, in summary fashion, what the ultimate destiny of the wicked will be: "Then he will say to those on his left, 'Depart from me, you cursed, into the eternal fire prepared for the devil and his angels'" (Matt 25:41) and "These will go away into eternal punishment, but the righteous into eternal life" (25:46). The terms "punishment" and even "fire" can refer both to the intermediate state of the reprobate as well as to the final "lake of fire" destiny after their resurrection. In other words, "eternal fire" and "eternal punishment" are not technical terms for the destination of the resurrected wicked but general terms for the post-death state of condemnation of the wicked. Their usage does not preclude further "punishment" and "fire" after bodily resurrection.

Another question is whether "all the nations" included in this eschatological message warning refers to all people who have ever lived, thus reflecting something like the great white throne judgment in Revelation 20:11–15 that, like the judgment of Matthew 25:31–46, ends with the wicked cast into fire.[27] Some even read the passage as implying a general resurrection, though that feature is missing.[28] Other interpreters view "all the nations" as a reference to a judgment of all but Jews, whose judgment will somehow fall under the authority of the apostles rather than the Son of Man.[29] Another view sees "all the nations" as a reference to Gentiles who are judged after the coming tribulation period prior to the millennial kingdom: that is, the Gentiles of the future period of judgment who survive the Day of the Lord.[30]

How one determines the scope and scale of the judgment of the nations, then, is determined by one's overall eschatological scheme, which must be established on other grounds. The passage in Matthew 25:31–46 does not itself establish such a chronology. If one's eschatology involves a single resurrection/judgment event followed by the eternal state, as in classic amillennialism, then "all the nations" would include every person who has ever lived—likely resurrected for the purpose

---

27. Leon Morris writes, "That *all the nations* will come before him makes it clear that Jesus is speaking of the final judgment of the whole race." Leon Morris, *The Gospel according to Matthew*, The Pillar New Testament Commentary (Grand Rapids: Eerdmans, 1992), 635. The interpretation that Matt 25:31–46 has in view all humans who have ever lived seems to be the dominant view at least among modern commentators. See Sherman W. Gray, *The Least of My Brothers: Matthew 25:31–46: A History of Interpretation*, ed. Charles Talbert (Atlanta: Scholars, 1989), 257–72.

28. See Andreas J. Köstenberger, Alexander E. Stewart, and Apollo Makara, *Jesus and the Future: Understanding What He Taught about the End Times* (Bellingham, WA: Lexham, 2017), 147.

29. Harrington, *Matthew*, 310–12.

30. Barbieri, "Matthew," 80.

of eternal judgment or eternal blessing.[31] However, if one's eschatology accepts a future tribulation period with both Jewish and Gentile survivors, and if that period precedes an earthly millennial kingdom, as in classic Irenaean premillennialism, then "all the nations" would reasonably be limited to those survivors.[32] The wicked would be judged as part of the satanic regime (in terms of the book of Revelation, as the followers of the beast and false prophet). In that case, then, Jesus' statement that they will be consigned immediately to the eternal fire rather than await the second resurrection and the second death might be understood as a unique situation in which they share the same fate as the one they worshiped during the tribulation—"thrown alive into the lake of fire that burns with sulfur" (Rev 19:20). If, however, one's eschatological expectations exclude a future tribulation and millennium, the scene of Matthew 25:31–46 simply refers to the judgment of all the living at the return of Christ, likely coupled with a general resurrection unto judgment, though the latter is not mentioned in the text.

If one insists on treating "eternal punishment" and "eternal fire" in Matthew 25:41, 46 as more technical synonyms for the ultimate "lake of fire," then it should be noted that at least two figures at the physical return of Christ are banished immediately to the eternal fire at the beginning of the millennium—the beast and false prophet: "And the beast was seized, and with him the false prophet who performed the signs in his presence, by which he deceived those who had received the mark of the beast and those who worshiped his image; these two were thrown alive into the lake of fire, which burns with brimstone" (Rev 19:20). This could mean that the term "lake of fire" in Revelation is not a technical term for the final destination of the wicked, completely distinct from an intermediate condition. Rather, it would be a symbolic representation of the destiny of the wicked from which return is impossible. Simply put, the figure of being cast into "the lake of fire" is a symbol of one's final *destiny*, not one's final *destination*.[33]

Another possibility is that the wicked at the end of the tribulation and beginning of the millennium—those who, we are told in Revelation, worshiped Satan, the beast, and the false prophet—are actually included, along with the objects of their worship, in the lake of fire. That is, they—together with the beast and false prophet—are thrown into the lake of fire upon their deaths, reaching the ultimate place of torment one thousand years earlier than others because of the heinousness of their sin in worshiping the dragon, the beast, and false prophet. In fact, Irenaeus indicated those who served the antichrist would receive immediate banishment to the lake of fire (*Haer.* 5.30.4).

---

31. William Hendriksen, *Exposition of the Gospel according to Matthew*, New Testament Commentary (Grand Rapids: Baker, 1975), 885–86.

32. See a list of six views on the identity of "all the nations" in W. D. Davies and Dale C. Allison Jr., *A Critical and Exegetical Commentary on the Gospel according to Saint Matthew*, vol. 3, International Critical Commentary (London: T&T Clark International, 2004), 422. These include (1) all non-Jews, (2) all non-Christians, (3) all non-Jews who are not Christians, (4) all Christians, (5) Christians alive when Christ returns, and (6) all humanity. The seventh view, all Gentiles—Christian or non-Christian—alive when Christ returns, is a variation of #5. See Eugene W. Pond, "The Background and Timing of the Judgment of the Sheep and Goats," *BSac* 159 (April–June 2002): 215.

33. Cf. Pond, "Background and Timing," 219.

In sum, the eschatological message concerning the judgment of the sheep and the goats can accommodate any millennial position. The ways in which specific elements of the language and imagery are interpreted depend on prior eschatological decisions, which are then brought to the text. An amillennialist and the postmillennialist can see the stylized language as pointing to a single judgment concurrent with the return of Christ as judge, in which all nations (all people) are summoned before the Son of Man (by a general resurrection), resulting in a once-for-all separation to eternal life and eternal condemnation.

The premillennial futurist can interpret the stylized language and imagery as pointing to a judgment of the surviving nations that follows the events of the tribulation period—some believers, some unbelievers. Those who demonstrated their righteousness will be ushered into the kingdom, which commences in the millennium and continues into eternity. Those who demonstrated their unrighteousness will be sent to eternal punishment symbolized by fire—either immediately to what Revelation refers to as the "lake of fire" (at the same time as the beast and false prophet) or eventually after a period of waiting among the condemned, whose eternal judgment is "inevitable" but not "immediate."[34]

It is also possible (perhaps probable), however, that the language and imagery of Jesus' concluding eschatological discourse was never intended to provide basic data for an eschatological timeline but to underscore the inescapability of eschatological judgment and the reality of reward or punishment with reference to one's works of righteousness.[35] In any case, the fact that the language and imagery can accommodate diverse eschatological schemata reinforces the need to establish one's eschatological framework upon a broad biblical-theological-historical foundation.

John 5:28–29

Classic Augustinian amillennial interpreters have cited this passage as proof that the first resurrection in Revelation 20:4–5 is a spiritual resurrection (regeneration) rather than physical. John 5:25 says, "Very truly, I tell you, the hour is coming and is now here when the dead will hear the voice of the Son of God, and those who hear will live." That the phrase καὶ νῦν ἐστιν ("and is now") refers to the present spiritual resurrection is hardly disputed.[36] It should be noted, then, that "the hour" that "is now" (ὥρα . . . νῦν ἐστιν) is not a literal sixty minutes but a very long period

---

34. Pond, "Background and Timing," 219. For a discussion of various views on the identity of "all the nations," see Eugene W. Pond, "Who Are the Sheep and Goats in Matthew 25:31–46?," *BSac* 159.3 (July–September 2002): 288–301.

35. This is the approach taken by Kathleen Weber, "The Image of the Sheep and the Goats in Matthew 25:31–46," *CBQ* 59.4 (October 1997): 657–78.

36. Marcus Dods, *The Gospel of St. John*, vol. 1 (New York: George H. Doran, 1887), 740–41; Andrew T. Lincoln, *The Gospel according to Saint John*, Black's New Testament Commentary (London: Continuum, 2005), 204 (emphasis original); John Peter Lange and Philip Schaff, *A Commentary on the Holy Scriptures: John* (Bellingham, WA: Logos Bible Software, 2008), 190. Cf. J. C. Ryle, *Expository Thoughts on John*, vol. 1 (New York: Robert Carter & Brothers, 1879), 295–96.

of time. This is how the term is used elsewhere in John's Gospel: "Jesus said to her, 'Woman, believe me, the hour is coming (ἔρχεται ὥρα) when you will worship the Father neither on this mountain nor in Jerusalem'" (John 4:21). John 4:23 uses the same kind of statement as 5:25–29: "But the hour is coming (ἔρχεται ὥρα), and is now here (καὶ νῦν ἐστιν), when the true worshipers will worship the Father in spirit and truth" (John 4:23). And John 16:2 says, "They will put you out of the synagogues. Indeed, the hour is coming (ἔρχεται ὥρα) when whoever kills you will think he is offering service to God." In these instances, the term "hour" (ὥρα) indicates a "time" or "period of time"—in fact, an indeterminate period of time that can last days, years, even millennia in the case of John 5:25.

The insistence by amillennial or postmillennial interpreters that John 5:28–29 demands a single-moment general resurrection of the righteous does not follow from the text. If the ὥρα νῦν ἐστιν ("hour that now is") during which the unregenerate can experience spiritual resurrection has lasted nearly two thousand years, there is no reason why the ἔρχεται ὥρα ("coming hour") cannot last for a thousand years, with some resurrected unto eternal life at its beginning and some to eternal condemnation at its end.

In light of this, the hour "during which" (ἐν ᾗ) all will be resurrected simply refers to a "time period during which" resurrection will be accomplished—whether that is a short or long span of time. Jesus said, "Do not be astonished at this, for the hour is coming (ἔρχεται ὥρα) when all who are in their graves will hear his voice and will come out: those who have done good to the resurrection of life, and those who have done evil to the resurrection of condemnation" (John 5:28–29). His statement in John 5:28–29 does not settle any millennial position. He certainly affirms a difference between the present age of spiritual resurrection and a future time of bodily resurrection, but every millennial position already affirms that. Jesus' statement does not establish an eschatological timeline beyond these broad categories. That timeline must be established in passages intended to present an order of events with more precise chronological indicators (such as 1 Cor 15:20–28; Rev 20:1–10).[37]

Summary of Views: Amillennialism, Postmillennialism, and Premillennialism

At the risk of oversimplification, I present the following chart summarizing the general views on particular issues of premillennialists, postmillennialists, and amillennialists. I am aware that these are generalizations and that individuals within these broad perspectives may hold unique positions or even hybrid positions that do not exactly match this summary chart. Nevertheless, this does present a sort of "average" of each tradition with regard to certain issues for the purpose of comparison and contrast.

---

37. See entries for ὥρα in standard lexica like BDAG, 1102–3; Henry George Liddell, Robert Scott, and Henry Stuart Jones, *A Greek-English Lexicon* (Oxford: Clarendon, 1996), 2035–36.

Issue	Premillennialism	Postmillennialism	Amillennialism
Christ's physical return	Christ's physical return comes before the millennium.	Christ's physical return comes after the millennium.	Christ's physical return comes after the millennium.
Relationship between Rev 19:11–20 and Christ's return	The yet-future millennium is a long period between the return of Christ and physical resurrection of the righteous and physical resurrection of the wicked.	The yet-future millennium is a long period between the commencement of the earthly golden age accompanying the victory of the gospel and return of Christ and general resurrection.	The already-present millennium is a long period fixed between the first advent of Christ and the physical return of Christ and general resurrection.
Duration and timing of the millennium in Rev 20	The yet-future millennium is a long period between the return of Christ and physical resurrection of the righteous and physical resurrection of the wicked.	The yet-future millennium is a long period between the commencement of the earthly golden age accompanying the victory of the gospel and return of Christ and general resurrection.	The already-present millennium is a long period fixed between the first advent of Christ and the physical return of Christ and general resurrection.
Nature of the first resurrection in Rev 20	The first resurrection is physical, already begun with Christ's resurrection and completed with the righteous at Christ's return.	The first resurrection is spiritual (regeneration) or metaphorical (conversion of the world by the gospel).	The first resurrection is spiritual (regeneration) or related to the intermediate state.
Nature of the second resurrection in Rev 20	The second resurrection is physical and includes all the wicked to eternal condemnation.	The second resurrection is physical and includes all righteous to eternal life and all wicked to eternal condemnation.	The second resurrection is physical and includes all righteous to eternal life and all wicked to eternal condemnation.
Nature of the binding of Satan in Rev 20	Only partially restrained now, Satan will be fully bound and completely banished during the millennium.	Partially restrained now, Satan may be increasingly restrained and bound during the coming millennial age.	Satan's present partial restraint constitutes a fulfillment of his binding and banishing during the present age.

While all three views of Revelation 20 fall within the bounds of orthodox Christian theology and have enjoyed historical precedence, I have argued that the classic Irenaean premillennial view of the second-century fathers rests on the strongest exegetical foundations. In the next chapter we will take a step beyond the intermediate period of the millennium to the question of the ultimate renewal of creation—"the new heavens and the new earth."

13

THE MILLENNIAL RENEWAL OF HEAVEN AND EARTH[1]

But when this present fashion of things passes away, and
man has been renewed, and flourishes in an incorruptible
state, so as to preclude the possibility of becoming old,
then there shall be the new heaven and the new earth.

Irenaeus, *Against Heresies* 5.36.1

According to one popular view today, the present world will be annihilated. In its place, God will create a completely new heavens and new earth *ex nihilo*.[2] Those who propagate this view rely on a number of Old and New Testament passages that describe a time when heaven and earth will apparently "pass away" or "perish" (Ps 102:25–26 [quoted in Heb 1:10–12]; Matt 24:35; Mark 13:31; Luke 21:33). With vivid images, Isaiah 24:20 pictures the fall of the world: "The earth reels to and fro like a drunkard and it totters like a shack, for its transgression is heavy upon it, and it will fall, never to rise again." Perhaps the most powerful statements that seem to teach the ultimate destruction of the universe are found in 2 Peter 3:10 and Revelation 20:11 and 21:1.[3] On the surface, these Old and New Testament texts seem to carry a degree of finality—utter destruction of the present heavens and earth and a replacement with a completely new physical universe.

---

1. This section is adapted from material first appearing in my article, Michael J. Svigel, "Extreme Makeover: Heaven and Earth Edition—Will God Annihilate the World and Re-Create It *Ex Nihilo*?," *BSac* 171.4 (October–December 2014): 401–17.

2. See, e.g., Eric Fuchs and Pierre Reymond, *La deuxième épitre de saint Pierre, l'épitre de saint Jude*, 2nd ed., Commentaire du Nouveau Testament (deuxième série), vol. 13b (Genève: Labor et Fides, 1988), 121; Otto Knoch, *Der Erste und Zweite Petrusbrief, Der Judasbrief*, Regensburger Neues Testament, ed. Jost Eckert and Otto Kuss (Regensburg: Friedrich Pustet, 1990), 285; John MacArthur Jr., *2 Peter and Jude*, The MacArthur New Testament Commentary (Chicago: Moody, 2005), 125; Grant R. Osborne, *Revelation*, Baker Exegetical Commentary on the New Testament, ed. Moisés Silva (Grand Rapids: Baker, 2002), 730; and John F. Walvoord, "Revelation," in John F. Walvoord and Roy B. Zuck, *The Bible Knowledge Commentary: New Testament Edition* (Wheaton, IL: Victor, 1983), 983.

3. Robert L. Thomas, *Revelation 8–22: An Exegetical Commentary* (Chicago: Moody, 1995), 440, notes that the language of 20:11 and 21:1 "is the decisive contextual feature that determines this to be a reference to an entirely new creation." Some also regard Rev 16:12–16 to be a summary of the final judgment, which contains language and imagery reiterated in Rev 20:11. See G. K. Beale, *The Book of Revelation*, The New International Greek Testament Commentary, ed. I. Howard Marshall and Donald A. Hagner (Grand Rapids: Eerdmans, 1999), 398–99.

Yet others come to completely opposite conclusions. Instead of expecting an annihilation of the present universe followed by a recreation out of nothing, they anticipate a "*transition* not extinction" of creation.[4] In this view, "neither heaven nor earth will be annihilated,"[5] but the coming judgment will purify, change, and renew the world.[6] The renewalists also cite passages that appear to indicate a continued existence of the physical creation, which will be redeemed and renewed but not annihilated and recreated (Gen 8:21–22; 48:4; Ps 15:5; 89:36–38; 119:90; 148:3–6; Eccl 1:4; Matt 19:28; Rom 8:19–22; Acts 3:21).[7]

So, which is it? Will this present creation be utterly annihilated and replaced by a new creation *ex nihilo* as some insist? Or will the present creation, subject to corruption, be purged, purified, and regenerated by the redemptive work of God, as the renewalists argue?

The Fathers and the Future of Creation

Around the year AD 180, Irenaeus of Lyons wrote:

> Neither is the substance nor the essence of the creation annihilated (for faithful and true is He who has established it), but "the fashion of the world passes away;" [1 Cor. 7:41]. . . . But when this present fashion of things passes away, and man has been renewed, and flourishes in an incorruptible state, so as to preclude the possibility of becoming old, then there shall be the new heaven and the new earth, in which the new man shall remain continually, always holding fresh converse with God. (*Haer.* 5.36.1)

Irenaeus's amillennial counterpart, Origen of Alexandria, held an identical view. Writing around AD 220, he also explicitly rejected the idea of a complete annihilation of the universe. After quoting 1 Corinthians 7:31 and Psalm 102:26, he wrote:

> For if the heavens are to be changed, assuredly that which is changed does not perish, and if the fashion of the world passes away, it is by no means an annihilation or destruction of their material substance that is shown to take place, but a kind of change of quality and transformation of appearance. Isaiah also, in declaring prophetically that there will be a new heaven and a new earth, undoubtedly suggests a similar view. For this renewal of heaven and earth, and this transmutation of the form of the present world, and this changing of the heavens will undoubtedly

---

4. Joseph A. Seiss, *The Apocalypse: Lectures on the Book of Revelation*, 6th ed. (New York: Charles C. Cook, 1900; repr., Grand Rapids: Zondervan, 1950), 484.

5. Henry C. Thiessen, *Lectures in Systematic Theology* (Grand Rapids: Eerdmans, 1949), 516.

6. Wayne Grudem, *Bible Doctrine: Essential Teachings of the Christian Faith*, ed. Jeff Purswell (Grand Rapids: Zondervan, 1999), 467; cf. Anthony A. Hoekema, *The Bible and the Future* (Grand Rapids: Eerdmans, 1994), 39.

7. Philip Edgcumbe Hughes, *The Book of Revelation* (Grand Rapids: Eerdmans, 1990), 221–22.

be prepared for those who are walking along that way which we have pointed out above. (*Princ.* 1.6.5 [*ANF* 4])

Likewise, around AD 300, Methodius of Olympus wrote:

But it is not satisfactory to say that the universe will be utterly destroyed, and sea and air and sky will be no longer. For the whole world will be deluged with fire from heaven, and burnt for the purpose of purification and renewal; it will not, however, come to complete ruin and corruption. . . . God therefore ordered the creation with a view to its existence and continuance. (*Res.*1.8 [*ANF* 6])

Perhaps the best representative of patristic amillennial eschatology, Augustine of Hippo, wrote in the fifth century:

For when the judgment is finished, this heaven and earth shall cease to be, and there will be a new heaven and a new earth. For this world shall pass away by trans-mutation, not by absolute destruction. And therefore the apostle says, "For the figure of this world passeth away. I would have you be without anxiety." The figure, therefore, passes away, not the nature. . . . And by this universal conflagration the qualities of the corruptible elements which suited our corruptible bodies shall ut-terly perish, and our substance shall receive such qualities as shall, by a wonderful transmutation, harmonize with our immortal bodies, so that, as the world itself is renewed to some better thing, it is fitly accommodated to men, themselves renewed in their flesh to some better thing. (*Civ.* 20.14, 16 [*NPNF¹* 2])

Rather than a cherry-picking from the patristic period, these voices from the second through fifth centuries actually represent a unified chorus of fathers who shared the view that this created universe would not cease to exist in a final conflagra-tion.[8] Instead, the fires of judgment will purge and purify the present material world, renewing and readying it for eternal life.[9] Indeed, to find contrary voices during the patristic period, one has to peer across the boundary line of orthodox Christianity and look to the gnostics who delighted in an eschatology that anticipated the total annihilation of the physical universe.[10] Craig Blaising notes, "The idea of cosmic an-nihilation properly belongs to Gnostic eschatology."[11] The patristic theme of renewal, however—whether expressed by premillennialists or amillennialists—resounded

8. Cf. especially the "capstone" of Eastern Orthodox theological thought, John of Da-mascus, *Fid. Orth.* 2.6, who in the eighth century wrote, "Wherefore it has been said, *They will perish, but Thou dost endure*: nevertheless, the heavens will not be utterly destroyed. For they will wax old and be wound round as a covering, and will be changed, and there will be a new heaven and a new earth."

9. Cf. 2 Clem. 16.3.

10. Cf., e.g., *On the Origin of the World* (NHL II, 5 125.32–127.17), in James M. Robin-son, ed., *The Nag Hammadi Library in English*, 3rd. ed. (San Francisco: HarperSanFrancisco, 1990), 188–89.

11. Craig A. Blaising, "The Day of the Lord Will Come: An Exposition of 2 Peter 3:1–18," *BSac* 169.4 (2012): 398.

with regularity throughout not only the medieval but also the Protestant periods.[12] Few details of eschatology can claim such historical tenacity as the expectation of a renovated rather than a recreated universe. In fact, in the late nineteenth century, Charles Hodge could still call the view of the "renovated earth" the "common opinion," though he pointed to post-Reformation Lutheran scholars who introduced the interpretation of "the absolute annihilation of the world."[13]

Today, the ancient and longstanding tradition of a renewed creation has waned in some circles. Whereas most fathers, theologians, and reformers read relevant "new creation" Scripture in light of the Bible's overarching narrative of creation, fall, and redemption, some modern scholars began to deconstruct this narrative based on what they regarded as more literal readings of the texts, especially Revelation 20:11 and 21:1.[14] Also, whereas proponents of the majority view of a renewed creation strived for theological consistency with the orthodox doctrine of a resurrection body that stood in full continuity with the body that had died, some modern theologians have felt no obligation to retain this doctrinal correspondence.[15] Finally, while classic commentators strived to interpret Scripture within a decidedly anti-gnostic worldview, some twentieth-century evangelicals were not afraid to come to gnostic-like conclusions in their interpretations regarding anthropology,[16] soteriology,[17] or eschatology. The gnostic view of an annihilated universe due to its essential wickedness once again became a viable option.

Earlier in this book, I touched on the issue of the renewal of creation in connection with other passages of Scripture, especially in discussions on Isaiah 11:6–9; 35:6–7; 43:19–20; 51:11, Matthew 19:28; and Acts 3:21. In keeping with the overall strategy of this book, this chapter defends the second-century Irenaean premillennial understanding of the "new heavens and new earth" as a renovation of the present physical universe. I argue that this interpretation of the millennial period

12. Cf. Daniel Keating, *First and Second Peter, Jude*, Catholic Commentary on Sacred Scripture, ed. Peter S. Williamson and Mary Healy (Grand Rapids: Baker, 2011), 185. See Anselm, *Cur Deus Homo* 1.18; Aquinas, *Summa Theologica*, Part 3 (Supp.) Q. 91, Art. 1. On the Protestant side, see Martin Luther, *The Epistles of St. Peter and St. Jude*, trans. John Nicholas Lenker (Minneapolis: Lutherans in All Lands, 1904), 365; John Calvin, *Commentary on the Book of the Prophet Isaiah*, vol. 4, trans. William Pringle (Edinburgh: Calvin Translation Society, 1853), 398–99; John Calvin, *Commentaries on the Catholic Epistles*, trans. John Owen (Edinburgh: Calvin Translation Society, 1855), 421.

13. Charles Hodge, *Systematic Theology*, vol. 3 (New York: Scribner, 1872), 854.

14. Cf. John F. Walvoord, *Revelation*, The John Walvoord Prophecy Commentaries, ed. Philip E. Rawley and Mark Hitchcock (Chicago: Moody, 2011), 317, 326.

15. Or they have used the correspondence to argue in a different direction. See Murray J. Harris, *Raised Immortal: Resurrection and Immortality in the New Testament* (Grand Rapids: Eerdmans, 1983), 168–71.

16. See the helpful summary and critique of the evangelical tendency toward the classically gnostic "trichotomy" anthropology in Kim Riddlebarger, "Trichotomy: A Beachhead for Gnostic Influences," *Modern Reformation* 14.4 (1995): 22–26.

17. See Earl D. Radmacher, *Salvation*, Swindoll Leadership Library, ed. Charles R. Swindoll and Roy B. Zuck (Nashville: Word, 2000), 107–9, where the discussion of the "new person inside" created by the divine "seed" in regeneration is sharply contrasted with the "old man," the former being sinless, the latter the source of sin.

as a progressive realization of the "new heavens and new earth" reflects a better canonical and theological reading of the relevant biblical texts. By tracing the theme
of the "new heavens and new earth" from its original Old Testament context to its
final articulation in Revelation 21, I will argue that a canonical reading of these passages favors the view of the renewalists. Recreationists, on the other hand, overturn
the classic reading with a rebuttable exegesis of one or two selected texts.

Isaiah's Instructive Imagery

The first place in which we find a description of the "new heavens and new earth"
is Isaiah 65:17–25. In this passage, the Lord God declares, "For I am about to
create new heavens and a new earth; the former things shall not be remembered
or come to mind" (Isa 65:17; cf. 66:22). Shed of its context, this verse could be
interpreted as creation *ex nihilo* following an annihilation of the universe, but in
its context the passage emphasizes the new *quality* of the world, not a new world
per se.[18]

Isaiah 66:15–22 also refers back to this renewal of the current heavens and earth
under the messianic reign. Following a period of judgment by fire (Isa 66:15–16),
nations will be converted and Israel will be regathered (Isa 66:17–21). Then God
swears by the new conditions of the world described earlier in Isaiah 65: "For as
the new heavens and the new earth, which I will make, shall remain before me, says
the Lord, so shall your descendants and your name remain" (66:22). Nothing in
the "new heavens and new earth" prophecy of Isaiah suggests an annihilation and
new creation *ex nihilo*. In fact, the symbol of fiery judgment described in 66:15–16
anticipates survivors and a continuation of the world after the fire (66:17, 19–20).

According to the classic interpretation, Isaiah's imagery of the new heavens and
new earth as the renewed condition of this world after a purifying conflagration
stands as the background of later canonical development. Therefore, whenever
the phrase "new heavens and new earth" appears in the canon, these subsequent
references find their inspiration and point of departure from the original use in
Isaiah 65:17–25.[19]

This kind of renewalist reading is confirmed in the next place that "new creation" language appears in the canon: 2 Corinthians 5:17. In keeping with this same
kind of "new creation" idea of redemption and renewal, Paul writes, "So if anyone is
in Christ, there is a new creation: everything old has passed away; look, new things
have come into being!" Here, believers have not ceased to exist only to be re-created

---

18. Cf. Beale, *Revelation*, 1043.

19. The principle of "prophetic telescoping" can be applied only when it fits an exegesis
of the passage, as in Dan 12:2, which lacks clear chronological indicators: the destinies of
the two groups in Dan 12:2, indicated individually as אלה, is distinguished by a vague ו,
which later revelation could separate with a greater span of time or with other events (cf.
similar minimal syntax in Isa 61:1–2; John 5:28–29). "Prophetic telescoping" is not a sound
explanation if it ignores the syntax and argument of the text, as in Isa 65:17–25, in which the
description of restoration that follows the introduction of the שמים חדשים וארץ חדשה is
a straightforward unpacking of the conditions of that new reality.

ex nihilo. Neither have their old ways entirely vanished. Rather, the salvation of a sinner is a regeneration, renewal, and redemption of the old and a transformation into something qualitatively new (Titus 3:5). This progressive sanctification in the present has a view toward entire sanctification upon the believer's resurrection, which itself is in continuity with the present physical life as a seed stands in continuity with its plant (1 Cor 15:42–44).

Peter's Apocalyptic Problem

The next appearance of "new creation" imagery is found in 2 Peter 3. At first glance, Peter seems to assert that the universe—even the *elements* themselves—will melt with intense heat prior to the creation of a new heavens and new earth (2 Pet 3:10). Is this not a clear support for an annihilation of the present creation in preparation for a completely new creation? To answer this, we need to examine Peter's entire argument more closely. Let me first set up the general context of the letter.

Throughout Peter's second epistle, he references the coming Day of the Lord—the judgment that culminates in the second coming of Christ (see discussion in chapters 15–17). In response to skepticism about the Lord's future return, Peter draws on the analogy of the flood in the ancient world—a world that was utterly destroyed by water: "The world of that time was deluged with water and perished" (3:6). So, just as the initial order of the world of humanity, animals, and even the earth itself was "destroyed" by the flood, leaving only a remnant to return and repopulate the earth, the future coming judgment of fire will similarly purge our present world of the godless (3:7).

Considering that Peter punctuates his end-times description with the "new heavens and new earth" language of Isaiah 65:17, it seems most likely that his source of inspiration for the judgment by fire comes from Isaiah 66:15–16, thus connecting God's coming judgment by fire in Isaiah with Christ's imminent judgment of the world at his return.[20] This, then, would correspond to the anticipated "day of the Lord," during which the current world system will be destroyed, just as the pre-flood world "passed away," having been replaced by a new order after the flood. Peter refers to this coming judgment as "the day of the Lord" that will come "like a thief" (3:10). There seems to be no reason for understanding this future judgment by fire as anything other than the early church's anticipated tribulation period, to which Jesus, Paul, and John already referred in similar terms (Matt 24:42–43; 1 Thess 5:2; Rev 3:3; 16:15). This coming judgment is what Peter describes with vivid terms of destruction in 3:10–12.

Several exegetically significant issues arise in this passage. First, who or what are the "elements" that will be destroyed in verse 10? The Greek word στοιχεῖα ("elements") must not be read anachronistically as "the basic atomic components that make up the universe."[21] Rather, three distinct interpretations have been

---

20. Louis A. Barbieri, *First and Second Peter* (Chicago: Moody, 1977), 122.
21. MacArthur, *2 Peter and Jude*, 124. See Gordon H. Clark, *1 & 2 Peter* (Phillipsburg, NJ: Presbyterian and Reformed, 1980), 72.

held.[22] One might understand στοιχεῖα as wicked angelic beings whose destruction will come at the return of Christ, reflecting the imagery of the removal of heavenly and earthly powers in Isaiah 24:21–22 or 34:4.[23] A majority of modern exegetes interpret the passage as celestial bodies like the sun, moon, planets, and stars,[24] or link the first and second views.[25] Still others see στοιχεῖα as referring to the "elements" regarded by the ancient philosophers as the building blocks of the world: earth, water, and air, with fire itself being the element used for purging the others.[26] At least one commentator suggests that Peter intended all three uses of στοιχεῖα to be understood.[27]

Regardless of which view one takes with regard to the meaning of the word στοιχεῖα, it is important to observe that 2 Peter 3:10 and 12 do not say that "*all* elements" or even "*the* elements" will be destroyed, but "elements." This lack of the article may very well indicate that the most severe fiery judgments of the coming day of the Lord, in which elements are destroyed, will be localized and limited, not universalized and total. In this case, Peter can be read in connection with the later revelation of the future judgment in Revelation 8:1–9:21; 16:1–21, wherein fire is used to judge various elements of this world.

This judgment will result in a radical change to the contents and appearance of the created order, but not its total annihilation. This drastic change—not annihilation—of elements in judgment is also seen in Wisdom of Solomon 19:18–20: "For the elements (στοιχεῖα) were changed in themselves by a kind of harmony, like as in a psaltery notes change the name of the tune, and yet are always sounds.

---

22. For historical supporters of each of the three views, see J. N. D. Kelly, *A Commentary on the Epistles of Peter and of Jude*, Harper's New Testament Commentaries, ed. Henry Chadwick (New York: Harper & Row, 1969), 364. Peter Davids writes, "All three of these suggestions have a *prima facie* validity and fit the culture in which 2 Peter was written." Peter H. Davids, *The Letters of 2 Peter and Jude*, The Pillar New Testament Commentary, ed. D. A. Carson (Grand Rapids: Eerdmans, 2006), 284.

23. Cf. 1 En 60.12, Jub. 2.2, Gal 4:3, 9; Col 2:8, 20. Modern proponents of this view are rare.

24. Paul Gardner, *2 Peter and Jude*, Focus on the Bible Commentaries (Geanies House: Christian Focus, 1998), 121; Keating, *First and Second Peter, Jude*, 181; A. R. C. Leaney, *The Letters of Peter and Jude*, The Cambridge Bible Commentary on the New English Bible (Cambridge: Cambridge University Press, 1967), 134; Robert Leighton and Griffith Thomas, *1, 2 Peter*, The Crossway Classic Commentaries, ed. Alister McGrath and J. I. Packer (Wheaton, IL: Crossway, 1999), 284; and Richard B. Vinson, Richard F. Wilson, and Watson E. Mills, *1 & 2 Peter, Jude*, Smyth & Helwys Bible Commentary, ed. R. Alan Culpepper (Macon, GA: Smyth & Helwys, 2010), 354.

25. Davids, *2 Peter and Jude*, 285; David G. Horrell, *The Epistles of Peter and Jude* (Peterborough, UK: Epworth, 1998), 180.

26. Fuchs and Reymond, *La deuxième épitre de saint Pierre, l'épitre de saint Jude*, 118. Some proponents of this interpretation include Clark, *1 & 2 Peter*, 72; George H. Cramer, *First and Second Peter* (Chicago: Moody, 1967), 121; and Jerome H. Neyrey, *2 Peter, Jude: A New Translation with Introduction and Commentary*, The Anchor Bible, vol. 37c (New York: Doubleday, 1993), 243.

27. Lewis R. Donelson, *1 & 2 Peter and Jude: A Commentary*, The New Testament Library, ed. C. Clifton Black, M. Eugene Boring, John T. Carroll (Louisville: Westminster John Knox, 2010), 277.

. . . For earthly things were turned into watery, and the things, that before swam in the water, now went upon the ground. The fire had power in the water, forgetting its own virtue: and the water forgot its own quenching nature." In any case, exegetes go far beyond what the text asserts when they conclude that Peter had in mind the absolute dissolution of all atomic particles in the universe when he referred to the destruction of the στοιχεῖα in 2 Peter 3:10 and 12. The text simply does not say this.

But what, then, does Peter actually teach?

He anticipates this judgment of fire as coming upon the present world system at the return of Christ: that is, during the coming day of the Lord. This period of judgment will destroy the present system, including evil and sin. It will also include the destruction of demons and a razing of the world's geography.[28] In fact, the fires pictured in 2 Peter 3:10, 12–13 are best interpreted as purifying fires, likely drawing on metallurgical imagery of heating for the sake of purifying and strengthening, not annihilating (Mal 3:2–4; 4:1–3).[29]

Peter describes the new world established after the return of Christ and his fiery judgment thusly: "But, in accordance with his promise, we wait for new heavens and a new earth," qualifying this statement with regard to its righteous quality, not its creation *ex nihilo*: "where righteousness is at home" (3:13). His reference to the "new heavens and new earth" must be understood in his own context of the anticipated coming of Christ in judgment of the present world during the tribulation and in light of the "new heavens and new earth" promises in Isaiah 65 and 66, both of which refer to the restoration of the world after the coming of the Lord "in fire" (Isa 66:15–16). Therefore, we must understand the destruction language of 2 Peter 3:10–13 as a vivid picture of judgment referring to the imminent day of the Lord and the coming of Christ preceding the regeneration of the world (Matt 19:28). This corresponds with Peter's earlier expectation of a universal restoration summed up in his message of Acts 3:19–21.

In sum, a contextual and canonical exegesis of 2 Peter 3 does not demand annihilation or "uncreation" of the universe and its physical elements. Nor is the "new heavens and new earth" in 2 Peter 3 a reference to a re-creation *ex nihilo* of a world that has no relationship to the present physical world. Just as the pre-flood earth was renewed after the judgment of water, so the current world will be renewed after a judgment of fire. However, Peter's language implies that the coming judgment at the return of Christ will be analogous to the world-altering flood of Noah, as Henry Alford says, "The flood did not annihilate the earth, but changed it; and as the new earth was the consequence of the flood, so the final new heavens and earth shall be of the fire."[30]

---

28. H. A. Ironside, *Lectures on the Book of Revelation* (New York: Loizeaux Brothers, 1930), 344.

29. See the excellent discussion in Blaising, "The Day of the Lord Will Come," 395–99.

30. Henry Alford, *Alford's Greek Testament: An Exegetical and Critical Commentary*, 5th ed., vol. 4, part 2 (Grand Rapids: Guardian, 1976), 418.

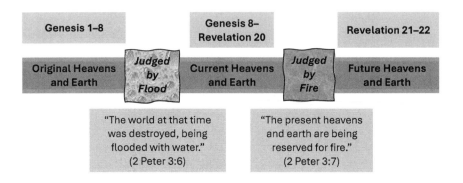

How "New" Are the New Heavens and Earth?

It is a general methodological assumption of the early church fathers, as well as those modern renewalists, that John's vision of the new heavens and new earth in Revelation 21 must be read in light of Isaiah 65–66.[31] To read this as annihilation and re-creation *ex nihilo* is to read into it meanings for "pass away" and "new heavens and new earth" that are foreign to the sum of biblical teaching.

The original terms often translated in the New Testament as "to pass away" do not mean "to be annihilated."[32] The terms are neutral, referring simply to "going away," or "departing." The term ἀπέρχομαι means "go away, depart" from a person or thing.[33] Jesus uses it of his ascension to heaven: "It is to your advantage that I go away (ἀπέλθω), for if I do not go away, the Advocate will not come to you" (John 16:7). And elsewhere in Revelation, it is used of one of the woes simply coming to an end: "The first woe has passed (ἀπῆλθεν)" (Rev 9:12; cf. 11:14). In 18:14 and 21:4, the term refers to previous conditions of the world that had come and gone.

The other term, παρέρχομαι, can mean "to come to an end and so no longer be there, pass away, disappear."[34] Drawing on language describing the transformation of creation during the messianic age in Isaiah 65:17, Paul uses the term παρέρχομαι to refer to the old things of the believer's life that have "passed away" (2 Cor 5:17). This indicates a transformation and renewal of a person's life and character, not an annihilation of the old person and a replacement by the new. First Peter 4:3 uses the same term in a similar sense: "For the time already past (παρεληλυθὼς) is sufficient for you to have carried out the desire of the Gentiles" (NASB). The time of former sin has "passed away." Jesus uses the term to describe the "passing away" of heaven and earth in contrast to the words of the law and his own words, which will never pass away (Matt 24:35; Mark 13:31; Luke 16:17; 21:31). It is likely

---

31. Cf. Beale, *Revelation*, 1041.

32. The text of Rev 21:1 contains a variant reading here, with 𝔓²⁴ and some other later manuscripts along with the Vulgate and other early Latin witnesses reading ἀπέρχομαι, while other early witnesses read παρέρχομαι. Regardless of which reading is accepted, neither refer to "annihilation" or "destruction."

33. BDAG, 102.

34. BDAG, 776.

Jesus used the passing away of "heaven and earth" in the same sense as intended in Revelation 21:1.

Even if we understand the vision of passing away to have a direct correspondence with the anticipated events, the image is not necessarily picturing annihilation of the old to make way for the ontologically new.[35] The uses of the Greek terms for "pass away" in 2 Peter 3:10 and Revelation 21:1 could refer to a radical transformation of the quality of something rather than to its absolute destruction. This is consistent with the general meaning of καινός, "new," which "usually indicates newness in terms of quality, not time."[36] Read in this light, two of the passages that seemed to suggest annihilation actually fit the perspective of a qualitative redemption, not quantitative substitution.

We finally arrive at Scripture's last reference to the new heaven and new earth. Revelation 21:1 says, "Then I saw a new heaven and a new earth, for the first heaven and the first earth had passed away, and the sea was no more." John said he saw the first heaven and first earth pass away,[37] which was part of the vision of the heaven and earth fleeing from the presence of God in Revelation 20:11. Remembering that John saw a series of symbolic visions throughout the book, we must allow the text itself to interpret what John was seeing here.[38] Though it is possible that the symbolic vision was meant to represent a complete annihilation and re-creation, it is just as possible that it symbolized an "extreme makeover" of the present creation: a "new and improved" version that bears little resemblance to the past order of things.[39]

It is my contention that immediately following John's vision of the fleeing of heaven and earth and its replacement by a new creation, the voice in Revelation 21:3–5 actually interprets the vision for us in keeping with the idea of qualitative renewal and redemption similar to Isaiah and 2 Peter.[40]

> And I heard a loud voice from the throne saying, "See, the home of God is among mortals. He will dwell with them; they will be his peoples, and God himself will be with them and be their God; he will wipe every tear from their eyes. Death will be no more; mourning and crying and pain will be no more, for the first things have passed away." And the one who was seated on the throne said, "See, I am making all things new." Also he said, "Write this, for these words are trustworthy and true." (Rev 21:3–5)

---

35. See Seiss, *Apocalypse*, 484.

36. Beale, *Revelation*, 1040; Hoekema, *The Bible and the Future*, 280.

37. If ἀπέρχομαι is the original reading in Rev 21:1, 4, then the translation "passed away" gives a wrong impression; a better rendering would be "the first heaven and the first earth had passed" and "the first things have passed"—that is, the former conditions of the creation will be a thing of the past when the conditions of Rev 21 are reached.

38. The symbolic vision of a vanishing creation and the symbolic appearance of a new creation need not be taken any more literally than the vision of a seven-headed monster (Rev 13) or a seven-eyed lamb (Rev 5). John's symbolic visions must be interpreted contextually and canonically. See discussion on preinterpretive issues related to the book of Revelation in Go Deeper Excursus 16. The interpretation of this vision must be the decisive factor, not the uninterpreted vision itself (contra Thomas, *Revelation 8–22*, 440).

39. See Beale, *Revelation*, 1040.

40. Beale, *Revelation*, 1046.

Revelation 21:4 interprets the symbols of the vision that heaven and earth "passed away": "the first things have passed away." What things are these? Not elements, atoms, or molecules, but the evil order of things have "passed away (ἀπῆλθαν)": death, wickedness, grief, suffering, pain, degeneration, and deterioration that had long held all physical and spiritual elements in bondage. Thus the vision of Revelation 21:1–2 and its God-breathed interpretation in verses 3–5 neatly build on, tie up, and complete the "new creation" theme developed throughout the Old and New Testaments, including Paul's own anticipation of cosmic redemption in Romans 8, when "the creation itself will be set free from its enslavement to decay and will obtain the freedom of the glory of the children of God" (8:21), which will coincide with the bodily resurrection of the saints at the return of Christ (8:23).

Renewal of Heaven and Earth as Paradise Unleashed

Many writers from the patristic, medieval, and Reformation eras advanced a view of the new heavens and new earth as cosmic renewal following purifying fire rather than cosmic recreation *ex nihilo* following an annihilating holocaust. I have demonstrated that such a reading is not only allowed by a careful exegesis of the relevant texts, but that it also presents a more cogent picture of the canonical reading from Isaiah, through Paul and Peter, and into the book of Revelation.[41] It also represents a reading of the texts that is more consistent with the redemptive themes of Scripture and an orthodox emphasis on the cleansing and restoration of creation rather than the gnostic notion of utterly annihilating an unredeemable creation that is evil per se. And it is consistent with the expectations of both Jews and Christians in the first century. Göran Lennartsson notes, "Jews did not view the future as the end of human history but rather as the beginning of a restoration. In this restoration Israel is a part, and has a role to play, which will finally result in full restoration of nature and the universe. In this process, when the covenant promises to Israel are fulfilled, parts of the future blessings and bliss are already experienced. However, the major fulfilment, when the messianic era breaks through, is a direct intervention by God with cosmic dimensions in a new paradise creation."[42]

The classic renewalists have always insisted that God's plan is not to surrender to the destructive work of Satan, but to reverse the degeneration of creation through resurrection and regeneration.[43] As our human bodies have been redeemed and will be resurrected and glorified, so the physical world will be redeemed, restored, and glorified at the return and reign of Christ (Rom. 8:18–25).[44]

---

41. See Ironside, *Lectures on Revelation*, 350–52, who notes that Rev 21:1 "reminds us of Isaiah's prophecy" and says, "It is to these promises that the apostle Peter refers in his second epistles" (351). Ironside applies all of these passages to the millennium (350).

42. Lennartsson, *Refreshing & Restoration*, 163.

43. See R. C. Sproul, who appeals to God's overall plan of redemption: "God has no design to annihilate this present world. His plan is to redeem it." In *1–2 Peter*, St. Andrew's Expositional Commentary (Wheaton, IL: Crossway, 2011), 285.

44. G. B. Caird, *The Revelation of Saint John*, Black's New Testament Commentary 19 (London: Black, 1966), 265–66.

The third-century Christian Latin poet Commodianus put it beautifully: "He who made the sky, and the earth, and the salt seas, decreed to give us back again ourselves in a golden age" (Commodianus, *Instructions* 29 [*ANF* 4:208]). And in the second century, Theophilus of Antioch anticipated a restoration of paradise on earth and a return of humanity to this Edenic state, improved by resurrection and immortality, which will occur "after the resurrection and judgment" (*Ad Autolycum* 2.26).

In keeping with this expectation, in the early fathers, there is a direct connection between the Edenic paradise of Adam and Eve, the superterrestrial paradise of departed saints, and the future earthly paradise of the millennial kingdom, during which creation will be progressively renewed. In our discussion of the biblical concept of the kingdom of God, we have already seen that when Adam and Eve were created, they were placed in paradise that God had planted and that was distinct from the rest of the world in its superior quality (see chapters 2 and 4 above). Joachim Jeremias notes:

> The hope of a future time of bliss, which is commonly attested in the OT, may be traced back to long before the Exile. The depiction of this age uses paradise motifs. The last time is like the first. . . . The site of reopened paradise is almost without exception the earth, or the new Jerusalem. Its most important gifts are the fruits of the tree of life, the water and bread of life, the banquet of the time of salvation, and fellowship with God. The belief in resurrection gave assurance that all the righteous, even those who were dead, would have a share in reopened paradise.[45]

In the apocryphal 2 Enoch (or *The Book of the Secrets of Enoch*) composed between AD 30 and 70, the author describes Enoch's fantastical and speculative journey through the various levels or chambers of the heavenly realm.[46] The text describes in vivid details—paralleling the account of Genesis 1—the creation of the heavens and the earth and all things in them (2 En. 23–29). According to this retelling, when God planted paradise on the third day, he "created renewal" (2 En. 30.1).[47] This renewal appears to be in contrast to the fall of Satan, which the text asserts occurred on the previous day. On the sixth day, God created Adam and Eve and placed them as custodians and rulers of the earth; but because of the seduction of Satan, they spent only five and a half hours in paradise (2 En. 30.8–32.2). From 2 Enoch, then, we see a first-century speculative theology in which paradise, planted on the earth on the third day of creation, was intended not only to be the

---

45. Joachim Jeremias, "Παράδεισος," in *Theological Dictionary of the New Testament*, vol. 5, ed. Gerhard Kittel, Geoffrey W. Bromiley, and Gerhard Friedrich (Grand Rapids: Eerdmans, 1967), 767.

46. This is not to be confused with the description of paradise in 1 En., for which see Eibert J. C. Tigchelaar, "Eden and Paradise: The Garden Motif in Some Early Jewish Texts (1 Enoch and Other Texts Found at Qumran)," in Gerard P Luttikhuizen, ed., *Paradise Interpreted: Representations of Biblical Paradise in Judaism and Christianity*, Themes in Biblical Narrative (Leiden: Brill, 1999), 38–49.

47. All quotations from 2 En. rely on the translation from the Slavonic text in R. H. Charles, ed., *Pseudepigrapha of the Old Testament*, vol. 2 (Oxford: Clarendon, 1913).

medium for access to the heavenly realm but also the source of renewal of the world in contrast to the evil that had entered with the fall of Satan and his angels.

We have already seen in chapter 4 that early Christians believed "that paradise still existed as a place where the just awaited the resurrection and final judgment."[48] That is, the historical, earthly paradise had been take into the heavenly realm after the fall of Adam and Eve.[49] Again, 2 Enoch provides a window into the first-century Jewish understanding of the fate of paradise, for when Enoch is ushered into the "third heaven," he enters paradise (2 En. 8.2). In this paradise of the third heaven stands the tree of life, "adorned more than every existing thing" (8.3). Enoch also describes paradise as "between corruptibility and incorruptibility"—that is, both physical and spiritual, mortal and immortal (8.5). When Enoch comments on the sweetness of paradise, the angels respond, "This place, O Enoch, is prepared for the righteous . . . for eternal inheritance" (2 En. 9.1).

In 2 Enoch, after the account of the creation of the world, angels, paradise, humanity, and of the fall (2 En. 20–32), God reveals to Enoch that the days of creation also anticipate periods of a thousand years, with the eighth period representing "a time of not-counting, endless, with neither years nor months nor weeks nor days nor hours": in other words, eternity (2 En. 33.1). At the completion of Enoch's preaching, he notifies them that he is about to be taken to heaven "to the uppermost Jerusalem to my eternal inheritance" (2 En. 55.2; cf. 1 En. 60.8; Jub. 4.23).

To this same paradise, righteous saints are taken when they depart this world. Irenaeus of Lyons writes: "Wherefore also the elders who were disciples of the apostles tell us that those who were translated [Enoch and Elijah] were transferred to that place (for paradise has been prepared for righteous men, such as have the Spirit; in which place also Paul the apostle, when he was caught up, heard words which are unspeakable as regards us in our present condition), and that there shall they who have been translated remain until the consummation [of all things], as a prelude to immortality" (*Haer.* 5.5.1). Irenaeus says that Elijah was caught up "in the flesh" and that those translated to paradise presently continue to live "as an earnest of the future length of days" (5.5.2): that is, their catching up to paradise is a prophetic type of the eschatological catching up to paradise of the saints in the future.

What is to become of this paradise preserved in the heavenly realm? Paradise will return to earth with the coming of Christ, and its boundaries will fill the earth and transform it. This process of edenification—or terraforming the world to become like the Garden of Eden—is what we mean by the renewal of heaven and earth, resulting in what is called "the new heavens and the new earth." During the coming millennial messianic kingdom, this world will be characterized temporarily by both conditions simultaneously—the old and the new—but these will not, strictly speaking, occupy the same space. Everything within the boundaries of the continuously expanding paradise-on-earth can be considered the "new heavens and new earth"; everything outside the boundaries of that paradise is the old creation ripe for renewal.

---

48. Jean Delumeau, *History of Paradise: The Garden of Eden in Myth and Tradition*, trans. Matthew O'Connell (New York: Continuum, 1995), 23.

49. Jeremias, "Παράδεισος," 767–68.

The paradise of Genesis 2, the paradise in the third heaven, and the paradise of the future age of restoration are not three separate realities; they are one reality. Jeremias writes: "That we do not have three distinct entities in the paradise of the first, the last, and the intervening time, but one and the same garden of God, may be seen quite indubitably from both the terminology and the content of the relevant statements. . . . As regards the content, identity is proved [especially] by the common mention of the tree of life in statements about the intervening and the eschatological paradise."[50]

Isaiah 51:3 looks forward to a time of restoration in Zion when the land will be made like Eden and like the garden of the Lord. The LXX of this verse uses the word παράδεισος. This corresponds with the messianic age or coming kingdom, which Isaiah calls the "new heavens and new earth" (Isa 65:17). According to Irenaeus, the "disciples of the apostles" taught that in the future the saved will experience different abodes, depending on their degrees of faithfulness in this life (*Haer.* 5.36.1–2). During that future kingdom, the saints grow in their immortality, advancing into the presence of the Father: this is known as "the beatific vision." So, during the reign of Christ over the earth, "those who are saved" will "advance through steps" (*Haer.* 5.36.2): they will grow in their immortality by the Spirit, through the Son, and to the Father. The millennial reign of Christ as an "edenification" of the world—paradise unleashed upon the earth—represents the means by which both the resurrected saints and those who are "still in the flesh" advance in their immortality toward the beatific vision of the Father and their dwelling in the renewed heavens and earth.

---

50. Jeremias, "Παράδεισος," 768.

14

The Character of the Coming Kingdom and Its Implications

The righteous will rule in the earth, growing greater by the vision of the Lord, and through him they will become accustomed to receive the glory of God the Father, and, with the holy angels, they shall receive in the kingdom conversation and fellowship and union with spiritual beings.

Irenaeus, *Against Heresies* 5.35.1

In the preceding chapters of this book, I presented the biblical, theological, and historical case for an Irenaean premillennial eschatology in which the coming of Christ would usher in a distinct intermediate era between a first resurrection of the righteous to eternal life and a second resurrection of the wicked to eternal condemnation. During this period, the world as we know it with its sin, suffering, death, and the devil will pass away while the paradise of God is restored to this creation and gradually encompasses the globe. During this period, the world will be transformed and released from its bondage to corruption, not through a natural evolutionary process and not instantly through a divine snap of the finger, but progressively through the co-laboring of humanity—indeed, through the second Adam and the new humanity—as they finally fulfill the *imago Dei* mission in being fruitful, multiplying, filling the earth, subduing it, and expanding the boundaries of Eden to the four corners of the earth.

In the present chapter, I will explore a handful of implications of an Irenaean premillennialism that have sometimes caused confusion or even led to objection. I will begin by describing how Irenaean premillennialism reflects the strengths of other millennial perspectives while avoiding their weaknesses. Second, I will address the issue of the restoration of Israel and the nations in the millennial age. Then, I will briefly explore the intermediate state as understood in Irenaean premillennialism and how it relates to personal eschatology: that is, what happens to a person when they die. Next, I will describe the Irenaean vision of the millennial age, offering a few thoughts on "Monday morning in the millennium," including a few matters of informed speculation.

Irenaean Premillennialism as an Eclectic Eschatology

If it has not become clear by this point, the basic tenets and many of the details of an Irenaean premillennial eschatology enjoy some overlap with what have traditionally been regarded as mutually exclusive views of the millennial kingdom. Though the Irenaean perspective is clearly chiliastic in its basic orientation, it can draw on elements of amillennialism, postmillennialism, and the recent (re-)emphasis on new creationism without fully adopting all elements of any one of these.

Like amillennialism, Irenaean premillennialism affirms some kind of spiritual, heavenly form of the kingdom in the present age. Christ is the anointed king, and the church is—in the present age—the spiritual kingdom, the spiritual "seed of Abraham," and even, at least in the words of later church fathers, spiritual "Israel." As the ultimate fulfillment of the new covenant and the messianic age are coterminous, the new covenant is also a present spiritual reality. Similarly, to the degree that the spiritual kingdom is more or less present and manifests itself more or less in the life and witness of the church, Satan is more or less restrained. In some places, in fact, where the church's power is most readily manifest, the restraint of Satan is more apparent. Thus the present spiritual application of the binding and banishment of Satan is affected through the ministry of the Spirit through the church. Likewise, just as a literal, bodily resurrection will occur in the future messianic age, so the present spiritual age of the kingdom is marked by spiritual resurrection, not as a full spiritual fulfillment of the "first resurrection" in Revelation 20:4–6 but as a spiritual sign and symbol of that future bodily resurrection. In classic Irenaean premillennialism, Old Testament passages describing in figurative language the conditions of reconciliation and restoration in the coming kingdom have spiritual applications in the church today. For instance, the spread of the gospel and church from Jerusalem to Judea, to Samaria, and to the ends of the earth (Acts 1:8) anticipates the future edenification and transformation of the world during the messianic age. The reconciliation between men and women of radically different ethnic, social, cultural, and economic backgrounds in the present age anticipates the literal reconciliation of all creation in the future age. Thus Irenaean premillennialism and many elements of amillennialism do not necessarily stand in stark contrast and conflict with each other but in a dialectical relationship.

Like postmillennialism, Irenaean premillennialism views the advance of the kingdom in the world as progressive—both the present spiritual form of the kingdom and the future earthly manifestation of the kingdom upon the return of Christ. That is, it anticipates an advance and partial victory of the gospel between the first and second advents of Christ. It anticipates that victories will be won as the kingdom progresses, though it also anticipates that ground will be lost as conflict ensues. It need not have a pessimistic and fatalistic expectation of the failure of the gospel in the world, but its optimistic expectations are tempered by a sober acceptance that the fullness of the kingdom will not be realized until the return of Christ. Irenaean premillennialism also allows for real theological and doctrinal development to occur in the church age, with advances becoming part of the treasury of truth bestowed on each generation of saints. With regard to the future age, too, Irenaean premillennialism shares with postmillennialism the mediated nature of the future messianic reign. Just as postmillennialism expects the world to be transformed through the agency of believing humans exercising dominion as image-bearers on behalf of Christ and his kingdom, so does Irenaean premillennialism. In fact, Christ's future reign, centered in Jerusalem, will be administered through resurrected saints, and Christ's cosmic-redemptive program over the course of the millennial era will be implemented by the means of human beings. It will not be an instantaneous transformation of all creation at the moment of the second coming but a long, slow, steady process of progress as the earth is gradually transformed into its Edenic condition.

Finally, Irenaean premillennialism is similar to new creationism in that the future millennial age—ruled by Christ through the agency of his co-regents and image-bearing co-laborers—represents the first phase of the "new heavens and new earth" as the Edenic condition progressively swallows up mortality and corruptibility throughout the world. The millennium-long renewal of heaven and earth culminates in the renewed heavens and earth, and after a brief testing and victory of the second Adam over the Serpent, sin and death will ultimately be destroyed and the renewal of all creation will continue, likely throughout the universe. In Irenaean premillennialism, the "millennium" and the "new creation" are not separated by a thick line, and they are even less quantitatively different things by virtue of annihilation and a second creation *ex nihilo* (see chapter 13). No, the millennium *is* the new creation, and the new creation is accomplished by means of the millennial age. With new creationism, there are no peoples of God assigned to a mere spiritual or heavenly existence. Despite the reality of the beatific vision and admittance into the very presence of the Father in glory, this is not the eternal habitation of the people of God. Rather, "God with us"—God's will being done on earth as it is in heaven—is the ultimate goal of God's plan of redemption.

Thus Irenaean premillennialism finds some common ground with certain key features of amillennial, postmillennial, and new creational models without fully adopting any of these. While these other approaches to eschatology definitely address some aspects of God's revelation, they do not adequately address all of them. Irenaean premillennial eschatology is flexible enough to accommodate valid exegetical and theological insights in amillennial, postmillennial, and new creational models.

The Future of Ethnic Israel in Irenaean Premillennialism

Osborn summarizes the point of the millennium in Irenaeus's eschatology: "Prospectively, the resurrection of the just into an earthly kingdom marks a transition into incorruption where those who shall be worthy will be gradually accustomed to partake of the divine nature. Retrospectively, they receive a reward for passing the trials of their former lives. It is right that in that very creation in which they were tested by labours and manifold suffering, they should receive the reward of their afflictions."[1] Beyond these purposes for the believers themselves, however, we should not lose sight of several purposes for the millennial phase of the coming kingdom related to historical-redemptive themes left unresolved in the overarching story of creation-fall-redemption. One of these relates to the unresolved promises regarding the repentance and restoration of the literal seed of Abraham: that is, "ethnic Israel."[2]

---

1. Eric Osborn, *Irenaeus of Lyons* (Cambridge: Cambridge University Press, 2001), 139.
2. This term is used in contrast to "spiritual Israel," which becomes a theological concept early in the history of the church.

Just as Irenaean premillennialism embraces a both/and approach to prophecies of the coming kingdom, the new covenant, the resurrection, and the binding of Satan, so it also holds a both/and approach to the future repentance and restoration of the nation of Israel. The issue of God's eschatological promises to ethnic Israel and the expectation of their future fulfillment have been repeatedly addressed in important works in recent years, and I do not intend to supplant or even supplement these.[3] In the preceding biblical, theological, and historical studies, I have already touched on a number of considerations that directly or indirectly point to a future restoration of a repentant, regathered Israel to the promised land under the Messiah. In Go Deeper Excursus 21, *The Future Restoration of Israel in the Early Church*, I present some of the historical indications of this expectation consistent with classic Irenaean premillennial eschatology.

Go Deeper Excursus 21

The Future Restoration of Israel in the Early Church

Though the earlier premillennialists in the tradition of Irenaeus embraced an earthly millennium and a real future repentance, regathering, and restoration of ethnic Israel, they rejected what has come to be known as the "carnal chiliasm" of the late first-century heretic Cerinthus and those who followed his extreme views. The third-century antichiliast Dionysius of Alexandria described the objectionable chiliastic teachings of Cerinthus this way: "That the kingdom of Christ will be terrestrial, and comprised of things Cerinthus himself enjoyed. Because he was a lover of corporeality and entirely fleshly, this is what he dreamed it will be like: full of things that satiate the belly and the regions of below the belly, that is, food, drink, sexual intercourse and (because he aimed to procure what was just mentioned by giving it all a more respectable name) festivals, sacrifices, and sacred sacrificial victims" (quoted in Eusebius, *Hist. eccl.* 7.25.3 [Schott]).

While the classic Irenaean premillennial eschatology certainly allowed for a repentance, regathering, and restoration of ethnic Israel as well as a rebuilding of the city of Jerusalem, the idea of a reinstitution of animal sacrifices during the millennium appears to be found only among the carnal chiliasts. Justin Martyr writes, "And do not suppose that Isaias or the other Prophets speak of sacrifices of blood or libations being offered on the altar at His second coming, but only of true and spiritual praises and thanksgivings" (*Dial.* 118 [Falls]).

The detailed description of a restored temple and sacrificial worship in Ezekiel 40–48 has drawn a lot of attention in the debate of a future millennial intermediate kingdom, especially one in which a restored Israel and Jerusalem play a central role. Ezekiel received this vision at a time when the people of Israel were in exile, their temple and city destroyed, and hope of restoration bleak. In that context, Ezekiel's intricate description of the new temple marking a new era of prosperity was meant to shame the rebellious people for their sins and to motivate them to repent (Ezek 43:10–11).

---

3. See especially Stanley E. Porter and Alan E. Kurschner, eds., *The Future Restoration of Israel: A Response to Supercessionism*, McMaster Biblical Studies Series, vol. 10 (Eugene, OR: Pickwick, 2023); and Michael J. Vlach, *Has the Church Replaces Israel? A Theological Evaluation* (Nashville: B&H Academic, 2010).

Despite the detailed plans for its construction, furnishing, and sacrifices, most commentators understand the imagery along the lines of "a typological vision of the present church age." However, Vlach observes, "Ezekiel 40–48 lists great architectural details for this temple and it is difficult to spiritualize these details."[4] Michael Vlach notes three interpretive options. [5] These are (1) a historical fulfillment (albeit in an underwhelming sense) in the return from exile and rebuilding of the temple under Joshua and Zerubbabel (cf. Ezra 1–6; Hag 1–2); (2) a figurative or spiritual fulfillment in Christ and the church;[6] or (3) a literal future temple in the millennial kingdom.[7] Vlach himself opts for a literal understanding not only of the structure but also of the animal sacrifices, noting that "just as sacrifices under the Mosaic Covenant were *typological*, pointing forward to Christ's ultimate sacrifice, the sacrifices described with Ezekiel's temple could be *retrospective*, drawing attention to Christ's completed sacrifice."[8]

I would offer a different understanding of the imagery of Ezekiel 40–48, which takes the imagery literally, understands that it has never been fulfilled historically, but also concludes that it will not be fulfilled in the future millennial period. Before I briefly set forth my current position on the matter, however, I want to state that I affirm, with Vlach and many other premillennialists, that "when Israel is restored there will be a restored temple in Jerusalem . . . which will be a center of Israel's expression of worship to the Lord."[9] I affirm this because of the numerous Old Testament passages that speak of a restored city, the centrality of the mountain of the house of the Lord, an actual place where worshipers come, and the overall incarnational understanding of the kingdom in the early premillennialists that also see the throne of that kingdom established in Jerusalem (see detailed discussion in chapters 5–6). However, the establishment of a place as the center of worship, devotion, and instruction does not necessitate the reestablishment of animal sacrifices. Even the reestablishment of a priesthood would not require such sacrifices per se, as the role of the priest even in the Old Testament also involved instruction: "For the lips of a priest should guard knowledge, and people should seek instruction from his mouth, for he is the messenger of the Lord of hosts" (Mal 2:7).

We have already seen in our survey of Old Testament images of the coming kingdom that while a temple and offerings are mentioned as part of the expectation, the specific idea of a sacrificial system of animals was not emphasized. Isaiah 2:1–4 indeed tells us that as the center of God's universal rule through the Messiah, Jerusalem will be the source of instruction of all the nations. Although the "house of the God of Jacob" is mentioned (2:3), the Gentiles are not coming to Jerusalem

4. Michael J. Vlach, *He Will Reign Forever: A Biblical Theology of the Kingdom of God* (Silverton, OR: Lampion, 2017), 203.
5. Vlach, *He Will Reign Forever*, 203.
6. Keith A. Mathison, *Postmillennialism: An Eschatology of Hope* (Phillipsburg, NJ: P&R, 1999), 91–92.
7. J. Dwight Pentecost, *Things to Come* (Grand Rapids: Zondervan, 1958), 517–19.
8. Vlach, *He Will Reign Forever*, 205–6.
9. Vlach, *He Will Reign Forever*, 205.

to offer sacrifices but to receive instruction and hear the word of the Lord.[10] In Jeremiah 3:13–15, the prophet points forward to a time when the ark of the covenant "shall not come to mind or be remembered or missed, nor shall another one be made." This may serve as a synecdoche for the system of animal sacrifices, which would suggest the changing of the entire old covenant. This is consistent with the fact that none of the Isaianic kingdom oracles placed an emphasis on a restoration of animal sacrifices in the restored place of worship and instruction.[11] When we reach Ezekiel 40–48, though, contrary to the deemphasis on temple and sacrifices in the oracles in Isaiah and Jeremiah and the rest of the prophets, Ezekiel presents a detailed expectation of a temple with sacrifices.

My solution to this problem does not fit exactly with any of Vlach's three options. Rather, I would argue that the picture of the restored temple described in Ezekiel 40–48 was intended to be taken entirely literally.[12] However, the image was meant to function the same way Moses' vision of the temple on the mountain functioned: as the "pattern (תבנית)" for the tabernacle on earth (Exod 25:9, 40). At the time of Ezekiel's vision, there was no temple in Jerusalem, so God showed Ezekiel a grand vision of a temple that far out-scaled Solomon's Temple and said, "As for you, mortal, describe the temple to the house of Israel, and let them measure the pattern (תכנית), and let them be ashamed of their iniquities. When they are ashamed of all that they have done, make known to them the plan of the temple, its arrangement, its exits and its entrances, and its whole form—all its ordinances and its entire plan (צורתיו) and all its laws; and write it down in their sight so that they may observe and follow the entire plan (צורתו) and all its ordinances" (Ezek 43:10–11). Had the people of Israel repented fully—including a full return from exile—they would have followed precisely the pattern and form as presented in Ezekiel's vision for the building of a new mega-temple. Schnittjer observes, "There is a strong continuity between the requirements of priests in the tabernacle in Leviticus and priests in Ezekiel's temple. In the case of differences, Ezekiel strengthens measures to preserve the holiness of the temple."[13]

Had all Israel turned in full repentance and returned to the land of promise, and had they followed the instructions as required in the great act of penance that was the reconstruction of the temple and establishment of its holy regulations, then God himself would have dwelled among them and blessed them beyond measure, just as the old covenant promised. In fact, the language of restoration echoes

---

10. Later, Isa 43:22–25 tells us that although Israel failed to honor God with the stipulations of the covenant, the Lord would forgive them: "I alone am the one who blots out your transgressions for my own sake, and I will not remember your sins" (v. 25). This contrast between their failure to offer sacrifices and God's gracious forgiveness apart from sacrifices may point to a time when the sacrifices will have passed away and a new covenant takes its place.

11. For a discussion of the possible reference to burnt offerings during the new covenant period, see comments in chapter 6 and Go Deeper Excursus 11 on Jeremiah 33:1–26.

12. For a comparison of the instructions for Ezekiel's temple and the tabernacle and temple described in Exod 25–31; 35–40; 1 Kgs 6; 8, see Gary Edward Schnittjer, *Old Testament Use of Old Testament: A Book-by-Book Guide* (Grand Rapids: Zondervan Academic, 2021), 337 47.

13. Schnittjer, *Old Testament Use of Old Testament*, 344.

Edenic imagery (Ezek 47:3–12),[14] suggesting that God's presence in Zion would have brought heaven to earth so the realm of heaven would have mingled with the earthly sanctuary. The twelve tribes would be restored and the land finally divided even greater than anybody could have dreamed (47:13–48:35).

However, Israel saw no such mass repentance, no complete return from exile, and no grandiose building project that followed Ezekiel's specific pattern. And with the construction—an outward sign of total devotion of the entire nation, its people, its resources, and its priorities to God—they would have also received a complete fulfillment of the blessings that would have come from total conformity to the old covenant. But it was not meant to be. Instead, only a small remnant of people returned—hardly enough even to conceive of a massive project envisioned by Ezekiel. When the temple was completed by the remnant under Joshua and Zerubbabel, it paled in comparison to even the Temple of Solomon (Hag 2:2–3). Though in the first century AD, with the beautification of the temple complex by Herod, the temple would finally rival Solomon's Temple, at no time did Israel follow the instructions and plans set forth in Ezekiel 40–48. As a result, the fullest manifestation of blessing possible under the old covenant was never realized. This solution allows us to take the details literally, understands the full blessing as contingent upon Israel's repentance and obedience to the instructions in Ezekiel 43:10–11, places the unrealized construction in the old covenant era when sacrifices were very much in place, and explains the lack of emphasis on animal sacrifices in a future millennial temple and the theological and practical problems such a scenario brings.

In short, in keeping with the classic Irenaean premillennial eschatology, I do not anticipate a restoration of animal sacrifices in the future temple in Jerusalem, though I do expect a rebuilt city and sanctuary for the purpose of instruction and worship. The new covenant worship, however, is markedly different from that of the old.

"Monday Morning" in the Millennium

Clement of Alexandria understood by Jesus' statement regarding the resurrection in Luke 20:34–36 that the present social distinctions between the sexes will not be maintained in the age to come. He does not appear to hold that humans will be genderless, neutral beings, but he sees "the sexual desire which divides humanity being removed" (*Instructor* 1.4). In any case, there will be neither sex nor marriage in the resurrection. That the resurrection body will not engage in sexual intercourse or sexual reproduction has been the view of orthodox Christians from the beginning. In a defense of the resurrection often attributed to Justin Martyr, the author asserts that sexual intercourse will be abolished, citing Luke 20:34–35 (Ps. Just., *Fragments on Resurrection* 3).

---

14. Jean Delumeau, *History of Paradise: The Garden of Eden in Myth and Tradition*, trans. Matthew O'Connell (New York: Continuum, 1995), 4.

However, in classic Irenaean premillennialism, not all who live during the millennium will be resurrected and glorified. We have seen that at the time of the coming intermediate kingdom, children will be born to the mortal survivors of the tribulation, who will thrive on the earth in a blessed state. The question of whether these mortals will experience the decline of aging and death has been answered in various ways. My own view, adopted from Irenaeus of Lyons, is that no righteous (regenerate) mortal will die. He writes, "For in the times of the kingdom, the righteous man who is upon the earth shall then forget to die" (*Haer.* 5.36.2). In the same way, I believe those righteous mortals will also forget to sin.

The progressive sanctification of the righteous will gradually transform them into an immortal condition, no longer suffering the effects of corruption and mortality. This, I believe, will come by means of the transformation of nature itself as the world is progressively edenified—made like paradise. This will include the propagation of the tree of life, the leaves of which are used "for the healing of the nations" (Rev 22:2). Though many view the vision of the descent of the New Jerusalem from heaven as a vision that follows the millennium and therefore the conditions of that New Jerusalem to apply only to the eternal state, I believe the symbolic imagery of the descent of the heavenly city is a picture of the return of paradise to this world, which begins at the return of Christ and finds its climax at the end of the millennial phase of the eternal kingdom. In the Testament of Dan, which likely precedes the imagery of the book of Revelation by at least a century, the "New Jerusalem" is associated with the future rest in Eden: "And the captivity shall he take from Beliar, and turn disobedient hearts unto the Lord, and give to them that call upon him eternal peace. And the saints shall rest in Eden, and in the New Jerusalem shall the righteous rejoice, and it shall be unto the glory of God for ever. And no longer shall Jerusalem endure desolation, nor Israel be led captive; for the Lord shall be in the midst of it, and the Holy One of Israel shall reign over it" (T. Dan 5.11–13; cf. Apoc. Mos. 42.3–5). Thus John sees a symbolic vision that represents the progressive transformation of creation as God takes his abode among humanity and gradually drives out the old and ushers in the new (Rev 21:1–5).[15] This means, then, that the tree of life is present in the world from the first day of the millennium forward. And those who partake of that tree of life will receive the physically regenerating power of its fruit: they will never die.

But the descendants of the mortal survivors of the tribulation will not necessarily be regenerate. They may harbor resentment, envy, and mutiny in their hearts, though outright revolt would be impossible in the millennial kingdom. If outward rebellion were to occur, it would be met with swift and just punishment (Isa 65:20). This means that though death is possible during the millennium, the renewal of creation and the edenification of the world will greatly diminish its

---

15. It is certainly true that in the vision itself, the heavenly Jerusalem descends to the earth, and many have taken this as literally referring to some kind of solid city that is placed on this globe; see Vlach, *He Will Reign Forever*, 518–20. Though I certainly hold to a literal Jerusalem on a literal earth, the symbolic nature of apocalyptic visions does not require that the fulfillment of the New Jerusalem is exactly as described in Rev 21–22, though nothing necessarily rules out an exact correspondence.

presence. It is likely that many living throughout the millennium will never know a person who has died.

As the population grows and the nations flourish on the earth, there is no reason to believe this world will mark the limit of humanity's exercise of dominion over all creation. While it is certainly an area of speculation, the idea that humans have always been destined to explore other planets and galaxies is not absurd. After all, God created a vast universe for a reason. After God's co-regents tasked with the mission to be fruitful, multiply, fill the earth, and subdue it accomplish that mission on a global scale, what prevents humanity from expanding the kingdom of God among the stars? Only the physical limitations associated with space travel prevent the realization of such a vision. With those physical limitations removed in resurrection and glorification, all obstacles for exercising dominion throughout the universe will also be removed. Ray Stedman has famously mused:

> The new universe will surely be as big or bigger than it is now—and it is mind-blowing in its immensity now! Billions of galaxies, far larger than our own galaxy of the Milky Way, fill the heavens as far as the eye can see by means of the greatest telescopes we have, and still we have not reached the end. That means that there will be new planets to develop, new principles to discover, new joys to experience. Every moment of eternity will be an adventure of discovery.[16]

Though I cannot prove it, I suspect the universe is filled with all manner of life—plants, animals, and other creatures perhaps too astonishing to imagine. Though Scripture certainly speaks of both benevolent and malevolent spirit beings in the universe, it is silent on the idea of other life forms. Yet neither does Scripture rule out the possibility. I would suspect that if life did exist on other planets, it would not be what we call "intelligent" life—though what we mean by "intelligent" is not easy to explain. Certainly, humans created according to the image of God—then glorified to conform to the image of God, Christ—will always occupy the chief place in the universe of created beings. The *imago Dei* mission to exercise dominion over all living things would include any life forms—plant or animal—on other worlds.

What of animal life on this world? Surely, our planet with its countless forms of animal life will continue to flourish. While the imagery of wolves, lambs, leopards, goats, calves, and lions dwelling in harmony paints a compelling picture of peace and harmony in the new world, we have no reason to assume that God will give up on animal life in the new creation any more than he would give up on plant life. However, it is highly unlikely that these animals will serve as food for humans or for one another.

But what about *our* pets? You do not have to be in ministry long before somebody asks you whether a beloved dog or cat will be in heaven. The answer to that, I believe, is no. There is no biblical, theological, or historical reason to believe that animals have enduring souls that continue after death and depart to paradise. However, this does not mean our pets are lost forever. I find it entirely possible that as

---

16. Ray C. Stedman, "The City of Glory," *Authentic Christianity*, April 29, 1990, https://www.raystedman.org/new-testament/revelation/the-city-of-glory.

part of the authority granted to resurrected, glorified saints, equipped to mediate the blessings of the new covenant in the new creation, that we will be delegated authority to lift life from the coils of death. Though I do not believe every animal that has ever existed will be restored to life, those beloved creatures with whom we have forged real relationships, who were once a part of our family, to whom we were both "master" and "friend"—these may one day hear us cry with a loud, familiar voice, "Come forth!" and find their way darting into our arms, perhaps unaware they had ever gone.

Is Premillennialism Fatalistic, Pessimistic, and Bad for the World?

It is often alleged that premillennialism—or at least its most popular forms—is essentially fatalistic and pessimistic, owing to its tendency to view the present age as getting progressively worse leading up to the coming of Christ as judge. As Kenneth Newport puts it:

> In general, premillennialists held (and hold) to a very negative view of humankind. They generally consider that humanity and/or human society is rotten to the core, and that this state of things can be overcome only by the direct, cataclysmic intervention of God. Things are bad and will get worse. Individuals at large will slip further and further into the moral chaos until this world is so totally wicked that God will himself act (as he did in Noah's day) to put things right.[17]

However, nothing in the premillennial scheme itself demands a belief in a steady, hopeless, and pessimistic deterioration of the world leading to the eschatological climax of history. In fact, a premillennial outlook can comfortably coexist with a view of the present age as either advancing in progress and human flourishing (similar to some forms of postmillennialism), remaining in a steady state of constant conflict (similar to most forms of amillennialism), or deteriorating toward chaos and destruction.

One's outlook on the condition of the world has far less to do with one's view of the millennium and more to do with one's understanding of the book of Revelation and the concept of "tribulation" as it relates to the present inter-advent period. Regardless of how figuratively or literally one takes the imagery of the Apocalypse of John, the great majority of commentators see in it a general deterioration of conditions accompanying an intensification of the judgments as the means of God's wrath. If one understands the book of Revelation in a historicist sense in which the whole book outlines in advance the period of history between the first and second advents, then one would expect to see the conditions of the world deteriorating. However, if one understands Revelation in a consistent futurist sense, then the period of the intensification of judgments would be limited to the coming Day

---

17. Kenneth G. C. Newport, *Apocalypse and Millennium: Studies in Biblical Eisegesis* (Cambridge: Cambridge University Press, 2000), 12–13.

of the Lord, yet future. In the meantime, the present age could see improvement, deterioration, a steady state, or all of these in different parts of the world and at different times in human history.

At the same time, though, it is also not the case that the postmillennial view necessarily expects the present age to experience a progressive improvement in religion, society, and government, which will then give way to a golden age. While this could be the position adopted by some forms of postmillennialism, others may allow for a gradual deterioration or a steady state of affairs that will then give way to a rapid victory of the gospel in a relatively short period of time, which will then usher in the millennial golden age. That is, the victory of the gospel pictured in Revelation 19 as understood by many postmillennialists could come as a result of a sudden future great awakening and revival accomplished in a single generation or even in the span of a few short years. Until that awakening, the world could spiral toward chaos or plug along as it has for centuries. In short, one's outlook on the world and expectations for improvement or deterioration is more logically connected to one's view of the book of Revelation. Premillennialism is not, necessarily, pessimistic or fatalistic.

But does premillennialism, with its hope heavily weighted in the future, let Christians off the hook for investing time and energy improving this world? Does it excuse us from caring for the environment, seeking cures for cancers, fighting against political corruption, taking a stand against injustice, and addressing problems like homelessness, hunger, and human trafficking? Not at all. Remember, we defined the "kingdom of God" in chapter 4 as "God's will being done on earth as it is in heaven." Though classic premillennialists in the Irenaean tradition believe the full manifestation of that kingdom cannot be realized until Christ returns, we believe that by the coming of the Spirit, the values, priorities, and even the power of the coming kingdom can be partially manifested in the world today. The fruits of Spirit (Gal 5:22–23) are a real present manifestation of the virtues of the coming kingdom in our present lives.

If our citizenship is in heaven (Phil 3:20), then the rules of heaven should be our rules on earth. And if the values of heaven are love, joy, peace, patience, kindness, goodness, faithfulness, gentleness, and self-control, then we should be representatives of those virtues in this present dark world. As Paul said, "Be blameless and innocent, children of God without blemish in the midst of a crooked and perverse generation, in which you shine like stars in the world" (Phil 2:15). If we are heirs of the coming kingdom, then we should advance the priorities of the kingdom: truth, justice, righteousness, holiness, faith, and hope. It does no good to claim these things are impossible until Christ returns, that if we cannot live them perfectly now, then we should not live them at all. And to say that way of kingdom living doesn't work in the real world is valid only if it can *never* work in the real world. Premillennial eschatology demonstrates that even mortal humans can live the values of the coming kingdom in the real world, because one day they will.

The glorious image of the coming kingdom—that ideal world that seems so far from possibility, nay, nearly impossible—should motivate us to labor. The fact that one day, *this world will* be made new means that it *can* be made new. And if it can be made new *perfectly* in the coming age, then it can be improved *imperfectly* in the present age. The vision of the millennium should encourage, not discourage us.

Let me clarify this with an illustration. Imagine if, in 1890, somebody said, "We'll never be able to cure polio. It's a lost cause. We might as well just give up and let it take its course. It's here to stay." Then imagine somebody traveled backward in time from the year 2024 to the year 1890 and said, "In the future, polio is cured." Without sharing the formula for the vaccine, without explaining the science, without any hints or clues on how to cure that dreaded disease, the people in 1890 would be motivated to work hard for a cure simply by knowing their labor is not in vain.

I often hear from eschatological pessimists that we are fighting a losing battle, that we can only expect trial, tribulation, persecution, and defeat on this side of the second coming. They suggest we should focus our time and energy not on making the world a better place, not on advancing causes that relieve human suffering and injustice, not on improving educational institutions, the arts, and the sciences. Rather, we should invest only in people's immortal souls. Why? Everything else is like polishing the chrome on a sinking ship, they say, or like investing our retirement funds in a company that just announced they're closing all their stores.

No, we are not fighting a losing battle. The classic Irenaean eschatology tells us that we are fighting a winning battle, and it encourages us to keep fighting.

Let me illustrate this with a scene in Tolkein's *The Two Towers* at the climax of the battle of Helm's Deep. Saruman's Orc army has broken through all the concentric barriers of that seemingly impenetrable fortress and are about to breech the very doors of the innermost fortress. A despondent King Théoden of Rohan appears to have surrendered in his heart. Despite a vigorous defense of the keep, by every measure they have been fighting a losing battle. But Aragorn knew better. He knew that at any moment Gandalf would arrive with an army of the exiled riders of Rohan. Aragorn pleads with the king to ride out against the enemy one last time. With new resolve, the king determines he will lead the few riders he has left against the army of wickedness, even though he rides out to his doom. Little does he know that the desperate final flex of hope will result in absolute victory. Because at the break of dawn, as he opens the doors and meets the dark army, a horn blasts through the vale and the army of Rohan appears on the mountaintop. What had been just a moment earlier a losing battle had in the blink of an eye been turned to victory, redeeming from futility every flash of the sword and twang of the bow expended against the enemy.

This is our motivation to press on against seemingly overwhelming odds. We ride out against the enemies of faith, love, hope, truth, justice, grace, and righteousness because the battle is ours. We may face setbacks, bear the wounds of enemies, and experience casualties that lead us to believe the battle has been lost. But we nevertheless press on, knowing that the Spirit of truth is waging God's own war through us: convicting the world of sin, of righteousness, and of judgment. As we fight, we keep an eye on the horizon for the break of dawn, when the hero of heaven will descend with his armies and put an end to the conflict once and for all.

In the meantime, as we await the coming of Christ as judge and king, we are to be preaching the gospel and calling people to live as citizens of that heavenly

kingdom, which will one day break fully into our earthly realm. Irenaeus sums up
the church's present responsibility well:

> Firm is our faith in Him and true is the tradition of preaching, that is, the witness
> of the apostles, who, sent by the Lord, preached to the whole world the Son of God
> come unto His Passion, endured for the destruction of death and the vivification of
> the flesh, so that, by putting aside enmity towards God, which is iniquity, we may
> receive peace with Him, doing that which is pleasing to Him. (*Epid.* 86)

15

The Day of the Lord in the Old Testament

*"For, behold," says Isaiah, "the day of the Lord cometh
past remedy, full of fury and wrath, to lay waste the
city of the earth, and to root sinners out of it."*

Irenaeus, *Against Heresies* 5.35.1

In our survey of Old Testament passages related to the coming kingdom in chapter 6, we observed that the times of eschatological restoration and renewal of Israel, the nations, and all creation frequently follow a season of judgment commonly known as the "Day of the Lord." So, for example, the first major prophecy concerning the coming restoration (Isa 2:1–5) is couched in a context of destruction (Isa 1:2–31; 2:6–4:1). Out of such judgment emerges the "remnant," the survivors of God's people, who are cleansed of wickedness "by a spirit of judgment and by a spirit of burning" (Isa 4:4). Throughout the prophets, the theme of judgment followed by restoration is repeated.[1]

In short, the collage of the coming kingdom portrayed in figurative language in the prophets is constantly framed by the coming judgment. The prophets look forward to a time when God's people Israel, having suffered the effects of covenant unfaithfulness, will return to God, who will call them back from their places of exile and restored to their own land. So, too, the wicked nations will be judged for their failure to abide by God's moral law that is written on their hearts (Rom 2:14–16). Judgment comes before blessing, purification before restoration.[2]

In the previous chapters of this book, we focused on the stunning biblical imagery of restoration, filling in the basic framework of the Irenaean premillennial understanding of the coming kingdom. With this picture before us, we can now step back and place the coming Day of the Lord in context. How one answers some of the interpretive and theological questions related to the millennium affects how one frames the questions regarding the preceding time of future judgment—the ultimate Day of the Lord.

---

1. See, e.g., Isa 26:1–27:13; 30:9–26; 31:6–32:5; 32:6–18; 65:1–25; Jer 4:13–27; 16:4–21; 30:1–31:26; Ezek 20:1–44; Dan 7:1–27; Joel 2:1–3:1; Mic 1:2–4:8.

2. Robin Routledge, *Old Testament Theology: A Thematic Approach* (Downers Grove, IL: InterVarsity, 2012), 273.

Introductory Questions Regarding the "Day of the Lord"

Meir Weiss argues that the varieties of events associated with the phrase "Day of the Lord" (יום יהוה) in the Old Testament prophets suggest that this was not a firm formula and was much more flexible.[3] This critique is important and cautions against a hasty reductionism in which the phrase is defined so narrowly that it allows for no development of meaning and significance. However, others suggest that the phrase does, in fact, have a fairly stable technical meaning, even if contextual usage must determine just how the technical term is being employed in various rhetorical situations.

Related to this issue is an important methodological question in determining the meaning of the "Day of the Lord" as a technical term. Do we limit ourselves only to passages that use the specific phrase יום יהוה?[4] Or should we think of the Day of the Lord less as a technical *term* and more as a technical *concept* that can be communicated with several terms pointing to the same general referent? In general agreement with the methodological approach of Yaim Hoffmann, I believe any definition of the Day of the Lord must begin with passages using the phrase יום יהוה itself; then, using parallel phrases in those יום יהוה passages, we may form a cluster of synonymous terms that help us construct the technical concept.

We must also keep in mind that the concept grew in the course of the many centuries of Old Testament canonical development and experienced continued change during the period of Second Temple Judaism in its various apocryphal and apocalyptic iterations.[5] Ultimately, the question for us will be rather narrow: Is there a technical (or even quasi-technical) meaning of the "Day of the Lord" prevalent among Jewish thinkers during the first century that will inform our understanding of the New Testament usage?

Hoffmann notes that "many scholars insist that the phrase was a well-known term already in Amos's time, but they are divided over the question of whether or not it was an eschatological term."[6] He concludes that although the יום יהוה in Amos's day was not yet a technical term, it was a well-known concept to which Amos assigns the phrase יום יהוה.[7] However, as we see in our detailed survey of the canonical and extracanonical literature, we must agree with Vander Hart, who says, "Because the phrase is used by the earliest writing prophet as well as by the last writing prophet, the phrase takes on importance as something of a *terminus technicus* in the Old Testament history of revelation."[8] Perhaps his phrasing "something of a *terminus technicus*" expresses the proper nuance in this discussion.

---

3. Meir Weiss, "Origin of the 'Day of the Lord'—Reconsidered," *HUCA* 37 (1966): 45.

4. See Yair Hoffmann, "The Day of the Lord Concept and a Term in the Prophetic Literature," *ZAW* 93.1 (1981): 37.

5. Hoffmann, "Day of the Lord Concept," 38–39.

6. Hoffmann, "Day of the Lord Concept," 40.

7. Hoffmann, "Day of the Lord Concept," 41.

8. Mark D. Vander Hart, "The Transition of the Old Testament Day of the Lord into the New Testament Day of the Lord Jesus Christ," *MAJT* 9.1 (1993): 6.

Is the "Day of the Lord" a Single Day?

Borrowing from "a number of disparate Sumerian, Hittite, Egyptian, and semitic texts from a variety of places and times," Douglas Stuart appeals to an "apparently widespread tradition" that "a truly great king or sovereign possessed such universal power and authority that he could complete a military campaign, or even an entire war of conquest against his enemies in a single day."[9] However, the actual Old Testament passages Stuart cites as evidence for depicting the Day of the Lord "in terms associated with warfare and its catastrophic results" (e.g., Isa 2; Jer 46, 47; Ezek 7, 30; Amos 5; Zeph 1; Mal 3, etc.) depict the Day of the Lord in terms of God mediating his judgment through earthly military exploits, the details of which occupy more than a single twenty-four-hour period.[10] Stuart then concludes, "This limited selection of texts should be sufficient to demonstrate the predominance of conquest or military victory language in the Old Testament describing the content of the *Day* of Yahweh."[11]

However, even considering the figurative nature of the language, these passages set forth earthly—indeed, *human*—military conquests and destruction orchestrated and governed by God, not a glorious personal appearance as a divine warrior. This is not symbolic anthropomorphic language casting God's sudden coming in terms of human military exploits; this is symbolic imagery of human military campaigns viewed as God's mediated intervention into human history as judge. In fact, this idea of God mediating his vengeance and wrath through a human army is explicitly spelled out:

> "Woe to Assyria, the rod of my anger; the staff in their hands is my fury! Against a godless nation I send him, and against the people of my wrath I command him." (Isa 10:5–6 ESV)[12]

> "I myself have commanded my consecrated ones, and have summoned my mighty men to execute my anger, my proudly exulting ones." (Isa 13:3)

Furthermore, whereas Stuart's references to a sovereign king's single-day victory explicitly boast that an entire war over the king's enemies was accomplished in a single day, none of the Old Testament texts actually make this same assertion. Quite the contrary: they describe a series of events that imply a prolonged period of warfare and its lingering, disastrous consequences like famine and disease (cf. Ezek 7:15–16). The fact that the attacks on Jerusalem or other fortified cities in Israel and Judah involved siege warfare means the "Day" was never a single day; sieges last months or even years.[13]

---

9. Douglas K. Stuart, "The Sovereign's Day of Conquest," *BASOR* 221 (1976): 160.

10. Stuart, "Sovereign's Day of Conquest," 160–61.

11. Stuart, "Sovereign's Day of Conquest," 161.

12. Unless otherwise noted, in this chapter and its accompanying excursus, I am using the English Standard Version (ESV) as the translation for two reasons: its more literal rendering of יוֹם as "day" as opposed to the more paraphrastic "time" (as in the NRSVue), and its use of lowercase rather than uppercase at the start of lines of prophetic poetry (as in the NASB).

13. Israel Eph'al, *The City Besieged: Siege and Its Manifestations in the Ancient Near East*, Culture and History of the Ancient Near East, vol. 36 (Leiden: Brill, 2009), 2.

Had the Old Testament prophets intended to draw on this non-Israelite figure of a sovereign defeating his enemies in a single day, they could easily have used that specific language. Even when Isaiah 2:12 seems to come close, when read in light of the further explication of the coming judgment in 3:1–26, the "day" in view involves a complex series of disastrous events over a prolonged period of time, not a single twenty-four-hour day. In fact, Isaiah 34:8 even parallels "day of vengeance" with "year of recompense"; at least in this instance the notion of a battle won by YHWH in a single day is simply not in the intention of the writer. In Amos 8, YHWH says, "And on that day (ביום) . . . I will make the sun go down at noon and darken the earth in broad daylight" (8:9); but he continues, "Behold, days (ימים) are coming . . . when I will send a famine on the land—not a famine of bread, nor a thirst for water, but of hearing the words of the Lord" (8:11).

Finally, "in that day" language is used even in restoration (not warfare) passages—"in that day I will raise up the booth of David that is fallen and repair its breaches, and raise up its ruins" (Amos 9:11). This, too, is paralleled with a reference to plural "days": "Behold, the days are coming . . . when the plowman shall overtake the reaper and the treader of grapes him who sows the seed" (9:13). Thus the language of "the day" or "that day" is not used exclusively for warfare, nor is it used literally as a twenty-four-hour period. Simply put, Stuart provides no clear instance in which the language of winning a battle "in a single day" is used for YHWH, he disregards passages in which "day" involves events that take place over the course of a period of time as God mediates his warfare through human agents, and he does not account for passages in which "that day" is paralleled with "year" or "days."

It is not the case that ancient Near Eastern hyperbole of sovereigns defeating their enemies "in a single day" stands as the background for the Day of the Lord language. Rather, the imagery related to the Day of the Lord points most often to the events and effects of sieges and invasions by human armies summoned to exercise God's judgment upon a nation. The staging and execution of such invasions as symbolized by the Day of the Lord take a long time. Fabrice De Backer notes several phases of a siege in the ancient Near East: both leading up to and including direct military aspects. These include investigation, preparation, and infiltration, all of which could last several years.[14]

Eph'al notes two military aspects of siege warfare in the ancient Near East: the blockade and the breakthrough. He notes, "The effect of a blockade is cumulative, so it must be continuous and generally extended in time."[15] He cites an Egyptian royal inscription regarding the siege of Megiddo by Thutmose III (fifteenth century BC), which lasted seven months.[16] Other examples describe sieges that lasted for five months.[17] This period of several months appears to fall on the short side of things. In Josephus *A.J.*, 9.14.2, we read Menander of Ephesus's report on the

14. See Fabrice De Backer, *L'art du Siège Néo-Assyrien*, Culture and History of the Ancient Near East, vol. 61, ed. M. H. E. Weippert, Thomas Schneider, et al. (Leiden: Brill, 2013), 273–82.

15. Eph'al, *City Besieged*, 35.

16. Eph'al, *City Besieged*, 36.

17. Eph'al, *City Besieged*, 39.

eighth-century siege of Tyre by Shalmaneser V of Assyria, which lasted over five years.[18] He also reported that Nebuchadnezzar besieged the same city of Tyre for thirteen years (*A.J.* 10.11.1)![19]

The fact that many biblical texts related to the Day of the Lord refer to famine, thirst, and disease suggests that these normal effects of the blockade phase of siege warfare were regarded as themselves elements of the Day of the Lord.[20] In the early days of this siege, as fodder for animals is exhausted, the population of a city must rapidly consume their dying or dead cattle. Eph'al points to Isaiah 22, the Day of the Lord passage known as the "Valley of Vision Oracle," as an example of this phenomenon.[21] This confirms that even the blockade phase and its increasingly disastrous effects are regarded as aspects of the Day of the Lord (Isa 22:1–14). Other typical effects of famine caused by a city besieged as an aspect of the Day of the Lord are seen in Lamentations 2:11–12, especially starvation leading to the horrors of cannibalism (2:20). Texts that exhibit Day of the Lord language and imagery without the specific term יום also point to famine as an effect of God's wrath and anger (Isa 51:20; Jer 14:18; Lam 4:10).[22] Disease as an effect of siege warfare is also mentioned in numerous passages in this same connection (Jer 21:6–9; 32:36; 38:2; 44:13; Lam 1:20; Ezek 5:2, 12; 6:11–12; 7:15).[23]

After sometimes months or even years of blockade, the second military aspect of a siege was the attacker's breakthrough over the wall, under the wall, or through the wall. Even this process, of course, took time. Both undermining and overtopping walls was prolongedly frustrated by a city's defenders; and once a wall was breached, defensive measures continued to slow the offensive.[24] Such a defensive barricade is described in Ezekiel 13:4–5, noting that because of the false prophesying, the city had not prepared their defenses against the invasion: "You have not gone up into the breaches, or built up a wall for the house of Israel, that it might stand in battle in the day of the Lord."[25]

My point with this apparent overanalysis of elements involved in a military invasion in the ancient world is to drive home an important conclusion: the technical concept of the Day of the Lord communicated through the Old Testament imagery is a prolonged period of suffering, death, and destruction. The Day of the Lord, then, is mediated through seemingly natural means: siege, hunger, pestilence,

---

18. Eph'al, *City Besieged*, 40.

19. Eph'al, *City Besieged*, 41; see especially the varying lengths of sieges on 110–12.

20. Eph'al, *City Besieged*, 57.

21. Eph'al, *City Besieged*, 58.

22. Eph'al, *City Besieged*, 63

23. Eph'al, *City Besieged*, 66–67. Cf. De Backer's horrifying and bleak picture of the suffering of the besieged people even prior to an actual infiltration in *L'art du Siège Néo-Assyrien*, 281.

24. For detailed examples of several lengthy offensive and defensive measures in the classical period, see Gwyn Davies, "'Dig for Victory'! Competitive Fieldwork in Classical Siege Operations," in *The Art of Siege Warfare and Military Architecture from the Classical World to the Middle Ages*, ed. Michael Eisenberg and Rabei Khamisy (Oxford: Oxbow, 2021), 45–53.

25. See Eph'al, *City Besieged*, 96.

horror, destruction, invasion, sword, fire, and death. The period of the Day of the Lord lasted many months or many years, not days or even weeks.

The "Day of the Lord" as a Mediated Theophanic Visitation in Judgment

Several scholars have suggested that the language and imagery of the "Day of the Lord" point to a theophanic event—that is, a manifestation of God's glorious presence in judgment against the wicked and vindication of the righteous.[26] Passages cited for the idea that divine theophany involve acts of salvation include Judges 5:1–5; 6:12–13, Isaiah 40:10; 42:13; 52:8; and Habakkuk 3. However, to reduce these to the in-breaking of God's glorious, immediate manifestation as with Moses on Mount Sinai overlooks some details of these passages in their contexts.

The song of Deborah and Barak does not distinguish between God's theophanic warfare against his enemies and the earthly, physical means of Israelite warriors (Judg 5:12–15), natural phenomena like the flooding of the Kishon (5:21), and the role of Jael in assassinating Sisera (5:24). These seemingly natural means are regarded as "the help of the Lord against the warrior" (5:23). Similarly, Gideon's desire—and God's promise—that the Lord would again visit the people of Israel with deliverance (Judges 6:12–15) is fulfilled when God provides victory through the warriors of Gideon and decisive military exploits through God's providential power (6:34–35; 7:19–25). This amazing military defeat of Israel's enemies is viewed as God's miraculous deliverance through seemingly natural means. Gideon understood this: "If You will deliver Israel through me . . ." (6:36); and God told Gideon, "Go down against the camp, for I have given it into your hands" (7:9). Thus the act of God's deliverance of Israel from their enemies is understood as mediated through what appear to be natural means—actual physical battles between human warriors.

In Isaiah, too, the figurative theophanic language of God's glorious visitation is fulfilled by means of seemingly natural events. In Isaiah 42:13, we read, "The Lord goes out like a mighty man, like a man of war he stirs up his zeal; he cries out, he shouts aloud, he shows himself mighty against his foes." Yet this warrior imagery that appears theophanic is actually understood as fulfilled through earthly events orchestrated by God's providence: "Who gave up Jacob to the looter, and Israel to the plunderers? Was it not the Lord, against whom we have sinned . . . ? So he poured on him the heat of his anger and the might of battle" (Isa 42:24, 25).

From a theological-canonical reading of these texts, the reference to God acting through his "arm" may be understood as pointing to a messianic figure who mediates God's active presence. From the New Testament perspective, his actual divine presence is the person of Jesus Christ (cf. Isa 40:10; 52:8–10; 53:1). Likewise, the rich theophanic imagery in Habakkuk 3 expresses the prophet's longing for God to revive the kind of work he manifested during Israel's history. At times, it

---

26. Hoffmann, "Day of the Lord Concept," 42.

is a "recollection of Israel's past history," as in Habakkuk 3:2, 3, 7, 8–15.[27] Those past events involved miraculous manifestations of God's glory (as on Sinai) as well as his acts of military deliverance wrought through figures like Joshua. In all cases, the rich, figurative language of theophany does not preclude God's active presence through various natural and human means—all, of course, under God's providence and often enhanced through direct miraculous measures and divine empowerment.

Consider especially the language of God's conquest when Jeremiah speaks "concerning the army of Pharaoh Neco, king of Egypt, which was by the river Euphrates at Carchemish and which Nebuchadnezzar king of Babylon defeated in the fourth year of Jehoiakim the son of Josiah, king of Judah" (Jer 46:2). That passage is filled with the vivid imagery of human battle: buckler and shield, horses and riders, helmets, spears, and armor, invasion of warriors and destruction of cities (Jer 46:3–8). Here, the prophet writes, "Advance, O horses, and rage, O chariots! Let the warriors go out: men of Cush and Put who handle the shield, men of Lud, skilled in handling the bow" (46:9). No doubt, a historical, prolonged period of warfare is envisioned. Jeremiah then identifies this warfare: "That day is the day of the Lord GOD of hosts (היום ההוא לאדני יהוה צבאות), a day of vengeance, to avenge himself on his foes" (Jer 46:10). Thus God's "day" of vengeance is mediated through human armies and battles.

The point here is that viewing the Day of the Lord as theophanic visitation does not stand in contradiction to viewing the Day of the Lord as God acting through various seemingly natural means such as an invading army, a plague of locusts, sudden storms, or confusion on the battlefield. The typical language of theophany— with God twanging bows, wielding swords, and riding horses and chariots—is undoubtedly figurative. It may point to more obvious supernatural manifestations (as at Sinai) or to less obvious supernatural interventions like the victory over large armies through a small force aided by "fortuitous" happenstances of nature. In every case, the eyes of faith view these as God making his active presence known.[28]

The "Day of the Lord" as Historical, Iterative, and Eschatological

With regard to the earliest use of "Day of the Lord" in Amos, Hoffmann suggests "there is no evidence whatever to its being connected with any eschatological perception."[29] Rather, in its earliest iterations, the phrase refers to the general, popular concept that "on certain occasions God would appear as he already had in the past": an "appearance" characterized by "judgment, war, victory over the idols, and cosmic upheavals."[30] However, Hoffmann argues that in later prophecies

---

27. Carl E. Armerding, "Habakkuk," in *The Expositor's Bible Commentary: Daniel–Malachi*, rev. ed., ed. Tremper Longman III and David E. Garland, vol. 8 (Grand Rapids: Zondervan, 2008), 634.

28. Hoffmann, "Day of the Lord Concept," 44.

29. Hoffmann, "Day of the Lord Concept," 45.

30. Hoffmann, "Day of the Lord Concept," 45.

(particularly, Isa 13:6–8; Joel 1:15; 2:1–11; 3:4; 4:14–15; and Mal 3:23), the term "is very commonly used and except for one case it always has a clear eschatological meaning."[31] The exception he cites is Ezekiel 13:5, in which Hoffmann suggests Ezekiel applies the eschatological term to the destruction of Jerusalem for rhetorical effect.[32] Hoffmann classifies phrases related to יום יהוה into three categories as they relate to eschatological implications: (1) those with a clear eschatological context (Isa 2:12; 34:8; 63:3; Zech 14:1); (2) those with a noneschatological context (Jer 46:10; Isa 22:5; Ezek 39:3; Lam 2:23); and (3) those that are eschatologically ambiguous (Ezek 7:19; 61:2). By "eschatological," Hoffmann means the ultimate climax of human history.

But all this evidence could just as easily be read as indicating that the phrase "Day of the Lord" refers to any epic intervention of God in the judgment of wickedness through various means. Thus one could point backward to previous instances of the "Day of the Lord" (historical), expect other periods rightly called "Day of the Lord" in the normal flow of history (iterative), and look forward to an ultimate "Day of the Lord" in the future (eschatological). All these would share certain basic characteristics so that historical instances and repeated iterations serve to illuminate one another as well as establish an increasingly concrete concept of the future, eschatological Day of the Lord.

This approach to the Day of the Lord as having either an eschatological (ultimate, final fulfillment) or an iterative (near or far fulfillment) referent is similar to the treatment of such passages by rabbinical commentators. Moses ben Maimon (Maimonides or "Rambam"), around AD 1190, writes regarding the "Day of the Lord" prophecy in Joel 3:3–5, "I refer them [the words] to the defeat of Sennacherib near Jerusalem; but they may be taken as an account of the defeat of Gog and Magog near Jerusalem in the days of the Messiah, if this appears preferable."[33] Maimonides sees Joel's "Day of the Lord" as potentially having a near-fulfillment with the defeat of the Assyrian king Sennacherib around 701 BC, yet he is open to the possibility that it has a final fulfillment in the last great battle leading to the messianic reign (called the battle of "Gog and Magog"). It is important to note that in both cases, the "Day of the Lord" refers to a series of events and battles in which God judges, exercises vengeance, and delivers his people. It is also important to note that Maimonides is open to the idea that the "Day of the Lord" may have immediate (near), mediate (far), or ultimate (final) referents. In fact, he counters those who may object to a near fulfillment: "You must know that a day of great salvation or of great distress is called 'the great and terrible day of the Lord.' Thus Joel (ii. 11) says of the day on which the locusts came over the land, 'For the day of the Lord is great and terrible, and who can abide it?' "

William J. Dumbrell notes, "The concept of the day of the Lord, as considered by the prophets, is not singular in meaning; the connotation can be determined

---

31. Hoffmann, "Day of the Lord Concept," 45.
32. Hoffmann, "Day of the Lord Concept," 47.
33. Maimonides, *Guide for the Perplexed* 2.29. English translation: Moses Maimonides, *The Guide for the Perplexed*, trans. M. Friedländer, 2nd ed. (London: Routledge, 1919), 209.

only by examining each context in which the phrase appears."[34] Aernie and Hartley summarize the situation with regard to the varied use of the "Day of the Lord" in the prophets this way:

> The prophets refer to the day of the Lord from different vantage points: (1) The day is described in retrospect by referring to past events where the Lord has previously rendered punishment (e.g., exile). The prophets want their audience to interpret those past incidences as a warning to later generations regarding the future judgment. (2) Judgment may be more imminent in that the Lord will send foreign nations as his agents to carry out retribution on his people. (3) Judgment may be specifically eschatological in nature, looking forward to the consummate day when Yahweh renders the final verdict on all nations of either divine judgment or divine blessing.[35]

> **Go Deeper Excursus 22**
>
> *The Old Testament and the Day of the Lord*

It is sometimes suggested that the "Day of the Lord" as a technical concept involves both judgment and deliverance—a period of prolonged wrath followed by a period of even longer blessing. A detailed examination of Day of the Lord passages suggests a slightly more nuanced description. First, in all instances, "Day of the Lord" includes God's judgment. Second, many of the "Day of the Lord" passages also include hope of preservation, deliverance, and salvation for the righteous remnant. The two ideas are often woven together to form an inseparable link— judgment gives way to blessing. However, the two ideas should not be conflated. In no case does "Day of the Lord" refer only to blessing and salvation apart from judgment. This suggests that the phrase "Day of the Lord" primarily has judgment in view; yet theologically, judgment and restoration cannot be separated.[36]

As has been established by the detailed examination of the Day of the Lord language and imagery in the Old Testament prophets (see Go Deeper Excursus 22), by the close of this prophetic period, the "Day of the Lord" had become a technical concept that employs stock language and imagery to point to any period of God's mediated theophanic visitation in judgment against any nation. Images closely associated with the Day of the Lord include wrath, anger, judgment, destruction, fire, sword, invading armies, death, darkness, and trumpet blast. It is equated not only with other phrases using "day" but also with "tribulation."[37] In short, mere utterance of the phrase יהוה יום or its closely related phrases with יום would bring to mind

---

34. William J. Dumbrell, *The Search for Order: Biblical Eschatology in Focus* (Grand Rapids: Baker, 1994), 109; cf. A. Joseph Everson, "The Days of Yahweh," *JBL* 93.3 (1974): 331.

35. Matthew D. Aernie and Donald E Hartley, *The Righteous and Merciful Judge: The Day of the Lord in the Life and Theology of Paul*, Studies in Scripture and Biblical Theology (Bellingham, WA: Lexham, 2018), 38.

36. Yair Hoffmann, "Eschatology in the Book of Jeremiah," in *Eschatology in the Bible and in Jewish and Christian Tradition*, ed. Henning Graf Reventlow, JSOTSup, vol. 243 (Sheffield: Sheffield Academic, 1997), 79.

37. The phrase צרה יום (ἡμέρα θλίψεως) appears in Gen 35:3; 2 Kgs 19:3 (=Isa 37:3); Pss 20:1; 50:15; 77:2; 86:7; Prov 25:19; Jer 16:19; Nah 1:7; Hab 3:16; and Zeph 1:15.

any one of God's mediated theophanic visitations, always in judgment and often with the promise of deliverance for the righteous remnant.

Aernie and Hartley aptly sum up the situation with the Old Testament prophets:

> The Prophets interpreted the day of the Lord as a *terminus technicus* for the final day of judgment. But the Prophets also revealed that they understood there to be "days" of the Lord. The circumstances that affected God's people (famine, sickness, war, exile, etc.) were seemingly understood as typological patterns pointing to the consummate day of the Lord. The hardships that the covenant people faced were to be interpreted as warnings to repent of their sins and return to Yahweh before the ultimate day arrived and all the nations would appear before him at the final assize. For the Prophets, the day of the Lord describes imminent judgment, while in other passages the locution clearly refers to the final eschatological judgment when God will ultimately make all things right.[38]

The Day of the Lord in the Old Testament Apocrypha

Although the technical phrase "Day of the Lord" is not used in the Greek Old Testament Apocrypha composed between the time of the prophets and the New Testament, a handful of passages utilize the stock language and imagery of the "Day of the Lord." This includes the presentation of God as judge exercising wrath against his enemies in often dramatic, vivid language portraying mediated theophanic presence.

In the song of victory in Judith 16, the Lord's "Day of Judgment" (ἡμέρᾳ κρίσεως) refers to the Lord's theophanic visitation in judgment, expressed specifically in the deliverance from the Medes and Persians (Jdt 16:10–16), but it is applied generally to any who assert themselves against God's people: "Woe to the nations that rise up against my people! The Lord Almighty will take vengeance on them in the day of judgment (ἐν ἡμέρᾳ κρίσεως); he will send fire and worms into their flesh; they shall weep in pain forever" (Jdt 16:17 NRSVue).[39]

In a few instances in the early second-century BC book known as the Wisdom of Sirach or Ecclesiasticus,[40] the author alludes to an eschatological time of judgment in terms similar to the prophets' "Day of the Lord" imagery. In Sirach 5, we read: "Both mercy and wrath are with him, and his anger will rest on sinners. Do not delay to turn back to the Lord, and do not postpone it from day to day; for suddenly the wrath of the Lord (ὀργὴ κυρίου) will come upon you, and at the time of punishment (ἐν καιρῷ ἐκδικήσεως) you will perish. Do not depend on dishonest wealth, for it will not benefit you on the day of calamity (ἐν ἡμέρᾳ ἐπαγωγῆς)" (Sir 5:6–8 NRSVue). Besides these brief references, both the personal and cosmic eschatology of Sirach is undeveloped as a theological theme.[41]

---

38. Aernie and Hartley, *Righteous and Merciful Judge*, 53.

39. Unless otherwise noted, translations of the Apocrypha in this chapter are from the New Revised Standard Version Bible Updated Edition.

40. On the date, see R. J. Coggins, *Sirach*, Guides to Apocrypha and Pseudepigrapha (Sheffield: Sheffield Academic, 1998), 18–20.

41. Cf. Coggins, *Sirach*, 99–100.

The apocryphal Wisdom of Solomon—sometimes included in early Christian canon lists—contains a few passages that employ conventional "Day of the Lord" language and imagery without using the technical term itself. Wisdom 5 portrays God gearing up and waging a war against the wicked who had opposed him and his people:

> [The Lord] will take his zeal as his whole armor, and will arm all creation to repel his enemies; he will put on righteousness as a breastplate, and wear impartial justice as a helmet; he will take holiness as an invincible shield, and sharpen stern wrath for a sword, and creation will join with him to fight against his frenzied foes. Shafts of lightning will fly with true aim, and will leap from the clouds to the target, as from a well-drawn bow, and hailstones full of wrath will be hurled as from a catapult; the water of the sea will rage against them, and rivers will relentlessly overwhelm them; a mighty wind will rise against them, and like a tempest it will winnow them away. Lawlessness will lay waste the whole earth, and evildoing will overturn the thrones of rulers. (Wis 5:17–23 NRSVue)

Here we see classic language and imagery portraying God's mediated theophanic coming in judgment, meting out wrath by means of natural catastrophes, and mustering creation itself against his enemies. On this passage, Lester Grabbe notes, "Although this is a part of the judgment on them in this life, it does not preclude a later, post-mortem judgment as well."[42] Indeed, the use of the phrase "day of judgment" at times seems to refer primarily to ultimate punishment for sin in the afterlife, not to a period of time on earth during which wicked peoples and nations are judged. Wisdom 3:17–18 says, "Even if they live long they will be held of no account, and finally their old age will be without honor. If they die young, they will have no hope and no consolation on the day of judgement (ἐν ἡμέρᾳ διαγνώσεως). For the end of an unrighteous generation is grievous" (NASB).

The Day of the Lord at Qumran

The question of the eschatology (or "eschatologies") at Qumran is one of great scholarly discussion. However, scholars generally admit to several stable themes in the Qumran community. These include dualism between the "children of light" and the "children of darkness"—a conflict that will be resolved in the future (1QS 3:13–4:26; 1QM 1, 15–19).[43] Philip Davies notes, "This is reminiscent of the ongoing conflict between the righteous and the wicked in the Old Testament prophets, which will be resolved in the Day of the Lord, when the wicked are punished and the righteous vindicated. Another element relates to the restoration of Israel in covenant faithfulness and their exaltation over the nations (1QM 2–9; 1QSa)."[44] This seems to take up the common Old Testament theme of restoration of Israel

---

42. Lester L. Grabbe, *Wisdom of Solomon*, T&T Clark Study Guides, ed. Michael A. Knibb, A. T. Lincoln, and R. N. Whybray (London: T&T Clark, 1997), 57.

43. Philip R. Davies, "Eschatology at Qumran," *JBL* 104.1 (1985): 49.

44. Davies, "Eschatology at Qumran," 49.

in the coming age brought about by the purging and discipling judgment of the Day of the Lord. Davies describes the third element, "in which the present time is characterized as a 'time of wrath,' namely, God's continuing punishment of Israel for its past sins, the perpetual exiling of Israel from full enjoyment in the land. . . . Such an eschatological perspective is seen in the *Damascus Document*, the Songs of Heavenly Lights (4QDibHam) and the Melchizedek fragments."[45] This theme also touches on the Day of the Lord in that it is one of wrath and results in exile. It may be that the Qumran community's sense of imminence resulted in the concept that they were in the midst of the final, ultimate Day of the Lord or that it was extremely close.

The War Scroll mentions repeatedly a coming day of war and judgment in language and imagery similar to the Old Testament Day of the Lord: "And on the day on which the Kittim fall, there will be a battle, and savage destruction before the God of Israel, for this will be the day determined by him since ancient times for the war of extermination against the sons of darkness. On this [day], the assembly of the gods and the congregation of men shall confront each other for great destruction" (1Q33 1.9–10).[46] This upheaval and conflict between the "sons of light" and the "sons of darkness" is called the "day of calamity" (ליום הווה) and is characterized by suffering (צרה) (cf. Zeph 1:15; Dan 12:1). Almost certainly drawing on language from Daniel 12,[47] the War Scroll prophesies that "of all their sufferings, none will be like this, hastening till eternal redemption is fulfilled."[48]

In that same passage, the length of the period seems to consist of seven "lots" or "allotments" (גורלות): three to the sons of light, three to the sons of darkness, and the final in which God is victorious over Belial. "In the war, the sons of light will be the strongest during three lots, in order to strike down wickedness; and in three [others], the army of Belial will gird themselves in order to force the lot of [light] to retreat. There will be infantry battalions to melt the heart, but God's might will strengthen the [heart of the sons of light.] And in the seventh lot, God's great hand will subdue [Belial and all] the angels of his dominion and all the men of [his lot]" (1Q33 1.13–15).[49] This seven-year liberation will then be followed by successive periods of time during which the sons of light conquer the surrounding enemies of Israel. The entire "day" of judgment is expected to take forty years.[50]

Later, the War Scroll uses similar language and imagery common to the Old Testament prophets: "For this will be a time of suffering (צרה) for [Israel and a service] of war /against/ all the nations" (1Q33 15.1).[51] Still later: "All those who are

---

45. Davies, "Eschatology at Qumran," 49.

46. Florentino García Martínez and Eibert J. C. Tigchelaar, *The Dead Sea Scrolls Study Edition (Translations)* (Leiden: Brill, 1997–1998), 113–15.

47. See Jean Duhaime, *War Texts: 1QM and Related Manuscripts*, Companion to the Qumran Scrolls, vol. 56 (London: T&T Clark, 2005), 65–72; Geza Vermes, *Scrolls, Scripture, and Early Christianity*, Library of Second Temple Studies, vol. 56 (London: T&T Clark, 2005), 69.

48. Martínez and Tigchelaar, *Dead Sea Scrolls Study Edition (Translations)*, 115.

49. Martínez and Tigchelaar, *Dead Sea Scrolls Study Edition (Translations)*, 115.

50. See Vermes, *Scrolls, Scripture, and Early Christianity*, 71.

51. Martínez and Tigchelaar, *Dead Sea Scrolls Study Edition (Translations)*, 137.

[ready for] the war shall go and camp opposite the king of the Kittim and opposite all the army of Belial, assembled with him for the day of [vengeance] ([קם] נ[יום ליום]) by God's sword."[52] The Pesher to Habakkuk affirms that on the Day of Judgment (ביום המשפט) the wicked idolaters will not be saved (1Qphab 12.14); in fact, "on the day of judgment God will destroy all the worshippers of idols, and the wicked, from the earth."[53] At the same time, the theme of the righteous remnant being saved on the "Day of Judgment" is found in a fragmentary comment on Micah 1:5 (1Q14).[54]

What becomes clear in the Dead Sea Scrolls, even in the midst of much uncertainty in the details, is its general consistency with the Old Testament portrayal of the eschatological "Day of the Lord."[55] It will involve not only Israel but a number of surrounding nations. It will culminate in God's judgment against Israel's enemies as well as the wicked among Israel, resulting in the victory of the righteous and their reward of immortality.[56]

Summary and Conclusion: The "Day of the Lord" at the Brink of the New Testament

By the time we reach the first century, the "Day of the Lord" was already functioning as a technical term for centuries. Other phrases like "day of wrath," "day of judgment," and "tribulation"—as well as stock language and imagery like fire, darkness, smoke, sword, pestilence, vengeance, trumpet, warfare, and so on, would have been associated with the "Day of the Lord."[57] This "Day of the Lord" would have been generally thought of as God's mediated theophanic visitation in judgment. Depending on specific circumstances, the object of that judgment could be God's people, Israel, which would usually result in exile; or the objects of the day of wrath are the enemies of Israel, resulting in the protection, rescue, or deliverance of his people.

In all cases, the "Day of the Lord" is never a single day, nor is it primarily conceived of as occurring in the afterlife or in the spiritual realm—though it may result in eternal condemnation for some and eternal blessing for others. And it may

---

52. Martínez and Tigchelaar, *Dead Sea Scrolls Study Edition (Translations)*, 137.

53. Martínez and Tigchelaar, *Dead Sea Scrolls Study Edition (Translations)*, 21.

54. Geza Vermes, *The Dead Sea Scrolls in English*, 4th ed. (Sheffield: Sheffield Academic Press, 1995), 335.

55. J. J. Collins writes, "While the various models of eschatology found in the Scrolls do not yield a fully coherent system, some ideas may be characterized as typical of the sect. One such idea is the expectation of an eschatological war." See "The Expectation of the End in the Dead Sea Scrolls," in *Eschatology, Messianism, and the Dead Sea Scrolls*, ed. Craig A. Evans and Peter W. Flint, Studies in the Dead Sea Scrolls and Related Literature (Grand Rapids: Eerdmans, 1997), 86.

56. Craig A. Evans and Peter W. Flint, introduction in *Eschatology, Messianism, and the Dead Sea Scrolls*, ed. Craig A. Evans and Peter W. Flint, Studies in the Dead Sea Scrolls and Related Literature (Grand Rapids: Eerdmans, 1997), 5.

57. Vander Hart "The Transition of the Old Testament Day of the Lord," 8. Vander Hart underscores the fact that the Old Testament imagery has YHWH as the "sole Actor" as opposed to mediated by a messianic figure (8–9); this overlooks the fact that the imagery, though theophanic, portrays a mediated theophanic judgment.

involve forces of spiritual good (angels) and evil (demons). Primarily, the "Day of the Lord" is a way of describing a prolonged period of divinely orchestrated and providentially controlled judgment against a nation or nations in this world. The actual historical manifestation of these judgments would be seen as natural: famine, flood, storms, locusts, disease, earthquakes, military campaigns or sieges, and so on. Past manifestations of the Day of the Lord, then, might serve as types of imminent days of the Lord, which themselves would forewarn the world of a future ultimate Day of the Lord.

So, when the New Testament uses the term "Day of the Lord"—especially associated with some of the stock language and imagery of the Old Testament—we should think not of the moment of Christ's second coming or of some instantaneous, otherworldly posthumous judgment before God's throne. Rather, the Day of the Lord refers to a prolonged period of judgment exercised by and through the coming divine Judge, mediated by seemingly natural means.

Aernie and Hartley convincingly demonstrate that the New Testament "concept of the Day of the Lord is based solely on the Old Testament."[58] Also, it is clear that Paul understands that the future "Day of the Lord" is to be fulfilled "in Jesus Christ." However, I assert that all aspects of the anticipated "Day of the Lord," drawn from the entire Old Testament development of its import, are to be fulfilled *in and through* Christ. His future actions as avenging judge and conquering king are rightly regarded in theophanic terms as the God-man. Yet, just as the Day of the Lord in the Old Testament referred to a period of time (not a single day) during which God's wrath was mediated through human armies and divinely providential natural calamities, so will the future, ultimate Day of the Lord associated with the coming of Christ as judge and king.

We have in Jesus Christ a fulfillment in the most complete sense of that term. Fulfillment of the Day of the Lord in and through Jesus Christ means both the Day of the Lord as mediated calamities of judgment on the earth over a period of time and the Day of the Lord as an actual manifestation of God's glory to judge the wicked, deliver the righteous, and establish justice in the world. When we speak of the future coming of Christ as judge and king, we speak of the Day of the Lord—a *prolonged period of time* during which temporal judgments are issued by the sovereign authority of Christ, culminating in the eternal king taking inescapable control over the world.

---

58. Aernie and Hartley, *Righteous and Merciful Judge*, 25.

16

THE DAY OF THE LORD CONCEPT
IN THE NEW TESTAMENT

*And the judgement, which will come by fire, will be the
destruction of unbelievers, at the end of this world.*

Irenaeus, *Demonstration* 69

The technical phrase "Day of the Lord" in the New Testament is limited to a few
passages (Acts 2:20; 1 Thess 5:2; 2 Thess 2:2; 2 Pet 3:10). Another phrase, closely associated but distinct, is the "day of our Lord Jesus Christ" (1 Cor 1:8; 5:5; 2 Cor 1:14).
Besides these, however, many New Testament passages employ stock language and
imagery from Old Testament "Day of the Lord" passages.

In this chapter, we will first examine the exact "Day of the Lord" passages in
the New Testament and then visit key passages that use similar quasi-technical
terms and imagery to understand the New Testament eschatological expectations
regarding the coming period of judgment. Because
of the more technical nature of the relationship between Joel 2 and Acts 2, the first instance of "Day
of the Lord" in Acts 2:20 is discussed in Go Deeper
Excursus 23, *Joel 2 in Acts 2: The Day of the Lord in
Peter's Sermon.*

> **Go Deeper Excursus 23**
>
> *Joel 2 in Acts 2: The Day of
> the Lord in Peter's Sermon*

The "Day of the Lord" in 1 Thessalonians 5:2

While it would be wrong to categorize 1 Thessalonians as an apocalyptic text, eschatological themes are woven throughout the letter, often drawing on standard
apocalyptic language and images.[1] The use of the technical phrase "Day of the
Lord" occurs in a section particularly saturated with Old Testament apocalyptic
imagery—1 Thessalonians 4:13–5:11. Though Paul uses the transitional expression
περὶ δέ ("now concerning") in 5:1, he is not introducing a completely new subject
but shifting his emphasis within the broader subject of eschatological hope.[2] While

---

1. Charles A. Wanamaker, "Apocalyptic Discourse, Paraenesis and Identity Maintenance
in 1 Thessalonians," *NeoT.* 36.1–2 (2002): 134.

2. The construction περὶ δέ can, of course, be used to transition to a new topic. It is used
by the Didachist to transition from the Two Ways to a discussion of baptism (περὶ δὲ τοῦ
βαπτίσματος) (Did. 7.1) and then to a discussion of the Eucharist (περὶ δὲ τῆς εὐχαριστίας)
(Did. 9.1). Yet within the discussion of the Eucharist itself, the construction is used to tran-

the technical term is used only in 5:2, the entire passage exudes Day of the Lord imagery. Even when Paul finally uses the phrase ἡμέρα κυρίου, he does so to discuss the timing (περὶ δὲ τῶν χρόνων καὶ τῶν καιρῶν) of the events: that is, the timing of the coming Day of the Lord (cf. Acts 1:7). In the first part of this passage, Paul seeks to allay the concerns of some Thessalonians that their fellow believers who had died (περὶ τῶν κοιμωμένων, 4:13) would thus fail to take part in the blessings of the coming of Christ.[3] To clear up the matter and to alleviate their grief, Paul fills in details related to Christ's coming and the fate of both the living and dead saints (4:13).

Already in the letter, however, Paul has directly treated eschatological matters to instill hope, eager expectation, and godly living. In 1 Thessalonians 1:9–10, Paul writes, "For they report about us what kind of welcome we had among you and how you turned to God from idols to serve a living and true God and to wait (ἀναμένειν) for his Son from heaven, whom he raised from the dead—Jesus, who rescues us from the coming wrath (τὸν ῥυόμενον ἡμᾶς ἐκ τῆς ὀργῆς τῆς ἐρχομένης)." The phrase "the coming wrath" evokes images of the coming Day of the Lord (Isa 13:9; Zeph 1:15; etc.) (see chapter 15). This is not a reference to the abiding wrath of God revealed against all ungodliness: that is, eternal condemnation (Rom 1:18).[4] This is the wrath that is coming upon the world in connection with God's theophanic visitation in judgment.[5] Thus the "coming wrath" is another term for the coming "Day of the Lord" that Paul will describe directly in 1 Thessalonians 5.

The object of the Christian's eschatological hope is the parousia of Christ as rescuer from the coming wrath (Ἰησοῦν τὸν ῥυόμενον ἡμᾶς ἐκ τῆς ὀργῆς τῆς ἐρχομένης) (1 Thess 1:10). Paul again mentions that the Thessalonians themselves will be his hope, joy, and "crown of boasting before our Lord Jesus at his coming (ἔμπροσθεν τοῦ κυρίου ἡμῶν Ἰησοῦ ἐν τῇ αὐτοῦ παρουσίᾳ)" (1 Thess 2:19); and in 3:13, Paul prays that they would be holy and blameless before God "at the coming of our Lord Jesus with all his saints." This language of the coming of Christ with his "holy ones" or "saints" echoes Zechariah 14:5, which is itself firmly planted in the Day of the Lord imagery (14:1–5).[6] So, when we arrive at the focused treatment of eschatological themes in 1 Thessalonians 4:13–5:11, Paul is merely fanning into a blaze the flames he had already lit along the way.

---

sition from a discussion of the prayer for the cup to the prayer for the bread—merely two aspects of the same sacred meal (περὶ δὲ τοῦ κλάσματος) (Did. 9.3). Cf. Charles A. Wanamaker, *The Epistle to the Thessalonians: A Commentary on the Greek Text*, New International Greek Testament Commentary (Grand Rapids: Eerdmans, 1990), 176.

3. Leon Morris, *1 and 2 Thessalonians: An Introduction and Commentary*, Tyndale New Testament Commentaries, vol. 13 (Downers Grove, IL: InterVarsity, 1984), 87.

4. The specific term "wrath" (ὀργή) is never unambiguously used for eternal condemnation—that is, the fate of the wicked lost, though possibly John 3:36, Rom 1:18; and 9:22 might have this in mind. In passages explicitly referring to the state of the lost, ὀργή is never used.

5. Gene L. Green, *The Letters to the Thessalonians*, The Pillar New Testament Commentary (Grand Rapids: Eerdmans, 2002), 111; and Ben Witherington III, *1 and 2 Thessalonians: A Socio-Rhetorical Commentary* (Grand Rapids: Eerdmans, 2006), 75.

6. Zechariah 14:5 is also quoted in 2 Thess 1:7, 10 and Did. 16.7.

Paul rests the believer's personal hope on resurrection at Christ's return: "Through Jesus, God will bring with him (διὰ τοῦ Ἰησοῦ ἄξει σὺν αὐτῷ) those who have died" (1 Thess 4:14). This could mean that the departed spirits of those who died "in Christ" are now present with him (2 Cor 5:8; Phil 1:23) and will accompany Christ at his coming;[7] or, more likely, it could mean that the Lord will bring back from the dead those who are with Christ: that is, "those who belong to Christ" (cf. 1 Cor 15:23).[8] Either interpretation results in encouragement for the Thessalonians their departed loved ones, the saints, will return with Christ.

Paul then provides a strong basis for their hope that rests on a revelation from the Lord. The phrase ἐν λόγῳ κυρίου, "by a word of the Lord" (1 Thess 4:15), could refer to something Jesus himself taught or to a new revelation from the Lord: that is, a prophetic utterance.[9] In either case, the content of this teaching is clear: "We who are alive, who are left until the coming of the Lord (εἰς τὴν παρουσίαν τοῦ κυρίου), will by no means precede (οὐ μὴ φθάσωμεν) those who have died" (4:15). The term "parousia" here has the same meaning as earlier in connection to Christ's coming with all the saints (1 Thess 2:19; 3:13). But the phrase "will by no means precede" primarily refers to not "having an advantage over" or not "having precedence over." Paul assures the Thessalonians that they have lost nothing.[10] How so? Because at the coming of the Lord, their loved ones will be resurrected (4:16).

Verse 16 introduces powerful Old Testament imagery that connects this passage to the Day of the Lord, as well as to one of the clearest references to bodily resurrection in the Hebrew Scriptures. The Lord's descent from heaven (cf. 1 Thess 1:9–10) reminds us of the Son of Man coming on the clouds (Dan 7:13), which Jesus applied to his own second coming in glory (Matt 24:30). Paul modifies this descent of Christ from heaven with three prepositional phrases beginning with ἐν—ἐν κελεύσματι ("with a shout"), ἐν φωνῇ ἀρχαγγέλου ("with a voice of an archangel"), and ἐν σάλπιγγι θεοῦ ("with a trumpet of God"). The "shout of command" (κελεύσμα) naturally brings to mind a battle cry or military command.[11] It is used in the Septuagint in Proverbs 24:62 (30:27 MT): "the locust is kingless, yet at one command (κελεύσματος) he marches in an orderly manner." The next attendant preposition refers to the voice of an archangel (ἐν φωνῇ ἀρχαγγέλου), who may be thought of as the one calling out the battle command. Scripture names only one "archangel," Michael (Dan 10:13, 21; 12:1). Finally, the "trumpet of God" (ἐν σάλπιγγι θεοῦ) also draws on Day of the Lord imagery (cf. Joel 2:1,

---

7. See Gordon D. Fee, *The First and Second Letters to the Thessalonians*, The New International Commentary on the New Testament (Grand Rapids: Eerdmans, 2009), 169–70.

8. F. F. Bruce, *1 & 2 Thessalonians*, Word Biblical Commentary, vol. 45 (Grand Rapids: Zondervan, 1982), 97–98.

9. Cf. Fee, *Thessalonians*, 173–74; Grant R. Osborne, *1 & 2 Thessalonians: Verse by Verse*, ed. Osborne New Testament Commentaries (Bellingham, WA: Lexham, 2018), 107–8; Wanamaker, *Thessalonians*, 170–71; Witherington, *1 & 2 Thessalonians*, 134–36. That Paul had in mind Matt 24:30–31, though a common view, is based on a superficial comparison of the elements of these passages. See detailed discussion above in chapter 7.

10. Bruce, *1 & 2 Thessalonians*, 99.

11. BDAG, 538. Osborne, *1 & 2 Thessalonians*, 109–10.

15; Zech 9:14).[12] At that time, then "the dead in Christ will rise (ἀναστήσονται)" (1 Thess 4:16).

These images—a military command shouted by an archangel, a blast of God's trumpet, and the resurrection of the dead—all triangulate on Daniel 12:1–2, which itself incorporates Old Testament Day of the Lord imagery: "And toward that country, Michael, the great messenger (ὁ ἄγγελος ὁ μέγας) who stands over the sons of your people, will go by. That will be a day of affliction (ἡ ἡμέρα θλίψεως),[13] of a kind that never was from when there were nations until that day. And in that day all the people, whoever may be found inscribed in the book, will be lifted up. And many of those sleeping (τῶν καθευδόντων) in the breadth of the earth will arise (ἀναστήσονται),[14] some unto everlasting life, but some unto reproach, and some to dispersion and everlasting disgrace" (LXX, Brannan).

Having drawn together imagery that connects the coming of Christ with the tribulation of the last days in Daniel 12, Paul then addresses the main point of his passage: the hope of resurrection. Whereas some Thessalonians believed the dead were at a disadvantage, Paul ends verse 16 with the impression that the opposite is true because "the dead in Christ will rise first (πρῶτον)." Does this then mean that the living are actually at a disadvantage? No, because the living who remain until the parousia of the Lord (4:17; cf. 4:15) "will be caught up (ἁρπαγησόμεθα) in the clouds together with them (σὺν αὐτοῖς)." The mention of the "clouds" also conjures images of the coming of the Son of Man to execute judgment and establish his kingdom (Dan 7:13); it was often connected to Day of the Lord theophanic visitations in judgment (Isa 19:1). Both the dead saints raised and the living saints who are still alive will be reunited "to meet the Lord in the air" and all will "be with the Lord forever" (4:17). This news of a glorious resurrection and assumption and the grand reunion that accompanies the parousia is the basis for encouragement (4:18).

Paul then pivots with περὶ δέ to the question of the timing of the Day of the Lord. Yes, Christ is coming to rescue us from the coming wrath (1 Thess 1:9–10), but he also comes as judge. Paul reminds his readers that with regard to the "times and seasons" (τῶν χρόνων καὶ τῶν καιρῶν), they should be well aware that "the Day of the Lord (ἡμέρα κυρίου) will come (ἔρχεται) like a thief in the night" (5:1–2; cf. Luke 12:39–40; 2 Pet 3:10).

By employing the phrase "Day of the Lord," Paul associates the coming of Christ with the series of events related to the theophanic visitation in judgment—an indeterminately long period of tribulation that would begin at an unexpected moment. In fact, people will be announcing "peace and security" just at the time when "sudden destruction (αἰφνίδιος . . . ὄλεθρος) will come upon them, as labor pains

---

12. Wanamaker, *Thessalonians*, 173, notes, "The 'trumpet of God' is an image occurring frequently in the OT in contexts of theophany and eschatological judgment (cf. Ex. 19:16, 19; Is. 27:13; Joel 2:1; Zp. 1:14–16; Zc. 9:14) as well as in both Jewish and Christian apocalyptic traditions (cf. Pss. Sol. 11:1; 2 Esdr. 6:17–24; *Apoc. Mos.* 22, 37–38; Mt. 24:31; Rev. 8:2, 6, 13; 9:14)."

13. Cf. Obad 12, 14; Zeph 1:15;

14. Cf. Isa 26:19 and its Day of the Lord context in Gary Edward Schnittjer, *Old Testament Use of Old Testament: A Book-by-Book Guide* (Grand Rapids: Zondervan Academic, 2021), 624–26.

come upon a pregnant woman, and there will be no escape (οὐ μὴ ἐκφύγωσιν)" (1 Thess 5:3). The Old Testament Day of the Lord imagery employed all these terms. Obadiah 13 refers to "the day of their distresses (πόνων)," "the day of their ruin (ὀλέθρου)," and "the day of their destruction (ἀπωλείας)" (LXX, Brannan). And in the Psalms of Solomon 8:1, we read, "My ear heard affliction (θλίψιν) and the sound of war (φωνὴν πολέμου), the sound of the trumpet (φωνὴν σάλπιγγος) sounding slaughter and ruin (ὄλεθρον)" (LXX, Brannan). Also, the connection between birth pains and the Day of the Lord is firmly established in the Old Testament (Isa 13:8; Jer 4:31).

Recalling that Paul had already established the principle that Jesus in his parousia from heaven will rescue them from the coming wrath (1 Thess 1:10), he now comforts his readers with a contrast between the world's inability to escape the sudden period of tribulation and judgment and their own secure position. The Day of the Lord will not catch the believers off guard and unprepared because as those who belong to Christ, they are children of light, not of darkness (5:4–5). The use of "darkness" to describe the period of the Day of the Lord is also common in the Old Testament (Amos 5:18, 20; cf. Joel 2:31). Paul draws a moral and ethical distinction that applies to the believers' behavior in the present (1 Thess 5:6–7). He urges the Thessalonians to put on faith and love, and "for a helmet the hope of salvation (ἐλπίδα σωτηρίας)" (5:8). Paul has in mind salvation from the coming eschatological judgment, and he echoes the same thought as in 1 Thessalonians 1:10 that believers are "to await (ἀναμένειν)" the Son from heaven, who "rescues us from the coming wrath (ῥυόμενον ἡμᾶς ἐκ τῆς ὀργῆς τῆς ἐρχομένης)." In Louw and Nida, both ῥύομαι and σῴζω fall under the semantic domain of "cause to be safe, free from danger" as opposed to "save in a religious sense," which more consistently employs only σῴζω.[15] So, in context, when Paul says in 1 Thessalonians 5:9, "For God has destined us not for wrath (εἰς ὀργήν) but for obtaining salvation (εἰς περιποίησιν σωτηρίας) through our Lord Jesus Christ," this is the coming wrath of the Day of the Lord and this salvation is the rescue from it (1 Thess 1:10).[16]

Several elements aptly tie Paul's conclusion of this section (1 Thess 5:9–11) back to the first part of the eschatological passage, confirming that Paul is referring to rescue from the coming wrath through resurrection and assumption to heaven. He says we are appointed for obtaining salvation "through our Lord Jesus Christ (διὰ τοῦ κυρίου ἡμῶν Ἰησοῦ Χριστοῦ)" (5:9), which echoes 4:14. Paul repeats that our rescue rests upon the fact that Christ "died for us (τοῦ ἀποθανόντος)" so that we may "live with him (ἅμα σὺν αὐτῷ ζήσωμεν)" (5:10). This also recalls the language of 4:14 and 4:17. The terms "whether we are awake or asleep" do not refer to moral conditions of ethical slumbering or alertness,[17] but "the image here goes back to 4:13–18, where those awake are the saints still alive and those asleep are the deceased believers."[18] Paul then concludes the passage with another exhortation to encourage

---

15. L&N, 240–41.
16. Wanamaker, *Thessalonians*, 187. Cf. also Bruce, *1 & 2 Thessalonians*, 112–13.
17. Bruce, *1 & 2 Thessalonians*, 114, calls such a notion "ludicrous," and I must concur.
18. Osborne, *1 & 2 Thessalonians*, 128; Witherington, *1 & 2 Thessalonians*, 153.

one another with this promise of salvation from the coming wrath of the Day of the Lord (5:11), which mirrors 4:18.

In 1 Thessalonians 5:2, then, Paul uses the phrase ἡμέρα κυρίου "Day of the Lord" in its technical sense, drawing together unambiguous language and imagery from the Old Testament not only in chapter 5 but already in chapter 4. He therefore anticipated an ultimate eschatological Day of the Lord consistent with the pattern of days of the Lord throughout God's history of theophanic visitations in judgment. The "trumpet of God" refers to the announcement of this ultimate Day of the Lord that will come unexpectedly on the people of the world who are not only carousing in darkness but who will be completely oblivious when the time of coming judgment and destruction breaks into their lives. Yet, Christ will save the children of light from this coming wrath upon the earth.

In context, the means by which this salvation from the coming wrath of the Day of the Lord appears to be the resurrection and catching up of the saints described in 1 Thessalonians 4:16–17. We are told in 1 Corinthians, written a few years later, that those who are alive at the time of the resurrection will not simply remain in their mortal condition but will be transformed into immortal bodies like those who rise from the dead (1 Cor 15:51–52). Unless one argues that Paul has two completely different resurrections in mind, the mention of the "last trumpet," upon which the dead will be raised and the living will be changed into immortal, incorruptible bodies (1 Cor 15:53), must be identified with the "trumpet of God" in 1 Thessalonians 4:17. Paul calls this the "last (ἔσχατος)" because it is associated with the "last day" (cf. John 6:40, 54; 11:24; 12:48): that is, the "last Day of the Lord."

> **Go Deeper Excursus 24**
>
> *The Last Trumpet in*
> *1 Corinthians 15:52 vs. the Seventh*
> *Trumpet in Revelation 1:15*

One more consideration is worth exploring. In Philippians 3:20–21, Paul writes, "But our citizenship is in heaven (ἐν οὐρανοῖς), and it is from there (ἐξ οὗ) that we are expecting (ἀπεκδεχόμεθα) a Savior (σωτῆρα), the Lord Jesus Christ. He will transform (μετασχηματίσει) the body of our humiliation that it may be conformed to the body of his glory, by the power that also enables him to make all things subject to himself."[19] The anticipation of believers at the coming of Christ from heaven is the transformation of our lowly bodies to conform to Christ's glorious body. This aligns precisely with Paul's statement in 1 Corinthians 15:52–54, which is associated with Christ's return from heaven. Yet in 1 Thessalonians 1:10, Paul describes the expectation of the believer who had turned to God from idols to serve the living God thusly: "to wait for his Son from heaven (ἐκ τῶν οὐρανῶν), whom he raised from the dead—Jesus, who rescues us from the coming wrath." Thus the expectation of rescue in 1 Thessalonians 1:10 and the expectation of transformation in Philippians

---

19. Regarding the reference to citizenship (τὸ πολίτευμα) in Phil 3:20, Wright is correct when he notes, "Being citizens of heaven, as the Philippians would know, doesn't mean that one is expecting to go back to the mother city, but rather that one is expecting the emperor to come *from* the mother city to give the colony its full dignity, to rescue it if need be, to subdue local enemies and put everything to rights." See N. T. Wright, *Surprised by Hope* (London: SPCK, 2007), 145.

3:20–21 both look forward to the same future event, and Paul holds both expectations together in 1 Thessalonians 4:13–5:11 (cf. 1 Cor 15:51–53).

Philippians 3:20–21	1 Thessalonians 1:10
[20] But our citizenship is **in heaven, and it is from there that we are expecting a Savior, the Lord Jesus Christ**. [21] *He will transform the body of our humiliation that it may be conformed to the body of his glory . . .*	. . . and **to wait for his Son from heaven, whom he raised from the dead—Jesus,** who rescues us from the coming wrath.

1 Thessalonians 4:15–17; 5:9–10	
[4:15] . . . that we who are alive, who are left until **the coming of the Lord**, will by no means precede those who have died. [16] **For the Lord himself,** with a cry of command, with the archangel's call and *with the sound of God's trumpet,* **will descend from heaven,** *and the dead in Christ will rise first.* [17] *Then we who are alive, who are left, will be caught up in the clouds* together with them to meet the Lord in the air. . . . [5:9] For God has destined us not for wrath but **for obtaining salvation** through our Lord Jesus Christ, [5:10] who died for us, so that *whether we are awake or asleep* we may live with him.	

1 Corinthians 15:51–53	
[51] . . . *We will not all die, but we will all be changed,* [52] *in a moment, in the twinkling of an eye, at the last trumpet. For the trumpet will sound, and the dead will be raised imperishable, and we will be changed.* [53] *For this perishable body must put on imperishability, and this mortal body must put on immortality.*	

This correspondence of language and imagery suggests that Paul viewed the anticipated resurrection, transformation, and assumption of those who are Christ's to occur "at the last trumpet of God" (1 Thess 4:16; 1 Cor 15:52) upon Christ's descent from heaven (Phil 3:20; 1 Thess 4:16). Further, it appears that Paul viewed this transformation and assumption as the actual means by which Christ will rescue or save believers from the coming wrath (1 Thess 1:10; 5:9). In the Old Testament, the sounding of the trumpet is always pictured as preceding the period of judgment known as the Day of the Lord (Joel 2:1; cf. Jer 4:5, 19, 21).

The "Day of the Lord" in 2 Thessalonians 2:2

Already in 2 Thessalonians 1, Paul presents vivid imagery of a theophanic visitation in judgment in which Christ himself takes the place normally occupied by YHWH in the Old Testament (2 Thess 1:6–10). Here Paul employs classic imagery in terms of YHWH's theophanic visitation in judgment (Isa 66:14–16; cf. 2 Thess 1:8). While the wicked receive tribulation at the coming of Christ, believers will receive ἄνεσις, "relief" (2 Thess 1:7). When the Lord comes, his presence will bring eternal destruction for the wicked (1:9; cf. Ps 96:5 [LXX]; Pss. Sol. 12:6; 15:5) but seasons of refreshing and relief for the righteous (2 Thess 1:7; Acts 3:20–21).

Many fall into an interpretational pit at just this point, failing to recognize the Day of the Lord ("that Day") as a use of the technical concept from the Old Testament; this failure often results in picturing the coming tribulation (θλίψις) inflicted upon the wicked as a momentary flash of fiery judgment rather than a long period of mediated judgment meted out on the earth, which will involve both retribution as well as repentance. That is, the coming of God/Christ in judgment is not a single day or a single moment but a long period marked by distinct eschatological events, just as the Day of the Lord in the Old Testament (see chapter 15).

Then, in 2 Thessalonians 2:1–2, we discover that since Paul's visit to Thessalonica and the writing of his first letter,[20] something had gone awry with the eschatological expectations of some of the people in Thessalonica. Paul needs to revisit the themes covered already in his previous letter (1 Thess 4:13–5:11): "As to the coming (ὑπὲρ τῆς παρουσίας) of our Lord Jesus Christ and our being gathered together (καὶ ἡμῶν ἐπισυναγωγῆς ἐπ᾽ αὐτὸν) to him" (2 Thess 2:1).[21] Yet, in the time since they received that first letter, some had been "shaken in mind or alarmed, either by spirit or by word or by letter" (2:2). This false prophecy or forged writing, Paul says, claimed that "the day of the Lord is already here (ὅτι ἐνέστηκεν ἡ ἡμέρα τοῦ κυρίου)" (2:2).

Two issues are necessary to address before we can fully comprehend the error Paul was addressing. First, the term "Day of the Lord" has the same meaning as it had in 1 Thessalonians 5:2 (see above, pp. 201–7). By failing to understand the significance of this technical term, some assume that the "Day of the Lord" was simply the moment of Christ's second coming—that is, the literal day on which Jesus comes down from heaven.[22]

Second, the verb ἐνέστηκεν means "is already here" (see NRSVue). BDAG rightly notes that in past tenses, the verb ἐνίστημι means "be present, have come": that is, "to be present as condition or thing at the time of speaking, be now, happen now."[23] Of course, ἐνέστηκεν is in the perfect tense, so Paul is saying that the Thessalonians had been misled into thinking they were in the midst of the long period known as the Day of the Lord. Their misunderstanding was not that the return of Christ and the gathering of the church had already happened, as if the Day of the Lord were a momentary event, nor that the Day of the Lord had come and gone and was now in the past, as if ἐνέστηκεν meant "already happened." Rather, the

20. With the majority of scholarly opinion (and contra Wanamaker, *Thessalonians*, 37–45), I take the writing of the Thessalonian epistles to have been the same as the canonical order. On the issues and perspectives on the order of the books, see Bruce, *1 & 2 Thessalonians*, xxxix–xlvi.

21. Osborne, *1 & 2 Thessalonians*, 169; Witherington, *1 & 2 Thessalonians*, 212.

22. E.g., Green, *Letters to the Thessalonians*, 301–6.

23. BDAG, 337.

Thessalonian error was believing they were in the midst of the Day of the Lord.[24] Bruce notes, "It cannot be seriously disputed that 'is present' is the natural sense of ἐνέστηκεν."[25]

If readers fail to understand the technical meaning of Day of the Lord as a period of judgment rather than a moment, and if they fail to understand ἐνέστηκεν as "is present now," then they face another obstacle in verse 3 because the verb is not repeated in the Greek text but is assumed. Thus the reader of the English text ends up with a misleading scenario, as illustrated by the NIV: "asserting that the day of the Lord has already come. Don't let anyone deceive you in any way, for that day will not come until the rebellion occurs and the man of lawlessness is revealed" (2 Thess 2:2–3). This translation presents a compound problem: first, translating ἐνέστηκεν as "has already come" gives the impression that the Day of the Lord had been perceived by Paul's opponents as a thing of the past rather than a present reality. Second, the addition of the phrase "that day will not come," which is not in the original Greek text, makes it sound as if Paul is saying the "rebellion" and "revelation" of the man of lawlessness must come before the Day of the Lord. Then, it is often wrongly concluded that before the coming of Christ to gather the church, the events of the apostasy and the revelation of the lawless one and his establishment in God's temple and so on must first take place (2 Thess 2:3–4). Associated with this advent of the lawless one is also the working of Satan with signs and wonders, deceiving those who are perishing (2:9–10). So, the interpretation goes: only with the actual coming of Christ to earth after the reign of the man of lawlessness will the coming of Christ and gathering take place (2:8). This misreading all stems from the triple mistake of (1) failing to understand Day of the Lord as a technical term for the long tribulation period that is coming upon this earth, (2) misunderstanding ἐνέστηκεν as meaning "is present now," and (3) extending this mistranslation of ἐνέστηκεν to verse 3 when supplying the missing verb. This has resulted in an interpretation of 2 Thessalonians 2:1–12 that has Paul asserting the exact opposite of what he intended to say.

To review, Paul's eschatology regarding the rescue from the coming wrath and Day of the Lord in his previous letter (1 Thess 4:13–5:11) had been undone by some deceptive teaching (2 Thess 2:5, 15). This led some people to believe that they were, in fact, in the very midst of the Day of the Lord. If my reading of the argument in 1 Thessalonians 4–5 is correct, then this would have not only shaken the Thessalonians who had understood Paul to have taught that the Lord Jesus would rescue them from the coming wrath (1 Thess 1:10), but they would have lost hope in resurrection and lost overall confidence in the trustworthiness of Paul, Silas, and Timothy. In response, Paul could not have simply asserted the opposite of the false teaching, since his authority had already been undermined; some in Thessalonica had decided to believe the false prophecy or forged letter rather than Paul's teaching in 1 Thessalonians. So, to counter the eschatological error, Paul had to appeal to

---

24. The same verb, ἐνίστημι, is used as a perfect participle in Gal 1:4 in reference to the "present evil age" (τοῦ ἐνεστῶτος πονηροῦ); that is, the evil age was present, not come and gone. Cf. also 1 Cor 7:26; Heb 9:9.

25. Bruce, *1 & 2 Thessalonians*, 165.

classic Day of the Lord imagery from the Old Testament to demonstrate that they were not, after all, in the midst of the Day of the Lord.

To do this, Paul points to the telltale events of the coming "man of lawlessness," which draws imagery primarily from the book of Daniel. The key to understanding what Paul had in mind is the description of the man of lawlessness (2 Thess 2:4). His language echoes the imagery from the Septuagint of Daniel 11:36–37, which foretells the exploits of a "willful king" (Dan 11:36) whose end will be wrath and destruction (Dan 11:36, 45).[26] Though most commentators today identify this figure as Antiochus IV Epiphanes (who died in 167 BC), some, including early Christian commentators, assigned the passage starting at Daniel 11:36 to the end-times figure often called the antichrist, or at least they saw a dual referent, in which Antiochus was a historical figure who also served as a type for the coming antichrist. That there seems to have been some ultimate eschatological application is suggested by the fact that the time of the coming of that king is associated with the rising up of the archangel Michael, the coming of a great time of tribulation the likes of which has never been seen, and the resurrection of the dead (Dan 12:1–4). Daniel also provides mysterious chronological indicators related to the timing of these eschatological events (12:7, 11–12).

The mention of these events, then, refers us back to both Daniel 7 and 9. In Daniel 7, the little horn that comes up among the ten horns has a mouth uttering boastful things (7:8, 11) until the beast is slain by the judgment of the Ancient of Days (7:9–12). Later, in the interpretation of the fourth beast and especially its little horn, we read, "He will speak out against the Most High and wear down the saints of the Highest One, and he will intend to make alterations in times and in law; and they will be given into his hand for a time, times, and half a time. But the court will sit for judgment, and his dominion will be taken away, annihilated and destroyed forever" (7:25–26). Then, in Daniel 9, the cryptic discourse on the seventy weeks climaxes with a prophecy about a person, probably "the prince who is to come" (9:26), who will destroy the city (Jerusalem) and the sanctuary (the temple) in the midst of wars and desolations. Verse 27 says, "And he will make a firm covenant with the many for one week, but in the middle of the week he will put a stop to sacrifice and grain offering; and on the wing of abominations *will come* one who makes desolate, even until a complete destruction, one that is decreed, is poured out on the one who makes desolate." It should be observed that by dividing the week of seven years, Daniel 9:27 creates who half-weeks of three and a half years each, likely corresponding to the time, times, and half a time mentioned in Daniel 7:25 and 12:7.

It appears that Paul consciously draws together elements from these various passages in Daniel,[27] which may constitute for him the "apostasy (ἀποστασία)" in 2 Thessalonians 2:3 that will come first in the order of Day of the Lord events. It is not easy to identify exactly what Paul had in mind by this term. It could be that all the exploits of the man of lawlessness are seen as the ἀποστασία, or it may be as

---

26. Cf. Ernest Best, *The First and Second Epistles to the Thessalonians*, Blank's New Testament Commentary (London: Continuum, 1986), 288; Green, *Letters to the Thessalonians*, 310; and Witherington, *1 & 2 Thessalonians*, 218.

27. Morris, *1 and 2 Thessalonians*, 127.

simple as the action that commences Daniel's "seventieth week" in 9:27 when the prince who is to come
will "make a firm covenant with the many for one
week (והגביר ברית לרבים שבוע אחד)." In any case,
the apostasy the revelation of the man of lawlessness,

Go Deeper Excursus 25

*Who (or What) Is the Restrainer
in 2 Thessalonians 2?*

his self-aggrandizement, his signs and wonders, his setting himself up in the temple
of God,[28] and his ultimate destruction by the coming of Christ all point to an end-
times figure whose exploits mirror many elements of the wicked king who will arise
during the final Day of the Lord. Paul's argument, then, was that since the apostasy
had not occurred and the man of lawlessness had not been revealed in keeping with
the Old Testament, they could not be in the midst of the Day of the Lord as they
had been led to believe. Therefore, the anti-Pauline eschatology was proven false.

The Day of the Lord in 2 Peter 3:10

Second Peter 3 addresses those who were growing impatient with the earliest Christian expectation of a "soon" coming of the Lord,[29] challenging the notion that the
coming of Christ as judge and king would occur at all (2 Pet 3:4). Peter counters
the idea that the world has been going on just as it has been from the beginning by
pointing to the world-altering judgment of the flood (3:5–6). This, then, functions
as a precedence in Peter's argument, as the future coming judgment will similarly
destroy and purify the present world system—this time by fire (2 Pet 3:7).

Peter draws this imagery of destruction of the world by fire from Isaiah 66:15–
16,[30] which makes important verbal and visual connections with other common Day
of the Lord language and imagery without using the actual term "Day." It should be
recalled that this language is couched between two references in Isaiah—the first
two in Scripture—to the new heavens and new earth, to which Peter refers in 3:13

---

28. Morris, *1 and 2 Thessalonians*, 127, writes, "Some think that *God's temple* means 'the
church' (cf. 1 Cor. 3:16), but it is more likely that something like the temple in Jerusalem is
meant."

29. "Soon" or "speedily" (ταχύς) can mean "within a brief span of time" (Matt 5:25), but
it can also mean "quickly" (as the women in the tomb left "quickly" [ταχὺ] with fear [Matt
28:8]). In the LXX τάχος or ταχύς translates מהרה, which, as in Joel 4:4, can mean "suddenly"
rather than "immediately." Also note that "soon" (קרוב) translated as ἐγγύς in the LXX (Isa
13:6) does not guarantee immediate fulfillment but sudden fulfillment. That the Amidah
prayers call for God to restore Jerusalem and "quickly" and "soon" is a petition for urgency.
When the NT says judgment is coming "soon" and "quickly," it carries the same sense as the
Old Testament: suddenness.

30. Louis A. Barbieri, *First and Second Peter* (Chicago: Moody, 1977), 122. Cf. discussion of various sources of background imagery in Richard Bauckham, *Jude-2 Peter*, Word
Biblical Commentary, vol. 50 (Nashville: Thomas Nelson, 1983), 299–301. Bauckham's sup-
position, *Jude-2 Peter*, 284–85, that Peter depended on a lost Jewish apocryphal apocalyptic
work, the *Book of Eldad and Modad*, cannot be demonstrated nor rejected. Even if plausible,
the hypothesis is unnecessary, as the Old Testament itself provides all the language and
imagery necessary to explain Peter's meaning; cf. E. G. Martin, "Eldad and Modad," in J. H.
Charlesworth, ed., *The Old Testament Pseudepigrapha*, vol. 2 (Garden City, NY: Doubleday,
1985), 463–65.

of his second letter (see the further discussion in chapter 13 as well as in Go Deeper Excursus 22, *The Old Testament and the Day of the Lord*).

The image of judgment by fire is also found in Malachi. In 4:1 (3:19 in the Hebrew Bible), the description of the Day of the Lord involves a sharp distinction between the righteous and the wicked, as God spares the righteous on that day (4:1 [Heb 3:19]). In keeping with God's pattern of making a distinction between the righteous and the wicked, the righteous are promised deliverance from the Day of the Lord while the wicked are destroyed (4:2–3 [Heb 3:20–21]). Thus the coming day promises preservation and reward for the righteous while threatening destruction for the wicked.

In Peter's reckoning, the coming fire in the day of judgment is meant for "destruction of godless people" (2 Pet 3:7). This will give way to the "new heavens and a new earth" (3:13). This new creation, Peter says, is "in accordance with his promise," demonstrating that he had a particular divine oracle in mind, which can be none other than the promise of a new heavens and new earth associated with the coming kingdom that will be restored to this earth after the Day of the Lord (see Isa 65:17; 66:22).

Peter refers to this coming judgment that will make way for the restoration of creation as "the Day of the Lord (ἡμέρα κυρίου)" that will come "like a thief" (3:10). This is the same language Paul used in 1 Thessalonians 5:2. In keeping with the technical concept of the Day of the Lord as the period of judgment, wrath, retribution, and purification, Peter anticipates a protracted series of judgments coming upon the earth. This whole period of the Day of the Lord, then, can be understood as Christ's "coming" as judge to destroy the present system, including evil and sin. The language of fire, melting, and burning pictured in 2 Peter 3:10, 12–13 is best understood in the sense of metallurgical purification for the purpose of ridding something of impurities and strengthening the final product (cf. Mal 3:2–4; 4:1–3).[31] This expectation corresponds with Peter's earlier expectation summed up in his message of Acts 3:19–21. It also acknowledges that a Day of the Lord judgment is sure to occur prior to this period, as reflected in Peter's Pentecost sermon when he quoted Joel 2 (see Acts 2:17–21).

Peter then urges his readers to live holy lives while "waiting for and hastening (προσδοκῶντας καὶ σπεύδοντας) the coming of the day of God" (2 Pet 3:11–12). While the first term, "wait for," is related to a passive hoping and longing,[32] the second implies that something can be actively done to hasten the coming of the Day of the Lord.[33] It may be Peter had in mind the same idea as in his sermon in Acts 3:19–21, where he urged his Jewish listeners to repent and turn "so that (ὅπως)" Christ would be sent to restore all things. Peter could also have had in mind Paul's

31. See the excellent discussion in Craig A. Blaising, "The Day of the Lord Will Come: An Exposition of 2 Peter 3:1–18," *BSac* 169.4 (2012): 395–99.

32. BDAG, 877.

33. The marginal alternative in the NRSVue, "earnestly desiring," though less problematic theologically, is semantically indefensible. See Bauckham, *Jude-2 Peter*, 325; Thomas R. Schreiner, *1 & 2 Peter and Jude,* Christian Standard Commentary (Nashville: Holman Reference, 2020), 467.

reference in Romans that before the restoration of Israel prophesied in the Old Testament, "the full number of the gentiles" had to come into the church (Rom 11:25–27). Both of these suggest that, at least from the perspective of the church militant, their evangelistic efforts could "hasten" the coming of the Day of the Lord and the following restoration of all things.[34]

However, Peter employs severe imagery of the Day of the Lord, so how is it that believers are to be "waiting for and hastening" the "day of God"? The idea that the "Day of God" and "Day of the Lord" are separate events is untenable.[35] The brief description of what will happen with the coming of the "Day of God" matches exactly Peter's earlier description of the "Day of the Lord" (cf. 2 Pet 3:10, 12). Why, then, does Peter urge his readers to wait for and hasten this theophanic visitation in judgment?

The answer, I believe, comes from the previous chapter. Already in 2 Peter 2, he refers to the coming judgment that culminates in the establishment of Christ's kingdom upon this earth. In chapter 2, Peter uses past judgments as types of the coming judgment not merely to point out how God judged the wicked. Employing a protasis/apodasis (if . . . then) argument,[36] Peter uses past judgments as types of the coming judgment not merely to point out how God judged the wicked but to establish hope of rescue for the righteous.

Protasis (if . . .) (2 Pet 2:4–8)
[4] For if God did not spare the angels when they sinned but cast them into hell and committed them to chains of deepest darkness to be kept until the judgment; [5] and if he did not spare the ancient world, even though he saved Noah, a herald of righteousness, with seven others, when he brought a flood on the world of the ungodly; [6] and if by turning the cities of Sodom and Gomorrah to ashes he condemned them to destruction and made them an example of what is coming to the ungodly;[7] and if he rescued Lot, a righteous man greatly distressed by the debauchery of the lawless [8] (for that righteous man, living among them day after day, was tormented in his righteous soul by their lawless deeds that he saw and heard),

Apodosis (. . . then . . .) (2 Pet 2:9)
[9] then the Lord knows how to rescue the godly from trial and to keep the unrighteous until the day of judgment.

The seemingly long protasis of examples includes only two historical episodes: the judgment of the flood (2 Pet 2:4–5) and the judgment of Sodom and Gomorrah (2:6–8). The first involves two categories and two kinds of judgment—the spiritual beings who had been "cast into hell (lit. ταρταρώσας)" (2:4) and the world of the

---

34. Peter H. Davids, *The Letters of 2 Peter and Jude*, The Pillar New Testament Commentary (Grand Rapids: Eerdmans, 2006), 290–91.

35. Davids, *Letters of 2 Peter and Jude*, 290n59.

36. See Bauckham, *Jude-2 Peter*, 253; Schreiner, *1 & 2 Peter and Jude*, 401.

ungodly who were destroyed by the flood (2:5). In Peter's prophetic typology, the first probably informs us concerning the fate of those wicked who die prior to the coming Day of the Lord; do they somehow escape judgment? No, Peter indirectly argues; the angels who were cast into the abyss of Tartarus are examples of those who will still face a future "judgment" (2:4). The second category—the ancient world of the ungodly—then represents those wicked people who will be alive at the coming of the ultimate Day of the Lord in the future; they will be destroyed, as were those who were alive at the time of Noah. Yet at this point, Peter also draws in an example of the righteous remnant who are protected (ἐφύλαξεν): Noah and his family. Instead of being wiped out by the flood, they are preserved in the ark to repopulate the world after the flood subsided (2 Pet 2:5). The second historical episode is Sodom and Gomorrah. The pattern is similar. God renders the judgment of those cities an example to the ungodly in Peter's day as well as the future; they were judged by the fires from heaven (2 Pet 2:6). Yet Lot, who serves as a type of the righteous remnant in the ungodly world, was "rescued (ἐρρύσατο)" when he left the city before God poured out judgment upon the wicked (2:7–8).

Peter then applies the examples to believers in the present age facing the coming eschatological "day of judgment (ἡμέραν κρίσεως)" (2 Pet 2:9). Because in the history of redemption, God has "practice" at judging the wicked and rescuing the righteous, he "knows how" to do two things: "to rescue (ῥύεσθαι) the godly from trial (ἐκ πειρασμοῦ)" and to "keep the unrighteous until the day of judgment" (2:9). What does Peter mean that the godly will be rescued from trial? Depending on the context, the term πειροσμός can refer to a temptation or enticement to sin (Luke 4:13; Jas 1:12), a testing of the quality of something (1 Pet 4:12), or a temporal trial associated with judgment (Rev 3:10). The book of Revelation uses the term in reference to what appears to be a large-scale persecution (Rev 3:10). Whether this refers to a persecution close to the time of the writing of Revelation, to the eschatological "Day of the Lord," or to both, it is clear that the term refers to earthly trials and tribulations, not to moral dilemmas or personal struggles. Given the context of ultimate judgment in 2 Peter 2 and 3, it seems Peter's intention behind the term was a time of ultimate testing and trial upon the earth.[37] To suggest that Peter was simply promising victory over personal temptations or moral dilemmas, or even the enticement of the surrounding culture, fails to read this apodosis in its rhetorical context.[38] The "rescue" (ῥύομαι) of Lot referred to in the protasis was the physical removal from the place of judgment, not the preservation of his integrity during temptation.

---

37. It may be, too, that Peter had in the back of his mind the language of the Lord's Prayer (6:13). In the first-century Didache, the language in the final eucharistic prayer in 10.5–6 reflects the sentiments of the Lord's Prayer, interpreting the language eschatologically and calling for an end-times in-gathering of the church from throughout the world into the kingdom.

38. Davids, *Letters of 2 Peter and Jude*, 230–31; Michael Green, *2 Peter and Jude: An Introduction and Commentary*, Tyndale New Testament Commentaries, vol. 18 (Downers Grove: InterVarsity, 1987), 125–26.

Returning to 2 Peter 3:12 where believers are "waiting for and hastening" the "Day of God," which is the Day of the Lord judgment, if Peter really had in mind a rescue from the coming judgment upon the earth (2 Pet 2:4–9), then this would make sense of the hope and eager anticipation in 3:12. And the "waiting for (προσδοκῶντας)," then, would reflect Paul's own language in 1 Thessalonians 1:10: "to wait (ἀναμένειν) for his Son from heaven, whom he raised from the dead—Jesus, who rescues (ῥυόμενον) us from the coming wrath."

Conclusion: The Day of the Lord

Just as the Day of the Lord was a technical concept in the Old Testament and intertestamental literature, it also functions as a technical concept in the New Testament. The primary passages in which the phrase itself is used, read in their immediate contexts (Acts 2:20; 1 Thess 5:2; 2 Thess 2:2; 2 Pet 3:10), reflect the same notion as in the Old Testament: a protracted season of judgment and wrath for the purpose of removing the wicked from the world and purifying or refining the righteous. It is the period of judgment coming upon this earth that precedes the establishment of the coming messianic age.

Because Christ himself is portrayed as taking on the role usually associated with YHWH in the mediated theophanic visitation in judgment, the phrase "coming of Christ" or parousia is often used in place of the same theophanic coming of God in the Old Testament (cf. Isa 65:15; 2 Thess 2:7–8, 10). From this we see that the use of ἔρχομαι ("coming") of Christ in his capacity as judge is not to be understood as a momentary event. Rather, the coming of Christ is technically a process—in fact, the whole Day of the Lord is Christ "coming" in judgment. In light of Christ's role as the agent behind God's ultimate theophanic visitation in judgment during the coming Day of the Lord, we must expand our definition of the "second coming" to involve all aspects of the end-times events.

Besides the specific uses of the phrase "Day of the Lord" examined in this chapter, we also noted parallel phrases that refer to the same period of coming wrath and trial upon this earth: for example, the "Day of God" (2 Pet 3:12) and the "day of judgment" (2 Pet 2:9; 3:7). Other phrases like the "day of [our] Lord [Jesus] [Christ] (ἡ ἡμέρα τοῦ κυρίου [ἡμῶν] [Ἰησοῦ] [Χριστοῦ])" may also refer to the entire coming Day of the Lord judgment or to an aspect of it. We cannot automatically assume every reference to "day" necessarily carries the same technical meaning as the Old Testament "Day of the Lord." For example, 1 Corinthians 1:8 could reflect that aspect of the Day of the Lord longed for in 2 Peter 3:12—the rescue and vindication experienced by the righteous. In 1 Corinthians 5:5, Paul could refer to the whole Day of the Lord and thus anticipate some kind of eschatological purification during that period or to the vindication that will occur for believers, in which all who repent will participate. In any case, each of these and similar passages related to the eschatological "day" must be examined in their own contexts.

17

The Impending Day of the Lord

*But when this Antichrist shall have devastated all
things in this world, he will reign for three years and
six months, and sit in the temple at Jerusalem.*

Irenaeus, *Against Heresies* 5.30.4

In classic Irenaean premillennial eschatology, the coming ultimate tribulation period (Dan 12:1–12; Matt 24:21–22) is the same as the ultimate Day of the Lord
(1 Thess 5:1–9; 2 Thess 2:2–12), which is also the same period as the seventieth week
of Daniel 9:27, all of which are described in other passages related to the ultimate
coming judgment prior to the coming kingdom (e.g., Jer 30:7; Dan 7:25; Rev 7:14;
Rev 11–13).

In keeping with the Irenaean principle of both/and, however, a futurist view of
the impending Day of the Lord allows for numerous iterations of tribulations, false
christs, false prophets, and divine judgments from the first century to the twenty-
first. Yet the present rehearsals are mere "birth pangs" compared to the ultimate Day
of the Lord that will take place in that final seven-year period of this present world
system. Lactantius (c. 250–325), who lived during the last great Roman persecution
under Diocletian, put it starkly: "These times of ours, in which iniquity and impiety
have increased even to the highest degree, may be judged happy and almost golden
in comparison of that incurable evil" (Lactantius, *Divine Institutes* 7.15 [*ANF* 7]).

The purpose of the coming tribulation according to both the Old and New Testaments is not simply judgment of the wicked (Isa 26:21; Joel 2–3; 1 Thess 5:1–3; 2 Pet
3:7–10; Rev 6:12–17; 11:18; 15:1). Righteous judgment does not require a prolonged
period of intensifying tribulation over the course of years, as we see symbolized
by the increasingly severe trumpet and bowl judgments in Revelation 8–11 and 16.
Rather, the purpose of a protracted period of intensifying wrath is to allow time
for people to repent before the final sorting of the righteous and the wicked (Joel
2:12–14). We are reminded in the midst of the vision of the Day of the Lord's wrath
(Rev 6:12–17) that God has sealed the remnant of Israel for preservation and restoration (7:1–8; cf. 14:1–5) and "a great multitude which no one could count, from every
nation and *all the* tribes, peoples, and languages" are among those who "come out
of the great tribulation (ἐκ τῆς θλίψεως τῆς μεγάλης)" because they "washed their
robes and made them white in the blood of the Lamb" (7:9, 14 NASB).

In this chapter, I present the basic contours of the impending Day of the Lord
as presented in the early church with particular emphasis on the developed futurist eschatology of Irenaeus of Lyon. The purpose of this chapter is not to provide

a blow-by-blow timeline of future events; I leave that up to expositors of the book of Revelation. Rather, I will address major themes common in the earliest fathers, including the reign of the figure commonly known as the antichrist.

The "Antichrist" in the New Testament

The word *antichrist* itself appears only five times in four verses of the New Testament (1 John 2:18, 22; 4:3; 2 John 7). In all but one of those instances (possibly 1 John 2:18), the term ἀντίχριστος refers not to a specific end-times figure but to a type of false teacher who denies the messiahship of Jesus (1 John 2:22) or the incarnation (2 John 7). Or it refers to the "spirit" that provokes such false teaching that denies Jesus has come from God (4:3), which means there are many antichrists in the world (1 John 2:18).

The possible reference in 1 John 2:18 to an ultimate eschatological antichrist is not clear. John writes, "Children, it is the last hour! As you have heard that antichrist is coming, so now many antichrists have come. From this we know that it is the last hour." This could mean that the prediction of the coming antichrist was not an individual but a category, fulfilled in John's day and continually fulfilled in our own by new antichrists in every generation.

Another possibility is that John refers to well-known prophecies of an end-times false messiah figure who would oppose God and his people (e.g., 2 Thess 2:3–11). This well-known figure, given the title "antichrist" in 1 John 2:18, is indeed still "coming (ἔρχεται)," but even so, as a partial fulfillment and foreshadowing of that future ultimate antichrist, "many antichrists have [already] come (γεγόνασιν)." This present, partial realization manifested in many antichrists is due to the "spirit" of the antichrist currently at work in the world, i.e., Satan. This, then, would correspond to Paul's reference to the ultimate "man of lawlessness (ὁ ἄνθρωπος τῆς ἀνομίας)" described in 2 Thessalonians 2:3–11, who will be revealed only when the restraining power is removed. But until then, the "mystery of lawlessness is already at work" (2 Thess 2:7).

If 2 Thessalonians 2:3–11 indeed refers to a yet-future coming of an ultimate individual antichrist, then we see some basic characteristics of this future antichrist reflected already in the character and career of the boastful, arrogant enemy of God's people pictured in Daniel 7:8, 11, 25–26; 9:27–27; 11:36–45. His arrival on the world scene is presently prevented by a mysterious restraining power (2 Thess 2:6–7). His obvious presence in the world will be a defining characteristic of the period of trial known as the Day of the Lord (2:2–3). He will be associated with a great apostasy or "rebellion"—likely, the cause or even the embodiment of it (2:3). He will be revealed as a man of lawlessness (2:3). He will exalt himself against all religions and even against God himself (2:4). He will sit in the temple of God—likely, a rebuilt temple in Jerusalem—claiming to be God (2:4). He will be empowered by Satan to perform astonishing signs and wonders that will deceive those who reject the truth (2:9–10). And he will be destroyed by Christ at his coming (2:8).

Some forty years later, toward the end of the first century, the description of the "beast rising out of the sea" from Revelation 13 reflects much of the same language and imagery used to picture the man of lawlessness in 2 Thessalonians 2. The beast of Revelation 13 sums up and embodies the series of four beasts pictured in Daniel 7:2–8, which, if we count the heads and horns together, results in seven heads and ten horns (cf. Rev 13:1). Its monstrous mongrel form reflects the same animals used to describe successive empires in Daniel: a leopard, a bear, and a lion (Rev 13:2). The beast receives its power and authority from the dragon, a symbol for Satan (Rev 13:2; cf. 2 Thess 2:9–10). His seemingly miraculous healing from a mortal wound, or perhaps from death itself, will deceive the whole world into following the beast and worshiping the dragon (Rev 13:3–4, 8; cf. 2 Thess 2:9–12). The beast will be a great military leader who will spout boastful and blasphemous words (Rev 13:4, 6–7; 2 Thess 2:4; cf. Dan 7:8, 11, 20–21, 24–25). The reign of the beast after his full rise to power will be forty-two months (Rev 13:5; cf. Dan 7:25; 9:27).

Along with the first beast from the sea, the apostle John saw the second beast "out of the earth" (13:11). While the first beast incorporates traditional imagery drawn mostly from Daniel and 2 Thessalonians, the second beast is relatively unique. Later in Revelation, this figure is called the "false prophet" (16:13; 19:20; 20:10). He works in conjunction with the first beast—the military and political figure—by performing signs and wonders and deceiving the whole world by the power of Satan (13:11–14). He establishes some kind of image of the first beast that appears in the vision to come to life, an image that becomes the object of worship (13:14–15). It is this second beast, the false prophet, who famously forces all people to be branded with a mark "on the right hand or the forehead," which is required for buying or selling (13:16–17). This "mark of the beast" is a number that corresponds with the beast's name, which can therefore be calculated (13:17–18). By resisting the worship of the beast and refusing to receive its mark, those who are faithful to the testimony of Jesus will suffer persecution and martyrdom throughout the beast's three-and-a-half-year reign of terror (20:4).

Antichrist in Didache and Barnabas

The earliest references to an ultimate antichrist figure in the noncanonical Christian writings appear in Didache (c. 50–70) and the Epistle of Barnabas (c. 70–130). In the "mini-apocalypse" that concludes the Didache, we read:

> And then the deceiver of the world (ὁ κοσμοπλανὴς) shall appear (φανήσεται) as a son of God and he will perform signs and wonders, and the earth will be handed over into his hands and he will do incessantly vile things which have never happened before since time began. Then the creation of mankind shall come to the burning ordeal of testing (εἰς τὴν πύρωσιν τῆς δοκιμασίας). And many will be led astray and will be destroyed, but the ones enduring in their faith will be saved by the accursed one himself. (Did. 16.4–5 [Brannan])

In the same generation, the author of the Epistle of Barnabas wrote concerning the coming of Christ, "He will abolish the season of the lawless one (τὸν καιρὸν τοῦ ἀνόμου)" (Barn. 15.5). This image harkens back to earlier passing references to this eschatological antichrist figure: "Therefore, we must take heed in the last days (ἐν ταῖς ἐσχάταις ἡμέραις), for the whole time of our faith will not benefit us if not now, in the lawless season (ἐν τῷ ἀνόμῳ) and in the coming stumbling blocks (τοῖς μέλλουσιν σκανδάλοις), we resist as is fitting children of God, so that the black one (ὁ μέλας) may not have an opportunity to sneak in" (Barn. 4.9). The "lawless season" and "season of the lawless one" refer to the same period—the "last days"—during which the "coming stumbling blocks" will occur, associated with a particular "lawless one" (ἄνομος) or "black one" (ὁ μέλας), what we are calling the "antichrist."

It is entirely possible that the author of Barnabas was familiar with the content—if not the very text—of Didache 16. These passages from both the Didache and Barnabas also reflect language and imagery from 2 Thessalonians 2, where Paul describes the future coming of a "man of lawlessness (ὁ ἄνθρωπος τῆς ἀνομίας)" (2 Thess 2:3–10). Thus the language and imagery of 2 Thessalonians 2, Didache 16, and Barnabas 15—all possibly written within the same forty-year window (c. 50–90)—triangulate on an individual figure during a particular season of trial and tribulation at the end of the age. When John writes sometime in the 90s, "As you have heard that antichrist is coming" (1 John 2:18), it is entirely possible that the term "antichrist" was being used to name this figure who earlier was variously referred to with a number of other titles. This would explain the use of the title "antichrist" as an ultimate end-times enemy of God and his people in the second century. Yet the general use of the term for any false teacher who opposes Christ continued beyond the first century. Around the year AD 110, writing to the church in Philippi, Polycarp of Smyrna quotes loosely from 1 John 4:2–3, "For everyone who does not confess that Jesus Christ has come in the flesh is an antichrist" (Pol. *Phil.* 7.1 [Brannan]).

The Antichrist in the Second Century: Justin to Hippolytus

Around 160, Justin began his discussion with Trypho (his Jewish respondent) regarding the second coming of Christ by writing: "Just think how great shall be His power at His glorious Advent! For, as Daniel foretold, He shall come on the clouds as the Son of Man, accompanied by His angels" (*Dial.* 31 [Falls]). He then quotes extensively from Daniel 7:9–28. In the next chapter, Justin casts the fulfillment of the events in Daniel 7 into the imminent future:

> And he whom Daniel foretold would reign for a time, times, and a half, is now at the doors, ready to utter bold and blasphemous words against the Most High. In ignorance of how long he will reign, you hold a different opinion, based on your misinterpretation of the word "time" as meaning one hundred years. If this is so, the man of sin must reign at least three hundred and fifty years, computing the holy Daniel's expression of "times" to mean two times only. (*Dial.* 32 [Falls])

Of course, Justin's expectation that the fulfillment of these events was "at the doors" missed the mark. But we do see that he understood the three-and-a-half-year reign of the figure of Daniel 7 to be yet future (contra preterism). He also identified this figure from Daniel as Paul's "man of sin" in 2 Thessalonians 2. In these writings, however, he does not yet refer to this figure as the "antichrist."

Toward the end of the second century, Irenaeus, the personal disciple of Polycarp and probably Justin, described the beliefs and practices of the heretic Marcus, concluding, "In truth, he was the forerunner of the Antichrist (Ἀντιχρίστου/*Antichristi*)" (*Haer.* 1.13.1 [Unger]). Thus Irenaeus reconciled the various senses of the term "antichrist" in the New Testament by referring to a present manifestation of many antichrists as forerunners of the ultimate future antichrist. Later he writes, "When he [Paul] said of the Antichrist, *who opposes and exalts himself against every so-called god, or object of worship,* he pointed out those who are called gods, that is, idols, by those who are ignorant of God" (*Haer.* 3.6.5 [Unger]; italics original). Without question, Irenaeus calls the "man of lawlessness" in 2 Thessalonians 2 the "antichrist" proper, as he does in *Against Heresies* 3.7.2 (cf. 4.29.1).

Like Justin before him, Irenaeus expected the coming of the ultimate antichrist of 2 Thessalonians 2 to be a future event. Throughout his exposition of future things, Irenaeus discusses the coming of the antichrist in some detail: "By means of the events which shall occur (*quae erunt*) in the time of Antichrist is it shown that he, being an apostate (*apostata*) and a robber, is anxious to be adored as God" (*Haer.* 5.25.1 [*ANF* 1]). He then outlines the future career of this ultimate figure:

> For he [antichrist] being endued with all the power of the devil, shall come, not as a righteous king, nor as a legitimate king, in subjection to God, but an impious, unjust, and lawless one; as an apostate (*apostata*), iniquitous (*iniquus*) and murderous; as a robber, concentrating in himself satanic apostasy (*diabolicam apostasiam in se recapitulans*), and setting aside idols to persuade [men] that he himself is God, raising up himself as the only idol, having in himself the multifarious errors of the other idols. This he does, in order that they who do worship the devil by means of many abominations, may serve himself by this one idol, of whom the apostle thus speaks in the second Epistle to the Thessalonians [2:3–4]. (*Haer.* 5.25.1)

In this passage, Irenaeus places Paul's "man of lawlessness" in the future. Contrary to preterist interpreters, neither Justin nor Irenaeus (nor anybody else in the first or second century) saw 2 Thessalonians 2 as being fulfilled in the first century during the First Jewish Revolt (c. AD 70) or in the early second century during the Bar Kochba Revolt (c. AD 132). Perhaps more surprising, Irenaeus also refers to a literal future temple in Jerusalem in which the antichrist will one day sit. This is an interesting assertion, given that Irenaeus surely knew that no such temple existed in Jerusalem in AD 180:

> Moreover, he [the apostle] has also pointed out this which I have shown in many ways, that the temple in Jerusalem (*in Hierosolymis templum*) was made by the direction of the true God. For the apostle himself, speaking in his own person, distinctly called it the temple of God. . . . in which the enemy shall sit (*in quo adversaries sedebit*), endeavoring to show himself as Christ, as the Lord also declares: "But when you shall see the abomination of desolation, which has been spoken of by Daniel the prophet, standing in the holy place (let him that reads understand), then let those who are in Judea flee into the mountains (*fugiant in montes*); and

he who is upon the house-top, let him not come down to take anything out of his house: for there shall then be great hardship, such as has not been from the beginning of the world until now, nor ever shall be." (*Haer.* 5.25.2)

Irenaeus correlates the events of Matthew 24 in Jesus' Olivet Discourse with the future coming of the antichrist in the temple described in 2 Thessalonians 2. To this, he adds the "abomination of desolation" described in Daniel 9:27; 11:31; 12:11: "Daniel too, looking forward to the end of the last kingdom" (*Haer.* 5.25.3). In his interpretation of Daniel 7:25, Irenaeus regards the "time, times, and half a time" as referring to the length of the antichrist's reign: "for three years and six months, during which time, when he comes, he shall reign over the earth. Of whom also the Apostle Paul again, speaking in the second [Epistle] to the Thessalonians, and at the same time proclaiming the cause of his [Christ's] advent" (5.25.3).

Later, Irenaeus refers to the antichrist's reign from the temple of God in the "earthly Jerusalem (*id est terrena Jerusalem*)" (5.25.4). Irenaeus also applies the visions of Daniel 8 and 9 to the time of the antichrist (5.25.4). In this same argument, he assigns the seventieth week of Daniel 9:27 to the future, the second half of which will be marked by the antichrist's three-and-a-half-year reign:

He points out the time that his tyranny shall last, during which the saints shall be put to flight, they who offer a pure sacrifice unto God: "And in the midst of the week," he says, "the sacrifice and the libation shall be taken away, and the abomination of desolation into the temple: even unto the consummation of the time shall the desolation be complete." Now three years and six months constitute the half-week. (*Haer.* 5.25.4)

Later, Irenaeus refers to this same period of the reign of the antichrist in vivid terms: "But when this Antichrist shall have devastated all things in this world, he will reign for three years and six months, and sit in the temple at Jerusalem; and then the Lord will come from heaven in the clouds, in the glory of the Father, sending this man and those who follow him into the lake of fire" (5.30.4).

Not surprisingly, Irenaeus also identifies the man of lawlessness with the beast from the sea in Revelation 13:1–10. He calls the second beast, the false prophet, the "armour-bearer" (*Haer.* 5.28.2). Here, Irenaeus interprets the number of the beast, 666, as "a summing up of the whole of that apostasy which has taken place during six thousand years" (5.28.2). Thus the antichrist sums up all lawlessness, apostasy, and sinfulness of humanity, epitomizing these things at the end of history.

With respect to the manuscript variant on the number 666 as 616, Irenaeus regards it as obviously spurious, citing not only the best manuscripts and the significance of the number, but also the testimony known to him of "those men who saw John face to face" (*Haer.* 5.30.1). He has little patience especially for those who use the 616 number to identify persons of the past (e.g., Nero) as the referent, rather than the antichrist of the future. Irenaeus, therefore, has no preterist inclinations whatsoever and regards those who do as deceivers (*Haer.* 5.30.1).

Irenaeus also notes that the antichrist will arise from the tribe of Dan (*Haer.* 5.30.2), claiming that this is the reason the tribe of Dan is not mentioned among those who are saved from the tribes of Israel in Revelation 7:5–7. He does, however, warn against attempting to identify the antichrist prematurely: "It is therefore more certain, and less hazardous, to await the fulfilment of the prophecy, than to be making surmises, and casting about for any names that may present themselves" (*Haer.* 5.30.3).

In *Against Heresies* 5.25.2–3, Irenaeus connects the prophecies of the Olivet Discourse (Matt 24), the coming of the man of lawlessness (2 Thess 2), and the abomination of desolation in Daniel 9:27; 11:31; and 12:11. All of these, he says, will take place in a future literal period during which the antichrist will reign from Jerusalem for three years and six months (Dan 7:25; cf. *Haer.* 5.25.3). Irenaeus also links Christ's admonition to those in Judea to "flee into the mountains" (Matt 24:16) with Revelation 12:6—"And the woman fled into the wilderness, where she has a place prepared by God, so that there she can be nourished for one thousand two hundred sixty days." With this correlation, along with an identification of the "woman" in Revelation 12 as "the church," Irenaeus then refers to John's prophecy of the antichrist's kingdom in Revelation 17. In this context, he refers to the "church" being put to flight (*effugabunt*) by the work of the antichrist's multination confederacy: "And they shall lay Babylon waste, and burn her with fire, and shall give their kingdom to the beast, and put the Church to flight (*et effugabunt Ecclesiam*). After that they shall be destroyed by the coming of our Lord" (*Haer.* 5.26.1).

Because of these detailed events, as well as the mention of the half-week time indicator and the church being "put to flight" during the reign of the antichrist's confederacy, "putting the church to flight" most likely refers to the flight of the woman in Revelation 12:6 and 14. If so, then Irenaeus believed that this woman will be protected from the persecution of the dragon. The dragon, frustrated with his failure to destroy the woman, goes off to make war with "the rest of her children, those who keep the commandments of God and hold the testimony of Jesus" (Rev 12:17).

In any case, the woman is "put to flight" or "driven into exile," thus saved and preserved from the kingdoms and the antichrist. However, if Irenaeus is relying on the details of the flight in Revelation 12, then he would also have in mind a second group of saints—the "rest of her offspring"—who are not protected but become the victims of the antichrist's persecution during his forty-two-month reign.

What, then, is the purpose of the impending tribulation for Irenaeus? He writes:

> And therefore throughout all time (*in omni tempore*), man, having been molded at the beginning by the hands of God, that is, of the Son and of the Spirit, is made after the image and likeness of God: the chaff, indeed, which is the apostasy, being cast away; but the wheat, that is, those who bring forth fruit to God in faith, being gathered into the barn. And for this cause tribulation (*tribulatio*) is necessary for those who are saved, that having been after a manner broken up, and rendered fine, and sprinkled over by the patience of the Word of God, and set on fire, they may be fitted for the royal banquet. As a certain man of ours said, when he was condemned to the wild beasts because of his testimony with respect to God: "I am the wheat of Christ, and am ground by the teeth of the wild beasts, that I may be found the pure bread of God." (*Haer.* 5.28.4)

At first glance, this passage appears to indicate that Irenaeus believed the saved must necessarily go through the future period of tribulation under the antichrist in order to be purified. Yet, at the same time, Irenaeus refers to the historical tribulation that Ignatius of Antioch suffered at the hands of Trajan around AD 110 as having had that purifying effect (see Ign. *Rom.* 4.1). Either Irenaeus viewed the "tribulation" as an already/not-yet reality that every generation is expected to endure in anticipation of the ultimate apostasy at the time of the antichrist, or he was applying an argument of analogy: the same kind of tribulation that happened to Ignatius will certainly be true of those who will suffer under the antichrist. The answer lies in Irenaeus's "throughout all time (*in omni tempore*)." Throughout the entire human history of apostasy and wickedness, the saved have been separated as wheat from chaff; Ignatius of Antioch was a recent example of this purification through temporal tribulation. Irenaeus thus explains the recent tribulations in Vienne and Lyons (AD 177) and also anticipates the ultimate purification through tribulation under the antichrist.

In sum, Irenaeus articulated quite explicitly not only a futurist view of the impending Day of the Lord but also fleshed out details of the reign of antichrist, which will take place in a future seventieth week of Daniel 9.[1] This perspective, he says, he received not only from the Gospels, Paul's epistles, and the book of Revelation, but also from his own teachers who received this eschatology from the apostles themselves.

Hippolytus (born c. 170), heir to Irenaeus's eschatological tradition, straddled the second to third centuries and furthered the futurist cause in an age when the Irenaean approach was about to wane and the Alexandrian approach would take its place. Though we cannot be sure of personal contact or correspondence between Hippolytus and Irenaeus, their proximity in the Roman west makes it probable. Without doubt, though, Hippolytus relied upon Irenaeus's *Against Heresies* in his own works.

Hippolytus understood the vision of the four beasts in Daniel 7 as types of "the kingdoms of this world" (Hippolytus, *On Christ and Antichrist* 23–25 [*ANF* 5]). The lion refers to Babylon while the bear refers to the Persians; the third beast is the Greeks, and the fourth beast is Rome. This corresponds exactly to his interpretation of the four metals of the statue in Daniel 2; Hippolytus directly correlates the symbolism of these metals with the succession of four beasts in Daniel 7 (Hippolytus, *On Daniel* 2.1 [*ANF* 5]; *On Christ and Antichrist* 23–25, 28). He then understands the ten toes of the feet as representing "ten kings that rise out of that kingdom [of Rome]," corresponding to the ten horns of the fourth beast in Daniel 7 (Hippolytus, *On Daniel* 2.2). The little horn that springs up among the ten is "the antichrist that is to rise; and he shall set up the kingdom of Judah" (*On Daniel* 2.2 [*ANF* 5:178]).

Hippolytus's description of the future antichrist figure is rather typical of writings in the early church: "And when he has conquered all, he will prove himself a

---

1. See the summary of Irenaeus's eschatological perspective in John Behr, *Irenaeus of Lyons: Identifying Christianity*, Christian Theology in Context (Oxford: Oxford University Press, 2013), 181–82.

terrible and savage tyrant, and will cause tribulation and persecution to the saints, exalting himself against them" (*On Daniel* 2.2). As a futurist, Hippolytus then interprets the stone that comes from heaven and destroys the image at the ten toes as the future coming of Christ—not, as preterists would have it, as the first coming of Christ and the gradual growth of the church in the world (*On Daniel* 2.3). He states explicitly, "All these things, then, are in the future" (*On Christ and Antichrist* 26, 27).

From his perspective, Hippolytus also understands the abomination of desolation described in Matthew 24:15 as something that will not happen until the fourth beast, Rome, is removed: "Since then the abomination has not yet come, but the fourth beast has still the dominion, how can the appearing of the Lord take place?" (JHK 34).[2] Preterists often point to this passage as already fulfilled in the destruction of the temple in AD 70, but Hippolytus regards this as awaiting fulfillment with the future antichrist. At the same time, Hippolytus acknowledges that wars and rumors of wars (Matt 24:6) "already came to pass" but also that they "will come to pass" (JHK 34). The key phrase for him is that "these are merely the beginning of birth pangs" (Matt 24:8). In keeping with the classic both/and approach to prophecy, Hippolytus allows for a dual fulfillment of the Olivet Discourse, or at least a patterned fulfillment in which the devastation of AD 70 became a prophetic type for the future abomination of desolation in the end times.[3]

Like Irenaeus before him, Hippolytus understands the seventieth week of Daniel 9 as a future seven-year period during which the antichrist will reign (*On Daniel* 2.22). He explains, "By one week [Dan 9:27], therefore, he meant the last week which is to be at the end of the whole world of which week the two prophets Enoch and Elias will take up the half. For they will preach 1,260 days clothed in sackcloth, proclaiming repentance to the people and to all the nations" (*On Christ and Antichrist* 43).

Hippolytus sees the removal of sacrifice and oblation as a reference to the church's ministry "in every place," not to the desecration of a future temple in Jerusalem, though he does hold to a future rebuilt temple of the antichrist in Jerusalem as part of the antichrist's false messianic claims. This fact is also mentioned in his contrast between Christ and the antichrist: "The Saviour raised up and showed His holy flesh like a temple, and he [antichrist] will raise a temple of stone in Jerusalem" (*On Christ and Antichrist* 6). Though the antichrist will center his kingdom in Jerusalem as a kind of false messiah (*On Christ and Antichrist* 6, 25, 54), his kingdom will dominate the entire world (*On Christ and Antichrist* 52).

Like Irenaeus, Hippolytus makes the case that the antichrist will rise from the Hebrew tribe of Dan: "'Dan,' he says, 'is a lion's whelp'" (see Deut. 33:22) (*On Christ and Antichrist* 14; cf. Deut 33:22). Hippolytus interprets the second beast from the

---

2. "JHK" refers to J. H. Kennedy, *Part of the Commentary of S. Hippolytus on Daniel (Lately Discovered by Dr. Basilios Georgiades), with Introduction, Notes, and Translation* (Dublin: Hodges, Figgis, & Co., 1888). For Greek text, see Marcel Richard, Albrecht Dihle, and Gottlieb Nathanael Bonwetsch, eds., *Hippolytus Werke: Kommentar zu Daniel*, Die Griechischen Christlichen Schriftsteller, vol. 7 (Berlin: Akademie Verlag, 2000).

3. See David G. Dunbar, "Hippolytus of Rome and the Eschatological Exegesis of the Early Church," *WTJ* 45 (1983): 334.

earth in Revelation 13 as "the kingdom of Antichrist," and its two horns as the antichrist "and the false prophet after him" (*On Christ and Antichrist* 49). He interprets the mark of the beast as a symbol for a forced sacrifice made to the antichrist, without which a person will not be able to buy or sell (*On Christ and Antichrist* 49). Like Irenaeus, Hippolytus regards the number of the beast to be a name the letters of which add up to 666, acknowledging that "many names indeed we find, the letters of which are the equivalent of this number" (*On Christ and Antichrist* 50). Though he sets forth a few names that add up to 666—Teitan, Evanthas, and Latinus—he acknowledges that nobody knows what the name will be, concluding, "When the times advance, he too, of whom these things are said, will be manifested" (*On Christ and Antichrist* 50).

With regard to the detailed events of Daniel 11, Hippolytus considers verses 1–35 to refer to past events related to the rise of the Greek Empire, its division, and the subsequent conflicts in the intertestamental period (*On Daniel* 2.29–37). At Daniel 11:36, then, Hippolytus believes the prophet "points out the last times." He writes:

> Thus, then, does the prophet set forth these things concerning the Antichrist, who shall be shameless, a war-maker, and despot, who, exalting himself above all kings and above every god, shall build the city of Jerusalem, and restore the sanctuary. Him the impious will worship as God, and will bend to him the knee, thinking him to be the Christ. He shall cut off the two witnesses and forerunners of Christ, who proclaim His glorious kingdom from heaven, as it is said: "And I will give (power) unto my two witnesses, and they shall prophesy a thousand two hundred and threescore days, clothed in sackcloth." As also it was announced to Daniel: "And one week shall confirm a covenant with many; and in the midst of the week it shall be that the sacrifice and oblation shall be removed"—that the one week might be shown to be divided into two. The two witnesses, then, shall preach three years and a half; and Antichrist shall make war upon the saints during the rest of the week, and desolate the world, that what is written may be fulfilled: 'And they shall make the abomination of desolation for a thousand two hundred and ninety days.'"
> (Hippolytus, *On Daniel* 2.39; cf. *On Christ and Antichrist* 47)

Note that Hippolytus correlates the exploits of the end-times antichrist figure with Daniel's seventieth week, as well as with the description of the ministry of the two witnesses from Revelation 11. The two witnesses, he says, will prophesy for the first 1,260 days while the antichrist's war on the saints will take place during the second 1,260 days—thus filling the whole seven-year period. Also, in keeping with his position that the antichrist will be a false messiah, Hippolytus says that the antichrist will rule from Jerusalem and restore the temple (and presumably, its sacrificial rites). This would correspond, then, with the activities of the man of lawlessness in 2 Thessalonians 2. Like his contemporaries, Hippolytus understood the chronological indicators literally. He explains the phrase "a time, and times, and a half" of Daniel 12:7 this way: "He indicated the three years and a half of Antichrist. For by 'a time' He means a year, and by 'times' two years, and by an 'half time' half a year. These are the thousand two hundred and ninety days of which

Daniel prophesied for the finishing of the passion, and the accomplishment of the dispersion when Antichrist comes" (*On Daniel* 2.43).

In sum, Hippolytus detailed a futurist view of the ultimate Day of the Lord with numerous details concerning the reign of antichrist, which will correspond with the future seventieth week of Daniel 9. In all respects he continues Irenaeus's premillennial, futurist eschatology into the third century.[4]

Return to Revelation 13 and the Antichrist Figures

The futurist expectation of *the*—not just *a*—coming antichrist has been a common view for much of the church's history.[5] As we have seen, popular among some of the earliest expositors was the thought that the antichrist will be a false messiah originating from the tribe of Dan who will attempt to deceive and oppress the Jewish people.[6] Contemporaneous with this early view was the idea that the antichrist would be a Roman emperor, perhaps even a revived Nero, while Commodian in the third century combined the two into one, seeing both a revived Nero and a false messiah.[7]

---

4. See the summary of Hippolytus's eschatology in T. C. Schmidt, *Hippolytus of Rome: Commentary on Daniel and 'Chronicon,'* Gorgias Studies in Early Christianity and Patristics, vol. 67 (Piscataway, NJ: Gorgias, 2017), 17.

5. Both partial preterists and full preterists believe the events described in 2 Thess 2 were already fulfilled in the years leading up to and including the destruction of the temple in Jerusalem and the end of the age of Israel between the years AD 66 and 73. Though the prophecy was yet future from Paul's perspective when he wrote 2 Thess around AD 50, it was already fulfilled about twenty years later; cf. Keith A. Mathison, *Postmillennialism: An Eschatology of Hope* (Phillipsburg, NJ: P&R, 1999), 227–33. However, if we are right in coordinating the expectation of the coming of Christ, the resurrection of the dead in Christ, the assumption of the church, and the Day of the Lord judgment in 1 Thess 4:13–5:11 with the parousia of the Lord and our being gathered together to him in 2 Thess 2:1, then the fact that the resurrection and assumption of the church has not happened means 2 Thess 2:3–11 awaits a future fulfillment.

6. Cf. Irenaeus, *Haer.* 5.30.2; Hippolytus, *On Christ and Antichrist,* 6. Cf. Paschal Huchedé, *History of Antichrist,* trans. J. D. B. (New York: Nicholas Bray, 1884), 15; Gregory C. Jenks, *The Origins of the Early Development of the Antichrist Myth* (Berlin: Walter de Gruyter, 1991), 77, 83; Arthur W. Pink, *The Antichrist* (Swengel, PA: Bible Truth Depot, 1923), 43; Walter K. Price, *The Coming Antichrist* (Chicago: Moody Press, 1974), 22. This idea survived in the Russian Church and enjoyed a limited popularity in contemporary writing on the subject in the modern era. Cf. N. I. Saloff-Astakhoff, *Antichrist and the Last Days of the World* (Berne, IN: Berne Witness, 1941), 30. Also see the discussion in Vincent P. Miceli, *The Antichrist* (Harrison, NY: Roman Catholic Books, 1981), 112, who examines the work of the nineteenth-century theologian John Henry Newman, "Advent Sermons on Antichrist," in *Tracts for the Times,* vol. 5, 1838–1840 (London: J. G. F. & J. Rivington, 1840). The church in the Middle Ages saw a resurgence of the doctrine of the Jewish antichrist, which triggered an outbreak of anti-Semitism; see Richard Kenneth Emmerson, *Antichrist in the Middle Ages* (Seattle, WA: University of Washington Press, 1981), 79–83.

7. Commodian writes, "Nero shall be raised up from hell. . . . The whore of Babylon, being reduced to ashes, its embers shall thence advance to Jerusalem; and the Latin conqueror shall then say, I am Christ, whom ye always pray to; and, indeed, the original ones who were deceived combine to praise him." Commodian, *Instructiones* 41 (*ANF* 4). Cf. comments in Jenks, *Antichrist Myth,* 77.

For some time, the label "antichrist" was hurled at heretics outside the Roman Church and even to anti-popes within.[8] Not until the time of the Reformation was there virtual unanimity among Protestant Christian scholars from diverse theological backgrounds that the pope and the antichrist were one and the same. Today, a growing number of views exists concerning the antichrist, some reflecting historical positions and others presenting new perspectives.

Though the earliest expositors were fairly consistent in their approach to the issue of the antichrist and his future reign, commentators since then have fragmented into a wide diversity of opinions on these matters, especially as it relates to the identities of the two beasts in Revelation 13. Often, the interpretations are driven by whether a commentator understands Revelation as an idealist, a historicist, a futurist, or a preterist (see discussion of these various approaches and other introductory issues regarding Revelation in chapter 10).

The first beast, who is said to rise up out of the sea (Rev 13:1), has been interpreted by some as merely an antichristian world system[9] or a revived Roman Empire,[10] deemphasizing a personal, human antichrist figure. Others place more emphasis on the individual interpretation, seeing the beast as the Gentile leader of the consummate political system of the end times.[11] A compromise view sees a dual meaning in the symbolism of the beast as referring to both the revived Roman Empire and its eschatological emperor.[12] Avoiding any future eschatological significance, preterist interpreters see the beast as reflecting either *Nero redivivus* or some other historical occasion of the Roman Empire.[13]

---

8. Price, *Coming Antichrist*, 27–29. As a reaction to this, the papacy initially labeled the Reformers as "antichrists" but then attempted to resurrect the doctrine of the Jewish antichrist, only to rekindle anti-Semitism and harsh persecution of Jews. Price, *Coming Antichrist*, 36.

9. See, e.g., E. W. Hengstenberg, *The Revelation of St. John, Expounded for Those who Search the Scriptures*, vol. 2, trans. Patrick Fairbairn (Edinburgh: T&T Clark, 1852), 87–88; R. C. H. Lenski, *The Interpretation of St. John's Revelation* (Minneapolis: Augsburg, 1961), 388–89; and Robert H. Mounce, *The Book of Revelation*, The New International Commentary on the New Testament (Grand Rapids: Eerdmans, 1977), 251.

10. Walter Scott, *Exposition of The Revelation of Jesus Christ and Prophetic Outlines*, 6th ed. (London: Pickering & Inglis, c. 1900), 269.

11. George Eldon Ladd, *A Commentary on the Revelation of John* (Grand Rapids: Eerdmans, 1972), 177; Leon Morris, *The Revelation of St. John*, The Tyndale New Testament Commentaries (Grand Rapids: Eerdmans, 1969), 165; and Charles C. Ryrie, *Revelation*, Everyman's Bible Commentary, new ed. (Chicago: Moody, 1996), 95; Roy Yates, "The Antichrist," *EvQ* 46 (1974): 49.

12. Arno C. Gaebelein, *The Revelation* (New York: Loizeaux Brothers, 1961), 79; H. A. Ironside, *Lectures on the Book of Revelation* (New York: Loizeaux Brothers, 1930), 277; Joseph A. Seiss, *The Apocalypse*, vol. 2, 7th ed. (New York: Revell, 1900), 391–96; and John F. Walvoord, *The Revelation of Jesus Christ* (Chicago: Moody, 1966), 197–200.

13. Isbon T. Beckwith, *The Apocalypse of John* (New York: Macmillan, 1919), 633–36.

In keeping with the Irenaean tradition, I hold that the beast from the sea represents a single eschatological individual symbolized in terms of his empire.[14] There are two reasons for this. First, the language of Revelation 16:10 is strong evidence that the beast and his kingdom are distinct entities.[15] Second, if the beast is a world system, government, or empire, then Revelation 19:19 would create a logical problem: "Then I saw the beast and the kings of the earth with their armies gathered to wage war against the rider on the horse and against his army." If the beast is a symbol for the allied kings of the earth, distinguishing between it and them would be problematic. I therefore understand the beast from the sea (13:1–10) as an individual political and military leader (13:2, 4). He is reasonably identified with the "man of lawlessness," where the self-exaltation and worship of this man parallels many aspects of the description of the beast in Revelation 13:4–5.

John's description of the first beast from the sea reveals that the beast has a mortal wound that healed (Rev 13:3). This aspect of the description has been understood in a variety of ways, most of which depend on the commentator's initial interpretation concerning either the individual or corporate nature of the beast. Some, resting heavily on the use of the same phrase in Revelation 5:6 in reference to the death and resurrection of Jesus, argue that the beast—whatever his nature—is seen in the symbolic vision as having literally died and risen from the dead.[16] Other able commentators, often for theological reasons, either deny or downplay a literal resurrection, and they often suggest a pretended resurrection, miraculous healing of a wound that normally would result in death, or even a kind of miraculous political recovery.[17] Of those who assign a corporate identity to the beast, they often see this passage as symbolic of the restoration of the Roman Empire.[18] A more idealist approach to Revelation might see the symbol as the death-blow inflicted by Christ's victory over Satan.[19]

To me, the force of the language is so compelling that I must admit that if the beast represents an individual, then that individual is said to appear as one having been slain. Since the same descriptive phrase is used in the vision of the lamb representing Christ (Rev 5:6), who was truly killed, the same phrase applied to the beast from the sea (13:3) argues strongly for a similar interpretation. Although

---

14. Cf. Dan 4:20–22, where the tree is identified as Nebuchadnezzar himself though described in terms of his empire. The beasts in Dan 7 seem to represent kingdoms whose parts represents individual kings (Dan 7:23–27; cf. 8:20–22). In the interpretation of the beast in Rev 17, however, the angel equates the beast itself with the eighth king (17:11).

15. The phrase θρόνον τοῦ θηρίου, καὶ . . . ἡ βασιλεία αὐτοῦ distinguishes the person from the kingdom, the genitives understood as either subjective or possessive.

16. E.g., Hengstenberg, *Revelation of St. John*, 19–20; Ladd, *Revelation of John*, 178–79; Ryrie, *Revelation*, 96; Seiss, *Apocalypse*, 399–400; and Robert L. Thomas, *Revelation 8–22: An Exegetical Commentary* (Chicago: Moody, 1995), 158–59.

17. E.g., Ford C. Ottman, *The Unfolding of the Ages in the Revelation of John* (Grand Rapids: Kregel, 1967), 310; J. Dwight Pentecost, *Things to Come: A Study in Biblical Eschatology* (Grand Rapids: Zondervan, 1958), 335–36.

18. E.g., Scott, *Exposition of Revelation*, 273; Walvoord, *Revelation*, 199–200.

19. Lenski, *Interpretation of Revelation*, 394. If Christ's victory was the deathblow, then by what cosmic power could Satan have recovered, if such a power must by necessity be greater than the power of Christ's resurrection?

Revelation 13:3 seems to limit the deadly wound to only one of the heads of the beast, John later attributes the deadly wound to the whole beast (13:12).

In Revelation 17, the interpreting angel provides an explanation of the symbolism of the heads and the beast. The heads represent both seven hills (17:9) and also seven kings (17:10). The kings, probably representing kingdoms, are partially historical: five have fallen, one is living, the other has not yet come. The head that has not yet come "must remain only a little while (ὀλίγον . . . μεῖναι)." This "little while" could coincide with the "short season (ὀλίγον καιρὸν)" of the dragon in 12:12 and the forty-two months of the beast's reign in 13:5, identifying the seventh head as the beast and placing its reign in the time when Satan is cast down during the future tribulation.

The beast's relationship to the heads is somewhat complicated: "As for the beast that was and is not, it is an eighth, but it belongs to the seven, and it goes to destruction" (Rev 17:11). In the same line, the text seems to distinguish the beast from the kings: it is an eighth (αὐτὸς ὄγδοός ἐστιν), but it also includes him as part of the seven (ἐκ τῶν ἑπτά ἐστιν). The solution to this enigma probably comes by holding to a strict *individual* identification of the *beast as a whole*, the epitome of the Gentile nations of history bearing the image of Satan himself.[20] Throughout history, Satan has worked through Gentile powers against the people of God and will one day personally empower (embody or possess?) a single Gentile leader (the beast/ antichrist). Yet we must allow the heads of the beast to continue to symbolize kings and kingdoms (as they did in the dragon symbol for Satan) who are the beast's predecessors, allies, and subjects. The first stage of the beast's kingdom (before he is empowered by Satan in Rev 13:1) is represented by one of the heads. From John's perspective, five kingdoms have fallen: one is (Rome), the other has not yet come (the beast's future seven-year tribulation kingdom). The beast himself is *of the seven*, for the scene of Revelation 13 opens after the initial three-and-a-half-year phase of his kingdom is defeated and the leader slain. Yet, upon his restoration to life, both the king and the kingdom are immediately restored. Therefore, this second three-and-a-half-year phase of the antichrist's kingdom following the resuscitation of the king makes this head *the eighth*. He is related to the seventh in person but distinct from him in character.

Therefore, understanding the beast as an individual and then accepting the full force of one of his heads having received a "death blow (ὡς ἐσφαγμένην εἰς θάνατον)," we may conclude that the individual whom the beast represents is seen in the vision of Revelation 13 to have already been healed of his wound. At most, he has been brought back from the dead; at least, Satan has somehow deceived the modern world that the man has been resurrected.

The second beast who rises up from the earth has likewise received various interpretations. Some suggest that the beast from the earth is a great religious leader of a false religious system or apostate church who works in cooperation

---

20. Cf. Rev 12:3–17 where the dragon is identified as Satan (12:9), described as having seven heads and ten horns, and is pictured as the source of the beast's power and authority (13:2).

with the antichrist.[21] Others give him the label of "pseudo-christ," a man claiming to be the Jewish messiah.[22] Those who see the beasts as representatives of systems rather than individuals understand the second beast to be a false religious system or antichristian priesthood.[23]

For the sake of consistency—and in keeping with the classic Irenaean eschatology—it is best to understand the beast from the earth as an individual. If the first beast from the sea is an individual, as argued above, then so is the second. It is clear by comparing Revelation 13:11–18 and 19:20 that the second beast is called by John "the false prophet."

Though the passage in Revelation 13 does not reveal many certain details of the two beasts, the passage can be read in continuity with the early Irenaean understanding of the coming antichrist. The first beast is understood as an individual who is apparently the head of a world system, not simply a symbol for the system itself. If one accepts the chronological indicators in Revelation 12 and 13—as did Justin, Irenaeus, and Hippolytus—then it would appear that the scene opens up near the beginning of the last three and a half years of the seven-year ultimate "Day of the Lord" or "tribulation" period, which is the future seventieth week of Daniel 9:27. The beast from the sea has already been restored to life, though the specific means of death and resurrection are not revealed. The beast from the earth (the false prophet) also appears on the scene at this time and he, too, is best understood as an individual rather than merely a religious system. From this point on, both figures appear to work in cooperation with each other, though the political figure, the first beast, seems to be the center of worldwide attention.

> **Go Deeper Excursus 26**
>
> *The Mystery of*
> *Babylon the Great*

At the end of the antichrist's reign of terror, in which saints who defy his devilish regime are persecuted and martyred, Christ's heavenly armies break into the world (Rev 19:11–21), as Irenaeus describes: "But when this Antichrist shall have devastated all things in this world, he will reign for three years and six months, and sit in the temple at Jerusalem; and then the Lord will come from heaven in the clouds, in the glory of the Father, sending this man and those who follow him into the lake of fire" (*Haer.* 5.30.4).

---

21. Ladd, *Revelation of John*, 183; Seiss, *Apocalypse*, 418–19; and Walvoord, *Revelation*, 204–6.

22. Gaebelein, *Revelation*, 82–83; Ironside, *Lectures on Revelation*, 236.

23. Hengstenberg, *Revelation of St. John*, 169; Lenski, *Interpretation of Revelation*, 417; and Mounce, *Revelation*, 259.

18

IRENAEUS AND THE ASSUMPTION
OF THE CHURCH

*When in the end the Church shall be suddenly caught
up from this, it is said, "There shall be tribulation such
as has not been since the beginning, neither shall be."*

Irenaeus, *Against Heresies* 5.29.1

The issues related to eschatology in this book have been arranged not chronologically but topically, and even these have been treated in a somewhat cyclical fashion as inextricably related themes need to be revisited in different contexts. Like constructing a building, I first established the threefold foundation of eschatology—the return of Christ, the resurrection of the righteous and the wicked, and the restoration of all creation. Upon that foundation, I established the basic structure of the coming kingdom, a doctrinal question that has had a number of differing perspectives throughout history. Having made the case for a premillennial return of Christ in the classic Irenaean tradition, I then focused attention on the character of this intermediate form of the kingdom, the primary purpose of which will be to progressively edenify the world and gradually defeat chaos and advance the good order of the new creation, all through the colaboring of God's image-bearers under the headship of the second Adam.

With the foundation and basic structure in place, I furnished the construction with some of the more prominent elements of a futurist eschatology in the second-century Irenaean tradition. I first established the biblical concept of the Day of the Lord as a technical term for the coming period of testing, purification, and purging of the world, and then I showed how this technical concept related to the expectation of the Day of the Lord in the New Testament. The meaning of the technical phrase is the same in both testaments, but the agent in the New Testament moves from YHWH as the major figure executing the mediated theophanic visitation in judgment to Jesus Christ as the executer of the series of judgments. I also argued—consistent with the early transmitters of the faith like Justin, Irenaeus, and Hippolytus—that the expected ultimate Day of the Lord in the future will bring together all remaining prophecies and patterns set forth in both the Old Testament and the New regarding the coming antichrist figure (Dan 7, 9, 11, 12; Matt 24; 1 Thess 5; 2 Thess 2; Rev 13).

This, then, means that the future Day of the Lord will be a period of seven years, divided into two three-and-a-half-year periods, the first half characterized by the ministry of the "two witnesses" apparently during the rebuilding of a temple in Jerusalem under the direction of the antichrist figure, which may constitute the "apostasy" that brings "strong delusion" to the world (2 Thess 2:3, 9–12). The second half of this coming Day of the Lord will involve a time of unprecedented persecution as the antichrist and his empire take complete control by the power of Satan for forty-two months (Rev 13). This final manifestation of satanic power will be destroyed with the coming of Christ, the Son of Man, and his armies from heaven. Christ will then establish his true messianic reign on the earth and rescue an apostate Jerusalem from the antichrist to restore the city to its proper place of glory (Dan 7:9–14; 2 Thess 2:8; Rev 19:11–21).

A final matter must be addressed, however, before bringing this presentation of a contemporary Irenaean eschatology to a close: the question of the assumption of the church to heaven. That is, when should we expect the resurrection of the dead saints, the transformation of the living, and their catching up together as described in 1 Thessalonians 4:15–17 (supplemented by 1 Cor 15:51–52; Phil 3:20–21; 1 Thess 1:9–10; and 2 Thess 2:1)? Several of these passages and issues related to the question of the relationship of the resurrection/assumption and the coming Day of the Lord have already been treated as they related to the topic. In this chapter as well as the next two, I will attend to the matter directly and present my own answer in light of Scripture and the teachings of the early church. I will begin by addressing the general ambiguity and apparent inconsistencies in the earliest references to the assumption of the church in the second century as well as the church's relationship to the coming Day of the Lord. Throughout this discussion, I will depend on more foundational positions already asserted in previous chapters related to the coming kingdom and the Day of the Lord.

The Assumption of the Church in the Second Century

Approaches to the assumption of the church in the second-century fathers range from a maximalist to a minimalist approach. Usually by cherry-picking or ripping statements out of context, maximalists have tried to claim historical precedence for a full pre-tribulation rapture doctrine similar to the modern pre-seven-year rapture of the whole regenerate body of Christ. Minimalists, on the other hand, have either overlooked, downplayed, or denied the existence of passages in the fathers that seem to suggest some kind of connection between the assumption of at least some righteous prior to the coming tribulation. Having worked through numerous passages in the fathers for decades, I have concluded that both of these approaches fail to appreciate the actual texts in their contexts. Both maximalists and minimalists appear to be driven by their desires to see their view of the rapture in the early church fathers.

My own hypothesis, taking all the evidence into consideration, is that a diversity of perspectives existed in the second-century fathers regarding the relationship between the assumption of the church and the coming tribulation, none of which exactly match the clean-shaven four views we find in popular treatments of the rapture today. Most fathers simply do not address the question. Others suggest what can best be described as a "partial pre-tribulation" rapture without precisely defining what the period of "tribulation" entails. And some set forth a kind of post-tribulation or pre-wrath rapture. That the second-century fathers spoke univocally on the matter is a fiction that does not comport with a careful evaluation of the evidence. In the end, this means the question must be answered by exegesis of relevant passages of Scripture interpreted in light of previously established eschatological positions regarding the nature of the millennium and the Day of the Lord.

The Assumption of the Church in Irenaeus

We have already seen that Irenaeus's concept of the coming kingdom was an intermediate period of progress in the history of personal and cosmic redemption. As such, the millennial kingdom was the initial stage of the new heavens and the new earth. That intermediate kingdom, then, would be uniquely characterized by some elements of the present age and some of the future—particularly the presence in the same world of both immortal, glorified saints reigning with Christ and mortal humans repopulating the world and living under the reign of the saints. He sets forth this picture in *Against Heresies* 5.35.1. My own translation, with relevant Latin texts, follows to provide the reader with everything needed for a close analysis:

> For all these and others [passages of Scripture] were without controversy spoken with regard to the resurrection of the just [*Haec enim alia universa in resurrectionem justorum sine controversia dicta sunt*], which will happen after the advent of Antichrist [*quae fit post adventum Antichristi*] and the perdition of all nations existing under him [*et perditionem omnium genium sub eo existentium*]; at which time the righteous will rule in the earth [*in qua regnabunt justi in terra*], growing greater by the vision of the Lord [*crescentes ex visione Domini*], and through him they will become accustomed to receive the glory of God the Father [*et per ipsum assuescent capere gloriam Dei Patris*], and, with the holy angels, they shall receive in the kingdom conversation and fellowship and union with spiritual beings [*et cum sanctis angelis conversationem et communionem et unitatem spiritalium in regno capient*], and [the words of the prophecies about the Millennium were spoken with reference to][1] those whom the Lord shall find in the flesh [*et illos quos Dominos in carne inveniet*], expecting him from heaven [*exspectantes eum de coelis*], and suffered tribulation [*et perpessos tribulationem*], which also escaped the hands of the Wicked One [*qui et effugerint iniqui manus*]. For it is in reference to them [those in the flesh expecting him after the reign of antichrist] that the prophet says [*Ipsi autem sunt de quibus ait propheta*]: "And those that remain will multiply on the earth" [Isa 6:12] [*et derelicti multiplicabuntur in terra*]. And however many of the believers God has prepared for this [*Et quotquot ex credentibus ad hoc praeparavit Deus*], to multiply those remaining on the earth [*ad derelictos multiplicandos in terra*], and to both be under the rule of the saints [*et sub regno sanctorum fieri*] and to minister to this Jerusalem [*et ministrare huie Jerusalem*], and reigning in it [*et regnum in ea*], Jeremiah the prophet speaks about [*significavit Jeramias propheta*]. (*Haer.* 5.35.1)

---

1. Irenaeus here picks up the plural accusative again, *illos*, designating a new group different from the first category of people (*resurrectionem justorum*) that he just described.

We have already seen this passage in chapter 5 and noted that Irenaeus anticipated both resurrected, glorified humans reigning in the kingdom as well as mortal saints who survived the persecution under the antichrist. These mortal survivors of the tribulation—not the resurrected saints—will be the ones who reproduce and multiply the population of the earth. (*Haer.* 5.35.1). This idea of both mortal humans and immortal humans occupying the space of the millennial kingdom is also echoed by Commodian in the third century: "We shall arise again to Him, who have been devoted to Him. And they shall be incorruptible, even already living without death. And neither will there be any grief nor any groaning in that city. They shall come also who overcame cruel martyrdom under antichrist, and they themselves live for the whole time, and receive blessings because they have suffered evil things; and they themselves marrying, beget for a thousand years [*Et generant ipsi per annos mille nubentes*]" (*Instructiones*, 44 [*ANF* 4]).[2]

How can we best account for this view of two different groups of people— immortals and mortals—occupying the same world for the duration of the millennial kingdom? And how can this be reconciled with the view presented in 1 Thessalonians 4:15–17 that when Christ comes and resurrects the dead saints, all those who are alive at the time will be themselves transformed into immortal bodies (1 Cor 15:51–52; Phil 3:20–21) and caught up with them? Where, then, do the mortal surviving believers of the tribulation and antichrist come from, those who expect Christ from heaven (*exspectantes eum de coelis*) (*Haer.* 5.35.1)? If Irenaeus coordinated the resurrection, transformation, and assumption of the church with the precise moment of Christ's descent from heaven after the reign of antichrist, the wicked would be killed, the dead raised, the living righteous transformed, and no mortals would be left on the earth. Yet Irenaeus definitely expects mortals to be left upon the earth—the very saints who escaped the antichrist and await Christ's coming from heaven to save them.

We have already seen, too, that Irenaeus believed the antichrist and those kings who will rule with him will "put the Church to flight (*et effugabunt Ecclesiam*)," and "after that they shall be destroyed by the coming of our Lord" (*Haer.* 5.26.1 [*ANF* 1]). Thus in Irenaeus's mind, the "church" is definitely present during the second half of the tribulation period. Yet this makes Irenaeus's words in 5.29.1 all the more puzzling: "And therefore, when in the end the Church shall be suddenly caught up from this (*Et propterea cum in fine repente hinc Ecclesia assumetur*), it is said, 'There shall be tribulation such as has not been since the beginning, neither shall be (*erit, inquit, tribulatio quails non est facta ab initio, neque fiet*)' [Matt 24:21]. For this is the last contest of the righteous, in which, when they overcome they are crowned with incorruption" (*Haer.* 5.29.1). The term *cum* is used "in a designation of time with which some action concurs."[3] The *cum ... assumetur* (third-person singular, future passive indicative from *assumo*) qualifies the timing of *erit tribulatio*

---

2. It must be stated that such a notion of mortal and immortal humans occupying the same world during the same period of time is not at all absurd. Jesus walked and talked with his disciples in his immortal condition for forty days after his own resurrection (Acts 1:3).

3. Charlton T. Lewis and Charles Short, *Harpers' Latin Dictionary* (New York: Harper & Brothers, 1891), 489.

(third-person singular future active indicative of *sum*). Because both the verb of the temporal clause with *assumetur* and the main clause with *erit* are in the future indicative, the events should be regarded as occurring contemporaneously, that is, *cum . . . assumetur* indicates the time at which *erit . . . tribulation*: in other words, at the time the church is suddenly caught up from this, there will be the tribulation. The construction does not mean the church will be caught up after the tribulation, or even during it, but that the unprecedented tribulation will commence upon the assumption of the church "from this place" (*hinc*).[4]

This seems to present us with a conundrum: (1) Irenaeus seems to teach that the church endures persecution during the coming tribulation (*Haer* 5.26.1); (2) Irenaeus describes the church as being caught up before the tribulation (5.29.1); and (3) Irenaeus has mortal saints who survive the tribulation repopulating the world in the kingdom as well as immortal saints reigning during the same kingdom (5.35.1).

To sort this out in a plausible fashion—though likely unsettling for almost any "rapture" view today—we need to step back and understand Irenaeus's theology of the assumption of the church from the rest of *Against Heresies*. Earlier in Book 5, Irenaeus described the assumption of the church by appealing to the Old Testament types of the catching up of Enoch and Elijah. He writes,

> For Enoch, when he pleased God, was translated [μετετέθη / *translatus est*] in the same body in which he did please Him, thus pointing out by anticipation the translation of the just [τὴν μετάθεσιν τῶν δικαίων προμηνύων /*translationem justorum praemonstrans*].[5] Elijah, too, was caught up [ἀνελήφθη/*assumptus est*] [when he was yet] in the substance of the [natural] form; thus exhibiting in prophecy the assumption of those who are spiritual [τὴν ἀνάληψιν τῶν πνευματικῶν προφητεύων / *assumptionem patrum prophetans*], and that nothing stood in the way of their body being translated and caught up [τὴν μετάθεσιν καὶ ἀνάληψιν /*in translationem et assumptionem*]. For by means of the very same hands through which they were molded at the beginning, did they receive this translation and assumption [τὴν μετάθεσιν καὶ ἀνάληψιν /*assumptionem et translationem*]. (*Haer.* 5.5.1)

The Greek text and Latin translations diverge at one significant point. The Greek text—likely reflecting the original wording of Irenaeus—asserts that the catching up of Elijah to heaven is a prophecy of "the assumption of those who are spiritual" (τὴν ἀνάληψιν τῶν πνευματικῶν), while the Latin text refers it to "the assumption of the fathers" (*assumptionem patrum*). The Latin translation appears to interpret Irenaeus's "those who are spiritual" as a reference to the Old Testament saints—the "fathers"—thus indicating the place to which the departed saints went upon death. However, elsewhere, Irenaeus uses the phrase "those who are spiritual" in reference to the righteous,[6] who have received the Spirit of God: "A

---

4. Lewis and Short, *Harpers' Latin Dictionary*, 855.

5. On the use of μετάθεσις here, see G. W. H. Lampe, ed., *A Patristic Greek Lexicon* (Oxford: Clarendon, 1961), 851, s.v. μετάθεσις.

6. He also uses the term in the sense in which gnostics used it to refer to the adherents of esoteric knowledge; *Haer.* 1.6.1 (τὸ πνευματικόν / *spiritale*); cf. 1.6.2; 1.7.5; 1.8.3; 2.17.3;

spiritual disciple [*discipulus vere spiritalis*] of this sort truly receiving the Spirit of God [*recipiens Spiritum Dei*] . . . does indeed 'judge all men, but is himself judged by no man'" (*Haer.* 4.33.1). He refers to such mature believers as "those who are truly spiritual [*spiritalis vere qui est*]" (4.33.15). He says these people are called "spiritual" because "they partake of the Spirit, and not because their flesh has been stripped off and taken away" (*Haer.* 5.6.1). He explains: "But when the spirit here blended with the soul is united to [God's] handiwork, the man is rendered spiritual and perfect [*spiritualis et perfectus*] because of the outpouring of the Spirit, and this is he who was made in the image and likeness of God" (5.6.1). Relying on 1 Thessalonians 5:23, Irenaeus notes, "And for this cause does the apostle, explaining himself, make it clear that the saved man is a complete man as well as a spiritual man [*perfectum et spiritualem salutis hominem*]" (5.6.1). Further, he explains that the Holy Spirit "dwelling in us, renders us spiritual [*spirituales*] even now" (5.8.1).

In Irenaeus's soteriology, however, not all "Christians" can be rightly counted among this category of "the spiritual." He notes in 5.8.2: "Those persons, then, who possess the earnest of the Spirit, and who are not enslaved by the lusts of the flesh, but are subject to the Spirit, and who in all things walk according to the light of reason, does the apostle properly term 'spiritual,' [*spirituales*] because the Spirit of God dwells in them." In contrast to the "spiritual" are "those who do indeed reject the Spirit's counsel, and are the slaves of fleshly lusts, and lead lives contrary to reason, and who, without restraint, plunge headlong into their own desires, having no longing after the Divine Spirit, do live after the manner of swine and of dogs"; these are called "carnal" because "they have no thought of anything else except carnal things" (5.8.2).

That those who are reckoned among Christians (as well as unbelieving Gentiles and Jews) can be regarded as "carnal" rather than "spiritual" Irenaeus makes clear in 5.8.4: "For men of this stamp do indeed say that they believe in the Father and the Son, but they never meditate as they should upon the things of God, neither are they adorned with works of righteousness. . . . Justly, therefore, did the apostle call all such 'carnal' and 'animal,'—[all those, namely], who through their own un-belief and luxury do not receive the Divine Spirit, and in their various phases cast out from themselves the life-giving Word, and walk stupidly after their own lusts." Later, in 5.9.2, he describes the "spiritual" this way: "As many as fear God and trust in His Son's advent, and who through faith do establish the Spirit of God in their hearts,—such men as these shall be properly called both 'pure,' and 'spiritual,' and 'those living to God,' because they possess the Spirit of the Father, who purifies man, and raises him up to the life of God."[7]

According to Irenaeus, then, all humanity can be divided into two categories: the "spiritual" who not only believe but also walk in the Spirit and are adorned in works of righteousness; and the "carnal" who do not believe, had once believed but had apostatized, or who claim to believe but do not walk in the Spirit nor are

---

2.29.1; 2.30.1, 2.30.5; 2.30.8, 9; 3.15.2. These are also called the "spiritual and perfect"; *Haer.* 1.6.4 (πνευματικοῖς τε καὶ τελείοις / *spiritalibus et perfectis*).

7. Cf. also *Haer.* 5.10.1; 5.10.2; 5.12.2.

adorned in righteous works. Thus when Irenaeus describes "the assumption of those who are spiritual" (τὴν ἀνάληψιν τῶν πνευματικῶν) in 5.5.1, he is referring to true Christians who are living lives of righteousness in contrast to unbelievers and carnal Christians who are not living such lives. This, then, would lead one to conclude that the promise of being caught up in the likeness of Enoch and Elijah is limited to those who are "perfect and spiritual," while those who are imperfect and carnal will be left along with the unbelievers to endure the purifying trials of the tribulation.

Irenaeus uses both Enoch and Elijah as Old Testament types of a future "translation" and "taking up" (τὴν μετάθεσιν καὶ ἀνάληψιν /*assumptionem et translationem*), both words being treated as two aspects of the same event, indicated by the two nouns governed by the single article. Though Irenaeus does not use the biblical language of ἀλλάσσω ("to change," 1 Cor. 15:51–52) or μετασχηματίζω ("to transform," Phil. 3:21) and ἁρπάζω ("to snatch up," 1 Thess. 4:17), he uses language and imagery that points us forward to the events described in these resurrection/transformation/assumption passages. Irenaeus is not exegeting these passages. He is simply relaying Old Testament types of New Testament eschatological truths. Irenaeus says that Enoch kept his body but was translated, pointing out by anticipation the translation of the just. Elijah was "taken up" also as a prophetic type of "the taking up of those who are spiritual." This will happen to "the just" or "the spiritual." He goes on:

> Wherefore also the elders who were disciples of the apostles tell us that those who were translated were transferred [τοὺς μετατεθέντας ἐκεῖσε μετατεθῆναι / *qui translate sunt, illuc translatos esse*] to that place (for paradise has been prepared for righteous men, such as have the Spirit [δικαίοις ... ἀνθρώποις, καὶ πνευματοφόροις / *justis enim hominibus, et Spiritum habentibus*], in which place also Paul the apostle, when he was caught up [εἰσκομισθείς / *asportatus*], heard words which are unspeakable as regards us in our present condition), and that there shall they who have been translated [*translati sunt*] remain until the consummation [of all things], as a prelude to immortality. (*Haer.* 5.5.1)

Irenaeus says that those who were "translated and transferred" were taken to paradise, a place where they would remain until the final consummation. This, he says, is a "prelude to immortality." This text cannot be read as applying to anyone other than Enoch and Elijah. He appeals to the "elders" who were disciples of the apostles, a common authority for Irenaeus. We can assume that Irenaeus is referring to the oral teaching he received from people like Papias and Polycarp, not to written records. He says the church's common interpretation is that Enoch and Elijah did not go to the throne of God but to "paradise." The fact that he mentions Paul's catching up to "paradise" from 2 Corinthians 12:4 may suggest that the place was still regarded as the place of the righteous saints awaiting the consummation, though this is not completely clear as the immediate context refers to Enoch and Elijah.[8] In any case, Enoch and Elijah provide not merely types but anticipations of

---

8. Though paradise is seen as a place of "waiting," it is not a place of torment or punishment but of rest and repose—the heavenly destination of "righteous men, such as have the

the experience of the just and spiritual saints who will one day be "translated and transferred." Their experience is a "prelude to immortality."

In an earlier reference to Paul's assumption to paradise, Irenaeus writes, "Paul expressly testifies that there are spiritual things when he declares that he was caught up into the third heaven [*ad tertium cœlum raptum se esse*], and again, that he was carried away [*delatum esse*] to paradise, and heard unspeakable words which it is not lawful for a man to utter" (*Haer.* 2.30.7). Note that Irenaeus uses the term *rapere* to refer to Paul's snatching up, where 2 Corinthians 12:4 uses ἁρπάζω. In this same passage, Irenaeus also insists that Elijah was "caught up in the flesh" (ἔνσαρκον ἀναληφθῆναι/*in carne assumptum*) to paradise. Irenaeus sees the continued preservation of the flesh of Enoch and Elijah as "an earnest of the future length of days"—that is, those who would, in the future, experience resurrection in incorruptible bodies.

Having established the fact of a future assumption to heaven of the "just and spiritual," we can now ask when this will occur relative to the future tribulation reign of the antichrist. Returning to 5.29.1, then, the assumption passage in its context reads:

> Those nations however, who did not of themselves raise up their eyes unto heaven, nor returned thanks to their Maker, nor wished to behold the light of truth, but who were like blind mice concealed in the depths of ignorance, the word justly reckons "as waste water from a sink, and as the turning-weight of a balance—in fact, as nothing;" [Isa 40:15, 17] so far useful and serviceable to the just, as stubble conduces towards the growth of the wheat, and its straw, by means of combustion, serves for working gold. And therefore, when in the end the Church shall be suddenly caught up from this (*Et propterea cum in fine repente hinc Ecclesia assumetur*), it is said, "There shall be tribulation such as has not been since the beginning, neither shall be (*erit, inquit, tribulatio quails non est facta ab initio, neque fiet*)" [Matt 24:21]. For this is the last contest of the righteous, in which, when they overcome they are crowned with incorruption. (*Haer.* 5.29.1)

This can be read in a couple of ways, but given the immediately preceding context, I think the best way to read this is by understanding Irenaeus's view of "tribulation" as having both a present, partial realization, and a future fulfillment. Already, tribulations are being experienced by the church for the purpose of purification. At the hands of the wicked nations, the saved are purified through their tribulations. Keeping in mind that Irenaeus is referring primarily to the present tribulations of the church, he writes, "And therefore, when in the end the Church shall be suddenly caught up from this." We should probably understand "this" (*hinc*) to refer to the present world where we are experiencing current tribulations wrought by the

---

Spirit (δικαίοις γὰρ ἀνθρώποις, καὶ πνευματοφόροις ἡτοιμάθη ὁ παράδεισος/*justis enim hominibus, et Spiritum habentibus praeparatus est paradisus*)" (*Haer.* 5.5.1). It is worth noting that in the 2 Cor passage Irenaeus cites, Paul used the verb ἁρπάζω (Vulgata *raptus est*), and Paul expressed uncertainty whether that catching up to paradise occurred physically or spiritually—"whether in the body or apart from the body, I do not know (εἴτε ἐν σώματι εἴτε χωρὶς τοῦ σώματος οὐκ οἶδα)" (2 Cor 12:3).

wicked nations. What follows, then, is the ultimate tribulation for which Irenaeus quotes Matthew 24:21. Yet Irenaeus refers to this ultimate tribulation as "the last contest of the righteous, in which, when they overcome they are crowned with incorruption" (5.29.1). If the "church" has been caught up prior to the tribulation, then who are the "righteous" who endure that same tribulation?

Because of Irenaeus's assertion that the church will endure the times of the antichrist, many have resisted Irenaeus's assertion that the church will be taken up prior to the tribulation.[9] This is an instance of choosing one passage and neglecting another, the fallacy of selective evidence. Even after quoting the relevant portion of *Against Heresies* 5.29.1 that asserts an assumption of the church prior to the tribulation, Sung Wook Chung notes, "In terms of timeline and overall structure, Irenaeus's eschatology coincides with that of historic premillennialism."[10]

On the other hand, New Testament scholar Adela Yarbro Collins, who has no theological horse in the race, reads this text "as is," acknowledging a likely allusion to 1 Thessalonians 4:17. Collins writes: "The notion that 'the church will be taken up' may have been inspired by 1 Thess 4:17. This suggestion is supported by the fact that not long after that statement and in the context of a reference to οἱ χρόνοι καὶ οἱ καιροί and the Day of the Lord, Paul mentions the 'sudden destruction,' from which there will be no escape, that will come upon those who say, 'peace and security' (1 Thess 5:3)."[11] Collins, then, allows Irenaeus's statement to stand: in *Against Heresies* 5.29.1, the church is taken up before the tribulation just as in 1 Thessalonians 4:17 the church is taken up before the Day of the Lord.

Even so, this does not solve the problem of Irenaeus's apparent contradiction. The "church" also endures persecution under the antichrist. Rather than simply asserting that Irenaeus unwittingly contradicts himself (which is, nevertheless, a possibility), perhaps a better solution can be found. We have to realize that Irenaeus's

---

9. Failing to recognize that Irenaeus is referring here to general tribulation and persecutions at the hands of wicked nations experienced throughout history—distinct in severity from the unparalleled future tribulation—lies at the heart of Martin's argument that this passage cannot refer to anything like an assumption of some members of the church from the earth prior to that future tribulation. See Gordon Wood Martin, "Eschatology in the Early Church: with Special Reference to the Theses of C. H. Dodd and M. Werner" (PhD thesis, University of Edinburgh, 1971), 519. The same author also argues against the "pretribulation" position by pointing out that elsewhere in Irenaeus the church suffers under the coming antichrist. Yet this fact only rules out an assumption of the entire church in all its parts; it does not rule out what seems to be the case in Irenaeus's exposition—that the "spiritual" will experience an assumption prior to the tribulation, while the "carnal" must endure the persecutions for the purpose of purification.

10. Sung Wook Chung, "Historic Premillennialism," in Sung Wook Chung and David Mathewson, *Models of Premillennialism* (Eugene, OR: Wipf & Stock, 2018), 10. Note that Chung, "Historic Premillennialism," 10–11, adds an interpretive introduction to Irenaeus's quotation not found or even implied in the original quoted material: "regarding the church's being caught up in the air to receive the returning Lord." Nothing in the text links Irenaeus's description of the assumption of the church to the return of Christ after the tribulation.

11. Adela Yarbro Collins, "Paul in Irenaeus on the Last Things," in *Irenaeus and Paul*, ed. Todd D. Still and David E. Wilhite, Pauline and Patristic Scholars in Debate (London: T&T Clark, 2020), 260.

ecclesiology and soteriology are pre-Augustinian and certainly pre-Reformation. So, when he uses terms like "church," we cannot assume he means the same thing as later theologians do. For Irenaeus, as was typical in the second century, the "church" refers to those baptized into the new covenant community of the Spirit, and ultimate salvation comes not to every baptized person, nor even necessarily to anyone who has once experienced the transformative grace of God. Rather, salvation involves perseverance in baptism and continued communion with the Father, through the Son, and by the Spirit. Salvation was not merely a state of being, but a journey toward a destination, a journey that could go awry and end in tragedy through apostasy.[12] We have already visited these themes in Irenaeus above in our discussion of his distinction between the "spiritual" and "carnal."

The best solution, given Irenaeus's second-century ecclesiology and soteriology, is that the rescue from the coming tribulation was a special privilege not of all baptized Christians but of the "spiritual"—those ready and waiting, spiritually prepared in holy living. This makes the best sense of the appeal to Enoch and Elijah, who were taken not simply because they were believers but because they were especially holy and pure believers in their corrupt generation. Others were left to endure the hardships on earth in their day. In Irenaeus's mind, part of the church—the spiritual—will be assumed prior to the tribulation. The rest of the church will be tested and purified through the last contest of the righteous, having to face the ordeal of the antichrist.

Where did Irenaeus get this view of a partial assumption of the church prior to the coming tribulation? I suggest he adapted it from the eschatological sections of the late-first-century visions section of the Shepherd of Hermas, which Irenaeus not only knew but also quoted from in *Against Heresies* 4.20.2. Because of the deeply technical nature of the eschatology of the Shepherd of Hermas, this matter is treated in Going Deeper excursus, *Escape from the Coming Wrath in the Shepherd of Hermas*.

Reading Irenaeus in Light of Hermas

In light of the analyses of Visions 2–4 of the Shepherd of Hermas (Go Deeper Excursus 27), I suggest that Hermas's eschatology involves a scenario in which those who maintain single-minded repentance in this age, who are perfectly fitted into the tower of refuge—the church—will have a glorious destiny in company with angels, distinct from the sorry fate of lackluster believers. In the Shepherd of Hermas, though some are cast so far from the tower that they have no hope (Vis.

---

12. For a more thorough description of Irenaeus's soteriology, see Eric Osborn, *Irenaeus of Lyons* (Cambridge: Cambridge University Press, 2001), 117–40, 256–62. Osborn, *Irenaeus of Lyons*, 130, writes that in Irenaeus's soteriology, "our offerings to God have moral conditions, for it is the pure conscience of the offerer that sanctifies the offering (4.18.4). We are sons of God only through obedience and doctrine (4.41.2); those who disobey their parents do not inherit (4.41.3). The earnest of the spirit dwells in us to make us spiritual even now while the mortal is swallowed up in immortality. By the spirit we are no more slaves of fleshly lusts, but ruled by the spirit. Following the light of reason, we become spiritual men (5.8.1, 2)."

3), others are close to it and will therefore have a second chance. While those in the tower seem to be promised salvation and refuge from the Great Tribulation coming upon the earth that will destroy the wicked and purify the righteous, those who are close to the tower will have to endure the tribulation for the purification of their sins. However, even these will enter into eschatological reward, yet in a position subordinate to those in the tower who were incorporated while it was still being built prior to the appointed "Day" for repentance.

> **Go Deeper Excursus 27**
>
> *Escape from the Coming Wrath in the Shepherd of Hermas*

Hermas, then, becomes the interpretational key for understanding the conundrum posed by Irenaeus's apparent contradiction between the church caught up *prior to* the coming tribulation and the church purified *by* the coming tribulation. Irenaeus argued that he received the following from those elders that preceded him: "And as the presbyters say, 'Then those who are deemed worthy of an abode in heaven shall go there, others shall enjoy the delights of paradise, and others shall possess the splendor of the city" (*Haer.* 5.36.1). He continues, "They say [moreover], that there is this distinction between the habitation of those who produce a hundred-fold, and that of those who produce sixty-fold, and that of those who produce thirty-fold: for the first will be taken up into the heavens, the second will dwell in paradise, the last will inhabit the city. . . . The presbyters, the disciples of the apostles, affirm that this is the gradation and arrangement of those who are saved" (*Haer.* 5.36.2).

Recall that Irenaeus's premillennial eschatology even distinguishes between two different groups of people in the coming age, which corresponds well with Hermas's own categorization of those who were incorporated into the tower and those who are saved but relegated to a "much subordinate place" (Vis. 3.7.6). That is, the immortal, glorified saints are those who are rescued prior to the tribulation and the mortal survivors of the tribulation correspond to those Christians who were not spiritually prepared and go through the tribulation, some of whom survive and enter the kingdom in their moral bodies (*Haer.* 5.35.1).

Though Irenaeus does not delve into an explanation as to how he arrived at this distinction between the resurrected, glorified saints and those who are still in their mortal bodies, Hermas's description in Vision 4 of an escape from the beast for some while others are left to endure tribulation and his description in Vision 3 of those who occupy a much inferior place provides the clue to solving Irenaeus's puzzle. This also explains Irenaeus's apparent contradiction in his eschatology, wherein "the church" appears to be taken up from present persecutions inflicted on them by the nations prior to the tribulation while others endure the "last contest of the righteous" (*Haer.* 5.29.1).

In light of the previous chapter, for those who hold to the classic Irenaean premillennial eschatology, the question is not *if* the church will be resurrected and caught up to meet the Lord in the air but *when*. The question, of course, cannot even be asked unless one already accepts a future tribulation of some duration. The timing of the rapture is not really a question for idealists, partial preterists, or historicists who tend to see the passage as referring to the general resurrection at the end of the age, associated with a fairly momentary conflagration of the world or a sudden purification and establishment of the new creation. These approaches do not usually include a distinct future period of prolonged judgment upon the earth. Without a prolonged Day of the Lord, the question of when the rapture takes place relative to that period is absurd.

However, those who do believe in a future tribulation period, in keeping with second-century Irenaean premillennial eschatology, approach the question of the timing of the rapture in a number of ways. Those who hold to a "pre-tribulation rapture" argue that the catching up of the saints in 1 Thessalonians 4:17 will occur prior to ("pre") the coming Day of the Lord period as a means of rescuing the saints from the coming wrath (1 Thess 1:10; 5:9).[13] Proponents of a "mid-tribulation rapture" believe the resurrection, transformation, and catching up of the saints will occur sometime in the middle of the tribulation, perhaps at the actual midpoint itself, and may be associated with the ascension of the two witnesses in Revelation 11:11–12.[14] Supporters of the "pre-wrath rapture" position see the church suffering through most of the future tribulation period; but in keeping with the promise of rescue from the coming wrath in 1 Thessalonians 1:10 and 5:9, they generally view the rapture as occurring prior to the final bowls of wrath in Revelation 16.[15] Those who hold to the "post-tribulation rapture" position see the timing of the rapture as concurrent with the descent of Christ to establish his kingdom on earth, after the future Day of the Lord (1 Cor 15:23; 2 Thess 2:1; Rev 19:11–21).[16] Finally, the "partial rapture" proponents may share the same timing of the rapture with pre-tribulational, mid-tribulational, or even pre-wrath views (or even all of them in a kind of multistage rapture); but in the partial rapture view, only the truly faithful, spiritual saints will be raptured while the carnal or unprepared will be left behind to endure the tribulation.[17]

I argued in the previous chapter that Irenaeus held to a future seven-year tribulation/Day of the Lord period and that his teaching that the church will endure

---

13. E.g., John F. Hart, ed., *Evidence for the Rapture: A Biblical Case for Pretribulationism* (Chicago: Moody, 2015); Renald E. Showers, *Maranatha—Our Lord, Come!: A Definitive Study of the Rapture of the Church* (Bellmawr, NJ: The Friends of Israel Gospel Ministry, 1995); and John F. Walvoord, *The Rapture Question*, rev. and enl. ed. (Grand Rapids: Zondervan, 1979).

14. E.g., James O. Buswell, *A Systematic Theology of the Christian Religion*, vol. 2 (Grand Rapids: Zondervan, 1963), 456; Norman B. Harrison, *The End: Re-Thinking the Revelation* (Minneapolis: Harrison Service, 1948), 114–21.

15. E.g., Marvin J. Rosenthall, *The Pre-Wrath Rapture of the Church* (Nashville: Thomas Nelson, 1990); Robert D. Van Kampen, *The Rapture Question Answered: Plain and Simple* (Grand Rapids: Revell, 1997).

16. E.g., Craig L. Blomberg, "The Posttribulationism of the New Testament: Leaving 'Left Behind' Behind," in *A Case for Historic Premillennialism: An Alternative to "Left Behind" Eschatology*, ed. Craig L. Blomberg and Sung Wook Chung (Grand Rapids: Baker Academic, 2009), 61–88; and Robert H. Gundry, *The Church and the Tribulation: A Biblical Examination of Posttribulationism* (Grand Rapids: Zondervan, 1973).

17. E.g., Robert Govett, *Entrance into the Kingdom, or, Reward according to Works*, 2nd ed. (London: Thynne, 1922); George H. Lang, *The Revelation of Jesus Christ*, 2nd ed. (London: Paternoster, 1948).

persecution during the tribulation (*Haer.* 5.26.1; 5.35.1) as well as being caught up prior to the tribulation (5.29.1). He also taught that at the end of the tribulation, those saints who survive the persecution of the antichrist will enter the kingdom in their mortal bodies and repopulate the world (*Haer.* 5.35.1; cf. Commodian, *Instructiones,* 44), which will be ruled over by resurrected saints (*Haer.* 5:35.1). Reading Irenaeus's eschatological expectations in light of the eschatological teachings of the Shepherd of Hermas (Herm. Vis. 2, 3, 4), I suggested the best solution to this conundrum is that Irenaeus held to something like a partial pre-tribulation rapture of the "spiritual" or "repentant" Christians, while the "double-minded" or "carnal" Christians will be left to endure the purifying fires of the tribulation.

While it may be expected that I would adopt this partial pre-tribulation view because of my methodological presumption that Irenaeus was "more right than wrong in his basic eschatological outlook," I cannot accept it without an important modification. My view on the specific matter of who will be caught up prior to the tribulation is affected by my soteriology and ecclesiology, which differ from that of Irenaeus. Like many of the early church fathers, Irenaeus did not hold to the concept of an irrevocable election, which Augustine later articulates, along with Protestant reformers like Calvin, that distinguishes between the truly regenerate and the unregenerate, regardless of their membership in the visible church. An effect of an Augustinian/Calvinist soteriology is that within the visible church of the baptized (that is, among those called "Christians"), there are those who are truly regenerate: the elect. A distinction is often made between the visible church, which is comprised of both saved and unsaved. On the other hand, Irenaeus, like many others in his day, regarded salvation as more of a process, a journey, in which a person who comes to faith is baptized and continues to cooperate with the Spirit in a life of sanctification and holiness will ultimately be glorified. In that view, some who begin the Christian life of faith will apostatize or will live in such a way that they fail to make spiritual progress will find themselves in the category of "carnal" or "unrepentant" Christians.

Irenaeus's soteriology and ecclesiology, then, affect his view of those Christians who participate in the assumption of the church: when the rapture occurs, only the spiritual, prepared saints who are diligent in their walk in the Spirit will be rescued from the coming tribulation; those who are not prepared will endure the tribulation. However, if Irenaeus had a more Augustinian view of the nature of salvation and the church, then his pre-tribulation rapture would have had the full body of the elect—the "invisible church"—caught up prior to the tribulation, leaving behind only unregenerate unbelievers. Of course, in both cases, people can come to faith in Christ during the tribulation and be counted among the regenerate elect; and, depending on how technical one defines the "church," they would even be called the "church."

Because I hold to a view of soteriology and ecclesiology more in keeping with the Augustinian/Calvinist tradition, my post-Reformation variation of Irenaeus's eschatology does not involve a partial pre-tribulation rapture but a pre-tribulation rapture of the whole church. However, from a phenomenological perspective, Irenaeus and I appear to have the same view, because both positions understand that not everybody who is part of the visible church of baptized members are necessarily "saved." To an outside observer, the catching up of only the truly regenerated, invisible church may look like a partial rapture.

In the following chapters (19 and 20), I will present my biblical/exegetical arguments for the pre-tribulation rapture of the church, relying heavily on discussions related to the Day of the Lord earlier in this book as well as mentioning a handful of further considerations.

19

THE ASSUMPTION OF THE CHURCH
IN THE NEW TESTAMENT

*Trust in the Lord, you double-minded, because he is
able to do all things—he sends his wrath away from you
and sends out punishments upon you double-minded.*

Shepherd of Hermas, Vision 4.2.6

In the middle of the 1800s, after a few generations of a resurgence in a futurist view of eschatology, the modern "pre-tribulation rapture" emerged.[1] Some futurists embraced the doctrine while others rejected it.[2] Nevertheless, through the vehicle of popular preaching, teaching, and writing, the pre-tribulation rapture became a fixture in many churches and institutions and still enjoys a degree of popular support today.[3] Interest in and support for the pre-tribulation position among scholars has declined significantly in recent decades.[4] The perception among many appears to be that the doctrine rests on flimsy inferences drawn from unclear passages dependent upon peculiar presuppositions.[5] In short, many today believe that the

---

1. Portions of this chapter and the next are adapted, with permission, from Michael J. Svigel, "What Child Is This? A Forgotten Argument for the Pretribulation Rapture," in John F. Hart, ed., *Evidence for the Rapture: A Biblical Case for Pretribulationism* (Chicago: Moody, 2015), 225–53. The substance of that chapter was itself drawn, with permission, from two articles written, Michael J. Svigel, " 'What Child Is This?' Darby's Early Exegetical Argument for the Pretribulation Rapture of the Church," *TrinJ* 35.2 (2014): 225–51; and Michael J. Svigel, "The Apocalypse of John and the Rapture of the Church: A Reevaluation," *TrinJ* 22.1 (Spring 2001): 23–74.

2. See Clarence B. Bass, *Backgrounds to Dispensationalism: Its Historical Genesis and Ecclesiastical Implications* (Eugene, OR: Wipf & Stock, 2005), 40, 76–77; Richard Reitner, "A History of the Development of the Rapture Positions," in Stanley N. Gundry, ed., *Three Views on the Rapture: Pre-, Mid-, or Post-Tribulational*, Counterpoints: Bible and Theology (Grand Rapids: Zondervan, 1996), 13–21.

3. See Tim LaHaye, *The Rapture: Who Will Face the Tribulation?* (Chicago: Moody, 2003); Hal Lindsey, *Vanished into Thin Air: The Hope of Every Believer* (Los Angeles: Western Front, 1999); and Amy Fryckholm Johnson, *Rapture Culture: Left Behind in Evangelical America* (New York: Oxford University Press, 2004).

4. T. Van McClain, "The Pretribulational Rapture: A Doubtful Doctrine," in *Looking into the Future: Evangelical Studies in Eschatology*, ed. David W. Baker (Grand Rapids: Baker, 2001), 233–45; Gary DeMar, *End Times Fiction: A Biblical Consideration of the Left Behind Theology* (Nashville: Thomas Nelson, 2001), 36.

5. DeMar, *End Times Fiction*, 36; Robert H. Gundry, *First the Antichrist* (Grand Rapids: Baker, 1997), 140–41; Douglas J. Moo, "Response to 'The Case for the Pretribulational Rap-

doctrine of the church's assumption to heaven prior to a future seven-year tribulation simply has no clear exegetical basis.[6]

In light of Irenaeus's second-century teaching regarding the assumption of the "spiritual" church prior to the coming tribulation, read in light of the teaching that the fully repentant saints will be spared from the tribulation in the Shepherd of Hermas, this chapter will revisit the question of a pre-tribulation rapture, asking whether Scripture may be reasonably and responsibly read in harmony with the general notion of a rescue from the coming Day of the Lord.

The word *rapture* comes from the Latin word *rapere*, which translates the Greek term ἁρπάζω. Paul uses it in reference to his sudden assumption into the "third heaven" (2 Cor 12:2, 4), and it appears in 1 Thessalonians 4:16–17: "We who are alive, who are left, will be caught up (ἁρπαγησόμεθα) in the clouds together with them to meet the Lord in the air." This event of the catching up of resurrected saints and living saints (transformed into immortal bodies; 1 Cor 15:51–52; Phil 3:20–21) is what is meant by the term "rapture," or, in the words of Irenaeus, the "assumption," of the church.

That the word ἁρπάζω appears in the Bible is without dispute. What is disputed, however, are two questions. First, does this passage actually refer to a future event involving the literal snatching of glorified saints into the air? Second, if so, then when will that event take place relative to the future tribulation period? Because the first question involves several technical discussions, it is addressed in Go

> **Go Deeper Excursus 28**
>
> *The Rapture of the Church in 1 Thessalonians 4:17 as an Actual Event*

Deeper Excursus 28, *The Rapture of the Church in 1 Thessalonians 4:17 as an Actual Event*. Those who are persuaded that the "rapture" is merely a metaphor should attend to that excursus carefully before proceeding to the question of when that event will take place relative to the future tribulation.

Stipulating that the assumption of the church is an actual event pictured in 1 Thessalonians 4:17, the question that irks futurists who take the details of end-times prophecy seriously is the question of timing. That is, what is the relationship between the catching up of the church in 1 Thessalonians 4:17 and coming final Day of the Lord, which we have established as a future seven-year period of the career of the antichrist and its related judgments.

The Classic Arguments for the Pre-tribulation Rapture

In this section, I will present in summary fashion seven arguments that have been variously articulated in numerous sources. I begin with what I regard as the weightier arguments, many of which were discussed indirectly in connection with other

---

ture Position,'" in *Three Views on the Rapture: Pre-, Mid-, or Post-Tribulational*, ed. Stanley N. Gundry, Counterpoints: Bible and Theology (Grand Rapids: Zondervan, 1996), 87–101.

6. Barbara R. Rossing, *The Rapture Exposed: The Message of Hope in the Book of Revelation* (Cambridge, MA: Westview, 2004), 21–22; N. T. Wright, "Farewell to the Rapture," *Bible Review* 17 (August 2001): 8, 52.

issues earlier in this book. For these, I will simply summarize and cross-reference previous discussions. I will also acknowledge when a particular argument works equally well for other rapture positions besides the pre-tribulation view.

The Symbol of Last Trumpet

In chapter 16, in conjunction with the discussion of the Day of the Lord in 1 Thessalonians 4:13–5:11, I made the case that the "trumpet of God" (1 Thess 4:16) and the "last trumpet" (1 Cor 15:52) both refer to the same final trumpet announcing the time of the resurrection/transformation/rapture of the church (1 Thess 4:17). In Go Deeper Excursus 24, I also argued for a disassociation of the "last trumpet" with the seventh angel who sounds a trumpet in Revelation 11:15–18, while in chapter 7, I argued that the "great trumpet" in Matthew 24:31 draws from Old Testament and intertestamental language regarding the regathering of Israel from among the nations and their restoration in the land after the tribulation.

In an examination of the language of 1 Thessalonians 4 and 5 (chapter 16), I also demonstrated that Paul used imagery that connects the trumpet to the coming Day of the Lord. And in chapter 15, through a detailed survey of the Day of the Lord language and imagery from the Old Testament and intertestamental literature, we saw that the trumpet related to the Day of the Lord always preceded it (cf. Jer 4:5–6; Joel 2:1–2; Hos 5:8, 10; Pss. Sol. 8:1–2). Because the "Day of the Lord" is a technical term for what is elsewhere called the "tribulation" and ultimately corresponds to the seventieth week of Daniel 9:27 in classic Irenaean eschatology, the relationship between the trumpet of God/last trumpet and the rapture of the church places the event prior to the tribulation.

However, we must be careful not to overstate the case here, because nowhere in the New Testament do we see a clear, unambiguous identification between the coming Day of the Lord period of judgement and the entire seventieth week of Daniel 9:27. If one defines the Day of the Lord (1 Thess 5:2) as the whole seventieth week of Daniel, then the identification of the trumpet as the alarm preceding the Day of the Lord is a strong argument for pretribulationism. But if one were to define the Day of the Lord more narrowly as the second half of the seven-year tribulation (Rev 13), or even as the final months of the tribulation during the bowls of wrath (Rev 16), then a mid-tribulation or pre-wrath rapture would still be viable options. Only a strict post-tribulation rapture is disallowed by the fact that the trumpet always precedes—never follows—the Day of the Lord in the Old Testament.

However, I must also direct the reader to the discussion of the Day of the Lord in 2 Thessalonians 2:1–2 in chapter 16, where we saw that it will be characterized by an "apostasy" related to the revelation of the "man of lawlessness" (2:3–12)—i.e., the antichrist, whose career will extend throughout the entire seventieth week of Daniel (9:27), though it will be most fearsome during the last forty-two months of that period (Rev 13:1–10). In light of this, the Day of the Lord must be seen to extend at minimum through the second half of Daniel's seventieth week, and more likely the entire period. Limiting the Day of the Lord to the final months of the bowls of wrath in Revelation 16 or to the very moment of Christ's descent is arbitrary and inconsistent with the technical use of the term and its New Testament associations.

Thus, all things considered, the relationship between the trumpet and the Day of the Lord in 1 Thessalonians 4:13–5:11 (with 1 Cor 15:52) favors the pre-tribulation position, permits the mid-tribulation position, weakens the pre-wrath position, and rules out the post-tribulation position.

The Promise of Rescue from Wrath

The second classic argument for the pre-tribulation rapture is related to the promise that the saints will be rescued from the "coming wrath" (1 Thess 1:9–10; 5:9), which is always a reference to the coming period of wrath upon this earth associated with the Day of the Lord (see detailed discussions in chapters 15 and 16). The context for rescue from this wrath is the coming of the Son from heaven (1 Thess 1:10) and the rapture of the church (1 Thess 4:17; 5:1–10). Christians are to await the Son from heaven for this rescue (1 Thess 1:10), implying that this is the next event for which believers should hope. They are also to await the Son from heaven to transform their mortal bodies to conform to Christ's body—the transformation associated with the resurrection and rapture of the church (1 Cor 15:52; Phil 3:20–21; 1 Thess 4:16–17). Read together, the object of the Christian's hope is the coming of the Son to raise the dead, transform the living, and rescue them from the coming wrath, which is the Day of the Lord or tribulation period.

Other passages of Scripture make a clear distinction between the coming future tribulation for the wicked and unbelievers and the relief from present tribulations endured by believers (2 Thess 1:5–10; cf. Rom 2:5–10). Peter's discussion of the Day of the Lord also affirms that God established a pattern with Noah prior to the flood and with Lot prior to the judgment of Sodom and Gomorrah: he rescues the godly from trials and keeps the unrighteous for the day of judgment (2 Pet 2:4–9; cf. Rev 3:10). We already discussed these passages and their relationship to the coming wrath in detail in chapter 16.

Though God may certainly spare the church from the coming wrath by means of protection in the midst of the place of wrath (e.g., Daniel's friends in the furnace in 3:19–30), the examples Peter uses in 2 Peter 2:4–9 for rescue from the coming wrath involve a removal from the place of wrath: Noah is removed from the earth and floats above the flood waters, and Lot is removed from the city before it is destroyed. Also, the rescue from the coming wrath in 1 Thessalonians is directly related to the return of Christ from heaven and the rapture of the church (1 Thess 1:10; 4:13–5:11).

However, the argument for the pre-tribulation rapture based on the rescue from the coming wrath works only if the "wrath" from which the church is promised salvation includes the entire future seventieth week of Daniel. If one narrowly defines the "wrath" as the bowls of wrath in Revelation 16, then a pre-wrath rapture satisfies this promise. If one defines the "wrath" as the wrath associated with the full rule of the antichrist and his persecution of the saints for the second half of the tribulation (Rev 13), then a mid-tribulation rapture satisfies the rescue from wrath.

To arbitrate between these positions, we must first observe that the promises of rescue and salvation from wrath do not refer to "the wrath of God" but simply to "wrath" (1 Thess 1:10; 5:9)—probably because it is a reference to the coming Day of the Lord, also known in the Old Testament as the "day of wrath" (Zeph 1:15). In the book of Revelation, "wrath" is already mentioned in the opening of the sixth seal, where the vision portrays the people of the earth crying out, "Fall on us and hide us from the face of the one seated on the throne and from the wrath of the Lamb, for the great day of their wrath has come, and who is able to stand?" (Rev 6:16–17).

Many disputes have ensued among futurists regarding the chronology of the events portrayed in the various cycles of visions—seals, trumpets, and bowls. Some hold to a form of recapitulation (see discussion above in chapter 10 and Go Deeper Excursus 17), in which the seven seals in some sense overlap or parallel the seven trumpets and seven bowls. This could potentially place the events symbolically portrayed in the breaking of the sixth seal toward the end of the seven-year tribulation. However, the symbol of the seven-sealed scroll "written on the inside and on the back" suggests a different function of the scroll than a presentation of chronological events.

John Philip Garrow makes the case that the visions accompanying the breaking of the seven seals of the scroll do not represent the direct revelation of the contents of the scroll—that is, symbolic visions that refer directly to actual future events. Rather, the breaking of the seals serves as a kind of foreshadowing or summary of the revelations of future events.[7] In other words, the seals do not answer the question, "What events, in what order, will occur during the coming tribulation?" Instead, they answer the question, "What, in general, will the coming tribulation be like?" It functions like a teaser trailer that catches the essence of the story about to unfold; it does not set forth that story.

That the scroll is sealed but has writing on the outside suggests a kind of "table of contents," giving a summary or overview of what is found inside.[8] In the ancient world, a sealed legal document, such as a deed or testament meant to be opened under certain conditions or by certain people, would need to have some kind of brief description of the contents in order to identify it.[9] Garrow concludes, "The seal visions (6.1–17) function like a foreshadowing 'table of contents' in which some of the principal elements of the contents of the scroll are sketched in outline."[10]

In answer to the question "What will the future time of tribulation entail?," the general description of the contents of the scroll symbolized by each of the seven seals says that there will be deception (Rev 6:1–2; cf. Matt 24:4–5, 11–13), warfare

---

7. Alan John Philip Garrow, *Revelation* (London: Routledge, 1997), 14–35.

8. Most commentators take the writing inside and out as indicating the document's completeness—it has so many words that they cannot fit on one side of the scroll; e.g., Leon Morris, *Revelation*, rev. ed., Tyndale New Testament Commentaries (Grand Rapids: Eerdmans, 1987), 96; and Grant R. Osborne, *Revelation: Verse by Verse*, Osborne New Testament Commentaries (Bellingham, WA: Lexham, 2016), 110.

9. See G. K. Beale, *The Book of Revelation*, The New International Greek Testament Commentary, ed. I. Howard Marshall and Donald A. Hagner (Grand Rapids: Zondervan, 1999), 344–45.

10. Garrow, *Revelation*, 32.

(Rev 6:3–4; cf. Matt 24:6–7), famine (Rev 6:5–6; cf. Matt 24:7), death (Rev 6:7–8; cf. Matt 24:7, 21–28), and martyrdom (Rev 6:9–11; cf. Matt 24:9). With the sixth seal, we see classic Day of the Lord imagery indicating divine wrath; but in the midst of this period of wrath and judgment, God will also redeem Israel and countless people from among the nations (Rev 6:12–7:7; cf. Matt 24:13–14, 29–31). Only with the opening of the seventh seal (Rev 8) do the symbolic visions correspond to chronological events during the tribulation. The seals, then, including the sixth seal, provide a general description true of the entire tribulation period. In light of this, the statement of panic expressed by the people of the world in Revelation 6:17 that "the great day of . . . wrath has come, and who is able to stand?" refers not to a discrete portion of the end of the tribulation but to the whole tribulation as the Day of the Lord, the day of wrath.

Yet another problem with limiting the "wrath" of the Day of the Lord to the "bowls of wrath" in Revelation 16 presents itself upon close examination. In Revelation 15, as the angels solemnly prepare to pour out the golden bowls with the seven plagues, we read, "Then I saw another portent in heaven, great and amazing: seven angels with seven plagues, which are the last (πλαγὰς ἑπτὰ τὰς ἐσχάτας), for with them the wrath of God is ended (ὅτι ἐν αὐταῖς ἐτελέσθη ὁ θυμὸς τοῦ θεοῦ)" (Rev 15:1). Note that the seven bowls symbolize "seven plagues" and that these plagues are the "last," implying that several plagues had already been unleashed upon the earth. In fact, we see exactly that in previous passages: in Revelation 9:18, the judgment of the sixth trumpet unleashes a monstrous army spewing fire, smoke, and sulfur, which the text calls "plagues" (Rev 9:18, 20); and in 11:6, the two witnesses who prophesy during the first half of the tribulation for 1,260 days "have authority . . . with every kind of plague (πληγῇ) as often as they desire." The seven "bowls of wrath" are merely the end of a long series of judgments executed by God and mediated through various means. Alan Johnson notes:

> While these plagues may be the finale to the whole historical panorama of God's judgments, it would be exegetically preferable to find a connection with events related in Revelation itself. . . . After the interlude of the sealing of the saints from spiritual harm (ch. 7) the seven trumpets are sounded (8:6–9:21; 11:15–19). The sixth one involves three plagues that kill a third of mankind (9:18). The third woe (11:14) includes the bowl judgments that are called the "last" plagues. From this we may conclude that the trumpets begin the eschatological wrath of God that is finished in the seven bowls.[11]

This idea is reinforced by the fact that the text informs us that with these seven plagues, the wrath of God is "finished (ἐτελέσθη)" (15:1), not started. Swete writes, "Three πληγαί are named in 9:18, and in 11:6 the Witnesses are empowered to strike the earth ἐν πάσῃ πληγῇ; but the plagues now about to begin are distinguished from all that came before them as 'the last' (cf. 21:9), the final cycle

---

11. Alan F. Johnson, "Revelation," in *The Expositor's Bible Commentary: Hebrews–Revelation*, rev. ed., ed. Tremper Longman III and David E. Garland, vol. 13 (Grand Rapids: Zondervan, 2006), 729.

of such visitations."[12] This means God's wrath has already been meted out on the earth prior to the seven bowl judgments; these represent the completion of wrath already begun.

Though many try to distinguish between the wrath of Satan (Rev 12:12) or the "wrath of the antichrist" on the one hand and the "wrath of God" on the other, this is a false dichotomy according to Scripture. Rather, God's wrath in the world is mediated by allowing Satan to be unleashed for deception or by providentially orchestrating events like invasions of armies, natural disasters, or pestilence. The LXX of Isaiah 10:5–6 demonstrates this: "Woe to the Assyrians! The rod of my anger and the wrath (τοῦ θυμοῦ μου καὶ ὀργῆς) is in their hands. I will send my wrath (τὴν ὀργήν μου) against a lawless nation, and I will order my people to make spoils and plunder and to trample the cities and to make them into a cloud of dust" (Brannan) (cf. Isa 13:1–22; Zeph 1:14–18). Distinguishing between "man's wrath" and "God's wrath," assigning the former to the early part of the tribulation and the latter to the last part of the tribulation, does not actually fit Scripture's perspective on wrath as executed by God as the agent but mediated through various seemingly normal means (see chapter 15 of this book).

In sum, the "Day of the Lord" and the "day of wrath" are both references to the same period of time during which God's increasingly severe judgments are mediated through various means. All of it, though, constitutes God's wrath. The new covenant church, the body of Christ, is promised rescue from the coming wrath at the coming of Christ (1 Thess 1:10; 5:9), and this itself is associated with the rapture of the church (1 Thess 4:13–5:11). God's past rescue of the saints from the presence of God's temporal wrath is a model for the future rescue of the saints from temporal wrath (2 Pet 2:9; Rev 3:10), and this wrath appears to occupy the entire tribulation period. Taken together, these facts favor the pre-tribulation position, which rightly understands the whole Day of the Lord as a day of wrath. Nevertheless, the mid-tribulation would be a viable option if the Day of the Lord is limited to the second half of the seventieth week of Daniel 9:27. The pre-wrath is weakened by the fact that Revelation 15:1 implies that wrath had been ongoing much earlier in the book of Revelation, even in the plagues of the two witnesses during the first half. The strict post-tribulation rapture simply cannot affirm that the church is rescued from wrath in any meaningful sense that matches the language and imagery considered here.

The Problem of Mortals Repopulating the Millennium

In chapter 14 and 18, I demonstrated that classic Irenaean premillennial eschatology holds that at the end of the tribulation Christ will return to a multitude of saints who survive the tribulation still in their mortal bodies (*Haer.* 5.35.1). In a strictly post-tribulation rapture, in which all surviving saints are suddenly transformed into glorious bodies and caught up to greet the Lord and return immediately to earth while the wicked are destroyed (Rev 19:21), there will be no mortal survivors of the tribulation to repopulate the world during the kingdom.

---

12. Henry Barclay Swete, ed., *The Apocalypse of St. John*, 2nd. ed., Classic Commentaries on the Greek New Testament (New York: Macmillan, 1906), 190.

The view that these could be unsaved wicked simply does not work, as no unsaved wicked can enter the kingdom (Matt 25:31–46; 1 Cor 6:9; Gal 5:21). The idea that these could be last-second converts who repent and turn to Christ during the final weeks of the tribulation as the bowl judgments are being poured out on the earth does not fit the tenor of the Revelation 16. In response to the just judgments of God against the beast and his kingdom and all those who allied with him, "They cursed the name of God, who had authority over these plagues, and they did not repent and give him glory" (16:9; cf. 16:11). At some point in the tribulation, the fate of each person is sealed. In any case, the picture of endurance mentioned in Matthew 24:13 and Revelation 3:10 does not match the idea that the kingdom will actually be populated by a vast throng of people who had previously cursed Christ and worshiped the beast.

No, those who enter the kingdom, having survived the antichrist's reign of terror, must be saints who came to Christ during the tribulation period, both Jews and Gentiles (Rev 7:1–17; 13:7–10). Many of the "great multitude" will suffer martyrdom and be raised to reign with Christ at his coming at the end of the tribulation (Rev 6:9–11; 20:4). In the Irenaean premillennial view, the righteous survivors of the tribulation will enter the kingdom in their mortal bodies and will be the ones who repopulate the earth. The handful of unsaved descendants of these mortal survivors will be among those who rebel at the end of the millennium—not resurrected saints (Rev 20:7–10).

Only with a mid-tribulation or pre-tribulation rapture of the church could there be an actual righteous remnant of mortal humans who persevered under the antichrist to repopulate the world during the millennium. A pre-wrath view seems to require the first citizen of the coming kingdom to be last-minute converts. Though this is plausible, it does not match the picture we see of God's consistent rejection in the midst of the last plagues or of the endurance of the saints leading up to the return of Christ to earth. The post-tribulation view requires the first citizens of the millennium to be unbelievers (because all believers will have been raptured at the end), or it requires a kind of partial rapture at the end in which only a faithful remnant are raptured while others are left behind.

The Removal of the Restrainer

In Go Deeper Excursus 25, *Who (or What) Is the Restrainer in 2 Thessalonians 2:6–7?*, I presented a case for the restrainer in 2 Thessalonians 2:6–8 as the church empowered by the Spirit to hold back wickedness and promote righteousness, thus preventing Satan from fully unleashing his wicked designs. This, in turn, prevents the ultimate antichrist from being revealed and the final Day of the Lord from commencing. If this is the case, then the removal of the restrainer will coincide with the removal of the body of Christ, the church—which has a unique calling in the present age as the mediator of the coming kingdom and its partial restraining work against Satan and his kingdom. This means of this removal is the rapture of the church described in 1 Thessalonians 4:17.

If we allow this conclusion, then the rapture must happen at the very latest by the midpoint of the tribulation, because after that point there will be no question about the identity of the man of lawlessness (2 Thess 2). Yet it is also probable that enough clues have been given in Scripture (e.g., the number of the beast as 666, the "apostasy," and the confirmation of some covenant; cf. Dan 9:27) that will "reveal" the identity of the antichrist to the spiritually aware much earlier than the midpoint of the tribulation (Rev 13:18).

To summarize, exegetically, the identity of the restraining power/person in 2 Thessalonians 2 is not completely clear to us. In early Christianity, the Spirit working through the church to restrain Satan, evil, and the coming judgment was viewed as a restraining power. This may provide interpretive light for identifying the restrainer as the Spirit-empowered church. The removal of the church would be the end of the restrainer's work, allowing the antichrist to be revealed. This would only fit a pretribulational or, less likely but possible, mid-tribulational rapture.

Christ's Return "For" and "With" the Saints

Although I have mentioned this on several occasions through this book, it bears repeating, because it has led to all sorts of confusion, especially when those who reject anything but a post-tribulation rapture accuse proponents of the pre-tribulation, mid-tribulation, or even pre-wrath views as affirming "two second comings." The fact is, the terms used for what we call the "return of Christ" or "second coming" —ἔρχομαι ("coming"), ἐπιφάνεια ("appearing"), παρουσία ("presence"), and ἀποκάλυψις ("revelation")—are used variously in the New Testament. They may sometimes refer to a precise moment in the future related to particular end-times events. Thus the term παρουσία in 1 Thessalonians 4:15–17 refers specifically to the Lord descending from heaven (καταβήσεται ἀπ' οὐρανοῦ) to resurrect, transform, and catch up the church. This is a specific event—in fact, a moment (1 Cor 15:51–52)—in the future. Yet the terms ἀποκαλύψει . . . ἀπ' οὐρανοῦ and ἔλθῃ (ἔρχομαι) are used in 2 Thessalonians 1:5–12 in a passage that draws on an Old Testament Day of the Lord imagery—a mediated theophanic visitation in judgment—that involves many events over a long period of time, not just a momentary descent (see discussion in chapter 16). This "revelation from heaven" refers to the revelation of the judgments associated with the coming tribulation, described figuratively in Revelation, during which judgment extends over a period of years, not moments.

In light of this, it is best to understand the "coming of Christ" or "second coming" to involve a complex series of events that coincide with the coming of the Day of the Lord (1 Thess 5:2). It does not always entail his personal, bodily presence, but it can involve the effects of actions he takes as judge when he mediates judgment upon the world (symbolized in Revelation by the opening of the seven sealed scrolls and progressively taking his position as king over the world). The "second coming" in this sense would also involve the entire eternal reign of Christ after he steps foot on this earth and establishes his kingdom. If we can refer to the "first coming" of Christ as occupying the span of time from his incarnation to his ascension—that is, about thirty-three years—then it is arbitrary to insist on limiting the "second coming" of Christ to a single moment.

From a biblical-theological perspective, the "second coming" involves the entire period of the seven-year tribulation as well as the eternal reign of Christ on earth. His second coming is first manifested indirectly as he fulfills YHWH's role in a theophanic "coming" in judgment—that is, throughout the whole tribulation. This allows the catching up of the saints as a rescue from the coming Day of the Lord to be just as much an aspect of the one second coming as the rest of the events of the tribulation and the descent from heaven to earth itself when he establishes his kingdom. This is not an either/or matter but both/and. To demand that every use of one of the terms for the return of Christ refers only to the moment of visible, physical "touchdown" is to fall into the fallacy of "unwarranted restriction of the semantic field."[13] We must also avoid reading into every use of one of these terms all the details of the complex, prolonged process of the parousia and thus commit the opposite error: the unwarranted adoption of an expanded semantic field or "illegitimate totality transfer."[14] Immediate context as well as the biblical-theological context must determine the meaning of "coming" in each instance.

When we notice apparent distinctions between the coming of Christ "for" his saints (to resurrect, transform, and rescue them) and the coming of Christ "with" his saints (returning to earth to rule and reign), we are not technically speaking of two second comings or even a second and a third coming. Declaring that "there can be only one coming" or "the Bible only talks about one second coming" as a rebuttal to the distinction between coming "for" and coming "with" the saints is a strawman argument. The one second coming is not an instant but a process consisting of a series of events over a long period of time. Distinguishing between the distinct events revealed in Scripture—whether they happen within the course of hours, days, months, or years—does not imply multiple second comings.[15]

Some passages in the New Testament picture Christ coming for his church to transform their mortal bodies (Phil 3:20–21), to rescue them from the coming wrath (1 Thess 1:10), to catch them up into the air to be with Christ and one another (1 Thess 4:17), and to take them to be with him in the heavenly realm (John 14:1–3). Though John 14:1–3 has sometimes been taken as something other than the second coming, Kruse frames the passage well:

> Jesus' coming back has been variously interpreted: (1) his coming to the disciples following his resurrection (cf. 20:19–29); (2) his coming in the person of the Holy Spirit (cf. 14:15–21); (3) his second coming at the end of this age (cf. 14:28; 21:22–23); and (4) his "coming" to take his disciples to be with him when they die. The third alternative is the correct one: Jesus' going in this context is his return to the Father's presence in heaven (via his crucifixion, resurrection and ascension), and it is to

---

13. Carson, *Exegetical Fallacies*, 57–60.

14. Carson, *Exegetical Fallacies*, 60–61.

15. We have already shown that the category of "first resurrection" involves more than one event—at least Christ's and the saints at his coming (1 Cor 15:23; Col 1:18; Rev 1:5). Yet we believe in only one "first resurrection" (Rev 20:5).

heaven he will take his disciples when he returns for them. This did not occur when he came to them following the resurrection, nor with the coming of the Holy Spirit, but will occur at his second coming. (The fourth suggestion, comforting though it is to think of Christ "coming" for us when we die, is not something that receives any support in this passage.) . . . While the Fourth Gospel emphasizes the present experience of eternal life and the presence of Jesus with his disciples through the Holy Spirit, the hope of his return and of their being with him in the Father's presence still remains the ultimate goal.[16]

Of course, even believers who died enter into the place where Jesus went upon death: to paradise, for to "be away from the body" is to be "at home with the Lord" (2 Cor 5:8), and Paul's desire was "to depart and be with Christ" (Phil 1:23). We are told that paradise—in the "third heaven"—is able to accommodate people either "in the body" like Elijah and Jesus or "out of the body" like the departed saved (Luke 23:43). In the meantime, prior to bodily resurrection, that place where Jesus goes is occupied by the souls of departed saints who believed in him as the way, the truth, and the life (John 14:6). Yet the natural reading of John 14:1–3 suggests that upon resurrection, at least for a season, the glorified saints will join Jesus in the heavenly realm in paradise.

Yet the broader narrative of the Irenaean premillennial eschatology as well as the promises of Scripture tell us that the church will not remain in the heavenly realm forever. Rather, the saints will return with Jesus when he establishes his kingdom. Or, perhaps better, the heavenly realm of paradise will return with Jesus, transitioning the place of glory to earth (see discussions in chapters 2, 4, and 13). We also have passages that describe the coming of Christ "with" his saints. This is pictured in the vision of the coming of Christ to destroy the beast and false prophet in Revelation 19:11–14, which we discussed in some detail in chapter 10.

The armies of heaven returning victoriously with Christ are described as wearing "white, clean, fine linen," which is interpreted as "the righteous deeds of the saints (τὰ δικαιώματα τῶν ἁγίων ἐστίν)" (Rev 19:8). The armies are already interpreted in Revelation 17:14 as "Those with him are called and chosen and faithful." The terms κλητός and ἐκλεκτός are used elsewhere in the New Testament most commonly to refer to believers. In Revelation, πιστός describes Christ (Rev 1:5; 3:14; 19:11) and Christians (Rev 2:10, 13). Thus at least the redeemed saints constitute the armies of heaven in Revelation 17:14 accompanying Christ at his coming, which is pictured in the vision of 19:11.

Yet, we saw in chapter 10 in our discussion of Revelation 19 and 20 that after Christ returns with his armies of saints and destroys the beast and false prophet and binds the dragon (Rev 19:11–20:3) and then take their seats on thrones to rule (20:4), a resurrection of martyrs who died during the reign of the antichrist during the second half of the tribulation will occur: "those who had been beheaded for their testimony to Jesus and for the word of God" who "had not worshiped the beast or its image and had not received its brand on their foreheads or their hands"

---

16. Colin G. Kruse, *John: An Introduction and Commentary*, Tyndale New Testament Commentaries, vol. 4 (Downers Grove, IL: InterVarsity, 2003), 292–93.

(Rev 20:4). They also come to life and reign with Christ and the saints who return with him for a thousand years. Altogether, Christ, the armies of heaven, and the resurrected tribulation martyrs constitute the "first resurrection" (Rev 20:5–6).

In a strictly post-tribulational rapture as well as a pre-wrath rapture of the church, the distinction between Christ coming for the saints and taking them to heaven for what seems to be a prolonged period (John 14:1–3) is difficult to explain, as is the distinction between his coming for the saints to rescue them and coming with the saints at what is obviously the very close of the tribulation. A mid-tribulation view allows for this distinction, though a pre-tribulation view makes better sense of the sojourn in the heavenly paradise suggested by John 14:1–3.

Missing Mentions of "Church" in Revelation

A common argument advanced by those who hold to a pre-tribulation rapture is the observation that the word ἐκκλησία ("church") is not mentioned on earth after Revelation 3.[17] The term appears nineteen times in Revelation 1–3, so John obviously knew the word as a description of New Testament saints. Yet in the future-oriented visions (Rev 4–21), John never uses the word ἐκκλησία. It appears only once more at the very end of Revelation in a passage after the visions of the future tribulation have ended: "It is I, Jesus, who sent my angel to you with this testimony for the churches (ἐκκλησίαις)" (Rev 22:16).

However, besides being an argument from silence, this position can end up falling into the fallacy of question-begging. For example, in response to the claim that the term "saints" in Revelation 13:7 or "those who keep the commandments of God and hold the testimony of Jesus" (Rev 12:17; 20:4) demonstrate the presence of the church on earth during the tribulation, Showers argues for the possibility of making a technical distinction between "tribulation saints" and "church saints."[18] While the possibility for this distinction certainly exists, the only proof that such a distinction must be made is the demonstration that the pre-tribulation rapture is true. However, if the pre-tribulation rapture is not proved first, then the interpreter has no basis for distinguishing between tribulation saints and church saints.

The argument from the missing church also tends to depend on a chronological structure to the book of Revelation, which is not universally held. In fact, most futurist commentators hold that the book is comprised of distinct visions that likely involve some kind of chronological disjunction in the events to which they refer. That is, Revelation 4–22 is not a single vision presenting the events of the tribulation in a strict, blow-by-blow chronological order. I am unaware of any commentators who would argue that. Rather, like the visions in Daniel, the visions in Revelation likely refer to different aspects of the future tribulation period seen from different angles, sometimes rewinding and replaying various scenes, sometimes jumping forward to the end, sometimes presenting events chronologically within a vision. Context and careful analysis must determine to what events the vision is pointing.

---

17. E.g., Showers, *Maranatha*, 245; Walvoord, *Rapture Question*, 260.
18. Showers, *Maranatha*, 247–48.

One aspect of the argument from the missing word ἐκκλησία, though, is somewhat relevant. If John had just as consistently used the term ἐκκλησία throughout Revelation with reference to the saints being persecuted and martyred, this would become a steep hill to climb for pretribulationalists. That is, if Revelation 13 said the beast will make war on "the church" to overcome it, this would pose a problem to the pre-tribulation rapture view, unless one adopted a partial rapture as in Irenaeus or simply employed a less technical use of ἐκκλησία to simply mean a follower of Christ. In any case, even if the absence of the word ἐκκλησία in Revelation 4–21 is regarded as a strong argument (a "loud" silence), we are nowhere told that the rapture is the reason for this silence. That would have to be ascertained elsewhere.

The Argument from Imminency

Among pretribulationists, the doctrine of imminency means that "Christ can return for His Church *at any moment* and that no predicted event will intervene before that return."[19] That is, the next event in the timeline of future events is the coming of Christ for the church, which could be at any moment. As a result, Christians should be waiting eagerly from moment to moment, expecting that the event could happen in their lifetime, or even today. Thus passages like 1 Thessalonians 1:9–10 are often cited as teaching imminency: while the Thessalonians are serving the living and true God, they "wait for his Son from heaven . . . who rescues us from the coming wrath" (1:10). Also, 1 Thessalonians 5:2 warns that the period of the Day of the Lord could arrive "like a thief." If the period of wrath could come upon the unbelieving world suddenly without warning, and if the church is to await with anticipation the coming of Christ to rescue us from the coming wrath, then the convergence of these two promises entails an any-moment rapture that is preceded by no other events.[20] If the rapture were to occur halfway through the seven-year tribulation, then it would not be at any moment. And if the rapture were to occur prior to the final wrath or after the entire tribulation, then it would come as no surprise to the faithful.

Scripture, however, also mentions many signs and world conditions that will signal the coming of the Lord in judgment (Matt 24:3–31). Yet many of these likely relate to events of the first century and the judgments associated with the destruction of Jerusalem. Or they relate to conditions that will prevail in the world throughout the "last days" between Christ's ascension and his coming in judgment through the Day of the Lord. In the midst of these signs, too, Jesus does say, "But about that day and hour no one knows" (Matt 24:36), and he suggests the judgment will befall people at a time utterly unexpected (24:37–41). Believers are therefore to "keep awake" because "you do not know on what day your Lord is coming" (24:42) and "the Son of Man is coming at an hour you do not expect" (24:44). However, the context here is not really about the rapture of the church but the coming of Christ

---

19. John A. Sproule, *In Defense of Pretribulationism* (Winona Lake, IN: BMH, 1980), 12.
20. See other arguments in Wayne A. Brindle, "Biblical Evidence for the Imminence of the Rapture," *Biblotheca Sacra* 158 (April–June 2001): 138–51.

in judgment. That is to say, Christians should always be awake and alert because they do not know the moment the Day of the Lord will begin. As far as an argument for the pre-tribulation rapture, I regard it as somewhat weak.

One factor that does commend the doctrine of imminence, though, is the orientation of hope it instills in the believer. For those who embrace a pre-tribulation rapture, the expectation is hope in the coming of Christ to save them from the coming wrath. It is a Christ-centered hope. Those who hold to a post-tribulation rapture instead anticipate the commencement of the Day of the Lord and the advent of the antichrist; this is often accompanied by anxiety and fear as well as a tendency to look to current events as fulfillment of prophecies and signs that the tribulation has begun or will begin. If consistently applied, the pretribulational doctrine of imminence should rule out sign seeking and antichrist hunting. It should be a Christ-centered, hope-driven eschatology rather than an antichrist-centered, fear-driven eschatology.

Conclusions Regarding Classic Arguments for the Pretribulation Rapture

Taken together, the preceding evidences and arguments rule out the a strict post-tribulation rapture, greatly weaken the pre-wrath view, and cast some doubts on the mid-tribulation position. Especially strong are the arguments regarding the symbol of the eschatological trumpet and its relationship to the Day of the Lord and the rescue from wrath understood as a rescue from the period of wrath associated with the rapture. The arguments based on the need for saved mortal survivors of the tribulation in the Irenaean premillennial eschatology is strong for both mid-tribulational and pretribulational positions, as is the identification of the restraining force as the Spirit working through the church in the present age. The distinction between the return of Christ "for" and "with" the saints also makes a pretribulational or mid-tribulational view more likely, though a pre-wrath position could accommodate it. The arguments from the missing church and imminency are corroborative but not unreasonable.

At this point, though, the arguments for the pre-tribulation rapture have depended upon direct implications of Scripture, probable implications of Scripture, and inductive conclusions from Scripture.[21] In the next chapter, I will present the classic exegetical argument for a pre-tribulation rapture from a single passage in Revelation.

---

21. On these designations of degrees of authority of theological statements, see Millard J. Erickson, *Christian Theology*, 3rd ed. (Grand Rapids: Baker Academic, 2013), 65–66.

20

An Exegetical Argument for the Timing of the Assumption

*John speaks concerning things present and things
to come. But Christ, long ago conceived, was not
caught up to the throne of God when He was brought
forth, from fear of the serpent injuring Him.*

Methodius, *On Chastity* 8.7

Contrary to some popular treatments of the subject,[1] the doctrine of the pre-tribulation rapture in the modern era did not begin with Scottish preacher Edward Irving (1794–1834) and his followers. Irving seems to have held a partial pre-wrath rapture view, not a consistent pre-tribulation position as commonly understood today.[2] As such, Irving's view appears to have been closer to that of Irenaeus and the Shepherd of Hermas described in chapter 18 and Go Deeper Excursus 27.

The first person to articulate a pre-tribulation rapture of the entire regenerate church was John Nelson Darby, as this idea was more consistent with his Calvinistic soteriology that makes a clear distinction between the regenerate and nonregenerate. Since the idea of a pre-tribulation rapture of any sort was reintroduced in eschatological discussions in the nineteenth century, arguments both for and against the pre-tribulation rapture have been advanced (see chapter 19). However, one of the earliest arguments that settled the question for many in the nineteenth century was based on a detailed exegesis of Revelation 12:5—the catching up of the "male son" as it relates to the future tribulation period. The text itself says:

Καὶ ἔτεκεν υἱὸν ἄρσεν, ὃς μέλλει ποιμαίνειν πάντα τὰ ἔθνη ἐν ῥάβδῳ σιδηρᾷ. Καὶ ἡρπάσθη τὸ τέκνον αὐτῆς πρὸς τὸν θεὸν καὶ πρὸς τὸν θρόνον αὐτοῦ. (Rev 12:5)

And she bore a son, a male, who is to rule all the nations by a rod of iron, and her child was caught up to God and to his throne. (Rev 12:5, my translation)

The Go Deeper Excursus 29, *Diverse Interpretations of the Male Son of Revelation 12*, surveys various approaches in the history of interpretation of Revelation

---

1. Dave MacPherson, *The Rapture Plot* (Simpsonville, SC: Millennium III, 1995), 55–85. Early critics of the doctrine also mistakenly linked its origins to Irving; see William Reid, *Plymouth Brethrenism Unveiled and Refuted* (Edinburgh: Oliphant, 1875), 296; cf. Thomas Croskery, *Plymouth-Brethrenism: A Refutation of Its Principles and Doctrines* (London: William Mullen, 1879), 138.
2. James Bennett, *The Second Advent* (London: James Nisbet, 1878), 153, 154.

Go Deeper Excursus 29

Diverse Interpretations of the Male Son of Revelation 12

12:5. That essay demonstrates that although the interpretation of the male son as Christ alone has dominated modern interpretations of that text, the corporate interpretation of the male son has always had representatives and, at times, appears to have held a place of prominence.

Lutheran theologian and pastor Joseph A. Seiss (1823–1904) wrote that "the symbol of the Child represents the whole regeneration purchase of the Saviour's blood. . . . So, then, I take this Man Child, and know not how else it can be taken without a miserable emasculation of the whole representation, emptying it of every significance at all up to the subject, or demanded by the circumstances."[3] This is also the exegetical argument that originally convinced John Nelson Darby of the pre-tribulation rapture.[4] In the following pages, I present a fresh case for the corporate interpretation of the male son as the body of Christ, the church, in union with Christ and thus the catching up of the male son as the assumption of the church to heaven mentioned in 1 Thessalonians 4:17.

This argument, however, serves only as exegetical evidence for a pre-tribulation rapture if four presuppositions are held: (1) a consistent futurist interpretation of the book of Revelation—that is, these prophecies primarily point to future (not past, present, spiritual, or ideal) realities; (2) a robust doctrine of the mystical union between Christ and the body of Christ, the church; (3) an openness to (though not a precommitment to) a distinction between Old Testament Israel, the New Testament church, and a future restored Israel, especially allowing for different symbols in Revelation to refer to these two different groups of saints; and (4) a literal understanding of the order of events and chronological indicators in Revelation 11–13.

Seven arguments lead me to conclude that the event of the catching up of the male son in Revelation 12:5 refers to the catching up of the church. The heart of the argument lies in the Old Testament language and imagery used to point us to the fact that the male son represents a corporate body, not an individual. The seven arguments are (1) the consistency in symbolism, (2) the allusion to Isaiah 66:7–9, (3) the background of Daniel 7, (4) the use of Psalm 2:9, (5) the allusion to Isaiah 26:16–27:1, (6) the use of ἁρπάζω, and (7) the missing death and resurrection.

The Consistency in Symbolism

Identifying the male son as the body of Christ is consistent with the symbolism of the vision recorded in Revelation 12:1–6. Introduced in Revelation 12:1, the woman is "clothed with the sun, with the moon under her feet, and on her head a crown of twelve stars." Her condition follows: "She was pregnant and was crying out in

---

3. Joseph A. Seiss, *The Apocalypse: A Series of Special Lectures on the Revelation of Jesus Christ with Revised Text*, vol. 2, 11th ed. (New York: Charles C. Cook, 1913), 331.

4. Michael J. Svigel, "What Child Is This? A Forgotten Argument for the Pretribulation Rapture," in John F. Hart, ed., *Evidence for the Rapture: A Biblical Case for Pretribulationism* (Chicago: Moody, 2015), 225–51.

birth pangs, in the agony of giving birth" (12:2). Some identify this woman as the church of both the Old and New Testaments.[5] Others, especially those who assert a distinction between Israel of the Old Testament and the church of the New, see the woman as representing national Israel alone.[6] Still others lean toward the Israel view but with a caveat: the woman is "ideal" Israel.[7]

Recognizing that the woman is, in fact, a symbol rather than a literal individual female in cosmic clothing, it seems most probable that the symbol represents Israel or, more specifically, the elect "remnant chosen by grace" (Rom 11:5).[8] When we compare the Greek of Revelation 12:1 and the Septuagint of Genesis 37:9, we see an unmistakable correspondence. Revelation 12:1 reads: "A great portent appeared in heaven: a woman clothed with the sun (τὸν ἥλιον), with the moon (ἡ σελήνη) under her feet, and on her head a crown of twelve stars (ἀστέρων)." In Genesis 37, Joseph relays the symbolic dream he had to his brothers: "As though the sun (ὁ ἥλιος) and the moon (ἡ σελήνη) and eleven stars (ἀστέρες) were prostrating themselves to me" (Gen 37:9 LXX, Brannan).[9] The sun, moon, and stars correspond to the symbols in Joseph's dream, where they represent the patriarch, matriarch, and the sons of Jacob; i.e., the father, mother, and twelve tribes of the nation of Israel, respectively.[10] In further support of this interpretation, the symbol of a woman for the nation of Israel is found throughout the Old Testament's prophetic literature.[11]

Though Revelation 12:9 calls the dragon "that ancient serpent, who is called the devil and Satan," the symbolism in the vision points to more than merely an individual wicked spirit. Because the dragon and the beast of Revelation 13 are distinguished

---

5. George H. Lang, *The Revelation of Jesus Christ: Select Studies*, 2nd ed. (London: Paternoster, 1948), 198–201.

6. John F. Walvoord, *The Rapture Question*, rev. and enl. ed. (Grand Rapids: Zondervan, 1979), 188.

7. George E. Ladd, *A Commentary on the Book of the Revelation of John* (Grand Rapids: Eerdmans, 1972), 167; Robert H. Mounce, *The Book of Revelation*, The New International Commentary on the New Testament (Grand Rapids: Eerdmans, 1977), 23.

8. This does not necessarily preclude the possibility that the symbol includes a second referent with Mary as the mother of Jesus fulfilling historically some aspect of the vision and embodying personally corporate Israel; see G. K. Beale, *The Book of Revelation*, The New International Greek Testament Commentary, ed. I. Howard Marshall and Donald A. Hagner (Grand Rapids: Zondervan, 1999), 628.

9. The only passages in the Old Testament where the sun, moon, and stars appear together are Gen 37:9; Deut 4:19, Eccl 12:2; Isa 13:10; Jer 8:2; 38:36; Joel 4:15; and the apocryphal Sir 50:6–7. None of these supplies a plausible background for identifying the woman except for Gen 37:9, which leads to the conclusion that the woman represents the people of Israel.

10. See Jacob B. Smith, *A Revelation of Jesus Christ: A Commentary on the Book of Revelation*, ed. J. Otis Toder (Scottdale, PA: Herald, 1961), 181.

11. J. Massyngberde Ford, *Revelation*, The Anchor Bible, ed. W. F. Albright, and David Noel Freedman (Garden City, NY: Doubleday, 1975), 195: "Although the woman may be an individual, a study of the OT background suggests that she is a collective figure. . . . In the OT the image of a woman is a classical symbol for Zion, Jerusalem, and Israel, e.g. Zion whose husband is Yahweh (Isa. 54:1, 5, Jer. 3:20, Ezek. 16:8–14, Hos. 2:19–20), who is a mother (Isa. 49:21, 50:1, 66:7–11, Hos. 4:5, Baruch 4:8–23), and who is in the throes of birth (Mic. 4:9–10, cf. Isa. 26:16–18, Jer. 4:31, 13:21, Sirach 48:19[21])." See G. K. Beale, *Revelation: A Shorter Commentary* (Grand Rapids: Eerdmans, 2015), 243; Mounce, *Revelation*, 231.

(Rev 13:3–4; 16:13), the symbolism of the seven heads and ten horns is not intended to identify him as the beast of the next chapter. The beast is later established in the image of the dragon; he is not identical to him. The dragon's symbolism leads to a corporate identification as the nations of the world who are opposed to God and his people. This is indicated by the correspondence between the seven heads and ten horns of the dragon and the same gruesome anatomy of the four beasts of Daniel 7:1–8. In that Old Testament symbolic vision, Daniel sees four beasts with a total of seven heads and ten horns. The first beast (Babylon) has one head (7:4), the second beast (Medo-Persia) has one head (7:5), the third beast (Greece) has four heads (7:6), and the fourth beast (Rome) has one head and ten horns (7:7). Incidentally, all these beasts are corporate identities referring to the characteristics of empire leaders and incorporating the historical political system as well. So, in Revelation 12:9, drawing on this principle of corporate identity in Daniel 7, the vision of the dragon sums up the totality of Satan's political opposition to God and his people throughout history. That is the meaning of the seven heads and ten horns.[12]

Thus the symbol of the dragon in Revelation 12 is best seen as Satan working through world empires. In the second half of the tribulation, the beast from the sea looks like the dragon, having seven heads and ten horns and also sharing some physical features of the four world powers of Daniel 7:1–7 (cf. Rev 13:1–2). So, the dragon symbolizes a corporate entity: both the world system as the great enemy of God's people throughout history and the secret ruler of that world system, Satan himself.

Finally, we come to the symbol of the male son. Because both the woman and the dragon are described with Old Testament symbols that point us to corporate identities, the consistent interpreter should consider whether the male son is also more than just an individual.[13] As was the case with the dragon—and even with the original beasts of Daniel 7—the corporate interpretation of the male son does not deny that the individual, Jesus Christ, also plays a part of the symbolism. However, if the symbolism is consistent in the vision, then Christ is not alone; the church, the body of Christ in spiritual union with him by the baptism of the Holy Spirit (1 Cor 12:13–14) are part of the intended meaning of the image.[14] This mysterious spiritual union of Christ with his body, the church, is one of the great, unique doctrines of the New Testament (e.g., Acts 9:4; Rom 12:5; 1 Cor 12:27; Eph 4:15–16). Therefore, the corporate identification of the male son in Revelation 12:5 does not discount the notion that Christ is also in view, informing the symbolism and underscoring the fact that this male son is more than just a corporate body: he is the body *of Christ*.

---

12. Beale, *Revelation: A Shorter Commentary*, 245–46, is instructive here: "Without exception, the imagery of the dragon is used throughout the OT to represent evil kingdoms who persecute God's people. 'Dragon' is in the OT another word for the evil sea monster which is symbolic of evil kingdoms who oppress Israel. . . . Yet the dragon is more than a mere metaphor for an evil kingdom. It also stands for the devil himself as the representative head of evil kingdoms. . . . The devil is the force behind wicked kingdoms which persecute God's people."

13. Lang, *The Revelation of Jesus Christ*, 198.

14. H. A. Ironside, *Revelation*, Ironside Commentaries, rev. ed. (Neptune, NJ: Loizeaux Brothers, 1996), 140.

The Allusion to Isaiah 66:7

Revelation 12:5 reads: "And she bore a son, a male (ἔτεκεν υἱὸν ἄρσεν) who is to rule all the nations by a rod of iron."[15] Most modern commentators identify the male son as none other than Jesus Christ.[16] Certainly, a cursory reading of the passage (especially in translation) lends itself to this interpretation.

However, in Revelation 12:5, the neuter ἄρσεν ("male" or "masculine") modifies the noun υἱόν ("son"). Even before recognizing the intended allusion back to Isaiah 66, a casual reader of the Greek text would have found the expression strange. It would be like somebody saying in English, "She had a son—a male." Why would John point out that the son is male? In the book of Revelation, such strange, unexpected uses of grammar and imagery provide interpretive keys, usually parallel passages from the Old Testament. The discordant grammar and the strange phrase "male son" force readers to pause and proceed carefully to catch what the vision is trying to communicate.

John's strange language of "male son" in Revelation 12:5 points the reader back to Isaiah 66:7,[17] which reads: "Before the one in labor gave birth, before the distress of birth pangs arrived, she escaped and bore a male child (καὶ ἔτεκεν ἄρσεν)" (LXX, Brannan). The next verse demonstrates that the woman and child of Isaiah 66:7–8 are not intended to represent individuals but rather corporate bodies: "Who has heard such a thing, and who has seen *something* like this? Has the earth labored in a single day, or was a nation brought forth all at once? For Zion was in labor and brought forth her children (ὤδινεν καὶ ἔτεκεν Σιὼν τὰ παιδία αὐτῆς" (Isa 66:8 LXX, Brannan). The parallelism in the passage identifies the "male (ἄρσεν)" in verse 7 with the plural "children (τὰ παιδία)" in verse 8, describing Zion giving birth to a to corporate body.

John usually uses Old Testament imagery in Revelation in one of two ways: either to say, "This *is* that," or, "This *is like* that." John either makes an exact equation, so the Old Testament image has the same referent as the image in Revelation:

OLD TESTAMENT IMAGE = IMAGE IN REVELATION[18]

Or John draws a meaningful parallel between the two, so the Old Testament helps inform our understanding of the image in Revelation in some way:

OLD TESTAMENT IMAGE ‖ IMAGE IN REVELATION[19]

---

15. After the word *male*, the NASB includes the word *child* in italics to avoid the phrase "male son," which is an awkward clarification even in English. What other kind of son is there besides a "male" son?

16. See Pierre Prigent, *Apocalypse 12: Histoire de l'exégése*, Beiträge zur Geschichte der Biblischen Exegese, ed. Oscar Cullmann, Ernst Käsemann, et al., vol. 2 (Tübingen: Mohr, 1959), 145.

17. See a full discussion in G. K. Beale, *John's Use of the Old Testament in Revelation*, Journal for the Study of the New Testament Supplement Series 166, ed. Stanley E. Porter (Sheffield: Sheffield Academic, 1998), 341–43.

18. An example would be the allusions to the imagery of the seraphim or cherubim from Isa 6:2–3 and Ezek 1:10–14; 10:14–14 used in Rev 4:6–8. The intention is to identify the angelic beings seen in the Old Testament with the angelic beings seen in the throne room of Revelation.

19. An example would be the identity of the two witnesses in Rev 11:3–6, where the text uses imagery from passages like Exod 7:14–25; 1 Kgs 17:1; and Zech 4:2–3. The intention is

It seems that John alludes to Isaiah 66:7–8 not to *equate* (=) the passages but to draw an important parallel (‖) necessary for us to interpret the image of Revelation 12:5.[20] The point of the parallel is that the male son is not intended to be understood as an individual. Instead, in light of the background of the corporate "male" born to corporate "Zion" in Isaiah 66:7–8, the male son in Revelation 12:5 should also be understood as a corporate body.

The Allusion to Daniel 7:13

In Isaiah 66:7, the woman gives birth to a male: ἔτεκεν ἄρσεν ("she bore a male"). This is interpreted in Isaiah 66:8 as Zion giving birth to her children: ἔτεκεν Σιὼν τὰ παιδία αὐτῆς ("Zion bore her children"). Nowhere in Isaiah 66:7–8 is the word υἱός ("son") used. But John inserts this word in Revelation 12:5: "And she bore a son, a male (ἔτεκεν υἱὸν ἄρσεν)." If John is pointing to Isaiah 66:7, why did he insert υἱόν ("son") into the phrase ἔτεκεν ἄρσεν, creating the grammatical dissonance and the puzzling tautology of the "male" son?

Isaiah 66:7	ἔτεκεν ἄρσεν bore a male
Revelation 12:5	ἔτεκεν υἱὸν ἄρσεν bore **a son**, a male

Considering the allusions to Daniel 7 already present in both Revelation 12 and 13 (in the symbolism of the dragon as well as the beast), the best explanation for John's insertion of the word υἱόν ("son") is to point the reader back to another vision from the Old Testament: the "son of man" (υἱὸς ἀνθρώπου) in Daniel 7:13–14.

In both Daniel 7:13–14 and Revelation 12:5, the "son" (υἱός) is destined to rule the nations; he is brought into the presence of God; and he is presented before his throne (see Dan 7:9, where the Ancient of Days is seated on a throne). Thus John

---

not to identify the two witnesses as Zerubbabel and Joshua or as Moses and Elijah, but to communicate that these two witnesses are similar to these Old Testament figures in some way. Thus the symbolism informs our interpretation by drawing parallels.

20. It is admittedly possible that John meant that the birth of the corporate male son in Rev 12:5 is, in fact, a direct fulfillment of the prophecy of Isa 66:7–8. In that original context, God promised Israel a miraculous restoration and renewal (66:10–24), as well as an ingathering of people from every nation to see the glory of the Lord (66:18–19). It is in this context that God establishes "the new heavens and the new earth" (66:22). While this regeneration of the new heavens and new earth is portrayed in Revelation as yet future (cf. Rev 21:1–22:5), the regeneration is seen in the church in promissory form (Rom 8:20–22). If the male son of Rev 12:5 is understood as the body of Christ, the church, and if John is making an equation with the imagery of Isa 66:7–8 instead of a parallel, then the point of the allusion would be that Israel is the source of the messianic community (what we know as the church) as well as the relationship between the messianic community and the eschatological regeneration (in the millennium, which will be reigned over by the church).

inserted the term υἱός into his quotation of the phrase ἔτεκεν ἄρσεν from Isaiah 66:7 to make a further connection between the male son and the "son of man" in Daniel 7:13–14.

Though some might hastily see this as proof that Jesus, the "Son of Man," is the sole referent in the image of the male son, the allusion to Daniel 7 actually strengthens the corporate identification. When the angel (Dan 7:16) interprets the vision of the "son of man," he explains the vision corporately.[21] He says, "And it will succeed to the kingdom, the holy ones (ἅγιοι) of the most high, and possess the kingdom unto the ages of ages!" (Dan 7:18 LXX, Brannan). In verse 22, "the saints (τοῖς ἁγίοις) of the most high" are given the kingdom (cf. vv. 26–27). Thus the "son of man" figure in the vision is interpreted corporately as the Messiah and his saints in Daniel 7:18, 22, 26–27, not as a lone individual. One commentator notes, "If the humanlike figure [the son of man] balances the [four] creatures [of Daniel 7], it would not be surprising if, like them, it could have both individual and corporate reference."[22] Seow puts it simply: "The one is the many; the many are the one."[23]

For this reason, John uses the term "son" (υἱός) in Revelation 12:5 to point readers back to the "son of man" vision of Daniel 7 and its corporate identification as Messiah and his saints, which we know from the New Testament to be the church. The corporate understanding of the "son of man" was common both in Jesus' time and thereafter, making a reference to "son of man" imagery from Daniel 7 almost certain to conjure up corporate identifications.[24] John's allusion to the vision of the son of man in Daniel 7 further strengthens the identity of the male son in Revelation 12:5 as the corporate body of Christ, the church, which is to rule over the nations with their head, Jesus Christ, after being presented before the throne of God to receive the reward of the kingdom.

The Allusions to Psalm 2:9

Identifying the male son as the body of Christ best explains Revelation's three allusions to Psalm 2:9—a messianic psalm. In Psalm 2:8–9, God tells the Messiah, "Ask of me, and I will make the nations your heritage and the ends of the earth your

---

21. Towner writes, "These three texts [Dan. 7:18, 21–22, 27] make clear that he [the Son of Man] has now been radically interpreted as an identifiable and specific collective entity." W. Sibley Towner, *Daniel*, Interpretation: A Bible Commentary for Teaching and Preaching, ed. James L. Mays, Patrick D. Miller, and Paul J. Achtemeier (Louisville: John Knox, 1984), 105.

22. John E. Goldingay, *Daniel*, Word Biblical Commentary, vol. 30, ed. David A. Hubbard, John D. W. Watts, and Ralph P. Martin (Dallas: Word, 1989), 170. Towner *Daniel*, 106, notes, "In the same way in which the beasts represent both kingdoms and their kings, so the son of man could represent the coming fifth monarchy even though he might remain an individual figure."

23. Choon-Leong Seow, *Daniel*, Westminster Bible Companion, ed. Patrick D. Miller and David L. Bartlett (Louisville: Westminster, 2003), 16.

24. Maurice Casey, "The Corporate Interpretation of 'One Like a Son of Man' (Dan. vii 13) at the Time of Jesus," *Novum Testamentum* 18 (1976): 179.

possession. You shall break them with a rod of iron and dash them in pieces like a potter's vessel."

Psalm 2:9 is first quoted in Revelation 2:26–28 where Christ broadens the promise of the psalm to believers: "To everyone who conquers and continues to do my works to the end, I will give authority over the nations, to rule them with an iron scepter, as when clay pots are shattered—even as I also received authority from my Father." In the vision of Christ's return to earth recorded in Revelation 19:14–15, the passage is quoted again, this time applied to Christ: "And the armies of heaven, wearing fine linen, white and pure, were following him on white horses. From his mouth comes a sharp sword with which to strike down the nations, and he will rule them with a scepter of iron; he will tread the winepress of the fury of the wrath of God the Almighty."

In Revelation 12:5, the psalm is applied to the symbol of the male son, "who is to rule all the nations with a scepter of iron." Identifying the male son as the corporate body of Christ, the church in union with Christ, is most consistent with the application of the promise of Psalm 2:9 that applies both to Christ (Rev 19:14–15) and to the church (Rev 2:26–28) in the book of Revelation. This also mirrors the same individual-corporate identification of the son of man in Daniel 7.[25]

The Allusion to Isaiah 26:16–27:1

Early in the Christian tradition, about the time of the composition of the book of Revelation, Isaiah 26:19–20 was associated with the return of Christ. Clement of Rome (c. AD 95) wrote: "All the generations from Adam until this day have passed away, but those who were perfected in love according to the grace of God have a place among the godly who shall be revealed when the kingdom of Christ comes. For it is written, 'Enter into the inner rooms for a very short while, until my anger and wrath pass away. And I will remember a good day and will raise you up out of your grave'" (1 Clem. 50.3–5 [Brannan]). Tertullian also interprets Isaiah 26:20 as referring to the time of God's final wrath during the reign of antichrist, but he understands the "closets" (ταμιεῖα) to refer to the grave where the bodies are to rest until after the future tribulation, after which the resurrection will take place (Res. 27).

Though these fathers offer different applications of the passage, in both Clement and Tertullian the time spent in the chambers of protection corresponds with the fury poured out on the antichrist. Irenaeus assigns the resurrection of the dead, described in Isaiah 26:19 as referring at least in part to Christ's first coming, when Jesus raised some people from the dead during his earthly ministry (Haer. 4.33.11). In keeping with his both/and approach, however, he also uses Isaiah 26:19 in refer-

---

25. The use of Ps 2:9 in Revelation also argues to some degree for an identification of the "armies of heaven" in Rev 19:14 with overcoming believers of the church (Rev 2:26–28). It is the armies who actually break to pieces the nations. This would suggest then that the church, the body of Christ, is raptured, resurrected, and glorified before the return of Christ to earth described in Rev 19:11–21.

ence to the ultimate bodily resurrection when God will confer immortality upon them (5.15.1; 5.34.1).

When we look at the Septuagint passage of Isaiah 26:16–27:1 through the lens of Revelation 12, we see striking verbal and thematic parallels. In fact, some of the terms occur together only in these two passages, rendering intentional verbal allusions beyond dispute. The following comparison chart places side by side Brannan's English translation of the Septuagint, the Greek text of the same, and the relevant passages from Revelation 12 in Greek and English.

Isaiah 26:16–27:1 LXX		Revelation 12	
26:16 Lord, in distress I remembered you; with a little distress *was* your discipline toward us.	16 κύριε, ἐν θλίψει ἐμνήσθην σου, ἐν θλίψει μικρᾷ ἡ παιδία σου ἡμῖν.		
17 And as the woman in labor approaches childbirth, *and* cries out at her pangs, this is how we have become *to* your beloved.	17 καὶ ὡς ἡ ὠδίνουσα ἐγγίζει τεκεῖν, ἐπὶ τῇ ὠδῖνι αὐτῆς ἐκέκραξεν, οὕτως ἐγενήθημεν τῷ ἀγαπητῷ σου.	2 καὶ ἐν γαστρὶ ἔχουσα, καὶ κράζει ὠδίνουσα καὶ βασανιζομένη τεκεῖν. . . . 4 . . . τῆς γυναικὸς τῆς μελλούσης τεκεῖν . . .	2 She was pregnant and was crying out in birth pangs, in the agony of giving birth. . . . 4 . . . the woman who was about to deliver a child . . .
18 Because of fear of you, O Lord, we conceived in the womb and had pangs and gave birth; we made a wind of your deliverance on the land, but all those who dwell on the land will fall.	18 διὰ τὸν φόβον σου, Κύριε, ἐν γαστρὶ ἐλάβομεν καὶ ὠδινήσαμεν καὶ ἐτέκομεν· πνεῦμα σωτηρίας σου ἐποιήσαμεν ἐπὶ τῆς γῆς, ἀλλὰ πεσοῦνται οἱ ἐνοικοῦντες ἐπὶ τῆς γῆς.		
19 The dead will rise, and those in the tombs will be raised, and those in the earth will rejoice; for the dew from you is a remedy for them, but the land of the impious will fall.	19 ἀναστήσονται οἱ νεκροί, καὶ ἐγερθήσονται οἱ ἐν τοῖς μνημείοις, καὶ εὐφρανθήσονται οἱ ἐν τῇ γῇ· ἡ γὰρ δρόσος ἡ παρὰ σοῦ ἴαμα αὐτοῖς ἐστιν, ἡ δὲ γῆ τῶν ἀσεβῶν πεσεῖται.	12 διὰ τοῦτο εὐφραίνεσθε, [οἱ] οὐρανοὶ καὶ οἱ ἐν αὐτοῖς σκηνοῦντες. οὐαὶ τὴν γῆν καὶ τὴν θάλασσαν, ὅτι κατέβη ὁ διάβολος πρὸς ὑμᾶς ἔχων θυμὸν μέγαν, εἰδὼς ὅτι ὀλίγον καιρὸν ἔχει.	12 "Rejoice then, you heavens and those who dwell in them! But woe to the earth and the sea, for the devil has come down to you with great wrath because he knows that his time is short!"

Isaiah 26:16–27:1 LXX		Revelation 12	
20 Go, my people, enter into your chambers; shut your door; hide a little while until the wrath of the Lord passes.	20 Βάδιζε, λαός μου, εἴσελθε εἰς τὰ ταμεῖά σου, ἀπόκλεισον τὴν θύραν σου, ἀποκρύβηθι μικρὸν ὅσον ὅσον, ἕως ἂν παρέλθῃ ἡ ὀργὴ Κυρίου.	[Rescue and protection from coming wrath envisioned in Revelation 12:5?]	
21 For look, the Lord is bringing from the holy *place* the wrath against those dwelling upon the land; and the land will uncover its blood, and it will not cover up the slain.	21 ἰδοὺ γὰρ Κύριος ἀπὸ τοῦ ἁγίου ἐπάγει τὴν ὀργὴν ἐπὶ τοὺς ἐνοικοῦντας ἐπὶ τῆς γῆς· καὶ ἀνακαλύψει ἡ γῆ τὸ αἷμα αὐτῆς, καὶ οὐ κατακαλύψει τοὺς ἀνηρημένους.		
27:1 On that day God will bring the holy and great and mighty sword against the dragon, a fleeing serpent, against the dragon, a twisted serpent; he will slay the dragon.	27:1 Τῇ ἡμέρᾳ ἐκείνῃ ἐπάξει ὁ θεὸς τὴν μάχαιραν τὴν ἁγίαν καὶ τὴν μεγάλην καὶ τὴν ἰσχυρὰν ἐπὶ τὸν δράκοντα ὄφιν φεύγοντα, ἐπὶ τὸν δράκοντα ὄφιν σκολιόν, ἀνελεῖ τὸν δράκοντα.	3 καὶ ὤφθη ἄλλο σημεῖον ἐν τῷ οὐρανῷ, καὶ ἰδοὺ δράκων μέγας πυρρός. . . . 7 Καὶ ἐγένετο πόλεμος ἐν τῷ οὐρανῷ, ὁ Μιχαὴλ καὶ οἱ ἄγγελοι αὐτοῦ τοῦ πολεμῆσαι μετὰ τοῦ δράκοντος. καὶ ὁ δράκων ἐπολέμησεν καὶ οἱ ἄγγελοι αὐτοῦ, 8 καὶ οὐκ ἴσχυσεν οὐδὲ τόπος εὑρέθη αὐτῶν ἔτι ἐν τῷ οὐρανῷ. 9 καὶ ἐβλήθη ὁ δράκων ὁ μέγας, ὁ ὄφις ὁ ἀρχαῖος, ὁ καλούμενος Διάβολος καὶ ὁ Σατανᾶς, ὁ πλανῶν τὴν οἰκουμένην ὅλην, ἐβλήθη εἰς τὴν γῆν, καὶ οἱ ἄγγελοι αὐτοῦ μετ᾽ αὐτοῦ ἐβλήθησαν.	3 Then another portent appeared in heaven: a great red dragon. . . . 7 And war broke out in heaven; Michael and his angels fought against the dragon. The dragon and his angels fought back. 8 but they were defeated, and there was no longer any place for them in heaven. 9 The great dragon was thrown down, that ancient serpent, who is called the devil and Satan, the deceiver of the whole world—he was thrown down to the earth, and his angels were thrown down with him.

The correspondences in language and imagery between the Septuagint of Isaiah 26:16–27:1 and Revelation 12 are too numerous and specific to be coincidental. The imagery of Isaiah 26–27 begins with God's people crying out in "tribulation," but it is comparatively "light tribulation (ἐν θλίψει μικρᾷ)" for the purpose of discipline (Isa 26:16). The people liken their afflictions to the pains of labor (26:17) in which they cry out (ἐκέκραξεν); this language is paralleled in Revelation 12:2, where the woman cries out in labor pains in giving birth (καὶ κράζει ὠδίνουσα). We have already seen that this language is used in Isaiah 66:7, to which Revelation 12:5 refers with the woman (Zion) giving birth to a male son (a "people").

Returning to Isaiah 26, in the midst of their affliction, they bring forth not a literal child but: πνεῦμα σωτηρίας σου ἐποιήσαμεν ἐπὶ τῆς γῆς: literally, "We made upon the earth a spirit [or breath] of your salvation" (Isa 26:18). It is not difficult to imagine how early Christian readers of this passage might find echoes of the coming of the Spirit at Pentecost on the small remnant of Jewish followers of Jesus; in their affliction, that community brings forth the Spirit—which is tantamount to the birth of a new community, a new people—indeed, a new humanity (Eph 2:15).

This bringing forth of a "spirit of salvation" is contrasted with the doomed fate of the wicked: "But all those who dwell on the land will fall" (Isa 26:18). In that same breath, the speakers confess the resurrection of the dead as well as a second warning to the impious dwelling upon the earth: "The dead will rise (ἀναστήσονται οἱ νεκροί), and those in the tombs will be raised, and those in the earth will rejoice (καὶ εὐφρανθήσονται οἱ ἐν τῇ γῇ); for the dew from you is a remedy for them, but the land of the impious will fall" (Isa 26:19). Note the contrast between those who dwell "upon the earth (ἐπὶ τῆς γῆς)" who will fall and those who dwell "in the earth (ἐν τῇ γῇ)" who will rise (26:18, 19). In fact, verses 18 and 19 present an intriguing parallel between giving birth and bringing forth the "spirit of salvation" upon the land (26:28) on the one hand and the resurrection of the dead (26:19) on the other, demonstrated by the contrast with the fate of the godless remaining in the land who will fall in judgment. The parallel and contrast may extend even into verse 20, where people are protected from the coming wrath in the ταμιεῖα.[26]

The term ταμιεῖον in Isaiah 26:20 refers to an innermost, windowless chamber, like a storehouse or cellar—a place to hide from a coming storm or an impending disaster (cf. Gen 43:30; Judg 16:9, etc.).[27] Isaiah 26:16–27:1 is already employing rich metaphorical language, so it is likely that ταμιεῖοα does not refer to literal places of hiding but to a state of protection. In the parallels with verses 18 and 19, it could be a reference to the protection experienced by those who fear God, who brought

---

26. In Zeph 2:1–3, the prophet also offered deliverance through repentance: the hope that the Day of the Lord may be averted or escaped if sinners gather in humility before the day of the Lord's anger begins (2:1–2). Clearly, once the day comes, it will be too late, for then the "burning anger (חֲרוֹן אַף־יהוה, ὀργήν Κυρίου) of the Lord" will come upon them, "the day of the anger of the Lord (יוֹם אַף־יהוה, ἡμέραν θυμοῦ Κυρίου)" (2:2). Verse 3 even inspires the law-keepers, who seek God in righteousness and humility, with the hope that they "may be hidden (תִּסָּתְרוּ, σκεπασθῆτε) on the day of the anger of the Lord" (2:3). This imagery is suspiciously similar to that of Isa 26:20–21.

27. Henry George Liddell, Robert Scott, and Henry Stuart Jones, *A Greek-English Lexicon* (Oxford: Clarendon, 1996), 1754.

forth the spirit of salvation, and who are raised from the dead. These experience God's protection for "a little while" until the wrath of the Lord passes.[28]

In any case, closely associated with the resurrection of the dead, God's people are hidden from the Lord's wrath (ἡ ὀργὴ Κυρίου), which is brought against "those dwelling upon the land (ἐπὶ τοὺς ἐνοικοῦντας ἐπὶ τῆς γῆς)" (Isa 26:21)—the same group who will "fall" (26:18–19). Here, the coming wrath is directed toward the impious who still dwell on the land, who have not been hidden in the "inner chambers." Isaiah 27:1, then, introduces the "dragon": that is, "the serpent." On the day that God brings wrath upon those who dwell on the land, he also brings his sword of judgment "against the dragon, a fleeing serpent, against the dragon, a twisted serpent; he will slay the dragon." The two terms δράκων and ὄφις appear together only in Revelation 12:9 in the New Testament and only in Isaiah 27:1 in the Old Testament. In light of the other verbal and thematic parallels, it seems virtually impossible that this clustering of words and images is coincidental. Therefore, Revelation 12 appears to be intentionally drawing attention to Isaiah 26:16–27:1.

To what end? The imagery of Isaiah 26:16–27:1 involves a woman in birth pains (Israel), giving birth to a spirit of salvation, resurrection from the dead resulting in rejoicing, protection from wrath by hiding in inner chambers, doom and wrath on those who are upon the earth, and warfare against a serpent-like dragon. Altogether, this is a clue that we are to understand the catching up of the male son in Revelation 12:5 in connection with giving birth to the "spirit of salvation (πνεῦμα σωτηρίας)"—that is, the spiritual birth that begins at Pentecost and extends to the end—and the resurrection from the dead, which leaves the impious behind to suffer wrath and judgment.

If this is the case, and the catching up of the male son refers to the rescue of the church from coming wrath, then the song of rejoicing in Revelation 12:12 makes perfect sense. Those who dwell in the heavens would be the corporate body of Christ, the church, caught up in the vision of the male son and rescued from the dragon, who is cast down to the earth for a "short time."

The Language and Imagery of "Snatching" (Ἁρπάζω)

John describes the destiny of the male son in the following way: "And her child was caught up (ἡρπάσθη) to God and to his throne" (Rev 12:5). Most readers who interpret the male son as only Christ identify the catching up of the child to the throne of God as the ascension (cf. Acts 1:9). However, such a view creates an intractable problem. Simply put, the verb ἁρπάζω ("to snatch") is completely inappropriate for describing the ascension of Christ.

---

28. One wonders, then, whether Jesus' reference to the "many dwelling places (μοναὶ πολλαί)" in his Father's house, where Jesus is going to prepare a place (τόπον) and from which he will come again to take them there (John 14:1–3), may be related to the same promise.

The word ἁρπάζω always includes the notion of "snatching," not merely relocating an object from one location to another.[29] In the thirty-nine occurrences of ἁρπάζω in the Septuagint, the New Testament, and the writings of Josephus, they all refer to a sudden, unexpected snatching, often within the context of a robbery or a violent attack. Never does ἁρπάζω refer to a neutral relocation from one place to another. In the New Testament, the word occurs fourteen times. Setting Revelation 12:5 aside, every occurrence in the New Testament refers to the same type of sudden, unexpected removal. In no instance does it refer to a neutral relocation. After examining all eighty-six occurrences of ἁρπάζω in the works of Josephus, Ernest Moore concluded that ἁρπάζω "is most often used in a bad sense—of seizing or snatching the persons or property of others."[30] When used in a good sense, it is used often in contexts of rescuing something or someone from a perilous situation (e.g., Josephus, B.J. 2.291; 4.71; 5.522; A.J. 12.113).

For the ascension of Christ, the New Testament authors consistently use neutral terms of spatial relocation in an upward trajectory. Some of these terms are used with Jesus as the actor (John 20:17; Eph 4:8–10), not simply as a passive object of the action. Jesus was actively involved in his own ascension, which is portrayed as a gradual upward action. In Acts 1:10, the combination of the imperfect of ἦσαν with the present parenthetical participle ἀτενίζοντες ("as they were gazing") and the present participle πορευομένου ("while he was going") makes best sense if the ascension of Christ is seen as a gradual rather than sudden event.

Besides using the word ἀναβαίνω ("to ascend") for the ascension of Christ in John 20:17, John himself used the exact word some twelve times in Revelation. Especially noteworthy is how John used ἀναβαίνω just twelve verses earlier in describing the ascension of the two resurrected witnesses to heaven (Rev. 11:12). Though he had this ascension vocabulary fresh in his mind, John instead used ἁρπάζω ("to snatch") in Revelation 12:5. If the snatching of the male son to God's throne was meant to represent the ascension of Christ, why did John not use established ascension terminology, which would have identified most clearly that the male son was, in fact, Christ alone. The simplest solution to this puzzle is that the catching up of the male son was not, in fact, intended to refer to the ascension of Christ but to the rapture (ἁρπάζω) of the church. Thus Ford writes, "The verb *harpazo*, 'snatch,' is never used of the ascension of Christ, although *anabaino*, 'ascend,' used of the two witnesses in 11:12, does have this connotation, and is used in relationship to the ascension of Jesus. But in our present text there seems to be no Christological reference. In the LXX and the NT *harpazo* means to take away by force, usually with the implication that resistance is impossible."[31]

Some have tried to solve this dilemma by suggesting that the snatching is not the ascension but some other event in Christ's life. For example, Caird suggests the snatching away is unto *death*, that the entire scene in Revelation 12:1–6 is a recasting

---

29. One lexicon, BDAG, 134, defines ἁρπάζω in the following ways: "*snatch, seize*, i.e., take suddenly and vehemently, or take away in the sense of 1. *steal, carry off, drag away.* . . . 2. *snatch* or *take away*—a. forcefully. . . . b. in such a way that no resistance is offered."

30. Ernest Moore, "ΒΙΑΖΩ, ΑΡΠΑΖΩ and Cognates in Josephus," *NTS* 21.4 (1975): 525.

31. Ford, *Revelation*, 200.

of Psalm 2.[32] Osborne argues that the snatching away is an image of the resurrection, snatching Jesus from the grave.[33] The problem with such views is that the destination of the snatching is "to God and to his throne." But Christ's ascension took place some forty days after the resurrection.[34] These views also fail to consider the corporate identification of the male son supported by the allusions to Isaiah 66:7, Daniel 7:13, and Psalm 2. If the corporate identification defines the symbol, then identifying this with any specific event in the life of Christ (death, resurrection, or ascension) fails exegetically.

Yet another factor to be considered is the fact that ἁρπάζω is used in a rescue context in Revelation 12:5—a rescue from the jaws of the dragon in order to prevent being devoured. Sometimes the term ἁρπάζω is used to connote rescue (Acts 23:10; Jude 23). In fact, in his study of the term in Josephus's writings, Moore concludes, "The rare occurrences of ἁρπάζω in a good sense serve to emphasize the general meaning of 'robbery with violence,' for they are usually in a context of violence. Even in a good sense, the suddenness of the action which ἁρπάζω denotes, and which is conveyed in the word 'snatching,' is rendered necessary by the violence of others.'"[35] That is, the term tends to be used positively as a rescue from a dangerous situation.

Revelation 12:1–4 sets up such a perilous situation in which the dragon stands with open jaws ready to devour the male son when he is born. Thus the term ἁρπάζω is used in a rescue context. Such a rescue nuance is incompatible with the New Testament portrayal of the ascension of Christ, not to mention his crucifixion. Jesus Christ was not snatched away to God to escape any threat, either from Satan or from any other.[36] Ladd emphasizes this problem when he writes, "This can hardly be an allusion to the ascension of Christ, for his rapture did not have the purpose of escaping Satan's hostility."[37]

At this point, the problems associated with maintaining an identification of the male son as Jesus Christ alone and his catching up to the throne as death, resurrection, or ascension seem insurmountable. The interpretation that the male son represents only Jesus is unsupported by the use of ἁρπάζω in a rescue context to the throne of God, in which the dragon's desire to harm the child is actually thwarted by the snatching; that interpretation is, in fact, contradicted by the meaning of ἁρπάζω.

---

32. G. B. Caird, *The Revelation of Saint John*, Black's New Testament Commentary, Henry Chadwick, ed. (London: Black, 1966; repr., Peabody, MA: Hendrickson, 1993), 149–59.

33. Grant R. Osborne, *Revelation*, Baker Exegetical Commentary on the New Testament, ed. Moisés Silva (Grand Rapids: Baker, 2002), 463.

34. See John 20:17; Acts 1:1–11.

35. Moore, "BIAZΩ, ΑΡΠΑZΩ and Cognates," 525–26.

36. Lang, *Revelation*, 198.

37. Ladd, *Revelation*, 170. Ladd does not, however, conclude that the male son is the church, but "John's vivid way of asserting the victory of God's anointed over every satanic effort to destroy him," an interpretation that neglects all the evidences of a corporate identification of the male son.

The Omission of Death and Resurrection

If one identifies the male son in Revelation 12:5 as Christ alone, then how do we explain the omission of his death and resurrection?[38] Often, the idea of foreshortening is invoked, a solution to which every view must appeal.[39] However, it still seems strange—though admittedly not impossible—that these essential elements of the work of Christ (cf. 1 Cor 15:3) would be missing without a hint.

This peculiarity is resolved if the male son does not refer to Christ alone but to the corporate body of Christ, the church. At the coming of Christ, not all believers will have experienced physical death, though all will experience transformation and translation from earth to heaven (1 Cor 15:51–52; 1 Thess 4:15–17). Of course, this argument can be called an "argument from silence," so it is introduced here as merely corroborative. If the description of the male son had said, "and her child suffered, died, rose again, and ascended to God and to this throne," there would be no mystery about the male son. That those elements are missing opens the possibility that the male son is not Jesus alone.

Conclusion: The Male Son and the Assumption of the Church

Considering all the evidence set forth above, I offer the following conclusions.

First, there is no good reason to reject the view that the male son represents the church in union with Christ. Nothing in the corporate identification contradicts the text. The appeal to Psalm 2:9 as messianic is rebutted by Jesus himself, who applies the promise of Psalm 2:9 to the church in Revelation 2:26–27. The distinct vision of Revelation 12 using a "male" son as the church is consistent with other analogies and imagery of the church in the New Testament; Ephesians 4:13 says that we are to grow up into a "mature man (εἰς ἄνδρα τέλειον)." The similar imagery of the male son is used to describe the church in Revelation 12:5 because of the connection made to Isaiah 66:7, Daniel 7, and the corporate image of the body of Christ.

Second, the common identification of the male son as Christ alone results in the fallacy of selective evidence. The "Jesus only" interpretation tends to ignore the allusion to Isaiah 66:7–8 and Daniel 7:13–14, which point to a corporate identification. It also neglects the strong allusions to Isaiah 26:16–27:1, which point to a context of resurrection and protection from wrath. The interpretation of the catching up of the male son as Christ's ascension disregards the meaning of ἁρπάζω, and the interpretation of the catching up as Christ's resurrection contradicts the destination of the action as the throne of God.

Third, the identification of the male son as the corporate body of Christ, the church in union with Christ himself, incorporates all the evidence. No evidence

---

38. Cf. J. Ramsey Michaels, *Revelation*, The IVP New Testament Commentary Series, ed. Grant Osborne (Downers Grove: InterVarsity, 1997), 149. He explains the difficulty by suggesting that (1) John consistently uses other symbols (such as a Lamb) for the death of Christ, and (2) that the emphasis in Rev 12:5 is on Jesus' identification with the "seed" of Gen 3:15.

39. Beale, *Book of Revelation*, 639.

is ignored by the interpretation of the male son as the body of Christ and the snatching up as the rapture. The evidence and arguments presented here may seem complicated on the surface, but opting for a simpler explanation that does not account for all the evidence is irresponsible. If interpreters reject this explanation of the male son, then they are responsible for providing a reasonable explanation for the clear allusions to passages that point to a corporate identification of the male son as well as the use of ἁρπάζω.

Therefore, the best interpretation of Revelation 12:5 is that the male son is a symbol for the corporate body of Christ, the church, and the catching up of the male son is the assumption of the church to heaven. Because 1 Thessalonians was one of the first (if not the actual first) New Testament book written, the use of ἁρπάζω for the rapture of the church would have already been in use between forty and fifty years before the vision of Revelation 12 was written down. Thus, by using ἁρπάζω in Revelation 12:5, the inspired text points the diligent reader back to the passage in which the corporate body of Christ, the church, is resurrected/transformed, and caught up to God, thereby rescued from the coming wrath, until that corporate body returns with Christ, their head, as the armies of heaven in Revelation 19:11–16 to "rule all the nations with a rod of iron" (Rev 12:5; cf. 2:26–27; 19:15).

The Timing of the Assumption in Revelation 12:5

Having identified the male son as the corporate body of Christ and the snatching up as the rapture, the next issue is whether this vision presents a pre-tribulation rapture. There is a simple answer to the question of the timing of the catching up of the male son. We start with the fact that today most modern commentators take the male son in Revelation 12:5 to be a reference to Christ in his birth and ascension to heaven.[40] So, for the sake of argument, let us assume that the identification of the male son as "Christ alone" is correct. If so, then the timing of Christ's ascension relative to the future seven-year tribulation is obvious: Christ ascended to the throne of God nearly two thousand years ago. Since the seven-year tribulation has not yet commenced, the ascension is without controversy regarded as pre-tribulational (by about two thousand years) by nearly every modern interpreter of that passage. Commentators who hold Revelation 12:5 to be Christ at his ascension have absolutely no problem seeing in Revelation 12 an order of events that places the catching up of the male son *prior to* the entire seven-year period described with chronological indicators in Revelation 11–13.

If upon a reexamination of the evidence, we simply modify our identification of the symbol of the male son from Christ to the corporate body of Christ and conclude that the arguments are stronger for seeing his snatching up as the rapture of the church, there is no justification for adjusting our understanding of the order of the event as it relates to other events in Revelation 12. That is, whether the symbol of Revelation 12:5 refers to Christ's ascension or to the church's assumption, the order

---

40. This interpretation, in fact, is often taken for granted with no attempt made to defend it. Many commentators appear unaware that there was ever any other view.

of events in Revelation 12 is not changed. It remains an event that takes place prior to the seven-year period described in Revelation 12. Simply put, if the catching up is pre-tribulational for the one identification of the male son, then it must remain pre-tribulational for the other.

Yet a close examination of the chronological indicators and an understanding of the events that follow the snatching of the male son also confirm that this is a pre-seven-year event. After the male son is caught up (Rev 12:5) there is war in heaven. Michael the archangel and his army fight the dragon, who is cast down to the earth (12:7–9). We should recall that 1 Thessalonians 4:16 says that the archangel is also associated with the rapture of the church, which, given the identification of the male son, had just occurred prior to the outbreak of this heavenly war (see discussion of the Day of the Lord imagery in 1 Thessalonians 4–5 in chapter 16).

We can confidently assume that the war in heaven portrayed in 12:7–9 takes some time. An intriguing episode in Daniel 10 reveals that conflict between angelic and demonic forces takes real time reflected in the physical world (Dan 10:12–13).[41] Thus conflict between only two angelic/demonic beings delayed angelic activity for three weeks. We may assume that a final battle between the forces of Satan and the forces of the archangel Michael described in Revelation 12:7–9 will take some time as well. This means that one unspecified period of time elapses in the narrative following the catching up of the church to God and the casting down of the devil and his angels to the earth. In the context of Revelation 12, this unspecified period of time follows the rapture, but it takes place before the woman's (the righteous remnant of Israel's) 1,260-day (i.e., three-and-a-half year) protection from the dragon. So, the war in heaven must take place during the first half of the future tribulation period.

When the dragon is at last cast down after the prolonged conflict, a song of victory breaks forth in heaven (Rev 12:10–12). If we read the words of this song of praise in light of the church having recently been resurrected/transformed and assumed to heaven, the song makes perfect sense. Those who dwell in heaven, then, are the recently raptured saints. In this action, the kingdom of Christ begins to manifest itself in the heavenly realm; finally, the judgments of the Day of the Lord described in the book of Revelation begin to affect both the spiritual and physical realms. Note also that those who had once been accused by the devil "day and night" are now said to have overcome him. No longer is there a basis for accusation against the saints, for they have been transformed immortal, resurrected, and glorified at the rapture of the church (1 Thess 4:17; 1 Cor 15:52; Phil 3:20–21). Those who remain on the earth, however, are about to face "great wrath" of the devil, whose time is now short. The church, though, has been saved from this wrath associated with the Day of the Lord (1 Thess 1:10; 5:9).

After the dragon is cast down, he immediately pivots to attack the woman, the faithful remnant of Israel, reconstituted at the beginning of the tribulation period (see Rev 7:1–8). Before the woman is preserved in the wilderness for 1,260

---

41. See Peter R. Schemm Jr., "The Agents of God: Angels," in *A Theology for the Church*, ed. Daniel L. Akin, Bruce Riley Ashford, and Kenneth Keathley, rev. ed. (Nashville: B & H, 2014), 252; and Henry C. Thiessen, *Lectures in Systematic Theology* (Grand Rapids: Eerdmans, 1949), 207.

days, however, the dragon—working through the world powers in keeping with his symbolism (see above)—launches an attack on Israel with an army (Rev 12:13–16). The image of the flood in Old Testament prophecy is that of a military invasion, another aspect of the Day of the Lord (Isa 8:7–8; Jer 46:7–8; 47:2; Dan. 9:27; 11:10, 40). The vision pictures the dragon's first attempt to destroy the woman (Israel) with an invasion during the first half of the tribulation, after the war in heaven. But the army is defeated. Then the woman flees to be protected in the wilderness for 1,260 days during the second half of tribulation. This earthly warfare that leads to the woman's flight also takes time, during which the woman is miraculously protected from the fierce wrath of the dragon.

Utterly frustrated in his repeatedly failed plans at destroying the woman, Israel, the dragon next turns his attention to the "rest of her children (τῶν λοιπῶν τοῦ σπέρματος αὐτῆς), those who keep the commandments of God and hold the testimony of Jesus" (Rev 12:17). The symbol of "the rest of her children" likely refers to the same group called the "great multitude" of Revelation 7:9–17 saved during the tribulation "from every nation, from all tribes and peoples and languages" (7:9). These come to faith through the testimony of the remnant of Israel symbolized in the vision of Revelation 7 as the 144,000 (7:1–8). During the future Day of the Lord, the remnant of Israel will fulfill its calling to be a kingdom of priests, a beacon of light for the nations. However, for Satan to accomplish his worldwide persecution of the tribulation-period saints, he turns to a different means of combating the people of God: the beast from the sea, commonly known as the antichrist (Rev 13). It is at the midpoint of the seven-year tribulation period that the forty-two months of the beast's authority begins (Rev 13:5).

To sum up, the catching up of the male son is immediately followed by time-consuming events before the midpoint of the tribulation: spiritual warfare in heaven resulting in the casting down of Satan (Rev 12:7–12), and warfare on earth by which the dragon attempts to destroy Israel (12:13–16). All of this must take place during the first half of the tribulation, during which the remnant of Israel is saved and sealed (7:1–8), the temple in Jerusalem is rebuilt (11:1–2), and the two witnesses carry out their 1,260-day ministry prior to the rise of the beast and their martyrdom (11:3–7). The forty-two-month reign of the beast and false prophet then take place during the second half of the tribulation (Rev. 13) (see discussion in chapter 17 of this book).

Given the chronological indicators in Revelation 11–13, the catching up of the male son, the church, takes place prior to the seven-year tribulation.

Conclusion

C. S. Lewis, arguing for the absurdity of concluding that an old idea had been discredited simply because it had "gone out of date," once urged his readers, "You must find why it went out of date. Was it ever refuted (and if so by whom, where, and how conclusively) or did it merely die away as fashions do? If the latter, this tells us nothing about its truth or falsehood."[42] The doctrine of the pre-tribulation rapture is often criticized for its novelty (though I have shown that this point is overstated), lampooned for its idiosyncrasy, and even set aside as an irrelevant obsession in light of more enlightened modern scholars happy to do away with the event of the rapture altogether—a novelty far newer than the pre-tribulation rapture itself (see Go Deeper Excursus 28).

In this chapter and the last, I revisited the question of the end-times assumption of the church to heaven, hoping to shed some new light on old arguments. Admittedly, the arguments for a pre-tribulation rapture are complicated. They require the interpreter to deal with original Greek texts, the use of the Old Testament in the New, several symbols and allusions important to deciphering puzzling elements, and an ability to keep all the evidences and arguments together. In fact, the complexity of the arguments—not their naive simplicity—may be one of the reasons why the pre-tribulation rapture has fallen out of favor in the last several decades.

Nevertheless, in keeping with several issues surfaced in the Irenaean premillennial eschatology—with necessary modifications in light of a more Augustinian soteriology and ecclesiology—the pre-tribulation rapture is not absurd. Despite the rhetoric of some, it is not true that the pre-tribulation rapture lacks any plausible exegetical support whatsoever. And it is a gross exaggeration to say that all of church history is uniformly against anything like a pre-tribulation rapture. The fact is, there is no *clear* evidence of anybody directly timing 1 Thessalonians 4:17 relative to the future tribulation prior to the end of the second century, though Irenaeus comes closest with what looks like a partial pre-tribulation rapture (*Haer.* 5.29.1). Tertullian, in the early years of the third century, is the first to tie 1 Thessalonians 4:17 to the end of the tribulation period, after the time of antichrist. To claim posttribulationism as "historic premillennialism" is an overstatement. History is not that simple.

Though many facts could contribute to a general understanding of the rapture as a rescue from coming wrath, the specific timing of the rapture relative to the two halves of the seven-year tribulation were not revealed until the 90s with the book of Revelation (Rev 12:5). This timing appears in a highly symbolic vision that would have likely been challenging for many to interpret. In any case, few would have a chance to do so, as futurist premillennialism like that of the fathers of the second century came under attack in the third century and dropped out of favor by

---

42. C. S. Lewis, *Surprised by Joy: The Shape of My Early Life* (New York: Harcourt, 1955), 207–8.

the fourth, leaving little interest in reflecting on the doctrine of the rapture until a premillennial and futurist resurgence in the nineteenth century. We should not be at all surprised, therefore, that the doctrine of the pre-tribulation rapture—along with numerous other eschatological "novelties"—would arise in the wake of a resuscitation, nay, a resurrection of a futurist, premillennial eschatology similar in many respects to the classic premillennialism of Irenaeus of Lyons.

21

Remembering the Future

*For in the times of the kingdom, the righteous man
who is upon the earth shall then forget to die.*

Irenaeus, *Against Heresies* 5.36.2

Death is not our friend. Death is the enemy (1 Cor 15:26). This fact is often forgotten in many Christian circles, especially when funerary sentimentality gets in the way of sound doctrine—when statements abound like "Don't cry for him; he's more alive than ever" or "She's finally been made fully whole" or "That body isn't him, he's in heaven." Some of our beloved hymns reinforce the celebration of death as a mere doorway to true life. For example:

> *Some glad morning when this life is o'er, I'll fly away;*
> *To a home on God's celestial shore, I'll fly away.*
> *I'll fly away, O glory, I'll fly away;*
> *When I die, hallelujah, by and by, I'll fly away.*

> *When the shadows of this life have gone, I'll fly away;*
> *Like a bird from prison bars has flown, I'll fly away. . . .*
> *Just a few more weary days and then, I'll fly away;*
> *To a land where joys shall never end, I'll fly away.[1]*

Yes, in our fallen world of suffering, death can bring an end to often excruciating physical pain, but that does not make death your "friend" any more than passing through a doorway engulfed in flames to escape a burning building makes the wall of flame your friend. It is a painful reality of the messed-up world in which we live.

Scripture and traditional Christian faith are clear that death is the enemy of humanity. In fact, death is the enemy of all creation; the victory over death is resurrection and restoration of all creation (Rom 8:18–25). Christ's death and resurrection defeated death in that microcosm of his own history. His glorification and ascension embody the promise that the same transformation from death to life through resurrection and glorification will be the experience of all who are in Christ and through them to the whole world. But the death, resurrection, and ascension of Christ did not transform death itself into something good, something harmless.

---

1. Albert E. Brumley, "I'll Fly Away," *The Hymnal for Worship and Celebration* (Waco: Word Music, 1986), no. 554.

Death is not a tamed monster. Death is a ferocious enemy whose defeat at Christ's empty tomb anticipates an ultimate vanquishing in the coming kingdom.

Yet for centuries, the church has been plagued by eschatological schemes that have somehow, through an unfortunate series of theological bad turns and doctrinal missteps, rendered death the friend of the Christian. By jettisoning God's plan of progressive glorification in connection with progressive edenification of all creation, many—if not most—have undermined God's plan of redemption. In such a scheme, even resurrection is sometimes conflated with death.[2] Eschatology has too often been reduced simply to "dying and going to heaven."

We encounter countless truncated eschatological expectations like those of the English Puritan Thomas Watson (1620–1686): "Death to a believer is *crespusculum gloriæ*,—the day-break of eternal brightness."[3] By seizing the eschatological promises of the future new creation and conscripting them into the service of an over-realized, over-personalized, and over-spiritualized eschatology, Watson exults over eight reasons why "to die is gain" for the Christian (Phil 1:21–23).[4]

1. Believers at death shall gain a writ of case from all sins and troubles.

2. Believers at death shall gain the glorious sight of God.

3. The saints at death shall not only have a sight of God, but shall enjoy the love of God.

4. Believers at death shall gain a celestial palace—an house not made with hands.

5. Believers at death shall gain the sweet society of glorified saints and angels.

6. Believers at death shall gain perfection of holiness.

7. At death the saints shall gain a royal magnificent feast.

8. Believers at death shall gain honour and dignity, they shall reign as kings.

I do not mean to pick on Watson, but most readers will recognize echoes of these kinds of statements in songs we sing, sermons we hear, and sayings repeated in Christian circles, in which death for the Christian means we are now "more alive than ever," we have finally entered into our full inheritance, walking the streets of gold, basking in the presence of God, and reigning as kings. The result? Well, in the minds of many, death is not the enemy; death is their friend.

---

2. Recall, for example, Riddlebarger's assertion, *A Case for Amillennialism*, 247, that "for Christians, death is really a resurrection unto life." See discussion in chapter 12 and Go Deeper Excursus 20.

3. Thomas Watson, *The Select Works of the Rev. Thomas Watson, Comprising His Celebrated Body of Divinity, in a Series of Lectures on the Shorter Catechism, and Various Sermons and Treatises* (New York: Robert Carter & Brothers, 1855), 193.

4. Watson, *Select Works*, 194–95.

What Happens When We Die?

A handful of passages of Scripture have been bandied about in support of the idea that death itself is good. These include Psalm 116:15, Ecclesiastes 7:1, 2 Corinthians 5:1–5; and Philippians 1:21–23. Most translations of Psalm 116:15 read something like this: "Precious in the sight of the Lord is the death of his faithful ones" (NRSVue). On the surface (and taken out of context), this verse looks like the death of the faithful is pleasing to God; that is, a good thing. Why? Because they go to heaven to be with him. Rather, "it seems more in keeping with the context of the psalm and of other passages in the Old Testament to take the word *precious* here to mean 'costly.'"[5] The term יקר ("precious") has the sense of "costly," which can be taken positively (e.g., a costly gem) or negatively (e.g., a costly war). The context of the psalm and the overall teaching of Scripture should move us to understand the term in its negative sense: "Costly in the sight of the Lord is the death of his saints." Therefore, as the psalmist prays, God delights in delivering his people from death.

In Ecclesiastes 7:1, we read, "A good name is better than fine perfume, and the day of death better than the day of birth." Does this mean the day we die is better than the day we were born? No, the context of Ecclesiastes 7:1–4 suggests the author is referring to funerals (the day of death) and birthdays (the day of birth): two different opportunities to reflect on different aspects of one's life. One commentator puts it in simple terms: "As inner character is more crucial than outer fragrance, so it is the funeral, not the rowdy birthday party, that poses the ultimate questions about life. . . . Death brings us to think about life (cf. Ps. 90:12). . . . A party has no such effect. Every funeral anticipates our own."[6] On the day of death, people reflect on the person's whole life, ponder their own mortality: "Death is the destiny of everyone; the living should take this to heart" (Eccl 7:2).

In 2 Corinthians 5:1–5, Paul addresses the question of what happens to believers when they die. Reflecting ideas found in Romans 8, Paul contrasts the "light and momentary troubles" and the "eternal glory that far outweighs them all," which prompts us to "fix our eyes not on what is seen, but on what is unseen, since what is seen is temporary, but what is unseen is eternal" (2 Cor 4:17–18; cf. Rom 8:18). In the context of hoping for this eternal inheritance—unseen by us in the present—Paul says, "For we know that if the earthly tent we live in is destroyed, we have a building from God" (2 Cor 5:1). It is contrary to everything we have seen regarding resurrection (cf. chapters 3 and 12 above) to assert that Paul is speaking about receiving resurrection bodies immediately upon death. Resurrection bodies are not—as many second-century gnostics taught—merely spiritual in substance; rather, resurrection bodies are those physical bodies that had died, now risen, re-

---

5. Robert G. Bratcher and William David Reyburn, *A Translator's Handbook on the Book of Psalms*, UBS Handbook Series (New York: United Bible Societies, 1991), 983. Cf. also Derek Kidner, *Psalms 73–150: An Introduction and Commentary*, Tyndale Old Testament Commentaries, vol. 16 (Downers Grove, IL: InterVarsity, 1975), 446; and S. Edward Tesh and Walter D. Zorn, *Psalms*, The College Press NIV Commentary (Joplin, MO: College Press, 1999), 359.

6. Michael A. Eaton, *Ecclesiastes: An Introduction and Commentary*, Tyndale Old Testament Commentaries, vol. 18 (Downers Grove, IL: InterVarsity, 1983), 125.

stored, and glorified (see chapter 3). The fact that we have physical remains after death is *prima facie* proof that resurrection does not occur at death; anything else is a rejection of the classic Christian view of resurrection (see Go Deeper Excursus 3).[7] It is better to understand Paul's use of the present tense "we have" as indicating the absolute certainty of our resurrection into glorious bodies, which will occur when Christ returns and he "will transform our lowly bodies so that they will be like his glorious body" (Phil 3:20–21).[8]

However, what happens when believers die prior to Christ's return to transform our mortal bodies into immortal bodies (1 Cor 15:51–52)? During that period between a believer's death and resurrection, Paul says, we are "away from the body" but "at home with the Lord" (2 Cor 5:8). Philippians 1:23 expresses the same clear hope: "I desire to depart and be with Christ, which is better by far" than "to go on living in the body," considering Paul was in chains and had experienced extreme physical and emotional suffering in ministry (cf. 2 Cor 11:23–28). It is no wonder that Paul could say, given the magnitude of his pain, that to depart and be with Christ would be "gain" (Phil 1:21). This does not make the death itself "good." Paul was not saying the ultimate, final goal of the Christian is to "die and go to heaven" and to life with Christ eternally in a spiritual realm. Rather, he did not want to remain "unclothed" (that is, without a body) but "clothed instead with our heavenly dwelling, so that what is mortal may be swallowed up by life" (2 Cor 5:4).

In referring to our "heavenly dwelling," Paul probably also had in mind more than just a new, glorified body. He likely had in mind the new creation that, quite literally, presently exists in the heavenly realm (1 Pet 1:3–4)—in fact, in the third heaven, in paradise. This is why he could say in Philippians 3:20 that "our citizenship is in heaven." Wright correctly observes that in the first-century way of thinking, "being citizens of heaven . . . doesn't mean that one is expecting to go back to the mother city, but rather that one is expecting the emperor to come *from* the mother city to give the colony its full dignity, to rescue it if need be, to subdue local enemies and put everything to rights."[9]

In our discussion in chapter 5 of Irenaeus's overarching premillennial eschatology, we saw that he taught that disciples of Jesus "go away into the invisible place allotted to them by God, and there remain until the resurrection . . . then receiving their bodies, and rising in their entirety, that is bodily, just as the Lord arose, they shall come thus into the presence of God" (*Haer.* 5.31.2). In the classic premillennial view, upon death, we are absent from the body and present with the Lord. But where? Not basking in the resplendent glories of the Father in the highest heavens but in the third heaven, paradise. This is a place of rest and repose, a heavenly place invisible to us today, where we stay until the resurrection. Irenaeus's teacher, Polycarp of Smyrna, also had an expectation that the faithful were in the presence

---

7. Contra, e.g., David E. Garland, *2 Corinthians*, The New American Commentary, vol. 29 (Nashville: Broadman & Holman, 1999), 252–55.

8. Cf. also 1 John 5:12–13 and 2 Tim 4:8, where the present tense is used to indicate the certainty of future reward.

9. N. T. Wright, *Surprised by Hope* (London: SPCK, 2007), 145.

of the Lord. Polycarp urged the Philippians to practice patient endurance in imitation of those who had paid the ultimate price—Christians like Ignatius of Antioch, other martyrs, and the apostles of Christ—"having confidence that none of them ran in vain but in faith and righteousness, and that they are with the Lord (παρὰ τῷ κυρίῳ) in the place (τόπον εἰσί) which they are due, who they also suffered with" (Pol. *Phil.* 9.2).[10]

So, the classic Christian view on "life after death" involves the conscious continued existence of the immaterial part of a person—the "soul" or "spirit." To be absent from the body is to be present with the Lord (2 Cor 5:6–8; Phil 1:21–24). However, this condition is temporary as we await the resurrection of our bodies, which is the ultimate hope of the Christian. In that intermediate state—in paradise—we are not yet "fully alive." We are, as Paul says, "the dead in Christ (οἱ νεκροὶ ἐν Χριστῷ)" (1 Thess 4:16). The fact that Moses (with Elijah) was able to appear and speak with Jesus (Luke 9:30–31) demonstrates that the souls of the departed saints continue after death in that heavenly realm. What we do not know, however, is the exact nature of that realm. In chapter 4, we saw that this heavenly realm is the place of paradise (Luke 23:43), a realm wherein both physical and spiritual beings can reside (2 Cor 12:3–4). But what is the passage of time like in such a place? Does a day on earth equal a day in paradise? Could it be that a hundred years on earth is experienced as a mere moment in paradise? Or could it be the other way around? We cannot answer these questions with any certainty. All we know is that the time between death and resurrection involves what we call "life after death"; therefore, the resurrection is "life after life after death."[11]

Until that resurrection, we are still longing for something more in that intermediate state, yearning for the completion of our salvation. Charles Spurgeon puts it well:

> You know there are some in heaven who have not yet waked up in God's likeness. In fact, none of those in heaven have done so. They never did sleep as respects their souls; the waking refers to their bodies, and they are not awake yet—but are still slumbering. . . . The righteous still sleep; and they are to be satisfied on the resurrection morn, when they awake. "But," say you, "are they not satisfied now? They are in heaven: is it possible that they can be distressed?" No, they are not; there is only one dissatisfaction that can enter heaven—the dissatisfaction of the blest that their bodies are not there.[12]

---

10. In this passage, Polycarp mentions that only certain people—martyrs who were faithful to the end and did not love the present age—were present with the Lord upon death. However, Polycarp, Pol. *Phil.* 9.1, also used the example of those famous martyrs who had won the prize to encourage endurance among the Philippians, which implies that they, too, can inherit this place with the Lord for their faith and righteousness.

11. See discussion on early Jewish, pagan, and Christian views of "life after death" in N. T. Wright, *The Resurrection of the Son of God*, Christian Origins and the Question of God, vol. 3 (Minneapolis: Fortress, 2003), 32–206.

12. Charles H. Spurgeon, "The Hope of Future Bliss," Sermon 25 (May 20, 1855), in *The New Park Street Pulpit Sermons*, vol. 1 (London: Passmore & Alabaster, 1855), 194.

What Happens When We Rise?

Eric Osborn writes,

> Irenaeus' eschatology is not an embarrassing postscript but a necessary conse-
> quence of a creator God who so surrounds all things (*concludens omnia*) and
> loves his creature that he becomes incarnate to restore its failings. That restoration
> completed, Christ inaugurates for ever the renewal of all creation. The restoration
> of human lives, which is the present concern of the church, will be complete in
> a restored universe. The inauguration of a new humanity is fed by the hope of
> final glory.[13]

I believe we need to understand our "personal eschatology"—that is, what happens
when we die and what we have to look forward to in "life after death"—in light of
our general eschatology—that is, what God is doing in the world. As a basic narrative framework, I understand creation to have been made good (but not perfect),
humans to have been fashioned out of the earth, which was subject to corruption,
and then placed in the garden of Eden: that is, paradise on earth. This place is the
intersection or meeting between the heavenly realm and the earthly, and it is this
earthiness that has been transformed and perfected through its union with the
heavenly. This in-between realm, known as the Garden of Eden, could accommodate both physical Adam and Eve as well as spiritual beings—even a manifestation
of God himself who fellowshipped with humans there in that temple-like realm.

When Adam and Eve sinned and were cast from the garden, this place of
heavenly fellowship was no longer accessible to them. However, it is clear in intertestamental literature as well as in the New Testament that when saints (the "saved")
die, though they are absent from their bodies, their immaterial souls are granted
access to the heavenly realm—into the "third heaven," to "paradise," which is the
same spiritual realm that had at one time intersected with Eden. We know from
further revelation that this spiritual existence in the heavenly realm is not permanent but temporary: one day, the saints will be physically resurrected, reunited to
their physical bodies, which will be glorified and immortalized, taking on a spiritual
and heavenly quality. They will become like the quality of the world once kissed by
heaven—the garden of Eden.

But we also know that cosmically the heavenly realm of paradise will also return to earth, eventually transforming not just one high mountain in the east but
the entire globe. Ultimately, all creation will become like the quality of Eden. We
do not leave the heavenly inheritance received first in our spiritual sojourn in the
third heaven and then in our resurrection into immortal life; rather, that heavenly
inheritance returns to earth with us at Christ's second coming and the whole earth
is transformed because of our own adoption into immortality (Rom 8).

To be specific, when we think of our "heavenly inheritance" (1 Pet 1:3–4) we
should think of the kinds of things promised to those who overcome in Revelation

---

13. Eric Osborn, *Irenaeus of Lyons* (Cambridge: Cambridge University Press, 2001),
139–40.

2–3: those things "kept" for us in the present time in the heavens, which will one day be unleashed in this world. This includes not only Jesus himself, who is the literal embodiment of our inheritance, but also, specifically, the promises to Abraham (Gal 3:18; Heb 11:18). We know that this ultimate inheritance is not only something for which we have a sort of down-payment through the Spirit (Eph 1:14), but also something we will experience much more in the heavenly realm (1 Pet 1:4), which will ultimately be experienced by the saints in the edenification of the earth (Rom 8). Though we speak of "going to heaven" to begin experiencing this inheritance kept for us, most New Testament authors were probably thinking less about that interim period and more about the inheritance that will come to us from heaven with Jesus when we are raised to life by resurrection.

Colossians 3:24 is of the same nature. The "reward of the inheritance" relates to the blessings we will receive in the kingdom, primarily after the resurrection when we receive in the body according to what we have done in the body. In 2 Corinthians 5:1–3, Paul is not talking about being "naked" (free from our bodies), but clothed fully in immortality—that is, receiving our immortal, glorious body, conformed to Christ's own body and fit for the kind of creation established by God during the millennium.

Though not ultimately accepted universally as canonical, the first-century BC Wisdom of Solomon was highly regarded by the early church and accepted by some Christian traditions as part of the deuterocanonical literature.[14] It was certainly known and even used by early Christians as at least insightful and inspiring literature. As such, it serves as a kind of window into the theology of early Jewish and Christian thinkers regarding death, the afterlife, and the restoration. Wisdom describes the destiny of the righteous thusly: "But the souls of the righteous are in the hand of God, and no torment will ever touch them. In the eyes of the foolish they seemed to have died, and their departure was thought to be a disaster, and their going from us to be their destruction; but they are at peace. For though in the sight of others they were punished, their hope is full of immortality" (Wis. Sol. 3:1–4 NRSVue). A few verses later, the same passage describes an ultimate hope: "In the time of their visitation (ἐν καιρῷ ἐπισκοπῆς αὐτῶν) they will shine forth, and will run like sparks through the stubble. They will govern nations and rule over peoples, and the Lord will reign over them for ever. Those who trust in him will understand truth, and the faithful will abide with him in love, because grace and mercy are upon his holy ones, and he watches over his elect" (Wis 3:7–9). On the reference to the saints shining forth, Lester Grabbe suggests, "This seems to presuppose what has sometimes been referred to as 'astral immortality.' . . . This is the view that the righteous became like the stars of heaven at death. The concept is evidently first attested in Dan. 12:3."[15]

---

14. Cf. Roger T. Beckwith, *The Old Testament Canon of the New Testament Church and Its Background in Early Judaism* (Eugene, OR: Wipf and Stock, 2008), 2; and J. N. D. Kelly, *Early Christian Doctrines*, 5th ed. (New York: HarperOne, 1978), 53.

15. Lester L. Grabbe, *Wisdom of Solomon*, T&T Clark Study Guides, ed. Michael A. Knibb, A. T. Lincoln, and R. N. Whybray (London: T&T Clark, 1997), 56.

These words of Wisdom transition us into another area often misunderstood in Christian circles: the destiny of the righteous after they rise. In what is sometimes called "folk theology," it is often thought that at some instant in the future—upon death or the return of Christ—all the righteous will be suddenly transformed into glorious beings. They will be made "perfect" in the sense of having everything ever promised, knowing everything there is to know, being everything they were meant to be. At that moment, it is often said, humans will become like angels, and while love continues, faith will come to an end because it will be replaced by sight, and hope will cease because all hope will be fulfilled.

Yet, this is not the "end" envisioned in classic Irenaean eschatology. Rather, what is often called "the end" is really the beginning. For the Christian, resurrection from the dead is an entrance into eternal life—and "life" in the sense of learning, doing, growing, being transformed forever and ever. Contrary to popular belief, we do not suddenly become everything we were meant to be. Resurrection begins an eternal progressive process of growing from glory to glory. Just as we could never count to infinity, so we can never grow to "perfection." Only God himself is perfect and without the capacity for growth and change per se; humans, as finite beings, will always have new experiences, which will transform them; and as they grow in knowledge of, love for, and relationship with God, that experience will make them ever new. Therefore, the capacity for our growth in relationship with one another is limitless.

We may call this "eternal progressive glorification" or "eternal christification"— that is, being eternally conformed to the image of God, Jesus Christ. For all eternity, we will be forever growing toward—but never fully attaining—the full likeness of the incarnate God-man.[16] James Payton puts it simply:

> Sometimes . . . the way we talk about salvation makes it sound like little more than a get-out-of-hell-free card. With our emphasis on what sinners like ourselves are saved from, do we know what we are saved for? Is salvation solely about us and our need to be forgiven and born again, or is there a deeper, God-ward purpose?

> The leaders of the ancient church thought so, speaking regularly of salvation in a way that may sound strange to many evangelicals. . . . In particular, they envisioned salvation as *theosis,* an ongoing process by which God's people becoming increasingly 'partakers of the divine nature' (2 Pet. 1:4), formed more and more in God's likeness. As the 2nd-century theologian Irenaeus urged in *Against Heresies*, "Through his transcendent love, our Lord Jesus Christ became what we are, that he might make us to be what he is."[17]

---

16. Nellas explains, "The Lord redeemed man from slavery to sin, death and devil, but He also put into effect the work which had not been effected by Adam. He united him with God, granting him true 'being' in God and raising him to a new creation. Christ accomplishes the salvation of man not only in a negative way, liberating him from the consequences of original sin, but also in a positive way, completing his iconic, prelapsarian 'being.' His relationship with man is not only that of a healer. The salvation of man is something much wider than redemption." Panayiotis Nellas, *Deification in Christ: Orthodox Perspectives on the Nature of the Human Person*, Contemporary Greek Theologians, vol. 5 (Yonkers, NY: St. Vladimirs Seminary Press, 1987), 39.

17. James R. Payton Jr., "Keeping the End in View: How the Strange Yet Familiar Doctrine of Theosis Can Invigorate the Christian Life," *CT* 52.10 (October 2008): 66–67.

As Payton mentioned, Irenaeus—along with the majority of Christian thinkers throughout history—affirmed the eternal progressive glorification of the saints after their resurrection. Irenaeus ties this real existence of humanity to the real existence of the universe: "For since there are real men, so must there also be a real establishment (*plantationem*), that they vanish not away among non-existent things, but progress among those which have an actual existence" (*Haer.* 5.36.1). We see further glimpses of the eternal growth in relationship with God: "But when this [present] fashion [of things] passes away, and man has been renewed, and flourishes in an incorruptible state, so as to preclude the possibility of becoming old, [then] there shall be the new heaven and the new earth, in which the new man shall remain [continually], always holding fresh converse with God" (5.35.1). Yet, Irenaeus also notes that some of the saved will dwell in heaven, some in paradise, and others in the holy city (5.35.1). In other words, drawing on imagery of different places, he asserted that there will be a distinction of reward in eternity based on differences in faithfulness and fruitfulness (5.35.2).

This leads to the concept of the "beatific vision" or the ability to stand in the presence of God the Father and perceive God's glory when we have been made able to do so. Irenaeus writes that "the resurrection and kingdom of the just"—that is, the millennium—"is the beginning of incorruption (*principium incorruptelae*), by which kingdom those who will be worthy, are progressively accustomed to comprehend God (*paulatim assuescunt capere Deum*)" (*Haer.* 5.32.1 [my translation]). In classic Irenaean eschatology, the resurrection and kingdom of the just (i.e., the millennium) is the stage for the gradual, progressive glorification of redeemed humanity, during which they grow deeper and deeper in their grasp of God. Irenaeus adds: "It behooves the righteous first to receive the promise of the inheritance which God promised to the fathers, and to reign in it, when they rise again to behold God in this creation which is renovated" (5.32.1).

In the Irenaean vision of the eschaton, in which cosmic and personal eschatology converge, the believers upon death do not immediately find themselves basking in the glory of the Father, surrounding the throne of God in the highest heavens—what is commonly called by theologians "the beatific vision."[18] Though some have argued that experiencing God's presence "face to face" (cf. 1 Cor 13:12) will always be mediated through the person of Christ (that is, all theophanies are really Christophanies), Gavin Ortlund defends the traditional view that "we will indeed see God's essence in heaven."[19] Ortlund demonstrates that the view of the eschatological "beatific vision"—beholding the essence of God face to face—is not a "catholic" view but the view of historic Protestant theology, and it is also biblical (Ps 11:7; 17:15; 27:4; 1 John 3:2; Rev 22:3–4).[20]

The Irenaean approach, the beatific vision—or what people often refer to colloquially as "basking in God's glory"—awaits the resurrection, when "our face shall

---

18. There may have been an exception for some martyrs who were granted a "fast pass" to the beatific vision.

19. Gavin Ortlund, "Will We See God's Essence? A Defence of a Thomistic Account of the Beatific Vision," *SJT* 74.4 (2021): 324.

20. Ortlund, "Will We See God's Essence?," 327–29, 330–31.

see the face of the Lord, and shall rejoice with joy unspeakable—that is to say, when it shall behold its own Delight" (*Haer.* 5.7.2). Again, though the departed saints are present with Christ in the spiritual realm of paradise, they are not yet admitted into the highest heavens, into the presence of the invisible Father. That experience awaits resurrection. Even then, the resurrected, immortal saints will experience growth from glory to glory as they gradually become more and more partakers of the divine nature and eventually reach such a state of glory that they are able to enter into the presence of the Father.

The beatific vision, then, comes after a period of progressive glorification that takes place during the millennium. Yet Irenaeus understood that some people have made more progress in the journey of this present life than others—what we often call "progressive sanctification." Those who have reached a greater level of maturity in this life will experience the beatific vision sooner than those who have made less progress. In this way, the various "abodes" or levels of reward are sorted out in the eschaton.

There is continuity between our present progressive sanctification and our future progressive glorification. The two are not unrelated.[21] Brian Arnold notes that in Irenaeus's eschatology, "believers already see God in this temporal life through the spirit, but believers do not yet see God as they will when they physically encounter him face-to-face."[22] For Irenaeus, Arnold says, "the purpose of the millennial reign is not so much rewards for the faithful, but rather a preparation for the glory that will be revealed in the final state. . . . Even as believers reign during the thousand years alongside Christ, the primary goal remains the preparation for glory that is still yet to come."[23]

The classic concept of "progressive glorification" and gradual growth after resurrection prior to admission to the beatific vision may sound strange—even heterodox—to those who have been taught since Sunday school that the moment we die and go to heaven, we will bask in the glory of God, sit at the feet of Jesus, and have all our questions answered, all our desires fulfilled, and all our joys completed. Too often, we rip the verses out of context that tell us, "For we know only in part, and we prophesy only in part, but when the complete comes, the partial will come to an end. . . . For now we see only a reflection, as in a mirror, but then we will see face to face" (1 Cor 13:9–10, 12). This is not speaking about conditions we experience when we go to heaven, but when "the perfect thing comes" (13:10). Paul

---

21. Widdicombe observes that in *Haer.* 4.20.5, Irenaeus "indicates that there is a progression in how God is seen both in this life and from this life to the next. To those who love him, God grants the power 'to see' him. God was first seen prophetically through the Spirit, then adoptively through the Son, and he shall be seen 'paternally [*paternaliter*] in the kingdom of heaven,' the Spirit preparing the believer in the Son of God, and the Son leading them to the Father, who confers incorruption and eternal life on them, which, as Irenaeus explains, results from seeing God." Peter Widdicombe, "Irenaeus and the Knowledge of God as Father: Text and Context," in *Irenaeus: Life, Scripture, Legacy*, ed. Sara Parvis and Paul Parvis (Minneapolis: Fortress, 2012), 148.

22. Brian J. Arnold, "'To Behold Its Own Delight': The Beatific Vision in Irenaeus of Lyons," *Perichoresis* 17.2 (2019): 34.

23. Arnold, "'To Behold Its Own Delight,'" 37.

is speaking of the eschaton. When he says we will "know fully" (13:12), that must be understood as a contrast to the imperfect, partial knowledge to which we have access in the present age. God has given us everything necessary and sufficient for life and godliness, yet we have countless questions unanswered. We have, as it were, an obscured vision of all reality, with no direct access to perfect knowledge. In the eschaton, when Christ returns, we will have an unobstructed access to knowledge of all things, able to grow in infinite leaps and bounds with nothing holding us back.

The classic Irenaean vision of growth in glory presents a completely different ending to the story of creation, fall, and redemption. In fact, it is not an ending but a beginning. It starts with God reversing the effects of death and the curse on creation throughout the millennium, liberating all things from their bondage to corruption as they themselves embark on a journey of forever growing toward—but never fully attaining—the full likeness of the incarnate God-man, Jesus Christ. What he is by nature, we will never be: that is, we will never become divine. However, what he is by nature, we finite beings can progressively grow toward by God's grace, invited into the life of immortality purely by the mercy and power of God.

Eternal Life as Unending Growth in Glory

In one sense, we "have" eternal life through our adoption as children of God. John makes this present reality clear: "God gave us eternal life, and this life is in his Son. Whoever has the Son has life; whoever does not have the Son of God does not have life. I write these things to you who believe in the name of the Son of God, so that you may know that you have eternal life" (1 John 5:11–13). We have experienced a spiritual rebirth, resurrection, and regeneration that transfers us from death to life (Eph 2:1–10; Col 1:13; 2:13; 1 Pet 1:23). And we have the firstfruits of the Spirit, a down payment and promise of much more in the future (Rom 8:23; 2 Cor 1:22; 5:5). However, in another sense, the full experience of "eternal life" awaits our resurrection from the dead, when the essential physical part of our human nature—our bodies—are raised anew and bestowed with immortality, incorruption, and an incapacity to sin (Matt 19:29; 25:46; Rom 2:7; 6:22).

Though dying and going to paradise where Jesus has prepared a place for us may be a next step in our experience of the life we have in his Son, it is not the final step. As we have seen in the preceding discussion, even our resurrection from the dead is not the final step. In fact, when it comes to eternal life, there is no "final step." There is a first step and then an unending journey. Eternal life is not a state but a trajectory. It is not something we have but something we experience. Eternal life is an unending ascent into the infinite heights of the divine, a boundless venturing into the profundities of the universe. Eternal life is ever growing in the inexhaustible knowledge of and love for God, being transformed more and more like him (1 John 3:2). As individual humans are perpetually transformed, our capacity for ever-renewed knowledge of and love for one another will see no end.

In short, the journey of eternal life will never have an end. The English playwright, poet, and politician Joseph Addison (1672–1719) puts this idea beautifully:

There is not, in my opinion, a more pleasing and triumphant consideration in religion than this, of the perpetual progress which the soul makes towards the perfection of its nature, without ever arriving at a period in it. To look upon the soul as going on from strength to strength, to consider that she is to shine for ever with new accessions of glory, and brighten to all eternity; that she will be still adding virtue to virtue, and knowledge to knowledge—carries in it something wonderfully agreeable to that ambition which is natural to the mind of man. Nay, it must be a prospect pleasing to God himself, to see his creation for ever beautifying in his eyes, and drawing nearer to him by greater degrees of resemblance.[24]

In "Heaven Below," his 1884 sermon on Revelation 7:16–17, the great English preacher Charles Spurgeon paints an awe-inspiring picture of that grand tour of eternity:

Now, even in heaven the holy ones need guiding, and Jesus leads the way. While he is guiding, he points out to his people the secret founts and fresh springs which as yet they have not tasted. As eternity goes on, I have no doubt that the Saviour will be indicating fresh delights to his redeemed. "Come hither," saith he to his flock, "here are yet more flowing streams." He will lead them on and on, by the century, aye, by the chiliad, from glory unto glory, onward and upward in growing knowledge and enjoyment. Continually will he conduct his flock to deeper mysteries and higher glories. Never will the inexhaustible God who has given himself to be the portion of his people ever be fully known, so that there will eternally be sources of freshness and new delight, and the Shepherd will continue to lead his flock to these living fountains of water.[25]

And perhaps none casts the image with such rich imagination as C. S. Lewis. In "Farewell to Shadowlands," chapter 16 of *The Last Battle*, his simple yet profound final book of *The Chronicles of Narnia* saga, he writes:

And for us this is the end of all the stories, and we can most truly say that they all lived happily ever after. But for them it was only the beginning of the real story. All their life in this world and all their adventures in Narnia had only been the cover and the title page: now at last they were beginning Chapter One of the Great Story which no one on earth has read: which goes on forever: in which every chapter is better than the one before.[26]

Finally, Irenaeus in *Against Heresies* 5.36.2—the concluding chapter of his epic defense of the Trinitarian creation-fall-redemption narrative centered on Christ's person and work in his first *and second* coming—sums up well the glorious destiny and destination of the saints:

24. Joseph Addison, "Immorality of the Soul, and Future State," *The Evidences of the Christian Religion* (London: Allman, 1825), 188.
25. Charles H. Spurgeon, "Heaven Below," Sermon 1800 (September 21, 1884), *The Metropolitan Tabernacle Pulpit Sermons*, vol. 30 (London: Passmore & Alabaster, 1884), 515–16.
26. C. S. Lewis, *The Last Battle* (New York: Macmillan, 1956; repr., New York: HarperCollins, 2007), 210–11.

The presbyters, the disciples of the apostles, affirm that this is the gradation and arrangement of those who are saved, and that they advance through steps of this nature; also that they ascend through the Spirit to the Son, and through the Son to the Father, and that in due time the Son will yield up His work to the Father, even as it is said by the apostle, "For He must reign till He hath put all enemies under His feet. The last enemy that shall be destroyed is death." For in the times of the kingdom, the righteous man who is upon the earth shall then forget to die.

Bibliography
(Includes Go Deeper Excurses)

Adams, Jay E. *The Time Is at Hand*. Philadelphia: P&R, 1970.

Addison, Joseph. "Immorality of the Soul, and Future State." *The Evidences of the Christian Religion*. London: Allman, 1825.

Aernie, Matthew D., and Donald E Hartley. *The Righteous and Merciful Judge: The Day of the Lord in the Life and Theology of Paul*. Studies in Scripture and Biblical Theology. Bellingham, WA: Lexham, 2018.

Aldridge, Robert E. "The Lost Ending of the *Didache*." *VigChr* 53 (1999): 1–15.

Alexander, Ralph H. "Ezekiel." Vol. 7 of *The Expositor's Bible Commentary: Jeremiah–Ezekiel*, edited by Tremper Longman III and David E. Garland. Grand Rapids: Zondervan, 2010.

Alford, Henry. *Alford's Greek Testament: An Exegetical and Critical Commentary*. 5th ed. Vol. 4. Part 2. Grand Rapids: Guardian, 1976.

———. *The Greek Testament*. Vol. 4. Boston: Lee and Shepard, 1878.

Allen, Leslie C. *Ezekiel 1–19*. Vol. 38, in Word Biblical Commentary, edited by David A. Hubbard, Glenn W. Barker, and John D. W. Watts. Grand Rapids: Zondervan, 1987.

Anonymous. *The Retrospect, Being an Enquiry into the Fulfillment of Prophecy during the Last Twenty Years*. London: Painter, 1845.

Anonymous ("A Graduate of the University of Cambridge"). *The Rule, Based on the Word of God, for the Calculation of Time in the Prophecies of the Old and New Testament*. London: Simpkin, Marshall, and Co., 1843.

Armerding, Carl E. "Habakkuk" and "Obadiah." Vol. 8 of *The Expositor's Bible Commentary: Daniel–Malachi*, edited by Tremper Longman III and David E. Garland. Grand Rapids: Zondervan, 2008.

Armstrong, A. H. "Dualism: Platonic, Gnostic, and Christian." *Neoplatonism and Gnosticism*. Vol. 6 of *Studies in Neoplatonism: Ancient and Modern*, edited by Richard T. Wallis and Jay Bregman. Albany: State University of New York Press, 1992.

Arnold, Bill T. "Old Testament Eschatology and the Rise of Apocalypticism." In *The Oxford Handbook of Eschatology*, edited by Jerry L. Walls. Oxford: Oxford University Press, 2008.

Arnold, Brian J. "'To Behold Its Own Delight': The Beatific Vision in Irenaeus of Lyons." *Perichoresis* 17.2 (2019): 27–40.

Audet, Jean-Paul. *La Didachè: Instructions des Apôtres*. Paris: Gabalda, 1958.

Augustine. *The City of God, Books XVII–XXII*. Translated by Gerald G. Walsh and Daniel J. Honan. The Fathers of the Church. Washington, DC: The Catholic University of America Press, 1954.

Aune, David. *Revelation 1–5*. Vol. 52A of Word Biblical Commentary. Dallas: Word, 1997.

———. *Revelation 17–22*. Vol. 52C of Word Biblical Commentary. Grand Rapids: Zondervan, 2016.

Austin, Benjamin M. "Afterlife." In *Lexham Theological Wordbook*, edited by Douglas Mangum et al. Lexham Bible Reference Series. Bellingham, WA: Lexham, 2014.

Ayroulet, Élie, and Marie L. Chaieb. "Quelle fin des temps? L'eschatologie d'Irénée de Lyon." *NRTh* 143.1 (2021): 34–45.

Baines, T. B. *The Revelation of Jesus Christ*. 2nd ed. New York: Loizeaux Bros., 1911.

Baker, David W. *Nahum, Habakkuk, Zephaniah*. Vol. 23B of Tyndale Old Testament Commentaries. Downers Grove, IL: InterVarsity, 1988.

———. "Obadiah." In *Obadiah, Jonah and Micah: An Introduction and Commentary*, edited by David W. Baker, T. Desmond Alexander, and Bruce K. Waltke. Vol. 26 of Tyndale Old Testament Commentaries, edited by Donald J. Wiseman. Reprint, Downers Grove, IL: IVP Academic, 2009.

Baldwin, Joyce G. *Daniel: An Introduction and Commentary*. Vol. 23 of Tyndale Old Testament Commentaries. Downers Grove, IL: InterVarsity, 1978.

Baldwin, Joyce G. *Haggai, Zechariah and Malachi: An Introduction and Commentary*. Vol. 28 of Tyndale Old Testament Commentaries. Downers Grove, IL: InterVarsity, 1972.

Barbieri, Louis A. *First and Second Peter*. Chicago: Moody, 1977.

Barbieri Jr., Louis A. "Matthew." Vol. 2 of *The Bible Knowledge Commentary: An Exposition of the Scriptures*, edited by John F. Walvoord and Roy B. Zuck. Wheaton, IL: Victor, 1985.

Barker, Kenneth L. *Micah, Nahum, Habakkuk, Zephaniah*. Vol. 20 of The New American Commentary. Nashville: Broadman & Holman, 1999.

Barnard, Leslie W. "The 'Epistle of Barnabas' and Its Contemporary Setting." In *Aufstieg und Niedergang der Römischen Welt Part II, Principat*, edited by Wolfgang Haase. Vol. 27.1 of *Religion (Vorkonstantinische Christentum: Apostolischen Väter und Apologeten)*. Berlin: De Gruyter, 1993.

———. "The Problem of the Epistle of Barnabas." *ChQR* 159.2 (1958): 211–30.

———. "The Shepherd of Hermas in Recent Study." *Heythrop Theological Journal* 9.1 (1968): 29–36.

Barrett, C. K. *A Commentary on the First Epistle to the Corinthians*. New York: Harper & Row, 1968.

———. "The Eschatology of the Epistle to the Hebrews." In *The Background of the New Testament and its Eschatology*, edited by W. D. Davies and D. Daube. Cambridge: Cambridge University Press, 1956.

Bass, Clarence B. *Backgrounds to Dispensationalism: Its Historical Genesis and Ecclesiastical Implications*. Eugene, OR: Wipf & Stock, 2005.

Bauckham, Richard J. *Jesus and the Eyewitnesses: The Gospels as Eyewitness Testimony*. 2nd ed. Grand Rapids: Eerdmans, 2017.

———. *Jude–2 Peter*. Vol. 50 of Word Biblical Commentary. Nashville: Thomas Nelson, 1983.

———. "Sabbath and Sunday in the Post-Apostolic Church." In *From Sabbath to Lord's Day: A Biblical, Historical, and Theological Investigation*, edited by D. A. Carson. Grand Rapids: Zondervan, 1982.

Beach, J. Mark. "The Kingdom of God: A Brief Exposition of Its Meaning and Implications." *MAJT* 23 (2012): 53–76

Beale, G. K. "Adam as the First Priest in Eden as the Garden Temple." *SBJT* 22.2 (2018): 9–24.

———. *The Book of Revelation: A Commentary on the Greek Text*. The New International Greek Testament Commentary, edited by I. Howard Marshall and Donald A. Hagner. Grand Rapids: Eerdmans, 1999.

———. *John's Use of the Old Testament in Revelation*. Sheffield, UK: Sheffield Academic, 1998.

———. *A New Testament Biblical Theology: The Unfolding of the Old Testament in the New*. Grand Rapids: Baker Academic, 2011.

———. *Revelation: A Shorter Commentary*. Grand Rapids: Eerdmans, 2015.

Beasley-Murray, G. R. *The Book of Revelation*. New Century Bible Commentary, edited by Ronald E. Clements, Matthew Black. London: Marshall, Morgan & Scott, 1974. Reprint, Grand Rapids: Eerdmans, 1981.

Beckwith, Isbon T. *The Apocalypse of John*. New York: Macmillan, 1919.

Beckwith, Roger T. *The Old Testament Canon of the New Testament Church and Its Background in Early Judaism*. Eugene, OR: Wipf and Stock, 2008.

Behr, John. *Irenaeus of Lyons: Identifying Christianity*. Christian Theology in Context. Oxford: Oxford University Press, 2013.

Ben Hyrcanus, Rabbi Eliezer. "The History of Jonah." In *Pirke de Rabbi Eliezer*, edited and translated by Gerald Friedlander. New York: Bloch, 1916.

Bennett, James. *The Second Advent*. London: James Nisbet, 1878.

Berchman, Robert M. "Origen and the Reworking of the Legacy of Greek Philosophy." In *The Oxford Handbook of Origin*, edited by Ronald E. Heine and Karen Jo Torjesen. Oxford: Oxford University Press, 2022.

Berkhof, Louis. *The History of Christian Doctrines*. Carlisle, PA: Banner of Truth Trust, 1969.

Best, Ernest. *The First and Second Epistles to the Thessalonians*. Blank's New Testament Commentary. London: Continuum, 1986.

Beukin, Willem A. M. *Jesaja 1–12*. Herders Theologischer Kommentar zum Alten Testament. Freiburg: Herders, 2003.

Blaising, Craig A. "The Day of the Lord Will Come: An Exposition of 2 Peter 3:1–18." *BSac* 169.4 (2012): 387–401.

———. "Early Christian Millennialism and the Intermediate State." *BSac* 177.2 (2020): 221–33.

Blass, Friedrich, and Albert Debrunner. *A Greek Grammar of the New Testament and Other Early Christian Literature*. Translated and revised by R. W. Funk. Chicago: University of Chicago Press, 1961.

Block, Daniel I. *The Book of Ezekiel*. The New International Commentary on the Old Testament Grand Rapids: Eerdmans, 1997.

Blomberg, Craig. *Matthew*. Vol. 22 of The New American Commentary. Nashville: Broadman & Holman, 1992.

———. "The Posttribulationism of the New Testament: Leaving 'Left Behind' Behind." In *A Case for Historic Premillennialism: An Alternative to "Left Behind" Eschatology*, edited by Craig L. Blomberg and Sung Wook Chung. Grand Rapids: Baker Academic, 2009.

Boase, Charles William. *The Elijah Ministry: Tokens of Its Mission to the Christian Church Deduced from the Ministry of John the Baptist to the Jews*. Edinburgh: Robert Grant & Son, 1868.

Bock, Darrell L. *Acts*. Baker Exegetical Commentary on the New Testament. Grand Rapids: Baker Academic, 2007.

Boethius. *The Theological Tractates: The Consolation of Philosophy*. Translated by H. F. Stewart and E. K. Rand. The Loeb Classical Library. London: Heinemann, 1918.

Boettner, Loraine. *The Millennium*. Phillipsburg, NJ: P&R, 1957.

Bonura, Christopher. "Eusebius of Caesarea, the Roman Empire, and the Fulfillment of Biblical Prophecy: Reassessing Byzantine Imperial Eschatology in the Age of Constantine." *CH* 90.3 (2021): 509–36.

Böttrich, Christfried. "The 'Book of the Secrets of Enoch' (2 EN): Between Jewish Origin and Christian Transmission. An Overview." In *New Perspectives on 2 Enoch: No Longer Slavonic Only*, edited by Andrei Orlov and Gabriele Boccaccini. Leiden: Brill, 2012.

Bowdler, Henrietta Maria. *Practical Observations on the Book of the Revelations*. Oxford: J. Fletcher, 1787.

Boxall, Ian. *The Revelation of Saint John*. Black's New Testament Commentary. London: Continuum, 2006.

Brannan, Rick, trans. *The Apostolic Fathers in English*. Bellingham, WA: Lexham, 2012.

Bratcher, Robert G., and Howard Hatton *A Handbook on the Revelation to John*. UBS Handbook Series. New York: United Bible Societies, 1993.

Bratcher, Robert G., and William David Reyburn. *A Translator's Handbook on the Book of Psalms*. UBS Handbook Series. New York: United Bible Societies, 1991.

Bredero, Adriaan H. *Christendom and Christianity in the Middle Ages: The Relations between Religion, Church, and Society*. Translated by Reinder Bruinsma. Grand Rapids: Eerdmans, 1994.

Bredin, Mark. *Jesus, Revolutionary of Peace: A Nonviolent Christology in the Book of Revelation*. Milton Keynes, UK: Paternoster, 2003.

Bright, John. *The Kingdom of God: The Biblical Concept and Its Meaning for the Church*. New York: Abington-Cokesbury, 1953.

Briley, Terry R. *Isaiah*. Vols.1–2 of The College Press NIV Commentary. Joplin, MO: College, 2000.

Brindle, Wayne A. "Biblical Evidence for the Imminence of the Rapture." *BSac* 158.2 (2001): 138–51.

Brock, Rita Nakashima, and Rebecca Ann Parker. *Saving Paradise: How Christianity Traded Love of This World for Crucifixion and Empire*. Boston: Beacon, 2008.

Brouwer, Wayne. "Understanding Chiasm and Assessing Macro-Chiasm as a Tool of Biblical Interpretation." *CTJ* 53.1 (2018): 99–127.

Brown, Francis, Samuel Rolles Driver, and Charles Augustus Briggs. *Enhanced Brown-Driver-Briggs Hebrew and English Lexicon*. Oxford: Clarendon Press, 1977.

Brox, Norbert. *Der Hirt des Hermas*. Vol. 7 of Kommentar zu den Apostolischen Vätern. Göttingen: Vandenhoeck & Ruprecht, 1991.

———."Die weggeworfenen Steine im Pastor Hermae Vis III,7,5." *ZNW* 80.1–2 (1989): 130–33.

Bruce, F. F. *1 & 2 Corinthians*. The New Century Bible Commentary. Grand Rapids: Eerdmans, 1971.

———. *1 & 2 Thessalonians*. Vol. 45 of Word Biblical Commentary. Grand Rapids: Zondervan, 1982.

Brueggemann, Walter A. *To Build, to Plant: A Commentary on Jeremiah 26–52*. International Theological Commentary. Grand Rapids: Eerdmans, 1991.

———. *Isaiah 1–39*. Westminster Bible Companion, edited by Patrick D. Miller and David L. Bartlett. Louisville: Westminster John Knox, 1998.

Brumley, Albert E. "I'll Fly Away." In *The Hymnal for Worship and Celebration*. Waco, TX: Word Music, 1986.

Buie, Caroline P., and Michael J. Svigel. *The Shepherd of Hermas: A New Translation and Commentary*. The Apostolic Fathers Commentary Series. Eugene, OR: Cascade, 2023.

Burkett, Delbert. *The Son of Man Debate: A History and Evaluation*. Cambridge: Cambridge University Press, 1999.

Burnet, Thomas. *The Sacred Theory of the Earth*. London: Walter Kettilby, 1690.

Burnett, Fred W. "Παλιγγενεσία in Matt. 19:28: A Window on the Matthean Community?" *JSNT* 5.17 (1983): 60–72.

Burton, Ernest De Witt. *Syntax of the Moods and Tenses in New Testament Greek*. 3rd ed. Edinburg: T&T Clark, 1898.

Buswell, James O. *A Systematic Theology of the Christian Religion*. Vol. 2. Grand Rapids: Zondervan, 1963.

Butler, Trent C. *Luke*. Vol. 3 of Holman New Testament Commentary. Nashville: B&H, 2000.

Caird, G. B. *The Revelation of Saint John*. Black's New Testament Commentary. London: Black, 1966. Reprint, Peabody, MA: Hendrickson, 1993.

Calvin, John. *Commentary on the Book of the Prophet Isaiah*. Vol. 1. Translated by William Pringle. Bellingham, WA: Logos, 2010.

———. *Commentary on the Book of the Prophet Isaiah*. Vol. 4. Translated by William Pringle. Edinburgh: Calvin Translation Society, 1853.

———. *Commentaries on the Catholic Epistles*. Translated by John Owen. Edinburgh: Calvin Translation Society, 1855.

———. *Commentary on the First Book of Moses Called Genesis*. Vol. 1. Translated by John King. Bellingham, WA: Logos, 2010.

———. *Institutes of the Christian Religion*. 2 vols. Translated by Henry Beveridge. Grand Rapids: Eerdmans, 1989.

Campbell, R. Alastair. "Triumph and Delay: The Interpretation of Revelation 19:11–20:10." *EvQ* 80.1 (2008): 3–12.

Carlson, Stephen C. "Fragments of Papias." In *The Cambridge Companion to the Apostolic Fathers*, edited by Michael F. Bird and Scott D. Harrower. Cambridge: Cambridge University Press, 2021.

Carpenter, Eugene. *Exodus*. Vol. 2 of Evangelical Exegetical Commentary, edited by H. Wayne House and William D. Barrick. Bellingham, WA: Lexham, 2012.

Carson, D. A. *Exegetical Fallacies*. 2nd ed. Grand Rapids: Baker, 1996.

———. "Matthew." In *Matthew–Mark*. Vol. 9 of *The Expositor's Bible Commentary*, edited by Tremper Longman III and David E. Garland. Grand Rapids: Zondervan, 2010.

Casey, Maurice. "The Corporate Interpretation of 'One Like a Son of Man' (Dan. vii 13) at the Time of Jesus." *NovT* 18.3 (1976): 167–80.

———. *The Solution to the 'Son of Man' Problem*. New York: T&T Clark, 2009.

Chadwick, Henry, ed. *Alexandrian Christianity*. The Library of Christian Classics. Philadelphia: Westminster, 1954.

Charles, Robert Henry. *A Critical and Exegetical Commentary on the Revelation of St. John*. Vol. 1 of International Critical Commentary. Edinburgh: T&T Clark, 1920.

———, ed. *Pseudepigrapha of the Old Testament*. Vol. 2. Oxford: Clarendon, 1913.

Charles, Robert Henry, and W. O. E. Oesterley. *The Book of Enoch*. London: SPCK, 1917.

Charlesworth, James H., ed. *The Old Testament Pseudepigrapha*. Vol. 1 of *Apocalyptic Literature and Testaments*. Garden City, NY: Doubleday, 1983.

Chester, Andrew. "The Parting of the Ways: Eschatology and Messianic Hope." Vol. 66 of *Jews and Christians: The Parting of the Ways AD 70–135*, edited by James D. G. Dunn. WUNT. Tübingen: Mohr Siebeck, 1992.

Chilton, Bruce D. "The Transfiguration: Dominical Assurance and Apostolic Vision," *NTS* 27.1 (1980): 115–24.

Chisholm, Robert B. *Handbook on the Prophets*. Grand Rapids: Baker Academic, 2002.

Chouinard, Larry. *Matthew*. The College Press NIV Commentary. Joplin, MO: College Press, 1997.

Christian, Ed. "A Chiasm of Seven Chiasms: The Structure of the Millennial Vision, Rev 19:1–21:8." *AUSS* 37.2 (1999): 209–25.

Chung, Sung Wook. "Historic Premillennialism." In *Models of Premillennialism*, edited by Sung Wook Chung and David Mathewson. Eugene, OR: Wipf & Stock, 2018.

Clark, Gordon H. *1 & 2 Peter*. Phillipsburg, NJ: Presbyterian and Reformed, 1980.

Clarke, Adam. *The New Testament of Our Lord and Saviour Jesus Christ with Commentary and Critical Notes*. Philadelphia: Thomas, Cowperthwait & Co., 1844.

Coggins, R. J. *Sirach*. Guides to Apocrypha and Pseudepigrapha. Sheffield, UK: Sheffield Academic, 1998.

Collins, Adela Yarbro. "Paul in Irenaeus on the Last Things." In *Irenaeus and Paul*, edited by Todd D. Still and David E. Wilhite. Pauline and Patristic Scholars in Debate. London: T&T Clark, 2020.

Collins, Brian C. "Were the Fathers Amillennial? An Evaluation of Charles Hill's *Regnum Caelorum*." *BSac* 177.2 (2020): 207–20.

Collins, J. J. "The Expectation of the End in the Dead Sea Scrolls." In *Eschatology, Messianism, and the Dead Sea Scrolls*, edited by Craig A. Evans and Peter W. Flint. Studies in the Dead Sea Scrolls and Related Literature. Grand Rapids: Eerdmans, 1997.

Colman, Benjamin. *Some of the Glories of Our Lord and Saviour Jesus Christ, Exhibited in Twenty Sacramental Discourses, Preached at Boston in New England*. London: Ford and Farmer, 1728.

Constable, Thomas L. *Notes on Isaiah*. https://planobiblechapel.org/tcon/notes/pdf/isaiah.pdf.

Conzelmann, Hans. *1 Corinthians*. Hermeneia: A Critical and Historical Commentary on the Bible. Philadelphia: Fortress, 1975.

———. *Acts of the Apostles*. Hermeneia: A Critical and Historical Commentary on the Bible. Minneapolis: Augsburg Fortress, 1988.

Cope, Lamar. "Matthew XXV: 31–46 'The Sheep and the Goats' Reinterpreted." *NovT* 11.1–2 (1969): 32–44.

Cortez, Marc. *Theological Anthropology: A Guide for the Perplexed*. London: T&T Clark, 2010.

Cramer, George H. *First and Second Peter*. Chicago: Moody, 1967.

Croskery, Thomas. *Plymouth-Brethrenism: A Refutation of Its Principles and Doctrines*. London: William Mullen, 1879.

D'Alès, A. *L'èdit de Calliste: Ètude sur les origines de la pènitence Chrètienne*. Bibliothèque de théologie historique. 2nd ed. Paris: Beauchesne, 1914.

Daley, Brian E. *The Hope of the Early Church: A Handbook of Patristic Eschatology*. Grand Rapids: Baker Academic, 1991.

Dallaire, Hélène M. "Joshua." Vol. 2 of *The Expositor's Bible Commentary: Numbers–Ruth*, edited by Tremper Longman III and David E. Garland. Grand Rapids: Zondervan, 2012.

Daniélou, Jean. *The Theology of Jewish Christianity*. London: Barton, Longman & Todd, 1964.

Daniélou, Jean. "La Typologie millénariste de la semaine dans le christianisme primitive." *VC* 2.1 (1948): 1–16.

Darby, John Nelson. *Lectures on the Second Coming*. London: Morrish, 1909.

———. *Notes on the Book of Revelations; to Assist Enquirers in Searching into That Book*. London: Central Tract Depot: 1839.

Davids, Peter H. *The Letters of 2 Peter and Jude*. The Pillar New Testament Commentary, edited by D. A. Carson. Grand Rapids: Eerdmans, 2006.

Davies, Gwyn. "'Dig for Victory'! Competitive Fieldwork in Classical Siege Operations." In *The Art of Siege Warfare and Military Architecture from the Classical World to the Middle Ages*, edited by Michael Eisenberg and Rabei Khamisy, 45–53. Oxford: Oxbow, 2021.

Davies, Philip R. "Eschatology at Qumran." *JBL* 104.1 (1985): 39–55.

Davies, W. D. *Paul and Rabbinic Judaism.* 3rd ed. London: SPCK, 1970.

Davies, W. D., and Dale C. Allison Jr. *A Critical and Exegetical Commentary on the Gospel according to Saint Matthew.* Vols. 2–3 of International Critical Commentary. London: T&T Clark, 2004.

Deane, Sidney Norton, trans. *St. Anselm: Proslogium; Monologium; An Appendix in Behalf of the Fool by Gaunilon; and Cur Deus Homo.* Reprint, Chicago: Open Court, 1926.

De Backer, Fabrice. *L'art du Siège Néo-Assyrien.* Vol. 61 of Culture and History of the Ancient Near East, edited by M. H. E. Weippert, Thomas Schneider, et al. Leiden: Brill, 2013.

De Jonge, H. J. "BOTRYC BOHCEI: The Age of Kronos and the Millennium in Papias of Hierapolis." In *Studies in Hellenistic Religions*, edited by M. J. Vermaseren, 37–49. Leiden: Brill, 1979.

De Jonge, Marinus. "The Expectation of the Future in the Psalms of Solomon." *Neot* 23.1 (1989): 93–117.

Delumeau, Jean. *History of Paradise: The Garden of Eden in Myth and Tradition.* Translated by Matthew O'Connell. New York: Continuum, 1995.

DeMar, Gary. *End Times Fiction: A Biblical Consideration of the Left Behind Theology.* Nashville: Thomas Nelson, 2001.

Dibelius, Martin. *Der Hirt des Hermas.* Vol. 4 of Apostolischen Väter. HNT. Tübingen: Mohr, 1923.

Dillon, John M. *The Middle Platonists, 80 B.C. to A.D. 220.* Ithaca, NY: Cornell University Press, 1996.

Dodd, C. H. *The Parables of the Kingdom.* London: Nisbet, 1935.

Dods, Marcus. *The Gospel of St. John.* Vol. 1. New York: George H. Doran, 1887.

Donelson, Lewis R. *1 & 2 Peter and Jude: A Commentary.* The New Testament Library, edited by C. Clifton Black, M. Eugene Boring, and John T. Carroll. Louisville: Westminster John Knox, 2010.

Draper, Jonathan A. "The Didache." In *The Apostolic Fathers: An Introduction*, edited by Wilhelm Pratscher. Waco, TX: Baylor University Press, 2010.

Duhaime, Jean. *War Texts: 1QM and Related Manuscripts.* Vol. 6 of the Companion to the Qumran Scrolls. London: T&T Clark, 2005.

Dumbrell, William J. *The Search for Order: Biblical Eschatology in Focus.* Grand Rapids: Baker, 1994.

Dunbar, David G. "Hippolytus of Rome and the Eschatological Exegesis of the Early Church." *WTJ* 45.2 (1983): 322–39.

———. "The Problem of Hippolytus of Rome: A Study in Historical-Critical Reconstruction." *JETS* 25.1 (1982): 63–74.

Dunn, Geoffrey D. *Tertullian.* The Early Church Fathers. New York: Routledge, 2004.

Dyer, Charles. *Future Babylon: The Biblical Arguments for Rebuilding Babylon.* Taos, NM: Dispensational, 2017.

Eaton, Michael A. *Ecclesiastes: An Introduction and Commentary.* Vol. 18 of Tyndale Old Testament Commentaries. Downers Grove, IL: InterVarsity, 1983.

Edwards, James R. *The Gospel according to Luke.* The Pillar New Testament Commentary, edited by D. A. Carson. Grand Rapids: Eerdmans, 2015.

Edwards, Lyford Paterson. "The Transformation of Early Christianity from an Eschatological to a Socialized Movement." PhD diss., University of Chicago, 1919.

Elwell, Walter A., and Barry J. Beitzel. "Magog." In *Baker Encyclopedia of the Bible.* Grand Rapids: Baker, 1988.

Emmerson, Richard Kenneth. *Antichrist in the Middle Ages.* Seattle, WA: University of Washington Press, 1981.

Eph'al, Israel. *The City Besieged: Siege and Its Manifestations in the Ancient Near East.* Vol. 36 of Culture and History of the Ancient Near East. Leiden: Brill, 2009.

Erickson, Millard. *A Basic Guide to Eschatology: Making Sense of the Millennium.* Grand Rapids: Baker, 1998.

———. *Christian Theology.* 3rd ed. Grand Rapids: Baker Academic, 2013.

Eusebius of Caesarea. *Commentary on Isaiah.* Translated by Jonathan J. Armstrong. Edited by Joel E. Elowsky. Ancient Christian Texts, edited by Thomas C. Oden and Gerald L. Bray. Downers Grove, IL: IVP Academic, 2013.

Evans, Craig A., and Peter W. Flint. Introduction to *Eschatology, Messianism, and the Dead Sea Scrolls,* edited by Craig A. Evans and Peter W. Flint. Studies in the Dead Sea Scrolls and Related Literature. Grand Rapids: Eerdmans, 1997.

Everson, A. Joseph. "The Days of Yahweh." *JBL* 93.3 (1974): 329–37.

Faber, George Stanley. *A Dissertation on the Prophecies, That Have Been Fulfilled, Are Now Fulfilling, or Will Hereafter Be Fulfilled.* Vol. 1. Boston: Andrews and Cummings, 1808.

Fairweather, Eugene R., ed. and trans. *A Scholastic Miscellany: Anselm to Ockham.* The Library of Christian Classics, edited by John Baillie, John T. McNeill, and Henry P. Van Dusen. Louisville: Westminster John Knox, 1956.

Falls, Thomas B. *Justin Martyr: The First Apology, the Second Apology, Dialogue with Trypho, Exhortation to the Greeks, Discourse to the Greeks, the Monarchy or the Rule of God.* Vol. 6 of The Fathers of the Church: A New Translation. Washington, DC: Catholic University of America Press, 1948.

Fanning, Buist M. *Revelation.* Zondervan Exegetical Commentary on the New Testament. Grand Rapids: Zondervan, 2020.

Farrer, Austin. *The Revelation of St. John the Divine.* Oxford: Oxford University, 1964.

Fee, Gordon D. *The First Epistle to the Corinthians.* New International Commentary on the New Testament. Grand Rapids: Eerdmans, 2014.

———. *The First and Second Letters to the Thessalonians.* The New International Commentary on the New Testament. Grand Rapids: Eerdmans, 2009.

———. *Revelation: A New Covenant Commentary.* New Covenant Commentary Series Eugene, OR: Cascade, 2011.

Ferguson, Everett. "Was Barnabas a Chiliast? An Example of Hellenistic Number Symbolism in *Barnabas* and Clement of Alexandria." In *Greeks, Romans, and Christians: Essays in Honor of Abraham J. Malherbe,* edited by David L. Balch, Everett Ferguson, and Wayne A. Meeks. Minneapolis: Fortress, 1990.

Finkelstein, Louis. "The Development of the Amidah." *JQR* 16.1 (1925): 1–43.

Ford, Josephine Massyngberde. *Revelation: Introduction, Translation and Commentary*. Vol. 38 of the Anchor Bible, edited by William Foxwell Albright and David Noel Freedman. Garden City, NY: Doubleday, 1975.

France, R. T. *The Gospel of Matthew*. In The New International Commentary on the New Testament, edited by Gordon D. Fee. Grand Rapids: Eerdmans, 2007.

———. *Matthew: An Introduction and Commentary*. Vol. 1 of Tyndale New Testament Commentaries. Downers Grove, IL: InterVarsity Press, 1985.

Friesen, Ivan D. *Isaiah*. In Believers Church Bible Commentary. Scottdale, PA: Herald, 2009.

Frye, Northrop. "Typology: Apocalypse." In *The Revelation of St. John the Divine*, edited by Harold Bloom. Modern Critical Interpretations. New York: Chelsea House, 1988.

Fuchs, Eric, and Pierre Reymond. *La deuxième épitre de saint Pierre, l'épitre de saint Jude*. 2nd ed. Vol. 13b of Commentaire du Nouveau Testament (deuxième série). Geneva: Labor et Fides, 1988.

Fuller, Michael E. *The Restoration of Israel: Israel's Re-gathering and the Fate of the Nations in Early Jewish Literature and Luke-Acts*. BZNW 138. Edited by James D. G. Dunn et al. Berlin: de Gruyter, 2006.

Funk, Franz Xaver, Andreas Lindemann, Henning Paulsen, et al., eds. *Die Apostolischen Väter: Griechisch-deutsche Parallelausgabe*. Tübingen: Mohr Siebeck, 1992.

Gaebelein, Arno C. *The Revelation*. New York: Loizeaux Brothers, 1961.

Gallusz, Laszlo. *The Throne Motif in the Book of Revelation*. Library of New Testament Studies 487. London: Bloomsbury T&T Clark, 2014.

Gardner, Paul. *2 Peter and Jude*. Focus on the Bible Commentaries. Fearn, UK: Christian Focus, 2001.

Gardner, Richard B. *Matthew*. Believers Church Bible Commentary. Scottdale, PA: Herald, 1991.

Garland, David E. *1 Corinthians*. Baker Exegetical Commentary on the New Testament. Grand Rapids: Baker Academic, 2003.

———. *2 Corinthians*. Vol. 29 of The New American Commentary. Nashville: Broadman & Holman, 1999.

Garrow, Alan John Philip. *Revelation*. London: Routledge, 1997.

Geldenhuys, Norval. *Commentary on the Gospel of Luke: The English Text with Introduction, Exposition and Notes*. The New International Commentary on the Old and New Testament. Grand Rapids: Eerdmans, 1952.

Gentry Jr., Kenneth L. *Before Jerusalem Fell: Dating the Book of Revelation*. Tyler, TX: Institute for Christian Economics, 1989.

———. *He Shall Have Dominion: A Postmillennial Eschatology*. 2nd ed. Tyler, TX: Institute for Christian Economics, 1997.

Gentry, Peter J., and Stephen J. Wellum. *Kingdom through Covenant: A Biblical-Theological Understanding of the Covenants*. Wheaton, IL: Crossway, 2012.

George, Timothy. *Theology of the Reformers*. Nashville: Broadman & Holman, 1988.

Giesen, Heinz. "Symbole und mythische Aussagen in der Johannes-Apokalypse und ihre theologische Bedeutung." Vol. 29 of *Studien zur Johannes-apokalypse*. Stuttgarter Biblische Aufsatzbände, Neues Testament, edited by Gerhard Dautzenberg and Norbert Lohfink. Stuttgart: Katholisches Bibelwerk, 2000.

Giet, Stanislas. *Hermas et les Pasteurs: les trois auteurs du Pasteur d'Hermas*. Paris: University of France Press, 1963.

Godet, Frédéric Louis. *Commentary on St. Paul's First Epistle to the Corinthians*. Vol. 2, translated by A. Cusin. Edinburgh: T&T Clark, 1893.

———. *A Commentary on the Gospel of St. Luke*. Vol. 2, translated by Edward William Shalders and M. D. Cusin. New York: Funk, 1881.

Goldingay, John E. *Daniel*. Vol. 30 of Word Biblical Commentary, edited by David A. Hubbard, John D. W. Watts, and Ralph P. Martin. Dallas: Word, 1989.

———. *Isaiah*. Understanding the Bible Commentary Series. Grand Rapids: Baker, 2012.

———. *Miracle in Isaiah: Divine Marvel and Prophetic Word*. Minneapolis: Fortress, 2022.

Goldsworthy, G. "Kingdom of God." In *New Dictionary of Biblical Theology*, edited by T. Desmond Alexander and Brian S. Rosner, 615–20. Downers Grove, IL: IVP, 2000.

Goodman, Martin. "Paradise, Gardens, and the Afterlife in the First Century CE." In *Paradise in Antiquity: Jewish and Christian Views*, edited by Markus Bockmuehl and Guy S. Stoumsa. Cambridge: Cambridge University Press, 2010.

Goodwyn, Henry. *The Judgment Seat of Christ*. London: Elliot Stock, 1876.

Govett, Robert. *Entrance into the Kingdom, or, Reward according to Works*. 2nd ed. London: Thynne, 1922.

———. *Govett on Revelation*. Vol. 2. Miami Springs, FL: Conley & Schoettle, 1981.

Gowan, Donald E. *Eschatology in the Old Testament*. 2nd ed. Edinburgh: T&T Clark, 2000.

Grabbe, Lester L. *Wisdom of Solomon*. T&T Clark Study Guides, edited by Michael A. Knibb, A. T. Lincoln, and R. N. Whybray. London: T&T Clark, 1997.

Grant, Robert M. *Irenaeus of Lyons*. The Early Church Fathers. London: Routledge, 1997.

Gray, George Buchanan. *A Critical and Exegetical Commentary on the Book of Isaiah, I–XXXIX*. International Critical Commentary. New York: Scribner's, 1912.

Gray, Sherman W. *The Least of My Brothers: Matthew 25:31–46: A History of Interpretation*, edited by Charles Talbert Atlanta: Scholars, 1989.

Green, Gene L. *The Letters to the Thessalonians*. The Pillar New Testament Commentary. Grand Rapids: Eerdmans, 2002.

Green, Michael. *2 Peter and Jude: An Introduction and Commentary*. Vol. 18 of Tyndale New Testament Commentaries. Downers Grove, IL: InterVarsity, 1987.

Greenside, S. L. *Early Latin Theology: Selections from Tertullian, Cyprian, Ambrose and Jerome*. The Library of Christian Classics. Ichthus Edition. Louisville: Westminster, 1956.

Gribben, Crawford. *Evangelical Millennialism in the Trans-Atlantic World, 1500–2000*. New York: Palgrave Macmillan, 2011.

Grogan, Geoffrey W. "Isaiah." Vol. 6 of *The Expositor's Bible Commentary: Proverbs–Isaiah*, edited by Tremper Longman III and David E. Garland. Grand Rapids: Zondervan, 2008.

Grudem, Wayne. *Bible Doctrine: Essential Teachings of the Christian Faith*. Edited by Jeff Purswell. Grand Rapids: Zondervan, 1999.

Gumerlock, Francis X. "Cassiodorus: *Brief Explanations on the Apocalypse*." In *Cassiodorus, St. Gregory the Great, and Anonymous Greek Scholia: Writings on the Apocalypse*, translated by Francis X. Gumerlock, Mark Delcogliano, and T. C. Schmidt. The Fathers of the Church: A New Translation, edited by David H. Hunter et al. Washington, DC: The Catholic University of America Press, 2022.

———. "Millennialism and the Early Church Councils: Was Chiliasm Condemned at Constantinople?" *FH* 36.2 (2004): 83–95.

Gumerlock, Francis X., Francesca Lecchi, and Tito Orlandi. *Pseudo-Cyril of Alexandria: Commentary on the Apocalypse*. Middletown, RI: Stone Tower, 2021.

Gundry, Robert H. *The Church and the Tribulation: A Biblical Examination of Post-tribulationism*. Grand Rapids: Zondervan, 1973.

———. *First the Antichrist*. Grand Rapids: Baker, 1997.

Guthrie, Donald. *New Testament Introduction*. Downers Grove, IL: InterVarsity, 1990.

———. *The Relevance of John's Apocalypse*. The Didsbury Lectures. Grand Rapids: Eerdmans, 1987.

Gwatkin, Henry Melvill. *Selections from Early Writers Illustrative of Church History to the Time of Constantine*. London: Macmillan, 1897.

Hagner, Donald A. *Matthew 14–28*. Vol. 33B of the Word Biblical Commentary. Grand Rapids: Zondervan, 2018.

Hahn, Roger L. *Matthew: A Commentary for Bible Students*. Indianapolis: Wesleyan, 2007.

Hall, Christopher A. "Christ's Kingdom and Paradise." *CT* 47.11 (November 2003): 79.

Hall, Thomas. *A Practical and Polemical Commentary or, Exposition upon the Third and Fourth Chapters of the Latter Epistle of Saint Paul to Timothy*. London: John Starkey, 1658.

Halton, Thomas P. *Saint Jerome: On Illustrious Men*. Vol. 10 of The Fathers of the Church: A New Translation. Washington, DC: Catholic University of America Press, 1999.

Harnack, Adolf von. *History of Dogma*. Vol. 1. 3rd ed. Translated by Neil Buchanan. Boston: Little, Brown, and Company, 1902.

Harrington, Daniel J. *The Gospel of Matthew*. Vol. 1 of the Sacra Pagina Series. Collegeville, MN: Liturgical, 2007.

Harris, J. Rendel, ed. and trans. *The Apology of Aristides on Behalf of the Christians*. 2nd ed. Cambridge: Cambridge University Press, 1893.

Harris, Murray J. *Raised Immortal: Resurrection and Immortality in the New Testament*. Grand Rapids: Eerdmans, 1983.

Harrison, Norman B. *The End: Re-Thinking the Revelation*. Minneapolis: Harrison Service, 1948.

Hart, Ian. "Genesis 1:1–2:3 as a Prologue to the Book of Genesis." *TynBul* 46.2 (1995): 315–36.

Hart, John F., ed. *Evidence for the Rapture: A Biblical Case for Pretribulationism.* Chicago: Moody, 2015.

Hartog, Paul A. "Patristic Era (AD 100–250)." In *Discovering Dispensationalism: Tracing the Development of Dispensational Thought from the First to the Twenty-First Century,* edited by Cory M. Marsh and James I. Fazio. El Cajon, CA: SCS Press, 2023.

Hendriksen, William. *Exposition of the Gospel according to Matthew.* New Testament Commentary. Grand Rapids: Baker, 1975.

———. *More Than Conquerors: An Interpretation of the Book of Revelation.* Grand Rapids: Baker, 1967.

Hengstenberg, E. W. *The Revelation of St. John, Expounded for Those who Search the Scriptures.* Vol. 2. Translated by Patrick Fairbairn. Edinburgh: T&T Clark, 1852.

Henne, Philippe. "Canonicité du 'Pasteur'd'Hermas." *RThom* 90.1 (1990): 81–100.

———. *L'unité du Pasteur d'Hermas: tradition et redaction.* Paris: Gabalda, 1992.

Hermans, Albert. "Le Pseudo-Barnabé Est-il Millénariste?" *ETL* 35.4 (1959): 849–76.

Hilber, John W. "Theology of Worship in Exodus 24." *JETS* 39.2 (1996): 177–89.

Hill, Andrew E. *Haggai, Zechariah and Malachi: And Introduction and Commentary.* Vol. 28 of Tyndale Old Testament Commentaries, edited by David G. Firth and Tremper Longman III. Downers Grove, IL: IVP Academic, 2012.

Hill, Charles E. "The Debate over the Muratorian Fragment and the Development of the Canon." *WTJ* 57.2 (1997): 437–52.

———. *The Johannine Corpus in the Early Church.* Oxford: Oxford University Press, 2004.

———. "Paul's Understanding of Christ's Kingdom in 1 Corinthians 15:20–28." *NovT* (1988): 297–320.

———. *Regnum Caelorum: Patterns of Millennial Thought in Early Christianity.* 2nd ed. Grand Rapids: Eerdmans, 2001.

Hodge, Charles. *Systematic Theology.* Vol. 3. New York: Scribner, 1872.

Hoegen-Rohls, Christina. "Κτίσις and καινὴ κτίσις in Paul's Letters." In *Paul, Luke and the Graeco-Roman World: Essays in Hon our of Alexander J. M. Wedderburn,* edited by Alf Christophersen, Carsten Claussen, Jörg Frey and Bruce Longenecker, 114–22. JSNTSup. 217. London: Sheffield Academic, 2002.

Hoekema, Anthony A. *The Bible and the Future.* Grand Rapids: Eerdmans, 1979.

Hoeksema, Herman. *Behold, He Cometh!* Edited and revised by Homer C. Hoeksema. Grand Rapids: Reformed Free, 1969.

Hoffmann, Yair. "The Day of the Lord Concept and a Term in the Prophetic Literature." *ZAW* 93.1 (1981): 37–50.

———. "Eschatology in the Book of Jeremiah." In *Eschatology in the Bible and in Jewish and Christian Tradition,* edited by Henning Graf Reventlow. JSOTSup. 243. Sheffield, UK: Sheffield Academic, 1997.

Hogeterp, Albert L. A. *Expectations of the End: A Comparative Traditio-Historical Study of Eschatological, Apocalyptic and Messianic Ideas in the Dead Sea*

Scrolls and the New Testament. Studies on the Texts of the Desert of Judah.
Vol. 83. Leiden: Brill, 2009.

Holmes, Michael W., ed. *The Apostolic Fathers: Greek Texts and English Translations of Their Writings.* 3rd ed. Grand Rapids: Baker, 2007.

Hopkins, Samuel. *A Treatise on the Millennium.* Edinburgh: John Ogle, 1794.

Horner, Barry E. *Future Israel: Why Christian Anti-Judaism Must Be Challenged.* NAC Studies in Bible and Theology. Nashville: B&H Academic, 2007.

Horrell, David G. *The Epistles of Peter and Jude.* Peterborough, UK: Epworth, 1998.

Horsley, Richard A. *Jesus and the Powers: Conflict, Covenant, and the Hope of the Poor.* Minneapolis: Fortress, 2011.

Hort, Bernard. "Millénarisme ou amillénarisme? Regard contemporain sur un conflit traditionnel." *RL* 31 (2000): 33–42.

House, H. Wayne. "Premillennialism in the Ante-Nicene Church." *BSac* 169.3 (2012): 271–82.

Howes, Llewellyn. "Judging the Twelve Tribes of Israel: Q 22:28, 30 in Light of the Psalms of Solomon and the Community Rule." *VE* 35.1 (2014): 1–11.

Hubbard, David Allan. *Joel and Amos: An Introduction and Commentary.* Vol. 25 of Tyndale Old Testament Commentaries, edited by Donald J. Wiseman. Downers Grove, IL: IVP Academic, 1989.

Huchedé, Paschal. *History of Antichrist.* Translated by J. D. B. New York: Nicholas Bray, 1884.

Hughes, Philip Edgcumbe. *The Book of Revelation.* Grand Rapids: Eerdmans, 1990.

———. "The First Resurrection: Another Interpretation." *WTJ* 39.2 (1977): 315–18.

Hughes, R. Kent. *Genesis: Beginning and Blessing.* Preaching the Word. Wheaton, IL: Crossway, 2004.

Instone-Brewer, David. "The Eighteen Benedictions and the Minim before 70 CE." *JTS* 54.1 (2003): 25–44.

Ironside, H. A. *Lectures on the Book of Revelation.* New York: Loizeaux Brothers, 1930.

———. *Revelation.* Ironside Commentaries. Neptune, NJ: Loizeaux Brothers, 1996.

Isenberg, Wesley W. "The Gospel According to Philip: Introduction." In *Nag Hammadi Codex II,2–7, together with XIII,2, Brit. Lib. Or. 4926(1), and P. Oxy. 1, 654, 655,* edited by Bentley Layton. Vol. 1 of *Gospel According to Thomas, Gospel According to Philip, Hypostasis of the Archons, and Indexes.* Vol. 20 of Nag Hammadi Studies, edited by Martin Krause, James M. Robinson, and Frederik Wisse. Leiden: Brill, 1989.

Jefford, Clayton N. *The Sayings of Jesus in the Teaching of the Twelve Apostles.* VCSup. 11. Leiden: Brill, 1989.

Jenks, Gregory C. *The Origins of the Early Development of the Antichrist Myth.* Berlin: de Gruyter, 1991.

Jeremias, Joachim. "Παράδεισος." Vol. 5 of *Theological Dictionary of the New Testament,* edited by Gerhard Kittel, Geoffrey W. Bromiley, and Gerhard Friedrich. Grand Rapids: Eerdmans, 1967.

———. *The Parables of Jesus.* Translated by S. H. Hooke. New York: Charles Scribner's Sons, 1963.

Jervell, J. *Luke and the People of God.* Minneapolis: Augsburg, 1972.

Johnson, Alan F. "Revelation." Vol. 13 of *The Expositor's Bible Commentary: Hebrews–Revelation*, edited by Tremper Longman III and David E. Garland. Grand Rapids: Zondervan, 2006.

Johnson, Amy Fryckholm. *Rapture Culture: Left Behind in Evangelical America.* New York: Oxford University Press, 2004.

Johnson, Dennis E. *Triumph of the Lamb: A Commentary on Revelation.* Phillipsburg, NJ: P&R, 2001.

Joly, Robert. "Le milieu complexe du 'Pasteur d'Hermas.'" Vol. 27 of *Aufstieg und Niedergang der Römischen Welt Part II, Principat.* 1: *Religion (Vorkonstantinische Christentum: Apostolischen Väter und Apologeten)*, edited by Wolfgang Haase. Berlin: De Gruyter, 1993.

Jones, Beth Felker. *Practicing Christian Doctrine: An Introduction to Thinking and Living Theologically.* Grand Rapids: Baker Academic, 2014.

Josephus. *The Works of Josephus: Complete and Unabridged.* Translated by William Whiston. Peabody, MA: Hendrickson, 1987.

Kaiser Jr., Walter C. "Exodus." Vol. 1 of *The Expositor's Bible Commentary: Genesis–Leviticus*, edited by Tremper Longman III and David E. Garland. Grand Rapids: Zondervan, 2008.

Kalvesmaki, Joel. *The Theology of Arithmetic: Number Symbolism in Platonism and Early Christianity.* Washington, DC: Center for Hellenic Studies, 2013.

Kapelrud, Arvid S. *The Message of the Prophet Zephaniah: Morphology and Ideas.* Oslo: Universitetsforlaget, 1975.

Keating, Daniel. *First and Second Peter, Jude.* Catholic Commentary on Sacred Scripture, edited by Peter S. Williamson and Mary Healy. Grand Rapids: Baker, 2011.

Kellum, L. Scott. *Acts.* B&H Exegetical Guide to the Greek New Testament, edited by Andreas J. Köstenberger and Robert W. Yarbrough. Nashville: B&H Academic, 2020.

Kelly, J. N. D. *A Commentary on the Epistles of Peter and of Jude.* Harper's New Testament Commentaries, edited by Henry Chadwick. New York: Harper & Row, 1969.

———. *Early Christian Doctrines.* 5th rev. ed. New York: HarperOne, 1978.

Kennedy, J. H. *Part of the Commentary of S. Hippolytus on Daniel (Lately Discovered by Dr. Basilios Georgiades), with Introduction, Notes, and Translation.* Dublin: Hodges & Figgis, 1888.

Keil, Carl Friedrich, and Franz Delitzsch. Vol. 1 of *Commentary on the Old Testament*, translated by James Martin. Edinburgh: T. & T. Clark, 1866. Reprint, Peabody, MA: Hendrickson, 1996.

Kidner, Derek. *Psalms 73–150: An Introduction and Commentary.* Vol. 16 of Tyndale Old Testament Commentaries. Downers Grove, IL: InterVarsity, 1975.

Kik, Marcellus J. *An Eschatology of Victory.* Phillipsburg, NJ: P&R, 1971.

Kimelman, Reuven. "The Daily Amidah and the Rhetoric of Redemption." *JQR* 79.2–3 (1988–1999): 165–97.

King, Greg A. "The Message of Zephaniah: An Urgent Echo." *AUSS* 32.2 (1996): 211–22.

Kirkland, Alastair. "The Literary History of the Shepherd of Hermas." *SC* 9.2 (1992): 87–102.

Kistemaker, Simon J. *Revelation*. New Testament Commentary. Grand Rapids: Baker, 2001.

Kleist, James A., ed. and trans. *The Didache, The Epistle of Barnabas, The Epistles and the Martyrdom of St. Polycarp, The Fragments of Papias, The Epistle of Diognetus*. New York: Newman, 1948.

Kline, Meredith G. *Axis of Glory: A Biblical and Theological Analysis of the Temple Motif in Scripture*. New York: Peter Lang, 2010.

———. "The First Resurrection." *WTJ* 37.3 (1975): 366–75.

———. "The First Resurrection: A Reaffirmation." *WTJ* 39.1 (1976): 110–19.

Kidner, Derek. *Genesis: An Introduction and Commentary*. Vol. 1 of Tyndale Old Testament Commentaries. Downers Grove, IL: InterVarsity, 1967.

Kissling, Paul J. *Genesis*. The College Press NIV Commentary. Joplin, MO: College Press, 2004.

Knibb, Michael. *Essays on the Book of Enoch and Other Early Jewish Texts and Traditions*. SVTP 22. Leiden: Brill, 2008.

Knoch, Otto. *Der Erste und Zweite Petrusbrief, Der Judasbrief*. Regensburger Neues Testament, edited by Jost Eckert and Otto Kuss. Regensburg: Friedrich Pustet, 1990.

Knollys, Hanserd. *An Exposition of the Whole Book of the Revelation*. London: Hanserd Knollys, 1689.

Koehler, Ludwig, et al. *The Hebrew and Aramaic Lexicon of the Old Testament*. Leiden: Brill, 1994–2000.

Koester, Craig R. *Revelation: A New Translation with Introduction and Commentary*. The Anchor Yale Bible. New Haven: Yale University Press, 2015.

Köstenberger, Andreas J., Alexander E. Stewart, and Apollo Makara. *Jesus and the Future: Understanding What He Taught about the End Times*. Bellingham, WA: Lexham, 2017.

Köstenberger, Andreas J., Benjamin L Merkle, and Robert L. Plummer. *Going Deeper with New Testament Greek: An Intermediate Study of the Grammar and Syntax of the New Testament*. Rev. ed. Nashville: B&H Academic, 2023.

Kraft, Robert A. *The Apostolic Fathers: A New Translation and Commentary*. Vol. 3 of *Barnabas and the Didache*, edited by Robert M. Grant. Camden, NJ: Nelson, 1965.

Kreitzer, L. Joseph. *Jesus and God in Paul's Eschatology*. JSNTSup. 19. Sheffield, UK: JSOT, 1987.

Kromminga, D. H. *The Millennium in the Church*. Grand Rapids: Eerdmans, 1945.

Krüger, Paul, and Matthew Haynes. "Creation Rest: Genesis 2:1–3 and the First Creation Account." *OTE* 30.3 (2017): 663–83.

Kruse, Colin G. *John: An Introduction and Commentary*. Vol. 4 of Tyndale New Testament Commentaries. Downers Grove, IL: InterVarsity, 2003.

Kugler, Robert. *The Testaments of the Twelve Patriarchs*. Guides to the Apocrypha and Pseudepigrapha. Sheffield, UK: Sheffield Academic, 2001.

Kurschner, Alan E. *A Linguistic Approach to Revelation 19:11–20:6 and the Millennium Binding of Satan.* Vol. 23 of Linguistic Biblical Studies. Leiden: Brill, 2022.

Kurschner, Alan E., and Michael J. Svigel. "Who Sat on the Thrones in Revelation 20:4? Ἐκάθισαν and Its Implications." Paper Presented to the Annual Meeting of the Evangelical Theological Society, November 17, 2021, Fort Worth, Texas.

Kurz, William S. *Reading Luke-Acts: Dynamics of Biblical Narrative.* Louisville: Westminster/John Knox, 1993.

Ladd, George Eldon. *A Commentary on the Revelation of John.* Grand Rapids: Eerdmans, 1972.

———. *The Gospel of the Kingdom: Scriptural Studies in the Kingdom of God.* Grand Rapids: Eerdmans, 1959.

———. "Kingdom of God (Heaven)." In *Baker Encyclopedia of the Bible*, 1269–78. Grand Rapids: Baker, 1988.

LaHaye, Tim. *The Rapture: Who Will Face the Tribulation?* Chicago: Moody, 2003.

Lake, Kirsopp, and J. E. L. Oulton, trans. *Eusebius: The Ecclesiastical History.* Vol. 2 of LCL. Cambridge, MA: Harvard University Press, 1926–1932.

Lampe, G. W. H., ed. *A Patristic Greek Lexicon.* Oxford: Clarendon, 1961.

Lang, George H. *The Revelation of Jesus Christ.* 2nd ed. London: Paternoster, 1948.

Lange, John Peter, and Philip Schaff. *A Commentary on the Holy Scriptures: John.* Bellingham, WA: Logos Bible Software, 2008.

Langen, Joseph. "Das älteste christliche Kirchenbuch." *HZ* 53.2 (1885): 193–214.

Lawson, John. *The Biblical Theology of Saint Irenaeus.* London: Epworth, 1948. Reprint, Eugene, OR: Wipf & Stock, 2006.

Leaney, A. R. C. *The Letters of Peter and Jude.* The Cambridge Bible Commentary on the New English Bible. Cambridge: Cambridge University Press, 1967.

Le Goff, Jacques. *The Birth of Purgatory.* Chicago: University of Chicago Press, 1984.

Leighton, Robert, and Griffith Thomas. *1, 2 Peter.* The Crossway Classic Commentaries, edited by Alister McGrath and J. I. Packer. Wheaton, IL: Crossway, 1999.

Leith, John H., ed. *The Creeds of Christendom: A Reader in Christian Doctrine from the Bible to the Present.* 3rd ed. Louisville: John Knox, 1982.

Leithart, Peter J. *Revelation 12–22.* International Theological Commentary. London: Bloomsbury T&T Clark, 2018.

Lennartsson, Göran. *Refreshing & Restoration: Two Eschatological Motifs in Acts 3:19–21.* Lund, SE: Lund University Center for Theology and Religious Studies, 2007.

Lenski, R. C. H. *The Interpretation of St. John's Revelation.* Columbus: Lutheran Book Concern, 1935.

———. *The Interpretation of St. Matthew's Gospel.* Minneapolis: Augsburg, 1961.

Lewis, C. S. *The Last Battle.* New York: Macmillan, 1956. Reprint, New York: HarperCollins, 2007.

———. *Surprised by Joy: The Shape of My Early Life.* New York: Harcourt, 1955.

Lewis, Charlton T., and Charles Short. *Harpers' Latin Dictionary.* New York: Harper & Brothers, 1891.

Liddell, Henry George, Robert Scott, and Henry Stuart Jones. *A Greek-English Lexicon*. Oxford: Clarendon, 1996.

Lietzmann, Hans. *An die Korinther I/II*. HNT 9. Tübingen: Mohr Siebeck, 1949.

Lindemann, Andreas. *Der Erste Korintherbrief*. HNT 9/1. Tübingen: Mohr Siebeck, 2000.

Lindsey, Hal. *Vanished into Thin Air: The Hope of Every Believer*. Los Angeles: Western Front, 1999.

Lincoln, Andrew T. *The Gospel according to Saint John*. Black's New Testament Commentary. London: Continuum, 2005.

Lioy, Daniel T. "The Garden of Eden as a Primordial Temple or Sacred Space for Humankind." *Conspectus* 10 (2010): 25–57.

Loman, Janni. "The *Letter of Barnabas* in Early Second-Century Egypt." In *The Wisdom of Egypt: Jewish, Early Christian, and Gnostic Essays in Honour of Gerard P. Luttikhuizen*, edited by Anthony Hilhorst and George H. van Kooten. Vol. 59 of Ancient Judaism and Early Christianity. Leiden: Brill, 2005.

Longman III, Tremper. "The Divine Warrior: The New Testament Use of an Old Testament Motif." *WTJ* 44.2 (1982): 290–307.

Lookadoo, Jonathan. *The Epistle of Barnabas: A Commentary*. Apostolic Father Commentary Series. Eugene, OR: Cascade, 2022.

Louw, Johannes P., and Eugene Albert Nida. *A Greek-English Lexicon of the New Testament: Based on Semantic Domains*. New York: United Bible Societies, 1996.

Luther, Martin. *The Epistles of St. Peter and St. Jude*. Translated by John Nicholas Lenker. Minneapolis: Lutherans in All Lands, 1904.

MacArthur Jr., John. *2 Peter and Jude*. The MacArthur New Testament Commentary. Chicago: Moody, 2005.

Macaskill, Grant. "Paradise in the New Testament." In *Paradise in Antiquity: Jewish and Christian Views*, edited by Markus Bockmuehl and Guy S. Stoumsa. Cambridge: Cambridge University Press, 2010.

MacLeod, David J. *Seven Last Things: An Exposition of Revelation 19–21*. Eugene, OR: Wipf & Stock, 2003.

MacPherson, Dave. *The Rapture Plot*. Simpsonville, SC: Millennium III, 1995.

Maimonides, Moses. *The Guide for the Perplexed*. Translated by M. Friedländer. London: Routledge, 1919.

Malinowski, Cościwit. "Septimontium (Seven Hills) as *conditio sine qua non* for a City to Pretend to Be a Capital." *Horizons* 8.1 (2017): 3–26.

Martin, E. G. "Eldad and Modad." Vol. 2 of *The Old Testament Pseudepigrapha*, edited by J. H. Charlesworth. Garden City, NY: Doubleday, 1985.

Martin, Gordon Wood. "Eschatology in the Early Church: with Special Reference to the Theses of C. H. Dodd and M. Werner." PhD diss., University of Edinburgh, 1971.

Martínez, Florentino García, and Eibert J. C. Tigchelaar. *The Dead Sea Scrolls Study Edition (Translations)*. Leiden: Brill, 1997–1998.

Mathews, Kenneth A. *Genesis 1–11: An Exegetical and Theological Exposition of Holy Scripture*. Vol. 1A of the New American Commentary. Nashville: Holman Reference, 1996.

Mathison, Keith A. *Postmillennialism: An Eschatology of Hope*. Phillipsburg, NJ: P&R, 1999.

McClain, Alva J. *The Greatness of the Kingdom: An Inductive Study of the Kingdom of God*. Chicago: Moody, 1968.

McClain, T. Van. "The Pretribulational Rapture: A Doubtful Doctrine." In *Looking into the Future: Evangelical Studies in Eschatology*, edited by David W. Baker. Grand Rapids: Baker, 2001.

McConville, J. Gordon. *Isaiah*. Baker Commentary on the Old Testament Prophetic Books, edited by Mark J. Boda and J. Gordon McConville. Grand Rapids: Baker, 2023.

McGinn, Bernard. *Antichrist: Two Thousand Years of the Human Fascination with Evil*. San Francisco: HarperCollins, 1994.

McGrath, Alister E. *Christian Theology: An Introduction*. Oxford: Blackwell, 1994.

Mealy, J. W. *After the Thousand Years: Resurrection and Judgment in Revelation 20*. JSNTSup. 7. Edited by Stanley E. Porter. Sheffield, UK: JSOT Press, 1992.

Meier, John P. *Matthew*. Collegeville, MN: Liturgical, 1980.

Ménard, Jacques-É. "La notion de 'résurrection' dans l'Épître à Rhèginos." Vol. 6 of *Essays on the Nag Hammadi Texts in Honour of Pahor Labib*, edited by Martin Krause, Nag Hammadi Studies, ed. Martin Krause, James M. Robinson, and Frederik Wisse. Leiden: Brill, 1975.

Merkle, Benjamin L. "Old Testament Restoration Prophecies Regarding the Nation of Israel: Literal or Symbolic?" *SBJT* 14.1 (2010): 14–25.

Merrill, Eugene H. "Malachi." Vol. 8 of *The Expositor's Bible Commentary: Daniel–Malachi*, edited by Tremper Longman III and David E. Garland. Grand Rapids: Zondervan, 2008.

Miceli, Vincent P. *The Antichrist*. Harrison, NY: Roman Catholic Books, 1981.

Michaels, J. Ramsey. "First Resurrection: A Response." *WTJ* 39.1 (1976): 100–09.

————. *Revelation*. The IVP New Testament Commentary Series. Downers Grove, IL: InterVarsity, 1997.

Middleton, J. Richard. *A New Heaven and a New Earth: Reclaiming Biblical Eschatology*. Grand Rapids: Baker Academic, 2014.

Milavec, Aaron. *The Didache: Faith, Hope, and Life of the Earliest Christian Communities, 50–70 CE*. New York: Newman, 2003.

Miller, Yonatan S. "Sabbath-Temple-Eden: Purity Rituals at the Intersection of Sacred Time and Space." *JAJ* 9.1 (2018): 50–51.

Minns, Denis. Irenaeus: An Introduction. New York: T&T Clark, 2010. Mitchell, Andrew. "Your Kingdom Come, Your Will Be Done: A Study of Matthew 6:10." *Bulletin for Biblical Research* 30.2 (2020): 208–30.

Moo, Douglas J. "Response to 'The Case for the Pretribulational Rapture Position.'" In *Three Views on the Rapture: Pre-, Mid-, or Post-Tribulational?*, edited by Stanley N. Gundry. Counterpoints. Grand Rapids: Zondervan, 1996.

Moore, Ernest. "ΒΙΑΖΩ, ΑΡΠΑΖΩ and Cognates in Josephus." *NTS* 21.4 (1975): 519–43.

Morgan, Christopher, and Robert A. Peterson, eds. *The Kingdom of God*. Theology in Community. Wheaton, IL: Crossway, 2012.

Morris, Leon. *1 Corinthians: An Introduction and Commentary*. Vol. 7 of Tyndale New Testament Commentaries. Downers Grove, IL: InterVarsity, 1985.

———. *1 and 2 Thessalonians: An Introduction and Commentary*. Vol. 13 of Tyndale New Testament Commentaries. Downers Grove, IL: InterVarsity, 1984.

———. *The Gospel according to Matthew*. The Pillar New Testament Commentary. Grand Rapids: Eerdmans, 1992.

———. *Revelation*. Tyndale New Testament Commentaries. Grand Rapids: Eerdmans, 1987.

———. *The Revelation of St. John*. The Tyndale New Testament Commentaries. Grand Rapids: Eerdmans, 1969.

Motyer, J. Alec. *Isaiah: An Introduction and Commentary*. Vol. 20 of Tyndale Old Testament Commentaries. Downers Grove, IL: IVP Academic, 1999.

Motyer, Stephen. *Come, Lord Jesus! A Biblical Theology of the Second Coming of Christ*. London: Apollos, 2016.

Moulton, James Hope, and Nigel Turner. *Syntax*. Vol. 3 in *A Grammar of New Testament Greek*. Edinburgh: T&T Clark, 1963.

Mounce, Robert H. *The Book of Revelation*. The New International Commentary on the New Testament. Grand Rapids: Eerdmans, 1977.

———. *The Book of Revelation*. The New International Commentary on the New Testament, edited by Gordon D. Fee. Grand Rapids: Eerdmans, 1997.

———. *Matthew*. Understanding the Bible Commentary Series. Grand Rapids: Baker, 1991.

Mulholland Jr., M. Robert. *Revelation: Holy Living in an Unholy World*. Francis Asbury Press Commentary, edited by M. Robert Mulholland Jr. Grand Rapids: Francis Asbury, 1990.

Müller, Mogens. *The Expression 'Son of Man' and the Development of Christology: A History of Interpretation*. New York: Routledge, 2008.

Mussies, Gerard. *The Morphology of Koine Greek as Used in the Apocalypse of St. John: A Study in Bilingualism*. NovTSup. Leiden: Brill, 1971.

Napiórkowski, Andrzej. "Is the Kingdom of Heaven the Church of Jesus Christ?" *Vox Patrum* 33 (2013): 547–57.

Navtanovich, Liudmila. "The Provenance of 2 Enoch: A Philological Perspective. A Response to C. Böttrich's Paper 'The "Book of the Secrets of Enoch" (2 EN): Between Jewish Origin and Christian Transmission. An Overview.'" In *New Perspectives on 2 Enoch: No Longer Slavonic Only*, edited by Andrei Orlov and Gabriele Boccaccini. Leiden: Brill, 2012.

Nebeker, Gary L. "John Nelson Darby and Trinity College, Dublin: A Study in Eschatological Contrasts." *Fides et Historia* 34.2 (2002): 87–108.

Nel, W. A. G. "Amos 9:11–15—An Unconditional Prophecy of Salvation during the Period of the Exile." *OTE* 2 (1984): 81–97.

Nellas, Panayiotis. *Deification in Christ: Orthodox Perspectives on the Nature of the Human Person*. Vol. 5 of Contemporary Greek Theologians. Yonkers, NY: St. Vladimirs Seminary Press, 1987.

Nevins, David Lord. *An Exposition of the Apocalypse*. New York: Harper and Brothers, 1847.

Newell, William R. *Revelation: Chapter-by-Chapter*. Grand Rapids: Kregel: 1994.

Newman, John Henry. "Advent Sermons on Antichrist." Vol. 5 of *Tracts for the Times*. London: Rivington, 1840.

Newport, Kenneth G. C. *Apocalypse and Millennium: Studies in Biblical Eisegesis*. Cambridge: Cambridge University Press, 2000.

Newton, Thomas. *Dissertations on the Prophecies, Which Have Remarkably Been Fulfilled, and at This Time Are Fulfilling in the World*. Vol. 2. New York: William Durrell, 1794.

Neyrey, Jerome H. *2 Peter, Jude: A New Translation with Introduction and Commentary*. The Anchor Bible. New York: Doubleday, 1993.

Nicholson, E. W. "The Interpretation of Exodus XXIV 9–11." *VT* 24.1 (1974): 77–97.

Nickelsburg, George W. E., and James C. VanderKam. *1 Enoch: The Hermeneia Translation*. Minneapolis: Augsburg Fortress, 2012.

Njeri, George. "Surprise on the Day of Judgment in Matthew 25:31–46 and The Book of the Watcher." *Neot* 54.1 (2020): 87–104.

Noē, John. "An Exegetical Basis for a Preterist-Idealist Understanding of the Book of Revelation." *JETS* 49.4 (2006): 776–96.

O'Hagan, Angelo. *Material Re-Creation in the Apostolic Fathers*. TUGAL 100. Berlin: Akademie Verlag, 1968.

O'Loughlin, Thomas. *The Didache: A Window on the Earliest Christians*. Grand Rapids: Baker Academic, 2010.

Olson, Daniel Olson. *A New Reading of the Animal Apocalypse of 1 Enoch: All Nations Shall Be Blessed*. Vol. 24 of Studia in Veteris Testamenti Pseudepigrapha. Leiden: Brill, 2013.

Orelli, Conrad von. *The Old Testament Prophecy of the Consummation of God's Kingdom, Traced in Its Historical Development*. Translated by J. S. Banks. Edinburgh: T&T Clark, 1892.

Orlov, Andrei A. "The Sacerdotal Traditions of 2 Enoch and the Date of the Text." In *New Perspectives on 2 Enoch: No Longer Slavonic Only*, edited by Andrei Orlov and Gabriele Boccaccini. Leiden: Brill, 2012.

Ortlund, Gavin. "Will We See God's Essence? A Defence of a Thomistic Account of the Beatific Vision." *SJT* 74.4 (2021): 323–32.

Osborn, Eric. *Irenaeus of Lyons*. Cambridge: Cambridge University Press, 2001.

———. *Tertullian: First Theologian of the West*. Cambridge: Cambridge University Press, 1997.

Osborne, Grant R. *1 & 2 Thessalonians: Verse by Verse*. Osborne New Testament Commentaries. Bellingham, WA: Lexham, 2018.

———. *Matthew*. Vol. 1 of Exegetical Commentary on the New Testament, edited by Clinton E. Arnold. Grand Rapids: Zondervan, 2010.

———. *Revelation*. Baker Exegetical Commentary on the New Testament. Grand Rapids: Baker Academic, 2002.

———. *Revelation: Verse by Verse*. Osborne New Testament Commentaries. Bellingham, WA: Lexham, 2016.

Osei-Bonsu, J. "The Intermediate State in the New Testament." *SJT* 44.2 (1991): 169–94.

Osiek, Caroline. *The Shepherd of Hermas: A Commentary*. Hermeneia, edited by Helmut Koester. Minneapolis: Fortress, 1999.

Oswalt, John N. *The Book of Isaiah, Chapters 1–39*. The New International Commentary on the Old Testament Grand Rapids: Eerdmans, 1986.

Ottman, Ford C. *The Unfolding of the Ages in the Revelation of John*. Grand Rapids: Kregel, 1967.

Page, Sydney H. T. "Revelation 20 and Pauline Eschatology." *JETS* 23.1 (1980): 31–43.

Paget, James Carleton. *The Epistle of Barnabas: Outlook and Background*. WUNT. 2 Series. Vol. 64. Tübingen: Mohr Siebeck, 1994.

———. "The *Epistle of Barnabas*." In *The Writings of the Apostolic Fathers*, edited by Paul Foster, 72–80. London: T&T Clark, 2007.

Papaioannou, Kim. *The Geography of Hell in the Teaching of Jesus: Gehenna, Hades, the Abyss, the Outer Darkness Where There Is Weeping and Gnashing of Teeth*. Eugene, OR: Pickwick, 2013.

Pareus, David. *A Commentary upon the Divine Revelation of the Apostle and Evangelist John*. Translated by Elias Arnold. Amsterdam: C. P., 1644.

Park, John Ranicar. *A Concise Exposition of the Apocalypse*. 2nd ed. London: James Duncan, 1825.

———. *A New Exposition of the Apocalypse*. 3rd ed. London: Smith, Elder, and Co., 1832.

Parvis, Paul. "Who Was Irenaeus? An Introduction to the Man and His Work." In *Irenaeus: Life, Scripture, Legacy*, edited by Sara Parvis and Paul Parvis, 13–24. Minneapolis: Fortress, 2012.

Patterson, Richard D. "Joel." Vol. 8 of *The Expositor's Bible Commentary: Daniel–Malachi*, edited by Tremper Longman III and David E. Garland. Grand Rapids: Zondervan, 2008.

Paul, Ian. "Introduction to the Book of Revelation." In *The Cambridge Companion to Apocalyptic Literature*, edited by Colin McAllister. Cambridge: Cambridge University Press, 2020.

Payton Jr., James R. "Keeping the End in View: How the Strange Yet Familiar Doctrine of Theosis Can Invigorate the Christian Life." *CT* 52.10 (October 2008): 66–68.

Peel, Malcolm L. "The Treatise on the Resurrection: Introduction." In *Nag Hammadi Codex I (The Jung Codex): Introductions, Texts, Translations, Indices*, edited by Harold W. Attridge. Vol. 22 of Nag Hammadi Studies, edited by Martin Krause, James M. Robinson, and Frederik Wisse. Leiden: Brill, 1985.

———. "The Treatise on the Resurrection: Notes." In *Nag Hammadi Codex I (The Jung Codex) Notes*, edited by Harold W. Attridge. Vol. 23 of Nag Hammadi Studies, edited by Martin Krause, James M. Robinson, and Frederik Wisse. Vol. 23. Leiden: Brill, 1985.

Pelikan, Jaroslav. *The Christian Tradition: A History of the Development of Doctrine*. Vol. 3 of *The Growth of Medieval Theology (600–1300)*. Chicago: University of Chicago Press, 1978.

———. *The Christian Tradition: A History of the Development of Doctrine*. Vol. 4 of *Reformation of Church and Dogma (1300–1700)*. Chicago: University of Chicago Press, 1983.

———. "The Eschatology of Tertullian." *CH* 21.2 (1952): 108–22.

Pentecost, J. Dwight. *The Parables of Jesus: Lessons in Life from the Master Teacher.* Grand Rapids: Kregel, 1998.

———. *Things to Come.* Grand Rapids: Zondervan, 1958.

Pietersma, Albert, and Benjamin G. Wright, eds. *A New English Translation of the Septuagint (Primary Texts).* Translated by Kenneth Atkinson. Oxford: Oxford University Press, 2007.

Pink, Arthur W. *The Antichrist.* Swengel, PA: Bible Truth Depot, 1923.

Polhill, John B. *Acts.* Vol. 26 of The New American Commentary. Nashville: Broadman & Holman, 1992.

Pond, Eugene W. "The Background and Timing of the Judgment of the Sheep and Goats." *BSac* 159.2 (2002): 201–220.

———. "Who Are the Sheep and Goats in Matthew 25:31–46?" *BSac* 159.3 (2002): 288–301.

Porter, Stanley E., and Alan E. Kurschner, eds. *The Future Restoration of Israel: A Response to Supersessionism.* Vol. 10 of McMaster Biblical Studies Series. Eugene, OR: Pickwick, 2023.

Porter, Stanley E., and Jeffrey T. Reed. "Philippians as a Macro-Chiasm and Its Exegetical Significance." *NTS* 44 (1998): 213–31.

Poschmann, Bernhard. *Paenitentia Secunda: die kirchliche Busse im ältesten Christentum bis Cyprian und Origenes: eine dogmengeschichtliche Untersuchung.* Bonn: Peter Hanstein, 1940.

———. *Penance and the Anointing of the Sick.* Translated and revised by Francis Courtney. New York: Herder and Herder, 1964.

Powell, Charles E. "Progression versus Recapitulation in Revelation 20:1–6." *BSac* 163.1 (2006): 94–109.

Poythress, Vern S. "Johannine Authorship and the Use of Intersentence Conjunctions in the Book of Revelation." *WTJ* 47 (1985): 350–69.

Price, Walter K. *The Coming Antichrist.* Chicago: Moody Press, 1974.

Prigent, Pierre. *Apocalypse 12: Histoire de l'exégèse.* Vol. 2 in Beiträge zur Geschichte der Biblischen Exegese, edited by Oscar Cullmann, Ernst Käsemann, et al. Tübingen: Mohr, 1959.

———. *Les Testimonia dans le christianisme primitif: L'épître de Barnabé I–XVI et ses sources.* Études bibliques. Paris: Gabalda, 1961.

Prostmeier, Ferdinand-Rupert. *Barnabasbrief.* Vol. 8 of Kommentar zu den Apostolischen Vätern, edited by Norbert Brox, G. Kretschmar, and Kurt Niederwimmer. Göttingen: Vandenhoeck & Ruprecht, 1999.

Pyle, Thomas. *A Paraphrase, with Notes, on the Revelation of St. John.* 2nd ed. London: Robinson, 1795.

Radmacher, Earl D. *Salvation.* Swindoll Leadership Library, edited by Charles R. Swindoll and Roy B. Zuck. Nashville: Word, 2000.

Rauschenbusch, Walter. *A Theology for the Social Gospel.* New York: Macmillan, 1922.

Redford, Douglas. *The Pentateuch.* Vol. 1 of Standard Reference Library: Old Testament. Cincinnati: Standard, 2008.

Reed, Annette Yoshiko. *Fallen Angels and the History of Judaism and Christianity: The Reception of Enochic Literature.* Cambridge: Cambridge University Press, 2005.

Reeve, J. J. "Gog." In *The International Standard Bible Encyclopaedia*, edited by James Orr et al. Chicago: Howard-Severance, 1915.

Reid, William J. *Lectures on the Revelation.* Pittsburgh, PA: Stevenson, Foster & Co., 1878.

———. *Plymouth Brethrenism Unveiled and Refuted.* Edinburgh: Oliphant, 1875.

Reitner, Richard. "A History of the Development of the Rapture Positions." In *Three Views on the Rapture: Pre-, Mid-, or Post-Tribulational?*, edited by Stanley N. Gundry. Counterpoints Grand Rapids: Zondervan, 1996.

Resseguie, James L. *The Revelation of John: A Narrative Commentary.* Grand Rapids: Baker, 2009.

Rhodes, James N. *The Epistle of Barnabas and the Deuteronomic Tradition: Polemics, Paraenesis, and the Legacy of the Gold-Calf Incident.* WUNT 188. Edited by Jörg Frey. Tübingen: Mohr Siebeck, 2004.

Rhodes, Ron Rhodes. *The Popular Dictionary of Bible Prophecy.* Eugene, OR: Harvest House, 2010.

Richard, Marcel, Albrecht Dihle, and Gottlieb Nathanael Bonwetsch, eds. *Hippolytus Werke: Kommentar zu Daniel.* Vol. 7 of Die Griechischen Christlichen Schriftsteller. Berlin: Akademie Verlag, 2000.

Richards, E. Randolph. *The Secretary in the Letters of Paul.* WUNT 42. Tübingen: Mohr Siebeck, 1991.

Richardson, Peter. *Israel in the Apostolic Church.* SNTSMS 10. Cambridge: Cambridge University Press, 1969.

Ridderbos, Herman. *The Coming of the Kingdom.* Translated by H. de Jongste. Edited by Raymond O. Zorn. Philadelphia: P&R, 1962.

Riddlebarger, Kim. *A Case for Amillennialism: Understanding the End Times.* Grand Rapids: Baker, 2013.

———. "Trichotomy: A Beachhead for Gnostic Influences." *Modern Reformation* 14.4 (1995): 22–26.

Roberts, Francis. *Clavis Bibliorum: The Key of the Bible, Unlocking the Richest Treasury of the Holy Scriptures.* 4th rev. ed. London: Peter Parker and Thomas Guy, 1675.

Robertson, O. Palmer. *The Books of Nahum, Habakkuk, and Zephaniah.* New International Commentary on the Old Testament. Grand Rapids: Eerdmans, 1990.

Robinson, James M., ed. *The Nag Hammadi Library in English.* 3rd. ed. San Francisco: Harper San Francisco, 1990.

Robinson, John A. T. *Redating the New Testament.* Philadelphia: Westminster, 1976.

Robinson, Theodore H. *The Gospel of Matthew*, edited by James Moffatt. Moffatt's New Testament Commentary. New York: Harper, 1928.

Roloff, Jürgen. *Die Offenbarung des Johannes.* Vol. 18 of Zürcher Bibelkommentare NT, edited by Hans Heinrich Schmid and Siegfried Schulz. Zürich: Theologischer Verlag, 1984.

Roop, Eugene F. *Genesis.* Believers Church Bible Commentary. Scottdale, PA: Herald, 1987.

Rordorf, Willy. *Sunday: The History of the Day of Rest and Worship in the Earliest Centuries of the Christian Church.* Philadelphia: Westminster, 1968.

Rordorf, Willy, and André Tuilier, eds. *La doctrine des douze apôtres (Didachè): Introduction, texte critique, traduction, notes, appendices, annexe et index.* 2nd ed. Paris: Cerf, 1998.

Rosenthall, Marvin J. *The Pre-Wrath Rapture of the Church.* Nashville: Thomas Nelson, 1990.

Rossing, Barbara R. *The Rapture Exposed: The Message of Hope in the Book of Revelation.* Cambridge, MA: Westview, 2004.

Routledge, Robin. *Old Testament Theology: A Thematic Approach.* Downers Grove, IL: InterVarsity, 2012.

Ruiz-Ortiz, Francisco Javier. "'Battle Is Over, Raise We the Cry of Victory': Study of Revelation 19:11–21." *Isidorianum* 29.2 (2020): 37–60.

Ryken, Leland, James C. Wilhoit, and Tremper Longman III, eds. *Dictionary of Biblical Imagery.* Downers Grove, IL: InterVarsity, 1998.

Ryle, J. C. *Expository Thoughts on John.* Vol. 1. New York: Robert Carter & Brothers, 1879.

Ryrie, Charles C. *Revelation.* Everyman's Bible Commentary. Chicago: Moody, 1996.

Sailhamer, John H. *Biblical Prophecy.* Grand Rapids: Zondervan, 1998.

———. "Genesis." Vol. 1 of *The Expositor's Bible Commentary: Genesis–Leviticus*, edited by Tremper Longman III and David E. Garland. Grand Rapids: Zondervan, 2008.

Saloff-Astakhoff, N. I. *Antichrist and the Last Days of the World.* Berne, IN: Berne Witness, 1941.

Sandy, D. Brent. *Plowshares and Pruning Hooks: Rethinking the Language of Biblical Prophecy and Apocalyptic.* Downers Grove, IL: IVP Academic, 2002.

Sarna, Nahum M. *Genesis.* The JPS Torah Commentary. Philadelphia: Jewish Publication Society, 1989.

Savage, John J. Introduction to *St. Ambrose: Hexameron, Paradise, and Cain and Abel*, translated by John J. Savage. Vol. 42 of The Fathers of the Church: A New Translation. Washington, DC: The Catholic University of America Press, 1961.

Schachter, Lifsa. "The Garden of Eden as God's First Sanctuary." *JBQ* 41 (2013): 73–77.

Schaff, Philip, ed. *The Creeds of Christendom with a History and Critical Notes.* Vol. 3 of *The Evangelical Protestant Creeds, with Translations.* 4th ed. Bibliotheca Symbolica Ecclesiae Universalis. New York: Harper & Brothers, 1877. Reprint, Grand Rapids: Baker, 1977.

———. *The Oldest Church Manual Called the Teaching of the Twelve Apostles.* New York: Scribner's, 1885.

Schaff, Philip, and David Schley Schaff. *History of the Christian Church.* Vol. 2. New York: Scribner's, 1910.

Schaller, Maria Emilia. Ἄβυσσος: *Un estudio en contexto: El significado del término "abismo" en el libro de Apocalipsis.* Serie Tesis de la Escuela de Graduados de la Facultad de Teología Universidad Adventista del Plata. Libertador San Martín, AR: Editorial Universidad Adventista del Plata, 2017.

Schemm Jr., Peter R. "The Agents of God: Angels." In *A Theology for the Church*, edited by Daniel L. Akin, Bruce Riley Ashord, and Kenneth Keathley. Rev. ed. Nashville: B & H, 2014.

Schenck, Kenneth. *1 & 2 Corinthians: A Commentary for Bible Students*. Indianapolis: Wesleyan, 2006.

Schillington, V. G. *2 Corinthians*. Believers Church Bible Commentary. Scottdale, PA: Herald, 1998.

Schmidt, T. C. *Hippolytus of Rome: Commentary on Daniel and 'Chronicon.'* Vol. 67 of Gorgias Studies in Early Christianity and Patristics. Piscataway, NJ: Gorgias, 2017.

Schneemelcher, Wilhelm. *New Testament Apocrypha*. Vol. 2 of *Writings Relating to the Apostles; Apocalypses and Related Subjects,* translated by R. M. Wilson. Louisville, KY: Westminster/John Knox, 1992.

Schnittjer, Gary Edward. *Old Testament Use of Old Testament: A Book-by-Book Guide*. Grand Rapids: Zondervan Academic, 2021.

Schoene, Alfred, ed. *Eusebi: Chronicorum Libri Duo*. Vol. 2. Berlin: Wiedemann, 1866.

Schreiner, Patrick. *The Kingdom of God and the Glory of the Cross*. Short Studies in Biblical Theology. Wheaton, IL: Crossway, 2018.

Schreiner, Thomas R. *1 & 2 Peter and Jude*. Christian Standard Commentary. Nashville: Holman Reference, 2020.

Scott, Thomas. *Commentary on the Holy Bible*. Vol. 6. 5th ed. London: Seeley, Hatchard, & Son, 1822.

Scott, Walter. *Exposition of the Revelation of Jesus Christ*. London: Pickering & Inglis, c. 1900.

Seiss, Joseph A. *The Apocalypse*. Vol. 2. 7th ed. New York: Revell, 1900.

———. *The Apocalypse: A Series of Special Lectures on the Revelation of Jesus Christ with Revised Text*. Vol. 2. 11th ed. New York: Cook, 1913.

———. *The Apocalypse*. Vol. 3. 9th ed. New York: Cook, 1906.

———. *The Apocalypse: Lectures on the Book of Revelation*. 6th ed. New York: Charles C. Cook, 1900. Reprint, Grand Rapids: Zondervan, 1950.

Shea, William H. "The Sabbath in the Epistle of Barnabas." *AUSS* 4.2 (1966): 149–75.

Shelton, W. Brian. *Martyrdom from Exegesis in Hippolytus: An Early Church Presbyter's Commentary on Daniel*. Paternoster Studies in Christian History and Thought. Eugene, OR: Wipf & Stock, 2008.

Shoemaker, Stephen J. *The Apocalypse of Empire: Imperial Eschatology in Late Antiquity and Early Islam*. Philadelphia: University of Pennsylvania Press, 2018.

Showers, Renald E. *Maranatha—Our Lord, Come!: A Definitive Study of the Rapture of the Church*. Bellmawr, NJ: The Friends of Israel Gospel Ministry, 1995.

Sim, David C. "The Meaning of παλιγγενεσία in Matthew 19:28." *JSNT* 15.50 (1993): 3–12.

Smalley, Stephen S. *The Revelation to John*. Downers Grove, IL: IVP Academic, 2012.

Smith, Billy K., and Frank S. Page. *Amos, Obadiah, Jonah*. Vol. 19B of The New American Commentary. Nashville: Broadman & Holman, 1995.

Smith, Christopher R. "Chiliasm and Recapitulation in the Theology of Ireneus." *VC* 48.4 (1994): 313–31.

Smith, Gary V. *Isaiah 1–39*. Vol. 15A of The New American Commentary, edited by E. Ray Clendenen. Nashville: B&H, 2007.

———. *Isaiah 40–66*. Vol. 15B of The New American Commentary. Nashville: B&H, 2009.

Smith, J. M. Powis, William Hayes Ward, and Julius August Bewer. *A Critical and Exegetical Commentary on Micah, Zephaniah, Nahum, Habakkuk, Obadiah and Joel*. International Critical Commentary. New York: Scribner's Sons, 1911.

Smith, Jacob B. *A Revelation of Jesus Christ: A Commentary on the Book of Revelation*. Edited by J. Otis Toder. Scottdale, PA: Herald, 1961.

Smith, T. C. "Claims of Christ: The Parable of the Sheep and the Goats; an Exegesis of Matthew 25:31–46." *Foundations* 19.3 (1976): 204–22.

Smith, William, ed. *A Dictionary of the Bible, Comprising Its Antiquities, Biography, Geography, and Natural History*. Philadelphia: Penn, 1884.

Snyder, C. Arnold. *Anabaptist History and Theology*. Kitchener, Ontario: Pandora, 1997.

Song, Seung-In. "Seeing the Johannine Last Meal as a Covenant Meal (John 13 and Exodus 24)." *Bib* 100.2 (2019): 286–87.

Spence-Jones, H. D. M., ed. *Exodus*. Vol. 2 of The Pulpit Commentary. London: Funk & Wagnalls, 1909.

———, ed. *Revelation*. The Pulpit Commentary. New York: Funk & Wagnalls, 1909.

Sproul, R. C. *1–2 Peter*. St. Andrew's Expositional Commentary. Wheaton, IL: Crossway, 2011.

Sproule, John A. *In Defense of Pretribulationism*. Winona Lake, IN: BMH, 1980.

Spurgeon, Charles H. "Christ with the Keys of Death and Hell." Sermon 894, October 3, 1869. Vol. 15 of *The Metropolitan Tabernacle Pulpit Sermons*. London: Passmore & Alabaster, 1869.

———. "The First Resurrection" Sermon 391, May 5, 1861. Vol. 7 of *The Metropolitan Tabernacle Pulpit Sermons*. London: Passmore & Alabaster, 1861.

———. *The Gospel of the Kingdom: A Commentary on the Book of Matthew*. London: Passmore and Alabaster, 1893.

———. "Heaven Below." Sermon 1800, September 21, 1884. Vol. 30 of *The Metropolitan Tabernacle Pulpit Sermons*. London: Passmore & Alabaster, 1884.

———. "The Hope of Future Bliss." Sermon 25, May 20, 1855. Vol. 1 of *The New Park Street Pulpit Sermons*. London: Passmore & Alabaster, 1855.

St. Clair, Michael J. *Millenarian Movements in Historical Context*. Vol. 763 of Garland Reference Library of Social Science. New York: Garland, 1992.

Stedman, Ray C. "The City of Glory" (April 29, 1990). https://www.raystedman.org/new-testament/revelation/the-city-of-glory.

Steenberg, Matthew C. *Irenaeus on Creation: The Cosmic Christ and the Saga of Redemption*. Leiden: Brill, 2008.

———. "Tracing the Irenaean Legacy." In *Irenaeus: Life, Scripture, Legacy*, ed. Sara Parvis and Paul Parvis. Minneapolis: Fortress, 2012.

Storms, Sam. *Kingdom Come: The Amillennial Alternative*. Fearn, UK: Mentor, 2013.

Stott, John R. W. *The Message of Acts: To the Ends of the Earth*. The Bible Speaks Today. Downers Grove, IL: IVP Academic, 1990.

Strand, Kenneth. *Interpreting the Book of Revelation*. 2nd ed. Naples, FL: Ann Arbor, 1979.

Strauss, David Friedrich. *The Old Faith and the New: A Confession*. 2nd English ed. Translated from the 6th German ed. by Mathilde Blind. London: Asher, 1873.

Stuart, Douglas K. "The Sovereign's Day of Conquest." *BASOR* 221 (1976): 159–64.

Stuart, Moses. *Hints on the Interpretation of Prophecy*. 2nd ed. Andover: Allen, Morrill, and Wardwell, 1842.

Svigel, Michael J. "The Apocalypse of John and the Rapture of the Church: A Reevaluation." *TrinJ* 22.1 (2001): 23–74.

———. *The Center and the Source: Second Century Incarnational Christology and Early Catholic Christianity*. Piscataway, NJ: Gorgias, 2016.

———. "*Didache* as a Practical Enchiridion for Early Church Plants." *BSac* 174.1 (2017): 77–94.

———. "The End Times in Retrospect." In *Exploring Christian Theology*. Vol. 3 of *Church, Spiritual Growth, and the End Times*, edited by Nathan D. Holsteen and Michael J. Svigel, 180–91. Minneapolis: Bethany House, 2014.

———. "Extreme Makeover: Heaven and Earth Edition—Will God Annihilate the World and Re-Create It *Ex Nihilo*?" *BSac* 171.4 (2014): 401–17.

———. "The Phantom Heresy: Did the Council of Ephesus (431) Condemn Chiliasm?" *TrinJ* 24.1 (2003): 105–12.

———. "'What Child Is This?' Darby's Early Exegetical Argument for the Pretribulation Rapture of the Church." *TrinJ* 35.2 (2014): 225–51.

———. "What Child Is This? A Forgotten Argument for the Pretribulation Rapture." In *Evidence for the Rapture: A Biblical Case for Pretribulationism*, edited by John F. Hart. Chicago: Moody, 2015.

———. "When He Returns: Resurrection, Judgment, and the Restoration." In *Exploring Christian Theology*. Vol. 3 of *The Church, Spiritual Growth, and the End Times*, edited by Nathan D. Holsteen and Michael J. Svigel. Minneapolis: Bethany House, 2014.

Sweeney, Marvin A. *Isaiah 1–39 with an Introduction to Prophetic Literature*. Vol. 16 of The Forms of the Old Testament Literature. Grand Rapids: Eerdmans, 1996.

Sweet, John. *Revelation*. TPI New Testament Commentaries. Philadelphia: Trinity Press International, 1990.

Swete, Henry Barclay. *The Apocalypse of John*. 2nd. ed. Classic Commentaries on the Greek New Testament. New York: Macmillan, 1906.

———. *The Apocalypse of John: The Greek Text with Introduction, Notes, and Indexes*. 3rd ed. London: Macmillan, 1911.

Tabory, Joseph. "The Rabbinic Traditions about the Establishment of the Amidah: Some Observations." In *On Wings of Prayer: Sources of Jewish Worship: Essays in Honor of Professor Stefan C. Reif on the Occasion of His Seventy-Fifth Birthday*, edited by Nuria Calduch-Benages, Michael W. Duggan, and Dalia Marx. Vol. 44 of Deuterocanonical and Cognate Literature Studies. Berlin: De Gruyter, 2019.

Tannehill, Robert C. "The Functions of Peter's Mission Speeches in the Narrative of Acts." *NTS* 37 (1991): 400–14.

———. "Israel in Luke-Acts: A Tragic Story." *JBL* 104.1 (1985): 69–85.

———. *A Narrative Unity of Luke-Acts: A Literary Interpretation.* Vol. 2. Philadelphia: Fortress, 1994.

Tanner, J. Paul. *Daniel.* Evangelical Exegetical Commentary, edited by H. Wayne House and William D. Barrick. Bellingham, WA: Lexham, 2020.

Taylor, Richard A. *Interpreting Apocalyptic Literature: An Exegetical Handbook.* Handbooks for Old Testament Exegesis, edited by David M. Howard Jr. Grand Rapids: Kregel Academic, 2016.

Terblanche, M. D. "An Abundance of Living Waters: The Intertextual Relationship between Zechariah 14:8 and Ezekiel 47:1–12." *OTE* 17.1 (2004): 120–29.

Tesh, S. Edward, and Walter D. Zorn. *Psalms.* The College Press NIV Commentary. Joplin, MO: College Press, 1999.

Thiessen, Henry C. *Lectures in Systematic Theology.* Grand Rapids: Eerdmans, 1949.

Thiselton, Anthony C. *The First Epistle to the Corinthians.* New International Greek Testament Commentary. Grand Rapids: Eerdmans, 2000.

Thomas, Robert L. *Revelation 1–7: An Exegetical Commentary.* Chicago: Moody, 1992.

———. *Revelation 8–22: An Exegetical Commentary.* Chicago: Moody, 1995.

Thomson, William. *The New Testament, with Some Preliminary Observations and Notes Critical and Explanatory.* Vol. 3. Kilmarnock: Crawford, 1816.

Tigchelaar, Eibert J. C. "Eden and Paradise: The Garden Motif in Some Early Jewish Texts (1 Enoch and Other Texts Found at Qumran)." In *Paradise Interpreted: Representations of Biblical Paradise in Judaism and Christianity,* edited by Gerard P Luttikhuizen. Themes in Biblical Narrative. Leiden: Brill, 1999.

Townter, W. Sibley. *Daniel.* Interpretation: A Bible Commentary for Teaching and Preaching, edited by James L. Mays, Patrick D. Miller, and Paul J. Achtemeier. Louisville: John Knox, 1984.

Tromp, Johannes. "Taxo, the Messenger of the Lord." *JSJ* 21.2 (1990): 200–209.

Tyconius of Carthage. *Exposition of the Apocalypse.* Translated by Francis X. Gumerlock. Vol. 134 of The Fathers of the Church: A New Translation. Washington, DC: Catholic University of America Press, 2017.

Ulrich, Dean R. "How Early Judaism Read Daniel 9:24–27." *OTE* 27.3 (2014): 1060–83.

Vander Hart, Mark D. "The Transition of the Old Testament Day of the Lord into the New Testament Day of the Lord Jesus Christ." *MAJT* 9.1 (1993).

VanderKam, James. "1 Enoch, Enochic Motifs, and Enoch in Early Christian Literature." In *The Jewish Apocalyptic Heritage in Early Christianity,* edited by James C. VanderKam and William Adler, 33–59. Section 3, vol. 4 of Compendia Rerum Iudaicarum ad Novum Testamentum. Minneapolis: Fortress, 1996.

Van Kampen, Robert D. *The Rapture Question Answered: Plain and Simple.* Grand Rapids: Revell, 1997.

Van Vleet, Jacob E. *Information Logical Fallacies: A Brief Guide.* Lanham, MD: Hamilton, 2021.

Verheyden, Joseph. "The *Shepherd of Hermas.*" In *The Writings of the Apostolic Fathers,* edited by Paul Foster. London: T&T Clark, 2007.

Verhoef, Pieter A. *The Books of Haggai and Malachi*. The New International Commentary on the Old Testament. Grand Rapids: Eerdmans, 1987.

Verme, Marcello Del. *Didache and Judaism: Jewish Roots of an Ancient Christian-Jewish Work*. New York: T&T Clark, 2004.

Vermes, Geza. *The Dead Sea Scrolls in English*. Rev. 4th ed. Sheffield, UK: Sheffield Academic, 1995.

———. *Scrolls, Scripture, and Early Christianity*. Vol. 56 of Library of Second Temple Studies. London: T&T Clark, 2005.

Vinson, Richard B., Richard F. Wilson, and Watson E. Mills. *1 & 2 Peter, Jude*. Smyth & Helwys Bible Commentary, edited by R. Alan Culpepper. Macon, GA: Smyth & Helwys, 2010.

Vlach, Michael J. *Has the Church Replaces Israel? A Theological Evaluation*. Nashville: B&H Academic, 2010.

———. *He Will Reign Forever: A Biblical Theology of the Kingdom of God*. Silverton, OR: Lampion, 2017.

Vos, Geerhardus. *The Pauline Eschatology*. Grand Rapids: Eerdmans, 1952.

Wace, Henry, and C. A. Buchheim, eds. and trans. *First Principles of the Reformation or the Ninety-five Theses and the Three Primary Works of Dr. Martin Luther*. London: Murray, 1883.

Wainwright, A. W. "Luke and the Restoration of the Kingdom to Israel." *ExpTim* 89.3 (1977): 76–79.

Walker, Larry L. "Zephaniah." Vol. 8 of *The Expositor's Bible Commentary: Daniel –Malachi*, edited by Tremper Longman III and David E. Garland. Grand Rapids: Zondervan, 2008.

Wall, William. *Brief Critical Notes, Especially on the Various Readings of the New Testament Books*. London: William Innys, 1730.

Wallace, Daniel B. *Greek Grammar Beyond the Basics: An Exegetical Syntax of the New Testament*. Grand Rapids: Zondervan, 1996.

Wallis, Wilber B. "The Problem of an Intermediate Kingdom in 1 Corinthians 15:20–28." *JETS* 18.4 (1975): 229–42.

Waltke, Bruce K. "The Kingdom of God in the Old Testament: Definitions and Story." In *The Kingdom of God*, edited by Christopher W. Morgan and Robert A. Peterson. Theology in Community. Wheaton, IL: Crossway, 2012.

Walvoord, John F. *The Rapture Question*. Grand Rapids: Zondervan, 1979.

———. *Revelation*. The John Walvoord Prophecy Commentaries, edited by Philip E. Rawley and Mark Hitchcock. Chicago: Moody, 2011.

———. "Revelation." In *The Bible Knowledge Commentary: New Testament Edition*, edited by John F. Walvoord and Roy B. Zuck. Wheaton, IL: Victor, 1983.

———. *The Revelation of Jesus Christ*. Chicago: Moody, 1966.

Wanamaker, Charles A. "Apocalyptic Discourse, Paraenesis and Identity Maintenance in 1 Thessalonians." *NeoT* 36.1–2 (2002): 131–45.

———. *The Epistle to the Thessalonians: A Commentary on the Greek Text*. New International Greek Testament Commentary. Grand Rapids: Eerdmans, 1990.

Warfield, Benjamin B. *Biblical Doctrines*. New York: Oxford University Press, 1929.

———. "The Millennium and the Apocalypse." *PTR* 2 (1904): 599–617.

Watson, Thomas. *The Select Works of the Rev. Thomas Watson, Comprising His Celebrated Body of Divinity, in a Series of Lectures on the Shorter Catechism, and Various Sermons and Treatises*. New York: Robert Carter & Brothers, 1855.

Waymeyer, Matt. "The Binding of Satan in Revelation 20." *MSJ* 26.1 (2015): 19–46.

Webb, Barry G. *The Message of Isaiah: On Eagles' Wings*. The Bible Speaks Today. Downers Grove, IL: IVP Academic, 1996.

Weber, Kathleen. "The Image of the Sheep and the Goats in Matthew 25:31–46." *CBQ* 59.4 (1997): 657–78.

Weber, Stuart K. *Matthew*. Vol. 1 of Holman New Testament Commentary. Nashville: B&H, 2000.

Weber, Timothy P. "Millennialism." In *The Oxford Handbook of Eschatology*, edited by Jerry L. Walls. Oxford: Oxford University Press, 2008.

Weidner, Franklin. *Annotations on the Revelation of St. John the Divine*. Vol. 12 of The Lutheran Commentary, edited by Henry Eyster Jacobs. New York: Christian Literature, 1898.

Weiss, Johannes. *Der erste Korintherbrief*. Kritisch-exegetischer Kommentar über das Neue Testament. Göttingen: Vandenhoeck & Ruprecht, 1910.

Weiss, Meir. "Origin of the 'Day of the Lord'—Reconsidered." *HUCA* 37 (1966): 29–71.

Wengst, Klaus. *Tradition und Theologie des Barnabasbriefes*. Vol. 42 of Arbeiten zur Kirchengeschichte. Berlin: De Gruyter, 1971.

White, R. Fowler. "Death and the First Resurrection in Revelation 20: A Response to Meredith G. Kline." Paper Presented at the Eastern Regional Evangelical Theological Society Meeting, Capital Bible Seminary, Lanham, MD, April 3, 1992.

———. "On the Hermeneutics and Interpretation of Rev 20:1–3: A Preconsummationist Perspective." *JETS* 42.1 (1999): 53–66.

———. "Reexamining the Evidence for Recapitulation in Rev 20:1–10." *WTJ* 51 (1989): 319–44.

Widdicombe, Peter. "Irenaeus and the Knowledge of God as Father: Text and Context." In *Irenaeus: Life, Scripture, Legacy*, edited by Sara Parvis and Paul Parvis. Minneapolis: Fortress, 2012.

Wikenhauser, Alfred. "Weltwoche und tausendjähriges Reich." *TQ* 127.4 (1947): 399–417.

Wilcke, Hans-Alwin. *Das Problem eines messianischen Zwischenreichs bei Paulus*. ATANT 51. Zürich: Zwingli, 1967.

Wilhite, Shawn J. *The Didache: A Commentary*. Vol. 1 of Apostolic Fathers Commentary Series, edited by Paul A. Hartog and Shawn J. Wilhite. Eugene, OR: Cascade, 2019.

Williamson, H. G. M. *A Critical and Exegetical Commentary on Isaiah 1–27*. Vol. 1 of *Commentary on Isaiah 1–5: The International Critical Commentary on the Holy Scriptures of the Old and New Testaments*. New York: T&T Clark, 2006.

Williamson, Peter S. *Revelation*. Catholic Commentary on Sacred Scripture. Grand Rapids: Baker Academic, 2015.

Wilson, John Christian. *Five Problems in the Interpretation of the Shepherd of Hermas: Authorship, Genre, Canonicity, Apocalyptic, and the Absence of the Name "Jesus Christ."* Vol. 34 of Mellon Biblical Press Series. Lewiston, NY: Mellen, 1995.

Wilson, Thomas. *A Complete Christian Dictionary.* Edited by Thomas Wilson and John Bagwell. 3rd ed. London: William Iaggad, 1622.

Windisch, Hans. *Die Apostolischen Väter.* Vol. 3 of *Der Barnabasbrief.* HNT. Tübingen: Mohr, 1920.

Witherington III, Ben. *1 and 2 Thessalonians: A Socio-Rhetorical Commentary.* Grand Rapids: Eerdmans, 2006.

Wood, Arthur Skevington. "The Eschatology of Irenaeus." *EvQ* 41.1 (1969): 30–41.

Wood, Hans Wood. *The Revelation of St. John Considered as Alluding to Certain Services of the Jewish Temple.* London: Payne & Son, 1787.

Woods, Andrew M. "Have the Prophecies in Revelation 17–18 about Babylon Been Fulfilled? Part 1." *BSac* 169 (2012): 79–100.

Wordsworth, Christopher. *Lectures on the Apocalypse: Critical, Expository, and Practical.* 2nd ed. London: F. & J. Rivington, 1849.

Worthington, John. *Miscellanies.* London: John Wyat, 1704.

Wright, N. T. *1 & 2 Thessalonians.* N. T. Wright for Everyone Bible Study Guides. Downers Grove, IL: InterVarsity, 2009.

———. "Farewell to the Rapture." *BRev* 17.4 (2001): 8, 52.

———. *The Resurrection of the Son of God.* Vol. 3 of Christian Origins and the Question of God. Minneapolis: Fortress, 2003.

———. *Surprised by Hope.* London: SPCK, 2007.

Yarbrough, Robert W. "The Kingdom of God in the New Testament: Matthew and Revelation." In *The Kingdom of God,* edited by Christopher W. Morgan and Robert A. Peterson. Theology in Community. Wheaton, IL: Crossway, 2012.

Yates, Roy. "The Antichrist." *EvQ* 46 (1974): 42–50.

Zahn, Theodor. *Introduction to the New Testament.* Vol 3. Translated by John Moore Trout et al. Edinburgh: T&T Clark, 1909.

Zvi, Ehud Ben. *A Historical-Critical Study of the Book of Obadiah.* BZAW 242. Edited by Otto Kaiser. Berlin: de Gruyter, 1996.